WHERE TO WATCH BIRDS IN DEVON & CORNWALL

SIXTH EDITION

SARA McMAHON & KEVIN RYLANDS

WITH A CONTRIBUTION FROM
DAVID NORMAN & VIC TUCKER

H E L M
LONDON • OXFORD • NEW YORK • NEW DELHI • SYDNEY

HELM
Bloomsbury Publishing Plc
50 Bedford Square, London, WC1B 3DP, UK
Bloomsbury Publishing Ireland Limited,
29 Earlsfort Terrace, Dublin 2, D02 AY28, Ireland

BLOOMSBURY, HELM and the Helm logo are
trademarks of Bloomsbury Publishing Plc

First published in the United Kingdom 1984
This sixth edition published 2026

Author copyright © Sara McMahon and Kevin Rylands, 2026

Contributor copyright © David Norman and Vic Tucker, 2026

Sara McMahon and Kevin Rylands have asserted their rights under the Copyright, Designs and Patents Act, 1988, to be identified as Authors of this work.

All rights reserved. No part of this publication may be: i) reproduced or transmitted in any form, electronic or mechanical, including photocopying, recording or by means of any information storage or retrieval system without prior permission in writing from the publishers; or ii) used or reproduced in any way for the training, development or operation of artificial intelligence (AI) technologies, including generative AI technologies. The rights holders expressly reserve this publication from the text and data mining exception as per Article 4(3) of the Digital Single Market Directive (EU) 2019/790

Bloomsbury Publishing Plc does not have any control over, or responsibility for, any third-party websites referred to or in this book. All internet addresses given in this book were correct at the time of going to press. The authors and publisher regret any inconvenience caused if addresses have changed or sites have ceased to exist, but can accept no responsibility for any such changes

A catalogue record for this book is available from the British Library
Library of Congress Cataloguing-in-Publication data has been applied for

ISBN: PB: 978-1-4729-8821-8; ePub: 978-1-4729-8822-5;
ePDF: 978-1-4729-8823-2

2 4 6 8 10 9 7 5 3 1

Typeset in the UK by Mark Heslington
Maps by Brian Southern, with updates to the sixth edition
by Julian Baker and Leanne Kelman

Printed and bound in Great Britain by Clays Ltd, Elcograf S.p.A.

To find out more about our authors and books visit
www.bloomsbury.com and sign up for our newsletters
For product safety related questions
contact productsafety@bloomsbury.com

Cover photographs. Front: Cirl Bunting (t), Ben Lucking; Choughs (b), David Dray/Alamy; Back: Avocet (l), W. de Vries/Shutterstock; Dipper (c), Erni/Shutterstock; Buzzard (r), Tamsin Hemming (CapKern Photography); Spine: Balearic Shearwater, Mark Darlaston

Due to a production error, this book printed with an incomplete contents list. The corrected contents with page numbers is below.

Acknowledgements	6
Foreword	7
Introduction	8
How to use this book	11
Key to the maps	14
Map of the region	15

DEVON (SOUTH COAST AND DARTMOOR)

1 Axe Estuary area, Seaton and Beer Head	17
1A Trinity Hill, Axminster	25

Site cluster: Exeter area   *27*

2 Otter Estuary Nature Reserve	28
3 Pebblebed Heaths	31
4 Exe Estuary: general introduction	36
4A Exmouth	37
4B Bowling Green Marsh, Topsham and the Clyst areas	39
4C Exminster Marshes and the canal	40
4D Powderham Marshes	43
4E Powderham and the park	43
4F Dawlish Warren	45
5 Stoke Canon Meadows and Stoke Woods	53
6 Haldon Woods and Little Haldon	56
6A Chudleigh Knighton Heath and Hennock	60

Site cluster: Torbay area   *64*

7 Teign Estuary and Newton Abbot district	65
7A Labrador Bay	69
7B Stover Country Park	70
8 Hope's Nose, Torquay	73
9 Torbay and Berry Head	77
10 Dartington and the Lower Dart	86

Site cluster: South Hams coast   *89*

11 Slapton Ley and district (including Beesands and Hallsands)	90
12 Start Point	96
13 Prawle Point	99
14 Kingsbridge Estuary	104
15 Soar area including Bolt Head to Bolt Tail	108
16 Thurlestone Area	111
17 South Efford Marsh, Avon Estuary and Water Meadows	115

Site cluster: Plymouth area   *119*

17A Stoke Point	120
18 Wembury and Bovisand	121
19 Plymouth area	124
20 Plymbridge Woods	130

Site cluster: Dartmoor   *133*

21 Dartmoor area: general introduction	134
21A Haytor, Emsworthy Mire and Yarner Wood	135
21B Venford-Swincombe	139
21C Soussons and Postbridge district	143
21D Fernworthy Reservoir and Plantation	147
21E Okehampton: high moors around Cranmere and Okement Valley Woods	149
21F Tavy Cleave, West Dartmoor	153
21G Burrator Reservoir and woodlands	154
21H Piles Copse, Harford Moor and Three Barrows	157
21J Steps Bridge and Dunsford Woods	159
21K Hembury Woods	162

CORNWALL

22 St John's and Millbrook Lakes, Lynher and Tamar Estuaries: general introduction	164
22A St John's Lake and Millbrook Lake	164
22B The Lynher	166
22C The Tamar	167
22D Lopwell and Upper Tavy Estuary	171
23 Rame Head, Whitsand Bay and Looe	173

Site cluster: Bodmin Moor and central Cornwall	*179*

24 Siblyback and Colliford Lakes	180
25 Upper Fowey Valley, Dozmary Pool and Moorland	184
26 Crowdy Reservoir and Davidstow Airfield	188
26A Goss Moor	192
27 Par Beach and Pool	193
27A Porthpean, St Austell Bay and Pentewan	197

Site cluster: Lizard Peninsula and Fal Estuary	*199*

28 Gerrans Bay and Nare Head	200
29 Fal Estuary, Carrick Roads complex	203
29A Boscawen Park, Truro	207
30 Falmouth, The Bay and Rosemullion	209
30A Argal and College Reservoirs	213
31 Stithians Reservoir	215
32 The Lizard	219
32A Loe Pool	228

Site cluster: West Cornwall	*231*

33 Marazion Marsh, Mount's Bay and waterfront to Newlyn and Mousehole	232
33A Drift Reservoir	238
34 Porthgwarra and Land's End area	240
34A Sennen area	248
35 The Isles of Scilly	250
35A Pelagic seabird trips (other than those launched from Scilly)	260
36 St Ives Island and Bay	261
37 Pendeen Watch	266
38 Hayle Estuary (including Carnsew Pool and Copperhouse Creek)	269

Site cluster: North Cornwall coast	*274*

39 Newquay district	275
39A Trevose Head	280
40 Camel Estuary, Treraven Meadow, Clapper and Amble Marshes	284

Site cluster: Bude and north-west Devon	*290*

41 Bude district	291

CORNWALL/DEVON BORDER

42 Tamar Lakes	297

DEVON (NORTH COAST AND INLAND)

43 Roadford Reservoir	301
44 Hartland Point and district	305
45 Lundy	311

Site cluster: North Devon	*318*

46 Taw – Torridge Estuary	319
47 North Devon Coast (Morte Point – Lynton)	328
48 Rackenford, Knowstone and Hare's Down	334
49 Meeth Quarry, Hatherleigh	335
49A Shobrooke Park, Crediton	337

Top sites for disabled access	**339**
Top sites for public transport	**340**
Thirty species to see in Devon and Cornwall	**341**
List of organisations	**347**
References	**347**
Glossary	**348**
Code of conduct for birdwatchers	**351**
Devon, Cornwall and the Isles of Scilly bird list	**353**
Index to species	**359**

CONTENTS

Acknowledgements	00
Foreword	00
Introduction	00
How to use this book	00
Key to the maps	00
Map of the region	00
DEVON (SOUTH COAST AND DARTMOOR)	00
1 Axe Estuary area, Seaton and Beer Head	00
1A Trinity Hill, Axminster	00
Site cluster: Exeter area	*00*
2 Otter Estuary Nature Reserve	00
3 Pebblebed Heaths	00
4 Exe Estuary: general introduction	00
4A Exmouth	00
4B Bowling Green Marsh, Topsham and the Clyst areas	00
4C Exminster Marshes and the canal	00
4D Powderham Marshes	00
4E Powderham and the park	00
4F Dawlish Warren	00
5 Stoke Canon Meadows and Stoke Woods	00
6 Haldon Woods and Little Haldon	00
6A Chudleigh Knighton Heath and Hennock	00
Site cluster: Torbay area	*00*
7 Teign Estuary and Newton Abbot district	00
7A Labrador Bay	00
7B Stover Lake and Woods	00
8 Hope's Nose, Torquay	00
9 Torbay and Berry Head	00
10 Dartington and the Lower Dart	00
Site cluster: South Hams coast	*00*
11 Slapton Ley and district (including Beesands and Hallsands)	00
12 Start Point	00
13 Prawle Point	00
14 Kingsbridge Estuary	00
15 Soar area including Bolt Head to Bolt Tail	00
16 Thurlestone Area	00
17 South Efford Marsh, Avon Estuary and Water Meadows	00
Site cluster: Plymouth area	*00*
17A Stoke Point	00

Contents

18	Wembury and Bovisand	00
19	Plymouth area	00
20	Plymbridge Woods	00

Site cluster: Dartmoor   00

21	Dartmoor area: general introduction	00
21A	Haytor, Emsworthy Mire and Yarner Wood	00
21B	Venford-Swincombe	00
21C	Soussons and Postbridge district	00
21D	Fernworthy Reservoir and Plantation	00
21E	Okehampton: high moors around Cranmere and Okement Valley Woods	00
21F	Tavy Cleave, West Dartmoor	00
21G	Burrator Reservoir and woodlands	00
21H	Piles Copse, Harford Moor and Three Barrows	00
21J	Steps Bridge and Dunsford Woods	00
21K	Hembury Woods	00

CORNWALL   00

22	St John's and Millbrook Lakes, Lynher and Tamar Estuaries: general introduction	00
22A	St John's and Millbrook Lake	00
22B	The Lynher	00
22C	The Tamar	00
22D	Lopwell and Upper Tavy Estuary	00
23	Rame Head, Whitsand Bay and Looe	00

Site cluster: Bodmin Moor and central Cornwall   00

24	Siblyback and Colliford Lakes	00
25	Upper Fowey Valley, Dozmary Pool and Moorland	00
26	Crowdy Reservoir and Davidstow Airfield	00
26A	Goss Moor	00
27	Par Beach and Pool	00
27A	Porthpean, St Austell Bay and Pentewan	00

Site cluster: Lizard Peninsula and Fal Estuary   00

28	Gerrans Bay and Nare Head	00
29	Fal Estuary, Carrick Roads complex	00
29A	Boscawen Park, Truro	00
30	Falmouth, The Bay and Rosemullion	00
30A	Argal and College Reservoirs	00
31	Stithians Reservoir	00
32	The Lizard	00
32A	Loe Pool	00

Site cluster: West Cornwall   00

33	Marazion Marsh, Mount's Bay and waterfront to Newlyn and Mousehole	00
33A	Drift Reservoir	00
34	Porthgwarra and Land's End area	00
34A	Sennen area	00

Contents

35	The Isles of Scilly	00
35A	Pelagic seabird trips (other than those launched from Scilly)	00
36	St Ives Island and Bay	00
37	Pendeen Watch	00
38	Hayle Estuary (Including Carnsew Pool and Copperhouse Creek)	00

Site cluster: North Cornwall coast — 00

39	Newquay district	00
39A	Trevose Head	00
40	Camel Estuary, Treraven Meadow, Clapper and Amble Marshes	00

Site cluster: Bude and north-west Devon — 00

41	Bude district	00

CORNWALL/DEVON BORDER — **00**

42	Tamar Lakes	00

DEVON (NORTH COAST AND INLAND) — **00**

43	Roadford Reservoir	00
44	Hartland Point and district	00
45	Lundy	00

Site cluster: North Devon — 00

46	Taw – Torridge Estuary	00
47	North Devon Coast (Morte Point – Lynton)	00
48	Rackenford, Knowstone and Hare's Down	00
49	Meeth Quarry, Hatherleigh	00
49A	Shobrooke Park, Crediton	00

Top sites for disabled access — **00**

Top sites for public transport — **00**

Thirty species to see in Devon and Cornwall — **00**

List of organisations and other useful links — **00**

References — **00**

Glossary — **00**

Code of conduct for birdwatchers — **00**

Devon, Cornwall and Isles of Scilly bird list — **00**

Index to species — **00**

ACKNOWLEDGEMENTS

We would like to thank the following people for their invaluable help, expertise, kindness, suggestions and patience with us while updating this version of *Where to Watch Birds in Devon and Cornwall*: Paul Boulden, Bob Bosisto, Darrell Clegg, Pete Combridge, Phil Edmonds, Alison Hill, Adrian Langdon, John Rance, Steve Rogers, Mike Simmonds, Vic Tucker, Mike Langman, Will Salmon, Chris Townend and Steve Wait.

FOREWORD

When the late Dave Norman and I first pitched our idea of a regional site guide for birdwatchers to (then) Croom Helm way back in the early 1980s, we could never have envisaged it would endure into a sixth edition, nor spawn a whole series of titles covering all the regions nationwide: such is the popularity of our original concept.

The first edition printed in hardback dealt with relatively few sites. The second edition was paperback, greatly expanded the original and also introduced new ideas. Our continuous desire to improve, innovate and introduce new or (more rarely) delete sites as circumstances demand while keeping information current and as reliable as possible has, I believe, been a cornerstone in contributing to the success of this – and indeed all the other titles in this informative series.

Our successors Sara (Cornwall) and Kevin (Devon) have, where required, updated all aspects of the text, including adding new sites, information and, yes, omitting a few others while implementing other changes to the format. It never fails to amaze me just how many truly significant changes occur throughout our region between each edition. This edition, 16 years on since the fifth, is no exception. Sara and Kevin are also acknowledging modern technology by introducing 'what3words', a free app which can be used on a mobile phone to help locate venues and car parks. When used in conjunction with the book and the detailed access section, this makes for a helpful addition to the sixth edition of the book, which will also be available as an ebook.

It is with confidence I feel the baton has been passed, so you the reader can benefit from the invaluable information contained within the following pages. I wish you all the very best of birding from here in the far South West.

Vic Tucker

INTRODUCTION

The object of this book is to guide the reader to areas of ornithological interest in the two counties of the extreme south-west of Britain, Devon and Cornwall, and their offshore islands. The information contained in the text is the distillation of thousands of hours of birdwatching experience in the region by the four authors. Our aim has been to make this book really useful by including local knowledge, the tricks of the trade, developed over the years with a 'feel' of when and in what conditions an area is most worth visiting.

Information on occurrences is based on events over the first two decades of this century, during which birdwatching has continued to develop as a mass hobby, although we have also tried to indicate the latest trends and discoveries. We have selected areas which have proved consistently worth visiting. Many species are widespread, but our chosen locations are based on the following rules.

1. Those which hold a high density of birds, whether breeding, migrating or wintering.
2. Those which form a specialised habitat where bird species occur which might not be found elsewhere.
3. Areas which are representative of their type, e.g. a wood with a good range of birds which might also occur in less accessible areas nearby.

Despite more than 40 years passing since the first edition, there remains ample scope for discovery in the region by visiting little-studied districts, or by visiting well-known sites during different conditions or times of year from other bird-watchers. Knowledge of the distribution and movements of birds can progress only if someone is prepared to try out ideas. It is not enough to know that a locality is good for seeing birds. At most birdwatching sites, factors such as tides and winds, as well as season, are of paramount importance in planning your visit. Much valuable information is obtained from county bird reports, but these assume quite a high degree of knowledge. It is not their function to explain in detail the background behind records, or to cover ancillary factors such as timing a wader-watch for high tide. Birdwatching visitors with limited time to spare will find our treatment of these topics particularly useful in planning their stay.

County bird reports, detailing annual occurrences are produced by Devon Birds and the Cornwall Bird Watching and Preservation Society (CBWPS), two parallel organisations through which regular birdwatching excursions take place in both counties. The national Royal Society for the Protection of Birds (RSPB) also has branches throughout the country that are particularly helpful to children, and beginners of all ages, the Wildlife Trusts similarly. Membership of any of these organisations furthers conservation efforts, helping to protect both the birds themselves and the habitats on which they rely.

FEATURES OF THE REGION'S BIRDLIFE

As the mildest part of Britain, the region plays host to many wintering birds which normally move further south, including waders and regular Firecrest, Blackcap and Chiffchaff; in severe winters, large numbers of birds can arrive from the east coast to seek ice-free conditions. Areas of extensive farming with overgrown hedges remain, especially in coastal areas, holding a good variety of small birds.

Introduction

Extensive valley woodlands, particularly on moorland fringes, hold many breeding residents and summer migrant songbirds, plus a healthy population of larger birds such as Buzzard, Sparrowhawk and Raven. Many once widespread species, such as Cuckoo and Willow Warbler, are now best found in these upland areas. The higher moors form a southern outpost of several breeding species usually found in Scotland and the Pennines, although for how much longer is uncertain. The moors are the source for much of the freshwater habitat in the region, with fast-flowing rivers a feature, but lowland lakes and reservoirs are scarce. Hundreds of miles of rocky coast with offshore islands hold a number of seabird colonies, while protruding headlands near feeding and migration routes enable a wide range of these birds to be seen passing in spring and autumn. In winter sheltered bays hold populations of grebe and diver species. Our southerly position means that spring often arrives early (from late February) and that autumn birds linger well into November; it also makes the region an arrival point for southern migrants such as Golden Oriole and Hoopoe in small numbers each spring. As we stand facing the New World, American vagrants are noted most autumns after westerly winds, while eastern species drop in before running out of land.

POPULATION CHANGES

Since the first edition, one of the most visible changes in the region's birdlife has been the establishment of the graceful Little Egret, formerly a rarity. At some of our larger estuaries night roosts exceed 100 birds, with breeding now widespread. Initially mass post-breeding dispersals of young birds from northern France arrived from late summer and stayed to winter, a pattern more recently repeated by Cattle Egret, which has bred in both counties. Great White Egret and Glossy Ibis may be on the same path ...

The natural return of the Cornish Chough has been a much-celebrated conservation and cultural event, with more than 50 pairs now present and a return to Devon imminent. Also making a comeback thanks to farmers and conservationists is the rare Cirl Bunting, found in no other part of Britain, with more than 1,000 pairs in south Devon and a reintroduced population thriving in south Cornwall. Another reintroduced species, Red Kite, is now a familiar sight although still a very rare breeder. The spring movement through the region is so great that any location could see a bird overhead, with hundreds congregating in west Cornwall.

Mediterranean Gull, another previously rare visitor, has become ever more widespread as breeding colonies develop in other regions of the UK.

Dartford Warbler, benefiting from mild winters, has also greatly increased its range and numbers throughout the region, despite being knocked back by cold periods in 2010 and 2011.

The globally critically endangered Balearic Shearwater is a regular visitor to south-west coastal waters, chiefly in summer and autumn, with warming seas bringing with them larger numbers of Cory's and Great Shearwater and increasing records of previously extremely rare seabirds. Rat eradication from Lundy and St Agnes has led to significant increases in breeding Manx Shearwater, European Storm Petrel and Puffin.

On the debit side, Wood Warbler, Ring Ouzel, Lapwing and Curlew, species listed with conservation concern in previous editions, are now precariously hanging on as breeding species, with many of our most anticipated summer migrants such as Cuckoo, Spotted Flycatcher and Swift suffering long-term declines. These declines are mirrored among many of our marine, woodland and farmland species, but as is highlighted above, conservation actions show recovery is possible. Many of our sites are fantastic nature reserves protecting rare and specialised species but for common species to remain common, conservation is need across the landscape.

The words below are from the first edition, written more than 40 years ago; they unfortunately still ring true.

'Oil pollution at sea is sadly regular, with every year bringing threats of major spillages, while the continued washing out of waste oil from ships' tanks, less noticed by the media, ensures regular seabird casualties. We also see river pollution by agricultural and industrial waste products; some lakes and waterways suffer toxic algal blooms caused by nitrate concentrations. Mass tourism has driven breeding terns and waders off mainland beaches; other large-scale amenity developments from water sports in estuaries to proposed woodland leisure parks all threaten valuable habitats, and firm conservation policies are ever more vital. Some local authorities, as well as the traditional conservation bodies, have, however, seen the benefits of positive habitat creation and management to attract both wildlife and visitors to their districts.'

CLIMATE AND GEOGRAPHY: SOME GENERAL POINTS

Geographers separate Devon and Cornwall from the rest of southern England by the 'Tees–Exe line' drawn on a map from Teesmouth in north-east England to the Exe Estuary in south Devon. To the west and north of the line lie upland regions with hills, rocks and deep offshore seas; to the east and south lie mainly lowlands and shallow muddy coasts. The peninsula is therefore classed with Wales, northern England and Scotland as a hill area. The hills and the position facing the Atlantic ensure a mild, damp and windy climate; severe gales are frequent in winter on exposed coasts and high hills, limiting tree growth and leading to boggy ground conditions because of the high rainfall. Snow and ice can occur on the mainland, particularly on the moors where snowfalls are sometimes very large, but thaws usually arrive swiftly, especially in the coastal lowlands. Prolonged hard frosts are increasingly rare in the region, although always uncommon in the far west of Cornwall and very rare on the Isles of Scilly. Most of the region's rivers are short and fast-flowing, with few forming large coastal estuaries and others flowing into flooded rias; the weathered granite masses of Bodmin Moor in Cornwall and Dartmoor in Devon are the origin of most of the larger rivers. High Willhays on Dartmoor (about 627m) is the region's highest point. Exmoor, which lies across the north Devon–Somerset boundary, falls partly within our scope. The sandy heathland ridges, valleys and chalk cliffs of east Devon are geographically distinct from the rest of the region.

HOW TO USE THIS BOOK

As with the authors of this book's previous editions, we often meet inexperienced but keen birdwatchers, though these days they may be more reliant on apps and the internet than field guides. Many are still frustrated and disappointed by inadequate and out-of-date information; for instance, if a book says, 'Chough found on Cornwall's cliffs', that leaves 422 miles of Cornish coast to search – and where do you start looking in 400 square miles of heather, rocks and bog to find a Cuckoo on Dartmoor? They are also given the impression that there will always be birds at a particular area in all conditions – yet very few spring migrants, for example, will be seen arriving at southerly coastal watchpoints in an opposing northerly gale, or sometimes even in ideal conditions! Birds undertake complex movements influenced by many factors such as weather, tides and seasons; human disturbance may also cause them to change quarters (for example, a group of ducks flying from one lake to another when disturbed by sailing). We have set out to highlight these factors to give you the best chance of success at each area you visit.

Throughout the text we have given measurements in those units most readily understood by the majority of English readers. Longer distances are normally stated in miles, followed by the metric equivalent in kilometres; shorter distances are stated in metres. Altitudes are given in metres, as on all modern Ordnance Survey maps. For surface areas, we have given the imperial measurement, followed by the metric one. For parking areas, what3words and some post codes have been added to make it easier to find places using today's available technology.

HABITAT

This section aims to paint a 'word picture' of each area and its scenery. The extent of the area covered and main bird habitat zones are indicated. Where the birdwatcher is likely to see other easily visible wildlife, such as dolphins, seals or scarcer butterflies, a brief note is often included.

SPECIES

This section does not list every species found in an area; for reasons of space, common birds are usually excluded. We have aimed to give a sample of the main species of interest, and what they are doing (breeding, moving through or turning up in cold weather). Frequency of occurrence and scale of numbers involved will guide the visitor on what to expect – whether single birds, small parties or flocks of hundreds of a particular species. A few ornithological 'goodies' which might be encountered are also mentioned.

The text is arranged in broadly chronological order to help the reader to follow the pattern of bird events through the year. At the start of the section, some reference is made to the general ornithological importance of the area. No attempt is made to give specific dates, as the 'Calendar' section gives further details on when each species usually occurs.

TIMING

How to avoid a wasted visit! How to judge appropriate weather conditions for what you hope to see; bird migration is heavily dependent on weather and a mass of birds along the coastline one day may all have departed by next morning if

How to use this book

conditions change. How to judge when particular groups of species will be most active; a dawn watch, for instance, often yields rich results. How to plan your visit to avoid human disturbance which may frighten birds off or make them difficult to see (do not forget that one form of disturbance is thoughtless birdwatchers!). How to pick tides to see roosting or feeding waders on different estuaries. Accurate use of this section is essential if you want best results from the book.

ACCESS

How to get there from main towns and A-roads, down minor roads, and what paths to take when you arrive. Often a maze of country roads leads to a birdwatching site; we have described one practical route. Use this section in conjunction with the map provided. Note: Special access restrictions, such as a military firing range or a wardened nature reserve, may mean that you need to plan your visit in advance, so check this section for possible problems beforehand. If visiting in a group as part of an organised club, contact should be made with wardens of protected areas before arranging visits, as these may lead to overcrowding or disturbance at popular visiting seasons. A visit may also be spoilt if viewing hides are overcrowded.

Addresses and organisations responsible for these sites are listed in the text. It should also be recognised that Forestry England plantations do not necessarily have public access or rights of way, except where stated.

Some private sites also accept visits by lone birdwatchers but should be consulted to check suitability for organised visits, e.g. some public houses situated by riverbanks accept casual use of their car parking by birdwatchers but would not expect large numbers to use the site without consultation. If an area includes private farmland, you should in all cases seek permission from the farmer before deviating from public footpaths.

To follow detailed directions, a 1:50,000 Ordnance Survey map will be a great help; the number of the appropriate map and a four-figure grid reference for the particular area described are given beside the heading for each locality. With many walkers now using digital maps on mobile phones, we have also included what-3words information to make it easier to find places without needing to carry bulky paper maps. However, phone signal can be limited in some areas of the region, so it's a good idea to check before going that you know exactly how the apps work and that you have the places marked.

In recent years, accelerated erosion of coastal land by high tides and storms has caused access difficulties at a number of sites; these have been indicated in the text where information was available at time of writing. Updates should be sought locally to ensure that footpaths are open at these localities. The effects forecast from climate change suggest this will be a continuing feature of coastal birdwatching.

CALENDAR

This is a quick-reference summary section, so all information has been condensed and abbreviated as much as possible. The calendar year has been split into seasons which relate to the majority of ornithological events, although obviously some species will not fit this pattern exactly. Winter is December–February as far as the larger numbers of winter bird visitors to our region are concerned; spring is March–May as far as most arriving migrants are concerned; summer, in terms of maximum breeding activity and little migration movement, can be extended only over June and July, with some species starting to move even in the later part of this period; autumn is protracted, with migration from August to November, although different groups of species peak at different periods within this. These are not, it should be noted, the same as normal human definitions of seasons. Many people, for example, might take a 'summer holiday' in late August, but if they visited a Guillemot or other seabird colony then they would find that the birds had finished breeding and moved far out to sea. To avoid confusion, we have repeated these groupings of months by name in each Calendar section.

Within the section we have included the most likely peak periods for each species or group of species; if no further qualifying comment is made, the bird concerned may be looked for with equal chance of success at any time during the season, or peak numbers may occur randomly whenever conditions are most suitable during these months.

KEY TO THE MAPS

- ⓟ Car park
- ⓗ Hide
- ⓧ Viewpoint
- ⓥ Visitor Centre
- ⓟⒽ Public house
- 🗼 Lighthouse
- ⓦⒸ Public toilet
- ⒸⒼ Coastguard
- ⒼⒸ Golf course
- ✝ Church
- Towns
- Conifers

- Deciduous
- Marsh
- Scrub
- Reedbeds
- Lakes
- Sea
- Railway
- Main road
- Minor road
- Track
- Footpath
- Embankment

MAP OF THE REGION

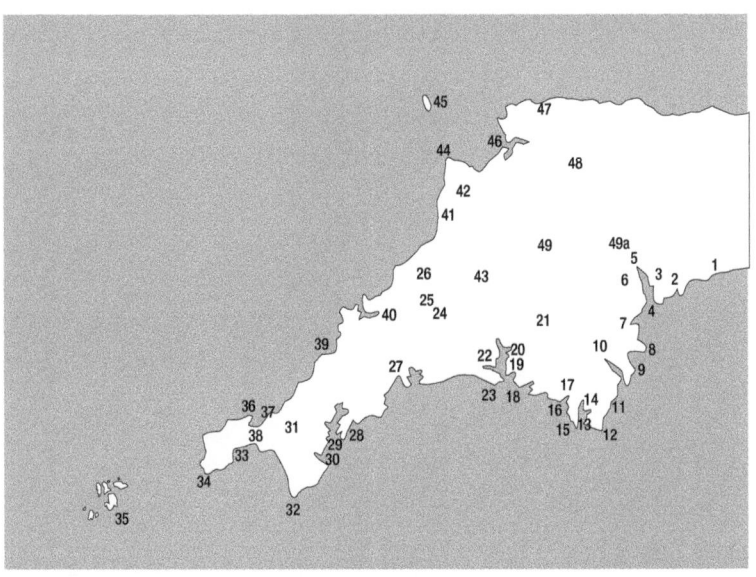

DEVON (SOUTH COAST AND DARTMOOR)

1 THE AXE ESTUARY AREA, SEATON AND BEER HEAD

OS grid ref: SY2590
Postcode: EX12 (for more detail and what3words, see Access section)

HABITAT
In the south-eastern corner of Devon, the Axe Valley provides extensive grazing meadows, wetlands and raised saltmarsh, alongside a 1 mile (1.6km) long open estuary. The mudflats are about 200m wide, with the Seaton Wetlands and extensive grazing marshes on the west side separated from the estuary by an old railway embankment now used for tourist trams. The tram company also runs birdwatching trips, providing unique views of the area.

The marshes are criss-crossed with a series of ditches and pools, with larger wetlands at Black Hole Marsh and the Borrow Pit. To the north of the estuary are numerous drainage channels and several small reedbeds, bordered at the north side by the A3052 main road. The estuary narrows towards a harbour and the open sea, with high chalk cliffs rising to the east. This area, which features 6 miles (9.6km) of coastline where large sections of rock strata have slid towards the sea, is the largest coastal landslip in Europe and is of great botanical and entomological interest. To the west of the estuary is the town of Seaton, overlooked by the bulk of Beer Head. The cove at the west end of the town's seafront is known as Seaton Hole. The small, partly enclosed bay of Beer is bordered on the east side by sloping Jubilee Gardens. Beer Head is a 130m-high chalk cliff; at the foot, adjacent to the shore, lies a collapsed landslip area of boulders and dense scrub. The east flank of the headland, slightly sheltered from prevailing winds, is bordered by hedgerows and small bushy areas. Beyond Beer Head, high exposed clifftops backed by agricultural land extend west towards Sidmouth, interrupted after 2km by the steep-sided Branscombe Valley.

North of the grazing marshes and the A3052, Lower Bruckland Farm contains an area of artificial fishponds that attracts species otherwise rare in the valley, along with dragonfly species including Scarce Chaser and Small Red-eyed Damselfly.

East Devon District Council, working with local conservation bodies, has carried out considerable work to improve this area for wildlife and visitors, and the whole area is designated as Seaton Wetlands Local Nature Reserve. There are five bird hides and nearly 2.5 miles (4km) of level trails and boardwalks suitable for wheelchairs, bikes and pushchairs. The reedbeds and grazing marshes on the east bank remain private, with some wildfowling in winter.

Devon (south coast and Dartmoor)

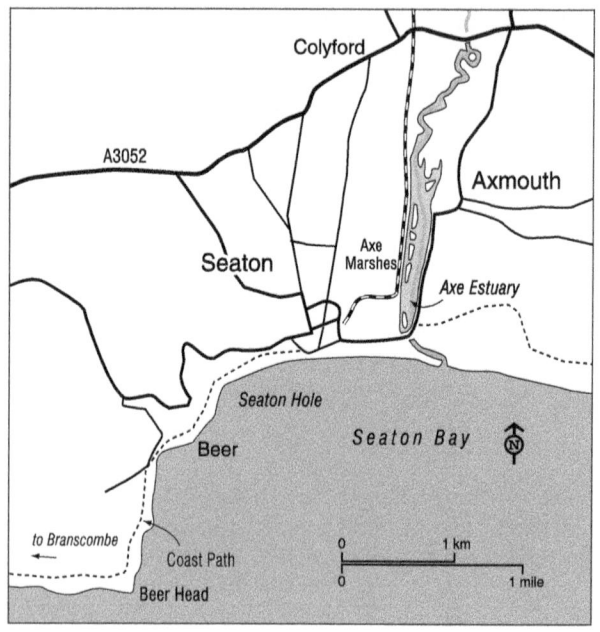

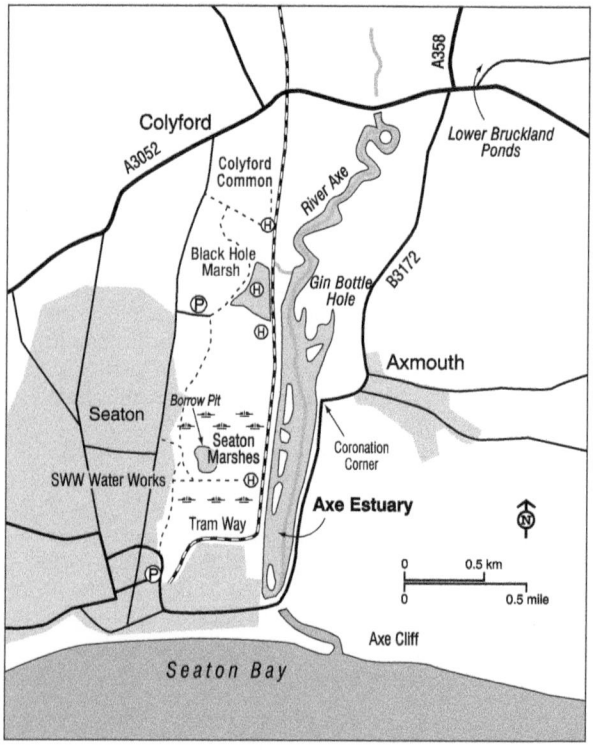

SPECIES

Around 200 species a year are typically recorded within a 3.1-mile (5km) radius of the estuary mouth. The estuary and marshes always attract attention, with further interest including offshore wintering populations of waterbirds, gale-blown seabird passage and passerine arrivals along the clifftops. Spring records have included Purple and Night Herons, White Stork, Spoonbill, Long-tailed Skua, Gull-billed Tern and a trio of roosting Alpine Swifts, and that was just in one year!

The estuary attracts a variety of wintering wildfowl and waders. The wide grazing meadows hold dabbling ducks, with up to 500 Wigeon and 100 Teal. Lapwing, Curlew and Black-tailed Godwit are conspicuous, Snipe and Jack Snipe less so, occurring among the reeds and in the ditches. Water Rail and Reed Bunting, joined by a few Cetti's Warbler, share these habitats. Sheltered bushes such as those near the Borrow Pit and sewage works harbour Common and, occasionally, Siberian Chiffchaffs at the end of the year. Water Pipit is seen throughout winter, especially on Colyford Marshes; although numbers vary, the Axe is one of the most reliable locations in the region to find them. There may be half a dozen Water Pipit in a good winter, with one or two staying to assume pink-breasted spring breeding plumage. Beware confusion with Scandinavian Rock Pipit, which also winters in numbers. One winter, two Asian rarities appeared: an Isabelline Wheatear and an Eastern Yellow Wagtail.

Cold weather brings flocks of Fieldfare and Redwing into the valley. Open meadows may hold one or two Ruff, and in prolonged freezing spells they may be joined by wild swans or 'grey' geese. On the open estuary, Shelduck, gulls and common waders such as Redshank and Curlew are easily seen, while several Little Grebe, Cormorant, Little Egret and Grey Heron hunt in the main channel. Various other dabbling ducks and waders drop in, especially on Black Hole Marsh, with Goosander on the estuary. Diving ducks are not usually found here but occasionally arrive at Lower Bruckland. Gatherings of gulls on the estuary are always worth scanning, with increasing numbers of Mediterranean present. Caspian, Glaucous and Iceland Gulls are virtually annual, and occasional rarities have included American Herring, Bonaparte's and Laughing Gulls. The gulls often bathe and preen on available mudflats, visible from the Tower Hide and roadside viewpoints. At the west end of the area, Beer and the coast towards Branscombe can prove interesting in winter. Black Redstart may be found anywhere along the coast, with Beer beach and Seaton Hole favoured locations. The ornamental Jubilee Gardens at Beer seafront may shelter a Firecrest or two. At sea, a few Shags feed and winter visitors can include Great Crested Grebe and parties of Common Scoter, which have been joined by Velvet and Surf Scoters. From here westward towards Branscombe various divers, grebes or seaducks might also be found. Red-throated Divers can occasionally number dozens in midwinter, with Great Northern Divers more numerous towards spring.

Spring brings a chance of a scarce heron such as Spoonbill, but Night and Squacco Herons have also been recorded. Garganey may arrive with other migrant ducks such as Gadwall or Pintail, and Shelduck prospect nest-burrows on nearby hillsides. Little Ringed Plover is one of the earlier migrant arrivals, with small parties turning up every spring. Common Sandpiper is often seen on the estuary, while flocks of Whimbrel and breeding-plumaged Dunlin drop in on the wetlands. Wheatear and a few Whinchat stop off, Sand Martin move through to their colonies upriver, while Reed and Sedge Warblers arrive in the reedbeds, alongside noisy Cetti's Warbler. Increasing numbers of Red Kite pass over, with several records annually of Osprey and Marsh Harrier. Although these species do not usually linger in spring, an Osprey often remains to feed for longer in autumn.

Midsummer is not a very active time on the estuary, although piebald juvenile Shelduck feature, a few non-breeding Black-tailed Godwits remain, and Green Sandpiper start to pass through. Devon's other larger resident species are always visible, including Raven, Kestrel, Buzzard and Sparrowhawk soaring overhead. A dusk visit should be rewarded by a ghostly Barn Owl. Little Grebe, a scarce breeder in Devon, usually nests at the Borrow Pit. The woods behind Axmouth hold a nesting colony of Grey Heron and Little Egret, with Cattle Egret an increasing possibility. The cliffs hold a few Fulmar and Shag, with Yellowhammer on the farmland.

At the end of summer and early autumn the area's migrant interest picks up again. The development of Black Hole Marsh has increased the variety and numbers of waders reported, although birds can be found throughout the valley. At peak periods both godwits, Greenshank and Ruff may all feed with commoner waders, and a Wood Sandpiper may be present among the Green Sandpipers; an exceptional 44 Wood Sandpipers were present one August. The very rare Solitary Sandpiper, from America, has been recorded with Western, Least, Semipalmated and Baird's Sandpipers also hailing from across the Atlantic. In late summer, Water Rails, and perhaps a Spotted Crake, may emerge from the reeds, and juvenile Yellow-legged Gulls start to arrive, especially after poor weather. Such conditions brought an Audouin's Gull to the marshes one August afternoon, one of the area's premier rarity sightings. Overhead, large numbers of hirundines, thousands at times, gather to feed before migration, perhaps attracting a passing Hobby. Once they were joined by another American vagrant, a Chimney Swift. Migrant Yellow Wagtails gather in the meadows prior to roosting in the reedbeds, with high *sweep* calls at dusk, but most leave by mid-autumn. A few other migrants such as Wheatear and Whinchat are seen passing through the marshes.

At migration periods Axe Cliff and Beer Head can be worth checking, with passerine migrants passing overhead and using clifftop fields and bushes. In an otherwise straight stretch of coast, Beer Head is the only natural focal point for birds moving through. The eastern slope of the headland, containing some partly sheltered vegetation, is most likely to hold any warblers or flycatchers that have made overnight arrivals. Those arriving in the dense landslip bushes at the foot of the high cliffs may be hard to locate, but they tend to filter up along the clifftop hedgerows during the morning. Rare migrants may include a Hoopoe, with Great Spotted Cuckoo, Iberian Chiffchaff and Blyth's Reed Warbler all having been discovered. Small numbers of a range of warblers may be joined by Whinchat, Redstart and Pied Flycatcher on spring and autumn migrations. Firecrests are occasional in spring and more likely during the second half of autumn. The same applies to Ring Ouzel, very localised coastal migrants in our region, which favour the cliff slopes. Small parties may occur in autumn, but spring records are most likely to be of single birds.

Open fields behind the clifftops provide good habitat for buntings and passing chats, wagtails and pipits, perhaps chased by a Merlin. Buff-breasted Sandpiper, Dotterel and Ortolan Bunting have all been seen. Peak overhead passage on late autumn mornings may include hundreds of finches and pipits, generally moving west or south-west. Warblers and flycatchers have also been found in the trees around the waterworks at the bottom of Branscombe Valley west of Beer; Yellow-browed Warblers have overwintered here.

Seawatchers mainly view from shelters in Seaton, picking up seabirds predominantly moving west through Lyme Bay. While totals do not match those from the region's major headlands, regular watches in rough weather have produced a range of species, especially from late summer onwards. Onshore gales and rain may produce something of interest at any season, spring skuas for example. A telescope is essential here as moving birds are not necessarily close to the shore. Viewpoints lower down near the beach are likely to be easier for picking out seabirds than watching from the high clifftops, although some elevation is helpful to search for wintering divers. Manx Shearwaters visit from late spring, occasionally in their hundreds, and a few Balearic Shearwaters are recorded on most watches between July and September. Larger shearwaters are very rarely seen at this site, as Lyme Bay is too sheltered to pick up these deepwater visitors. Occasional storm-blown European or Leach's Storm Petrels occur. Skuas are regular in single figures, usually Arctic or Great (Pomarine are occasional, mainly in late spring) along with a trickle of the commoner terns. Scarcer visitors in late autumn might include a Little Gull or Grey Phalarope.

TIMING

There is something of interest all year. The marshes can produce large numbers of wildfowl and open-ground species driven from further north and east by ice and snow, particularly when this lasts for more than a few days. Thousands of birds may then shelter in the valley. Most of the unusual wildfowl recorded here come at such times, although periods of extensive flooding can also produce species not normally present. Southerly winds in spring produce the chance of 'overshooting' rarities such as Spoonbill or Hoopoe. For gulls, later afternoons and states of the tide when some mud is exposed, are usually best. On sunny days try to avoid looking westward across the mudflats against late afternoon glare. Evening viewing across the meadows might still produce a sighting of a scarce Barn Owl. Avoid highest tides on the estuary, when birds tend to gather on Black Hole Marsh, although a rising tide pushes waders up towards Axmouth, and ducks, Wigeon in particular, might be seen at close range swimming in the estuary.

As usual, migrant songbirds are best sought in the early mornings. The normal conditions for migration apply to passerine 'falls' on Beer Head: high pressure and winds with a southerly or easterly element to bring in chats, warblers and flycatchers overnight, with reduced visibility encouraging them to land and remain in the area. On mornings when an overnight arrival of small migrants has taken place, two or three hours may be needed to allow those birds that have landed in bushes at the foot of the cliff to work their way upwards onto the Head itself. Light to moderate headwinds and reasonably clear visibility enable overhead coasting passage of day-flying migrants along the clifftops in autumn. Mist and/or rain, combined with strong (force 6 upwards) winds with a southerly element, are likely to drive seabirds in off Seaton front. In such conditions a sheltered viewpoint is required. In other conditions passing seabirds are most likely to be too far out to watch. Early mornings are generally the most productive for seawatches.

For wintering divers and seaducks off the cliffs west of Beer, a fairly calm sea is needed, with overcast conditions ideally giving flat, even light, enabling more distant birds on the sea to be picked out by telescope. The high line of cliffs provides coastal waters with some shelter from northerly winds.

ACCESS

Axe Estuary The coastal town of Seaton, adjacent to the estuary, lies off the A3052 between Sidmouth and Lyme Regis. To reach the east bank of the estuary, continue east along the main A3052 to cross the Axe at the north end of the marshes near Colyford. Beyond the bridge take the B3172 south towards Axmouth. Stop and view the meadows at convenient points along this road; there are very few public footpaths through the meadows on this eastern side. Roadside lay-bys adjacent to farm gateways enable some scanning but vehicles should not be left there because of the need for access. From Axmouth village the road runs directly beside the mudflats down to the beach, giving easy car-window views all the way, suitable for disabled visitors. Pull-in points are present every few hundred metres. Axmouth bend, known locally as **Coronation Corner (EX12 4AE, ignites.wipe.regret)**, level with the top of the estuary, can be productive as views can also be obtained upriver, especially of gulls bathing and loafing. It can also viewed from the Tower Hide (see below).

Seaton Marshes (EX12 2LQ, instincts.open.smaller) For the southern section of grazing marshes, cross the bridge at the lower end of the estuary and continue along Harbour Road into Seaton town. After 400m turn right at the roundabout and then next right into the large, signposted Harbour Road pay-and-display car park. Follow the roadside pavement beyond the far end of the car park and adjoining children's play area; a public footpath is signposted to the right. This leads onto the level path overlooking the grazing marshes, following the marked route of the Wessex Cycle Track. After 800m the path reaches a small lane adjoining the perimeter fence of the sewage works. Turn right and walk through the wooden gate into the signposted Seaton Marshes Local Nature Reserve. From here, a level permissive path (suitable for disabled access), screened by blinds to prevent disturbance of birds feeding on the marshes, runs across the meadows to the hide at the end, which has a ramped entry. Gaps in the blinds along the pathway provide close views of duck and wader flocks on flooded areas in winter.

A hide is situated beside the tramway embankment, permitting wide views across both the adjacent estuary and saltmarsh ahead, and the adjoining freshwater pools in the meadows. At the start of the Seaton reserve path, adjacent to the South West Water treatment works, a side path leads past the Borrow Pit area and provides views into areas of wet vegetation.

For those with limited mobility, a small parking area has been provided opposite the water treatment works, next to the start of the reserve path. To reach this by road, continue north from the Harbour car park, turning right at the roundabout onto Colyford Road. Keep on this road until you see to the right signs for Axe Vale Caravan Park and the football ground; here, turn right into Hillymead residential cul-de-sac. Bear left down the narrow Salt Pan Lane for 50m until you reach the parking spaces marked on the right, opposite the waterworks entrance.

The area of grazing marshes with lagoons and scrapes, together with improved access managed by East Devon District Council, gives much better potential for birdwatching visitors than previously existed. Views across the area might also be obtained from the Seaton–Colyton tramway, which hosts birdwatching 'specials' as well as running daily between April and October (with a reduced service at other times of the year). For more information see tram.co.uk or telephone 01297 20375. The tram entrance is immediately adjacent to Harbour Road car park. Arranged birdwatching trips on this line, accompanied by local observers, are advertised to the general public. Seaton Tramway have also opened their new Wetlands Halt, allowing direct access from the trams to Seaton Wetlands, ideal for those with limited mobility.

Black Hole Marsh (EX12 2XA, solves.glows.wrenching) This recently created wetland is connected to the estuary, with a tidal gate allowing water levels to be managed. The Tower Hide in the south-east corner allows for views across this area and the top of the estuary, while the Island Hide is located in the centre of the marsh and provides panoramic, 360-degree views. There is no path between Seaton Marshes and here. To travel between the two you will need to use the Seaton to Colyford Road (via car or on foot), approximately 0.6 miles (1km). Heading north from Seaton to Colyford, turn into Seaton Cemetery on the right and continue through to use the reserve's car park.

Colyford Common This reserve is best reached by following the cycleway north from Black Hole Marsh but can also be reached from the road north towards Colyford village. Near the minor junction with Pope's Lane on the south side of the village is a small roadside lay-by, for no more than three or four cars. The signposted reserve entry is opposite here, across the road. Alternatively, park on the roadside in the village where unrestricted, taking care not to block entrances. Walk back 200m along the road. Follow the signposted reserve path which borders the first field, pass through a gate then continue along a boardwalk across flood meadows to the hide near the tramway bank. Beside the hide entrance another path leads north for 200m to a raised viewing platform, providing a different view of the marsh and pools. This area of saltmarsh is regularly flooded by high tides.

Beer and Beer Head (EX12 3AG, crawler.freezing.undertone) can be reached from the west end of Seaton, following signs from the end of the seafront, or direct from A3052 coast road from Exeter towards Seaton, turning south on B3174 into Beer. For **Beer Head**, in the village street turn right towards Beer Clifftop car park on the west side of the town. From there, walk uphill following the lane past a caravan site, over a cattle grid and bear left to follow public bridleway signs across open, grassy fields to the clifftop. Here you connect with the South West Coast Path, which follows the open, exposed cliff edge and borders arable fields. Turning right, at migration times it is worth continuing west for a couple of fields, past the prominent Old Lookout building, scanning fields for open-ground species such as chats, pipits and larks. The kissing gate on the coast path is a convenient finish point if just checking the Head.

After a mile (1.6km) the coast path descends steeply to Branscombe Cove, an area of grassland, scrub and a small waste treatment works, where there is a National Trust car park. Return to the path junction by Beer Head clifftop. Below here a winding path gives access down to the foot of the cliffs and landslip scrub. Most birdwatchers scan the vegetated slopes from here rather than make the descent to the undercliff bushes. Birds tend to move up the slope after arrival. From the clifftop walk back east along the coast path (completing the circuit towards the car park), viewing the partly sheltered area of hedges and bushes on the eastern flank of the headland. **Beer seafront** can be reached by walking down from the car park into the main street, reaching the cove after 100m. Jubilee Gardens are on the left slope. In wet weather the covered shelter next to the gardens provides a good lookout point over the bay.

Lower Bruckland Farm ponds are at the northern edge of the area, north of the A3052 Exeter–Lyme Regis road. After crossing the River Axe eastward at Colyford Bridge, take the second, smaller turn on the left, along minor roads for a mile

(1.6km) to the fish farm. Public footpaths cross the site and there is limited roadside parking on the approach lane.

Seawatching is carried out from various points. At the west end of Seaton seafront, after a roundabout the road rises at Castle Hill. Next to the slope is a thatched public shelter, which provides a vantage point over the bay. Street parking nearby is available at Seafield Road or for limited periods at Sea Hill. Alternatively continue west, turning left towards Beer at the first junction, then left again onto a minor road (Old Beer Road), to reach Seaton Hole at the end of the bay. Limited roadside parking is available near the café. From here, steps lead down through a small copse (which has held migrants, including a Hume's Warbler) towards sea-level rocks. Seabirds may be forced to shelter in the bay in the lee of Beer Head in severe conditions. This end of the area has suffered from cliff subsidence at times and some paths may be closed. The road from here links to the B3174 towards Beer. Seabirds might also be seen from the shelter at Beer seafront and perhaps from Branscombe cove mouth further to the west.

CALENDAR

Resident: Shelduck, Little Grebe, Cormorant, Shag, Grey Heron, Little Egret, Buzzard, Water Rail, Sparrowhawk, Stock Dove, Barn Owl, Kingfisher, Cetti's Warbler, Reed Bunting, Yellowhammer.

December–February: Possible 'grey' geese or wild swans in hard weather, occasional Gadwall, Pintail, Tufted Duck, Wigeon, Teal, Shoveler, Fulmar, Cattle Egret possible at roost, Oystercatcher, Black-tailed Godwit, Curlew, Dunlin, Redshank, Snipe, Green Sandpiper, possible Common Sandpiper, Ruff, Jack Snipe, gulls, Water Pipit, Grey Wagtail, winter thrushes, Black Redstart, Chiffchaff and Firecrest.

March–May: Winter visitors to early April in reduced numbers. Migrants include chance of Garganey; Sand Martin, Wheatear (mid-March onwards), occasional Spoonbill (April–May), Common Sandpiper, Bar-tailed Godwit and Whimbrel (late April onwards), Yellow Wagtail, Reed and Sedge Warblers. Passerine migrant arrivals possible, including warblers and flycatchers along clifftops or in the valley, chiefly April–early May; shearwaters and other seabirds possible later in spring; migrant raptors such as Marsh Harrier and Red Kite.

June–July: Rarer European migrants still possible in June. Black-tailed Godwit, Grey Heron, Shelduck, Sand Martin, Kingfisher, Barn Owl and Little Egret; passage waders return from July.

August–November: Fulmars depart from late September; Hobby and Osprey (August–September), wader passage including Wood Sandpiper mostly August–September, often a Little Stint in September; hirundines and Yellow Wagtail (peak late August); winter visitors arrive from October; migrant passerines possible in coastal bushes; a Pallas's Warbler was once at Coronation Corner and a Dusky Warbler has been trapped on Seaton Marshes; occasional seabird passage offshore in suitable conditions.

Devon (south coast and Dartmoor)

1A TRINITY HILL, AXMINSTER

OS grid ref: SY3196
Postcode: EX13 5SL
what3words: bother.crackles.really

HABITAT
About 2 miles (3.2km) south of Axminster, Trinity Hill is 200m high, an area of heathland with extensive pinewood plantations on its southern and eastern slopes. It is managed by East Devon District Council as a Local Nature Reserve and its crest provides extensive views across the Axe Valley.

SPECIES
Birdwatchers chiefly visit the reserve in summer to seek characteristic heathland nesting species. Nightjar are usually well represented with several breeding pairs. Grasshopper Warblers, patchily distributed breeding birds in the region, can be heard singing in spring, though most will just be pausing on migration. A few pairs of Tree Pipit are generally located around the edge of the heath alongside Stonechat and Linnet. Winter visits can be quiet, but Ravens may *cronk* overhead and the Reed Bunting roost has held wintering Little Bunting.

TIMING
Fine weather without strong winds encourages birds on territory to sit out on exposed stems. Sunset visits, preferably on warm evenings when insect activity is high, are required to watch the Nightjars displaying and feeding.

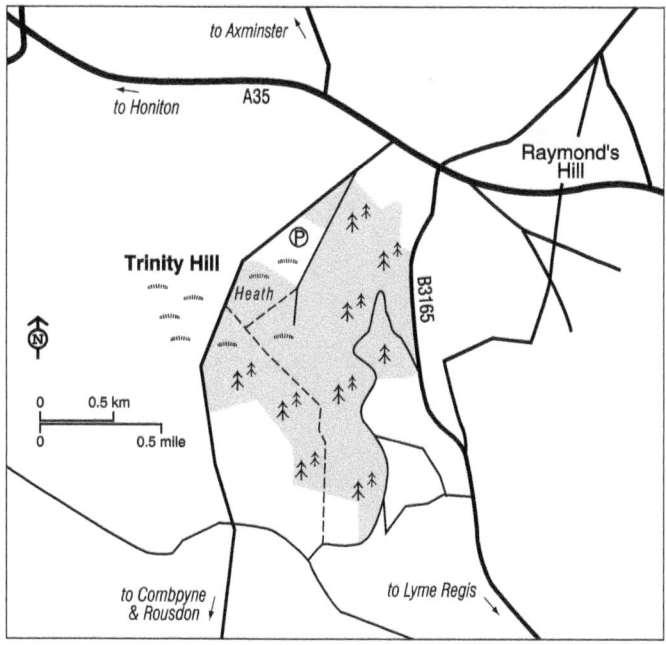

Devon (south coast and Dartmoor)

ACCESS

From Axminster take the A35 east towards Lyme Regis. Just before Raymond's Hill, as you approach the 40mph speed limit sign, turn right along Trinity Hill Road. The turning is signposted to Combpyne and Rousdon. After 0.6 miles (1km) you arrive on the open heath, and the car park is on the left. A network of paths leads around the perimeter of the hill and across the heath on both sides of the road. More gorse clumps are found on the right-hand (west-facing) slope. Take care to avoid disturbance to ground-nesting species.

CALENDAR

Resident: Reed Bunting, Meadow Pipit, Stonechat, Raven.

Summer: Tree Pipit and Nightjar likely from mid- to late spring; Grasshopper Warbler possible, especially Apr–May.

Devon (south coast and Dartmoor)

SITE CLUSTER: EXETER AREA

- **2** Otter Estuary Nature Reserve
- **3** Pebblebed Heaths
- **4** Exe Estuary
- **4A** Exmouth
- **4B** Bowling Green Marsh, Topsham and the Clyst areas
- **4C** Exminster Marshes and the canal
- **4D** Powderham Marshes
- **4E** Powderham and the park
- **4F** Dawlish Warren
- **5** Stoke Canon Meadows and Wood
- **6** Haldon Woods and Little Haldon
- **6A** Chudleigh Knighton Heath and Hennock (see Dartmoor map on page 133)

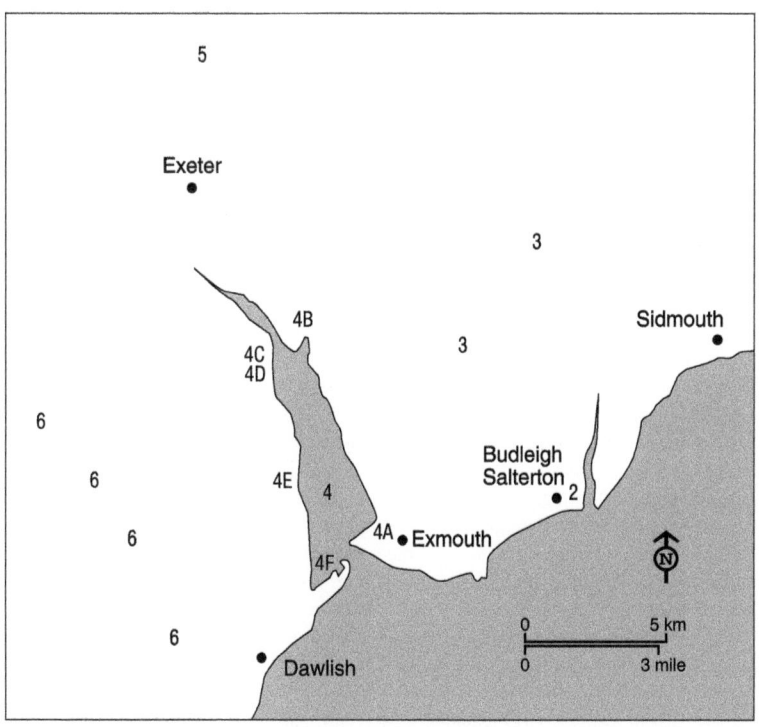

Devon (south coast and Dartmoor)

2 OTTER ESTUARY NATURE RESERVE

OS grid ref: SY0782
Postcode: EX9 6BG
what3words: sunshine.degrading.melt

HABITAT
The east Devon coast between the Axe and Exe valleys chiefly comprises sandstone cliffs up to 170m high, with numerous small coves and coastal stream valleys. The only low-lying area is the Otter, an 800m estuary and raised saltmarsh next to the town of Budleigh Salterton. The pebble beach forms a bar across most of the estuary mouth. Newly created reedbeds and saltmarsh, backed by trees and thickets, border the west side of the river north to White Bridge. Immediately above the open estuary, moving north towards Otterton village, the river is far narrower, with shallow, clear stretches and gravel bars. The Lower Otter Restoration Project has rejuvenated the old riverside fields west of the river, which is bringing considerable benefits for wildlife and visitors alike. Budleigh Salterton itself is well wooded, with large mature gardens and ornamental conifers.

SPECIES
This is a well-known area locally, with a good cross-section of the region's waterside and farmland birds, although none is restricted to this area alone. Interesting residents include Barn Owl, which might be seen over the meadows at dusk, and Kingfishers, which are seen regularly; they move upriver to breed but frequent the saltmarsh channels at other seasons. Grey Wagtails are also widespread here and Dippers are resident on faster-flowing stretches around Otterton and above. The same stretch hosts a reintroduced population of Beavers as well as the river's namesake Otters.

In winter the estuary usually shelters half a dozen Little Grebes, while Cormorants and Grey Herons stand sentinel along the banks, joined by up to 30 Little Egrets. Duck numbers are lower than adjacent estuaries, but up to 400 Wigeon and Teal are present, with smaller numbers of Shoveler and Goosander on occasion. Canada Geese often graze on saltmarsh islands, and flocks of over 300 may visit the flood meadows. Water Rails squeal from the reedbeds. On the narrow mudflats, waders are limited, but numbers are increasingly using the new saltmarsh since the breach in October 2023; Black-tailed Godwit, Dunlin, Oystercatcher, Lapwing, Redshank and Curlew overwinter, with Snipe and perhaps a Common Sandpiper, flying off low with stiff, flickering wingbeats when disturbed. The estuary gull roost may contain one or two Mediterranean Gulls among the Black-headed Gulls, with American Herring, Bonaparte's, Caspian and Glaucous Gulls also recorded. A scan off the beach can be worthwhile; Red-throated and Great Northern Divers are reported in most winters, Shag is present and parties of seaducks may be found. Numbers are now much lower they once were, but up to 100 Common Scoter may be present in a tight black raft, with scarcer Velvet Scoter, Eider and Long-tailed Duck sometimes joining them. The flocks are mostly east of the river and often gather off rocky coves towards Sidmouth. Divers, peaking at 15–20, regularly winter off the coast around Brandy Head and Chiselbury Bay to the east of the estuary;

Devon (south coast and Dartmoor)

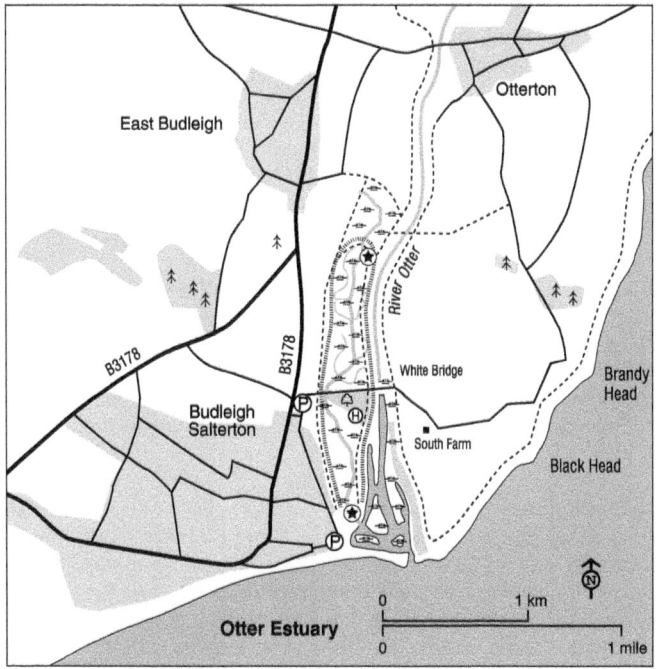

Red-throated is the main species involved and these birds may link with the Exe Estuary/Dawlish Warren population. Nearer, look across to Otterton Ledge rocks, which project seaward on the east side of the river mouth; a few Purple Sandpiper may feed here (although they prefer the rocks off Sidmouth), with Great Northern Diver sometimes close offshore.

Passerine species by the estuary include Meadow and Rock Pipits, with Water Pipit often on Little Marsh, a newly created habitat above White Bridge at the far north of the restoration area. Occasionally Bearded Tits have been found in the small reedbeds, where Reed Buntings are often seen and Cetti's Warblers heard. The town parks and gardens are shelters for Blackcap, Chiffchaff or Firecrest most winters, with Black Redstart another possibility, Ladram Bay being a favoured location.

In spring, as few other gaps occur in the coastal cliffs, the estuary and surrounding fields and bushes attract passerine migrants. Yellow Wagtail and Wheatear turn up in the wetland habitats, while Blackcap, Whitethroat, Willow Warbler and Chiffchaff follow riverbank path bushes and nearby hedges. The district attracts a few rarer migrants: Hoopoe has occasionally been seen, Serin has bred and both Bee-eater and the extremely rare Blue-cheeked Bee-eater have been reported. As with most of Devon's estuaries, spring may also bring a Spoonbill or rarer vagrant of the heron family. Autumn visitors have included flocks of Glossy Ibis and increasing numbers of Cattle Egret. Cliffs east of the Otter as far as Ladram Bay hold breeding seabirds: up to 15 pairs of Fulmar and 30–40 each of Shag and Cormorant.

Cirl Bunting on the farmland, and Grey Heron around the estuary, have recently started breeding as a result of the improved habitats. Inland, small Sand Martin colonies, together with resident Kingfishers, Dippers and Grey Wagtails, make an interesting upriver walk. Autumn brings more varied migration, with two or three Greenshank, their *tew-tew* flight calls ringing over the estuary, and Common and Green Sandpipers and small flocks of species such as Ringed Plover and Turnstone. As with the Axe Estuary, the new wetlands are, however, rapidly changing wader numbers for the better. Offshore, migrant Sandwich Terns move west and other seabirds such as skuas may be driven in by rough weather. The fields above Ladram Bay often hold flocks of Skylarks, with Corn, Lapland and Snow Buntings, and – from further east – Richard's Pipit all recorded.

TIMING

Wader watching on the estuary is easiest away from high tide, but as other wetland habitats develop this is beginning to change. Early mornings following south-east breezes are best for spring arrivals, especially on weekdays as many walkers use the riverbank paths on fine weekends. Autumn seawatching benefits from south-west gales. Flattish sea conditions are needed to spot divers from the beach. Gulls gather to bathe in the evening before roosting offshore.

ACCESS

Budleigh Salterton, on the A376 south-east of Exeter, can be reached via Exmouth along the coast, or inland over Woodbury Ridge on minor roads. The estuary mouth car park is at the far east end of the seafront, and birds can often be seen from the car. From here, walk along the pebble ridge for views out to sea and up the estuary between the raised saltings. Then take the raised estuary bank path northward; there is easy walking for 800m up to the minor road at White Bridge at the head of the estuary. Raised wooden screens are built beside the path, enabling views over the estuary channels and newly created saltmarsh for wheelchair birdwatchers. Note the path here is a little rough for wheelchair access, although the new paths to the west are better suited. From White Bridge either continue upriver towards Otterton, about 1.5 miles (2.4km) away, for riverside birds, or cross the bridge and turn right down the partly wooded east bank towards the sea. From the seaward end you can continue eastward on the coast footpath towards Ladram Bay, 3 miles (4.8km) away, for passerines, winter seaducks or summer seabirds.

From White Bridge, turn back left along the minor road to view the new saltmarsh to the north, or take the diversion south to The Island, a viewing screen overlooking reedbed and saltmarsh. After crossing another road bridge, just before the small car park, a footpath leads back south towards the beach car park. Another footpath heads north along the west side to Little Marsh. However, be aware this path floods on high spring tides. For small birds in the town, look for well-timbered parks and avenues; there are many suitable localities. Do not trespass onto private property.

Birdwatching and Beaver tours are available: devonbeavertours.co.uk.

CALENDAR

Resident: Goosander, Shag, Cormorant, Grey Heron, Little Egret, Sparrowhawk, Kestrel, Stock Dove, Barn and Tawny Owls, woodpeckers, Kingfisher, Rock Pipit, Stonechat, Cetti's Warbler, Grey Wagtail, Dipper, Reed Bunting, Raven.

December–February: Shelduck, Wigeon, Teal, Common and possibly Velvet Scoter, Red-throated and Great Northern Divers, Little Grebe, Water Rail,

Oystercatcher, Dunlin, Ringed Plover, Redshank, Black-tailed Godwit, Curlew, Snipe; likely wintering Black Redstart, Chiffchaff, Firecrest, Water Pipit.

March–May: Little Grebe (March), Fulmar, Wheatear and Sand Martin (mid-March on), Sandwich Tern (late March on), migrant waders, e.g. Greenshank, Little Ringed Plover, Whimbrel (mostly mid-April–May), breeding gulls and other seabirds on cliffs, chance of Hoopoe, commoner small migrants peak late April.

June–July: Breeding residents and seabirds, Shelduck, Reed and Sedge Warblers, waders and Sandwich Tern in July.

August–November: Waders, including Ruff and Little Ringed Plover, in small numbers mainly August–September; terns and maybe skuas to October; passerine migrants to end October; winter visitors return by November.

3 PEBBLEBED HEATHS

OS grid ref: SY0690
Postcodes: EX5, EX9, EX10 (for more detail and what3words, see Access section)

HABITAT

Also known as the East Devon Commons, this area of sand- and pebble-based lowland heathland lies on the ridge between the valleys of the lower Exe and the lower Otter. About 7 miles (11km) from north to south, this is the largest contiguous area of lowland heathland outside the New Forest. It reaches a height of around 180m, sloping gently to the east and more steeply to the west. It varies in width from just a few hundred metres to nearly 2 miles (3.2km), and is broader in the central and southern parts. The vegetation consists of open heather, gorse and bracken, boggy hollows with birch and willows, and larger stands of woodland – predominantly conifer plantations with some Beech. The heaths provide good habitat for lizards, snakes, dragonflies and butterflies; more than 30 species of butterfly are seen annually at Aylesbeare Common, including Grayling and Silver-studded Blue, with a good range of dragonflies including Southern Damselfly and Keeled Skimmer.

The RSPB leases 166ha of Aylesbeare and Harpford Commons, and 48ha at Venn Ottery. DWT has a 25ha reserve at Venn Ottery, adjoining the RSPB site.

For convenience we have included the related area of Muttersmoor, across the Otter just west of Sidmouth.

SPECIES

Barn Owls haunt neighbouring farmland, Green Woodpeckers are a frequent sight and sound, and Stonechats can appear on any patch of gorse. Small numbers of Dartford Warblers have traditionally been present here, even when lost from elsewhere in the region. Their ability to reproduce quickly has returned them from the brink of oblivion after several harsh winters and in good years dozens can be found, Aylesbeare Common being particularly favoured. This district remains their main population centre in the region although they have

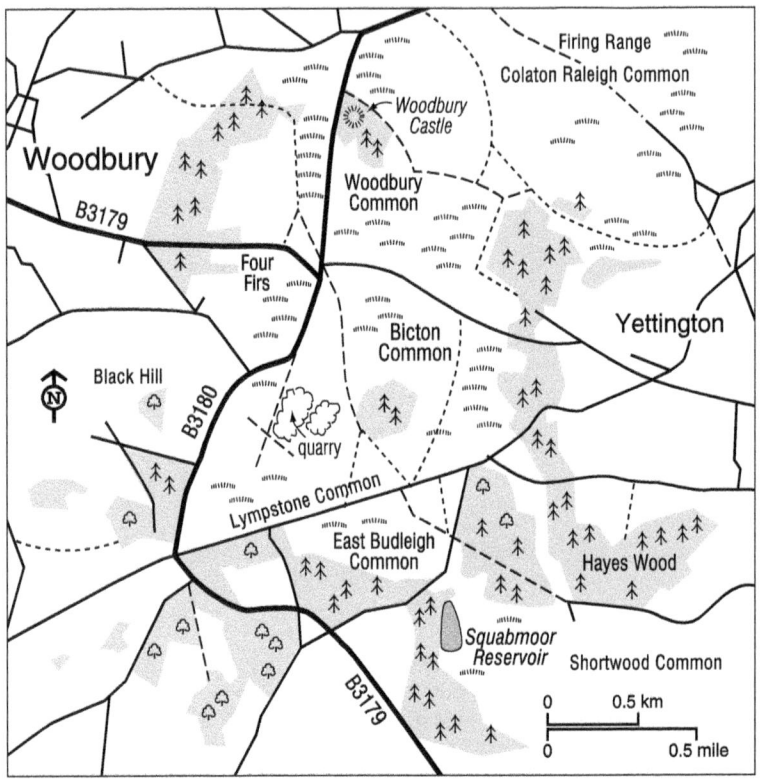

recolonised several other sites. Crossbill numbers vary annually; after an invasion year, when continental birds arrive, dozens forage through the pine clumps, but few are seen in other years.

In winter the commons hold several other species of interest but some luck is needed to find them. A passing Hen Harrier might be seen over larger open stretches, where Merlins also hunt intermittently. Woodcock occur in greater numbers than elsewhere in the region, particularly in cold spells when dozens may arrive. Among the Snipe in boggy hollows and streamside areas the scarcer Jack Snipe may be encountered; it is probably regular throughout the area in suitable habitat. Some years a Great Grey Shrike may winter on the heaths, its pale front prominent as it perches on some vantage point. This species now winters in very few locations in southern England, and the commons are probably among the more productive areas to search. In damp willows and birches, flocks of Siskins and a few Lesser Redpolls search for seeds, together with Reed Buntings. Bramblings are often found with Chaffinch flocks around large stands of Beech.

Siskins are also prominent in early spring, and as the season progresses, Sparrowhawk, Buzzard, Kestrel and Hobby may be seen, with Red Kite and a chance of other migrant raptors drifting over in fine weather. Other spring visitors have included Roller, Bee-eater and several singing Golden Orioles. Curlew and Turtle Dove have been lost as breeding species, but Nightjar remains well distributed, with churring males across the commons on summer evenings. Passerines in

Devon (south coast and Dartmoor)

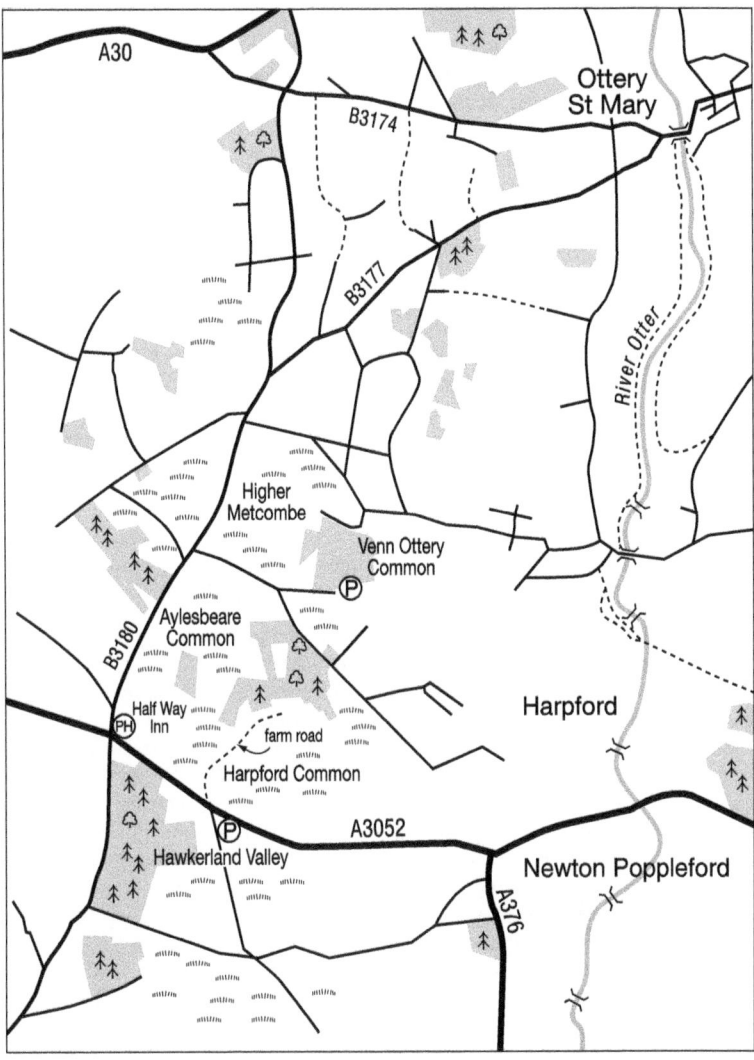

summer include resident specialities such as Dartford Warbler and Lesser Redpoll, with Tree Pipit on the larger heaths. A Cuckoo or reeling Grasshopper Warbler might be heard early in the morning.

After the breeding season the area can relatively quiet, but mixed flocks of tits and warblers should be checked for migrants such as Pied Flycatcher and Redstart, and a Wryneck might be picked out by keeping an eye on any agitated Stonechats. There are occasional sightings of migrant harriers, including Devon's first ever Pallid, and other raptors, including Red Kite.

TIMING

In winter avoid wet weather or high winds. Freezing conditions may bring an influx of Woodcock or other winter visitors. In summer, mornings and evenings are best, most specialised heathland visitors being crepuscular. A dusk visit is recommended for Nightjar and Grasshopper Warbler, and in midsummer Nightjars are unlikely to be active before 9.30 p.m. Fine anticyclonic days with south-easterlies are the most likely conditions for arrivals of migrants or raptors. The most accessible commons attract many walkers, so arrive early unless you are prepared to walk well away from the roads.

ACCESS

From the north end, the A30 Exeter–Honiton trunk road passes the area; the B3180 runs south down the ridge towards Exmouth; and the A3052 between Exeter and Sidmouth cuts across the centre at Half Way Inn. From the Exeter direction, the B3179 through Woodbury village gives access to the ridge at Four Firs. A maze of minor roads crosses the commons from east to west, the remotest areas from road access being the centre of Woodbury/Colaton Raleigh heaths and Aylesbeare Common.

Note: Parts of Colaton Raleigh Common in particular are sometimes used as a military training area; check gov.uk/government/publications/straightpoint-and-wcta-grenade-range-firing-times or call 01395 272972 for details.

Those with limited time will probably visit one of the following:

Venn Ottery To access the DWT reserve, from the A3052/B3180 junction at Half Way Inn, turn north up the B3180 northwards towards West Hill. Ignore the turning on the right to Venn Ottery after 1 mile (1.6km) and continue for a further 0.6 miles (1km), turning right at Tipton Cross. Continue for 0.6 miles (1km), passing a left fork, until you reach a crossroads signposted to Broad Oak and West Hill on the left and a public footpath along a rough track to the right. Park carefully on the road verge and walk down the public footpath. After 200m the track reaches a T-junction; the public footpath turns left, but turn right to access the reserve. Continue along track a further 200m and walk through the gateway to Furzelands. Turn left immediately before the next gateway and walk down the track into the reserve. Breeding Nightjars and Dartford Warblers are likely in summer, Snipe in winter.

To access the adjoining RSPB reserve, from Half Way Inn go north on the B3180 towards Ottery St Mary for 1 mile (1.6km) then turn right towards Harpford. After 800m, at the junction adjoining Otterdene riding stables, fork left and continue for 400m to reach the first parking spaces beside the reserve.

Aylesbeare/Harpford Commons (EX10 0HZ, overdone.probe.radiating) From Half Way Inn go east on A3052 towards Sidmouth (ignore signs for Aylesbeare village). Look immediately for a minor turning on the right marked to Hawkerland. Adjacent to the junction is a car park, beside main road. Stop here and explore around. The main heath lies on the north side of A3052 opposite the junction, signed to RSPB reserve. Dartford Warblers have their regional stronghold in deeper heather. A fine spring or summer morning walk down the tarmac track that crosses the reserve might produce a few sightings of these jerky, active, long-tailed little birds. If not in view they might be detected by watching Stonechats, as they often follow a foraging pair. RSPB reserve: open access at all times but please keep to paths.

Parties intending to visit should pre-book; contact the RSPB for details: rspb.org.uk/days-out/reserves/aylesbeare-common.

Fire Beacon Hill is an outlying high point on the edge of the commons. A Local Nature Reserve (LNR) managed by the RSPB and East Devon District Council, it contains a cross-section of the area's birds including Nightjar and Dartford Warbler, with good populations of Stonechat and Yellowhammer. Head east on the A3052 towards Sidmouth from Newton Poppleford; on reaching the Bowd Inn turn left towards Ottery St Mary. Immediately after the inn turn right onto Fire Beacon Lane. This narrow lane takes a sharp left turn after 100m. Continue uphill to reach a small parking area on the right designated for the LNR. Take the stony footpath up to the flat hilltop, which is crossed by minor trails and paths.

Woodbury Common (EX5 1JL, squashes.mediate.sunroof) About 800m north of the B3180/3178 junction at Four Firs, Woodbury Castle tumulus and pinewood is one of the highest points, with views over the surrounding commons and the Exe Valley; Brambling is often present in winter, and Nightjar in summer.

East Budleigh From Four Firs turn south on the B3180 and drive towards Budleigh Salterton for 2 miles (3.2km); the third minor road on the left leads up past woods and small lakes onto the common. Park in the dirt car park on the right at the hill crest. The slope below overlooks Squabmoor Reservoir, a good area for Nightjar in summer and Lesser Redpoll in winter. Explore left into Hayes Wood and along tracks on the far side of the road.

Muttersmoor (EX10 0NN, hiking.bunny.lots) From the A3052 into Sidmouth, reach the seafront and turn right; continue along the minor road west from the seafront up Peak Hill, stop in the car park at the crest and walk inland. Nightjar, together with Stonechat, Linnet and Yellowhammer, may be found, and this is also a good vantage point for displaying or migrant raptors. Access on foot is unrestricted on most heathland, which is crossed by numerous paths, but keep to existing pathways and be careful not to disturb ground-nesting birds.

CALENDAR

Resident: Sparrowhawk, Buzzard, Barn Owl, Green Woodpecker, Dartford Warbler, Stonechat, Lesser Redpoll, maybe Crossbill, Reed Bunting.

December–February: Possibly Hen Harrier, Merlin and Great Grey Shrike; Woodcock, Snipe and Jack Snipe, winter thrushes, Brambling, Siskin.

March–May: Most winter visitors leave by late March, when Yellowhammer move up from farmland. Summer visitors (most from late April) include Hobby, Cuckoo, Tree Pipit, warblers (possibly including Grasshopper), maybe Redstart in woods; Nightjar mostly from late May; occasional migrant raptors mostly May.

June–July: Breeding residents and summer visitors mostly singing in June, but Nightjar heard all summer. Still a chance of Red Kite or other migrants, e.g. Golden Oriole, into June.

August–November: Breeding species have parties of juveniles moving about in August. Otherwise relatively quiet, but Short-eared Owl and raptors might be noted; Hobby still present in September, Hen Harrier, Merlin and other winter visitors from October.

Devon (south coast and Dartmoor)

4 EXE ESTUARY: GENERAL INTRODUCTION

HABITAT

At the north-west corner of Lyme Bay, the estuary has 6 miles (9.6km) of tidal mudflats, more than 1 mile (1.6km) wide in places, between Exeter and the sea. Extensive *Zostera* (eelgrass) beds grow in sheltered areas. The tidal mud is sandier in the lower estuary, where Dawlish Warren extends eastward across the river mouth. The river is tidal up to Countess Wear on the edge of Exeter. Water meadows up to 1 mile (1.6km) wide flank the upper west bank, separated from the tides by the Exeter Canal. A tidal reedbed lies opposite Topsham at the head of the estuary. Both this area and the adjoining Old Sludge Beds to the north are leased by DWT as nature reserves. The RSPB manages much of Exminster Marshes, along with Powderham Marshes, Bowling Green Marsh near Topsham and Matford Marshes. Shooting is banned on much of the west bank. Dawlish Warren is a National Nature Reserve owned by DWT and Teignbridge District Council. North of the A38 at Countess Wear, much of the floodplain has been drained for development, but areas of wetland still exist and continue to be restored. The estuary mouth is heavily used by holidaymakers in summer and water sports, although zoned, are increasing. There is an excellent cycle path and train network adjacent to both sides of the estuary.

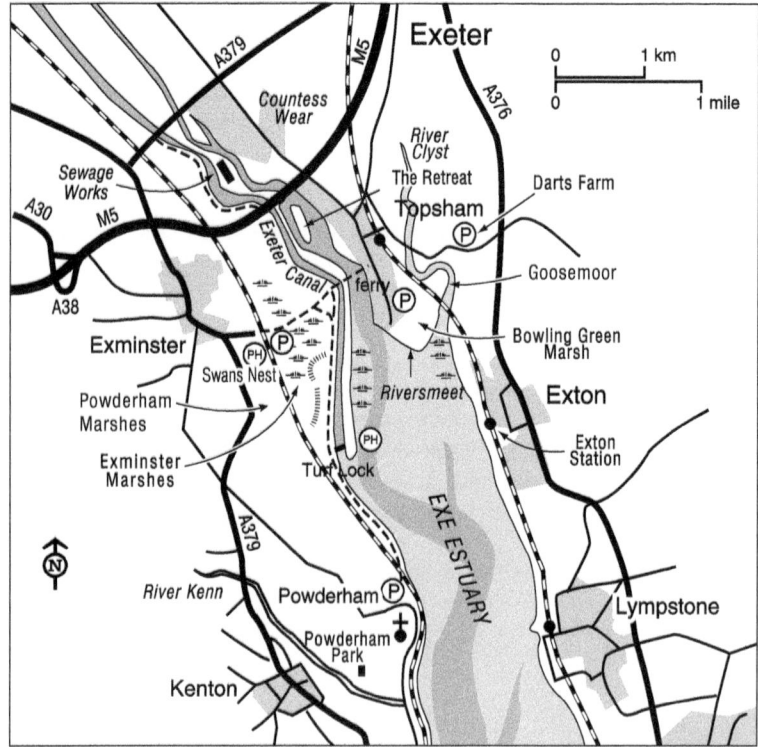

SPECIES

The estuary is one of south-west England's most important areas for waders and wildfowl in winter, with up to 8,000 waders of 20 species and several thousand ducks. Numbers of Black-tailed Godwit (of the Icelandic race) are present in internationally important numbers. Avocet form one of Britain's largest winter flocks and are relatively easy to see at the north end of the estuary, with Dark-bellied Brent Geese widespread. The shallow sea is attractive to passing gulls and terns, and to divers, grebes and seaducks in winter. Together with surrounding farmland, the area holds an extremely wide variety of birds, with over 330 species recorded over the years.

MAIN BIRDWATCHING ZONES

Because of the size and complexity of the area, the text divides it into zones, concentrating on those with the easiest access and most birds, although anywhere around the banks may repay investigation.

East bank: Exmouth, Exton, Darts Farm Wetlands; Bowling Green Marsh, Topsham and the Clyst.

West bank: Exminster Marshes, Exeter Canal, Matford Marshes and Riverside Valley Park, Powderham Marshes; Powderham and the Park; Dawlish Warren.

4A EXMOUTH

> OS LANDRANGER MAP 192
> OS grid ref: SY0081
> Postcode: **Mudbank** – EX8 1EN
> what3words: **Mudbank** – animal.armed.reds

HABITAT

At the east side of the estuary mouth, Exmouth waterfront gives views out to sea, across the fast-flowing channel to Dawlish Warren, and up the estuary mudflats. High cliffs rise from the east end of the seafront, continuing eastwards past Sandy Bay, where there is a large holiday park, and Straight Point, which is used as a military firing range. The habitat is mainly open clifftops with a few sheltered hedges and scrubby bushes. Behind the town lies Mudbank, a wide, sheltered estuary bay with beds of *Zostera*, an important food for wildfowl.

SPECIES

In winter, the bay to the west of the town is the estuary's main feeding zone for Brent Geese, Wigeon and Pintail; whistling rafts of up to 3,000 Wigeon can often be seen at close range. Brent Geese partially disperse as food runs short, while the graceful Pintail can exceed 100 in number. The deeper water of the main tideway is favoured by fishing Red-breasted Merganser; sometimes a Long-tailed Duck or Black-necked Grebe stays for a week or two, and Shags and auks are often present in small numbers after storms. At the southern end of town, seaweed-covered boulders attract a regular flock of around a dozen Purple Sandpipers, accompanied by Oystercatcher and Turnstone. Groups of Eider in

Devon (south coast and Dartmoor)

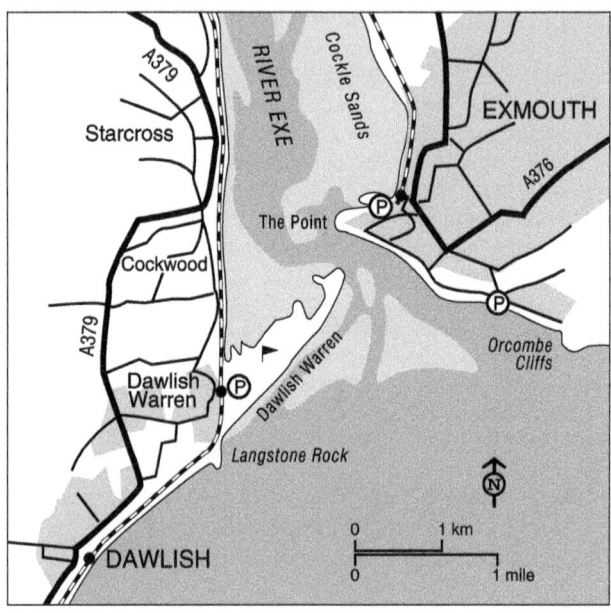

assorted plumages often swim near the rocks; further out there may be grebes, divers and scoter, sometimes including a few Velvet Scoter, but these move about between Exmouth and Dawlish Warren according to disturbance, wind and tide.

Spring brings large numbers of terns feeding offshore, often picking up sand-eels over sand bars or moving past the seafront into the estuary at high tide. They roost on Dawlish Warren but dozens may be seen off the east side, especially early in the morning. All the commoner sea terns occur here, with Roseate also possible. Terns are also an attraction in autumn, often chased by one or two Arctic Skuas. In stormy conditions larger movements of seabirds might be seen off Orcombe. When Balearic Shearwaters move west down the Channel coast in late summer/early autumn they can be seen passing or feeding offshore. Little Auk and Grey Phalarope have been seen off Orcombe in autumn.

In spring and summer, a further range of species can be viewed by following coast paths east from Orcombe Point. A range of commoner warblers might occur in the clifftop bushes on migration, with a Sardinian Warbler found one spring and Pallas's and Dusky Warblers in autumn. If the clifftop fields are left as stubble, large numbers of Skylarks may winter, and they have been joined briefly by scarce or rare migrants such as Red-throated and Richard's Pipits or Lapland Bunting. The projecting rock strata of Straight Point provide a nesting area for seabirds, including Kittiwakes, Cormorants and gulls. The Kittiwake colony here has increased, although others in the region have had mixed fortunes, and over 100 pairs have been recorded here.

Devon (south coast and Dartmoor)

4B BOWLING GREEN MARSH, TOPSHAM AND THE CLYST AREAS

OS grid ref: SX9787
Postcode: **Bowling Green Marsh** – EX3 0FP
what3words: **Bowling Green Marsh** – notes.ladders.dumpling

HABITAT

Topsham lies on the east side of the Exe at the head of the main estuary. Wide views over the upper Exe mudflats can be gained from the waterfront. The River Clyst flows into the estuary immediately below the village, the embanked Clyst grazing marshes extending several miles upstream. Bowling Green Marsh, a 14ha flood meadow leased by the RSPB, is immediately adjacent to the Clyst mouth. The mudflats off the Clyst mouth can also be seen from Exton station on the east bank of the main estuary.

North of the rail embankment, the wetland extending up towards the A377 is known as Goosemoor. This area has been restored to saltmarsh by the RSPB, adding to the wetland habitat available around the estuary.

SPECIES

Bowling Green Marsh is one of the easiest places on the Exe to see large numbers of birds at reasonable range (although a telescope is still desirable). Regular watching has produced a long list of species, with many wildfowl and waders coming in off the estuary at high tide. This has brought the opportunity to find some scarcer species normally undetectable far out on the main estuary. A typical winter visit to the reserve brings views of hundreds of Brent Geese and Wigeon, together with lesser numbers of Teal, Shoveler and Pintail. Rarer wildfowl have included American Wigeon, Green-winged Teal and once a Falcated Duck. Groups of noisy Canada Geese and a few feral Greylag Geese are also usually present. Common waders include dozens of Curlew, Redshank, Lapwing and Golden Plover, with large flocks of Black-tailed Godwit moving across from the estuary to roost at high tide. Greenshank reach double figures and Long-billed Dowitcher has twice overwintered. The large concentration of birds here often attracts a passing Peregrine or Marsh Harrier.

The south end of Topsham waterfront, known as the Goatwalk, overlooks the upper Exe mudflats where hundreds of Avocet feed in midwinter. Large numbers of other wintering waders may be seen here, while a Spotted Redshank may be found wading in the shallows around the Clyst mouth. Further up the Clyst, a wetland complex has been created at Dart's Farm; the fields here can hold large flocks of Brent Geese in winter, with small numbers of waders often present including perhaps a Green or Common Sandpiper. Kingfishers are often seen and three Penduline Tits once overwintered. The surrounding fields often hold winter flocks of finches and Reed Buntings.

The narrow Exe passage between Topsham and Exminster Marshes, on the west side of the village, is a favourite feeding area for Goldeneye, which are often joined by Red-breasted Merganser. The footpath north from the recreation ground at the north end of Topsham enables views of these plus roosting gulls; Water Pipits are sometimes seen along the shoreline in winter. Most other species of the canal bank area and the 'Retreat' reedbed to the north can be seen more conveniently from the Exminster side.

In spring, a Garganey usually drops into Bowling Green Marsh, plus a variety of waders including Whimbrel and Little Ringed Plover. Scarcer migrants to the region that might be found in spring include Wood Sandpiper, conspicuously pale-spotted compared with the dark-winged Green Sandpiper. Other spring surprises have included Temminck's Stint, Pectoral Sandpiper and a Terek Sandpiper – a major national rarity.

Large groups of hirundines hawk over the pools, and migrant Yellow Wagtails stop off to feed. Little Grebe and Tufted Duck have nested on the main pool. The summer season should not be ignored here: two of the best rarities, a breeding-plumaged Franklin's Gull and a smart Pacific Golden Plover (Devon's only record) were both seen in mid-summer. Late summer and early autumn bring more Green Sandpipers, together with further chances to find less common waders such as Wood Sandpiper, Little Stint and Curlew Sandpiper. Unseasonal Avocets are becoming more frequent in ones and twos. Gull flocks at rest may include Mediterranean Gull in smart summer plumage plus occasional terns, which have included Caspian, Gull-billed, Roseate and Arctic.

When autumn westerlies propel American waders across the Atlantic, this area is again worth a careful look, with several Lesser Yellowlegs, as well as White-rumped and Baird's Sandpipers recorded. Little Egrets often use the marsh, and if Spoonbills are visiting the estuary they are likely to roost here at high tide. The Goatwalk waterfront path can be a good lookout point for an Osprey; these often feed over the upper estuary in autumn, or even perch to digest a fish on one of the larger trees overlooking the Exe/Clyst junction, in full view of the hide.

4C EXMINSTER MARSHES AND THE CANAL

OS grid ref: SX9687
Postcode: EX6 8DZ
what3words: ducks.tigers.manage

HABITAT

A tract of wet grassland, up to 1 mile (1.6km) wide and intersected by drainage ditches, stretches along the west side of the upper estuary. The Exeter Canal, now used for angling and rowing, runs along the outer marsh, entering the estuary at Turf Lock. South of here, the estuary seawall embanks a smaller area towards Powderham. No shooting is permitted on the canal, but a private shoot operates on the marshes. Opposite Exminster Marshes, between the canal and Topsham village across the river, lies an extensive tidal reedbed through which the river flows before reaching open mudflats, which are particularly rich in food. At the north end of the marshes, between the canal and the river, are the Old Sludge Beds, a DWT reserve, and Countess Wear sewage works.

The RSPB manages much of the centre of Exminster Marshes and retains a range of freshwater pools. Further areas of freshwater have been enhanced by management to the north of the main road bridge at Countess Wear, both in Riverside

Devon (south coast and Dartmoor)

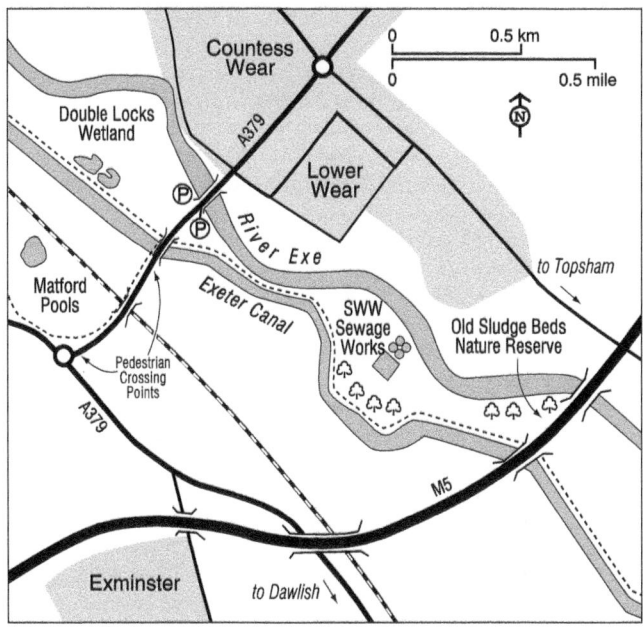

Valley Park near the canal and Matford Marshes by the main road junction a few fields away.

SPECIES

In winter, the grazing marshes' attractiveness to birds often depends on water levels. Scrapes and floods attract large flocks of ducks and waders, including thousands of Wigeon, with smaller numbers of Teal, Pintail and Shoveler; scores of Snipe are hidden away and cold spells often bring thousands of Lapwing, joining up with the regular wintering birds. Areas where closer watching is possible, such as pools in Riverside Valley Park, may bring sightings of Jack Snipe or even Bittern into early spring. The reservoir in the centre of the marshes attracts a wide variety of waterfowl, often including a few diving ducks; Devon's first Lesser Scaup was found here. Hundreds of Curlew and Black-tailed Godwit fly in off the estuary to roost at high tide and are often joined by flocks of Dunlin and a few Grey Plover and Knot. Some godwits feed as far up the estuary as Countess Wear, and were once joined by a wintering Hudsonian Godwit from North America. Several hundred Golden Plover, usually accompanied by one or two Ruff, stay all winter; in cold weather they may be joined by White-fronted or even Tundra Bean Geese and wild swans, now usually Whooper Swan. Fieldfare and Redwing can be seen in their hundreds in similar conditions.

The canal sometimes holds a surprise such as a Red-throated Diver or Long-tailed Duck, watchable at close range from reed-fringed banks. A Kingfisher can often be seen by Turf Lock. Rough fields might harbour a Short-eared Owl, rising to beat slowly across the marshes on a winter afternoons; Barn Owl might also be seen. Marsh Harriers may roost in Topsham reedbed, where the *ping* calls of Bearded Tit have been heard. On mild winter days the far-carrying song of Cetti's

Warblers can be heard from tangled vegetation all along the canal to the Old Sludge Beds north of the M5 flyover. Willows surrounding this sheltered area often hold wintering Chiffchaffs, sometimes joined by a Firecrest; Yellow-browed Warbler has been recorded several times. Reed Buntings are widespread residents along the ditches and reedbeds. The upper estuary flats are notable for flocks of wintering Avocet, reaching more than 1,000 at times. The main Exe flock may move between Turf, Topsham across the river, and Powderham, but by careful timing close views can be obtained of these elegant waders from both sides of the river. The mudflats are the site of a massive roost of Black-headed and Common Gulls from the Exe Valley farmland. Peregrines are often seen overhead or perched on pylons. Red-breasted Merganser frequents the main channel, and small numbers of Goldeneye still winter.

Spring's earliest arrival is often Garganey, with one or two of these scarce ducks on channels and pools in the marshes. This area, together with Bowling Green Marsh across the river at Topsham, is the most regular location in the region for them, although they can be very elusive. A few non-breeding Wigeon, Pintail and Shoveler remain most years. Wheatears and Sand Martins pass through the marsh in the first mild spring weather. From mid-spring, a variety of warblers, including Sedge, Reed and sometimes Grasshopper, arrive to sing alongside Cetti's Warbler in the ditches. Migrant flocks of Whimbrel, reaching 100 or more, rest on the meadows before continuing overland. Oddities can include a Spoonbill, while Marsh Harrier and Cattle Egret have become a regular sight, and one or two Short-eared Owls are noted most years on spring migration. Migrant Hobbies may number up to a dozen birds circling over the marshes on fine days; Exminster is one of the more reliable sites in the region to find them at this time, and once attracted a Red-footed Falcon. Perhaps unexpected is the passage of tern flocks moving north inland along the outer marsh edge on fine evenings and through the night; generally, they spiral high over the canal banks before flying north upriver. Groups of Sandwich, Common and even Arctic Terns have been seen passing, while the nesting Peregrines in Exeter have intercepted a couple of Roseate Terns! Flocks of Pale-bellied Brent Geese may also be seen following the same route. This is also a good time for waders such as Little Ringed Plover and Common Sandpiper, with the pools attracting rarer spring migrants such as Black-winged Stilt, Broad-billed Sandpiper and American Golden Plover alongside Wood Sandpiper and perhaps Temminck's Stint. Matford Marshes has hosted some interesting visitors including several Glossy Ibises and, from North America, Laughing Gull.

Breeding species include a couple of pairs of Lapwing, now virtually extinct as breeding birds in the region. Several pairs of Shelduck will also be present. Yellow Wagtails have ceased to breed, although they still turn up each spring. Common raptors, herons and egrets are frequent hunters in the fields while Red Kite may pass overhead. Swallows and House Martins nest around local farms; in late summer many feed over the marshes, joined by Sand Martins from further afield. The hirundines are often chased and frequently caught by unerringly accurate Hobbies. At the end of the breeding season, thousands of Swallows and martins roost overnight in Topsham reedbed. This concentration of birds attracts predators; two or three Hobbies may hunt here.

Autumn passage waders on the marshes often include Common and Green Sandpipers, while flocks of shanks and godwits return early to the mudflats. Rarities have included Wilson's Phalarope and increasingly, Glossy Ibis. Just north of the main marsh, the freshwater pools at Riverside Valley Park and Matford Marshes can also attract a similar selection of passage waders that are scarce in the region, including Little Ringed Plover, Wood Sandpiper and Ruff. Look also for the odd Little Stint or Curlew Sandpiper with the Dunlin. Early autumn can be productive around Turf, with a good chance of a fishing Osprey, causing the gulls and waders to fly up in unnecessary alarm. Black Terns or Little Gulls may dip over the canal's wider stretches, and there are various small migrants in reeds and bushes – once an American Robin. Late season has produced unexpected 'wrecked' seabirds during gales, such as exhausted skuas, Grey Phalarope and even Little Auk on the canal. It will be the end of autumn before most Avocets return, and a visit to see them should ideally be left until winter.

4D POWDERHAM MARSHES

OS grid ref: SX9586
Postcode: EX6 8DZ
what3words: ducks.tigers.manage

HABITAT/SPECIES

This area of previously arable farmland, to the west of the railway at Exminster, has been managed by the RSPB to return it to wet grassland, with a small area of spring barley still grown to provide habitat for resident Cirl Buntings. A large area of predator-fenced grazing marsh and pools holds the largest remaining breeding population of Lapwing in the region. The range of species to be found is similar to that on the adjacent Exminster Marshes, with many birds often moving between the two sites.

4E POWDERHAM AND THE PARK

OS grid ref: SX9784
Postcode: EX6 8JJ
what3words: inflating.folks.deprive

HABITAT

The 1 mile (1.6km)-wide central tidal flats of the Exe Estuary are bordered on the west by the wooded parkland and freshwater of Powderham Park, the Earl of Devon's estate. A herd of several dozen Fallow Deer grazes in the castle grounds. The small River Kenn runs through the estate into the estuary, the northern branch widened into a shallow mere, which often overflows onto nearby fields. North of the park, low-lying meadows behind the estuary wall slowly widen northward towards the Turf Inn and Exminster Marshes. The main deepwater channel of the estuary flows close to the embankment bend.

SPECIES

The park boundary and seawall running north towards Turf are one of the region's most popular areas for autumn and winter wader-watching. The meadows behind the seawall area are a high-tide roost for waders from nearby mudflats. The balance of species is different from that at Dawlish Warren, with more species adapted to probing softer mud. Curlew and up to 2,000 Black-tailed Godwit predominate; the latter, smart in flight with black and white wing-stripes, is one of Britain's largest gatherings. Brent Geese graze in meadows at high tide when other food becomes scarce. Rich mud off the embankment attracts many waders, including a few Greenshank and perhaps a paler Spotted Redshank. Avocet, usually further upriver, sometimes feed this far down the estuary and at high tide may be easily overlooked as they float buoyantly among Shelduck and Black-headed Gulls. Views may be distant, so telescopes are recommended.

Flocks of up to 1,000 dabbling ducks rest on mudbanks. Among hundreds of Mallard and Teal, the elegant shape of Pintail may be picked out; smaller numbers of Shoveler join them. Several Red-breasted Merganser may fish on deeper stretches, alongside plentiful Cormorants, with Grey Herons and Little Egrets poised along the water's edge. Sometimes the whole mass of birds erupts as a Peregrine dives to make a kill.

The park serves as a roost for shanks, which usually fly in to the River Kenn at high tide. These freshwater habitats hold dozens of wintering Teal, a few Pintail and Shoveler and often Egyptian Geese. Kingfishers may speed along the waterside, and sometimes a Green Sandpiper stays to winter on a sheltered channel. Recently, dozens of Cattle Egrets have wintered, joining Little Egrets at roost, with Great White Egrets seen increasingly.

Spring brings large flocks of Whimbrel and reddish, breeding-plumaged godwit dropping in on the mud. Sandwich and Common Terns, and sometimes Little Tern, follow the rising tide up the estuary. Greenshank, usually present only in twos and threes through winter, become more numerous. The park's large trees hold a heronry of up to 40 pairs and provide nesting habitat for many Stock Doves. Kestrel, Buzzard and Sparrowhawk are often seen circling overhead, while Great Spotted and Green Woodpeckers fly across the clearings and Mistle Thrush are regular. Open spaces are frequently dotted with pairs of Shelduck prospecting rabbit burrows in which to breed.

In autumn, the park is again home for waders, as several Greenshank join scores of Redshank. Two or three Green Sandpipers, and perhaps a Wood Sandpiper, may be present by freshwater pools in early autumn, with Common Sandpiper passage noticeable on the main estuary. Observations of gull flocks bathing at the stream mouths just off the park may include Mediterranean and Yellow-legged Gulls. Most watchers visit in hopes of an Osprey fishing off the seawall or even roosting in the park, with a couple often staying for several weeks. The upper part of the estuary is most favoured by fishing birds and the open estuary bank here offers a good vantage point. Sometimes a Hobby comes down from the marshes to try a small wader meal, and Dunlin flocks may host other migrant waders, such as Curlew Sandpipers.

Most wildfowl return in October, with numbers building in late autumn; in colder weather flocks of Tufted Duck, found in few places locally, may arrive on the pools.

Devon (south coast and Dartmoor)

4F DAWLISH WARREN

OS grid ref: SX9879
Postcode: EX7 0NF
what3words: caged.rephrase.frightens

HABITAT
This 1-mile-long (1.6km) sand dune spit projects eastward across the estuary mouth, the seaward side heavily used by the public. Offshore, the water is shallow, with extensive sand bars at low tide. The centre of the Warren is a dune slack with bushes, artificial pools and small reedbeds. The inner (upriver) side of the spit is a golf course, with *Spartina* saltings in the bay behind (no public access). The tip of the peninsula curves upriver, creating a sheltered tidal bay, The Bight, behind the dunes. To the west, along the seawall, Langstone Rock projects seaward. The Warren is well known botanically, supporting more than 760 species of plant; it is one of only two UK sites for Sand Crocus.

SPECIES
This excellent area for waders and waterbirds is much visited by birdwatchers, although sea-level rise means the hide is no longer publicly accessible. Winter brings large high-tide roosts of waders and hundreds of Brent Geese. Oystercatcher (usually more than 1,000), Dunlin (often more than 2,000) and several hundred Curlew, Bar-tailed Godwit and Grey Plover are the principal species, with 100 Knot and small numbers of Greenshank, Ringed Plover,

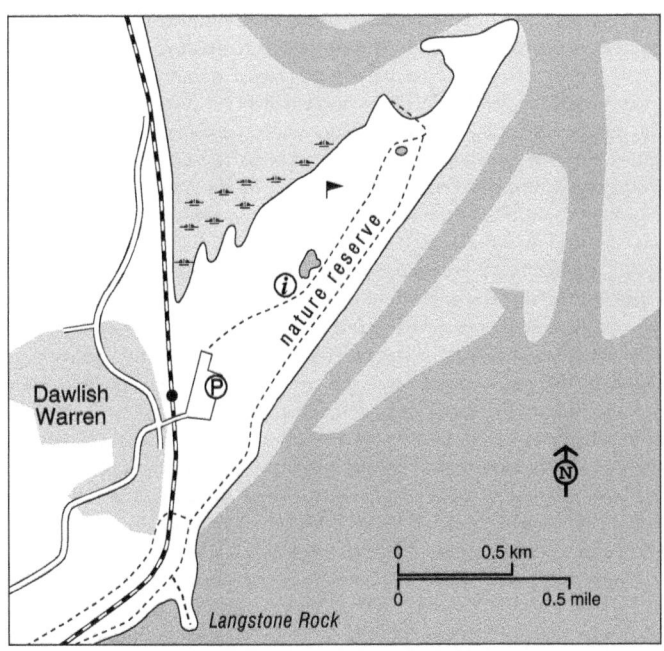

Sanderling and Turnstone. Generally, waders using the lower estuary are those adapted to coarse, sandy mud.

Red-breasted Merganser, occasionally accompanied by Goldeneye, fish on the estuary behind the Warren. Further in, behind the spit, hundreds of Wigeon and Teal graze among saltings, and Shelduck, Little Egret and Kingfisher may be found along muddy Shutterton Creek entering the main channel. Hunting Peregrines often take advantage of the concentration of birds.

Cirl Bunting and Stonechat can be found around the bramble scrub, with Shoveler on the Main Pond and Water Rail in the reeds. Common and Siberian Chiffchaffs and Firecrests often winter in the bushes in small numbers and a Black Redstart might be found along the seawall towards Langstone.

The sea off Dawlish Warren remains one of the region's main wintering areas for marine waterfowl although, as elsewhere, variety and numbers of divers, grebes and seaducks have declined. In most winters, up to 70 Great Crested Grebes and half a dozen Red-throated Divers are dotted across the Langstone Rock–estuary mouth area, joined by two or three Great Northern Divers. The relatively shallow, sheltered sea here suits Red-throated best; the population that feeds between here and the Otter cliffs is the most regular group on the south coast of the region. Once a key site for Slavonian Grebe, this species is now very rarely encountered. Small numbers of Eider, mostly brown or patchy immatures, are present in most winters, sometimes close in off Langstone, where Shags perch on the projecting jetty. Common Scoter numbers are variable; rafts may reveal the occasional white bar on an outstretched wing of a Velvet Scoter in their midst, although long-staying Velvet or even Surf Scoter are often on their own. Less frequent visitors such as a Black-throated Diver and Red-necked Grebe may join them in hard or stormy weather, with parties of Razorbills and Guillemots often feeding offshore. Check in winter for Turnstone and Brent Goose among the weedy rocks below Langstone at low tide. Watching off Langstone requires a scramble so the seawall is much preferred. From all locations views may be long-distance and a telescope is helpful. Seaducks, divers and grebes may pass by anywhere between Exmouth and Dawlish seafront to the south-west, depending on tides and weather.

Large numbers of gulls use the estuary mouth. After onshore gales, thousands may gather along the shore and seawall to scavenge cast-up marine life; commoner species may be joined by a Caspian, Glaucous or Mediterranean Gull. Occasionally after high winds, when the dunes and beach suffer severe erosion, a Little Gull may be seen fluttering over the breakers or a skua harrying gulls offshore.

In spring, the earliest Wheatears arriving along the spit are soon followed by the *kirrick* calls of the first Sandwich Tern. Later in the season, mixed flocks plunge for fish close off the beach or drop in to roost in the tidal bay among waders. Although Sandwich Terns are always most noticeable, migrant Little Terns, a dozen or more hovering over the sea on peak days, are more regularly present here than elsewhere in the region. Common Tern, sometimes joined by the more rakish Arctic, may be briefly numerous according to weather conditions, but soon continue their migration. In the second half of spring there is a good chance of a pale-backed Roseate Tern; two or three of this scarce species may arrive together. Other seabirds may include Arctic and Pomarine Skuas, while Kittiwakes and sometimes a flock of Great Crested Grebes remain offshore. Meanwhile, Willow Warblers and other spring migrants sing from scrub in the centre of the Warren, with Whitethroats and Reed Warblers staying to breed. A Red Kite or Osprey may drift overhead. A Garganey might stop off at the Main Pond, once visited by a Great Reed Warbler.

When breezes blow from the Continent, almost anything is possible. A Hoopoe may probe among the dunes, Great Spotted Cuckoo has appeared twice and Lesser Grey and several Woodchat Shrikes have also been found. On such days, the wader roost is a colourful sight, with resting northbound birds in breeding plumage including chestnut-fronted godwits, black-bellied Grey Plover and scurrying groups of Sanderling. This last species, a High Arctic breeder, is one of the latest to peak on spring migration. Many Whimbrel fly in off the sea, and it is worth searching among the smaller waders for an oddity such as a Kentish Plover. This pale, sandy continental relative of the Ringed Plover is seen as often here as anywhere in the region, although it is no longer annual. Many birdwatchers visited after careful observation detected a Semipalmated Plover from North America among the similar Ringed Plovers in 1997 and 1998. The larger Greater Sand Plover from Asia has also been a surprise arrival, and the stripe-crowned Broad-billed Sandpiper has been picked out among the Dunlin. Several Stone-curlew, very rarely found on migration, have also been seen.

Summer is quieter for birds, although Linnet, Skylark, Stonechat, Whitethroat and Cirl Bunting will be seen or heard, while a few terns remain offshore, sometimes chased by a skua. These drop in at the roost through summer and often include two or three Roseate Terns. This can be a difficult species to find away from its few breeding sites, and Dawlish Warren offers probably the best chance in our region.

The Main Pond hosts Little Grebe, a rather scarce local breeder in Devon, as well as the elusive Water Vole. Even while the beach is still thronged with holidaymakers, the first post-breeding terns and Arctic-nesting waders return. Around 200 Oystercatcher will have summered on the estuary. Late summer often produces Balearic Shearwater, with groups passing and occasionally lingering offshore, in rough weather a few feeding European Storm Petrels may join them.

Autumn is protracted, with large parties of waders and terns staying to feed around the estuary mouth for weeks at a time. Screaming juvenile Sandwich Terns fly in across the dunes pursuing parents which have caught sand-eels offshore; up to 200 are regularly present. Among several dozen Common Terns there may again be an Arctic or Roseate, and one or two Little Terns. Both the extremely rare Elegant and Lesser Crested Terns have been recorded, and Caspian Tern has stopped off for a few brief hours. Often a Black Tern joins them for a few days, while Mediterranean Gulls are regular with passage counts sometimes breaking three figures. This source of food attracts Arctic and Pomarine Skuas offshore. Osprey, which fish on the estuary for long periods in autumn, range widely and drift over the Warren at times, flushing roosting flocks; on one occasion the flush was created by a Short-toed Eagle. Waders can number more than a thousand, with an early passage of Ringed Plover, Curlew and Sanderling, the first sometimes reaching 350 birds. Through mid-autumn several Curlew Sandpiper and Little Stint may be picked out among the teeming Dunlin. After westerly gales, Baird's, Pectoral and Semipalmated Sandpipers have flown in to join the roost, and Buff-breasted Sandpiper has been seen. Wheatears are a familiar sight in the dunes, and small numbers of migrants feed in the scrub. The establishment of the Dawlish Warren Recording Group has produced increased numbers of scarcer species, including several Barred and Yellow-browed Warblers, as well as Dusky, Pallas's and Radde's. Even rarer was an American Red-eyed Vireo.

Terns move on from mid-autumn, although other seabirds may still gather offshore during gales later in the season. Large numbers have sometimes been seen (more than 300 Balearic Shearwaters, all four skua species and hundreds of Kittiwakes and Gannets in a single day); maybe even a Sabine's Gull or larger shearwater. After a really rough autumn spell, check in the lee of Langstone Rock for a sheltering ocean waif – a Grey Phalarope, perhaps, or a rotund Little Auk. Long-billed Murrelet, a small Pacific auk, made its only UK appearance here, moving between the Warren and Dawlish seafront to the joy of thousands from all over the country.

In autumn, the first Brent Geese and Wigeon drop in, occasionally bringing scarcer species such as American Wigeon, Black Brant and even Mandarin. Large wintering flocks of Oystercatcher, Dunlin and Bar-tailed Godwit may be chased by a Peregrine, with the diminutive Merlin preferring flocks of Linnet and other finches. A Short-eared Owl might be on Warren Point, which has hosted Great Grey Shrike and Short-toed Lark. Visible migration can produce notable movements of passerines; Brambling and Lesser Redpoll are often found among the Chaffinches, with rarer species such as Hawfinch, Woodlark, Richard's Pipit and Lapland Bunting also recorded. As the last summer migrants pass through, the passage returns to commoner species, with tens of thousands of Woodpigeons and hundreds of Jackdaws heading west. This spectacle over, birdwatchers turn their attention back to the sea for divers and grebes.

Information about the latest sightings can be found on the website of the Dawlish Warren Recording Group, at dawlishwarren.co.uk.

TIMING (ALL EXE ESTUARY SITES)

At low tide, most waders and ducks are a long way from the majority of observation points. The best watching is generally in the two or three hours before high tide, as birds move closer to the banks, and at main roosts such as Dawlish Warren for an hour or so across high tide. Tides reaching 3.1m and above will start to concentrate waders at roost sites, especially at the top end of the estuary. Quantities of birds feed in the creek behind Dawlish Warren at most tides and some roost in saltmarsh close to the railway embankment at high tide. The Avocets at Turf are best seen when feeding nearest to the bank about two hours before high water. They are visible from Topsham at most tides, but a rising tide pushes some birds closer. All times should be weighed against the height of the tide; spring tides may force birds to stop feeding sooner, and even to abandon normal roosts.

Terns tend to join the Warren roost when there is some mud left in the tidal bay, two or three hours before or after high tide, or on neap tides; rising tides encourage them to fly upriver as far as Turf. High-pressure conditions, with winds from a southerly quarter, are best for spring arrivals; more easterly species, such as Black Tern, arrive mostly in autumn easterlies. Strong south-west winds with rain battering the coast in autumn produce concentrations of seabirds off the coast and occasional 'wrecked' birds as far up as Turf. Freezing weather elsewhere brings influxes of wildfowl and open-ground species on the marshes. Periods of heavy rain, flooding meadows, may also encourage birds to come from the estuary to feed. Wildfowl and waders at Bowling Green Marsh are seen in highest numbers at high tide. Allow sufficient time to check thoroughly from the roadside as birds can easily be missed. The public hide can be busy on weekends. Short-eared Owls fly mostly in late afternoons. For raptors such as Peregrine or Osprey, a wait of at least two or three hours at vantage points along the estuary banks may be needed. For views of divers and grebes on the sea, choose a calmish sea; in a swell it is better to watch from Orcombe but there is little shelter there. Avoid watching the mudflats from the west bank in early mornings when light glare is against you and choose days when wind in these exposed spots will not prevent focusing on distant birds.

The reedbed roost at Exminster Marsh–Topsham should be watched from about two hours before dusk, in fine weather.

Coastal districts are heavily used by walkers at weekends, and by holidaymakers in summer; in July or August especially, early morning visits are best. Kitesurfers may disturb wildfowl offshore.

ACCESS (ALL EXE ESTUARY SITES)

All sites can be accessed from the Exe Estuary cycle trail.

Dawlish Warren is reached from the A379 Exeter–Dawlish road, turning south around Cockwood Harbour bridge, or east at the start of Dawlish town. Go under the railway bridge onto the Warren, then left towards the main estuary, and right for the seawall and Langstone. For sea views walk right along the seawall to the rock; some observers climb the worn steps (care required) and scan more widely from the top. A walk south towards Dawlish should produce more winter grebes, seaducks or divers.

For the wader roost and estuary mouth, turn left from the car park. Walk along the beach or past the central marsh and bushes, then drop to the beach before the golf course and walk to Warren Point, finally coming back to view the bay. Access or return is not possible on the highest tides, with some risk of being cut off around high water. Coastal erosion and a failed sea defence scheme mean public access to the hide is sadly no longer possible.

The Warren's sand dunes, seafront and central marsh are managed by Teignbridge District Council, who employ full-time wardens. Golf links and adjacent saltmarshes at the rear of the Warren are owned by DWT. Although the golf course can be overlooked from nearby paths, there is strictly no public access. Dogs are not allowed past groyne nine and must be kept on a lead when off the beach. Guided walks are available.

From the car park the path leads through the centre of the Warren, passing the visitor centre. Immediately beyond the next gateway you gain views of the Main Pond and reedbed, the main path skirting them on the right. A smaller path to the left leads round the north side of the wetland and through the rear of the willows. The warden can be contacted via teignbridge.gov.uk/sports-and-leisure/parks-and-open-areas/nature-reserves/dawlish-warren-national-nature-reserve or by calling 01626 863980.

The saltmarshes and mudflats behind the Warren can also be viewed from the north. Follow the main road north, turning right from the Dawlish Warren entrance. The road passes several holiday camps before running immediately adjacent to the high railway embankment. Pull in at the marked lay-by just south of Cockwood and use the pedestrian railway crossing. Large numbers of wintering ducks and waders can be viewed from the steps, especially at half-tide – but be sure to take extreme care crossing the busy railway line.

From here proceed 800m to Cockwood Harbour, a small enclosed tidal basin. A minor road on the left past the Ship Inn follows the Cockwood Valley. This habitat has turned up some unexpected rarities including Night Heron, Little Bittern and Marsh Warbler in spring. Sedge and Reed Warblers breed.

Following the A379 north between Cockwood Harbour and Starcross village, Oak Meadow Golf Course, adjacent to the road, can attract winter wildfowl, especially feeding flocks of Brent Geese, and waders. Parking is very difficult and it is best to walk from Cockwood Harbour. The golf course is only open in the summer season. At Starcross village a further vantage point is provided by the railway station platform, overlooking the estuary. Red-breasted Mergansers and other diving ducks often feed off here, and Turnstones roost on the old stone pier. Just north of the village a low-lying field when flooded can hold large numbers of waders and a few wildfowl, with egrets often gathering pre-roost.

Powderham From the A379, travelling north from Dawlish Warren, fork right at the north end of Starcross village on the minor road between the park and estuary. Stop and look across the park and pools from roadside lay-bys; a telescope is helpful. There is no public access into this side of the park. There is, however, a signposted public path across fields just south of the River Kenn outlet, which gives partial views across the wetter parts of the park. A pedestrian railway crossing gives good views across the centre of the estuary. Take great care when crossing the railway line. For the estuary bank, continue to the sharp bend beside the church; there is limited parking space here, although more is available around the corner under trees. Follow the cycle path north alongside the railway before going over the bridge leading to the estuary bank. A footpath leads to Turf Lock (see below) about 1.5 miles (2.5km) along the seawall.

Exminster Marshes From the A379, turn down the lane towards the Swan's Nest Inn at the south end of Exminster village. Bypass the inn entrance and continue over a humpbacked bridge across the railway; stop to check fields on either side if flooded. The RSPB car park is accessed by a sharp right turn immediately after crossing the bridge. An information board here shows the reserve and other local features. Visitors must decide whether to park here and explore the rest of the marshes on foot, or whether to continue to the fishermens' car park adjacent to the canal at the end of the unmade track, which is often flooded in winter. No parking is available in between. From the RSPB car park a footpath runs south, parallel to the railway, offering views over the lower marsh fields towards Turf Lock. Breeding Lapwing frequent this area.

Continuing along the central track, adjacent fields have shallow pools that hold waders and ducks; there is no access but they can be viewed well from the track or from the raised canal bank. Walk up onto the canal bank and head either north towards Countess Wear or south towards the Turf Lock/Turf Inn area (colloquially known as Turf), checking adjacent fields for Short-eared Owls in winter and Hobbies passing over in late spring/summer. About 300m along the canal bank towards Turf, a viewing platform looks out over scrapes and a large central storage pool in the middle of the marsh; close access is not available, but using a telescope you can check them from the bank. Avocet and other waders are on the estuary opposite in winter. For better views, continue to Turf, crossing the lock gates and watching upriver along the outer marsh, and looking down the estuary channel for diving ducks or Osprey in season.

To access the east bank, two passenger ferries operate between Topsham Lock Cottage and the Turf Inn. Timetables and further detail can be found at exeter.gov.uk/leisure-and-culture/sport-and-leisure/exeter-port-authority/topsham-ferry and topshamturfferry.com.

Powderham Marshes From the RSPB car park at Exminster walk back over the railway bridge, a good vantage point to scan for wildfowl or raptors, then walk behind The Swan's Nest pub to follow a footpath south and around the fields to a viewing area on higher ground overlooking the main marsh; a telescope is essential.

Exminster to Countess Wear section The cycle path and canal towpath head north past the reedbeds towards Exeter, reaching the A38 at Countess Wear Bridge. This route leads past the Old Sludge Beds, between the reedbed and the waterworks. You can pass the compound either on the west (canal) side, or on the east (river) side. The west side gives occasional views into pools inside the waterworks perimeter, a reliable location for Gadwall. In winter, the riverbank gives good views of any ducks in the channel, and sometimes a Kingfisher, while the outfall pipe may attract feeding Teal. This area can also be accessed direct off the A38 from the Countess Wear end, turning into a poorly marked entrance immediately between the main river bridge and the canal bridge when heading west. Beware fast-moving traffic and indicate to turn well before the entry. Park adjacent to the rowing club and walk south along the tarmac drive towards the waterworks. Large numbers of Cormorants roost on the power pylons across the river. Immediately to the north, the canal bank towards Exeter gives views over the **Riverside Valley Park** wetland. To park on the northern side of the carriageway, take the A38 west for 800m to the main roundabout and circle back eastwards; after the swing bridge pull into parking spaces on the left near the riverbank. Walk back north for 400m to join the canal path and view Riverside Valley Park pools through wooden blinds. Following the main roadside path, you can alternatively walk west for some hundreds of metres to view adjoining **Matford pools** for sandpipers, ducks and Little Egret. A public path and cycle track branches off and continues north past a series of pools and small fields.

Bowling Green Marsh, Topsham and the Clyst Topsham lies south of Exeter, approached via Countess Wear roundabout off the A38 or signposted from the main A376 Exmouth road. Follow the main road through the village and over the railway crossing before taking a right turn into Elm Grove Road after 300m. This becomes Bowling Green Road and opens up to give views across Bowling Green Marsh meadows to the left.

Note: There are parking restrictions along Bowling Green Road, and birdwatchers are advised to use the Holman Way car park (EX3 0AF, scared.ramp. free) adjacent to Topsham railway station. Alternatively, park at Darts Farm and follow the cycle path south before turning right, crossing the Clyst and continuing past Goosemoor. There are two parking spaces for disabled birdwatchers by the hide.

There is no access into the marsh, which can be scanned from the roadside or from the wheelchair-accessible RSPB hide overlooking the pool and other flooded areas. It is difficult to gain a complete view of the pools from any vantage point. After watching from the hide, walk on down the lane; a gated footpath on the left leads to a viewing area on a raised embankment overlooking the Clyst estuary mouth.

Continuing to the end of the lane, you reach the Riversmeet area, facing across the main Exe mudflats, a convenient point to view Avocet. From the end of the lane, the level Goatwalk path enables you to walk back towards Topsham centre. Scan downriver from here for Osprey in autumn.

For views of the Exe and the reedbed at the north end of Topsham, turn right into Follett Road when approaching the town centre from the Exeter direction. This is a few metres before the mini roundabout and is signposted to the ferry, riverside and recreation ground. Continue along the road, which bears right, and park at the roadside after about 200m then continue north towards the motorway bridge on foot. A long-staying Spotted Sandpiper was here one recent winter.

Devon (south coast and Dartmoor)

The embanked River Clyst and surrounding fields (which are private with no access, although open to view) can be seen along the road towards Exmouth where it crosses the river. They can also be viewed from Darts Wetland, which is accessed from the RSPB Exe Estuary Centre at Darts Farm south of Topsham. The wetlands have hosted wintering Penduline Tit and both Red-breasted Goose and Black Brant have been found in the Brent Goose flocks; Bramblings often frequent the weedy fields. Views of the upper Exe Estuary flats can be obtained anywhere along the cycle path and from Exton Station, 2 miles (3.2km) south of Topsham on the A376.

Exmouth Continue south on the A376, following signs through Exmouth to the seafront. For Eider and Purple Sandpiper, try Maer Rocks, at the far east end; a path leads up onto Orcombe cliffs. For the estuary, head back past the docks and turn left to Imperial Road car park (past the station), which gives open views over the mudflats. Good views of ducks and waders can be obtained from a parked car here if weather conditions are unfavourable. From the north end of the car park, the cycle path (part of the East Devon Way) runs north between the estuary and railway. This level path can afford very good views of winter duck flocks, including Wigeon and Pintail, especially on a rising tide when they come closer to the bank. The cycle path continues north toward Topsham while the East Devon Way turns inland towards Woodbury about a mile (1.6km) up the estuary.

For clifftop walks east of Exmouth, continue along the coast path from Orcombe Point along the National Trust's 'High Lands of Orcombe' area for a mile (1.6km) to Sandy Bay. The main coast path skirts the edge of a holiday camp. The seabird cliffs can be seen from the coast path by the front of the camp but there is no access onto Straight Point due to the presence of army firing ranges.

Exe Estuary birdwatching boat trips Winter birdwatching trips (often advertised as 'Avocet Cruises' but giving chances of seeing a wide range of species) start from Exmouth Dock; visit: stuartlinecruises.co.uk/guided-bird-watching-cruise.

CALENDAR

Resident: Shelduck, Eider (in some years), Grey Heron, Little Egret, Marsh Harrier, Coot, Water Rail, Lapwing, Oystercatcher, Black-tailed Godwit (non-breeders in summer), Stock Dove, Barn Owl, Cetti's Warbler, Stonechat, Mistle Thrush, Cirl and Reed Buntings.

December–February: Occasional Whooper Swan and 'grey' geese, Dark-bellied Brent Goose, Gadwall, Wigeon, Teal, Pintail, Shoveler, Tufted Duck, maybe Scaup, Common and perhaps Velvet Scoter, Goldeneye, possibly Long-tailed Duck, Red-breasted Merganser, occasional Goosander, divers (especially Red-throated) and Great Crested Grebe offshore, Little Grebe, Cormorant, Shag, Peregrine, Avocet, Ringed, Golden and Grey Plovers, Turnstone, Dunlin, Knot, Sanderling, Purple Sandpiper, Redshank, Greenshank, Common and Green Sandpipers, probably Ruff, Curlew, Bar-tailed and Black-tailed Godwits, Snipe and Jack Snipe, rarely skuas, gulls, including Mediterranean; Short-eared Owl, Kingfisher, Chiffchaff, Black Redstart, winter thrushes; maybe Bearded Tit.

March–May: By mid-March, Wheatear, Garganey on marshes; first Sandwich Tern by end of third week. Passage Great Northern and Red-throated Divers through to May. Whimbrel, Common Sandpiper and Little Ringed Plover on passage; migrant shanks pass from mid-April. Reed and Sedge Warblers arrive mid–late April. Hobby arrives from late April through May. Short-eared Owl occasional to early May. Main tern passage from mid-April to May, mostly end April and first half May, when Roseate usually seen. Arctic or Pomarine Skua possible in May. Occasional scarcer migrants, e.g. Osprey, Kentish Plover, Hoopoe or rare heron, late April through May. A few Great Crested Grebes, Common Scoter and auks on sea; Fulmar, Gannet and Kittiwake pass offshore.

June–July: From end June to early July, first waders return; a few terns arrive on passage, including one or two Arctic and Roseate; Mediterranean and Yellow-legged Gulls arrive. Sandpipers and other waders in breeding plumage appear late in period. Cirl Bunting on territory.

August–November: Balearic Shearwater offshore, especially in August, with occasional larger shearwaters. Common, Green, and maybe Wood Sandpipers from August to early September on marshes; migrant warblers, Wheatear and wagtails; hirundines roost in Topsham reedbed, with attendant Hobby and other raptors from August through September. Terns feeding in large numbers August to early September, perhaps with Black Tern in September. Arctic Skua frequent from mid-August. Small numbers of Little Ringed Plover, Little Stint and Curlew Sandpiper through September, and maybe Pectoral or another American sandpiper; several Osprey linger. Merlin and Short-eared Owl mostly October to November. Arctic, Great and other skuas, and Sabine's Gull offshore in gales September and October. Maybe Little Auks or Grey Phalarope October and November. Divers and grebes arrive from mid-October, mostly late November. Snow Bunting occasional, and Black Redstart and Yellow-browed Warbler often arrive late October and November. Wildfowl return from late September, but mostly in November. Few Avocet until November.

5 STOKE CANON MEADOWS AND STOKE WOODS

OS LANDRANGER MAP 192
OS grid ref: SX9397
Postcode: **Stoke Woods** – EX4 5BN
what3words: **Stoke Woods** – breakfast.sediment.chained

HABITAT

This site is approximately 2 miles (3.2km) of low-lying river valley north of Exeter, bordered along its eastern flank by Stoke Woods, mixed woodland on a steep hillside, designated as a country park. The River Exe meanders through meadows liable to flood, especially in winter. Above Stoke Canon, towards Brampford Speke village, the river is faster and shallower, with shingle bars. Below Stoke Canon, the Exe and Culm rivers converge; willow and alder trees line the banks, and at low river levels mud bars are exposed. White-legged Damselfly is particularly well represented in this area.

SPECIES

This is a good area, close to Exeter, to see woodland and waterside birds. The meadows attract different species depending on water levels. Flocks of up to 300 Canada Geese drop in to graze outside the breeding season, and occasionally

Devon (south coast and Dartmoor)

other geese have been found, including Tundra Bean and White-fronted. Winter floods bring varying numbers of dabbling ducks, with past reports of several hundred Wigeon, although there have been fewer records recently. Teal can occur in scattered parties of 20–30. Pintail and Shoveler have also been noted.

On the main river, a small group of Goosander might be encountered. Lapwing and Snipe feed in damp fields after cold weather, while Common and Green Sandpipers winter in ones and twos on sheltered riverbanks and pools. Up to 30 or more Little Egrets may feed in the water meadows, occasionally with rarer cousins. Large flocks of gulls feed in the wet meadows, Black-headed is usually the most numerous species, but Common, Lesser Black-backed and, increasingly, Mediterranean often join them.

The riverside is always worth watching, with Dippers bobbing in shallows near Brampford Speke, and Kingfishers and Grey Wagtails feed all the way along. Parties of Siskin forage in overhanging trees, and mixed flocks of other finches feed on stubble fields near Stoke Canon. Large groups of winter thrushes are often present. Woodcocks are sometimes flushed from quieter parts of the wood, where woodpeckers, thrushes, tits, Nuthatch and Treecreeper may be encountered.

Spring migrant arrivals can be noticeable as birds funnel up from the Exe Estuary. A Little Ringed Plover or other passage wader may stop off on a shingle bar beside noisy parties of Common Sandpiper. Large groups of Swifts and hirundines follow the valley. Canada Geese often breed, while pairs of Shelduck and Great

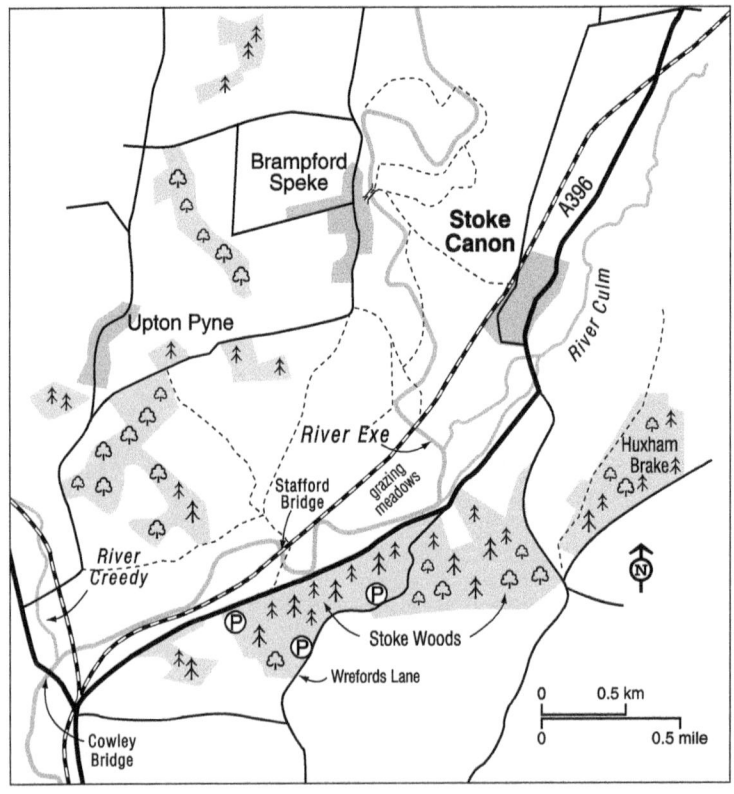

Black-backed Gulls, unusual this far inland, have been present in recent springs, as have Goosander. Kingfishers nest in the bigger riverbanks and Sand Martins can be watched entering nest-holes below Brampford, although their numbers fluctuate from year to year. Sometimes they lose their nests here when river levels rise.

One or two Sedge and occasionally Cetti's Warblers sing in damp thickets. The wood hosts summer visitors such as Redstart, Blackcap, Garden Warbler, Willow Warbler and Chiffchaff in varying numbers. Raven and Sparrowhawk also raise young.

Early autumn, with low river levels leaving exposed mud, is good for waders. Common and Green Sandpipers, as in spring, are the most frequent; twos and threes are usual but sometimes up to 10 Green Sandpipers rise from the mud with loud *tluee* calls. A Wood Sandpiper might also occur. Gulls flock in the fields, where various small migrants such as Yellow Wagtail and Whinchat might be found. Apart from frequent Sparrowhawks, predators hunting over the riverside may include Hobby.

TIMING

Duck numbers tend to increase when the meadows flood after heavy rain; there are partial floods most winters. Flood pools at migration periods may also attract waders. Frozen conditions can bring scarcer wildfowl in winter. Evening visits in late summer or early autumn can be good for waders on the move. Disturbance by the public can be a problem in the wood on fine summer weekends; try mornings for songbirds in spring. The attractive riverbank walks near Brampford Speke can become disturbed by public use at weekends.

ACCESS

The A396 Exeter–Tiverton road runs north from Cowley Bridge on the edge of Exeter. For the water meadows, continue for 1 mile (1.6km) and park beside the wood in a small lay-by on the right, after passing two signposted woodland entry points. Cross the main road, take the gated public footpath left across fields to Staffords Bridge, and scan from here. Alternatively, several roadside lay-bys on the left further up the main road give views over likely flood areas. Park near the foot of Wrefords Lane, which joins from the right halfway along the wood (do not park on main road), and look left across the Culm–Exe meeting point. In summer, check the wood near the lane; the small valley behind is good for most woodland birds. Try also turning right up the lane and stopping at car parks on the right for more mature stands of trees.

The north end of the valley can be viewed by continuing up the A396, crossing the River Culm at the start of Stoke Canon village. Turn immediately left down the lane past a bungalow estate and look across nearby fields. Follow the lane around to a rail signal box and gated crossing point, then take the public footpath (part of the Heart of Devon Way) for 400m to Brampford Speke riverside, and further north follow the riverbank path towards Thorverton for a longer walk. Alternatively, Brampford Speke village can be accessed directly via minor roads north off the A377 Exeter–Crediton road; leaving Exeter, turn left at Cowley Bridge crossroads, following Crediton signs; the Brampford Speke road is the first turning on the right. At Brampford Speke, park in the main street and follow signs on the right to a footbridge providing access to the riverbank meadows.

CALENDAR

Resident: Goosander, Sparrowhawk, Buzzard, Grey Heron, Little Egret, Stock Dove, Kingfisher, woodpeckers, Grey Wagtail, Marsh Tit, common woodland passerines, Dipper, Raven.

December–February: Flocks of dabbling ducks, Cormorant, Common and Green Sandpipers, Lapwing, Woodcock, Snipe, Stonechat, winter thrushes, Brambling, Siskin, Lesser Redpoll, other finches.

March–May: Chiffchaff and Sand Martin arrive by late March. Shelduck may be present. Migrant Little Ringed Plover, Common and Green Sandpipers, other passage migrants and summer visitors peak late April to May.

June–July: Breeding residents and summer visitors; hirundines, common warblers. Waders and gulls return from July.

August–November: Common, Green and occasional Wood Sandpipers, peaking August; Yellow Wagtail and other migrants pass August and September; Hobby. Most winter visitors return from late October, but duck numbers remain low unless cold weather.

6 HALDON WOODS AND LITTLE HALDON

OS LANDRANGER MAP 192
OS grid ref: SX8885
Postcode: **Haldon** – EX6 7XR **Little Haldon** – TQ14 9NY
what3words: **Haldon** – blown.regularly.couriers
Little Haldon – varieties.handsets.difficult

HABITAT

West of the Exe, Haldon is a conspicuous ridge extending about 6 miles (9.6km) north to south, rising above surrounding farmland to a height of 250m. The flat, sandy top is sadly covered largely by conifer plantations of varying ages, with small stands of Beech and other deciduous trees, including Hornbeam. Many small clearings, with a rich summer growth, vary the woodland habitat, and some original heathland survives along with areas of newly restored heath on the top of the ridge. The largest open area is the horse-racing track and surrounding heath in the centre of the ridge. Little Haldon is a smaller, detached block of similar terrain 2 miles (3.2km) further south, with areas of open heather and a golf course. Both hills afford panoramic views over lowlands and coastline, with Dartmoor tors on the western horizon.

The area harbours Fallow and Roe Deer, often glimpsed in quieter woodland areas at dawn or dusk. Adders and Common Lizards may be seen basking in open spaces in warm weather. The area is well known for butterflies, especially on the managed Butterfly Walks at the north side of the hills, an area of cleared glades under pylons. Grizzled Skipper, Pearl-bordered Fritillary and White Admiral can be expected in their appropriate flying seasons, among 35 butterfly species.

Devon (south coast and Dartmoor)

SPECIES

The large area of mature conifers means that most birds are those adapted to this specialised habitat, including a variety of both breeding and passing birds of prey. In winter the woods can appear lifeless, although the plentiful local Buzzards soar overhead on fine days, occasionally joined by a larger, longer-tailed Goshawk. This rare bird of prey, sadly persecuted, is resident in small numbers in Haldon district and starts to make display flights over the pinewoods from late winter. The full round-ended tail, sturdy build and heavier head help to distinguish it from the less powerful Sparrowhawk. If you *think* it was a Goshawk, it wasn't! You'll understand when you see the real deal.

Sometimes a Woodcock may be flushed beside the tracks or watched departing the woodland at dusk. A thorough search is likely to reveal parties of Siskin and Lesser Redpoll moving through treetops. Crossbills can also be found but are hard to locate, often swinging silently beneath pine cones or detected by repeated *chip* calls as parties fly overhead. In dry weather they often gather around any remaining water – even the car park puddles on a quiet day. Assorted finches feeding on fallen seeds or beechmast often include Brambling. Small groups of Hawfinch also occur in winter, mostly at the north end of the area. This elusive treetop species is often best detected by its sharp but quiet *tick* call.

As early spring comes, resident raptors tower and dive in display overhead, and woodpeckers eke out nest-holes in old timber. Coal Tit and Goldcrest are common in dense conifers with Siskin numbers increasing. Later spring brings a wide variety of breeding species, especially around pockets of heathland and where clearings or a mixture of tree species provide habitat variety; central areas of the densest plantations harbour very few species. Blackcaps are abundant, with Willow Warbler and Yellowhammer also present, while Tree Pipits are seen in song flight in many areas, particularly over younger plantings. In a few places Lesser Redpolls chatter in flight between mature conifers and the low bushes where they breed.

On the heaths, Stonechats may be encountered perched on gorse sprigs. Sadly, the once regular Honey Buzzards no longer breed, although an occasional migrant might still overfly the area in suitable passage conditions, along with Red Kite, Osprey or Marsh Harrier. A Hobby might be seen circling over the heaths and young plantations, catching and eating insects in flight, while the heavier-built Peregrine may also be sighted. Goshawks join the soaring Buzzards occasionally, and Sparrowhawks and Kestrels are frequent overhead. Close views cannot always be expected, however, as most raptors range over large areas and may soar up to a considerable height. Knowledge of shape and outline can be critical in identifying more distant birds.

It is usually the end of spring before the most distinctive breeding species are present, including the largest concentration of Nightjars in the region. Males are active each evening, churring loudly to establish territories in fern-covered clearings and clapping their wings together to deter intruding males; close views can be obtained by silent watchers as they glide low overhead in pursuit of moths. When the breeding season is in full swing, dense woods do not permit close views of passerines and few birds still sing. Nightjars continue to churr into late summer. Breeding raptors may be seen intermittently circling over their territories on fine days throughout the autumn. At the end of the season, large assorted parties of tits and warblers search the woods for food.

Devon (south coast and Dartmoor)

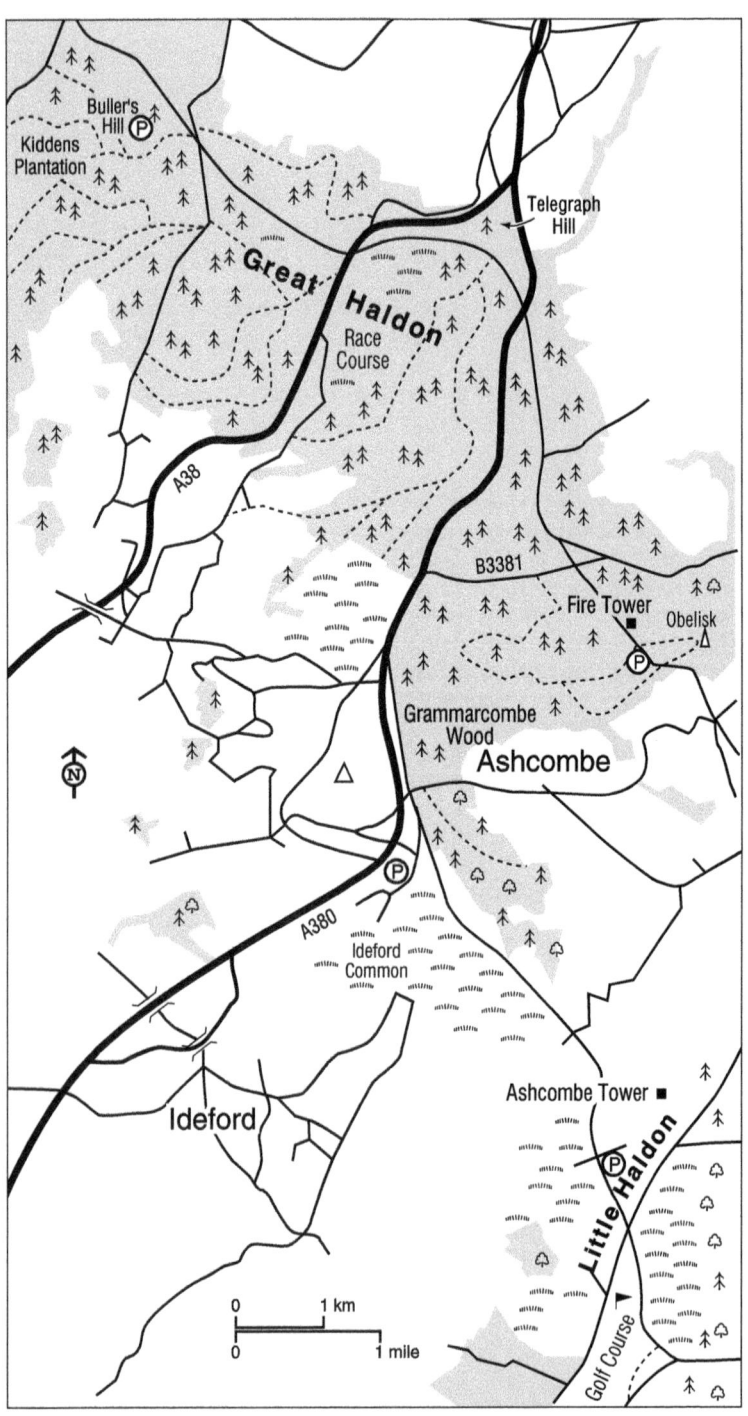

Devon (south coast and Dartmoor)

TIMING

Most species, especially larger raptors, keep under cover in poor weather; fine conditions without strong winds are best. Mornings and evenings are best for passerine activity; larger raptors do not soar until mid–late morning, when thermals start to form. In calm, clear conditions, Goshawks may display over the plantations at any time of day, even if temperatures remain low in late winter and early spring. Hobbies stay active later, towards sunset. High pressure weather with light east or south-east winds can bring soaring migrant raptors across from the Continent. Warm summer evenings with insects on the wing are best for Nightjars (which do not usually churr before 9.30 p.m.).

Those particularly keen to see raptors should be prepared to sit in a chosen vantage point for 3–4 hours at a time to gain good views. During these periods other species such as Lesser Redpoll, Siskin and Crossbill often fly over.

Public use has increased considerably within the area and can cause disturbance at weekends and holiday periods. Birdwatchers may wish to avoid peak periods or visit less frequented parts of the area at these times.

ACCESS

From Exeter, the A38 to Plymouth and A380 to Torquay cross the top of Haldon in parallel. Birds of interest are scattered widely in the extensive woods, most of which are relatively easily accessed by forest tracks and footpaths; paths can be steep and muddy at times. The following provide chances of some of the more distinctive species, although the age and suitability of planted stands changes over time.

Turn-off by racecourse At the crest of the ridge beside A38, turn left just before the course if approaching from the Exeter side, and use the underpass road to turn north towards Dunchideock. The lane gives views across the adjoining woods and hill slopes. Raptors circling up over the steep east side of the ridge may pass over here and Hobbies may hunt overhead. Stonechat and Tree Pipit are common. Stop by any gate leading into forest on the left and listen for Nightjar around clearings at last light.

Haldon Gateway (Buller's Hill) A mile (1.6km) further along the Dunchideock road is the Forestry Commission's central public car park (fee paying) on the left. Leaflets and general information about the area are available, as are toilets and refreshments, with rangers based here. This central area can be very busy, especially at weekends. From here there is access to the various marked trails, including walking down the west slope to the pylon line and Butterfly Walk.

From Buller's Hill continue on the road to the end of the ridge and down off the pine plantations, turning left towards Doddiscombsleigh, to check deciduous trees for Hawfinch in winter and listen for Firecrest song in spring and summer.

Butterfly Walk If Hawfinches are present, they often roost in late afternoon at the bottom end of Butterfly Walk trail. Take the signposted path from the main car park. Follow it down the valley parallel to the pylons for a mile (1.6km), passing a small pond. The Hawfinches may be seen in the next 200–300m, gathering to feed in Hornbeams on the hillside to the left prior to roosting in nearby thickets. Peak midwinter counts of 20–30 birds have occurred here in some cold spells, but in milder conditions they roost elsewhere.

Thorns Valley and the Obelisk From Exeter, take the A380 across the ridge and turn left on the B3381 towards Starcross and Mamhead. Stop by the gates to look right across the valley for soaring raptors. Continue 400m and turn right at a small

Devon (south coast and Dartmoor)

crossroads towards Ashcombe. Hillsides on the right have breeding warblers and Tree Pipit. Taller trees left of the road may have Lesser Redpoll or Siskin. At the end of the level stretch, park under trees; walk left through woods to Obelisk lookout for extensive views of the east flank of Haldon and the Exe Estuary.

Ideford Common Continue south on the A380 beyond the Starcross turning. Take the B3192 towards Teignmouth. Continue 800m to a minor road junction on the right. The car park is 200m along this road. Walk south from the car park to the open heath and views over Dartmoor.

Little Haldon Continue south on the A380 beyond the Starcross turning. Take the B3192 towards Teignmouth. Continue 2.3 miles (3.7km) to a car park on the left. The lane that forks right at the start of the golf course and runs along the west side has small pull-ins that provide good vantage points along the hillside and towards Dartmoor. Passing raptors might be seen from here. At migrant seasons, look across the golf course from roadsides; Wheatears, pipits and other open-ground species may occur.

CALENDAR

Resident: Sparrowhawk, Goshawk, Buzzard, Dartford Warbler, Stonechat, Marsh Tit, common woodland passerines, Crossbill, Bullfinch, Siskin, Lesser Redpoll.

December–February: Woodcock, Snipe, Brambling and other finches, possibly Hawfinch. Goshawk display by February.

March–May: Wheatear possible in open areas, Cuckoo in late April, Tree Pipit, common woodland warblers (including Garden), Hobby, passage raptors through May. Nightjar from late May.

June–July: Breeding summer visitors and residents sing in June but are generally quieter in July though Nightjar continue to churr.

August–November: Nightjar may still sing to mid-August. Most small migrants leave by late September. Scarcities such as Pied Flycatcher and Wryneck possible. Family parties of local breeders, chance of migrant raptors especially August–September. Woodcock and winter finches return from November.

6A CHUDLEIGH KNIGHTON HEATH AND HENNOCK

OS LANDRANGER MAP 191
OS grid ref: SX8477
Postcode: **Chudleigh Knighton** – TQ12 6RD
Hennock Reservoirs – TQ13 9NR
what3words: **Chudleigh Knighton** – madness.alleyway.wardrobe
Hennock Reservoirs – hobbyists.glorious.pines

HABITAT

Between the south-east fringe of Dartmoor and the Teign Estuary, the Teign/Bovey basin is a low-lying, poorly drained area of heath, thickets and copses. The

Devon (south coast and Dartmoor)

habitat has been fragmented by residential and industrial development, including extensive open claypits; Chudleigh Knighton Heath is the best remaining example of the original habitat. DWT has a 59ha reserve covering much of the heath, on lease from the clay company. The area is also well known for butterflies and orchids.

The land rises northward from the heath edge towards Hennock ridge, reaching 250–300m between the Teign and Bovey valleys. Three deep, narrow reservoirs – Kennick (18ha), Tottiford (14ha) and Trenchford (13ha) – are surrounded by forestry plantations; the rest of the ridge is occupied by small farms.

SPECIES

Although not visited by large numbers of birds, these areas are known for a few specialities, mostly breeding species.

In winter, the heath appears bleak, with few birds except for Meadow Pipit, a Stonechat or two, and seed-eaters such as Yellowhammer and Reed Bunting. Although the reservoirs hold very few ducks (single-figure counts of Tufted Duck or Goosander being normal), colder weather can bring a Pochard, Goldeneye or, on a couple of occasions, Ring-necked Duck. Such visits are usually brief, the narrowness of the reservoirs and frequent presence of dog walkers and anglers creating disturbance. Kennick Reservoir, the widest, and the wider central bay of Trenchford are most likely to hold visiting ducks.

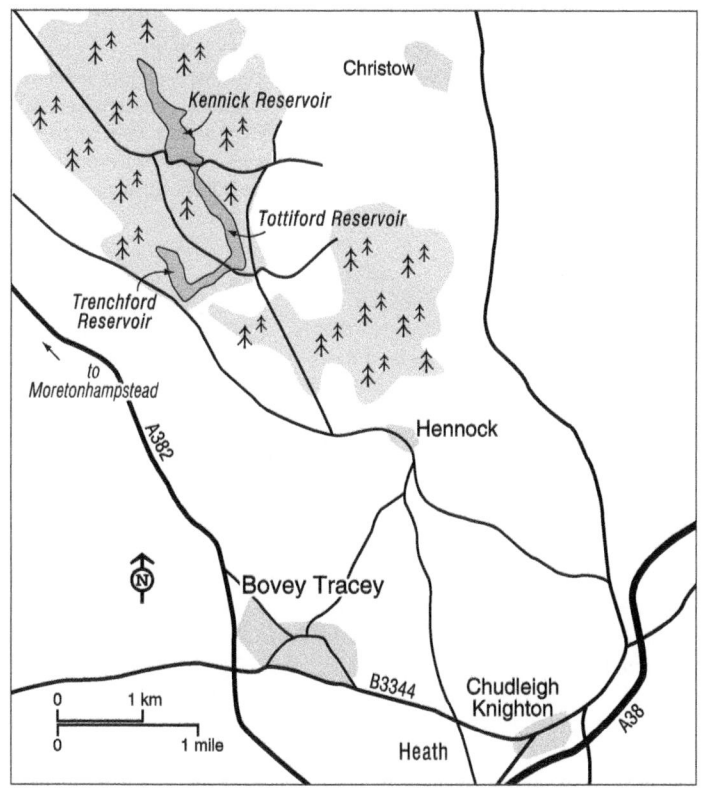

The conifer plantations may be more interesting, although as usual in this habitat, the variety of species is limited. In more mature sections, or under rhododendron cover, a Woodcock may be flushed. Small parties of Siskins, Lesser Redpolls or even Crossbills roam the treetops. As warmer weather arrives, Siskin gather in chattering pre-migration flocks, counts sometimes reaching hundreds, although many stay to breed.

Later spring brings summer migrants. Tree Pipits perform parachuting song flights, Stonechats perch on top of low thickets and the reel of a Grasshopper Warbler might be heard. Many passerine species use telephone wires stretching across the heath as song posts, including Linnet, Yellowhammer and Willow Warbler. A wide range of warblers includes numerous Whitethroats and Garden Warblers. Woodpeckers and common woodland passerines are seen in trees bordering the heath. Great Crested Grebe has bred on the reservoirs.

The heath and harvested woodland blocks hold several pairs of Nightjars, which fly out over adjoining heathland to feed. Sometimes a Hobby hunts insects or hirundines overhead.

Late summer is a more difficult time for locating birds, although parties of fledged young passerines move about the plantations and heath. As autumn approaches, young Wheatears and Redstarts hatched on higher ground filter down across the heaths. Common Sandpiper is an expected visitor along the stony banks of the reservoirs.

TIMING

Fine days without strong winds are needed to properly cover the areas mentioned for passerines. Ducks are most likely to be viewable on the Hennock reservoirs in cold weather, when numbers and variety may increase. Late afternoons and evenings are often most productive at the heath; the best chance of seeing Nightjar is in the last hour before dark, preferably on warm dry evenings – but note that the population here is tiny compared with that on Haldon and those wishing to see this species may do better there.

ACCESS

From the A38 Exeter–Plymouth road, turn off to Chudleigh and continue through to **Chudleigh Knighton** village. Take the B3344, which crosses the heath, towards Bovey Tracey and stop at roadside lay-bys to walk the paths. Take care to keep to existing paths so as not to damage plants and birds' nests. The best place to spend time is near the road junction at the centre of the heath (Dunley Cross). Turn left at the junction to park by the roadside on a wider stretch and explore the paths through the thickets opposite, beside the minor road.

For **Hennock**, turn east at the central crossroads instead of turning west to park. Drive north for 3 miles (4.8km) to Hennock village. In the village turn left, uphill, following signs for another 2 miles (3.2km) to the reservoirs. A network of roads crosses the three lakes and plantations adjoining, although the narrow, curving shape of the lakes makes overall views difficult. For Crossbill and Siskin, try a walk along forest tracks (public bridleways) on the east side of Kennick Reservoir, signposted from the banks.

Exploration of the Teign Valley can be done by continuing east past the foot of Kennick Reservoir and following narrow minor roads towards Christow or Bridford villages.

Devon (south coast and Dartmoor)

CALENDAR

Resident: Mistle Thrush, Stonechat, Marsh Tit, Raven, Bullfinch, Lesser Redpoll, Siskin, Yellowhammer, possible Crossbill, Linnet.

December–February: Goosander, Tufted Duck, Woodcock, winter thrushes.

March–May: Siskins concentrate in March, warblers and pipits arrive by May and Nightjar back by late May.

June–July: Breeding species, including Spotted Flycatcher; passerines harder to find by July.

August–November: Summer visitors leave and migrants pass through; quieter by November.

Devon (south coast and Dartmoor)

SITE CLUSTER: TORBAY AREA

7 Teign Estuary and Newton Abbot district
7A Labrador Bay
7B Stover Lake and Woods
8 Hope's Nose, Torquay
9 Torbay and Berry Head
10 Dartington and the Lower Dart

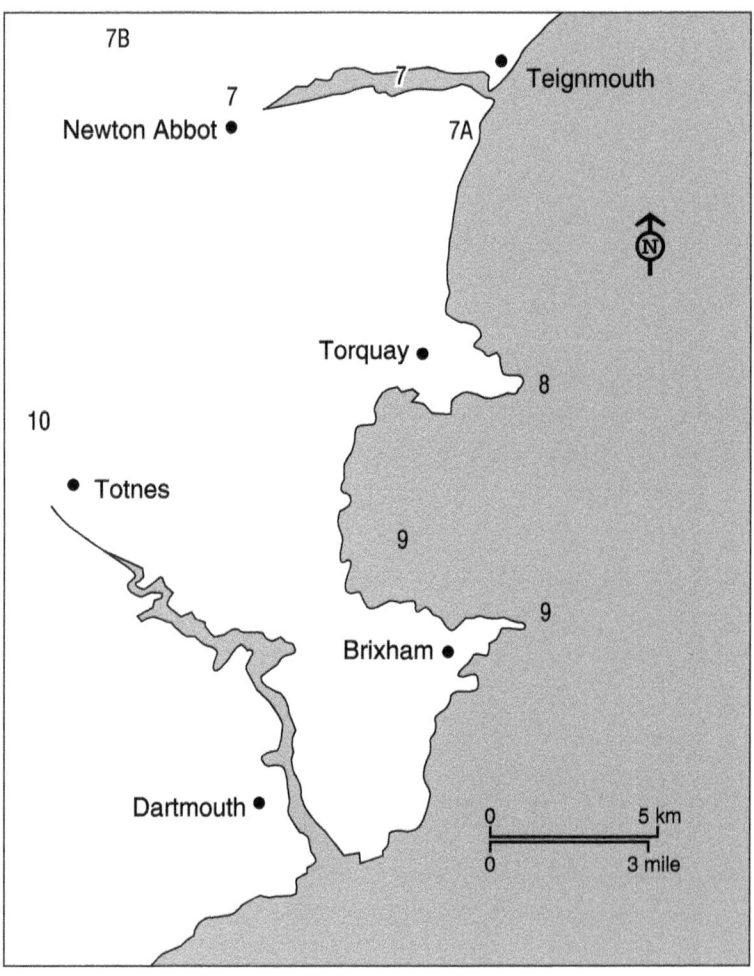

Devon (south coast and Dartmoor)

7 TEIGN ESTUARY AND NEWTON ABBOT DISTRICT

OS LANDRANGER MAPS 191/192/202
OS grid ref: SX8772
Postcodes: TQ12, TQ14 (for more detail and what3words see Access section)

HABITAT

The shallow, east-facing estuary basin is 3.7 miles (6km) long and up to 800m wide, with extensive mudflats at low tide. Teignmouth, a small port and holiday town, lies at the mouth, where a natural sand bar extends south across the estuary as it enters Lyme Bay. A bridge crosses the lower estuary to Shaldon on the south bank. The middle and upper estuary, flanked by fertile farmland, especially on the less steep north side, is muddier. The estuary head narrows sharply at Passage House Inn, where stretches of raised saltmarsh project into the mudflats, leaving sheltered channels between. Immediately inland from here, sandwiched by housing and the main railway track, lies a stretch of wet meadows, ditches and pools known as Hackney Marshes, managed by Teignbridge District Council as a Local Nature Reserve.

Inland from the estuary, the town of Newton Abbot is surrounded by low-lying land, much used for quarrying clay, especially to the east. Old quarries now form several lakes with overgrown perimeters. The main Newton Abbot sites are:

Jetty Marsh An area of reedbed and scrub along an old overgrown canal complex immediately east of Newton Abbot town centre. This is maintained as a Local Nature Reserve by Teignbridge District Council.

Decoy Country Park On the south-west side of Newton Abbot, a deep lake used for recreation and sailing, with a wooded hillside behind. Maintained by Teignbridge District Council.

Teigngrace Meadows and a riverbank walk where the River Teign is shallower and faster, just north of Kingsteignton.

Note: The former DWT reserve New Cross Pond near Kingsteignton has been filled in and no longer exists.

SPECIES

The lower Teign has a range of estuary, freshwater and woodland birds; the lakes are often best in midwinter. The upper estuary is an easy place to see wintering Common Sandpiper and year-round Little Egret. Gull flocks can be worth careful study with 16 species recorded so far.

At the start of the year, Red-breasted Merganser fishes in the lower estuary or middle reaches above Shaldon Bridge, where close views of 20–30 might be gained, the spiky crested drakes most conspicuous. They roost at sea off Teignmouth, joining dozens of Shags, which gather to catch flatfish off the estuary mouth. Great Northern Diver, Common Scoter and a few Guillemots and Razorbills may also be offshore with other diver species or the occasional Eider. The lower estuary is popular with Oystercatchers, which peak at 300–400, but is little used by other waders except a few dozen Turnstone.

On the upper estuary, the flats off the Passage House Inn host several hundred

Devon (south coast and Dartmoor)

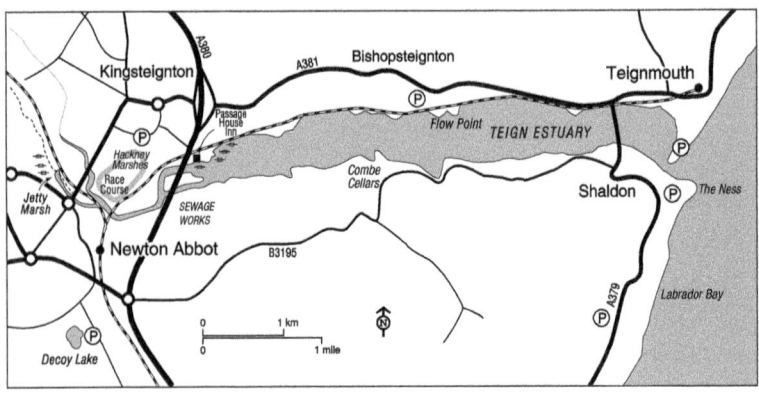

Black-headed and Herring Gulls at low tide, with a few Great Black-backed, Lesser Black-backed and Common Gulls. Other gulls such as Mediterranean, Glaucous and Iceland have been found among them, especially late winter–early spring. Close examination of this roost has produced several records of Ring-billed Gull. A Bonaparte's Gull returned for seven winters and both Franklin's and Laughing Gulls have visited. On high tides many gulls also rest downriver towards Shaldon Bridge. On mid-tide they might be seen from the Coombe Cellars pub car park on the south bank at Coombeinteignhead (long-distance telescope views, the river is wide at this point). On the middle and upper estuary Cormorant, Little Egret and Grey Heron feed. Dabbling ducks find little food here, although a few Mallard, Wigeon and Teal call in. Parties of Red-breasted Merganser range up to the estuary head at high tide, joining up to five or six Little and Great Crested Grebes, which dive in the main channel. Wild geese are unusual, but an occasional Brent Goose may fly across from the Exe. Dozens of Shelduck (peaking at around 50) and many Rooks and Carrion Crows forage over the mud as the tide recedes.

A few Oystercatchers feed at Passage House, roosting flocks of up to 100 Curlew are very noticeable, Redshank now number around 40 and Lapwing are now only seen in cold weather. These are joined by several wintering Greenshank and occasional godwits, and recently up to 20 Avocet have overwintered. Apart from a handful of Dunlin and Ringed Plover, smaller waders are limited in number and variety. Sheltered saltmarsh creeks around Passage House, where waders roost at high tide on grassy islands, hold a few Common Sandpiper each winter, flying off with characteristic stiff wingbeats if disturbed. A Spotted Sandpiper, its close American relative, has also wintered. Beside sheltered marsh channels a Kingfisher is often encountered. Bushes near the river may hold Cetti's Warbler and wintering Chiffchaff and Firecrest.

Inland at Decoy CP, Great Crested and Little Grebes may be seen, plus several Cormorants, which commute out to the estuary. Tufted Duck are regular, with occasional Pochard, Scaup and Mandarin. Great Northern Diver and rarer grebes have also occurred. Feral visitors include small groups of Canada Geese all over the district, sometimes holding a wild goose or two at Teigngrace. At this site, Green Sandpiper can be seen in flooded fields, with Cattle Egret in some winters.

Fieldfare and Redwing feed in flocks around farmland, while parties of Siskin and a few Lesser Redpoll chatter in the Alders. The loud song of Cetti's Warbler is heard at Jetty and Hackney Marshes all year.

In spring, a range of commoner waders visits the estuary, including passing Whimbrel flocks. Sandwich Terns fish off Teignmouth seafront, which is passed by Manx Shearwater and sometimes skuas in rough weather. Shelduck fly up from the estuary to nest-burrows in nearby farmland, where scattered pairs of Whitethroat and Cirl Bunting breed. Mute Swan and Coot breed at Decoy CP, with Kingfishers moving up to breed in sandbanks towards Teigngrace, where Sand Martins arrive to nest in riverbank holes; this colony of a declining species is now one of the largest in the region. Grey Wagtail, Dipper and Kingfisher may be seen by those prepared to take a longer walk upriver. In late spring several pairs of Reed and Sedge Warblers arrive to breed. On the upper estuary, Spoonbill has been recorded, with Night Heron once found at Jetty Marsh.

In summer, strings of young Shelduck are led across the estuary mudflats by volunteer 'aunties', and soon flocks of Curlew gather, joined by a few migrant godwits and Whimbrel. In late summer up to 20 Common Sandpipers and Greenshank, with other returning waders, gather at the estuary roosts. This period has produced high numbers of Little Egrets, with counts at their evening treetop roost on the south bank exceeding 100 birds. Some feed in brackish backwaters behind the railway track on the north bank.

Autumn may produce a Curlew Sandpiper or Little Stint among the Dunlin, and Greenshank mingling with the Redshank. A few Sandwich Terns forage well up the estuary, once joined by a Gull-billed Tern. Kittiwakes and Balearic and Manx Shearwaters move southward off Teignmouth, with terns and a few skuas. Raptors, aside from ubiquitous Buzzards, are not really a feature of the area, but a Peregrine may wander over outside the breeding season, and Ospreys are regular on passage. A few migrant Sedge Warblers feed in the small reedbed adjacent to Passage House car park, with the occasional Grasshopper Warbler.

TIMING

Species variety increases sharply in hard weather, when Decoy CP may come into its own. For the estuary, the last two hours of rising tide bring waders close enough to watch from the Passage House shore as they gather to roost. Best views are obtained from the steep track adjacent to the sewage works on the southern shore. Passage House can be visited at other tides to check saltmarsh channels but waders and gulls will be distant, necessitating a telescope. Strong onshore winds, especially southerlies and easterlies with poor visibility, may bring seabirds off Teignmouth. At Decoy CP, try to avoid sunny Sundays, when sailing and public use make watching more difficult.

ACCESS

Newton Abbot lies just off the A380 Exeter–Torquay road, which bypasses the town and crosses the estuary on a flyover near Passage House. Turn off the bypass at the Teignmouth (A381) sign from the dual carriageway just north of the flyover. For **Teignmouth**, follow the A381 from this roundabout, stopping in winter at Bishopsteignton where on the right before the garden centre is a public footpath to Flow Point, overlooking the middle estuary. Roadside lay-bys towards Teignmouth give further estuary views. For the estuary mouth and offshore, continue along Teignmouth seafront to a car park at the end **(TQ14 8BW, storeroom.meaning.probe)**.

For the **Upper Estuary**, turn back from the roundabout into Kingsteignton. Turn left at the second mini-roundabout and watch for a lane on the left after 100m to

Passage House Inn (TQ12 3QH. worms.reddish.skater). Follow the lane and view from the car park, adjacent to Passage House Inn, but note that it is intended only for patrons' use. Alternatively, access via the cycle path from Newton Abbot (closed on race days) giving views over the racecourse or park at Hackney Marshes – on the left 300m past the Passage House turning – and walk towards the estuary.

The flat, open area adjoining the upper estuary saltmarsh is an excellent viewpoint, providing car-window views of a variety of waders, Little Egret and other estuarine species at the right state of tide. Ease of access makes this area particularly useful in poor weather or for those with restricted mobility. A telescope is necessary to check gull roosts from here. A flat footpath leads upriver under the road flyover and may give views of Kingfisher and Water Rail. The path leads onto Hackney Marshes, a heavily used area of rough fields, scrub and pools; tracks circle the area.

For **Jetty Marsh**, continue along the main road to Newton Abbot, past the racecourse, to the next roundabout. Park nearby in a small safe-parking area alongside the road and walk back up the main road, crossing the reedy channel, then left onto a public footpath. The path continues through to Teigngrace.

For **Decoy CP (TQ12 1EP, trio.swear.class)**, go back onto the A380 flyover southward, continue across the estuary, then take the slip road before turning right into Newton Abbot at the roundabout. Take the first left on entering Newton Abbot into Keyberry Road. Drive through an urban area to the third roundabout, and turn right. The entrance is a few metres along on the left. Park in the car park and take signposted lakeside walks.

For **Teigngrace**, turn left at the junction at the far end of Broadway Road in Kingsteignton; continue until you have passed over a bridge with a car park on the left and take a public footpath on the right (north) side adjacent to the bridge.

The south side of the estuary is accessible at three main points, all needing a telescope for views across mudflats. From Newton Abbot cross the A380 roundabout on the filter lane marked towards Milber and Shaldon. Follow signs on the B3195 uphill towards Shaldon for about a mile (1.6km) then turn left down a minor road towards Lower Netherton. Park carefully at the first bend and walk down the track ahead for 400m to the estuary side. Scan from here, or at low tide, walk downriver (boots essential) towards Coombe Cellars waterfront pub along the muddy estuary bank. Alternatively go back onto the B3195 and drive another mile (1.6km) towards Shaldon, then just after Coombeinteignhead head left down the Coombe Cellars access lane. From here you can continue towards Shaldon and onto the coastal A379, which crosses the Teign towards Teignmouth. Stop at parking spot on the left just before the bridge to check the lower estuary flats.

CALENDAR

Resident: Canada Goose, Great Crested and Little Grebes, Shag, Grey Heron, Little Egret, Water Rail, Sparrowhawk, Buzzard, Coot, woodpeckers, Shelduck, Kingfisher, Grey Wagtail, Cetti's Warbler, Marsh Tit, Mistle Thrush, common woodland passerines, Cirl Bunting.

December–February: Tufted Duck and other diving ducks at times, Red-breasted Merganser, Cormorant, Oystercatcher, Curlew, Avocet, Redshank, Greenshank, Common Sandpiper, Turnstone, gull roost possibly including scarcer species, Great Northern Diver and auks on sea, winter thrushes, Chiffchaff, Firecrest, Siskin, Lesser Redpoll.

Devon (south coast and Dartmoor)

March–May: Most winter visitors leave by end of March. Sandwich Tern and Sand Martin arrive from late March. Gulls continue to pass through with occasional rarities. Terns and other seabirds late April–May. Whimbrel and other wader passage from late April. Whitethroat and Reed and Sedge Warblers from late April; chance of Spoonbill late season. Shelduck peak late spring.

June–July: Young Shelduck and passerines. Wader movements start again from late June, especially shanks and sandpipers; Curlew flocks on mud.

August–November: Most activity on estuary, including Osprey, with terns, Balearic Shearwater or maybe skuas offshore. Flocks of passage waders with chance of less common species; most migrants have moved on by mid-October. Common Sandpiper remains to overwinter but other visitors in low numbers in November unless cold weather.

7A LABRADOR BAY

OS LANDRANGER MAP 202
OS grid ref: SX9370
Postcode: TQ12 4QU
what3words: radar.stack.elbowing

HABITAT

Just south of Shaldon, this 25ha RSPB reserve consists of coastal mixed farmland with panoramic views across Lyme Bay and the distant tors of east Dartmoor. The sandstone cliffs are edged with dense scrub, with thick hedges dividing small arable fields and steep rough, scrubby pasture. The car park is managed by Teignbridge District Council. It is heavily used by the public, including dog walkers, but despite its small size the terrain keeps many visitors near the car.

SPECIES

This is an easily accessible area to see one the region's major specialities, the rare Cirl Bunting; numerous birds can often be heard in song from the car park.

In winter, in common with many non-wetland sites, birds may initially seem to be absent but small flocks of Skylark and Cirl Bunting will be well hidden across the stubble fields. A hunting Kestrel or other raptor will cause them to flush, the buntings taking refuge in the nearest hedge. A few Meadow Pipits and Linnets will likely be among them, perhaps with a Yellowhammer, scarce here. A look offshore will produce distant Shag, Gannet and auks, with a Great Northern Diver, Common Scoter or rarer seaducks sometimes present.

Male Cirl Buntings sing on fine days from midwinter but as spring arrives up to 30 may stake their territorial claims. Migrants start to move through with Wheatears pausing on the larger fields and Swallows and martins following the coastline north. Whitethroats sing from the scrub, sometimes joined by their Lesser Whitethroat cousin, its rattling song strangely similar to Cirl Bunting's. Green Woodpeckers are often heard and a Peregrine may join the local Buzzards and Ravens overhead.

Cirl Buntings breed late into the year, with family groups present through August.

Devon (south coast and Dartmoor)

September sees migrants start to move south, when Redstarts and Whinchats may be seen along the hedgerows, with pipits returning and the chance of a scarcer bunting in the stubbles. The build-up of smaller birds may tempt a migrant Merlin to stay a few days.

TIMING
Cirl Buntings sing for much of the year, quietest during August and September, in almost all weathers, but calm mornings offer the best chance of success. The area around the car park can be busy, especially at weekends.

ACCESS
The site is reached by heading south from Teignmouth over Shaldon bridge, following the A379 for 1.7 miles (2.8km) to the council car park on the left. Take the right path, level and parallel to the road, to the southern end for favoured stubble fields and scrub. A steep circular route is then possible using the South West Coast Path.

CALENDAR
Resident: Shag, Kestrel, Sparrowhawk, Buzzard, Green Woodpecker, Skylark, Mistle Thrush, Linnet, Bullfinch, Cirl Bunting.

December–February: Common Scoter, possibly other seaducks, Great Northern Diver, winter thrushes, Stonechat, Firecrest.

March–May: Most winter visitors have left by the end of March. Wheatears arrive from late March. Whitethroat and possibly Lesser Whitethroat from late April. Possible migrant passage including Willow Warbler, Spotted Flycatcher and hirundines.

June–July: Cirl Bunting families throughout.

August–November: Migrant activity including Garden Warbler; possible Whinchat and Redstart. Cirl Bunting and Skylark numbers start to build from October, when Meadow Pipit influxes may bring a hunting Merlin.

7B STOVER COUNTRY PARK

OS LANDRANGER MAP 191
OS grid ref: SX8375
Postcode: TQ12 6PW
what3words: reworked.input.awaited

HABITAT
Between Newton Abbot and Dartmoor this 42ha site on sandy soil contains a mixture of coniferous plantations and broadleaved woodland. Much of the understorey consists of rhododendron and small (but increasing due to management) pockets of lowland heath to the north of the lake. The centrepiece of the country park is 14ha Stover Lake, surrounded by well-developed marshland

habitat. General wildlife interest includes dragonflies and damselflies, for which the site is particularly well known. The area is managed by Devon County Council and is heavily used by the public, including dog walkers. The main A38 dual carriageway borders its northern side.

SPECIES

This is an easily accessible area to see a range of woodland and freshwater birds. Rarities are not expected, although one winter a Sora from North America joining the Water Rails by the lake attracted thousands of birdwatchers. Laughing Gull, Ring-necked Duck and Purple and Night Herons have also occurred. More expected sightings here include a variety of tits with Marsh Tit often prominent, woodpeckers, Nuthatch and Treecreeper. The feeding stations overlooked from the aerial walkway enable very close views of many of these woodland residents, including Jay.

On a winter day a walk around the network of paths is often enlivened by groups of Siskin and Lesser Redpoll chattering in waterside alders, while other seed-eaters may include a few visiting Crossbills; large numbers of finches also roost in the park. The lake itself is somewhat acidic but usually features a small wintering population of ducks. Numbers of Tufted Duck and Goosander can reach double figures, and it remains one of the few Devon sites to hold regular Pochard, occasionally joined by other diving ducks in cold weather. Dabbling ducks are also present, including a few Gadwall, Shoveler and Teal. More prominent residents are Mute Swan and Mallard waiting for food scraps, together with a score or more Coot and, recently,

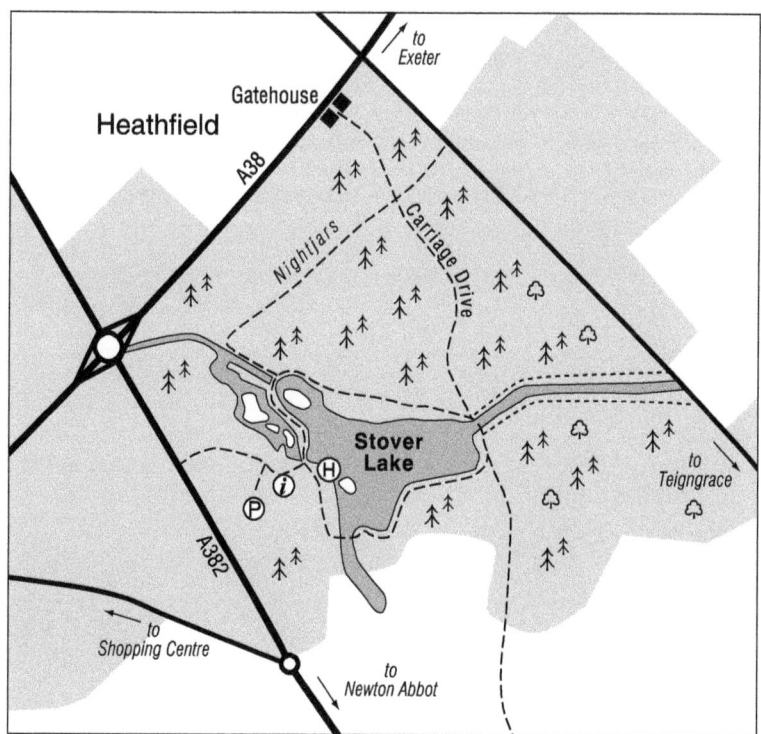

Mandarin. Little and Great Crested Grebes may be present outside the nesting season, the latter occasionally breeding. Small numbers of Cormorants are regularly seen perched on dead trees. Several Water Rails frequent the marshes during the autumn and winter, as well as a large daytime roost of Snipe which can number several dozen. The Snipe leave to feed on surrounding pasture at dusk and then return before dawn. They are best viewed from the south side of the lake as they sit along the marshy edge opposite. A few Woodcock, hidden in the dense woodland by day, may also be seen heading for the same feeding areas at dusk. Kingfisher is recorded every month, with two or three in the autumn. Bittern has overwintered.

Spring brings hirundines skimming over the lake, including Sand Martin from the nearby River Teign colonies, while widespread Chiffchaffs and Willow Warblers sing from the woods. Among a selection of expected summer migrants, more noteworthy are a few Spotted Flycatcher, plus Nightjars which favour the open areas.

TIMING

Calm mornings encourage activity among small woodland birds, and the presence of feeders means that birds such as tits and Nuthatch may be seen all day especially in winter. The site can be quite disturbed at weekends and school holidays. Midweek visits, or early and late in the day, may be quieter.

Waterfowl numbers and variety may be increased by arrivals in colder weather. Nightjar watches, as always, should be at last light on summer evenings in fine weather. The same applies for Snipe, Woodcock and roosting finches, but in winter.

ACCESS

The site is reached by turning off the A38 Exeter–Plymouth road; follow the A382 left at Drumbridges roundabout, signposted to Newton Abbot. After 200m, a signposted left turn (brown tourist sign) takes you into the country park car park (fee payable). A visitor centre and noticeboard display site details, with leaflets and maps available. A network of flat paths, suitable for wheelchair access, crosses the site. Most non-birdwatching visitors use the area near the lake. Further information devon.gov.uk/stovercountrypark or 01626 835236.

CALENDAR

Resident: Great Crested Grebe, Grey Heron, Cormorant, Mandarin, Kingfisher, woodpeckers, Marsh Tit, common woodland passerines, Siskin.

December–February: Gadwall, Shoveler, Tufted Duck, Goosander, maybe Pochard, Snipe, Woodcock, Water Rail, Brambling, Lesser Redpoll, possibly Crossbill.

March–May: Early hirundines arriving to feed over pools. Commoner warblers and Spotted Flycatcher arriving later in period, Nightjar by the end of May.

June–July: Breeding summer visitors as above, Nightjars active throughout.

Devon (south coast and Dartmoor)

8 HOPE'S NOSE, TORQUAY

> OS LANDRANGER MAP 202
> OS grid ref: SX9564
> Postcode: TQ1 2HT
> what3words: deed.desire.crust

HABITAT
Hope's Nose is the northern promontory of Torbay, the first large headland south of the Exe. Cliffs and a small disused quarry face Lyme Bay to the north. Offshore lie the rocky islets of Lead Stone (the smallest and nearest), Ore Stone, 800m out, and Thatcher Rock, 45m high, to the south. The peninsula is covered in bracken and scrub, with a small pine copse on the northern slope and management is restoring areas of more open grassland. A sewer outfall is situated near the tip of the point, but discharges should now only happen in flood conditions.

SPECIES
Hope's Nose is known mainly as a seawatching point. For skuas, and terns particularly, this is one of the better watchpoints in the region in the correct conditions, although the cessation of regular sewer discharges has meant birds tend to pass straight through and linger less frequently. Birds moving along the coast can pass close inshore, especially in reduced visibility or when blown by onshore winds; most movement is south out of Lyme Bay.

In the early part of the year it is worth checking for the occasional Little Gull dipping over the sea or, more likely, a Mediterranean among the Black-headed Gulls. Iceland and Glaucous Gulls may still occur, although they rarely linger since the sewage outfall was modernised. Birds not actively feeding may roost on Lead

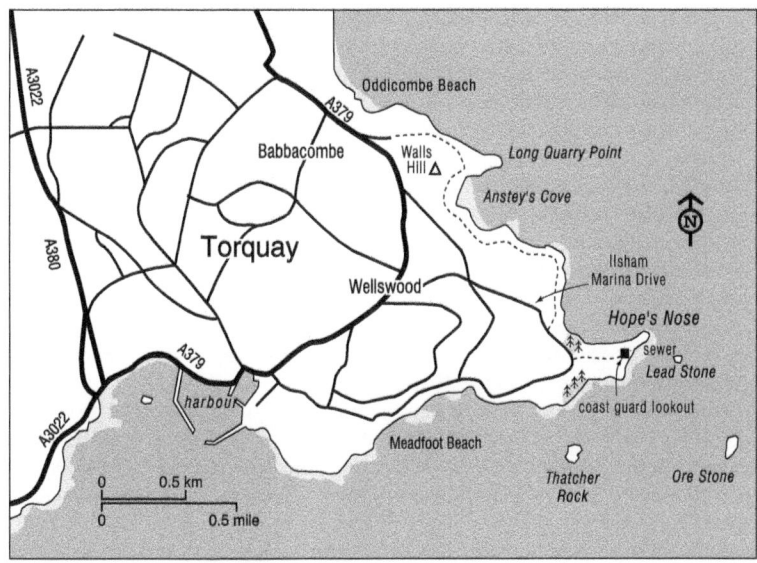

Devon (south coast and Dartmoor)

Stone or the rocky beach right of the point, where Oystercatcher and Turnstone search for food; Purple Sandpipers are regular in small numbers. Rock Pipits are always present near the shore, and often there is a wintering Black Redstart or two. Offshore, a few Gannets and Kittiwakes pass, with rough weather bringing increased numbers, alongside hundreds of auks, and sometimes a skua, most likely a Pomarine. One or two divers, grebes and seaducks feed in the area, often in the bay on the north side. The most likely diver on the sea is Great Northern, told by its steep, domed forehead; Red-throated Divers fly past, although passage of both species can occur. Ducks may include patchy brown and white immature Eider near Lead Stone or some passing Common Scoter.

As migration begins, small numbers of Chiffchaff, Wheatear, Firecrest and Black Redstart arrive. Later, a variety of small migrants feed in the thick bushes, while a singing Lesser Whitethroat may be heard. Numbers of most passerines are not usually large, but scarcer arrivals over the years have included Nightingale, Bee-eater, Woodchat Shrike and Ortolan Bunting. At sea, migrant Whimbrel as well as Sandwich and a few Common Terns pass north, with a chance of skuas. Northward movements in spring are generally small and not close to shore; the best watches are when strong onshore winds bring in south-moving birds as in autumn. Such conditions in May occasionally bring packs of skuas, including spoon-tailed Pomarine, accompanied by scores of Fulmars, Manx Shearwaters, Gannets, terns and auks.

Summer brings hundreds of breeding Herring Gulls, especially on Ore Stone and Thatcher Rock, with several pairs of Great and Lesser Black-backed Gulls. Several pairs of Shag breed, with white-thighed Cormorants choosing the highest pinnacles. A Kittiwake colony on the islets and nearby mainland cliffs was formerly one of the largest in southern England, with up to 500 pairs, but has now disappeared; a few may still breed on Ore Stone. Kittiwakes are still seen commonly around the point in spring and summer, as well as on passage. Careful inspection of Ore Stone ledges (a telescope will be useful) will reveal up to 50 pairs of Guillemot and probably two or three of Razorbill. Puffins may be seen on the sea or flying past at intervals in late spring and summer but are not known to breed. Fulmar breed along the cliffs to the north and frequently glide past the Nose. Whitethroat, Linnet and Stonechat can be found around the scrub.

Out at sea, parties of dozens of Manx Shearwaters regularly pass low over the waves at dawn and dusk through summer. Rough weather can drive a group of tiny European Storm Petrels within view of shore. Gannet and parties of Common Scoter are frequent in midsummer, with a chance of a passing skua. From late summer variety increases, and Manx Shearwaters are replaced by smaller numbers of other shearwaters. Late summer and autumn produce the dusky Balearic Shearwater, thicker set than Manx, often passing at close range. Birds move around Lyme Bay to feed and can be expected most days, but hundreds can pass through in the right conditions or when food is concentrated in the west of the bay. The larger Sooty Shearwater is seen annually, in late summer to early autumn, with increasing numbers of Cory's and Great reported.

As autumn progresses, a steady flow of terns moves south past the Nose in early mornings; Sandwich Terns are most evident at close range, with up to 100 passing on good days. Common Tern passage fluctuates more, depending on weather and food availability. When terns are passing, there will usually be a skua twisting in high-speed aerial pursuit; more than 20 Arctic Skuas pass on good autumn mornings. Small numbers of Pomarine Skua are regular, single figures being usual, and one or two Greats are anticipated but sadly can no longer be expected; the rare Long-tailed Skua has been seen in small numbers, some stopping to patter over the waves in a petrel-like manner, distinctly different from other skuas. Hope's Nose, and Berry Head across the bay to the south, are probably the best watchpoints in the English Channel for this species in autumn onshore winds.

After most terns have departed, skuas may still be blown in by adverse weather, along with a stray oceanic migrant such as a Grey Phalarope, Sabine's Gull or Little Auk; although virtually annual, these last species are seen in smaller numbers than at watchpoints in west Cornwall. Sabine's Gull are as regular here as anywhere in Devon; several have passed in a day, and tired birds may pause to rest offshore for hours, rarely even days. Prolonged gales have very occasionally brought in a dozen or more pale Grey Phalaropes, difficult to watch as they fly a few metres before dropping on the sea to feed; Little Auks are rarer, however. Parties of Brent Geese and Wigeon flying in to local estuaries, plus a few passing divers, mark the approach of winter.

On shore, a few commoner warblers move through the scrub; later in the season Firecrest may be detected. Wheatears and perhaps a Ring Ouzel flit around the rocks in small numbers, replaced later by Black Redstart. Regular watching here has produced records of rarer migrants including Lesser Kestrel, Barred Warbler and Wryneck. Overhead, circling local Ravens are often obvious, while a Peregrine occasionally flies out to attack passing migrants over the sea in autumn.

TIMING

Seabird movement depends heavily on weather conditions, but the largest numbers usually pass in the first three or four hours of daylight; some continue to pass all day if it stays dull, wet or misty but swing away from land once visibility has improved. Days when the horizon is clear and the coastline is seen well will not produce many seabirds. If mist or rain suddenly lifts, such as when a front passes over, there may be a large movement of seabirds out of Lyme Bay past Hope's Nose. Onshore winds (between east and south) give the best birdwatching, but strong south-westerlies may sweep birds up into Lyme Bay; they then seek to pass back southward. Evening watches may prove worthwhile at migration times and can bring summer sightings of Manx Shearwaters as they move up to feed overnight in Lyme Bay; try the last two or three hours of daylight. In fine, high-pressure conditions skuas and terns also tend to move right up to nightfall, the former roosting offshore. Gulls commute between here and the Teign Estuary to the north. After winter gales, check the bay on the north side for sheltering seabirds.

ACCESS

Hope's Nose is accessed from the top of Ilsham Marine Drive in the Babbacombe district of Torquay. From Torquay harbour, turn inland up Torwood Street then right at first traffic signals to Meadfoot Beach. Follow the beach and turn sharp right onto the winding, scenic Ilsham Marine Drive at far end. Park by the road at the highest point. From the road take the public footpath, very steep and muddy in places, down to the bottom of the Nose (unsuitable for less physically able watchers). Check bushes on the way down for warblers at appropriate seasons. Near the bottom, look left into the quarry and bay behind. Wintering grebes may shelter close under the cliff in rough weather. Continue to the end of the spit, where seabirds come in from the north parallel with the coast, a few pass directly

Devon (south coast and Dartmoor)

overhead. Try also walking right, overlooking the shore, for gulls and waders; this path leads back eventually to the top of the Nose.

The breeding birds of the islands, particularly Ore Stone, are hard to check from shore; wildlife boat trips run from Teignmouth (devonseasafari.com), Torbay (funfishtrips.co.uk/brixham-and-torquay-dolphin-wildlife-sea-fari-cruises) and Brixham (boatsafari.co.uk), with guided trips available (mikelangman.co.uk/guided-cruises).

CALENDAR

Resident: Shag, Sparrowhawk, Green Woodpecker, Rock Pipit, Stonechat, Raven.

December–February: Often Eider, Common Scoter, Great Northern, Red-throated and occasional Black-throated Divers, Great Crested and maybe Red-necked Grebe, Gannet, Oystercatcher, Turnstone, Purple Sandpiper, Mediterranean and possible Little Gull, Kittiwake (small numbers), rarely skuas, auks, Firecrest, maybe Black Redstart.

March–May: Fulmar, Cormorant, Kittiwake, larger gulls and auks start to breed. Gull passage (March) with chance of Glaucous or Iceland, diver passage starts; perhaps Puffin feeding offshore; Chiffchaff, Wheatear, Firecrest and Black Redstart late March, Sandwich Terns arriving. Manx Shearwater, Whimbrel and most terns after mid-April, small numbers of passage waders (check Lead Stone), diver passage and best chance of Arctic or Pomarine Skuas in first half of May. Whitethroat and Lesser Whitethroat, Grasshopper Warbler and other warblers end of April–May.

June–July: Common Scoter flocks, breeding seabirds, Manx and, later in period, Balearic Shearwater feeding movements, Gannets pass, chance of European Storm Petrel and skuas. Later Mediterranean Gull passage with returning Black-headed, and tern passage starts. Whitethroat breeds.

August–November: Shearwater passage mainly August–September, with Balearic, maybe Sooty, Cory's or Great Shearwaters. Terns August–mid-October, mostly Sandwich and Common, maybe Arctic or Black, peaking from late August–mid-September; Arctic, Great and Pomarine Skuas to early November, most end August–early October; chance of Long-tailed Skua, September–early November; warblers, mostly September; Firecrest from end September, Wheatear until October, maybe Ring Ouzel. Chance of European Storm Petrel or Sabine's Gull, September–October; first divers, generally Red-throated, end September; possible Grey Phalarope, October; Little Auk, November; Black Redstart and Purple Sandpiper from end October.

Devon (south coast and Dartmoor)

9 TORBAY AND BERRY HEAD

> OS LANDRANGER MAP 202
> OS grid ref: SX9060
> Postcodes: TQ1–TQ6 (for more detail and what3words see Access section)

HABITAT

The sea off Torquay, Paignton and Brixham is sheltered from prevailing south-westerly winds, with Berry Head protruding at the south end. Between the headlands of Hope's Nose to the north and Berry Head to the south, Tor Bay is particularly shallow with important seagrass beds off the Preston–Paignton–Goodrington stretch, a 2-mile (3.2-km) urban seafront backed by public lawns, with Roundham Head in the centre. Cockington is an extensive area of mature mixed woodland, park and pools set in a sheltered valley between Torquay and Paignton. Clennon Valley, behind Goodrington beach, has several sheltered pools, fringed with natural vegetation, which are managed by local volunteers to encourage wildlife. Broadsands beach, between Paignton and Brixham, has

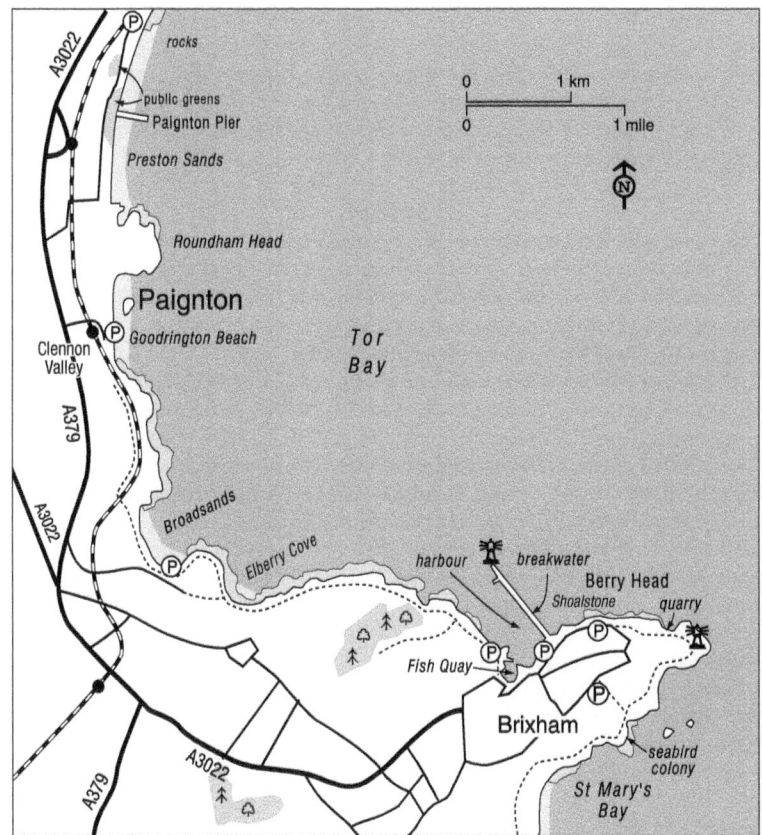

extensive car parking adjoining remnants of a former marsh which still has small areas of reeds and flooded, sheltered bushes. South from the beach lies an area of open grassland and Elberry Cove, giving extensive views of the southern half of Tor Bay.

Brixham, under the lee of Berry Head, still retains a trawling fleet and fish quay. Running into Tor Bay, an 800m stone breakwater projects out to sea, providing shelter for the harbour. Berry Head itself, a limestone mass 65m high, is flat-topped, with a disused quarry facing the sea on the north side. The top, a country park much used by walkers and dog owners, has grass, scrub and, around the hotel, sheltered woodland. At the end is the UK's shortest lighthouse, and behind the cliffs lie ruined fortifications. Berry Head is botanically important, with White Rockrose, Small Hare's-ear, Honewort, Small Restharrow and Goldilocks Aster among its nationally rare species. Orchids are well represented, with Bee, Green-winged, Southern Marsh, Pyramidal, Early Purple and, in late summer, Autumn Lady's-tresses. Butterflies include Small Blue and Wall. Greater and Lesser Horseshoe Bats use the caves in the quarry and can be seen departing in late summer evenings. Berry Head is designated a National Nature Reserve.

Beyond Berry Head southward the coast is mostly cliff-lined, with sheltered scrub around St Mary's Bay and Sharkham Point. Mansands Cove's shingle beach ridge is backed by a 1 mile (1.6km)-long marshy valley which at times floods partly, forming an extensive freshwater lagoon (Mansands Ley). Water levels vary considerably, and the shingle ridge collapses after severe storms, allowing much of the freshwater lake to drain away. The valley is managed by the National Trust. From here high coastal downs with open fields extend towards the Dart estuary.

The whole bay is heavily used by tourists during the summer, and offshore water sports are increasing throughout the year.

SPECIES

The bay is one of the best in the region for a variety of wintering grebes, divers and seaducks. Berry Head is known traditionally as a seabird breeding colony but has become a focus for seawatching, with rough conditions bringing large passages of shearwaters, skuas and other seabirds. A number of interesting migrant landbirds have also been detected on the Head.

Divers are regular on the sea, usually with two or three Great Northern – and sometimes up to 40 – wintering in the southern half of Tor Bay. Red-throated and Black-throated occur sporadically; twice a White-billed was seen, and once a Pacific Diver. Grebes are more widespread, and a telescope is helpful for detailed comparisons between species. Great Crested are scattered widely at times but favouring the Broadsands–Elberry Cove end of the bay. Red-necked Grebe, with its yellowish bill, is seen in most years, especially off the southern half of the bay (Broadsands–Brixham), although prolonged gales may increase sightings and drive birds close in to sheltered coves or harbours. Preston–Paignton is particularly recommended for Black-necked Grebe, but numbers of this species have dramatically declined in recent years.

Small groups of Eider and Common Scoter occur mainly off Elberry and Broadsands, with occasional Velvet and Surf Scoter. All these species may be forced to move around by wind, tide or water sports. The Torquay end is usually less frequented but can be productive when periods of north-easterly winds force birds to shelter here. Oystercatcher and Turnstone are seen mostly from Preston south, with Purple Sandpiper regular on Brixham breakwater and Haldon Quay, Torquay.

Gull roosts on Preston Rocks when the tide falls may include a Mediterranean Gull in addition to Common Gulls among the Black-headeds.

Pied Wheatear and Short-toed Lark have been surprise arrivals on Preston seafront, where Turnstones scurry among walkers. Rock Pipits and Grey Wagtails, sometimes joined by a Black Redstart, feed on tidewrack in sheltered coves. Peregrines occasionally patrol over the beaches.

Cockington Gardens, popular with the general public, is a good location for those starting to learn bird identification. In winter, when it is less crowded with visitors, birds are also easier to see in leafless trees. A wide range of common woodland passerines can be seen in a short circular walk, plus Mistle Thrush and winter thrushes, woodpeckers and common Devon raptors such as Buzzard and Sparrowhawk.

Clennon Valley Ponds form this urban district's main freshwater habitat; Teal, Gadwall and Tufted Duck generally winter in small numbers, although icy spells can bring influxes for short periods. Lying at low level and only a few hundred metres from the sea, the ponds are only likely to freeze over in exceptional conditions. Coot, several Moorhen, a few Water Rails and two or three Little Grebes (which may stay to breed) are also usually present, and warblers may be located in waterside bushes. Yellow-browed Warbler has appeared regularly in late autumn, Hume's Warbler has been recorded, and several have been detected wintering alongside Chiffchaffs, the latter including birds of the eastern *tristis* subspecies. Dusky Warbler has been found a remarkable four times, one staying to overwinter. Another rarity was a brief Penduline Tit found feeding on stands of bulrushes, with one wintering a few years later; both had been seen previously at Slapton Ley.

The larger ponds and nearby sports pitches, which can flood, are used extensively by gulls coming to drink and bathe, especially pre-roost, with the chance that a less common species might be spotted. A Franklin's Gull joined a group of Black-headed Gulls wintering here, and Mediterranean Gulls are regular. In the autumn, Yellow-legged Gulls (usually juveniles) can be found among the local Herring Gulls. Glossy Ibis and Cattle and Great White Egret have also stopped by on occasion. Kingfishers are regularly present by the pools in winter.

The tangle of flooded bushes behind Broadsands beach car parks is another sheltered location that can hold wintering Chiffchaff, Firecrest and occasionally a scarcer warbler. Water Rails winter by the stream, where Reed Warblers sing in spring. The stubble fields at the back of the car parks are a very good place in winter to see between 15–20 Cirl Buntings, a dozen or more Reed Buntings, the occasional Yellowhammer and once a Little Bunting; an RSPB feeding scheme encourages birds to gather.

Broadsands and Goodrington beach and low tide rocks are familiar places to gull enthusiasts. Both beaches have freshwater outflows that attract the gulls. Roosting gulls and terns, especially in mid to late summer, have included more than 100 Mediterranean, regular juvenile Yellow-legged and a few Caspian Gulls. In winter look out for Little, Iceland and Glaucous Gulls. Rare gulls have included Franklin's and Laughing Gull. Sandwich Terns are usually present on offshore buoys, sometimes joined by Common and Arctic, plus rarer Roseate and even an Elegant Tern!

Close observation of Brixham fish dock and the gull roost on the nearby marina pontoons in winter has led to a number of records of Glaucous, Iceland and Caspian Gulls. After its storm-blown arrival from North America, an obliging Laughing Gull remained for over three months around the Breakwater and harbourside. Mediterranean Gulls are usually present from late summer through winter. After southerly and easterly gales, Great Northern Divers, auks and sometimes grebes can be seen at close range feeding in the harbour in the colder months, once including a wintering White-billed Diver. Offshore, feeding parties of Gannet, Kittiwake and auks move about all winter, coming closer in poor weather. Occasionally a Little Auk or lingering Black Guillemot is found in a sheltered cove after rough seas. Behind the Breakwater car park a disused overgrown quarry face adjoins a multi-storey car park; the bushes here often shelter warblers and one or two Firecrests in winter.

Most divers and grebes leave in early spring, when other seabirds gather to breed on the south side of Berry Head; Guillemots may have returned to ledges on mild winter days, but from early spring to mid- or late summer up to 1,000 are present on the overhanging cliffs. Parties of dozens also gather to wash and preen immediately below the cliffs, where they can be watched more easily. Several cackling pairs of nesting Fulmar (plus numerous others patrolling past), Shag and Great Black-backed Gull, and a few Kittiwakes and Razorbills complete the summer scene. This is now the largest auk colony on the English Channel coast, and birds are easily viewable as they fly to and fro. Herring Gulls breed around the cliffs and quarry, where they are joined by additional noisy pairs of Fulmars; a few Sandwich Terns often fish off Tor Bay beaches, even in midsummer.

Cirl Buntings are found on open farmland around the edges of Torbay, often within metres of encroaching development. The southern edge of the area just outside Brixham has a good population, and several pairs breed at Berry Head. Clennon Valley usually holds a few breeding Reed Warblers, and Tufted Duck has bred.

The top of Berry Head attracts a number of migrants, and a few rarer species have occurred, many characteristic of open, rocky terrain. A magnificent white Greenland Gyr Falcon spent 10 days roosting in the quarry one spring, while Alpine and Pallid Swifts have frequented the area in early autumn, although Devon's second Chimney Swift did not linger. Wheatear, Redstart, Whinchat and commoner warblers are likely in small numbers in spring and autumn, joined by a few flycatchers. One or two Ring Ouzels occur late in the autumn migration, when berry-bearing bushes on the slopes below the café provide suitable food and cover. Dartford Warbler is seen annually, with Barred and Sardinian Warblers also noted. Occasionally a shrike might be seen on a prominent thorn bush lookout; Red-backed, Great Grey, Woodchat and two vagrant rufous-tailed 'Isabelline' Shrikes have been seen. A Desert Wheatear was once found here too. Overhead passage can be impressive with hundreds of hirundines, finches, pipits and the occasional Merlin, Hobby, Woodcock or Short-eared Owl. However, a good ear is essential to pick out the smaller numbers of Brambling, Crossbill, Woodlark and Tree Pipit. Scarcer species passing over have included Richard's and Red-throated Pipits, Shore Lark, Serin, Tree Sparrow and Hawfinch.

The tall Sycamore copse on the north side of Berry Head can hold scarcer migrants in late autumn. It has become known as one of the most regular localities in Devon for sightings of Pallas's and Yellow-browed Warblers, occasionally joined by a Red-breasted Flycatcher, although they can be difficult to see in these tall trees, or exceptionally Dusky or Radde's Warbler. Blyth's Reed and Western Bonelli's Warblers have also been found in low bushes in the quarry. An elusive Red-flanked Bluetail found during October easterlies remains Devon's only mainland sighting. In late autumn, Black Redstarts often flit around the quarry and ruined fort walls.

Shearwaters, petrels, skuas and terns are seen passing south off Berry Head's cliffs, occasionally in spring and summer, although the main passage is through autumn. A number of these will normally be individuals that have been recorded off Hope's Nose, visible 4 miles (6.4km) to the north, within the previous 20–30 minutes. However, when deep depressions pass up the English Channel, very large movements are often observed here which have largely avoided Hope's Nose. A September passage of over 700 skuas in a day, for example, far exceeded previous Devon counts and included several Long-tailed. Sabine's Gull and other scarce migrants have accompanied them, although phalaropes are more seen off Hope's Nose than here. Great Shearwaters, during their marathon annual feeding trip from the South Atlantic, can be pushed into the mouth of the English Channel by such conditions. In late summer and early autumn Berry Head has provided opportunities for seeing this species, with dozens occasionally recorded and once nearly 300 (although calm autumns may produce few or none). Lesser numbers of Sooty Shearwater, occasionally in double figures (but once a Devon record of 582), and a few Cory's are recorded on peak days. Balearic Shearwaters can be seen in a wide variety of conditions, even on calm, clear days, and are recorded passing most mornings in late summer and autumn. Sightings vary annually; some years flocks linger to feed, perhaps connected with the movements of fish shoals. This area provides some of Britain's highest Balearic Shearwater passage counts, with a record 1,978 in August 2025. Increased interest in this Critically Endangered seabird has led to careful logging of numbers for survey purposes and birds are being reported, albeit less regularly, through into winter. Observers have also been rewarded by the UK's first Yelkouan Shearwater, Little Shearwater and several Desertas-type petrels. However, Devon's first Brown Booby evaded them, being photographed from a passing wildlife cruise!

The lookout point at Berry Head quarry is higher than Hope's Nose rocks, giving better views over wavetops in rough seas. Fishing vessels may attract groups of shearwaters, occasionally even Great Shearwater, following incoming trawlers, and flocks of European Storm Petrel have been located similarly on a number of occasions by telescope observations of birds following passing boats. Even when other seabirds are not passing offshore, the arrival of an incoming trawler may stimulate interesting sightings among the gatherings of attendant seabirds, offering closer views as the trawler approaches. Passage seabirds might be detected beyond the expected migration periods during south-westerly gales in winter. Pomarine Skuas in particular, are likely to turn up harrying gulls throughout the winter when conditions move them in from open seas. Severe gales have also produced multiple counts of Great Skua, approaching 80 on one January day, but there have been very few since the devastation of avian flu. During heavy squalls, flocks of several hundred Gannets and Kittiwakes shelter in the bay.

Mansands Cove and its freshwater pool area (the pool is present some years, virtually dry in others) has attracted a distinctive bird population, although this depends greatly on water levels. During periods of extensive freshwater buildup, the 'Ley', as it became known, has attracted a regular population of wintering ducks, including 30 Teal, half a dozen Shoveler and Gadwall, Tufted Duck in single figures, a couple of Little Grebes and a wintering Blue-winged Teal. Hundreds of gulls, once including a Ring-billed, also come to bathe and preen. During migration periods a selection of waders visiting the muddy margins (although numbers are always small) has included Green and Wood Sandpipers, as well as Pectoral Sandpiper and Grey Phalarope. Cetti's Warbler, Snipe and Water Rail are generally present in the marginal vegetation in winter (even once joined by a Bittern) and Water Pipit has stayed. Spring sees breeding Coot and Moorhen, while hirundines feeding over the water are often chased by a Hobby. Fortunate observers have found a Red-rumped Swallow with them, a male Bluethroat in waterside bushes in spring and a Desert Wheatear around the Lifeguard Cottages one autumn, an area often frequented by Black Redstart in the same season.

Hedgerows behind the cove often have groups of Cirl Buntings in winter, and several pairs breed in the valley. Offshore, Razorbill, Great Crested Grebe and varying numbers of Common Scoter are regularly present in Mansands Cove in winter; Peregrines and Ravens fly over along the coast. The high area of clifftop fields towards Froward Point to the south is not much visited by birdwatchers, but records of Quail, Buff-breasted Sandpiper, Dotterel, Red-backed Shrike, Lapland Bunting and Common Rosefinch show the potential for migrants.

TIMING

Grebes and other waterbirds in Tor Bay are best picked out when cloudy skies cast pale grey 'flat' light on the sea. High tides with little wind and a calm sea are helpful; east winds usually churn up the surface, which makes watching difficult. The bay is very exposed to such conditions and, if these are prolonged, waterbirds may move off to areas further west. On fine weekends, water sports may cause disturbance unless you arrive early.

Cockington Gardens can be very crowded at weekends or holiday periods. This and Clennon Valley are best visited early morning or weekdays when public disturbance is less. A visit during a cold spell might bring increased numbers of all species.

At Brixham, a weekday visit when trawlers are unloading is likely to be best for gulls. Strong winds and rough seas in the bay can force wintering divers to shelter near the breakwater, or even inside the harbour. Try a seawatch for passing seabirds off Berry Head in strong south or south-west winds with mist or rain, particularly early in the morning when birds are first moving through, or late afternoon/evening when there can be some revival of passage if conditions are still rough. It is important for good movements that the coastline outside Tor Bay is obscured by mist, rain or low cloud; once the cliff line north-east towards Dorset is clearly visible, passage seabirds move much further out into Lyme Bay. It is also worth checking offshore whenever returning trawlers approaching Brixham attract flocks of Gannet, Kittiwake, gulls and other seabirds looking for scraps. Rarer species may be tempted to join them. When seawatching from the quarry be aware that some species, including Arctic Skua and Balearic Shearwater, may circle close in from the north-west after following the bay round, while others, including most larger shearwaters, will cut across the mouth of the bay in front – so watching in two directions is needed to gain views of all arrivals. In very heavy squalls skuas, Gannets and Kittiwakes build up in the bay north of Brixham, waiting for a gap in the weather before passing the headland. Heavy rain may cause all species to sit on the sea. Birds that have sheltered in the bay can also be watched leaving for the open sea from the Shoalstone car park on the edge of Brixham.

For passerine migrants, especially in south-east breezes, try early mornings on Berry Head before public disturbance is too great. There is limited cover and small passerines are hard to see on windy days. Observations of unusual autumn migrants in the Sycamores behind Berry Head Hotel have been mostly after south-east or easterly winds. Some migrants also shelter down in the quarry in strong winds with a southerly element. The auk colony can be seen at any time in the breeding season (but beware early July departure dates after breeding concludes). Autumn coasting movements of finches, pipits, larks and other day migrants are usually in the early to mid-morning and are most pronounced against a light to moderate headwind.

ACCESS

The A379 runs south from Torquay seafront through Paignton via Preston, with frequent signposts to the seafront and beaches; at the hilltop crossroads beyond Goodrington, the A3022 is signposted to Brixham. All seafront areas may be worth checking, but the main bird viewpoints are as follows:

Cockington Signposted right off the main road between Torquay and Paignton. A central car park is available. Tarmac paths run through the area.

Preston Between Torquay and Paignton. Follow the main road southward, left past the traffic lights and under the railway bridge. Turn left immediately onto a small promenade road. You can watch from car windows in bad weather. Wintering grebes are regular. Rocks at north end often have Turnstones (which forage in the car park at high tide), plus resting gull flocks. A Black Redstart is usually nearby in winter. The public footpath across the small headland to the north side leads to Hollacombe Cove and gardens about 300m away, where gulls may roost when disturbed from the main beach.

Paignton Pier This viewpoint can be reached by turning left across the public greens off the main seafront road. You can walk left along the front to Preston (10 minutes). Car-window views are possible here. You can also walk out onto the pier past amusement arcades to gain closer views of birds on the sea. Try elsewhere if water sports are in progress, as birds then usually move well out or feed in other parts of the bay.

Goodrington Signposted left off the Paignton–Brixham road at the mini-roundabout opposite the sports and leisure complex. Grebes and Great Northern Diver are often present in winter. The large ornamental pond may hold storm-blown seabirds among the Coot and Mallard, with Chiffchaff and Firecrest in the small marsh in winter.

Clennon Valley (TQ4 5HS, future.hungry.jump) Reached by turning right opposite the Goodrington entrance. Go left into the large car park by the sports and leisure centre (parking fee). Take the path from the rear of the car park across the full length of the sports fields; the pools are at the far end. Paths are level but muddy in places. At weekends, sports teams often use the fields. Occasionally, after heavy rains, floodwater remains on the fields and can be worth checking for interesting species among gull flocks.

Broadsands (TQ4 6HX, rags.remotest.monkeys) A sheltered cove between Paignton and Brixham, this has a sandy shoreline, extensively used by the public. It is reached by turning off the main Paignton–Brixham road at a minor crossroads at the top of the hill beside Churston library and shops, just before the traffic lights. Drive for 0.6 miles (1km) down Broadsands Road and under the viaduct. Park either in the car park on the left (for a fee) or by the roadside when permitted in the winter months. Rocks at the north and south sides of the cove are used by roosting gulls (often including Mediterranean), Oystercatcher and Turnstone. Divers or grebes may feed close offshore on quiet mornings. At the south side (there is a path from the right of the beach) there is open access along the low grassy clifftop, towards stony Elberry Cove. This 10-minute walk provides opportunities for wide scanning across the southern half of the bay, especially with a telescope, for feeding divers, grebes and seaducks. Behind the large tarmac Broadsands car park are reed-fringed ditches and an area of wet scrub and tangled trees; these can host wintering warblers, with winter buntings feeding in the second car park.

By returning north from Broadsands, it is possible to view the Saltern Cove/Three Beaches area of rocky foreshore and bays stretching towards Goodrington. Drive back up the hill from Broadsands, turn right on the A379 and down the hill for 800m until the row of shops appears on the right. Turn right between the row of shops and the large church, following Barn Road, then Horseshoe Bend residential street round two bends until arriving at a gap where a path leads between the houses. Park carefully along the street to avoid blocking residents' access. Follow the path across a bridge over a railway and out onto a grassy headland with gives good views over the sea between Broadsands and Goodrington. Evening gull roosts can often be seen well in winter, with the chance of less common species. Saltern Cove beach is reached by a flight of steps.

Brixham Harbour north side Obvious from the town centre, the fish dock at the north corner of the harbour is worth a look in winter, especially when trawlers are unloading and attracting hundreds of gulls. Roadside parking is very limited but there is a multi-storey car park just before you reach the harbour. Entry into the fish dock is not allowed but you can walk round the quayside path to the right of the dock entrance. From here you can look across the boundary fence to the fish quay a few dozen metres away, although boats coming in at the rear of the quay can only be seen from Freshwater car park, further along the road. Beyond the dock entrance the main road curves sharply uphill; a sharp right turn at the bend takes you to Freshwater car park, which overlooks much of the harbour and part of the fish quay. By walking north from the car park along the coast path for 300m you reach Battery Gardens lookout, which has partial views north-west towards Elberry and Broadsands.

Brixham Harbour south side For divers and auks in winter try the south side of the harbour (back from the fish quay to the top of the harbour, then turn sharply left instead of entering the main shopping street). Drive 800m to the Breakwater car park and walk along; good views of passing and sheltering birds can be obtained from the end, and grebes and divers may feed close in beside the wall. Purple Sandpipers are usually present in winter. From here you can also look across the Marina pontoons (private, no access), where gulls roost. Immediately behind the Breakwater (accessible by a tunnel) is the old ivy-covered quarry adjacent to Harbour East multi-storey parking; this is worth checking for Firecrest in winter. About 300m beyond the Breakwater car park towards Berry Head is Shoalstone Beach car park; skuas, shearwaters and petrels, and even a White-billed Diver have been seen from car windows here, although there is also a beach shelter below the car park.

Berry Head (TQ5 9AP, picnic.talker.reunion) This can be reached by continuing along beyond the Breakwater and Shoalstone. Past Berry Head Hotel the road swings up through a sheltered valley to the hilltop car park. If entering the town on the main road from Paignton, Berry Head is signposted to the right as you approach the built-up area. From the car park, head for the Northern Fort, turning right and going past the visitor centre to see the auk colony in spring/summer. For small migrants, check walls and bushes around the edges of the Head, which can be windswept on top. Bushes and thickets behind the car park, reached by a network of signposted paths, can be productive especially in a northerly or easterly wind. Try also the sheltered hedgerows, fields and clifftop bushes towards St Mary's Bay on the south side of the Head, reached by the same footpath network. Care is needed to avoid accidents. In late autumn also try the valley coming up from the direction of Berry Head Hotel and the adjoining Sycamore copse. View either from the lane or from well-marked footpaths leading through the wood – this area has been the most productive for Pallas's and Yellow-browed Warblers. Opposite the lower wood entrance another path branches off, opposite a parking place, leading past sheltered cottage gardens and walled areas. This area can also be productive for warblers in late autumn.

For passing seabirds, walk ahead from car park towards the end of the Head, then turn left down a gravel track before reaching the fortress wall. Follow this track around the perimeter fence of the disused quarry until you reach a metal gate and stile; you can walk down an old tarmac road towards the edge of the quarry, immediately below the tip of the Head, and seawatch in relative shelter, even in strong south-westerly winds. Black Redstarts are often present around the quarry from late autumn and other migrants shelter here.

Note: Owing to the potential for quarry floor subsidence, birdwatchers going out to the end of the quarry track beyond the concrete blockhouse are advised they do so at their own risk. Parties intending to visit should contact Torbay Coast & Countryside Trust: countryside-trust.org.uk.

Sharkham Point Beyond St Mary's Bay at the south side of Berry Head lies this little-watched area with bushes that can hold passerine migrants; both Hoopoe and Wryneck have been recorded. Walk south along the coastal path from Berry Head – around a mile (1.6km) – or drive back from the Head to the crossroads with the B3205 Brixham–Dartmouth road, turning left at the traffic lights towards Dartmouth for 800m, then turn left into Castor Road, towards St Mary's Bay through narrow lanes; turn right to a rough car park near the clifftop signposted to Sharkham Point and follow the gravelled paths to the right. When the path splits, fork left and down towards the tip of the Point. The narrow path can be muddy.

Mansands Cove and Marsh (TQ6 0EF, recline.prospers.punks) Those with time and energy to spare could walk the cliff path from Sharkham a mile (1.6km) further south to the beach and adjoining freshwater marsh. The area can also be reached from the Kingswear road. Drive south on the A379 from Torbay towards Kingswear and Dartmouth, ensuring you fork left onto the B3205 for Kingswear and Lower Ferry. After half a mile (800km), take a minor left turn towards Coleton Fishacre and Woodhuish. Bear left for Woodhuish along a narrow, twisting lane terminating in a National Trust parking area. Walk 800m down the rather steep track to the beach and marsh. Passage waders might be found on the beach or marsh, but are often frightened off by walkers or dogs.

The high, clifftop fields between here and the Dart can be viewed from the coastal footpath beyond Mansands or from the National Trust car park at Brownstone near the Coleton Fishacre estate, from which a mile (1.6km)-long track leads to the coast at Froward Point.

Bird and wildlife boat trips run regularly throughout the year but mostly summer to mid-autumn from Brixham, if the weather is good. Guided boat trips around Tor Bay and longer excursions out into Lyme Bay are available via mikelangman.co.uk/guided-cruises.

CALENDAR

Resident: Shag, Coot, Peregrine and other common raptors, Great Black-backed Gull, Raven, Stonechat, Rock Pipit, Cirl Bunting. Common woodland passerines at Cockington.

Devon (south coast and Dartmoor)

December–February: Gadwall, Tufted Duck, Great Northern, Red-throated and sometimes Black-throated Divers, Great Crested, Black-necked and maybe Red-necked Grebes; Gannet, Eider, Common Scoter, occasional Velvet Scoter, Oystercatcher, Turnstone, Purple Sandpiper, gulls including Mediterranean and maybe Iceland. Regular Kittiwake, Razorbill and Guillemot at sea. Small numbers of Firecrest and Black Redstart. winter thrushes. Wintering chiffchaffs in sheltered areas may include the eastern subspecies and be accompanied by rarer species.

March–May: Great Northern Diver stays to early April some years; Fulmars on cliffs from start of period, breeding Shag, larger gulls, Kittiwake, Guillemot, Razorbill. Migrant passerines on headlands late March–May; passing seabirds mostly from mid-April, e.g. Manx Shearwater, maybe skuas, terns, a few Puffin.

June–July: Tor Bay quiet except for the odd Sandwich Tern. Berry Head's breeding Fulmar, gulls, Kittiwake and auks most active to end of June; Manx Shearwater, Yellow-legged Gull and Gannet pass, with first Balearic Shearwater and occasional Puffin in July.

August–November: Fulmar and gulls still on cliffs in August. European Storm Petrel, Balearic and maybe larger shearwaters (mostly August–September), skuas to late October. Passerine migrants on headlands August–November, Black Redstart from mid-October. First divers and grebes in Tor Bay from mid-October but often scarce until November. Chance of scarcer warblers, e.g. Yellow-browed, Pallas's, end October–early November. Occasional Little Auk in November.

10 DARTINGTON AND THE LOWER DART

OS LANDRANGER MAP 202
OS grid ref: SX7962
Postcode: **Dartington** – TQ9 5HL **Stoke Gabriel** – TQ9 6RD
what3words: **Dartington** – squeaking.swerves.audibly
Stoke Gabriel – amplified.vanished.green

HABITAT

The River Dart flows south in a loop past the attractive mixed woods, parkland and farmland of the Dartington Estate near Totnes. On the north side, the river is shallow with gravel bars in places, but on the south side a wider slow-flowing stretch lies above Totnes weir. The estuary between Totnes and Dartmouth is scenic and winding, with wooded banks and sheltered creeks used extensively for boating.

Stoke Gabriel Millpond is a 400m-long semi-tidal lagoon, backed on one side by deciduous woods and on the other by houses.

SPECIES

The shallower stretches of the river are a regular haunt of Dipper and Grey Wagtail bobbing on waterside stones. Early in the year the wider stretches towards the weir are used by a variety of ducks, especially in cold weather, with Goosander often seen. A scattering of dabbling ducks includes regular Teal, one

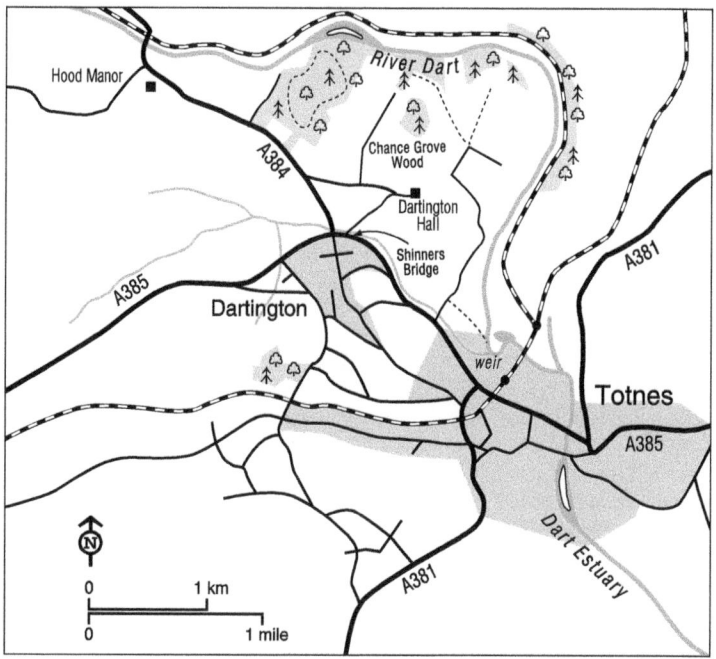

or two Gadwall and Mandarin. When disturbed, flocks may fly to south of the weir, near to Totnes. Little Grebe are also usually seen. The varied habitat and sheltered position ensure a wide variety of farm and woodland species such as woodpeckers, tits, Nuthatch and finches.

Summer migrants include woodland and hedgerow warblers such as Blackcap, Garden Warbler, Whitethroat and Chiffchaff, with hirundines around buildings. Having bred further up the Dart, a red-headed female Goosander with a brood of ducklings might be seen in the area. At the end of summer, Kingfishers often spend periods on this part of the river before moving down to the estuary to winter.

The tidal estuary, although scenic, lacks extensive mudflats or bordering marshes, meaning that wildfowl and waders are never numerous, although small numbers of common species occur. Scarce and rare birds have included Black Tern, Glossy Ibis, Spoonbill and Great White Egret. The estuary's winding course and many private estates make viewing difficult. The best way to watch the Dart estuary is by boat – regular guided wildlife boat trips are run during the summer and autumn. The upper, sheltered stretches may hold overwintering Common Sandpiper. Outside the breeding season, Kingfishers are often hidden amongst overhanging trees, where Mandarin Duck often associate with Mallards and Cormorants usually fish in the waterways, roosting beside Grey and Common Seals on rocks at low tide or on boating pontoons at high water. Shags and Great Northern Diver are regular around the lower stretches nearer Dartmouth, especially after storms. There are heronries near Sharpham on the west bank, as well as Maypool and Kingswear on the east bank; Little Egret now frequent these, often feeding upriver as far as Dartington. Shelduck breeds, and dozens are seen in spring and early summer, while Buzzards, Sparrowhawks and Ravens soar over the wooded banks. In autumn, a few Sandwich Terns follow the tide up the estuary, and there are regular sightings of Osprey fishing in the lower and middle reaches up to Sharpham. Stoke Gabriel Millpond has held a number of interesting species, despite disturbance. Smew and Scaup have been seen in severe cold weather, and once a spotty breeding-plumaged Spotted Sandpiper was found.

TIMING

Duck numbers are highest in cold winter weather, especially when lakes elsewhere are frozen, and mild winters may produce very few diving ducks. Early mornings in spring and summer are best for songbirds. The estuary has no central high-tide roost for waders; for these, visit at lower tide.

ACCESS

Dartington Estate is just east of the A385 Totnes–Buckfastleigh road. If leaving Totnes northbound, turn right at the roundabout in Dartington and right again at the next roundabout for parking. From here an all-access path runs east for 1.9 miles (3km) into central Totnes, passing alongside the River Dart and by Queen's Marsh and Bidwell Brook.

Stoke Gabriel village is reached down minor roads off the A385 between Torbay and Totnes; drive through the village until signs point right to the quay. Park by the quay and scan the pool; for further views cross the concrete weir which separates the pool from the main Dart estuary, take the well-marked paths to the left through the wood.

The estuary is difficult to cover from the banks; many visitors take scenic boat trips from Totnes or Dartmouth, available mainly from April to October (contact local tourist information offices for details). Some operators offer wildlife cruises with guided trips available: mikelangman.co.uk/guided-cruises.

CALENDAR

Resident: Cormorant, Shag, Grey Heron, Buzzard, Mandarin Duck, woodpeckers, Kingfisher, Grey Wagtail, common woodland passerines, Dipper, Raven.

December–February: Dartington – Goosander, possibly other diving ducks, Little Grebe, winter thrushes, Siskin, Lesser Redpoll. Estuary – Shelduck, Water Rail, Common Sandpiper, maybe Green Sandpiper, Greenshank, Redshank, Curlew, Snipe, Kingfisher, Chiffchaff.

March–May: Most ducks and waders leave by mid-March. Singing warblers mostly from mid-April at Dartington and Long Wood, Kingswear. A few migrant waders on the estuary and plentiful Shelduck.

June–July: Common breeding residents and summer visitors; Shelduck breeds and Goosanders might be seen with young.

August–November: Post-breeding flocks of tits and warblers (August), regular Osprey, terns and a few waders on the estuary (mostly mid-August–early September), winter visitors from end October.

Devon (south coast and Dartmoor)

SITE CLUSTER: SOUTH HAMS COAST

 11 Slapton Ley and district (including Beesands and Hallsands)
 12 Start Point
 13 Prawle Point
 14 Kingsbridge Estuary
 15 Soar area including Bolt Head to Bolt Tail
 16 Thurlestone area
 17 South Efford Marsh, Avon Estuary and Water Meadows

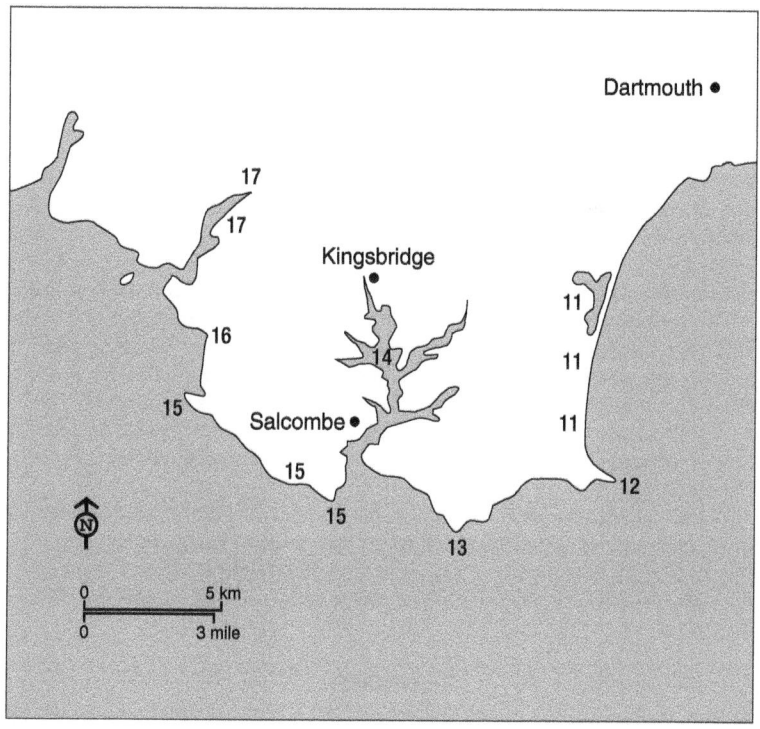

ds
11 SLAPTON LEY AND DISTRICT (INCLUDING BEESANDS AND HALLSANDS)

OS grid ref: SX8344
Postcode: **Slapton Ley** – TQ7 2TQ
what3words: **Slapton Ley** – hosts.snap.mailings

HABITAT

Start Bay faces eastward, sheltered from prevailing winds by the promontories of Start Point and Prawle Point, with high farmland behind. Slapton's diminishing shingle beach, facing the bay, runs south for 1.9 miles (3km). The freshwater lagoon of Slapton Ley lies behind the beach, parallel to the coast; halfway along, it is divided by a narrow neck into the northern Higher Ley, reed-choked with encroaching willow scrub and other bushes, and the open water of Lower Ley on the south side. Reeds fringe the Lower Ley, while shallow bays at the rear, where streams enter, have more extensive reedbeds. Along the inland side of the shingle ridge, runs a strip of thickets and brambles; the top of the beach is sandy turf, with a footpath and the main road running down its length. Slapton Bird Observatory maintains a ringing hut overlooking the bridge between Higher and Lower Leys. The Field Study Centre in Slapton village manages the area as a nature reserve on behalf of the owners, the Whitley Wildlife Conservation Trust.

The Leys, beach and surrounding area boast much rare and local flora and fauna. Strapwort *Corrigiola litoralis* grows nowhere else in Britain, Flowering Rush is another Ley-side rarity, with Yellow-horned Poppy and Viper's Bugloss growing along the beach. A wide variety of dragonflies and damselflies includes the recently arrived Norfolk Hawker, alongside Hairy Dragonfly and Beautiful Demoiselle. Otters, although often elusive, are present, and can sometimes be seen from Slapton Bridge.

The shingle beach extends south past Slapton towards Start Point, blocking the small, deep valleys of Beesands and North Hallsands. At Beesands an open 12ha lake, backed by fields, reeds and scrub, forms a sheltered miniature of Slapton Ley. At Hallsands a semi-dry reedbed with scattered pools and bushes extends 400m up the valley.

SPECIES

Slapton is an easy area to see winter wildfowl, marsh species and a variety of other birds, especially at migration seasons. Beesands and, particularly, Hallsands are much less watched.

In winter one or two Great Northern Divers, plus Shag, Eider and Common Scoter are seen regularly from Slapton and Beesands beaches; sometimes a Red-necked Grebe or group of Velvet Scoter may also be present.

Waders, including Turnstone, a few Dunlin and Ringed Plover, are often present on the shingle if undisturbed. Large gull flocks, sometimes including hundreds of Great Black-backed and a few Kittiwake, collect on quieter stretches of beach, flying over into the Lower Ley or the stream entering the sea just beyond Torcross cliff at the south end to drink and bathe. Little and Mediterranean Gulls are often found among the flocks. Notable sightings have included several Glaucous and Iceland Gulls and an adult Ross's Gull one February weekend.

Devon (south coast and Dartmoor)

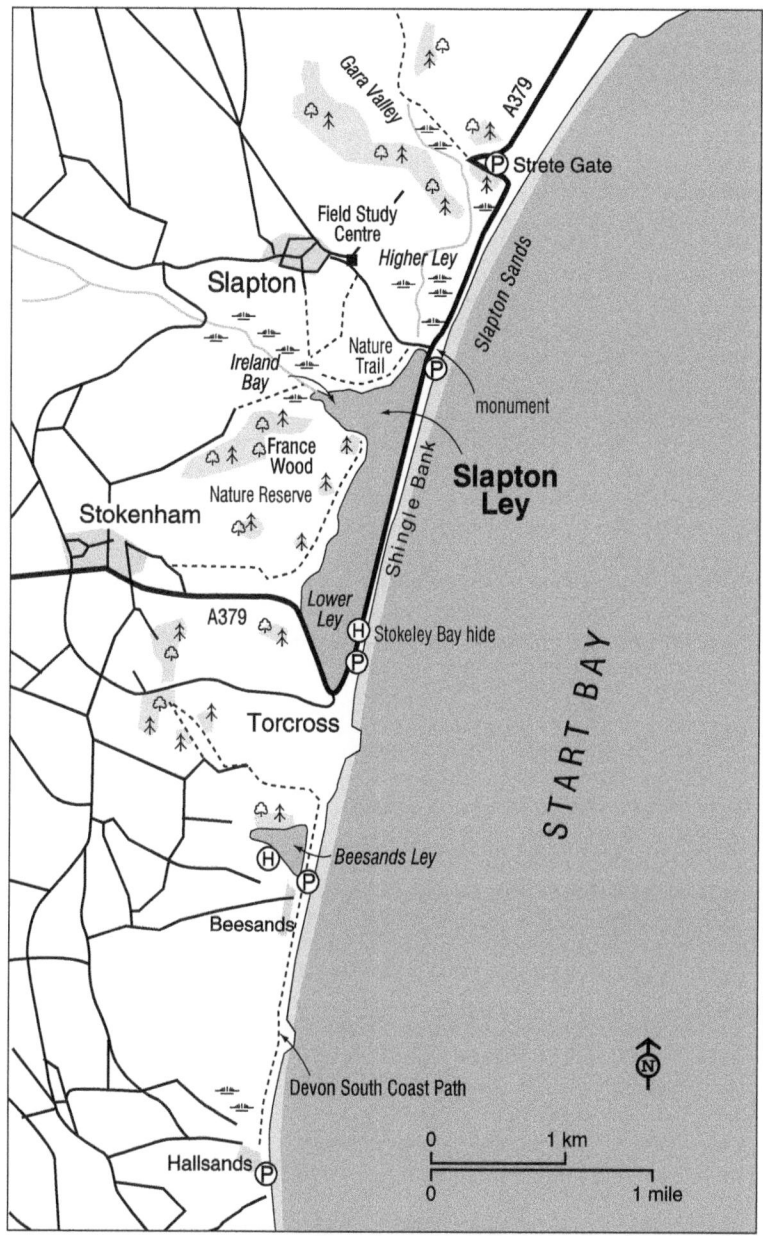

Several hundred wildfowl, chiefly diving ducks, use the leys in winter, with more than 100 Tufted Duck usually on the Lower Ley, many nearer Torcross. Once as numerous, Pochard now only winter in single figures, as do Goldeneye. Goosander are now regular and a Long-tailed Duck or Smew may turn up on sheltered parts of the Ley.

As one of the best locations in the region for diving ducks, Scaup are often picked out, and Ferruginous Duck has been recorded here more than anywhere else in the region, though the last record was in 2003. Ring-necked Duck, from North America, are more frequent with returning birds over many winters and a couple of times even small flocks. Dabbling ducks are not numerous apart from the bread-chasing Mallard at Torcross, but flocks of Wigeon and Teal may be present in reedy bays. Devon's only American Black Duck spent long periods here, moving between the leys and the Kingsbridge Estuary. Gadwall are now well established, with peaks of up to 50 and several breeding pairs.

Great Crested Grebe has one of its breeding strongholds in the region at Slapton, with increased numbers in winter. Black-necked Grebe also occurs on the Ley itself in most years, often staying to moult into smart breeding plumage. Coots remain in numbers, often feeding in tight flocks, but are 80 per cent down on previous peaks. The Higher Ley is more difficult to watch, but Cetti's Warblers are noticeably vocal among damp vegetation, their loud song carrying far across the ley on mild winter days. Especially in colder weather, which increases wildfowl numbers and may bring a party of wild geese, a Bittern may be seen over the reeds at dusk, and the metallic *ping* calls of Bearded Tit are heard in some winters, with the unrelated – and rarer – Penduline Tit also recorded. Chiffchaff and Firecrest often stay through the coldest months in sheltered corners at the back of both leys, with both Siberian Chiffchaff and Yellow-browed Warbler having overwintered. In some years an impressive Starling roost will gather as numbers of hidden Water Rails squeal from the reedbeds. These may attract a Marsh Harrier or Peregrine, and occasionally a Barn Owl may be seen hunting the ley fringes on a winter afternoon.

Beesands has similar birds to Slapton, with two or three Great Crested Grebes, Coots and Gadwall feeding on pondweeds, and parties of Tufted Duck and Pochard. There is much interchange between the sites and in some years, birds may favour one or other ley. Close views are possible on this relatively small lake. Rarer ducks, such as Ring-necked, may visit from Slapton, and several have been found here, as have three Lesser Scaup. Cetti's Warbler is present in waterside vegetation both here and at Hallsands; the latter has fewer attractions in winter, but Chiffchaffs reside in the valley, with a Black Redstart often flycatching along the beach.

Spring awakens with a sprinkling of shoreline Wheatears and the chance of an early Hoopoe on sandy turf at Slapton beach. Their arrival may coincide with an influx of diving ducks and Sand Martins circling over the ley. Garganey appear in the marshy bays and may stay for a week or two. Parties of migrant Common and Lesser Black-backed Gulls join flocks of other species roosting on the beach. Scarcer gulls may be recorded: a Caspian, or perhaps a Little or Glaucous. Later in spring a trickle of terns, mostly Sandwich, passes northwards, and small numbers of Red-throated, Black-throated and Great Northern Divers may be seen in breeding plumage offshore.

From mid-spring, migrants are often numerous. Large numbers of hirundines and warblers feed around the leys, with thousands of Swifts and Swallows hawking at head height in the right conditions, and many Reed and Sedge Warblers staying to breed in reedbeds, with Whitethroat also nesting. Falls of migrants among the scrub have included species such as Nightingale, Woodchat Shrike, and two Little Buntings one early spring, while Great Reed Warbler has been heard chuntering from the reedbeds. Warblers and flycatchers may also be seen around Hallsands as they filter off nearby Start Point and up the valley. Waders are not numerous generally in this area, but tired groups of migrants, especially Bar-tailed Godwit and Whimbrel, are often seen resting on quieter stretches of beach.

Warm winds, bringing the main arrival of summer migrants, also regularly carry overshooting marsh species from the Continent to the area. Species such as Night-Heron and Purple Heron are almost expected in spring with Cattle, Great White and Litte Egrets all now regular. Rarer species such as Squacco Heron, Little Bittern, Whiskered and White-winged Black Terns and Red-rumped Swallow have all occurred. Marsh Harriers quarter the reeds but are yet to stay to breed. Montagu's Harrier, Honey Buzzard and Black Kite have also passed through at this season. Warmer weather encourages Great Crested Grebes to court, with several pairs performing their elaborate 'weed-dance' displays. A few Gadwall and Tufted Duck stay and breed while any remaining Goldeneye start their head-jerking displays. Although common in winter, Water Rail is a scarce breeder, but Coot is more frequent. Raven and Hobby nest in surrounding woodlands.

Offshore, seabirds – including lines of Manx Shearwater and groups of Gannet and Kittiwake – feed throughout summer. Fulmars inhabit the cliffs south of Torcross. Late summer brings Balearic and perhaps rarer shearwaters feeding with the Manx, and Sandwich Terns fish off the beach, with Arctic, Little and Roseate Terns also recorded. Thousands of Swifts mass over the leys on humid days; a Little Swift once joined them for a couple of days. Early autumn may produce an Arctic Skua pursuing the seabirds, or a Black Tern dipping to catch insects over Torcross lily-pads, perhaps accompanied by a Little Gull or Common Tern. Waders such as Common Sandpiper and Greenshank feed on lagoon-fringe mud if the water level is low. Scarcer species seen in these conditions have included Pectoral Sandpiper, but in some seasons there is no wader habitat away from the beach. Thousands of Swallows and Starlings roost among Torcross reeds at dusk, the swirling flocks forming an attractive target for a Sparrowhawk or Hobby as they gather before dropping in. The pale juvenile Rose-coloured Starling has joined its commoner cousins on occasion. The bird observatory's ringing studies have shown that large numbers of warblers pass through the insect-rich reed fringes at this season, including the occasional Aquatic Warbler, and other uncommon migrants such as Bluethroats and Icterine and Melodious Warblers have also been recorded. Owing to the dense vegetation, few of these would have been recorded without the use of mist-nets, although Wryneck can be more cooperative.

Migrants continue to pass late in the year, with Snow Bunting possible along the beach and regular sightings of Swallow into November. It is always worth checking for a late Wheatear, and maybe another Desert Wheatear may turn up! Meanwhile, gales in the Channel may force a tired phalarope, skua or other stray seabird into the bay.

TIMING

Slapton's southerly position encourages large numbers of birds to shelter in cold winters when Bittern and large numbers of wildfowl and winter thrushes might be expected. Strong easterly winds, although they probably bring birds, create difficult viewing conditions; a seawatch from the beach car park might pay off, though. However, in gale-force east winds the seafront road is occasionally closed, because of the danger of flying stones and sand; this strip is very susceptible to erosion. The area is sheltered from most other winds. Sea conditions need to be fairly calm to maximise the chance of viewing divers and grebes from the low beach. For ducks on the ley, avoid high winds, when many shelter among reeds. Spring migrant arrivals are most noticeable on cloudy, humid days with winds between south-east and south-west; most rarer herons have arrived in mild south-westerlies. Easterlies in autumn will bring Little Gull and possibly Black Tern, and maybe an Aquatic Warbler or another scarce passerine. Strays such as phalaropes (which have included Grey, Red-necked and a Wilson's on the ley) arrive with prolonged south or south-west gales and rain. For the autumn hirundine and Starling roosts, the hour before darkness is best.

Slapton beach is very heavily used by the public on fine weekends all year.

ACCESS

Along the coastal A379 between Dartmouth and Kingsbridge. This road is subject to erosion and after winter storms can be impassable.

The main areas to watch are:

Strete Gate At the north end of Higher Ley. Park in the car park and look offshore for divers and seaducks in winter. Cross the road to view Gara Valley reedbed for harriers or herons.

Higher Ley Take the path along the road for rails, Cetti's Warbler, maybe Bittern, and a chance of other warblers and migrants at appropriate season. Purple Heron is occasional in spring. Permits are required from the Field Centre to access the inland side.

Monument Halfway down the bay, opposite the bridge between Higher and Lower Leys. This is a suitable seawatch point, but alternatively view from the beach car park nearby. Check scrub across the road for small passerines. Walk south along the beach crest for gull roosts and spring Wheatears, maybe Hoopoe.

Ireland Bay Across the bridge on the southern side, take the path through the gate. Continue on the bank path (which is narrow and uneven and may be muddy), checking scrub on the right for warblers and flycatchers at migration times. Scan across the bay for bathing gulls – and diving ducks in winter. If the water level is high, continue along the higher path; do not stray into private farmland above. After about 300m watch across the reeds to the left for herons, harriers and warblers. Follow the lake-shore path until a gated track turns left across the marsh towards France Wood. Check the pool ahead for herons, rails and ducks, including migrant Garganey. Look in the small overgrown quarry on the corner for wintering Firecrest and Chiffchaff.

Deer Bridge walk Instead of crossing into the reserve through the gate, continue along the public path following the marshy valley and sheltered bushes, which hold wintering warblers and a selection of summer breeding warblers. Cirl Buntings might be found. To reach Deer Bridge, some 250m along this path take a boardwalk on the left, just before a gate and stile. Continue along this often-muddy footpath for approximately 1 mile (1.6km) to Deer Bridge and a minor road. Return along the same route to rejoin the original path. This route offers shelter in windy conditions and an interesting, varied walk. Rejoining the original route, after 800m this path reaches the Slapton village road near the Field Studies Centre, enabling the completion of a circular walk back down the roadway verge towards the shore.

Scrub behind beach At migration times, try walking the length of the ley between the road and marsh for scattered passerine migrants and further views of the ley.

Torcross (TQ7 2TQ, surgical.fine.nurtures) At the south end of the ley. Ducks are numerous, and this area is also best for grebes, Little Gull and Black Tern. Divers may be seen off the beach, and gulls pass along the shore to drink from the stream beyond the rocks. Fulmars nest further on. In wet weather the ley can be viewed from roadside car parks. A public bird hide with wheelchair access overlooks the open ley from the rear of the main car park. Walk from here around the lower end of the ley, following the A379 road verges, for views of ducks at the rear of wide Stokeley Bay, which is sheltered from northerly winds. Once the road climbs away from the lakeside, after 100m you can scan over Stokeley Pond, a farm pool that often attracts egrets and ducks, including Gadwall.

At low tide you can walk south for 800m on shingle to Beesands from Torcross front.

Beesands (TQ7 2EL, proposals.plausible.started) On the A379, drive to Stokenham, west of Torcross; turn left towards Start Point then left down a steep, narrow road signposted Beeson and Beesands. Walk left to the lake. Devon Birds has erected a public hide on the southern side, reached by a good, level, gravelled path along the field edge which starts by the last cottages on the left. Extra parking has been made available at this point. The hide is accessible for disabled visitors including those using wheelchairs, although the path can flood in winter.

Hallsands (TQ7 2EN, attitudes.mildest.flipping) Continue past the Beesands turn, towards Start Point. Turn left to North Hallsands Valley and check the beach and nearby reeds, as well as the bushes and private pools along the length of the valley beside the road.

CALENDAR

Resident: Great Crested Grebe, Shag, Cormorant, Grey Heron, Little Egret, Sparrowhawk, Marsh Harrier, Gadwall, Water Rail, Coot, Barn Owl, woodpeckers, Cetti's Warbler, Stonechat, Cirl and Reed Buntings, Raven.

December–February: Wigeon, Teal, Shoveler, Tufted Duck, Pochard, Eider, Common Scoter, Goldeneye and Goosander, maybe Scaup or Smew in hard weather; Great Northern Diver, Black-necked and occasional Red-necked Grebe, Bittern, Kingfisher, Black Redstart, Chiffchaff, Firecrest; waders and gulls on beach.

March–May: Migrant gulls including uncommon species (March), Wheatear, Sand Martin, maybe Garganey and Hoopoe from mid-March; arrivals of summer migrants; Fulmars nesting; diver passage April–May, terns and Whimbrel mostly from mid-April, auks feeding offshore. From mid-April, a wide range of migrants including Yellow and White Wagtails, hirundines and warblers; chance of a rarer heron, raptor or other southern 'overshoot'.

June–July: Seabirds feeding, including Manx and in July Balearic Shearwater; breeding ducks and other residents, Reed and Sedge Warblers; Sandwich Terns return in July.

August–November: Sandwich, Common and occasional other sea terns to early October, with Black Tern and maybe Little Gull from late August–October; possibly skuas or Sooty Shearwater to end October; phalaropes end September–October but rare. Heavy migration of Swallows, martins, warblers and other passerines including rarer species, mostly August–September, peaking end of August. Swallows and other migrants to early November.

Devon (south coast and Dartmoor)

12 START POINT

OS LANDRANGER MAP 202
OS grid ref: SX8336
Postcode: TQ7 2EN
what3words: bulldozer.weaned.losing

HABITAT

The jagged, bracken-covered Start Point promontory, with a lighthouse and rocky islets at the tip, projects south-east into Start Bay. The ridge is a spine of rocks, one side of which is usually sheltered from the wind. On the eastern side a tarmac road leads to the lighthouse, where there is a small area of tamarisk. To the west an open, grazed valley leads inland to Start Farm, with often sheltered trees and bushes. Above the farm, fields lined with thick hedgerows head up onto an open plateau. West from Start a low strip of fields, punctuated by Lannacombe and smaller coves, borders the rocky shore towards Prawle, about 5 miles (8km) to the west. The coast includes several stretches owned by the National Trust, with some of the county's best cliff scenery.

The sea dominates with good feeding conditions offshore attracting cetaceans and Atlantic Blue-fin Tuna. Grey Seals are often hauled out onto the outer rocks off Peartree Point at lower tides; a few white pups may join adults through winter and spring in particular.

SPECIES

This is one of the region's best migration watchpoints, but most watchers tend to gravitate to Prawle Point, with its greater shelter and cover.

In winter, Start can be a quiet site with a few Stonechats and Rock Pipits on its slopes, and perhaps a Black Redstart at the lighthouse. Winter seabird movements are usually limited to Gannet, Kittiwake and auks, although Great Skua is possible. Shag feed in the ley of the ridge, often joined by a Great Northern Diver after south-westerly gales. Oystercatcher and Turnstone feed along the shore, with a Peregrine or Raven often patrolling overhead. Any crop fields are worth scanning in winter; flocks of Yellowhammer, Skylark and Linnet are often boosted in cold weather, when parties of thrushes may also arrive.

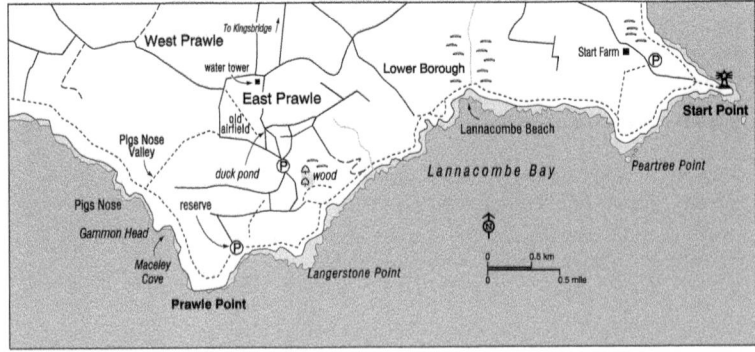

Spring can bring large numbers of migrants. Chiffchaffs and Goldcrests rarely pause on arrival, rapidly moving along the coast to more sheltered areas, whereas Wheatears are more suited to the terrain. The highly distinctive Hoopoe could be encountered as it probes areas of short turf on the first warm March days, as the first Swallows head north. Spring falls can occur in suitable weather, with Willow Warblers and Whitethroats most numerous. The lighthouse occasionally attracts large numbers of grounded migrants – once 300 Sedge and 40 Grasshopper Warblers together. Devon's first Iberian Chiffchaff held territory at the farm for a week, and Serin and Woodchat Shrike have been recorded on several occasions. The sea is less watched at this season, but waders and skuas pass through and diver passage once included a White-billed. European Storm Petrels, often reported by boatmen offshore around Skerries Bank north of Start, may be driven nearer by rain or wind, or seen following fishing vessels for scraps. Other summer birds include breeding Shag, Great Black-backed Gull and Oystercatcher. Black Guillemot has summered, appearing occasionally over several years. A walk to the headland is likely to produce sightings of Stonechat on the bracken-covered slopes, as Rock Pipits parachute overhead.

Although sheltered spots are hard to come by, Start is now recognised as a premier seawatching site in the region, as birds exiting Lyme Bay join with those passing further out in the Channel. As the summer draws on, Manx Shearwaters are largely replaced by Balearic, with hundreds of the latter recorded on peak days, occasionally with similar numbers of Cory's and Great. On such days rarities such as Little Shearwater, Wilson's Storm Petrel and Desertas-type petrel are also possible.

Early autumn brings peak numbers of migrant passerines, with warblers, Redstart, and Pied and Spotted Flycatchers feeding in the lighthouse compound or sheltered scrub. Rarer still, individual Booted and Arctic Warblers were the first of their species ever recorded in mainland Devon.

On fine days, Yellow Wagtails and Tree Pipits call frequently overhead, with up to 100 of each passing sometimes, the former often pausing among cattle. Ortolan Buntings are probably more frequent in stubble fields than the occasional records suggest, with shrikes a possibility along the hedgerows.

From mid-autumn, many more diurnal migrants move overhead. Movements of hundreds of hirundines are followed by Meadow Pipits and wagtails, frequently harassed by a dashing Merlin. Skylarks and finches, often totalling thousands, pour over on late autumn days, when the calls of northern migrants such as Brambling and Siskin can often be heard and a passing Short-eared Owl might be seen.

As numbers of common warblers drop, Firecrests can arrive in number and a Yellow-browed Warbler may be possible around the farm. Both Dusky and Radde's Warblers have been added to the site's impressive warbler list, and a couple of Eastern Stonechats have been picked out among their ubiquitous European cousins. Woodpigeons and Starlings are two of the last species to move overhead late into November, when late finch movements sometimes include Lapland Bunting and Hawfinch.

TIMING

Dawn and dusk are generally productive times for passerines; warblers especially are most active in the morning. Migrants that have dropped in on open terrain near the lighthouse on misty nights are best seen at first light. Although some remain at the point, many soon move along the promontory. The area around the valley below the farm will often hold migrants. Warblers are most numerous in typical fall conditions with high barometric pressure at the start of a night, encouraging them to commence their nocturnal migration journeys, and developing drizzle or mist that later disorientates them and causes them to land. Light southerlies often produce varied migrants, including occasional southern overshoots. Overcast days with easterlies can produce rarer species in late autumn, whereas departing diurnal migrants move south along the point in light to moderate westerly or south-westerlies. In strong easterly winds, the sheltered Start and Lannacombe valleys are worth searching.

The higher fields are often left unploughed in autumn, attracting large finch flocks to feed and encouraging raptors to exploit this food resource. Seawatching is usually productive after gales and when the horizon is obscured by mist or drizzle.

ACCESS

Start Point is reached via narrow lanes from the A379 Dartmouth–Kingsbridge road, south of Slapton Ley. Turn sharp south (left if coming from Slapton Ley) in Stokenham village. Passing Start Farm valley on the right, drive to the paying car park at the top of Start Point. Walk back and check roadside trees and field edges for migrants; Cirl Buntings are often present. Go through gate into the Start lighthouse access lane beyond the car park, turning immediately right down the coastal public footpath. Follow the valley down towards the sea; there are few trees or bushes in the lower half, however. For the Point, walk half a mile (800m) down the lighthouse lane, looking among boulders for rock-loving birds such as Black Redstart (at correct seasons). Kestrel and Raven are usual overhead. The lighthouse is now automated and private; look over from the wall at the tamarisk-edged lighthouse gardens close to sea level, where newly arrived migrants may shelter. Walk up over the ridge via a steep narrow track to see nesting seabirds. The area is heavily used by the public at weekends and in summer.

Another worthwhile area to check is the small Lannacombe Valley immediately to the west of Start, reached by turning off the coast path just beyond a sandy cove; this has held shrikes and scarce warblers. Some energetic watchers do the Start–Prawle walk by coastal path, with spectacular scenery, rock-pool waders, scattered migrants and Cirl Buntings en route, but most migrants occur near the headlands. The path, although basically level, may be very muddy in places.

CALENDAR

Resident: Shag, Oystercatcher, Great Black-backed Gull, Rock Pipit, Skylark, Stonechat, Cirl Bunting, Linnet, Raven.

December–February: Offshore movements of Gannet, gulls, Kittiwake, auks, occasional Great Skua. Lark and finch flocks, maybe Black Redstart, occasional hard-weather influxes.

March–May: Chiffchaff, Goldcrest, Firecrest, Wheatear and Black Redstart from mid-March, occasional Hoopoe. Wide range of passerines peaking late April–early May; Manx Shearwater and Fulmar in May, European Storm Petrel and Puffin possible from May; Whimbrel, Bar-tailed Godwit, a few Great, Arctic or Pomarine Skuas, Sandwich Tern, all mostly late April–May.

June–July: Feeding parties of seabirds, Manx and Balearic Shearwaters, European Storm Petrel, Gannet, Fulmar, breeding species.

August–November: Seabirds moving throughout; Balearic Shearwater mostly August–September, Great, Cory's and Sooty Shearwaters through August, peaking mid–late September. Warblers, flycatchers, Wheatear, Whinchat, Redstart peak late August–September; Firecrest (late September–early November), coasting hirundines, pipits, wagtails (mid-September–October); possibly Yellow-browed and other scarce migrants, lark and finch passage, October–November. Occasional Hen Harrier and Short-eared Owl; Black Redstart arrivals and winter thrushes (late October–November), large pigeon and Starling flocks, seabird passage including many auks.

13 PRAWLE POINT

OS LANDRANGER MAP 202
OS grid ref: SX7735
Postcode: **Prawle Point** – TQ7 2DF **East Prawle** – TQ7 2DB
what3words: **Prawle Point** – skinning.button.tidal
East Prawle – freshen.relishes.directly

HABITAT

Prawle Point projects southwards, reaching slightly further seaward than Bolt Head cliffs, which are visible to the west. Much of the eastern flank is farmland with stone walls and tall hedges. There are overgrown rocky outcrops a few hundred metres inland, and wartime bunkers overlook the shore. The National Trust car park lies in a sheltered hollow surrounded by scrub.

There is a dense Sycamore wood on the steep hillside below East Prawle village, and a tangle of damp vegetation grows behind the duckpond beside the road into the village. The top of the point, which provides a superb vista of cliffs and coves to the west, is largely covered by rough grass, gorse, bracken and boulders. A mile (1.6km) west is a deep valley, with a stream, trees and thickets, known as Pig's Nose Valley. Inland, west of the village near Vinivers Cross, lies open, flat fields once used as an airfield.

The sea can produce spectacular sightings of larger creatures such as massive but harmless Basking Sharks, which show as double triangular back and tail fins when circling lazily just below the surface on summer days. Rough vegetation in coves encourages concentrations of butterflies; residents include Green Hairstreak and Small Pearl-bordered Fritiilary, and the spectacular orange and black Monarch has visited from North America. The soft sand cliffs hold some of the most important solitary bee aggregations in the UK.

SPECIES

A major attraction for visiting birdwatchers is the resident Cirl Bunting, commoner here, in thickets and hedges near sea level, than anywhere else in Britain. The male's flat, trilling song, at times confusable with Lesser Whitethroat, is a familiar spring sound and up to 50 pairs breed in sheltered fields around Prawle. Outside the breeding season, parties can be detected as they perch in hedges or feed in field edges, giving quiet *sipp-sipp* notes; 60 or more may flock together. This has been a real success story for farming and conservation.

Devon (south coast and Dartmoor)

In winter, especially after storms, large numbers of Gannets, Kittiwakes and auks pass offshore, along with a few divers. Large movements of Great Northern and Black-throated Divers have been recorded. Wildfowl are occasionally seen passing offshore but are scarce. Flocks of up to 40 Turnstone and smaller numbers of Purple Sandpiper feed on the rocks at Langerstone Point or Maelcombe, together with vocal Oystercatcher and a few Redshank and Curlew. Rock Pipit are plentiful on sheltered beaches with Water Pipit occasional, and Devon's first American Buff-bellied Pipit was found here one winter. In sheltered bushes and coves, Chiffchaff, Firecrest and Black Redstart may overwinter. Stubble fields at the point and around the village are worth checking for lark and finch flocks. Golden Plover appear irregularly on the 'aerodrome' fields (part of a former RAF naval air base) and may be joined by other waders, particularly Lapwing, in hard weather.

Spring can bring large arrivals of migrants, the earliest being Wheatear or Black Redstart. Chiffchaff, Goldcrest and, often, Firecrest work their way along the hedges and away inland to more sheltered spots.

Later, mixed falls of migrants occur in suitable weather, with freshly arrived birds singing and feeding in every bush at dawn, although most soon move on. Willow Warbler usually predominates in these spring falls, accompanied by lesser numbers of Chiffchaff, Blackcap and Whitethroat. Other arrivals may include a few Lesser Whitethroats, and Reed, Grasshopper and Sedge Warblers. The last two species may stay to breed in damper areas, but the Reed Warblers that sing briefly in sheltered trees are purely migrants.

A good spring day is likely to reveal scattered Redstarts, flycatchers and other summer visitors. From mid-morning in fine weather, diurnal migrants including hirundines and finches may be seen arriving from France over the cliffs, with the chance of a raptor such as a Hobby. Buzzards are frequent, but any large raptors are worth checking for scarcer species at migration times. One spring, a young male Red-footed Falcon hunted insects along the coastal fields for over two weeks. Late spring is best for any chance of the now-rare Turtle Dove, and many other interesting migrants including Tawny Pipit, Squacco Heron, Common Rosefinch and Sardinian Warbler have also turned up. Prawle's potential for attracting southern migrants was amply demonstrated one May morning when Bee-eater, Black Kite, Woodchat Shrike and Serin were all present.

Poor visibility and onshore winds can bring large parties of commoner seabirds, with a few divers, waders such as Whimbrel or Bar-tailed Godwit, skuas and Sandwich Terns moving through. Manx Shearwaters are present most days, parties sometimes resting on the sea, and hundreds on fine evenings banking low over the waves as they fly up the Channel to feed overnight.

Other summer birds include breeding Fulmar, Shag and Lesser Black-backed Gull, with one or two pairs of Kestrel in most years. Shelduck and Oystercatcher also nest, the former choosing rabbit burrows along the shore.

A walk along the coastal footpath through gorse and bracken is likely to produce sightings of Whitethroats sounding a warning from deep cover, while bright cock Yellowhammers sing alongside Cirl Buntings. The density of breeding birds, apart from resident specialities, is relatively low, making migrant passerines easier to detect; many common woodland species are not usually resident.

Late summer brings Sandwich Terns moving westward in small groups, often totalling 60 in a morning, while Manx Shearwater is largely replaced by Balearic. Hundreds of the latter have appeared on peak days, together with longer-winged Sooty Shearwaters; the very rare Black-browed Albatross and Desertas-type petrel have been recorded. With major gales, hundreds of Gannets and other common seabirds pass west, with a variety of shearwaters and skuas; Sooty Shearwater is frequent in rough weather with both Cory's and Great Shearwaters increasing (all have peaked at over 100 in a day, but single figures are more usual). Skuas have also exceeded 100 in a day exceptionally, Arctic Skua appearing on most watches, with small numbers of Great and Pomarine Skuas and exceptionally a Long-tailed. Other pelagic species such as petrels may be seen, and a Grey Phalarope or Sabine's Gull may flash past. Most seabirds move straight past against the wind, so views tend to be brief. Later in autumn, Kittiwakes and auks may pass in thousands, and Little Auk has been reported on a number of occasions.

Early autumn brings peak numbers of migrant passerines, with a similar mix of species as found at Start Point. Warblers and flycatchers often remain for several days, feeding in bushy hollows and overgrown hedges and occasionally flicking out to snap up a passing insect. Often, more birds are present than first appears, so wait near suitable cover to see what pops out. Looking stocky among the *Phylloscopus* warblers, a scarce migrant Icterine Warbler or shorter-winged Melodious Warbler may be encountered.

Ortolan Bunting is occasionally located in stubble fields, with Wryneck and Red-backed Shrike found most years, and once a Rufous Bushchat. Dotterel may be present in the fields adjacent to Vinivers Cross; the rare Buff-breasted Sandpiper and other commoner waders have also been sighted here.

The small beach at Maelcombe Cove below Prawle Wood and the surrounding rock pools may hold a few passing waders, including Dunlin, Whimbrel and Bar-tailed Godwit in ones and twos; a Pectoral Sandpiper has visited, and a couple of Desert Wheatears have been seen (remarkably, one was a bird ringed in Suffolk, proving that some migrants filter across to our region from the east coast). The hedgerows bordering the cove often hold post-breeding parties of Cirl Bunting.

From mid-autumn, when temperatures start to drop, many diurnal migrants coast overhead. Movements of hundreds of hirundines can attract a Hobby, which might patrol the area for weeks to pick off passing birds. Meadow Pipits, sometimes joined by a lone Richard's or even an Olive-backed or Red-throated, also move west in hundreds, stopping to feed on open fields. One or two Merlin may stay all autumn, attracted by hundreds of Linnets and Goldfinches that swirl in pre-migration flocks on weedy stubble fields. Grey Wagtail, picked out by hard *chizz* calls, pass south-west, with up to 30 on some days. Among the pipits, wagtails, Skylarks and finches which pour over on late autumn days, often totalling thousands, calls of northern migrants such Brambling, Redpoll and Siskin can often be heard.

As warblers start to thin out, Ring Ouzels pass in small groups, favouring rocky outcrops. The lively Firecrest is often present on later autumn mornings, usually two or three but up to 30 on peak days. Late falls of Blackcap and Chiffchaff may include a Siberian Chiffchaff or Yellow-browed Warbler. Dusky and Radde's Warblers, often skulking and difficult to watch, have occurred along with the more showy and striking Pallas's Warbler.

After a strong Atlantic gale, there may be a chance of sighting a vagrant American passerine such as Red-eyed Vireo. Prawle has recorded more American passerines than the rest of mainland Devon combined. A Chestnut-sided Warbler was only the second record for Britain; this frustratingly brief visitor was seen by only a few fortunate observers. Prawle Wood might hold a few sheltering migrants, and in such conditions, extreme rarities such as Blackpoll or Black-and-white

Warbler have occurred. Black Redstarts are frequently seen around rock outcrops and coastal buildings, and Red-breasted Flycatcher has been found, while a few summer visitors put in late appearances. Sheltered areas may hold single summer migrants staying on into the start of winter.

TIMING

As at Start and elsewhere, dawn and dusk are generally productive for passerines. After a fall along the coast, migrants may continue to work their way up into areas of cover for another hour or two, so check main patches of vegetation regularly. In spring, diurnal coasting migrants such as hirundines and finches arrive from across the Channel four or five hours after daybreak; raptors take longer and may not make landfall until after midday, or up to late afternoon. Departing diurnal migrants in autumn move south-west out to sea, and movement often finishes by mid-morning. Seawatching is best avoided in strong sunlight as glare off the water can be a problem, but is usually worthwhile when the horizon is obscured by mist or drizzle. In the teeth of really strong south-westerly gales, seabirds do not pass, moving west only when the wind or rain slackens. Try fine high-pressure evenings for shearwaters and skuas moving up-Channel. Spring passages of skuas, terns and waders up the coast are enhanced during easterly winds. Force 9–10 westerlies in mid- to late autumn give the best chances of an American vagrant but little chance of the more usual migrants to appear. Watch out for reports of large, orange Monarch butterflies; these might precede transatlantic bird arrivals.

To check the car park area, avoid sunny midday periods at weekends or main holiday times, when there is more human disturbance. In strong easterly winds, the sheltered lowest part of Pig's Nose Valley often holds interesting migrants.

The high 'aerodrome' fields near Vinivers Cross, north-west of East Prawle, seem to attract waders and other open ground species in years when they are ploughed and rolled flat in September; this also enables views of more distant birds which are not concealed by plough furrows.

ACCESS

From the A379 Dartmouth–Kingsbridge road, south of Slapton Ley, via narrow lanes.

Prawle Point From the A379, turn south at Frogmore or Chillington along minor roads to East Prawle village. Approaching the village, the duck pond and thick bushes lie to the right. For the Point, continue into the village, past the green, and keep right down the 'no through road' to the National Trust car park at the bottom. This is a narrow, winding lane with limited parking at the end, which soon fills on fine weekends. There is also limited parking around the village green.

Car park area Check the surrounding bushes very thoroughly; many species occur here, and it is the easiest spot to find warblers, Firecrest and flycatchers. Most observers base themselves here and check again at intervals. Also look overhead for diurnal migrants moving towards the Point. The long list of species, including many rarities, seen within a few metres of the car park makes this a good spot for birdwatchers with limited mobility, despite the terrain.

Lower Fields Walk down from Prawle Point car park and turn left. Walk east along the coast path, which is level and well-marked in this area but often muddy. Check the beach for waders, and the gullies for sheltering migrants. Look in scrub around overgrown crags for warblers and Cirl Bunting. The land curves out to the low, turfy Langerstone Point, where any stubble fields are well worth checking in autumn.

Prawle Wood Continue east around the corner into the next cove, checking for waders sheltering on the small beach. Walk up the steep track to the wood edge, a very sheltered area for warblers. Watch the edges; the interior is dense and no access routes exist. This may be a productive area for sheltering migrants after a strong westerly gale. The steep track allows a return route to the village.

Top Fields From the wood turn left, back up to the lane. Walk back to the Point past open fields with overgrown stone hedges. Look in fields for pigeon flocks, finches, larks and other seed-eaters. Raptors may pass over. In windy weather, Redstarts and other migrants may shelter behind stone walls.

Top Track (Ash Lane) At the first corner of the lane below the village, a muddy track branches off to the right past a large house. Bushes along the right of this track are sheltered from north-east winds and often hold warblers; this track leads eventually to Pig's Nose Valley.

Point and Coastguard Cottages From the car park, walk down towards the sea and turn right uphill past the Coastguard Cottage gardens. Warblers may shelter here and Black Redstarts sometimes perch on buildings or rock outcrops. Grazing farm stock may attract migrant wagtails to the grass field and Whimbrel may feed here in spring groups. Cross the stile to the top of the heath and check for pipits and Wheatears; Hoopoe is occasional. Daytime migrants pass west low over here on autumn mornings.

Seawatching From near the memorial seat halfway down the right flank of the Point, or – if it rains – there is precarious shelter under nearby rocks.

West Cliffs From the heath, follow the scenic coast path west to Gammon Head and Pig's Nose Valley. This is good for small migrants in strong easterly winds, Raven and maybe raptors. Also, Grey Seal, Small Pearl-bordered Fritillary butterfly and spring flowers.

Vinivers Cross area and Pig's Nose Valley Walk At the top end of East Prawle village, take the small lane between the corner of the village and the duckpond, turning right if approaching from the north. After 100m, scan fields either side for winter plover flocks, finches and buntings. After another 200m, near a sharp bend, walk down the tree-lined public footpath through Pig's Nose Valley, towards Moorsands Cove, watching for warblers in the trees and possibly raptors passing over. Thickets near the stream can hold numerous warblers, but patience is required to observe them. In some autumns the large fields to the right, particularly when ploughed and rolled flat, have held rare species. Stop near the Vinivers Cross road junction at the end of the lane and can take the footpath crossing the fields diagonally towards the village.

CALENDAR

Resident: Shag, Sparrowhawk, Buzzard, Oystercatcher, Great Black-backed Gull, Stock Dove, Green Woodpecker, Rock Pipit, Stonechat, Cirl Bunting, Yellowhammer, Raven.

December–February: Eider (irregular), Common Scoter, divers (mostly Great Northern); offshore movements of Gannet, gulls, Kittiwake, auks, occasional skuas; Turnstone, Purple Sandpiper, Curlew; maybe Firecrest or Black Redstart; lark and finch flocks.

March–May: Much as Start Point; Firecrest and Black Redstart arrive from mid-March; chance of migrant raptors from late March, but especially April–May, including rarer species; Hobby late April–May; wide range of passerines peaking late April–early May; Manx Shearwater and Fulmar commonest May, with European Storm Petrel and Puffin possible from May; all three divers, Common Scoter, Whimbrel, Bar-tailed Godwit, a few Great, Arctic or Pomarine Skuas, Sandwich Tern, all mostly late April–May, although odd terns from late March; possibly Turtle Dove, Serin, maybe Woodchat Shrike or other rarities.

June–July: Feeding parties of seabirds, Manx and Balearic Shearwaters, European Storm Petrel, Gannet, Fulmar, breeding Shag, occasional late southern overshoots (June), breeding specialities, Shelduck; from mid-July, a few waders, Sandwich Tern.

August–November: The same range of birds seen at Start but usually in lower numbers, including Balearic and Sooty Shearwaters and possibly Great and Cory's; Arctic and Great Skuas mostly September–mid-October, some Pomarine especially later; a few terns to mid-October. Little Egret on shoreline. Yellow Wagtail, Tree Pipit, warblers, flycatchers, Wheatear, Whinchat, Redstart peak late August–September; occasional petrels, Grey Phalarope possible mid-September–October; chance of larger raptors in September, Merlin to November, Hobby to mid-October; Firecrest (late September–early November), coasting hirundines, pipits, wagtails possibly a Wryneck or shrike (mid-September–October), possibly Red-breasted Flycatcher or Barred Warbler late September–early November, with Melodious or Icterine Warbler possible to mid-October; lark and finch passage October–November, including scarcer species. Occasional Hen Harrier and Short-eared Owl; chance of Pallas's or Yellow-browed Warbler especially end October–early November; large pigeon and Starling flocks, divers, seabird passage including many auks, odd late summer visitors through November.

14 KINGSBRIDGE ESTUARY

OS LANDRANGER MAP 202
OS grid ref: SX7441
Postcode: **Bowcombe Creek –** TQ7 2DH **West Charleton Marsh –** TQ7 2AQ
what3words: **Bowcombe Creek –** patching.watches.land
West Charleton Marsh – fury.exist.tradition

HABITAT

This large south Devon estuary, technically a ria (a long, narrow, partially submerged river valley), extends from Salcombe at the mouth to Kingsbridge town at the head. Several large, sheltered creeks extend up to 1 mile (1.6km) east and west. The central basin of the estuary, more than a mile wide in places, is about 2 miles (3km) long. The waterways are flanked by farmland and houses; this, together with its shape and poor access points, makes easy checking impossible. The estuary is muddy rather than sandy, with weed-covered rocks bordering in places. Some parts are shot over by wildfowlers (except on Sundays) during

Devon (south coast and Dartmoor)

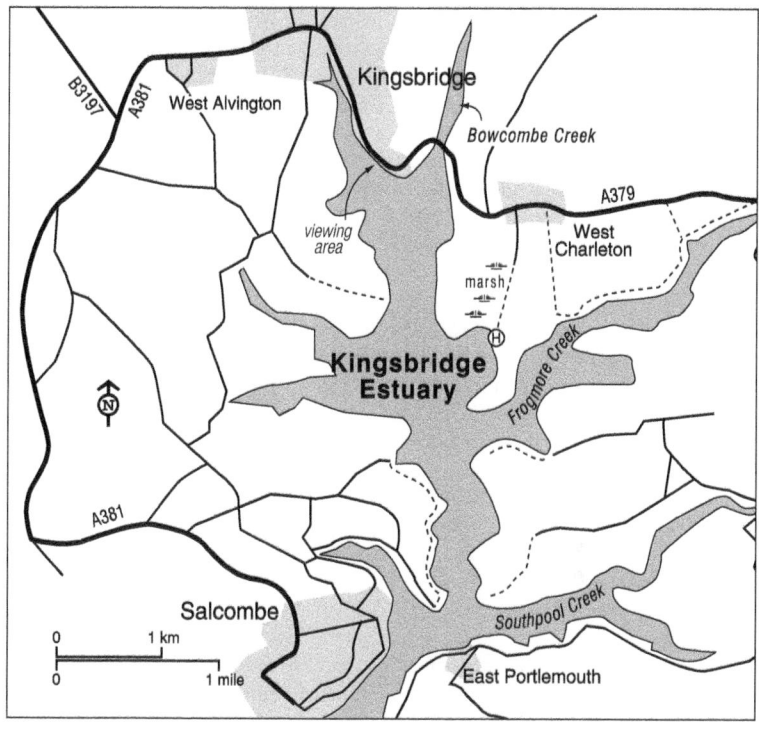

winter. Adjacent to the north-east side of the basin lies West Charleton Marsh, a small reserve of brackish grassland separated from the estuary by a seawall. On high tides, seawater can flow back up the central ditch, overflowing onto this very low-lying area and increasing its shallow muddy pools. There is a small stand of *Phragmites* reeds. A public hide is situated on the seawall between the marsh and estuary, with views over both.

SPECIES

This estuary is best known for grebes, ducks and larger waders. Divers, mostly Great Northern – once a celebrity albino bird – favour the central basin, often lingering after perhaps sheltering from bad conditions at sea. A few divers and grebes may also occur near the estuary mouth, where up to 100 Shags gather. On the creeks, the most numerous grebe is Little, with more than 20 commonplace, peaking in mid- to late winter, when a Black-necked may be present along with 10 or more Great Crested. Wildfowl are well represented. A wintering population of more than 100 Dark-bellied Brent Geese (once joined by a Black Brant) feeds on the mudflats at low tide. Wigeon is the most numerous species, with an average peak of over 800 in the early year, when parties of up to 40 Pintail might be expected. Mallard and Teal are regular but only in double figures. Devon's first American Black Duck was discovered here associating with Mallard. Red-breasted Merganser is the most numerous diving duck, with several Goldeneye often feeding alongside. Other diving ducks turn up on the estuary, especially after cold or rough weather, perhaps a Scaup among the Tufted Duck. There may also be a solitary Eider, Long-tailed Duck or Velvet Scoter; on two occasions, a Surf Scoter was seen. These often find a good supply of crabs and shellfish, even up the narrow muddy creeks, and can stay for weeks.

Grey Heron and Little Egret breed in adjacent woods and favour the sheltered creeks to feed. Spoonbills have been seen frequently, with Cattle and Great White Egrets increasingly appearing. Ospreys often linger for weeks in autumn, with Marsh Harrier also regular alongside the common resident raptors.

Wintering waders include over 400 Dunlin, 200 Oystercatcher and 150 Curlew, with smaller numbers of regular estuary species, especially during migration. Flocks of up to 1,000 Golden Plover, which may mass on the central estuary, also feed in nearby fields. Very hard weather causes plover numbers to rise dramatically.

Sheltered areas regularly produce one or two wintering Greenshank and Common Sandpiper and maybe a Spotted Redshank. These same areas are favoured by Kingfisher, often perching on overhanging branches. The lack of an easily viewable roost at high tide has probably limited observations of scarcer small waders, but sightings of Pectoral and White-rumped Sandpipers and American Golden Plover show the potential.

West Charleton Marsh can attract waders that prefer marshy rather than estuarine habitat, such as Ruff, Little Ringed Plover, and Wood and Green Sandpipers. Black-winged Stilt has visited. A few ducks such as Teal use the marsh. The tiny reedbed has hosted Bittern and other retiring marsh species such as Night Heron and Spotted Crake have been recorded. A smart male Black-headed Wagtail was a major rarity.

The estuary is situated in the midst of the Cirl Bunting's stronghold; thickets, hedgerows and stubble fields around the estuary fringes are an ideal home for this localised species.

TIMING

To watch waders on the estuary, the tide must be at least partly out. An incoming tide pushes them towards observation points near Kingsbridge. An ebbing tide allows waders to alight on freshly exposed mud in the same areas, enabling you to watch them; at low tide they may be too distant. A neap tide facilitates watching, as the area of exposed mud is less. With many scattered high-water roosting areas, however, only a portion of waders present will likely be seen on each visit. High tides may induce some waders to leave the estuary in favour of the marsh. When the tide is fully out, there still remains a substantial main channel stream, the basin, used by divers, grebes and diving ducks although they may drift downstream with the tide.

Any daylight hours will suffice for winter visits to the estuary, but very early mornings or evenings might prove quieter. During or after prolonged periods of gales and high seas, more sea species may shelter. When severe winter weather is worse in other regions of Britain, and on the near continent, many birds arrive here seeking milder conditions. Rarer herons and other unusual visitors are best looked for in southerly spring winds.

There is much disturbance from people and boats on the estuary in summer.

ACCESS

The A379 runs alongside the estuary adjacent to the town, and crosses Bowcombe Creek by a narrow stone bridge. This same road later, going east towards Slapton, passes through West Charleton village and skirts the tip of Frogmore Creek. To check this side of the estuary you can start in the town, although little apart from commoner gulls, Little Egret, and a few Redshank and Dunlin can be expected here. However, Laughing Gull has appeared, and Yellow-browed Warblers have been seen in the adjacent park.

As you drive out of town eastward and start to gain views of the wider estuary channel ahead, there is a potential viewpoint beside the small South West Water Pumping station at the water's edge. Park in steep residential Warren Road on the left, cross the A379 and walk down a concreted track opposite, following the public footpath sign. This leads to the waterside after about 50m. It is worth viewing from here as a rising tide brings birds closer. Some will still be distant, though, and a telescope is usually needed.

The Bowcombe Creek road is on the left immediately before crossing the bridge from Kingsbridge. In winter a good mix of ducks can be seen at close range, and there may be Blackcap, Chiffchaff or Firecrest in roadside bushes. Limited roadside parking is available along the small road by the creek. After 300m or so along this road, a lookout platform overlooking the mudflats has been created for bird-watchers. Greenshank are generally easily found in autumn and winter.

Just past the bridge, the estuary suddenly widens considerably alongside the main road, but there are no vantage points other than the roadside, where there are no parking facilities. When the tide is out, one can walk along this side of the estuary for a considerable distance. Take care that the tide is ebbing when setting out; there are low, sandy cliffs in many places bordering the mudflats, and if caught by a rising tide it is not easy to find a route back up.

Frogmore Creek meets the A379 at Frogmore village. There is little parking space on the main road before the turning towards Start and East Prawle, which crosses the top of the creek. From here either walk down the creek bank at low tide or walk back up the main road towards Kingsbridge for 100m until a gap between the cottages and a signposted public footpath to the creek.

For West Charleton Marsh, turn right in the middle of West Charleton village onto the very narrow, unmade Marsh Lane; past the last house, there is limited parking towards the lower end near the sewage plant (be very careful not to block entrances). A public footpath runs through the flat grassy field which contains the marshy land towards the far end. From this path, parts of the marsh are easily over-looked. Continuing a short distance along this path brings you to the estuary, overlooked by the public hide.

Off the A379 at Frogmore, take the Southpool road to look at the Southpool Creek area. From this village at the head of the creek, the road then continues to East Portlemouth near the estuary mouth, running along much of the creek's edge en route, giving intermittent views. The opposite side of the estuary is reached by the A381 from Kingsbridge to Malborough, but access is more difficult still. The best checking point is from Blanksmill Creek; walk out along the beach until you are able to see the main estuary. Only roadside parking is available. Checking the area from Salcombe town is easy, as roads run beside the waterfront; since there is more traffic, fewer birds occur, but divers, grebes, seaducks and terns are seen in small numbers.

CALENDAR

Resident: Shelduck, Cormorant, Shag, Grey Heron, Little Egret, Oystercatcher, common raptors, Grey Wagtail, Stonechat, Cirl Bunting, Yellowhammer, Raven.

December–February: Brent Goose, possibly other geese in hard weather; Teal, Gadwall, Wigeon, Pintail, Shoveler, Tufted Duck, Scaup, Goldeneye, Red-breasted Merganser, occasional Eider and Long-tailed Duck, divers, particularly Great Northern; Little, Black-necked and Great Crested Grebes; Golden and Grey Plover, Turnstone, Dunlin, Common Sandpiper, Greenshank, Bar-tailed Godwit, maybe Spotted Redshank; Kingfisher, wintering warblers, Firecrest, Black Redstart.

March–May: Most of the above depart by the end of March; migrant Whimbrel, Little Ringed Plover and Osprey pass through; Garganey and rarer herons possible in the right weather.

June–July: Heavy human disturbance. Little Egret build-up and return passage starts towards end of period.

August–November: Wader passage continues with Wood and Green Sandpipers, Ruff and Pectoral Sandpiper possible among commoner species; Osprey sightings increase in August–September, with ducks arriving later in season.

15 SOAR AREA INCLUDING BOLT HEAD TO BOLT TAIL

OS LANDRANGER MAP 202
OS grid ref: SX7037
Postcode: **East Soar** – TQ7 3DW
Bolberry – TQ7 3DY
Inner Hope – TQ7 3HG
what3words: **East Soar** – playfully.jiffy.thus
Bolberry – drove.darker.ultra
Inner Hope – lists.dabbling.blindfold

HABITAT

On the western side of the Kingsbridge estuary mouth (near Salcombe), opposite distant Prawle Point, lies this 5-mile (8km) stretch of rugged coast, extending from Sharpitor west to Bolberry Down. High cliffs owned by the National Trust back on to a plateau about 130m above sea level, especially between Bolt Head and Bolt Tail, giving spectacular coastal views. In the centre of the area, Soar Mill Valley cuts down through the high cliffs to form the relatively sheltered Soar Mill Cove.

Around Soar Mill Valley are rocky escarpments, partially clothed with bushes and bracken, while small trees are scattered throughout. A brook runs down the lower part of the valley, and in the wettest part there is a tiny reedbed, plus a stand of willows. Other parts of the area offer either less or too much cover, being rough sheep pasture or dense bracken. Located near Bolt Head and East Soar is a narrow belt of level, tightly grazed pasture called The Warren. Running parallel and adjacent to the clifftop, it extends for about 1 mile (1.6km) before reaching the edge of steep-sided Soar Mill Cove. A National Trust-owned farm allows a network of public paths throughout Soar district, including The Warren, also taking in arable fields and small pools at the head of craggy Starehole Valley. Through this valley flows a

Devon (south coast and Dartmoor)

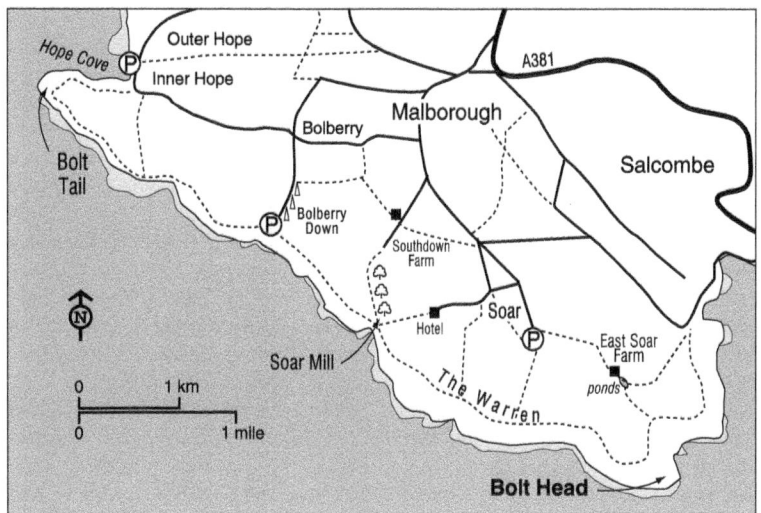

small brook with further bracken, trees and bushes scattered throughout. The National Trust gardens at Sharpitor (Overbecks) have sheltering trees, fringed by hedges.

Springtime witnesses cliffsides set ablaze with massed wild flowers. Among them are found particularly high populations of generally scarce butterflies such as Small Pearl-bordered Fritillary, Silver-studded Blue and Grayling.

SPECIES

The area's resident speciality is the Cirl Bunting. Up to 40 pairs breed here, while there are regularly counts of more than 100 across the area outside the breeding season, often associating with 80 or so Yellowhammers.

Birdwatchers chiefly visit the area searching for migrants, which in the main are the same species occurring at nearby Start and Prawle, and are seen at the same times and in the same conditions. This site, however, often produces larger numbers of those same species.

Wheatear is among the first spring migrants, and a pair or two may stay to breed. In autumn especially, up to 100 in a day is not unusual, and once more than 500 were seen; often the flocks contain examples of the larger Greenland form. The Warren area is particularly favoured by this and other open-ground species, such as wagtails and pipits. Other migrants, some of which stay to breed, include Grasshopper and Sedge Warblers, with higher numbers of Blackcap, Whitethroat, Willow Warbler and Chiffchaff. Migrants are usually present less consistently in spring, when they remain for a shorter time than in autumn. Frequently high numbers are confined to early mornings; even so, good numbers can occur. Apart from expected commoner passerine migrants, less common species have been seen; Hoopoe is regularly recorded in the area. Along the cliffs Kestrel, Fulmar, Stock Dove and Raven breed.

From Bolt Tail you can look into Thurlestone Bay, from which moving seabirds pass the headland. Little seawatching takes place here, which may prove to be a serious omission; in light southerly winds with poor visibility, terns, skuas and Manx Shearwater pass in good numbers in both seasons; similarly, try watching from Bolt

Head. Good seawatches have provided respectable numbers of the region's more sought-after species, including spring flocks of Pomarine Skua, Black Tern and Little Gull, with Leach's Storm Petrel in autumn, all observed in double figures.

In autumn, high numbers of diurnal migrants move along the coast or out to sea. Most numerous are Meadow Pipit, Yellow Wagtail and, later, Chaffinch and Linnet. Among later finch movements Brambling, Siskin, Lesser Redpoll and sometimes Hawfinch are recorded in smaller numbers. From mid-autumn, high numbers of migrant Goldcrest use Soar, peak numbers exceeding 100, with 10 or more brighter Firecrest (good numbers of both can pass through in spring, too). Black Redstarts, always arriving later than Redstart, can reach double figures. Check for them on rooftops and farm buildings, including houses and masts at Bolberry Down. Migrant Robins can also easily exceed 100. Ring Ouzels often fly from deep cover, giving harsh *chack* calls. This district is Devon's best site to look for them on migration; frequently a dozen or more occur together and 46 were once counted.

Scarcer migrants occur regularly, including Red-breasted Flycatcher, Red-backed Shrike and Melodious and Icterine Warblers. Earlier in autumn, one or two Wrynecks are anticipated every year. Dotterel have favoured the short turf of The Warren and the open fields at Soar, with Kentish Plover and Buff-breasted Sandpiper also having visited. Hen Harrier, Merlin and Short-eared Owl are likely but brief visitors in mid-autumn. The area's rarities have included Black Kite, Red-footed Falcon, Alpine Swift, and Aquatic, Pallas's, Radde's, Dusky and Western Bonelli's Warblers. Britain's first mainland Bobolink brought the area to national attention, with the area also yielding Devon's first mainland Yellow-breasted Bunting.

Unexpected spring scarcities have included Richard's Pipit and Short-toed Lark, both also turning up in autumn. Britain's latest autumn record of Woodchat Shrike was also here.

TIMING
Much as for Start/Prawle area; refer to those entries.

ACCESS
From the A381 at Malborough, between Kingsbridge and Salcombe, take the Bolberry road for Bolt Tail and continue through the village, following signs to the headland car park. Public footpaths extend along the clifftop from Bolt Tail to Bolt Head at the eastern end of the ridge, all under National Trust management. For Soar (sign reads Soar and Bolberry), the same exit is taken from Malborough, following signs to East Soar or Soar Mill Cove along narrow lanes.

You can follow public footpaths from Inner Hope to Bolberry (interesting migrants can be seen from this path around Hope Cove; a small wood contains a large Rookery). A public footpath runs through Soar Mill Valley to the tiny cove. Paths through high, steep grassy slopes near the cove connect the valley to Bolberry Down above, and eastwards towards Bolt Head, via The Warren. From the large car park at East Soar, public footpaths lead out to The Warren area, or towards and through the National Trust-owned farm, where further signs show paths leading to Sharpitor and Starehole Bay. Some public paths transect arable and newly ploughed fields; none lend themselves to access by those with limited mobility.

CALENDAR
Resident: Much as Start/Prawle areas.

December–February: Mainly small numbers of residents including Cirl Bunting, plus possible Woodcock in valley bottoms; offshore, Gannet, Fulmar and other seabirds.

March–May: Much as Start/Prawle areas.

June–July: Much as Start/Prawle areas.

August–November: Similar to the Start/Prawle areas, but numbers of various passerine migrants are consistently higher here, especially Wheatear and Ring Ouzel. The latter is seen more regularly here than any other coastal points in the region, especially in mid-October.

16 THURLESTONE AREA

OS LANDRANGER MAP 202
OS grid ref: SX6842
Postcode: **Thurlestone** – TQ7 3JU **South Huish** – TQ7 3JU
what3words: **Thurlestone** – asking.mimed.blush
South Huish – exhales.collide.according

HABITAT

Situated in a mild and drier part of south Devon, three major habitat zones are found in this interesting area: South Milton Ley, South Huish Marsh and Thurlestone Bay.

South Milton Ley is a Devon Birds reserve, comprising over 16ha and holding the second largest reedbed in Devon; there is no open standing water. Facing east–west, the reedbed lies in a shallow valley, with the narrow mouth of the marsh to the west, facing Thurlestone Bay. The Ley is regularly flooded by very high tides, especially during winter storms. When wave action piles sand high over its entrance, the sea water is not released until either internal water pressure or further storms break open the sand barrier. The highest reaches of the Ley remain as fresh water at all times. It is surrounded by farmland and, apart from hedgerows and some larger trees at its upper end, cover is minimal.

South Huish Marsh comprises at least 16ha of flat, flooded rough pasture, lying in a shallow open-sided valley among arable farmland. Running east-west and facing the sea, it runs parallel to South Milton Ley, which lies over the ridge to the north. The marsh is currently separated from the bay by low sand dunes and a National Trust car park. The marsh is interspersed with scrapes and drainage ditches; heavy winter rain partially floods it. Devon Birds and the National Trust manage the meadow and, with controlled drainage and new scrapes, the area's attractiveness to birds has been enhanced.

The bay is dominated by the remarkably shaped Thurlestone Rock, which projects from an otherwise mostly sandy shoreline. The bay faces west and is therefore sheltered from easterly and south-easterly winds.

It is worth checking the golf course and trees and scrub in the general area. All summer, the beach is a major tourist venue.

Devon (south coast and Dartmoor)

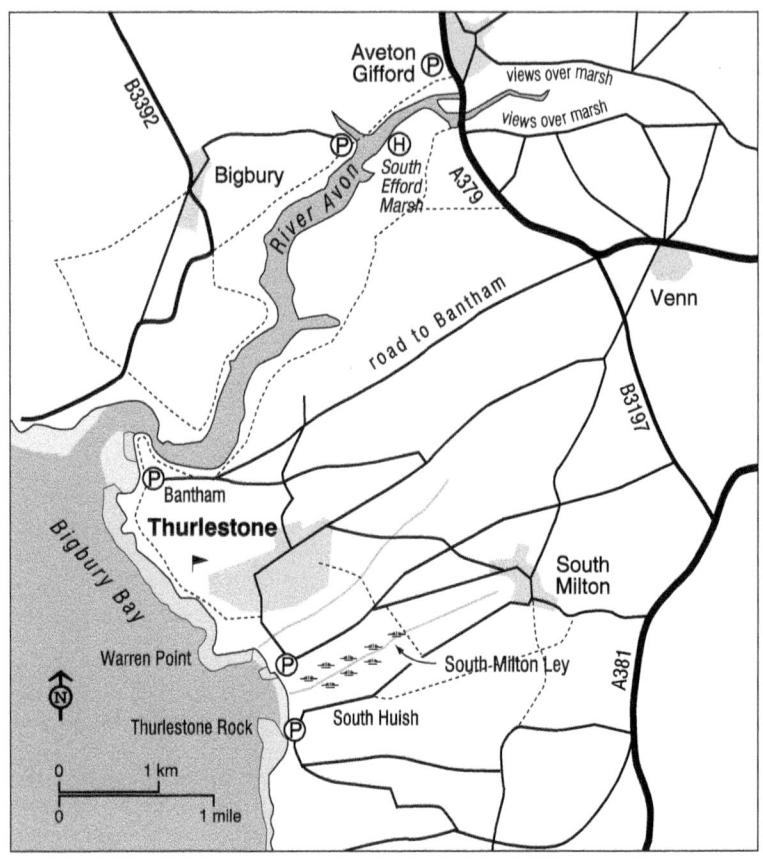

SPECIES

Because reed density is high at South Milton Ley, many rarer species are only seen when removed from a mist-net by ringers. Bearded Tits have visited the ley in winter and, especially on calm days, can be watched moving through reed tops giving their distinctive pinging calls. One of the resident Cetti's Warblers may burst into song despite the season, and wintering Chiffchaffs should be checked for the Siberian subspecies. Reed Buntings are present and have been joined by Little Bunting on three occasions. During winter, Jack Snipe regularly join Snipe foraging in the any open areas of the reedbed. Through the late spring, Reed and Sedge Warblers sing from reed tops. Water Rail may also be heard, rather than seen; it is present all year and breeding has been proven.

In autumn, the reedbed becomes a major roost site, with thousands of Swallows and Starlings forming the bulk, joined by several hundred Pied Wagtails, including the continental form, White Wagtail. Yellow Wagtails are less predictable, but early autumn usually witnesses large numbers for short periods. Ringing studies have produced occasional rarities, including Aquatic Warbler, Bluethroat and Penduline Tit (Devon's first).

Scarce raptors have flown over the area, including Red Kite, Osprey and

Goshawk. Marsh Harrier may linger on migration, hunting over the reedbed for a day or two. A summer-plumaged Least Sandpiper was an extreme early autumn rarity.

A very cold spell in winter makes South Huish Marsh especially attractive to dabbling ducks such as Mallard, Teal and Wigeon; numbers vary but 100 Teal and several hundred grazing Wigeon are not infrequent, and American Wigeon has twice been picked out within the flock. Geese, usually White-fronted or Brent, sometimes visit in hard weather and often stay for several weeks. Water Pipits are regularly present, although often well hidden. Gulls come to rest, bathe and preen by pools; unusual and rare species should be looked for, with a Ross's Gull once visiting.

In spring, returning waders such as Bar-tailed Godwit, which are seen in small groups, are often in summer plumage. Small parties of Whimbrel may stay for several days. Two or three Garganey may be attracted to the marsh, and an exceptional 65 were offshore one spring day. Early Wheatear can be looked for from the first spring days. Improved management of the marsh has benefited waterbirds and waders, attracting at times large numbers of species that previously visited only rarely, such as Dunlin. Records of Ruff, Little Ringed Plover and Wood Sandpiper have also increased. A pair of Black-winged Stilt graced the scrapes one spring, with another four arriving for a long sojourn several years later. Other lingering spring rarities have included Purple Heron and Red-rumped Swallow. Yellow Wagtail is an annual visitor, including regular Blue-headed and rarer Grey- and even Black-headed forms on occasion. In autumn, several Spotted Crake and Pectoral Sandpipers have been seen, as well as a very scarce species for the region, Red-necked Phalarope.

Little, Mediterranean, Sabine's, Glaucous and Iceland Gulls have all been recorded in Thurlestone Bay. Along the winter shoreline, Turnstones and maybe a few Purple Sandpipers are present, while Rock Pipits and Pied and Grey Wagtails feed together among the tidewrack. Grassy cliffs and clifftop buildings are favourite haunts of Black Redstarts. Divers, mostly Great Northern, occur offshore.

From early spring, Fulmar pass by the bay and the first Sandwich Terns are usually noted, often pausing to fish. Later, substantial numbers of Common Terns, and sometimes flocks of Arctic and Little Terns, may do the same. One or two Black Terns are seen regularly with the passing tern flocks. These often attract a few skuas, generally Arctic. Easterly winds encourage tern flocks to follow the coastline closely, when they may be joined by up-Channel northbound waders such as Whimbrel and Bar-tailed Godwit. Occasionally, hundreds of terns and thousands of waders move through in a day, often high overland across the marsh rather than flying around Bolt Tail – presumably not rejoining the sea again until reaching Lyme Bay.

In autumn, unusual waders may use the beach but are usually displaced by disturbance; Kentish Plover has been seen. Gales can produce unusual gulls, especially Little or Mediterranean. Autumn's westerly gales often produce Grey Phalarope; sometimes a small group bobs on the waves.

The golf course, although busy, is a specialised habitat used regularly by a few waders, pipits, wagtails and Wheatear, particularly in spring and autumn; Buff-breasted Sandpiper has been seen and two Desert Wheatears, including a wintering bird. Hedgerows, trees and scrub hold small numbers of passerine migrants, and possibly Cirl Bunting. Interesting species turn up in the whole complex around Thurlestone. For example, Hoopoe is recorded most springs and Wryneck nearly every autumn, while Great Reed and Icterine Warblers have been found in sheltered vegetation exceptionally late in the year. Spring records have included Whiskered Tern and Subalpine Warbler species, also recorded here in autumn. Several Woodchat and two Isabelline Shrikes have visited the area, while a Black Stork once rested briefly on South Huish.

TIMING

Not critical during winter. In spring and autumn, an early morning visit is best, partly because there is less disturbance and partly because bird movement is usually greater, or at least more observable, then. Easterly winds are best in spring for tern and wader movements in the bay. Late afternoon and evening checks have been productive, especially for seabirds and waders, which may use South Huish or the beach to rest or roost, pausing their migrations. At dusk in early autumn, hirundines and wagtails fly in to roost at the South Milton reedbed. In summer, most breeding birds in the reedbed are active in early mornings.

ACCESS

Approaching from the Plymouth direction, follow the A379 to the top of steep Aveton Gifford hill, then follow Thurlestone signs at the roundabout a few hundred metres after the hilltop. Take the first right off the B3197 after the roundabout, down narrow minor roads to Thurlestone. Either park in the pay-and-display at the golf course or drive past. On the brow of the hill towards South Milton, the road curves left; at this point there is a sharp right turn about 1 mile (1.6km) after Thurlestone village. This entrance leads to a pay-and-display car park overlooking the bay, a good place for viewing.

If approaching from Kingsbridge, take the A381 towards Salcombe then branch off to Thurlestone (this same road is also initially taken for South Milton Ley or South Huish); either route will bring you to the car park overlooking both South Huish Marsh and the bay. Access from South Milton village to overlook South Huish Marsh; turn sharp left where the minor road is signposted to South Milton Sands. From here, for South Milton Ley or Thurlestone village and golf course, walk north along the car park; a public footpath opposite public toilets leads across a footbridge over the mouth of the ley. From this point there are good views of the reedbed. The path continues past a small area of sand dunes before meeting the road which adjoins the Thurlestone car park.

Access into South Milton Ley reserve is limited to Devon Birds members. Wellingtons are usually essential, and there is limited access for the less physically mobile. There is no access onto South Huish Marsh, but birds can be seen well from the National Trust car park, especially with a telescope. Also, walk the minor road bounding its southern flank for intermittent but different views over the site; some birds may be hidden from view from the front of the marsh. The perimeter of the golf course has open access.

CALENDAR

Resident: Sparrowhawk, Buzzard, Water Rail, Rock Pipit, Cetti's Warbler, Stonechat, Reed Bunting, Raven, Cirl Bunting (scarce).

December–February: Wild geese may visit the South Huish Marsh; large numbers of Teal and Wigeon, a few Pintail, Shoveler and Gadwall, Water Pipit. Snipe in hundreds, Ruff in ones and twos. Possibly one or two divers, grebes and auks on sea; Bearded Tit in South Milton Ley (some years); sheltered places may hold a wintering Black Redstart, Chiffchaff or Firecrest; Merlin may hunt over area; scarce gulls, e.g. Glaucous or Iceland.

March–May: Garganey may visit the Marsh from April, also Whimbrel and godwits; Sandwich and other terns from April; Hoopoe possible from March, Wheatear from mid-March; Sedge and Reed Warblers in Ley from mid-April; commoner migrants may be joined by unusual species; White and Yellow Wagtails, Blue-headed possible.

June–July: Breeding species include Sand Martin, and Reed and Sedge Warblers; hirundines, Starlings and wagtails start to use the reedbed roost in late July.

August–November: Wagtail roost still heavily used to mid-September, when White Wagtail more evident; Yellow Wagtails often roost in reeds at South Milton Ley, gathering at South Huish prior to roosting, August–early September; return passage of migrant raptors, waders, seabirds and passerines; Grey Phalarope and Snow Bunting irregular from October; Black Redstart arrive late October; Mediterranean, Little or other unusual gulls.

17 SOUTH EFFORD MARSH, AVON ESTUARY AND WATER MEADOWS

OS LANDRANGER MAP 202
OS grid ref: SX6947
Postcode: **South Efford Marsh** – TQ7 4JL **Bantham** – TQ7 4AR
what3words: **South Efford Marsh** – chatters.uniform.artichoke
Bantham – rehearsed.probe.ripe

HABITAT

The Avon forms a narrow estuary in the South Hams of Devon, flanked by trees, including many oaks. Muddy areas towards the estuary head include saltmarsh and the recently enhanced South Efford Marsh. Adjacent to the head of the estuary, water meadows extend inland for about 1 mile (1.6km) and are up to 800m wide. The River Avon meanders throughout. Although potentially extensive, few areas remain permanently marshy.

In winter, on high tides and after prolonged heavy rainfall, the entire valley is liable to flood. This situation normally only lasts for a few days at a time but leaves the soil waterlogged, with many standing pools throughout winter until early spring. Along the riverbank grow clumps of alder; other riparian trees such as willows are scattered along this wide shallow valley.

South Efford Marsh is an area of saltmarsh and wet meadows on the south side of the estuary, opposite the tidal road. The installation of a tidal gate allows water to flow in at high tide, creating an area much favoured by waders.

Towards the river mouth (leading out into Bigbury Bay), the estuary is easily observed from Bantham. The central section of estuary is difficult to access, while its narrowness makes it less attractive to many species. Spring comes early to this part of south Devon, and Wild Daffodils, Snowdrops and Primroses grow among the hedgerows.

SPECIES

The sheltered estuary head attracts typical wintering species found on the region's south coast such as Greenshank, and Green and Common Sandpipers, usually in ones and twos. Kingfishers, which have probably only undertaken a local movement from breeding sites further up the Avon, are common in winter and may be seen resting on a stranded log in midstream or dashing from tree-lined banks. Cormorant, Grey Heron and Little Egret, like Kingfisher, may be seen up the river as well as the estuary. Cattle Egrets and Glossy Ibises, often several together, are now often seen in winter. Up to 10 wintering Little Grebes are usually present around the tidal road area, staying in the main channel when the tide is out.

At the head of the open estuary, gulls often congregate to bathe and preen in fresh water discharging from the river. A couple of hundred Black-headed may gather, joined in winter by 50 or more Common Gulls and perhaps a few Mediterranean Gulls.

Waders tend to be in small flocks. Ringed Plover is most numerous in autumn, with up to 100, but only a dozen remain through the winter. Oystercatcher and Curlew number about 50, Redshank, Dunlin and Turnstone usually 20 or so, often using South Efford at high tide. American rarities have included Pectoral Sandpiper and the elegant Lesser Yellowlegs, one of which over-wintered; even rarer was a Killdeer, an unexpected and all-too-brief wintertime find. Shelduck and Mallard are usually the most numerous ducks, with about 50 of each, and Teal vary in number, usually 40 or so, with fewer Wigeon. Mute Swan exceed 50 in winter and several pairs breed, but lack of suitable habitat means success rates are low.

Towards its mouth, the estuary widens, its proximity to the sea encouraging gulls to loaf or shelter and sea-going birds to wander into its sheltered entrance. Most species occurring elsewhere on the estuary will also occur around the mouth, but if small parties of Brent Geese arrive, they favour the mouth, likewise occasional divers or grebes.

Lesser Black-backed Gulls congregate in late winter–early spring, 100 or more in number. Later in spring, Whimbrel often gather around the mouth or on the beach if not disturbed, before migrating on. The shallow sandy bay itself is less used by interesting seabirds, although it is certainly worth checking if you are in the area. Terns can occur in good numbers and enter the estuary to fish or rest; among the commoner species, Roseate and Little have been noted.

The water meadows in winter attract various dabbling ducks, irregularly in small numbers, including Pintail and Gadwall. Over 100 Snipe are usually well hidden in harder weather, with Water Rail frequent but often impossible to see, their squealing calls revealing their presence. Green Sandpiper winter in ones and twos, although half a dozen at a time can pass through in autumn. Difficult to identify, Water Pipits favour this type of habitat and are seen here from time to time in early spring. When hard weather forces birds to change from their traditional wintering grounds elsewhere, wild geese, perhaps a group of White-fronted, or swans may visit for a short while; both Bewick's and Whooper Swans have been recorded. High in the Alders, a party of Siskins could be feeding on the tiny seeds, or a Barn Owl might be watched quartering the meadows in early mornings and late afternoons. Most years, by late in the winter period 'spring' weather arrives sufficiently for the regular ducks to depart, taking with them any other remaining wildfowl, which have included a wintering Blue-winged Teal. Above the incessant cawing of Rooks, a solitary, sonorous *kronk* will advertise the presence of a Raven as it performs mid-air rolls over its territory.

From early spring, the first Chiffchaffs are already singing among the Hazel catkins in the hedgerows. Because the area offers shelter, early songsters might be overwintering birds. Blackcap also winter here, although migrants arrive later. The flash of a white rump around the sand dunes heralds the arrival of the first sub-Saharan migrant, Wheatear. Sand Martins are also seen early on, following the river inland. Just after the first influx of Chiffchaffs, Willow Warblers begin to appear, the hedgerows briefly full of their musical, descending notes. Soon the first Swallows and House Martins are skimming in over the meadows. There is a chance of a rare heron arriving; Night, Purple and Squacco have been noted. The region's first Marsh Sandpiper once paused briefly on the mudflats.

In summer, there is little to be found on the estuary, with persistent disturbance from small boats and water-skiers. The heronry midway down the estuary in the woods is active, and a few Mallard and Shelduck breed, along with good numbers of common woodland passerines. A large breeding population of Spotted Flycatcher, unfortunately now much declined, was extensively studied here.

Some waders return early at the start of autumn and may still wear colourful summer plumage, with Curlew Sandpiper or Little Stint possible on South Efford. Hirundine numbers build up steadily in this favourite gathering area. Small flocks of migrant Yellow Wagtail intermingle with up to 100 Pied and White Wagtails. Passing raptors spending a few days hunting the water meadows have included Hen and Marsh Harriers; further down towards the estuary an Osprey may fish, with birds lingering in autumn.

TIMING

The upper part of the estuary cannot be checked until the tide is out, owing to access problems. When the tide has just dropped, very close views can be obtained by using your car as a hide along the tidal road. Any time of day is suitable to visit the water meadows and South Efford Marsh, although either side of high tide gives the best chance of seeing waders pushed from the estuary by the rising tide.

Hard weather can produce more and different birds. When there is little or no standing water, the meadows are unattractive to wading birds. In spring a visit on a quiet morning to either the water meadows or dune areas might be productive for newly arrived migrants.

All year round, when the surf is running, surfers may be present, pushing seabirds further out into the bay.

ACCESS

Checking the uppermost part of the estuary is via the narrow tidal road, located off the A379 roundabout adjacent to the Ebb Tide Inn at the south end of Aveton Gifford village. Several pull-in spots along its length allow close views, ideal for disabled drivers. A small car park is sited at its furthest end. This road is totally impassable at high tide.

South Efford Marsh can be reached by crossing south over the road bridge from the car park. An uneven, unsurfaced path leads around the perimeter of the reserve to a hide giving views across the marsh and estuary.

Devon (south coast and Dartmoor)

The water meadows are best checked by following either of the minor roads opposite one another at the south end of the road bridge, or one which starts in the village. On the south side (towards Kingsbridge), a minor road runs adjacent to the meadows downstream for a few hundred metres; park your car tightly beside the road when checking this area. This same minor road continues to follow the water meadows (now upstream) across the other side of the main road and is signposted to Venn, running the length of the water meadows, although they are often not in view. An unsigned steep turning in the middle of Aveton Gifford village (opposite the post office) leads to several points where the road overlooks the meadows; about halfway up their length is a better area for ducks and waders.

Public footpaths run either side of the estuary, one starting near the car park area at the bottom of the tidal road, the other on the far side of the road bridge at Bridge End. Although running the full length of the estuary, they lead some way off it in places.

Access for the estuary mouth and bay is from the A379 roundabout near the top of the steep Aveton Gifford hill south of the river. Take the minor road to Bantham. At Bantham, where the road ends, there is ample car parking, except during summer months when the privately owned car park will be crowded. This lower part of the estuary is easily watched over from the elevated roadside.

Note: The A379 Aveton Gifford bypass avoids the village.

CALENDAR

Resident: Shelduck, Grey Heron, Little Egret, Buzzard, Kestrel, Stock Dove, Barn Owl, Green and Great Spotted Woodpeckers, Rock Pipit, Grey Wagtail, Stonechat, Raven, Bullfinch, Reed Bunting.

December–February: Possibly Brent or 'grey' geese; Teal, Wigeon, Shoveler, Little Grebe, Water Rail, Oystercatcher, Ringed Plover, Turnstone, Dunlin, Redshank, Greenshank, Green and Common Sandpipers, Curlew, Snipe, Mediterranean Gull; Kingfisher, Water Pipit and Siskin; occasional divers, scarcer grebes or seaducks such as Common Scoter.

March–May: Possibly a rarer heron or Hoopoe from mid-April; Whimbrel, hirundines; commoner migrant passerines, e.g. Chiffchaff, Willow Warbler and Whitethroat, from April; Lesser Black-backed Gulls gather from end of previous period; terns, mostly Common and Sandwich, may include scarcer species especially towards end of period.

June–July: Breeding species, mostly common woodland passerines, including Spotted Flycatcher.

August–November: Returning waders, possibly including Little Stint, Curlew or Pectoral Sandpiper; migrant raptors, e.g. Osprey; Mediterranean Gull, Yellow Wagtail; terns, mostly Sandwich, but occasional other species. All the above mostly August–September. Later in period, ducks return and gales may produce sheltering seabirds.

Devon (south coast and Dartmoor)

SITE CLUSTER: PLYMOUTH AREA

17A Stoke Point
18 Wembury and Bovisand
19 Plymouth area
20 Plymbridge Woods

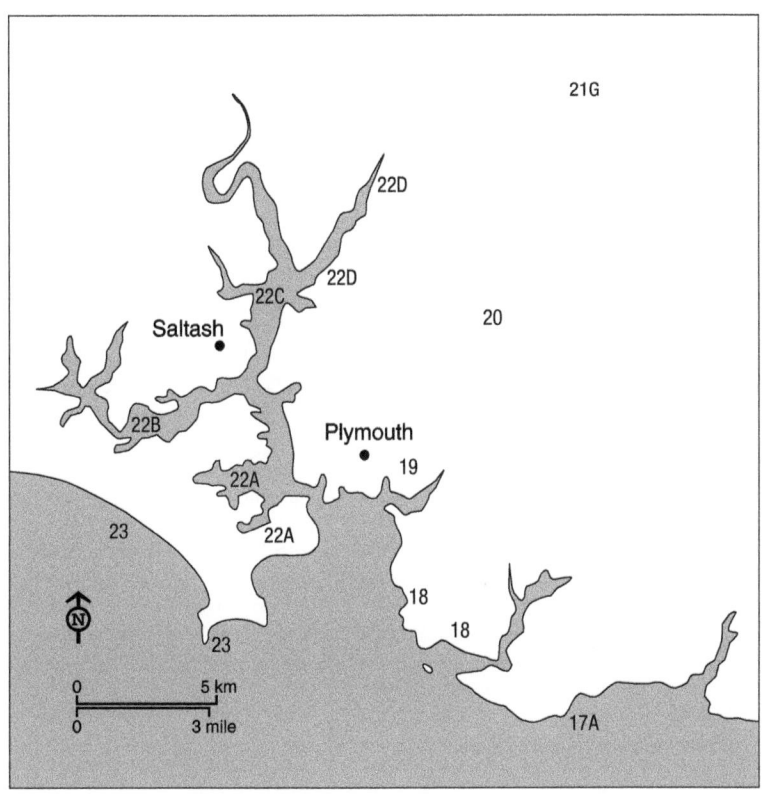

17A STOKE POINT AREA

OS LANDRANGER MAP 202
OS grid ref: SX5646
Postcode: PL8 1EL
what3words: waltz.holidays.speaker

HABITAT

A narrow coastal strip of mostly exposed land stretches between two river mouths, the Yealm and Erme. Backed by arable farmland, the greater part of the area is rough sheep-grazed pasture, sloping to a rocky coastline. At Carswell, near the east end, cliffs are high and precipitous.

The open sward is interspersed with patches of gorse. A small wood of mostly Sweet Chestnut grows at Stoke Point, adjacent to the caravan park, which has further trees and bushes. A tiny, willow-lined valley runs down from the bushy gardens at Warren Cottage. A relatively level coast footpath runs for virtually the whole length of the area, mostly along its highest points, allowing panoramic views of coastline and open sea.

SPECIES

Up to 30 pairs of Cormorant, and a dozen or more of Shag and Fulmar, breed on Blackattery and Carswell cliffs near Battisborough. Several pairs of Shelduck also nest in burrows along the coast. Kestrel are commonly met; in autumn, a Merlin may chase flocks of larks, pipits or Linnets. A few pairs of Oystercatcher nest on suitable sea-circled rocky outcrops, and Turnstone frequent the shoreline.

At migration seasons a variety of commoner passerines may be seen, such as flycatchers and warblers, chiefly in small numbers, and Woodchat Shrike has been recorded. Birds of open country regularly visit, including Meadow Pipit, Skylark, Whinchat and Wheatear; a pair or two of the last have bred. Resident Yellowhammers also like this exposed habitat, but not so much Cirl Buntings, which may be better sought near either of the river mouths and among sheltering trees and hedgerows around Stoke Point or Warren Cottage. Autumn/winter flocks of Cirls in stubble fields or weedy margins can number 20 or more.

During later autumn especially, the area around Stoke Point attracts more species requiring shelter, funnelling warblers such as Blackcap to feed on elderberries and blackberries. Thrushes, too, take advantage of this food supply, with perhaps a departing Ring Ouzel mingling with incoming Redwings. Foraging flocks of Goldcrests and Chiffchaffs often contain a few Firecrests and have produced Yellow-browed Warblers; other noteworthy species noted in this underwatched area have included Icterine Warbler, Tawny Pipit and passing Osprey.

TIMING

Birdwatchers will find most interest during migration periods. If the visit is specifically for migrants, favourable weather conditions are required, although Stoke Point itself is sheltered from northerly winds, so may be worth a check then for delayed migrants. Winds from southerly quarters can also produce some interesting seabirds such as Manx Shearwater, terns and skuas passing Stoke Point; misty conditions, even if winds are light, seem more productive than strong westerlies.

ACCESS

Travelling on the A379 Plymouth–Kingsbridge road, turn off at Yealmpton onto the B3186 signposted to Newton Ferrers and Noss Mayo. Continue past Noss Mayo village until about 800m past Netton Farm, reaching a National Trust car park, with public access paths to coastal walks. There is no access restriction throughout the total walk of over 5 miles (8km) from Ferry Wood at Noss Mayo east to Battisborough Cross.

Alternatively, follow signs to Stoke and Holbeton from Noss Mayo; when at a crossroads take a very narrow road signposted to Stoke Beach. There is a small visitors' car park at the entrance of a caravan park. Public footpaths from this car park allow you to walk westwards through the top part of the woods (an important area to check) or skirt the more sheltered lower edge of the wood through the caravan park, or eastwards past often-productive bramble patches and hedgerows, before either route returns to open land.

CALENDAR

Resident: Kestrel, Shag, Oystercatcher, Raven, Skylark, Linnet, Cirl Bunting, Yellowhammer.

December–February: Wintering flocks of finches and buntings, perhaps Lapwing and Golden Plover, more numerous in cold weather.

March–May: Commoner passerine migrants may include scarcer species.

June–July: Breeding species.

August–November: Returning commoner passerine migrants, with a chance of less common species among them; Merlin often later in period.

18 WEMBURY AND BOVISAND

OS LANDRANGER MAP 201
OS grid ref: SX5048
Postcode: **Wembury** – PL9 0HR **Bovisand** – PL9 0AT
what3words: **Wembury** – distract.frame.distorts
Bovisand – radically.correct.bath

HABITAT

This section of the south Devon coast follows from near where the Plymouth coast walk ends at Jennycliff (see site 19).

The Wembury side of the Yealm estuary has quite high cliffs, quickly losing height westward, then dropping almost to sea level near Wembury village. From then until Bovisand Bay, the cliffs remain mostly only 4–5m high, rising at Bovisand for a short distance to about 20m. The low, soft cliffs are prone to erosion; very high tides combined with storm force winds has caused major damage, and the public footpath has shifted several metres inland along much of its length. As the immediate coastal land is low-lying, the vegetation is generally taller. Bushes and trees

Devon (south coast and Dartmoor)

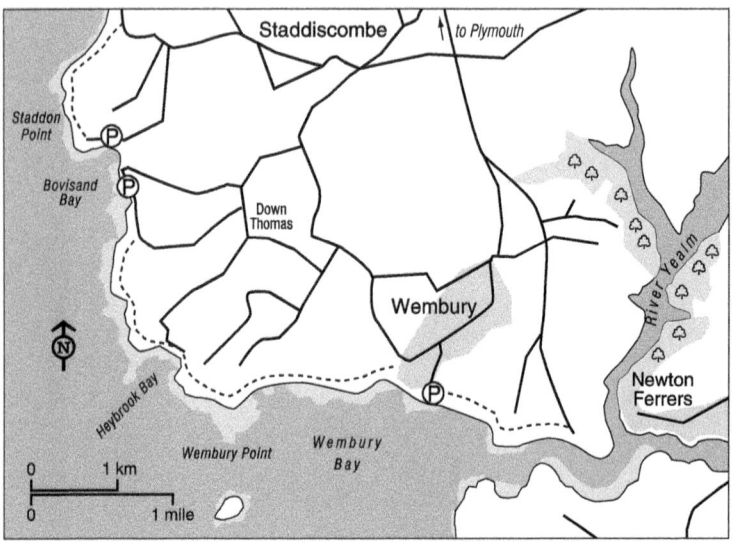

away from the shoreline are abundant, offering good cover. Areas owned by the National Trust are being partially cleared and managed as a more diverse wildlife habitat, including fields adjacent to what was the HMS *Cambridge* gunnery school prior to being returned to nature.

Mill Meadow is a small, wet, bushy area, offering shelter for birds; now made accessible, it is worth checking.

The whole of this rocky coastline is a marine sanctuary holding a varied shore and rock-pool fauna. This walk can offer something of interest all year, with hedgerows, brakes and arable fields forming an intermittent backdrop.

SPECIES

Probably the most interesting area in autumn and winter is that used by waders at Wembury Point. High tides and the action of the wind bring large quantities of rotting seaweed ashore, providing rich feeding areas for myriad tiny animals. Up to 100 Turnstones forage here in winter, with numbers dropping to 30 or fewer in midsummer, when they will be in full breeding plumage. During autumn, up to 30 Ringed Plovers may be present. Purple Sandpipers were previously winter regulars, usually around rocks at the Point, but nowadays there are generally only two or three birds. Waders seen occasionally, particularly in autumn, include Little Stint and Curlew Sandpiper, but only in ones and twos, while Sanderling, Common Sandpiper and Bar-tailed Godwit are regular in slightly larger numbers. Whimbrel pass through in spring and autumn in small groups. Through winter and early spring 20–30 Rock Pipit congregate, in some years with one or two Water Pipits among them. A few of the Scandinavian *littoralis* subspecies of Rock Pipit also occur; positive identification can be confirmed by colour-ringed Norwegian individuals.

Leaving the immediate shoreline, another speciality is the resident Cirl Bunting population. These birds can be seen among brakes and hedgerows or feeding, perhaps in the company of Yellowhammers, in stubble fields, especially near Wembury Point. Flocks of 25 or so are expected in winter, once joined by Devon's only Pine Bunting. At suitable times of year, commoner migrants such as 'crests' and warblers are found at Mill Meadow, which has also produced Yellow-browed Warbler. Black Redstart is frequent from later autumn, feeding in sheltered coves, particularly near Bovisand, and also around Wembury church. Rare later autumn visitors have included Britain's second Ovenbird, a sad roadside casualty, a Red-eyed Vireo in the brakes, and Isabelline and Woodchat Shrikes on thorn bushes. Richard's Pipit has been found in spring and autumn. Hoopoe, more likely in spring, has also been recorded.

Small numbers of wintering Firecrests are not unusual in the brakes around Wembury Point, where a winter roost of up to 100 Magpies has been recorded. Few interesting species are seen on the sea, although Cormorant, Shag, Fulmar, Shelduck and Herring and Great Black-backed Gulls breed on Great Mewstone rock, 1 mile (1.6km) off the Point. This rock also acts as the major winter night roost for thousands of Herring Gulls which scavenge the estuaries of Plymouth, and hundreds of Great Black-backeds that share their routine. Up to 10 pairs of Fulmar breed on the higher cliffs at Bovisand. Occasional divers, grebes and seaducks visit in ones and twos, very sporadically.

Scarcer visitors to the bay have included a white Greenland Gyr Falcon, which graced the top of the Mewstone for a few spring days (attracting an appreciative audience of birdwatchers). Black Guillemot, Glaucous and Iceland Gulls have been seen offshore, while storm-weakened individuals of both Long-tailed Skua and Sabine's Gull, normally true pelagic birds, have been found resting in fields overlooking the shoreline.

TIMING

A rising tide is required to concentrate waders onto the beach at the Point. Human disturbance can be a problem, especially on sunny afternoons, but less so on morning high tides.

ACCESS

The A379 Plymouth–Kingsbridge road is the best starting point. From Plymouth, turn right at the Elburton roundabout on the edge of the city (opposite Elburton Inn), through the village and along narrow country lanes. Head towards Staddiscombe for Bovisand and Wembury Point, or direct from Elburton to Wembury village. Continue through the village to the National Trust car park. Walk from there to the beach, then turn right following the mostly level but often muddy public paths to the Point, or continue west towards Bovisand. If preferred, there is a fee-paying car park at Bovisand, from where walking eastwards will again give views over the area.

At Wembury Point there is a small car park at the entrance to the former HMS *Cambridge* site. The Point can be reached by walking towards the sea from the car park or walking back up Spring Road 400m to a steep, often muddy, public footpath which leads down to the coast path; this area is often very good for birds. Views from the roadside are magnificent, the Mewstone leading your eye seawards.

The main wader area at Wembury Point is viewed very easily from the public footpath, which runs adjacent to the cliff edge throughout. The total length of the walk is about 3 miles (4.8km); access is unrestricted at any time. Eastwards, the coast path leads towards the Yealm estuary.

Paths surround Mill Meadow, the bottom of an open, shallow-sided valley heading north-east inland behind the beach.

Devon (south coast and Dartmoor)

Strictly no access is allowed on Great Mewstone without special permission from the National Trust, which owns the island.

CALENDAR

Resident: Shelduck, Cormorant, Shag, Sparrowhawk, Buzzard, Oystercatcher, Turnstone, Rock and Meadow Pipits, Stonechat, Cirl Bunting, Raven.

December–February: Grey Plover, Purple Sandpiper, Curlew, *littoralis* Rock Pipit and occasional Water Pipit, occasional Black Redstart and Brambling.

March–May: Early Chiffchaff and Wheatear, first Sandwich Terns often late March, also Willow Warbler; from mid-April, waders including Whimbrel.

June–July: Breeding species including Fulmar, Great Black-backed Gull, Blackcap, Whitethroat, Spotted Flycatcher, plus residents.

August–November: Waders, including Ringed Plover, Whimbrel, Dunlin, Redshank, Sandwich and Common Terns, less frequently other terns, August–September; general passage of departing summer migrants such as warblers, Wheatear, then Black Redstart, possibly scarcer species, October–November; early morning movements of Skylark, Chaffinch and Linnet.

19 PLYMOUTH AREA

OS LANDRANGER MAP 201
OS grid ref: SX4753
Postcodes: PL1–PL9 (for more detail and what3words see Access section)

HABITAT

Plymouth city lies on the Devon/Cornwall border, at the confluence of four rivers: the Lynher, Tamar, Tavy and Plym, all of which flow into Plymouth Sound. The city's waterfront has a rocky foreshore enclosed in a large bay (the Sound), protected from all but the roughest seas by a breakwater across the bay mouth. Following the South West Water 'Clean Sweep' operation, no sewage outfalls now discharge along the seafront. Consequently, gulls no longer assemble en masse, effectively removing a major facet of birding interest. Since the early 2000s, additional adverse changes to available gull food supplies have included the loss of several fish quays and the creation of more covered trawler unloading areas. Chelson rubbish tip is now a recycling point and only open to the public to deposit household waste, so there are only ever a handful of gulls present as their food source has now disappeared. All these factors have reduced gull activity and numbers enormously. It would appear Plymouth's heyday for vast numbers of gulls – and the annual occurrence of rarer species – has passed.

Tiny Drake's Island is situated in the Sound, surrounded by shallowly submerged rocks covered in seaweed. For those who wish to view deep-sea species, Plymouth is the departure point for Brittany Ferries trips to Santander in northern Spain, providing seabird and cetacean sightings across the Bay of Biscay (for details see 'Pelagic seabird trips', site 35A).

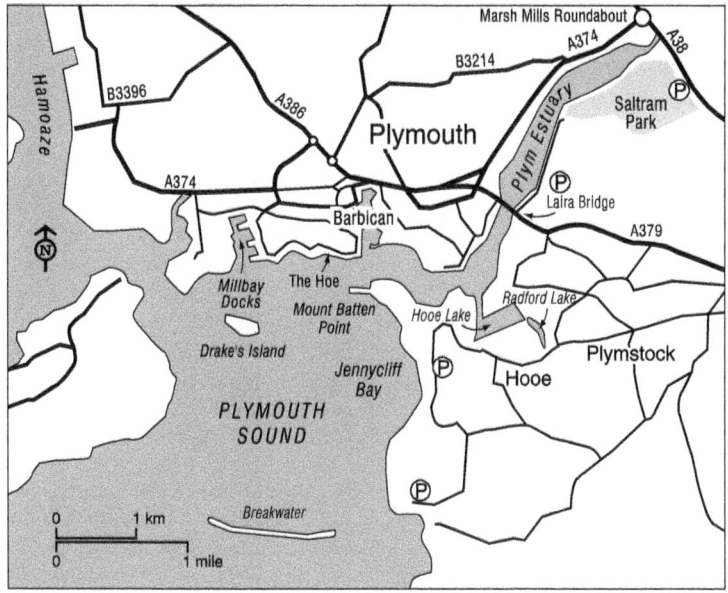

At Jennycliff on the eastern side of the bay, rocky cliffs and brakes reach a height of some 90m. The bay here is sheltered from north and east winds. Nearby Radford Lake is a suburban, Plymouth City-owned brackish lake in a parkland setting, and located at the head of Hooe Lake is a wide tidal creek leading towards the Plym Estuary on the city's eastern boundary. Fed from one end by a stream, 1ha Radford Lake is separated from Hooe Lake by a sluiced dam; at higher tides, sea water enters the pond. Hexton Woods are adjacent, with Radford Woods about 1 mile (1.6km) away. Jennycliff coastline, bordered by housing, lies about 1.6km off. No fishing or water sports are allowed on Radford Lake (also known as Radford Pond). This enclosed body of water is the only such habitat within the city boundaries capable of producing interesting waterbirds.

Chelson Meadow was the city rubbish tip until 2008, when it became a recycling centre. It is situated adjacent to the Plym Estuary. Blaxton Meadow, a 5ha site near Marsh Mills at the head of the estuary, has been transformed into a haven for wildlife since disturbance has been reduced by the closure of one of the footpaths. It can be viewed from the hide on the footpath around Saltram. The Tamar and Tavy rivers converge at their mouths, forming extensive mudflats.

There are 13 Local Nature Reserves (LNRs) in and around the city, 12 of which are owned and managed by Plymouth City Council in partnership with local communities. These provide a variety of habitats that are valuable for wildlife but support few noteworthy birds, although some less common species are found and at least two woodpecker species probably breed in them. Efford Marsh, with its fringing rough fields, hedges and trees, boasts one of the greatest habitat diversities in the area.

SPECIES

The coastal areas probably produce most of the interesting and rare birds. Every winter, through to early spring, one or two divers and grebes are found in the bay.

After prolonged gales or in very harsh, icy conditions, numbers and variety often increase as sheltering birds arrive. Up to 10 or more divers (mostly Great Northern) and similar numbers of grebes appear. Occasional Slavonian Grebes appear but cold-weather influxes are mostly of Great Crested and the occasional Red-necked Grebe; favourite areas are around Jennycliff in easterlies, and the lee of Drake's Island in westerlies. During very mild winters the bay is virtually ignored by these species, but occasional sightings are made of Eider, Common Scoter, Long-tailed Duck and Black Guillemot, which may stay for weeks. The Island can host a Little Egret roost, while a Glossy Ibis visited regularly one winter.

Severe weather conditions do not really influence the occurrence of uncommon gull species, for which Plymouth has had an enviable record. Lesser numbers of gulls than previously now gather in the area in winter. Plymouth once ranked as high as any conurbation in Britain for its variety of gull species (in season). During one period of only a few weeks, 13 species and four subspecies were present, with a Ross's, Bonaparte's, Ring-billed and Mediterranean Gull standing side by side! Plymouth has recorded 19 species of gull to date. The remaining fish quays, especially when trawlers are offloading, still attract gulls but in far smaller numbers. Among them may be one or two of special interest. Patience and expertise have resulted in many uncommon and a few rare gulls being seen. Mediterranean Gulls are present most of the year. Little, Iceland and Glaucous Gulls are now seen less than annually and in reduced numbers, Iceland and Glaucous mostly between late winter and early spring. Expert birders have found the difficult-to-identify Ring-billed Gull; these have occurred among flocks of migrant Common Gulls from late winter but are now once again a rare occurrence. Other American rarities have included Franklin's, Laughing and Kumlien's Gulls.

The Radford and Hooe area can be good for migrant and wintering species, although many commoner residents are present, including woodland passerines in the two wooded areas. The most productive periods are from autumn to spring. At Radford Lake small numbers of Little Grebe, Coot and Tufted Duck winter; several Tufted have summered and Little Grebe breeds there. Other diving species visit irregularly in ones and twos. The pond is unsuitable for most dabbling ducks, but Mallard feed on copious scraps and several pairs breed. Ten or more Shelduck winter on Hooe Lake. Moorhen and Mute Swan are resident and breed, while Kingfisher and Grey Wagtail winter.

At low tide in winter Herring and Black-headed Gulls feed across Hooe Lake's mudflats, joined by small numbers of Common Gull. Among the gull flocks, rarer Glaucous and Iceland Gulls have been recorded. More frequent on Radford has been Little Gull, including summer-plumaged spring arrivals. The gulls commute to Radford's fresher water frequently, especially at high tide. A White-winged Black Tern was a rare visitor. Waders are few on the mudflats, but Redshank and Turnstone are regular, as are wintering Common Sandpiper and Greenshank, with several Dunlin and Curlew. During hard or stormy winter weather, a diver, scarcer grebes or seaducks are occasional visitors to Hooe Lake.

Radford Lake and its surroundings are quite sheltered, and freshly arrived passerine migrants (especially in early spring) often work through from the exposed coastline, pausing here until able to move on. Considerable numbers of hirundines, Chiffchaff, Willow Warbler and Goldcrest can be gathered here, mixed with lesser numbers of other migrants. A very wide variety has been noted over the years. Spring movements have brought both Little Bittern and Night Heron to the lakeside, while a Woodchat Shrike appeared among a fall of summer migrant passerines at Jennycliff. Among an impressive list of 'fly-over' raptor species are two sightings of Black Kite, and Red Kite is seen increasingly. As with any coastal area, the entire district can produce small migrants at appropriate periods, including the scarce Yellow-browed Warbler, a rare Lesser Grey Shrike and even an autumn Desert Warbler in one urban garden.

Few waders are able to inhabit the bay's narrow, rocky shoreline. Oystercatcher usually feeds on limpet-strewn rocks, accompanied by Turnstone and an occasional Purple Sandpiper. Small parties of Whimbrel are brief spring visitors.

Among the bay's first spring migrants is Sandwich Tern, the most numerous tern species here. Terns use the bay in small numbers, pausing to rest and feed on both migrations. Spring sightings of other terns are unpredictable, usually only in ones and twos. On return passage, Sandwich are again often first to arrive, accompanied by their still semi-dependent juveniles. Common Terns are usually next. Arctic Terns, mostly juveniles, are latest to arrive in both spring and autumn, and autumn numbers are always higher than in spring. Scarce Black Terns mainly occur in ones and twos, while Roseate and Little Terns are rare.

The Plym Estuary, open to frequent disturbance, attracts few interesting waders or ducks. The large Canada Goose flock is worth checking for an unusual visitor such as Barnacle Goose. Shelduck and Mallard are the commonest wildfowl and both breed. Mandarin nests regularly, and up to 30 birds can be present after breeding. Teal are present in small numbers; other ducks include up to 20 Wigeon, around a dozen Goosander and fewer Red-breasted Merganser. Shoveler, Garganey and Goldeneye are very irregular visitors. Cattle Egrets are becoming frequent visitors to the area so check any cattle around Saltram Estate and Blaxton Meadow. Great White Egret has been recorded during the autumn, while Little Egret is present all year. Bar-tailed and Black-tailed Godwits are mainly passage birds; Golden Plover may visit briefly in cold weather. Dunlin are present in varying numbers for most of the year and 300–400 birds can be present in winter. Small numbers of Common Sandpiper and Greenshank are passage migrants and several often overwinter, twice accompanied by a Spotted Sandpiper from North America. Generally, though, autumn wader passage of more interesting waders is poor. Common species that overwinter can include up to 30 Turnstone, sometimes with a Purple Sandpiper or Ringed Plover. Grey Heron, Kingfisher and Dipper all breed locally and are resident.

The Plym is very good for gulls, many using it to loaf during the day when the tide is out. In winter, more than 100 Great Black-backed Gull may assemble at low tide and the Common Gull aggregations should be checked for Ring-billed Gull. Glaucous and Iceland Gulls are occasional visitors, usually singly. Mediterranean Gulls are ever more frequent – often one or two summer and from early autumn through to late spring they may be present in double figures. The large Herring Gull flocks are worth checking for Yellow-legged and Caspian Gulls, especially in autumn. Little, Bonaparte's and Ross's Gulls have all appeared on the Plym.

The paths from Chelson Meadow Recycling Centre car park and on through Saltram can give great views of many passerines, including Nuthatch, Treecreeper, Green and Great Spotted Woodpeckers and the noisy Ring-necked Parakeet.

Rarer sightings have included Spoonbill, Black-winged Stilt, Little Ringed Plover and Gull-billed Tern, while nearby cover has produced Red-backed Shrike, Melodious and Yellow-browed Warblers and Bluethroat.

The wide Tamar–Tavy Estuary is more difficult to watch, but many of its birds are similar. Ducks are more numerous; Tufted Duck with the occasional Scaup or Goldeneye may be present, as can the Wigeon flock that once held an American

Wigeon. Some grebes visit, maybe Slavonian but mostly Great Crested into double digits, more rarely Black-necked or Red-necked. It is possible to see Little, Great White and Cattle Egrets around the complex in varying numbers. Avocet can break away from the upper Tamar population and a handful may stay for much of the winter. One or two Greenshank and Common Sandpiper regularly overwinter. Every winter, at irregular intervals, a Peregrine spends time hunting in the area, concentrating on the estuaries.

Tamerton Creek and Warleigh Point are worth checking for Avocet, Spoonbill and commoner waders, and the creek has produced Spotted Redshank and Lesser Yellowlegs in the past. The tree-lined areas on the Tamerton Foliot side are good for commoner woodland birds, winter thrushes and Firecrest in winter. Warleigh Point offers one of the best vantage points to scan the Tamar and Tavy Estuaries for passing Osprey in August and September; sometimes as many as three birds can be seen fishing as the low tide turns.

The small, narrow marsh at Efford attracts a variety of interesting species, mostly in winter. Most winters, the marsh and surrounding areas attract the more unusual wintering passerines associated with the region, including a few Blackcaps and up to 20 Chiffchaffs, perhaps including some pale, grey-toned northern and eastern types. Both Goldcrest and Firecrest are regular, the latter often occurring in twos and threes. Rare and unexpected, Yellow-browed Warbler has wintered, as has Hume's Warbler.

TIMING

Tides are of little consequence if checking the bay and waterfront. Trawlers unloading in winter attract gulls to the fish quays. Otherwise, times of day are normally unimportant in the bay. Low winter sunlight, however, can make a check of the bay very difficult; an overcast day with good but flat light is ideal. Prolonged northerly winds, especially from midwinter onwards, can produce a Glaucous Gull. Gale-force southerly winds or fog in spring or early autumn may cause numbers of terns to shelter in the bay, perhaps accompanied by a Little Gull.

To check the estuaries for waders, it is essential that some mud is exposed. The main channels always flow, attracting ducks or grebes. The head of the Plym is less disturbed, although boating, paddle-boarding and bait-digging are year-round activities. Gulls in particular gather here, where they bathe and preen in fresh river water when the tide is out. Waders on the Plym cluster in the same upper area when an incoming tide pushes them up the estuary; another good time to check is just as the tide is ebbing, as birds are again forced to congregate in a restricted space. There are no central high-tide roosts on either estuary. Severe weather can increase numbers. Now Blaxton Meadow has been closed to the public, the area is used regularly at high tide by waders and gulls. The area can be viewed from the paths around Saltram, a National Trust property; a small hide overlooks the meadow.

Visiting Radford and Hooe areas on quieter mornings avoids public disturbance pressure. Foggy or inclement weather and cold winds force tired migrants to move short distances from the coast, seeking shelter; if such conditions persist, late morning, afternoon or evening could be productive. Hard winters cause the dispersal of unexpected species to new areas, such as the arrival of a Smew here once (although in very harsh conditions the pond can freeze over).

If hoping to watch a fishing Osprey, the hour before and after low tide is generally best, as younger, less experienced birds can see the fish more easily in the shallower waters. Adult birds are less predictable and, if present, may be seen at any state of the tide.

ACCESS

The **seafront (PL1 2PJ, fields.slices.intro)** is well signposted throughout the city centre, from which it is less than 800m. The Barbican is a popular tourist spot so apart from gulls, only occasional divers, grebes or seaducks venture into this area, where very close views can be obtained. Part of the bay is easily watched from a public walkway off the road at West Hoe, where it bends down towards nearby Millbay; this is a good place to check the sea for divers, grebes and auks around Drake's Island.

To reach Radford and Jennycliff from Plymouth city follow the A379 to Plymstock, where you take the Hooe road (pronounced 'who', this is a south-eastern outlier of Plymouth, not to be confused with The Hoe). This is also signposted to Mount Batten. At Radford, just before Plymstock merges with Hooe, at the bottom of a hill (Radford dip) turn off right into Mayers Way, where there is limited car parking for visiting **Radford and Hooe Lakes (PL9 9QQ, ears.pots.dairy)**. Walk through the adjoining parkland over good footpaths to Radford Lake, continuing on to overlook Hooe Lake, by itself of little merit but worth checking if you are visiting Radford. Continuing along the road, a left-hand fork at Hooe takes you up to **Jennycliff (PL9 9SW, foods.friday.happy)**, where there is a large free car park with toilets. From here, a scan of the sea takes in the whole eastern part of the Sound. Divers, grebes and seaducks can often be best seen from here, or from the pier at Mount Batten. The road continues from Jennycliff, following signposts, down to the free parking areas at Mount Batten where there are also toilets with disabled access. Passerine migrants might be seen along the clifftop in spring and autumn.

The **Plym Estuary (PL9 7JA, forks.taken.closer)** is very accessible, easily watched and can be checked from both sides. Immediately across Laira Bridge on A379, in the Plymstock direction, is a left-hand turn marked to Saltram. There is a small car park almost opposite the recycling centre, allowing you to walk the entire length of the estuary along good footpaths. This takes in the edge of the National Trust wood at Saltram, where there are further tracks through the wooded areas. Kingfishers may be seen perched on branches overhanging the estuary. Sunlight is always at your back, and the surroundings are more pleasant than on the opposite bank, where you can watch from the pavement on the extremely busy Embankment Road. Small, tidal Blaxton Meadow marsh is located at the top end of the estuary. If checking from the Embankment Road side, there are several car pull-ins when heading into Plymouth city centre.

To reach the lower Tamar Estuary at **Warren Point (PL5 2SH, fake.reader.direct)**, take the A38 to St Budeaux then the Budshead road on your left. Walk between factories on the industrial estate along often muddy public footpaths to the Point area. Access to **Warleigh Point (PL5 2SL, exit.newly.firms)**, opposite across the creek, is found by taking the exit to Budshead Road and Tamerton Foliot off the A386; at the first roundabout take the second exit onto Budshead Road, then at the second roundabout, after 500m, take the second exit onto Tamerton Foliot Road. Follow the road for 1.3 miles (2km) to Station Road in the village of Tamerton Foliot, then take Station Road to the parking area just before Warleigh Point. Follow the footpath until the River Tamar, and part of the River Tavy can be viewed from Warleigh Point.

For **Efford Marsh (PL3 6SE, puzzle.pinks.shape)**, turn from Eggbuckland Road into Deer Park Drive; access to the Local Nature Reserve is gained within 200m via Hamble Close or the Tay Gardens cul-de-sacs. Roadside parking is permitted. The footpath is often very muddy.

CALENDAR

Resident: Mute Swan, Mandarin, Shelduck, Moorhen, Sparrowhawk, Buzzard, Stock Dove, Kingfisher, common woodland passerines, Ring-necked Parakeet, Grey Wagtail, Stonechat, Rock Pipit, Raven.

December–February: On the waterfront and Sound, seaducks, divers and grebes are occasional; gulls, including rarer species; Purple Sandpiper; Black Redstart usually somewhere along the Hoe waterfront. On the estuaries, gulls, Goosander and Red-breasted Merganser, Wigeon, Teal, Tufted Duck, probably Peregrine, Black-tailed Godwit, possibly Avocet on the Tavy. Tufted Duck, possibly other diving ducks at Radford Lake.

March–May: All of the above seabird species may be present in fluctuating numbers, with Black-throated Diver possible through early part of period, plus Fulmars arriving to breed at Jennycliff; waders and ducks depart from early March; uncommon gulls may pass through in March–early April, particularly Iceland; Sandwich Tern from end March; Chiffchaff and Wheatear from mid-March; passerine migrants at Jennycliff and Radford from early April onwards in favourable conditions. Breeding summer visitors arrive in woods, where Blackcap and Chiffchaff might have overwintered. Red Kite possible anywhere, especially during anticyclonic conditions.

June–July: Mostly only breeding species including Rock Pipit and Little Egret. Sandwich Tern reappear in July; Red Kite possible.

August–November: Most waders reappear on estuaries from early August onwards, gradually increasing in number and variety. Osprey annual August or September on Plym/Tamar/Lynher/Tavy. Terns reappear in the Sound: Common from mid-August, Arctic and Black from late August–September. Passerine migrants especially at Jennycliff and Saltram; Black Redstart from October. Uncommon gulls, especially Little and Mediterranean, can occur throughout.

20 PLYMBRIDGE WOODS

OS LANDRANGER MAP 201 OR OS OUTDOOR LEISURE MAP 28
OS grid ref: SX5258
Postcode: **Estover Parking** – PL6 8AW **Plympton Parking** – PL6 8LL
what3words: **Estover Parking** – shift.pardon.fence
Plympton Parking – remain.tour.icon

HABITAT

On the northern outskirts of Plymouth, this is a large, 50ha mixed (mainly broadleaved) woodland, through which the River Plym flows. The lower section at Plymbridge Woods, which is owned by the National Trust, is an extremely popular picnic and recreation area for local residents. The woods, although dense in parts, have open glades and border onto rough meadows. The mixture of trees is excellent, with good numbers of oak and beech supporting many forms of wildlife. Other fruiting trees, such as Sweet Chestnut, Hazel and Rowan, are

Devon (south coast and Dartmoor)

abundant. Open glades with bushy fringes, the river and its banks, and damp meadows ensure a range of specialised natural history subjects to study.

Commoner wild animals are present in very good numbers and include Common Toads and Common Frogs. Grass Snakes and Adders are also present. Deer are best seen very early in the morning or at dusk. There are several species of bat, and one of the authors has seen 30 species of butterfly here, including Purple Hairstreak, Silver-washed Fritillary and White Admiral.

SPECIES

This is a good area to 'learn your birds' as all the commoner woodland passerine families are represented. During winter, the so-called 'winter thrushes' can be watched stripping Rowan and other berries from trees or searching among the understorey for food. Woodcock and Snipe may be flushed from wetter areas, and white-rumped Bramblings can be identified in flocks of Chaffinches feeding on fallen beechmast. Wintering Crossbills are possible among the conifers. Along the riverbanks, in some years, Lesser Redpoll and Siskin swing upside-down on Alder trees, while on the river Dipper and Grey Wagtail are commonly seen. The less turbulent stretches are favourite haunts of Kingfisher, which with luck may be seen for more than the usual few seconds of blue and orange blur. Several pairs of Mandarin Duck breed. Spring brings the return to the wood of common

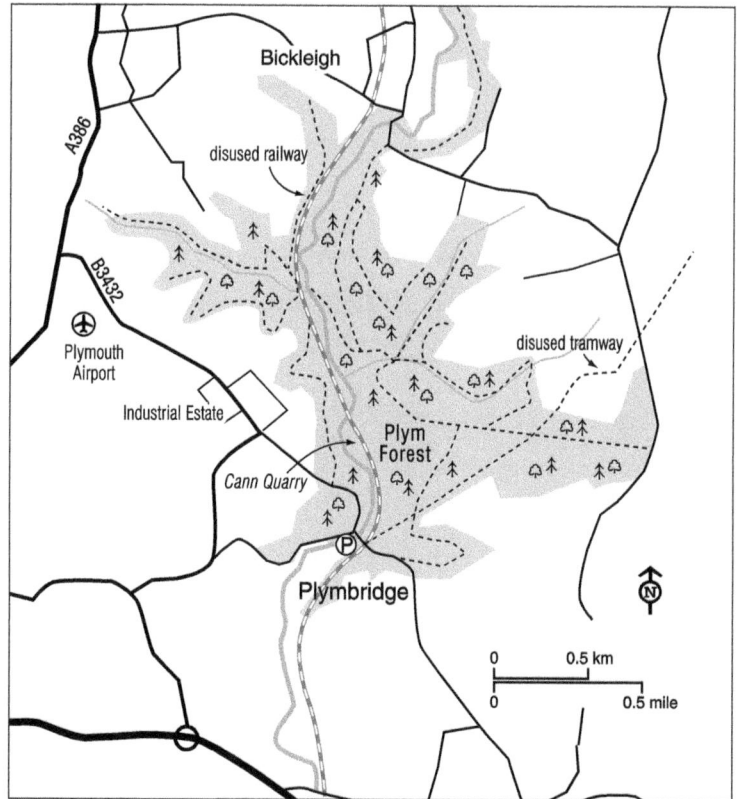

migrants, and the less common such as Garden Warbler. In summer, especially if an early start is made, breeding species can be watched feeding young, offering a further chance to widen your knowledge. At the end of summer, the phenomenon of irrupting Crossbill has resulted in flocks of these fascinating and colourful birds frequenting the woods. Autumn provides increasingly less-hindered views of resident species, as deciduous trees drop their leaves to reveal more birds.

For many years, a pair of Peregrines have nested in Cann Quarry, and a seasonally staffed observation post is operated by the National Trust, allowing superb public viewing facilities with telescopes provided. Areas of clearfelled conifer plantation and newly replanted conifers in the Cann Wood area have resulted in the return of breeding Nightjars.

TIMING

During summer, all woodland birds become more secretive, as they have nests and families to protect. Early morning is by far the most productive time. Later in the day, places where many birds were seen earlier may now appear almost birdless save for the occasional call. Human and dog disturbance can be heavy around the bridge area on fine days, but a mile (1.6km) or so upstream lies a wealth of interesting flora and fauna, which is less disturbed.

During winter, there is more or less constant daylight activity by birds, and less disturbance by humans.

ACCESS

At Estover roundabout, Plymouth (near the Wrigley company factory), take the narrow, rather steep Plymbridge Road. There is ample parking at the bottom of the hill, in the bridge area. Approaching from Plympton, you can pick up Plymbridge Road from either Plymouth Road or Glen Road. Your starting point for the walk will again be the bridge, closed to traffic. From here, follow various woodland paths or the disused railway track, which is now used as a cycle track, heading north. The walk from the bridge car parks to Bickleigh is about 5 miles (8km); alternatively, continue until Clearbrook village, fringing Dartmoor, where a pub offers food and facilities.

Cann Quarry is overlooked from the viaduct, which is now crossed by the busy cycle track.

CALENDAR

Resident: Mandarin Duck, Sparrowhawk, Buzzard, Kestrel, Peregrine, Stock Dove, Tawny Owl, Great Spotted and Green Woodpeckers, Kingfisher, Grey Wagtail, Dipper, Raven, Siskin, Goldcrest, common woodland passerines, such as Treecreeper, Nuthatch and Marsh Tit.

December–February: Grey Heron, Woodcock, Snipe, winter thrushes, possibly Brambling, Lesser Redpoll, Crossbill.

March–May: First migrant Cuckoo in late April, possibly Tree Pipit; Garden Warbler, Blackcap, Whitethroat.

June–July: Nightjar towards the moors and in recent clearfelled and newly planted conifer areas; maybe irrupting Crossbill, late July.

August–November: Redwing and Fieldfare return from October and feeding parties of small passerines (mixed species) roam through the woods.

Devon (south coast and Dartmoor)

SITE CLUSTER: DARTMOOR

21 Dartmoor area: general introduction
21A Haytor, Emsworthy Mire and Yarner Wood
21B Venford-Swincombe
21C Soussons and Postbridge district
21D Fernworthy Reservoir and Plantation
21E Okehampton: high moors around Cranmere, and Okement Valley Woods
21F Tavy Cleave, West Dartmoor
21G Burrator Reservoir and woodlands
21H Piles Copse, Harford Moor and Three Barrows
21J Steps Bridge and Dunsford Woods
21K Hembury Woods

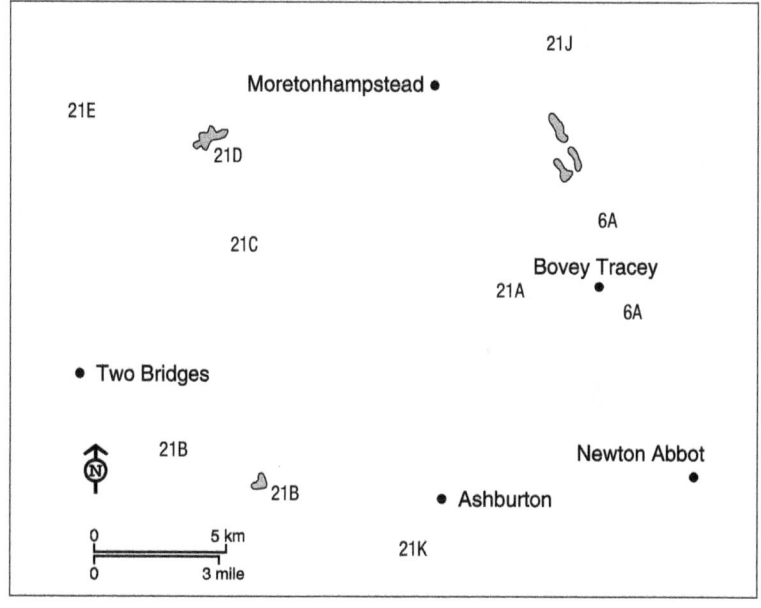

21 DARTMOOR AREA: GENERAL INTRODUCTION

HABITAT

Dartmoor is the only major area of high open moor in southern England, some 400 square miles (1,036km^2) of rough grassland, heather, tors, bog, streams and woodland, standing out above the surrounding fertile Devon lowlands. Underlying granite shows through characteristically as 'tor' rock formations on exposed moorland hilltops. The moor forms a steep-sided plateau from which many rivers and torrents flow, running down through deep scenic wooded valleys around the fringes of the area. The highest hills and main peat bogs, from which most of Devon's rivers originate within a few miles of each other, are on the northern moor, with High Willhays (621m) and Yes Tor (619m) forming a twin high point near Okehampton. The southern moors, south of Princetown, are characteristically 100m lower than those in the north, with less peat bog and more rough grassland. Gorse grows freely on better-drained slopes, with extensive bracken in summer and welcome scrub developing in areas. Most open ground on the central moor is relatively gently sloping, with broad marshy valleys and rolling hillsides.

Rainfall on high ground averages over 2,030mm per year, substantially higher than in the lowlands, resulting in waterlogged, acidic soil. A light covering of snow occurs most winters, although it often thaws in a day or two as milder air arrives from the sea. Gales are frequently recorded on open hillsides in autumn and winter, combining with cold and damp to give a high 'exposure factor', preventing natural deciduous tree growth over 400m altitude. A few Hawthorn and Rowan trees, often stunted and twisted by winds, grow along sheltered streams and hedge banks. Forestry England has conifer plantations of various ages on the centre and south-west moor. Some rivers have been dammed on the plateau edge to form reservoirs.

This whole open area, and much farmland and valley woods on the flanks, is incorporated into Dartmoor National Park. The moor acts as a centre for some very specialised wildlife and refuge for many species now lost in the lowlands. Adders are often encountered on sunny hillsides among gorse and bracken in summer. As well as rare wildlife, Dartmoor also boasts a rich abundance of archaeology such as burial cairns, hut circles and old farm buildings. Feral ponies are widespread; do not feed them, especially near roadsides, as serious accidents can occur; hardy sheep and beef cattle range over the unfenced hills. Many visitors come in summer, and hiking activities have increased, with parties now visiting even the remotest areas. The National Park authorities arrange guided walks over more accessible sections in summer.

Note: Parts of the moor, particularly on remoter northern sections, are closed to the public when used as Army firing ranges for a portion of the year. These areas are indicated by red flags flown from tors during live firing days; information should be sought on access. For more information: gov.uk/government/publications/dartmoor-firing-programme or 0800 458 4868. Of the sites listed below only the high moors above Okehampton, and Tavy Cleave (within Willsworthy range), are directly affected.

SPECIES

Open moorland holds many small breeding passerines in summer, although the number of species is limited. Skylark and Meadow Pipit sing constantly overhead and Wheatear are seen on many rocky slopes; Stonechat and Whinchat are encountered on gorse and bracken tops. The highest moors have very small, scattered numbers of specialised birds such as Red Grouse, with Snipe, the largest numbers in southern England, and breeding Dunlin at their most southerly global location. Steep valley woods on moor fringes hold many breeding summer visitors, including widespread Redstart and, especially where nest boxes are provided, Pied Flycatcher. Red-backed Shrike has bred recently, and any fortunate spring or summer sightings should be reported to the RSPB and Devon Birds, as egg-collectors still operate in the region. Moorland conifer plantations have encouraged specialised feeders such as Crossbill, Lesser Redpoll and Siskin, although the peaty waters of adjacent reservoirs are too barren to attract much birdlife except a few Goosander, which stay to breed in small numbers by moorland rivers, particularly the middle reaches of the Dart. Dipper and Grey Wagtail feed along many swift-flowing streams running off the moor, while Buzzard and Raven sail overhead. Migration times can bring large flocks of Golden Plover, halting on open slopes, and sometimes a passing raptor; scarce migrants overshooting the coast can turn up on the southern slope, even lost seabirds. In winter, hardy Red Grouse, occasional crows, Raven or raptors such as Hen Harrier and Merlin may be encountered on open moors. Winter visitors such as Fieldfare and finches tend to feed in less exposed moor valleys and fringes of high farmland.

Of the many sites on Dartmoor, the major birdwatching areas are given as follows.

21A HAYTOR, EMSWORTHY MIRE AND YARNER WOOD

> OS LANDRANGER MAP 191
> OS grid ref: SX7879
> Postcode: **Haytor** – TQ13 9XT **Emsworthy Mire** – TQ13 9XT
> **Yarner Wood** – TQ13 9LJ
> what3words: **Haytor** – concluded.trustees.listening
> **Emsworthy Mire** – yappy.headboard.richer
> **Yarner Wood** – coveted.derailed.otter

HABITAT

At the south-east edge of Dartmoor, the land rises very steeply. The most prominent landmark on this side of the moor is Haytor Rocks (457m), with wide views over south Devon. The vegetation in front of the rocks is heavily influenced by tourists, but behind them lie old mining gullies and relatively undisturbed open heath with scattered bushes. Just past Haytor to the south-west is the DWT reserve of Emsworthy Mire, a long-abandoned hill farm with open fields, bogs and lines of mature hawthorns and a vibrant display of Bluebells in late spring. On

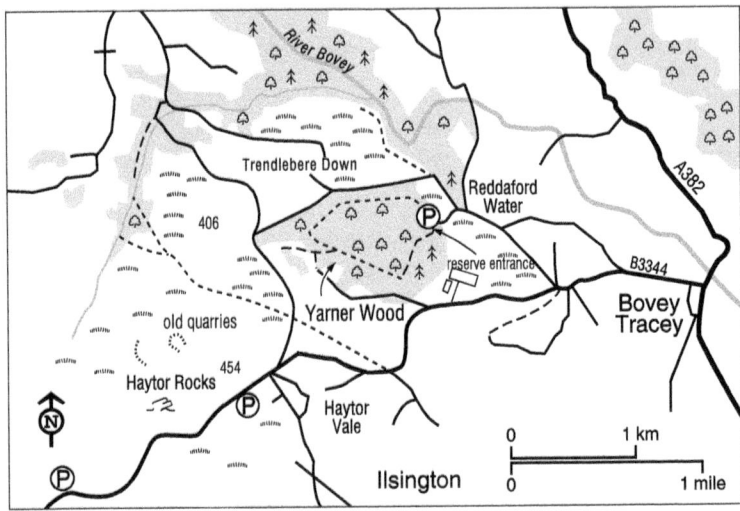

the east flank, overlooking the Bovey Valley, lies Yarner Wood, a mixed woodland with mostly oak trees above a ground covering of Bilberry. The wood is particularly rich in wildlife, including White Admiral and Purple and Green Hairstreak butterflies in open glades in summer; massive wood ant nests can be seen beside the paths. Trendlebere Down is an area of heathland to the north-west. The attractive, boulder-strewn Becky Falls lies in the wooded valley below the down. The area of Yarner Wood, Trendlebere and the Bovey Valley together make up the East Dartmoor National Nature Reserve, covering 356ha.

SPECIES

The area is relatively quiet early and late in the year, but wintering Woodcock may be found, and sometimes a flock of Lapwing or Golden Plover or a passing Hen Harrier or Merlin may be seen around Haytor. Yarner provides views of resident woodland birds – perhaps more easily in winter than in summer when leaf cover is thicker – and this is one of the last refuges for Lesser Spotted Woodpecker in the region. The thin *quee-quee-quee* calls of this tiny woodpecker call attention to its presence high in the canopy.

Spring migrant warblers arrive relatively late in these high woods, but the first good migration days may bring in Wheatear or Ring Ouzel on the moor around Haytor. In late spring, Yarner abounds with bird activity, a high density of small passerines singing and feeding overhead in the tree canopy. The trilling song of Wood Warbler once echoed through the wood, but sadly is now only heard rarely. Garden and Willow Warblers can also be found. Pied Flycatchers, which have flourished through the provision of nest boxes, are a major attraction. The smart black-and-white males are particularly noticeable, looping through the branches to catch tiny insects or singing their short scratchy series of notes from twigs above occupied nest boxes. Males may be polygamous, mated with females from two or three boxes. This species has increased in Dartmoor oakwoods in recent years, with hundreds of young fledged. Spotted Flycatchers also breed. Up to 20 pairs of Redstarts (some also in natural holes) and commoner tits have also made good use of boxes, and Marsh Tits are also present. More open areas at the top and edges of the wood attract a different range of species, with Tree Pipits song-flighting from treetops and Linnets and Yellowhammers atop gorse. Buzzards, Goshawks and Ravens may circle overhead.

The semi-open heathland bordering the wood has its own distinctive birds. In most years a pair or two of Nightjars can be found; Stonechat, Lesser Redpoll and Tree Pipit are also regular here. Hobbies may be seen hawking Fox Moths over the open ground. Three hundred metres below, characteristic hill-stream birds such as Dipper and Grey Wagtail may be seen close to tourist paths past Becky Falls.

Emsworthy and the other tors and valley bogs south and south-west of Haytor form a summer habitat for Grasshopper Warbler and Redstart, and a few pairs of nesting Snipe. It is probably one of the best places now to encounter Cuckoo in the region, and in autumn the berry-laden bushes regularly attract Ring Ouzel arriving with the first winter thrushes; over 20 of the former have been recorded in a day. In winter the same areas may form a hunting ground for one or two Merlins, sometimes joined by Short-eared Owl in years when vole populations are high. Great Grey Shrike has also visited this area.

TIMING

For raptors flying over at Haytor or Trendlebere, fine high-pressure conditions with light winds are needed. Yarner Wood can be watched in most weathers owing to its sheltered position and thick summer leaf canopy, but sunny mornings are best, as leaf cover cuts down available light on dull days. **Note:** The car park is closed to public access from dusk, reopening at 8.00 a.m.

For birds of prey on the moors south-west of Haytor in winter, a prolonged scan of at least an hour or two is needed, preferably on a fine afternoon. Emsworthy can be visited at any time, but an early May morning with the back drop of drumming Snipe and Cuckoo is hard to beat.

Avoid Haytor when heavily congested with tourists on peak summer weekends and holiday periods, unless an early morning start is planned.

ACCESS

From the A38 Exeter–Plymouth road, turn north on the A382 to Bovey Tracey. Take the first major road left when you reach Bovey Tracey, heading towards Haytor and Widecombe on the B3387. After half a mile (800m), fork left for Haytor or continue towards Manaton for Yarner Wood. From this fork, directions are as follows.

For **Haytor**, after about 5 miles (8km) stop in the roadside car park below the tor and walk up to the right; cross to the rear of the hill for heathland and old quarries.

For **Emsworthy Mire**, continue past Haytor for about 1.3 miles (2km) to a car park on the right and follow the stone wall down the slope to the old field network and barns.

For **Yarner**, after about 2 miles (3.2km) the road dips through Reddaford Valley, then climbs sharp right onto the moor. Turn left immediately on the bend, onto a tarmac lane into the wood. Pass the private cottages and park beyond. There are prepared nature trails and a noticeboard beside the car park. A hide has been erected which facilitates views of several surrounding nest boxes used by Pied Flycatchers and Redstarts, and also offers opportunities to see winter resident species at a feeding station. The 'Woodland Walk' encompasses a 3-mile (4.8km) circuit of the wood, while the 'Nature Trail' follows a 1.5-mile (2.4km) route. Both

Devon (south coast and Dartmoor)

take in an observation hide, which is found by walking back from the car park to a junction 100m towards the entrance, then following a steep major track up to the right. Two further hides, at the car park and at the top of the wood overlooking a small reservoir, may give good views of Grey Wagtail and Mandarin respectively.

The wood is managed by Natural England. Free access is given to individual visitors provided that they abide by the instructions posted and keep to the paths. Parties should book with the warden; May and June weekends are often booked well in advance. More information at eastdartmoorwoods.org or 01626 832330.

A minor road through Reddaford, just below the reserve, connects with Haytor route.

Trendlebere Down can be watched from roadside car parks on the moor above the Yarner Wood entrance, by continuing 800m up the road beyond the entrance or by taking paths leading out from the wood itself. Scan further across the valley slopes from here for raptors. For Becky Falls, continue up the road towards Manaton for another 2 miles (3.2km); park and walk down to the falls on the right.

In winter, turn south on the minor road towards Ashburton for 2 miles (3.2km), stopping at Coldeast Cross car park to scan the surrounding moors. The flat boggy Halshanger Common area on the east side of the junction can also be productive. This is also a suitable area for disabled and car-bound birdwatchers, as wide views can be obtained from the car. Indeed, it is not desirable to walk the hillsides and risk disturbing birds of prey.

CALENDAR

Resident: Sparrowhawk, Buzzard, Kestrel, woodpeckers including Lesser Spotted, Tawny Owl, Dipper, common woodland passerines, Marsh Tit, Grey Wagtail, Raven, Lesser Redpoll, Siskin.

December–February: Hen Harrier or Merlin possible over open land, Golden Plover, Woodcock, Snipe, feeding parties of common small birds.

March–May: Occasional raptors, Wheatear and passage Ring Ouzel (mid-March on); from late April many summer visitors, e.g. Cuckoo, Pied and Spotted Flycatchers, warblers including Garden, Grasshopper and possibly Wood; Redstart, Stonechat, Whinchat, good numbers of Tree and Meadow Pipits; Nightjar, Hobby (from late May).

June–July: Nightjar active, singing passerines in wood less vocal when busy feeding young.

August–November: Most summer visitors leave in August, so generally quiet until Ring Ouzel and winter thrushes start arriving.

21B VENFORD-SWINCOMBE

> OS LANDRANGER MAP 191/202
> OS grid ref: SX6871
> Postcode: PL20 6SE
> what3words: gets.brambles.inert

HABITAT

This attractive area on the south-east side of the high ground combines open moorland, conifer plantations and rhododendron thickets surrounding the 33ha Venford Reservoir, upland streams, and views over the steep, thickly wooded Dart Valley to the east. Below the reservoir dam lies a mixed woodland enclosure around the waterworks, and behind this a sheltered coombe with deciduous trees and bushy slopes carries Venford Brook down towards the Dart. The road through Venford follows approximately the edge of the open moor, which rises steeply to the west, Ryders Hill (515m) being one of the highest points of southern Dartmoor. The Swincombe Valley is a sheltered area of upland valley surrounded by rolling slopes of rough grass moorland grazed by cattle and ponies. The valley floor is occupied by the meandering Swincombe stream, a tributary of the Dart; scattered willow, hawthorn and gorse clumps provide limited cover. A wide, easily walkable track follows the valley floor; at the top of the valley is a small South West Water catchment pool. Above this, rough moorland slopes climb up towards the boggy expanse of rushy ground known as Fox Tor Mires.

Just north of the turning to Swincombe Valley is the Forest Inn, Hexworthy, a convenient stopping point. Adjacent scattered trees and hedges provide a further habitat worth inspection in spring and summer.

The wooded banks of the River Dart below Dartmeet towards Newbridge provide a sheltered walk for some miles nearby, partly through DWT and National Trust reserves. Dartmeet and Newbridge are both very popular summer tourist venues.

SPECIES

In winter the area may appear windblown and desolate, with just a few corvids feeding on open ground. On closer inspection, however, sheltered areas such as the Swincombe Valley may hold feeding flocks of both resident species and winter visitors. Fieldfare and Redwing may be present in hundreds, while flocks of Golden Plover use the open slopes. Large groups of Skylark and Meadow Pipit can be encountered, occasionally panicked by a hunting Merlin.

Venford Reservoir in midwinter is a key night roost site for Goosander on the eastern half of the moor, with other sites now also hosting birds as the population has increased. Venford, however, does not necessarily hold feeding Goosander during the day. Most feed on rivers and streams over a wide radius, often passing low over the dam as they return to Venford to roost; up to 55 birds have been seen flying in to roost at this season, although 20–30 is more typical. Other diving ducks are irregular visitors in ones and twos, seldom staying.

Spring brings a substantial breeding avifauna to the moorland valleys, including Wheatear and scattered pairs of Whinchat and Stonechat. Cuckoos perch hawk-like on isolated bushes or rocks, often mobbed by the pipits whose nests they are

Devon (south coast and Dartmoor)

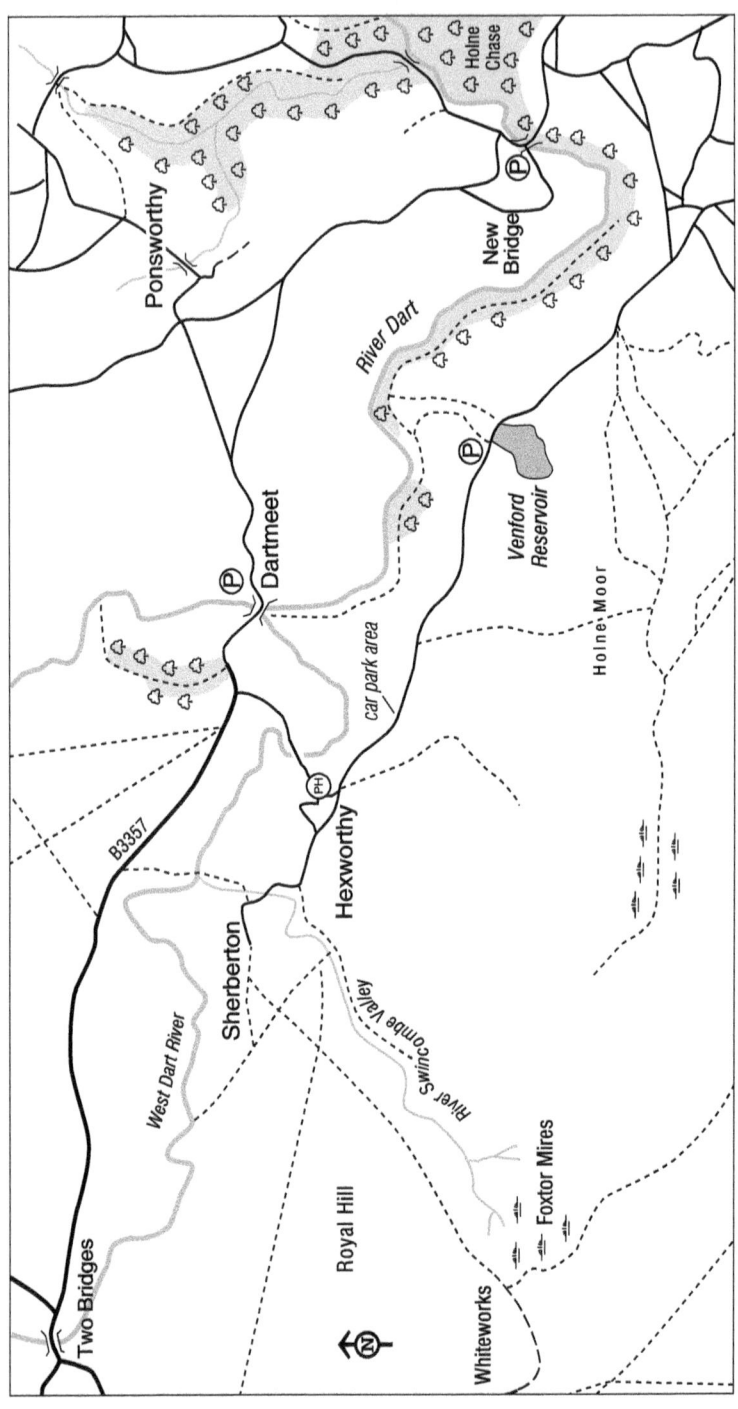

searching for. Tree Pipits often song flight where taller bushes occur. Where larger trees grow, Redstarts and Spotted Flycatchers may be found, together with a few pairs of Pied Flycatcher in more extensive deciduous woodland. Breeding visitors to damp streamside bushes include a few Reed Buntings, a species perhaps surprisingly found in a number of high moorland valleys. Grey Wagtails frequent larger streams, including Swincombe, and the banks of the Dart. At either locality Dippers might be seen carrying out their distinctive underwater feeding technique in the clear shallows. Goosander disappear to breed in well-wooded riverbanks in the Dart Valley. From later spring, adults with broods of young might be encountered on waterways or back on Venford Reservoir at times when the young can fly. Canada Geese and occasional Mallards are the only other waterfowl likely on the lake at this season, although Great Crested Grebes sometimes breed.

Large trees around the dam lodge are frequently used by Siskin and Lesser Redpoll, which both breed nearby and might be seen at eye level from the dam. Venford is probably the easiest site in the region to see breeding Siskin, the attractive yellow-green and black cock finches calling and display flighting in various places around the plantation or feeding on the ground nearby. Their high-pitched calls often first draw observers' attention. Lesser Redpolls, although usually present, are less noticeable. In late spring or summer, a Hobby might be seen feeding on dragonflies over the reservoir banks or taking day-flying moths over sheltered valley bottoms. North of the Swincombe–Fox Tor area is a rough grass moor at Royal Hill, where Dotterel have occasionally turned up in late spring. Areas of scattered trees anywhere on the edge of the moor, including those adjacent to the Forest Inn, hold good breeding populations of tits and warblers. Pied Wagtails are also conspicuous around stone walls and buildings, while clumps of trees often hold noisy Mistle Thrushes. Green Woodpeckers are met around the moorland fringe on open, close-cropped grassland. An early morning or evening walk up to Fox Tor Mires, beyond Swincombe, may bring Snipe 'drumming' in display flight. Lone Cormorants and Grey Herons visit waterways and pools in search of prey.

As with most parts of Dartmoor, breeding species move off this exposed terrain quickly in autumn, which is a quiet period, although occasionally an Osprey may visit the lake.

TIMING

As with all moorland habitats, higher ground is more strongly affected by wind, mist and rain, so fine settled days should be chosen. Early mornings in late spring and summer are ideal for viewing breeding species. Numbers of winter-roosting Goosander on Venford Reservoir may not build up fully until near nightfall. Breeding Snipe are more likely to display at dawn.

Venford dam car park, and more especially the parking facilities at Dartmeet and Newbridge on the main road, can become very busy with tourist cars on fine weekends and summer holidays. At these times an early morning visit is advised to avoid congestion and delays. At busy times, it may be necessary to walk some distance from the car parks to find quieter birdwatching areas.

Those who choose to undertake longer moorland hikes, such as across Holne Moor or around Fox Tor Mires, should check weather forecasts and allow time to complete journeys in daylight, as is usual for high moorland safety. Proper weatherproof clothing and a detailed map and compass are desirable. You should inform someone of your intended route.

Devon (south coast and Dartmoor)

ACCESS

The A384 road north from Ashburton passes through the east side of the area, crossing the Dart at the ancient stone bridges of Holne Bridge, Newbridge and Dartmeet. Following northward from Holne Bridge, the road rises steeply, then a left turn on a minor road signposted to Holne leads on towards Venford Reservoir. (Do not follow further signs to Holne village itself – there are brown tourist signs to Venford.)

On reaching Venford, the car park is a few hundred metres further on beyond the dam and is usually frequented by hand-tame Chaffinches. From this point walk back down the road a few metres to scan the lake and check the trees nearest to the dam. Below the dam, the waterworks and residential building are set down a private South West Water lane, in an enclosed woodland area that can be checked from the road above or from the surrounding moorland edges.

Cross the road from the car park and go through a gate which leads to a path around the reservoir perimeter. From here a 20–30 minute walk provides a complete circuit of the reservoir. Alternatively, having walked up to the top end of the reservoir, just before reaching the stream crossing, branch right through the pines on a small path and over a stile. From here it is possible either to strike out across higher ground to Holne Moor behind the reservoir, or return to the car park across the moor to gain an exterior view of the trees around the lakeside, plus adjacent moorland-edge habitat.

Starting again from the car park, another option is to check the waterworks enclosure and walk down the valley below, towards the main Dart Valley oakwoods. Corndon Tor provides the skyline focal point ahead and Bench Tor rises just to the right of the valley you are in, providing a home for Ravens most years. Our suggested route is to walk back across the dam and turn left along the perimeter fence at the far end. Having reached the sheltered area of streamside bushes at the far end below the waterworks, either cross the small stream and loop back steeply up the perimeter fence the other side towards the parking, or turn downhill. (Do not cross the stream if taking the downhill valley walk.) The line of an old granite trackway provides a path down the coombe; Tree Pipit can be found here. Further down, as the trees thicken, Redstart and Pied Flycatcher are likely; explore down into the coombe on the left for better views or walk on down until the track skirts the top of the very extensive oakwoods overlooking the Dart. There is no marked public path down to the riverside from here.

To reach Swincombe from Venford, drive on northward along the moorland minor road, and after 3 miles (4.8km) take a minor left turn to Sherberton, just before the Forest Inn. At the hilltop a gated access is marked to Sherberton Farm only. Park at the right-hand verge and continue on foot. It may be worth walking down the tarmac track as far as the bridge across the River Swincombe, where Dipper and Redstart are likely. Public footpaths are signposted further down this valley if desired. Most birdwatching visitors now fork left, back 200m from the stream bridge, and take the wide level track, walkable with no special footwear, up the Swincombe Valley floor. This continues for about 2 miles (3.2km), and although passing through privately owned grazing fields on the edge of the open moor, the National Park authorities have arranged for the track to have open pedestrian access. The track proper stops on reaching the small South West Water catchment pond at the head of the valley; beyond this it is possible with suitable footwear to progress on across the boggy hillside towards Fox Tor Mires. Alternatively, return to your vehicle, drive back down to the road junction, turn left and park near the Forest Inn, then explore sheltered trees and stone walls nearby.

Those who wish specifically to take longer moorland walks may find it easier to cross the footbridge halfway up Swincombe Valley towards the ruined cottages on the far bank. Well-used footpaths lead north and west from here, towards Royal Hill en route to Princetown, or keeping more to the left, skirting Fox Tor Mires basin and connecting with the minor lane from Princetown at Whiteworks Cottages after about 2 miles (3.2km).

Those who wish to approach Swincombe from the Fox Tor Mires end can take the turning off Two Bridges Road in the middle of Princetown and drive for 3 miles (4.8km) to the limited parking at the Whiteworks end of the lane. From here follow tracks to the left across the hillside towards Swincombe, keeping above the line of the bogs.

In windy conditions, the relatively sheltered walks through riverbank woods between Newbridge and Dartmeet can still be worthwhile.

Starting from the Dartmeet end, crossing the road from the main car park, try walking down the left hand riverbank for at least 300–400m for good views of feeding Dippers.

CALENDAR

Resident: Grey Heron, Cormorant (visiting), Buzzard, Mandarin, Dipper, Grey Wagtail, Siskin, Lesser Redpoll, Reed Bunting, Raven.

December–February: Goosander roost, maybe other diving ducks, possibly Peregrine or Merlin, Golden Plover, open-ground species, winter thrushes.

March–May: Breeding residents most active later in period (mainly May), Great Crested Grebe, Goosander (elusive), Snipe breeding in bogs; summer visitors including Cuckoo, common warblers, Grasshopper Warbler, Redstart, Whinchat, Pied and Spotted Flycatcher.

June–July: Breeding species as above, maybe Goosander broods on river, chance of Hobby throughout.

August–November: Generally quiet period but occasional Osprey at lake up to early October, and winter visitors around Swincombe Valley by November.

21C SOUSSONS AND POSTBRIDGE DISTRICT

OS LANDRANGER MAP 191 OR OS OUTDOOR LEISURE MAP 28
OS grid ref: SX6780
Postcode: **Warren House** – PL20 6TA **Postbridge** – PL20 6TH
what3words: **Warren House** – wanted.short.dispenser
Postbridge – hobble.regulates.smiling

HABITAT

Near Warren House Inn on the east side of the moors, the West Webburn brook runs through a sheltered valley overlooked by heather-covered hillsides and old,

Devon (south coast and Dartmoor)

overgrown tin-mining gullies. Scattered hawthorn bushes and ruins of old settlements stand along the stream banks. The lower valley is occupied by Soussons forestry plantation and the mine-furrowed hillside known as Vitifer. Mine gullies extend east across the ridge to Grimspound in the next valley. Unpolluted brook water contains abundant aquatic life in summer, and deep heather provides cover for animals such as Adders, Foxes and Stoats.

West of Soussons lies Postbridge, a small community on the upper East Dart River. North and west of the village are boggy riverside pastures, overlooked by high moorland. Sundew plants grow in the wet soil, and beech and willows line the riverbanks. Across the river is the large, mature Bellever Forest conifer plantation.

SPECIES

The Soussons area is one of the most productive moorland birdwatching sites in winter, the valley and plantation acting as a central roost for many species.

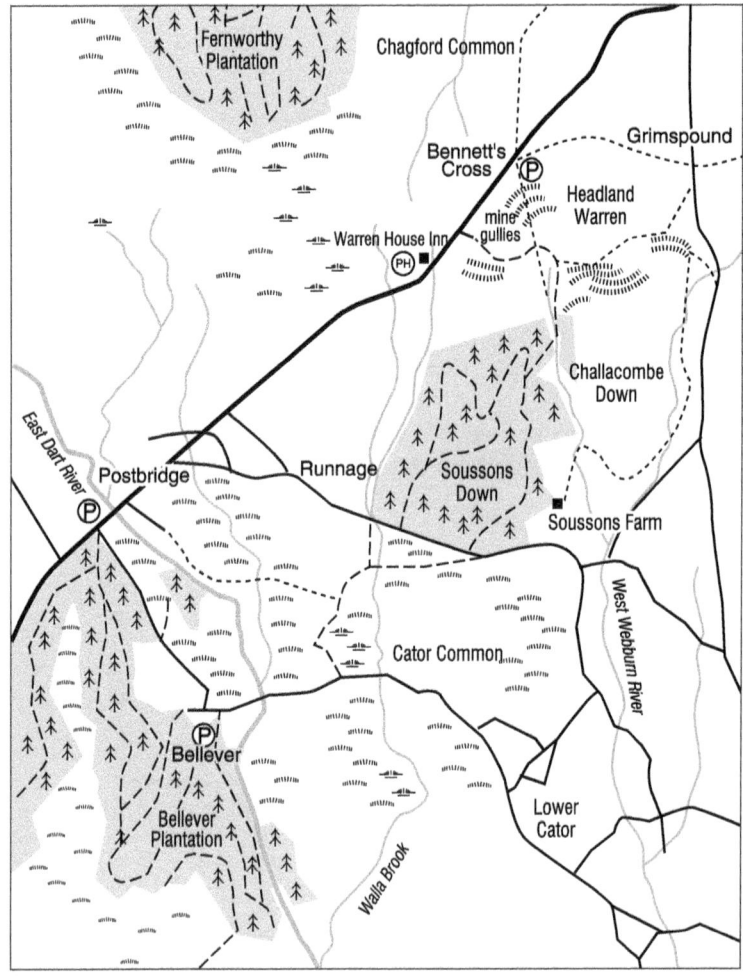

Woodpigeon, Fieldfare, Redwing and finches pass the night here in large numbers; Sparrowhawk and Merlin often chase flocks as they arrive to roost. Amongst areas of clearfell and thorn bushes near the stream, a Great Grey Shrike may be wintering.

Soussons plantation is often quiet on winter days except for a few Goldcrests and Coal Tits. Occasional Crossbills may *chip* overhead. Woodcock may rise from the side of tracks or fly out near dusk to feed on open boggy ground, while Snipe can be flushed near the stream. Larger residents such as Buzzards and Ravens are usually visible, circling overhead. On farmland edges south of the plantation the population is more varied, with flocks of Chaffinch and Brambling often appearing below Beech trees. Bellever can usually be relied on for parties of Crossbill, flying around high treetops above the visitors' car park or nearby rides with characteristic hard *chip* calls. In winter, Short-eared Owl and other predators sometimes hunt boggy pastures north of Postbridge, where Fieldfare and Golden Plover feed. Early spring, while snow still lies in some years, brings Wheatear back to their territories. The Warren House–Vitifer area was traditionally the easiest on Dartmoor for finding Ring Ouzel, their harsh *tack* alarm calls or piping song showing their presence along heather-clad gullies; they are now however only seen occasionally on migration. Open slopes support many Meadow Pipits in the breeding season, while Whinchats perch on bracken along the valley floor. Snipe perform drumming display flights over rushy pasture below the plantation and Grey Heron, Dipper and Grey Wagtail can be seen along the River Dart; a pair or two of herons often nest nearby, an unusually high site for this species. Reed Buntings are also present in wet scrubby vegetation, where two or three Grasshopper Warblers 'reel'.

Migrants passing up the Soussons Valley in later spring have included raptors such as Marsh and Montagu's Harriers. The rakish Hobby can quite often be seen circling above the heather slopes on a warm day, hunting for day-flying moths which it plucks and eats on the wing. Cuckoos are often seen, scouring the slopes for pipit nests to parasitise. In plantation clearings, Redstarts occur in small numbers, while calls overhead draw attention to Lesser Redpolls nesting in fir treetops; these diminutive finches fly out to feed in bushes overhanging nearby streams. Redstart is also likely along riverbank trees in Postbridge, where the songs of Garden and Willow Warblers can be heard. Stock Doves nest in the rocky areas and old mines, and diminutive Siskins, increasing in Dartmoor woods, breed in both Soussons and Bellever. Look for males delivering their jingling song from high conifer sprigs. Nightjars have moved into the plantations as areas are harvested and replanted.

Late summer sees parties of young birds foraging along the Soussons Valley, while occasional post-breeding flocks of Crossbill visit the taller trees. When most other species have departed, wintering thrushes may descend on the Rowan berries beside the stream; by the time frost returns to open slopes, Short-eared Owls are being seen in the valley again.

TIMING

On fine days, most winter-roost species spread widely to feed. Most birdwatchers concentrate on afternoons to see birds gathering before roosting. In the last hour before nightfall, especially on frosty evenings, pigeons, thrushes and other mass-roosting species fly to the south end of the plantation behind Soussons Farm; at this time Woodcock may fly out. Short-eared Owls are erratically present on marshy fields near Postbridge, especially in years of high rodent populations.

Snipe display over territory in early mornings, also the best time for songbirds. Hobbies are most likely feeding over the hillsides in later spring on dry fine days. Evening visits to plantation clearings in summer may produce the eerie churring of Nightjars on territory.

On fine weekends and at the peak summer season, there is often disturbance in the Warren House area, but as elsewhere this diminishes the further you get from parking spaces.

ACCESS

The B3212 Moretonhampstead–Postbridge road crosses the head of West Webburn Valley above Soussons. Birdwatchers often park by Bennett's Cross (an ancient stone monument), in the dip immediately east of Warren House Inn. To cover the valley and Vitifer gullies, walk down across the moor from here, or down the gravel track near the inn. Where the track overlooks the stream halfway along the valley is a good starting point to check if a shrike is in the area. If energetic, follow the mine gullies east across the ridge in summer for Whinchat; alternatively, continue to Soussons plantation and explore. For the lower end of the plantation continue west towards Postbridge by road, turning very sharply left just before the village; this minor road follows the plantation side. At the minor crossroads near Soussons Farm, turn left to watch over boggy ground to the wood edge.

Other minor roads skirt the flank of the moor and can provide views of summer breeding passerines around the rough pastures, stone walls and hawthorn hedges. Try for example continuing beyond Soussons Farm, turning left past the boggy pastures to Challacombe Farm and continuing up the valley, stopping at occasional roadside pull-ins to scan adjacent farmland for Cuckoo, Wheatear, Whinchat, Redstart, pipits and other species characteristic of the moorland edge. This road continues onto the open moor and eventually rejoins the B3212 Moretonhampstead–Postbridge road. On the way it passes Headland Warren Farm on the left, which lies on the edge of Vitifer tin mine gullies (across the hill from Soussons plantation). Public rights of way cross the moor from the Headland Warren road, past the farm buildings and mine gullies to Soussons plantation across the hill, and south towards the edge of the plantation where they link with woodland walks.

Three quarters of a mile (1.2km) west of Warren House Inn towards Postbridge on the B3212, the road crosses a shallow, boggy valley at Statts Bridge, with parking on the north side. This is a useful area to scan for a passing raptor on winter afternoons.

At Postbridge, cross the river on the B3212 westward and park near the road for views over boggy pastures. There are footpaths along riverbanks south past the stone clapper bridge. To reach Bellever, take the signposted lane left, adjacent to the plantation, following this for 1 mile (1.6km) to the car park.

CALENDAR

Resident: Grey Heron, Sparrowhawk, Buzzard, Kestrel, Snipe, Stock Dove, Mistle Thrush, Grey Wagtail, Goldcrest, Coal Tit, Dipper, Stonechat, Crossbill, Lesser Redpoll, Siskin, Reed Bunting.

December–February: Merlin, Golden Plover, Woodcock, occasional Short-eared Owl; roosting Woodpigeons, Fieldfare, Redwing, possibly a Great Grey Shrike, finches including Brambling.

Devon (south coast and Dartmoor)

March–May: Most winter visitors leave by mid-March. Wheatear and possibly Ring Ouzel arrive by late March. Cuckoo, Whinchat and Redstart, late April. Garden and Willow Warblers widespread by late April, Grasshopper Warbler in small numbers. Occasional migrant raptors late April–May, Hobby likely. Nightjar arrives by late May.

June–July: Breeding residents and summer visitors as above, Nightjar on territory, family parties of passerines in July.

August–November: Summer migrants move out during August. A few Wheatears to October. Passing Hen Harrier, Merlin, wintering thrushes from October.

21D FERNWORTHY RESERVOIR AND PLANTATION

OS LANDRANGER MAP 191 OR OS OUTDOOR LEISURE MAP 28
OS grid ref: SX6684
Postcode: TQ13 8EY
what3words: spoon.solicitor.seducing

HABITAT

This reservoir is adjacent to high moors on the east side of Dartmoor; to the west and north-west of the reservoir lies some of the highest peat bog. The 31ha reservoir is typical of the region's moorland waters, with brown, peaty, acidic water that sustains limited flora and fauna. The upper end, furthest from the dam, is fairly shallow, but still lacks muddy margins. A large forestry plantation surrounds much of the lake; within the forested area, near the lake, is a small area of deciduous trees, mainly Beech. From the dam end, views are panoramic, as sloping moorland gives way to farmland towards the town of Chagford.

SPECIES

The most numerous waterbird using the reservoir regularly in winter is Teal, with up to 30–40 often present around the boggy sides furthest from the dam, where a dozen or so Mallard usually reside. Tufted Duck usually number fewer; Goosander visit in ones and twos and local rarities such as Long-tailed Duck have been recorded. Cormorants call in to feed, as do Grey Herons. Small numbers of Common Gull join flocks of Black-headed Gull. During winter, small flocks of Crossbill may be seen, often first heard calling in the high conifer tops; their numbers depend on the amount of cone crop available for feeding. Lesser Redpolls and Siskins form winter flocks, with Bramblings among the Chaffinches. Migration does not usually bring many passing visitors, but Hoopoe has been found on the approach road and an Osprey occasionally calls in to fish. Lower water levels might tempt Common Sandpiper or scarcer waders such as a Greenshank to feed. Hobby are occasionally seen overhead.

Among the summer breeding migrants, Tree Pipits are noticeable and common. Several pairs of Pied Flycatcher breed among the Beeches, with Redstart and Spotted Flycatcher in suitable habitat. Chiffchaff and Willow Warbler are also

Devon (south coast and Dartmoor)

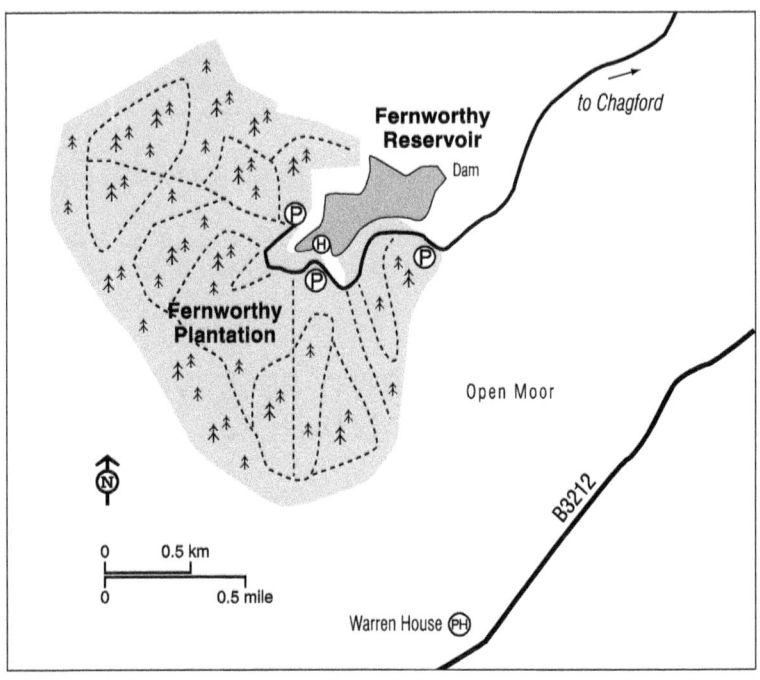

plentiful. Wheatear nests on the adjacent moors, where Snipe may be seen tumbling in display. Nightjar is a noteworthy summer visitor to the clearings in the wood. Unusually, pairs of Great Crested Grebe and Grey Heron have also stayed to breed at this high site.

TIMING

This site is far less visited by the general public than other sites at any season, permitting an interesting and scenic walk in comparative solitude. The only special timing needed is to watch Nightjars; the first churring will be heard less than an hour before sunset and views may be obtained. Still evenings from late spring to late summer are the times to try.

ACCESS

From the A384 at Two Bridges, near Princetown in the centre of the moors, take the B3212 eastward until signs show Fernworthy to the left on minor roads. Alternatively, leave the A382 at Moretonhampstead, travelling west on the B3212 until reaching signposted minor roads to the north. Car parking areas are provided by the reservoir, parts of which can be seen without leaving the car. A small bird hide overlooks the top (inlet) end of the reservoir, where an area of shallow water and marsh is kept as a nature reserve; there are parking areas by a hut on the left side of the road and by a grassy open stretch on the right. Beyond the grassy stretch is an entry gate to a footpath leading to the lakeside. The first hide, just beyond the entry gate, has disabled access. The second, smaller hide is nearer the water. There are open access paths throughout the plantation area. Try, for instance, parking at the far end of the reservoir perimeter road, then walking left uphill, which will lead you past some of the larger clearings. The Beech copse, a productive area for breeding summer migrants and wintering Brambling, is at the end of the perimeter road.

CALENDAR

Resident: Great Crested Grebe, Grey Heron, Dipper, Grey Wagtail, Raven, Coal Tit, Crossbill, Siskin, Lesser Redpoll.

December–February: Teal, Goosander, Woodcock, Golden Plover, passing raptors, winter thrushes, possibly Great Grey Shrike, Brambling.

March–May: Wheatear and hirundines arrive, most warblers and Redstart on territory by May; Hobby and Nightjar by end of period.

June–July: Summer visitors active and singing during June, quieter by July as young are fed; Snipe *chip* or drum in bogs north of the reservoir.

August–November: Generally quiet until winter thrushes and Woodcock arrive.

21E OKEHAMPTON AREA: HIGH MOORS AROUND CRANMERE, AND OKEMENT VALLEY WOODS

OS LANDRANGER MAP 191 OR OS OUTDOOR LEISURE MAP 28
OS grid ref: SX5993
Postcode: **Okehampton Camp** – EX20 1QR **Meldon Reservoir** – EX20 4LU
what3words: **Okehampton Camp** – banana.survey.landlords
Meldon Reservoir – sweetened.willpower.trooper

HABITAT

The highest part of Dartmoor forms a unique area in southern England. Uninhabited terrain stretches for more than 10 miles (16km) south of Okehampton. Rolling, open moorland and peat bogs form a desolate landscape, relieved by a few protruding tors and the white-tufted seed heads of Common Cotton-grass in summer. The ground, mostly 550–600m in altitude, is wet and uneven. Most of Devon's rivers originate here. Cranmere Pool is a small, seasonally flooded hollow in the centre, forming a landmark for hikers. On the edge of the high moor plateau, steep escarpments have rock scree and gorse thickets. The open moor is used as an army firing range for part of the year, with access restrictions (see Access note below).

At the foot of the northern escarpment, the East and West Okement rivers flow close past Okehampton, through a deep, sheltered valley with oakwoods and carpets of Bluebells in spring. The West Okement River is dammed at Meldon, on the edge of the high moor just west of the town, forming the steep-sided Meldon Lake. Above the lake, the river flows through a steep ravine which shelters Black Tor Copse (listed as Black-a-tor on some maps), one of the highest areas of natural woodland on the moor.

SPECIES

Both the high moor and the valley woods are best known for specialised breeding birds in late spring and summer. The desolate winter moorland environment, with frequent heavy rain or snow, supports few species except for hardy Red Grouse and a few Ravens and Carrion Crows. The few hardy wintering passerines such as Skylark and Meadow Pipit are sometimes pursued in low, twisting flight by a Merlin. Migration here has been little studied, but large passing groups of Golden Plover wheel over the tors at times, and other open-ground species such as Dotterel, or scarce raptors, have been seen on passage. Wheatears arrive early to breed on the high tors; later, Whinchats appear on thickets lower down near the moor edge, where Redstarts nest in stone walls.

In the breeding season, the moors abound with breeding Skylarks and Meadow Pipits. Buzzards, Kestrels and Ravens patrol the area regularly. With luck, the walker might be greeted by harsh *go-back* calls of Red Grouse as they whirr off low across heather slopes; the breeding population is small, widely scattered and rarely encountered these days. A handful of Dunlin nest each year in extensive bogs around the river sources, boosted by conservation work. Snipe inhabit rushy valleys a little below the sources, their presence revealed by repeated *chip* calls or display flights overhead. These boggy moorland valleys form the species' main summer home in the region. Grasshopper Warblers and Reed Buntings nest in some high bogs where tall, rushy vegetation exists. Dippers and Grey Herons may visit the high streams, but breed at lower altitudes.

Down in Okement woods, a nest-box scheme has encouraged a substantial summer population of the attractive little Pied Flycatcher, one of the largest colonies in the region, although some nests are disturbed by Hazel Dormice. Cold spring weather and heavy downpours, minimising insect availability, also reduce

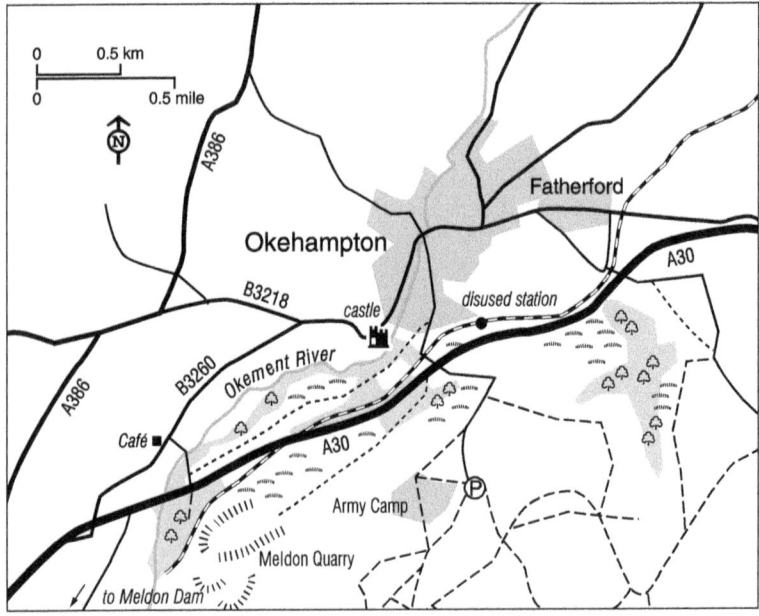

success. Other summer migrant songbirds include a scattering of Redstarts, while Dippers and Grey Wagtails can be found along the riversides.

Breeding species soon abandon the open moors once young have been reared, many moving back towards the coast. Although high moors are generally quiet at this period, passage birds might be seen, including a wandering raptor, moving flocks of Ring Ouzel or, as in spring, Golden Plover flocks or an occasional Dotterel. There is a chance of other strays such as Snow Bunting on high, rocky tors in late autumn/winter.

TIMING

Fine weather is essential to cover the moors properly; accurate weather forecasts should be sought. Do not attempt to walk across the moor in severe winter conditions or fog; every year walkers become ill with exposure (some die) and emergency rescues are needed. Allow sufficient time to reach civilisation before nightfall. Most birds on high ground can be seen at any time of day, but Snipe are most easily seen in the first three or four hours of daylight when display flights occur. The moor is best avoided on days when large-scale hiking events such as 'Ten Tors' (unfortunately around mid-May) are planned. See the Access section for army-range restrictions.

Mornings are best for singing Pied Flycatchers and other breeding birds in the valley, which can be fitted in after an early moorland trip.

ACCESS

From Okehampton, which can be reached by turning off the A30 by-pass, turn north at traffic lights (left if approaching from Exeter) in the town centre, along a minor road signposted 'Dartmoor National Park' and 'Battle Camp'. For the moors, drive up a steep hill, forking right at the signposted junction (Station Road) near the church, past the army camp and through a gate onto the roughly tarmacked military road.

Note: Army firing ranges operate some weeks; red flags fly from tors when firing commences. Do not continue beyond the gate before checking. Advance-warning notices are published in local newspapers or online. For more information visit gov.uk/government/publications/dartmoor-firing-programme or call 0800 458 4868. Do not touch metal objects found on the ranges.

Continue to the furthest point of the 'loop' road at Okement Hill, then explore southward across the bogs. Carry a compass and let someone know where you are going. Try also walking up larger tors and screes for rocky-ground species such as Wheatear. Boots and waterproof clothes are essential. The best area to cover for a range of species is between Okement Hill and Fur Tor (south of Cranmere) and around the upper Taw and Dart. A circular walk around these points could be interesting, although very arduous. Stay to tracks to avoid flushing birds from nest sites. The obvious rough track (not driveable) running south-east from Okement Hill army lookout point towards Hangingstone Hill is a useful start point; Red Grouse can be present on the heathery slopes.

Note: Severe winter conditions can cause considerable damage to the tarmac surface of the moor road; the west side of the loop is often badly rutted in places. The east side is generally more passable. (Turn left at the fork in road south of the army camp.) It contains a stream ford but this is usually driveable except after heavy rains.

For woodland species, several access points lead to paths through the East and West Okement valleys. Coming into Okehampton from the east, Fatherford viaduct is a good starting point; turn left down a poorly marked minor road immediately after the 'Welcome to Okehampton' sign, opposite Exeter Road Industrial Estate, just before the 40mph speed limit sign and motel on left. Drive 800m along the narrow lane to the corner where the footpath starts and park carefully on the verge. Footpaths lead both up- and downriver; by walking right you can walk through to the access point near the disused railway station, a distance of about 1 mile (1.6km). If driving up to the high moor, en route you can visit either Okement Castle (an English Heritage property) on the West Okement or the East Okement near the old railway station. To reach the castle, start off from Okehampton centre along the army-camp road, turning right after a short distance at the National Trust signposts. Try the wooded slopes behind the castle ruins and the woodland edge. For East Okement, continue up the moor access road for 800m, turn left along the residential street leading to the disused station and park (unrestricted) before the houses finish on the left. The public path, signposted back to Fatherford Viaduct, starts to the left just before the station entry. West Okement woods can also be entered to the west of the town; follow the main road up the hill to the west from the town centre, towards Launceston. After 2 miles (3.2km), you reach Betty Cottles Inn and the A30 Rescue Garage, where you can turn left onto a minor road to Meldon Quarry and Bluebell Wood opposite the inn. After 800m take signposted paths to the right into the woods, before the lane crosses the new bypass.

To reach Meldon Lake and the higher reaches of the Okement, continue 1 mile (1.6km) past the inn. The B3260 road, on which you are travelling, continues as a narrowing country road through Meldon hamlet (ignore the turn to A30 Launceston which takes you onto the main A30 bypass). At the top of Meldon hamlet, past the houses, follow brown tourist signs to Meldon Lake. The lake is deep and peaty, with few attractions to waterfowl except a few Canada Geese and Cormorants. By parking here and walking past the reservoir, it is possible to hike up to the upper West Okement ravine and Black Tor Copse ancient woodland (about an hour each way). The northern slope overlooking Meldon Lake, encircled by footpaths, often produces Cuckoo, Tree Pipit and Redstart.

CALENDAR

Resident: Red Grouse, Skylark, Carrion Crow, Raven on moors; Dipper, Mistle Thrush, Grey Wagtail and common woodland passerines in valley; Buzzard, Peregrine and Kestrel anywhere.

December–February: Generally quiet. Possibly Woodcock in woods or a passing raptor on moors.

March–May: Wheatear returns from late March, most other migrants from late April, including Cuckoo, Whinchat and breeding Snipe, passage plovers and maybe Dotterel (the latter most likely in May), passing Merlin or Hobby; in valley woods, Pied Flycatcher, Grasshopper and other warblers, Redstart.

June–July: Breeding species active through June but most have finished song and display by July when young being fed and post-breeding flocks start to form.

August–November: Summer breeding visitors departing. Chance of Dotterel, late August; possibly passing raptors, e.g. Hen Harrier and Merlin (mostly from October); chance of Snow Bunting, November; passing plover flocks.

Devon (south coast and Dartmoor)

21F TAVY CLEAVE, WEST DARTMOOR

OS LANDRANGER MAP 191 OR OS OUTDOOR LEISURE MAP 28
OS grid ref: SX5583
Postcode: PL19 9QG
what3words: sticking.bandaged.vaulting

HABITAT
The boulder-strewn River Tavy runs off the high moor plateau through a picturesque gorge. The valley floor contains scattered gorse and hawthorn bushes, while higher slopes are covered by rock screes from tors above, with isolated Rowans. An artificial leat (watercourse) carries drinking water from the Tavy across the lower moor slopes to nearby villages. Farmland with rough pasture, surrounded by high stone walls and small trees, lies adjacent to the open moor. Willsworthy firing range, used by the army, extends across the valley from the north (see Access note below).

SPECIES
This is a good area to sample typical moorland species in pleasant surroundings in the breeding season. Farmland fringes hold Redstarts, while numerous Wheatears dip off along the valley slopes and both Stonechat and Whinchat perch on gorse sprigs. Other summer migrant visitors include Cuckoo and Tree Pipit. The fast-flowing river is a regular haunt of Dippers and Grey Wagtails, while Buzzards and Ravens soar overhead. Hobbies, Kestrels and Peregrines may circle the gorge, and Stock Doves nest in small numbers in the valley. In autumn,

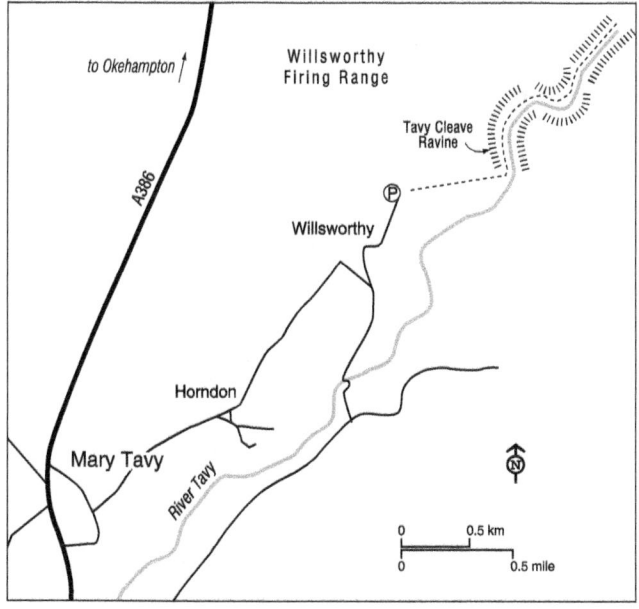

153

migrant Golden Plover flocks arrive on the open slopes, winter thrushes might be found feeding on Rowan berries and raptors such as Merlin occasionally pass over.

TIMING
Fine mornings produce maximum activity, but most breeding species might be seen at any time of day. As usual with moorland sites, those making a long hike should check weather conditions beforehand and let people know where they are going.

ACCESS
From the A386 Plymouth–Okehampton road, north of Tavistock, turn right at Mary Tavy village. Continue along narrow lanes up the Tavy Valley through Horndon towards Willsworthy and Lane End. At Lane End there is a car park near the gate onto the open moor. Walk to the right beside the leat (watercourse) and up into the valley for about 2 miles (3km).

Note: As usual with firing ranges nearby, watch out for red warning flags and avoid metal objects on the moor. For more information, check gov.uk/government/publications/dartmoor-firing-programme or call 0800 458 4868.

CALENDAR
Resident: Grey Heron, Sparrowhawk, Buzzard, Kestrel, Grey Wagtail, Raven.

December–February: Generally quiet. Possibly Woodcock in damp scrub, or a passing raptor on moors.

March–May: Wheatear returns from late March, most other migrants from late April, including Cuckoo, Redstart and possibly Grasshopper Warbler.

June–July: Breeding species as arrived above active through June but most finished song and display by July, when young being fed and post-breeding flocks start to form.

August–November: Summer breeding visitors departing. Chance of passing raptors, e.g. Hen Harrier and Merlin later.

21G BURRATOR RESERVOIR AND WOODLANDS

OS LANDRANGER MAP 202 OR OS OUTDOOR LEISURE MAP 28
OS grid ref: SX5669
Postcode: PL20 6PF
what3words: coach.daisy.tightest

HABITAT
Near Yelverton, on the south-west edge of Dartmoor, this 60ha reservoir lies in a steep-sided valley, overlooked by scree-covered tors reaching above a 300m

altitude. The lower slopes are tree-clad, mostly with Forestry England conifers; many trees are now reaching maturity and large tracts are being harvested and restocked, although there is also extensive replanting of native species. Small areas of mature broadleaf, mostly Beech, remain, and there are many Rowan trees, with bunches of scarlet fruits in autumn.

None of the Dartmoor reservoirs are very attractive to diverse plant or animal life, being steep-sided and often exposed. They lack muddy margins, unless water levels are exceptionally low, and peaty acidic water prevents many plants from growing. Burrator, however, has more varied habitat than other Dartmoor reservoirs, but it also attracts more public visitors.

SPECIES

This is Dartmoor's best reservoir for ducks, although few other specialities occur. Mallard and Teal often exceed 50, but Tufted Duck and especially Pochard are less frequent. Goosander use the lake as a night roost, flighting in late on winter afternoons from elsewhere on the moors. This attractive sawbill has reached two dozen on occasions, although about half that number is more usual. Other ducks, including several rare Ring-necked Ducks, have also visited, along with wind-blown or stray divers and grebes, but these are very infrequent. Coot assemble in small groups, and 10 or more Grey Heron may line the banks; there is a small heronry at nearby Meavy. Gulls use the reservoir to a greater extent in rough weather as a sheltered place to rest and preen. All the commoner species visit, but apparently do not roost overnight.

The conifers may hold Crossbills, whose presence is indicated by shredded cones littering the ground below. Siskins are also keen feeders on conifers; their

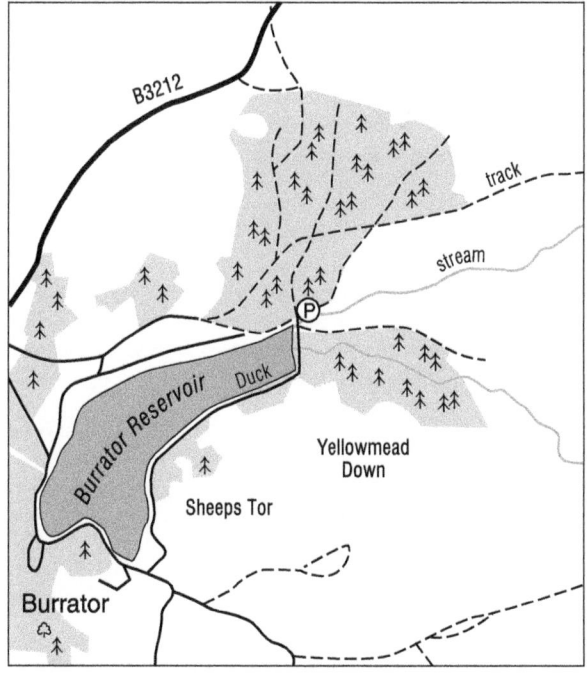

high-pitched wheezy *klee* calls help you locate them. Brambling mix with flocks of Chaffinch foraging among fallen beechmast. A portly, rufous Woodcock breaking daytime cover may be an added bonus while waiting for the last Goosander to fly in just before dusk. Dippers are more easily found along the streams in winter, when disturbance is less, sharing the habitat with Grey Wagtail.

When wildfowl depart northward as spring commences, there is normally little to see on the reservoir, although recent seasons have produced several Goosander, with females having been seen leading a brood of young. Common Sandpiper is possible when water levels are low. By mid-spring, attention switches to surrounding woodlands, where both Chiffchaffs and Willow Warblers sing; the latter is the commonest local warbler. Blackcaps and Garden Warblers breed, with a few Pied Flycatchers present in deciduous woodland. Redstarts can be found nesting among drystone walls and ruined farm buildings. Cuckoos call, and Tree Pipits parachute from perches on small moorland-fringe trees. These more open areas also hold a small population of Nightjars.

Summer finds both Sparrowhawks and Buzzards soaring overhead, ever watchful for prey. Family parties of residents such as Coal Tit and Nuthatch may include Siskins and their broods. These roving flocks are soon joined by earlier-breeding summer visitors and their first-brood fledglings. Goldcrests can be abundant, especially if winters have been mild and their population has remained high. Restless groups of irruptive Scandinavian-bred Crossbills may occur.

After a long dry spell in early autumn, the area furthest from the dam may have exposed mud. Very small numbers of waders such as Common and Green Sandpipers may then pass through. Ring Ouzels may be watched feeding on Rowan and hawthorn berries. By late autumn, waterfowl are returning.

TIMING

Human activity can be substantial around perimeter roads and verges on fine weekends, even in winter; in late spring and summer, it is busier still. Fortunately, the vast majority of daytrippers do not wander far from their cars.

In winter, mornings and late afternoons are quieter and also offer a better chance of seeing larger numbers of Goosander. Nightjars are most likely to be noticed when active at dusk.

ACCESS

Leave the A386 at Yelverton and take the B3212 to Dousland, 1 mile (1.6km) away. At the village crossroads, take a minor road signed to Burrator. Roads surround the lake and there are several parking spots. The reservoir can be checked from the roadside (at least when leaves are off the trees). Best views are from the road running along the south (Sheepstor) side; about halfway along is probably best for Goosander.

Surrounding woods and moorland have open access. Dogs must be kept on leads to prevent them chasing livestock. Tracks at the top end of the lake (furthest from dam) lead off left and right. The right-hand track is probably better. Along this, among walls and ruined buildings, watch for Redstarts. Most other species present in the area can be seen here too.

Devon (south coast and Dartmoor)

CALENDAR

Resident: Great Crested Grebe, Goosander, Grey Heron, Sparrowhawk, Buzzard, Kestrel, Tawny Owl, Dipper, woodpeckers, Grey Wagtail, Goldcrest, Coal Tit, Raven, Lesser Redpoll, Siskin.

December–February: Possible appearance of a diver or rare grebe; Teal, Tufted Duck, Goosander; other ducks including Pochard and Goldeneye in severe weather; Brambling.

March–May: By mid-March, most wildfowl have departed but Goosander may stay to breed; Cuckoo, House Martin, Tree Pipit, Redstart, Wheatear, Garden Warbler, Blackcap, Chiffchaff, Willow Warbler and Spotted Flycatcher arrive to breed, mostly from late April but Spotted Flycatcher mid-May.

June–July: Breeding species including Nightjar; Crossbill influx possible in July.

August–November: If any exposed mud, waders including Green and Common Sandpipers may visit. Waterfowl begin to return by end November.

21H PILES COPSE, HARFORD MOOR AND THREE BARROWS

OS LANDRANGER MAP 202 OR OS OUTDOOR LEISURE MAP 28
OS grid ref: SX6462
Postcode: **Piles Copse** – PL21 0JQ
what3words: **Piles Copse** – snore.pairings.adjusted

HABITAT

This sector of the southern moors encompasses most of the features associated with moorland bird habitats contained within a relatively compact area. Piles Copse is an example of stunted oakwood, a small remnant of once-extensive woodlands. The copse is situated on a steep west-facing bank in the River Erme Valley. Harford Moor consists largely of sheep-grazed moorland turf. Three Barrows, a high spot at 461m, consists mainly of bracken and rather poor quality heather, but provides wide vistas. The whole area contains steep, high, rocky banks, with Sharp Tor forming a focal point. The copse also contains a few Rowans and hawthorns, more frequently scattered along lower stretches of the river valley and found sparsely among stone-walled, rough grazing fields. The low trees and small extent of wooded area allow for relatively easy viewing of some species which can be difficult elsewhere.

SPECIES

Virtually all those species occurring on the lower moorland habitats are present; Dippers and Grey Wagtails both breed on the river, while Meadow Pipits nest abundantly on the open moors and Yellowhammers are present in bushy areas. Golden Plover are found in flocks of hundreds from autumn through to spring, once joined by a Dotterel. Breeding passerines arriving in spring include Tree Pipits, Willow Warblers and Redstarts around wooded areas, along with other

Devon (south coast and Dartmoor)

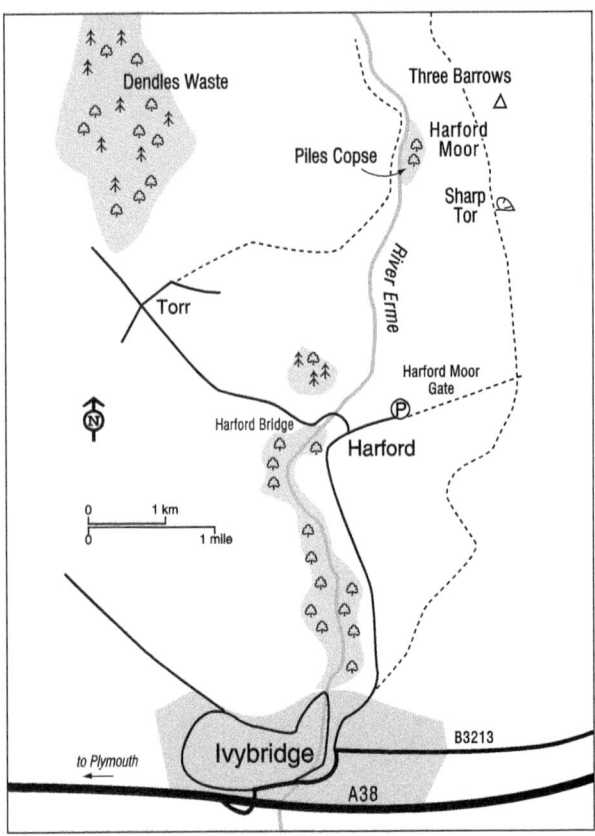

species such as Wheatears, Whinchats, Stonechats and ever-watchful Cuckoos on more open terrain. Raptor interest includes breeding Kestrels and Buzzards, while Hobbies are frequent visitors in season. From late autumn to early spring there is a good chance of a Merlin. This locality has produced several Red Kites and Hen Harriers; Golden Oriole has been found in the copse and notably a stunning male Rock Thrush was seen by a few fortunate observers one May evening.

TIMING

Although this is not the highest-elevation moorland, the same safety principles apply as to any other moorland site when walking; it is surprisingly easy to become disorientated in thick fog, for example. Rapid weather changes can occur, so usual precautions must be taken and appropriate clothing carried.

For breeding passerine species, early mornings in springtime are best, when the males are singing strongly and in immaculate breeding plumage. Anticyclonic fine weather systems at migration periods increase the chance of a passing raptor. Fine weather will obviously be desirable for birdwatching in open habitats at any time. Although this area suffers less human disturbance than some moorland venues, weekdays are quieter.

Devon (south coast and Dartmoor)

ACCESS

From the A38 turn into Ivybridge town and follow the narrow B3213 signposted to the hamlet of Harford. Once there, turn right at the church; after 800m the road ends at a small gated car park. From the car park walk left (northward) over high, turfy ground. Piles Copse soon becomes visible near the valley bottom, set among a virtually treeless hilly landscape, some 2 miles (3km) from the car park. Continue heading towards Higher Piles enclosures, crossing a small stream en route, then through a dilapidated wall. Keep to the higher parts of the steep slope below Sharp Tor, thus avoiding boggy conditions on the lower slopes. Head diagonally towards the copse along its eastern edge.

Covering the wood from its outer edges still allows you very good views into the trees for birds; there is no path through the rocky interior. At the furthest edge of the copse, following the inner face of the wall, descend a rough, little-used path to the riverside and a level grassy area, from which you can retrace your route.

For a longer, though more arduous, walk to Three Barrows starting from the top of Sharp Tor, walk out onto high ground for wide moorland vistas at least 2 miles (3.2km) from the car park and scan the surrounding country for raptors and a chance of grouse.

CALENDAR

Resident: Buzzard, Dipper, Raven

December–February: Occasional passing raptors; Golden Plover, Woodcock, winter thrushes.

March–May: Commoner summer migrants arrive, including upland specialities; chance of an uncommon overflying raptor or other less expected species later in the period.

June–July: Breeding species.

August–November: Generally quiet, but winter visitors arrive towards the end.

21J STEPS BRIDGE AND DUNSFORD WOODS

OS LANDRANGER MAP 191 OR OS OUTDOOR LEISURE MAP 28
OS grid ref: SX8088
Postcode: **Steps Bridge** – EX6 7EH
what3words: **Steps Bridge** – stitching.conga.skippers

HABITAT

At the eastern edge of Dartmoor, the River Teign flows through a deep, sheltered valley thickly covered in mature Sessile Oaks for several miles, with scattered areas of Ash and birch in flatter areas. In spring, the site is well known for woodland wild flowers, including a high concentration of Wild Daffodils. Higher slopes above are bracken-clad with rocky outcrops. Butterflies can be well represented

Devon (south coast and Dartmoor)

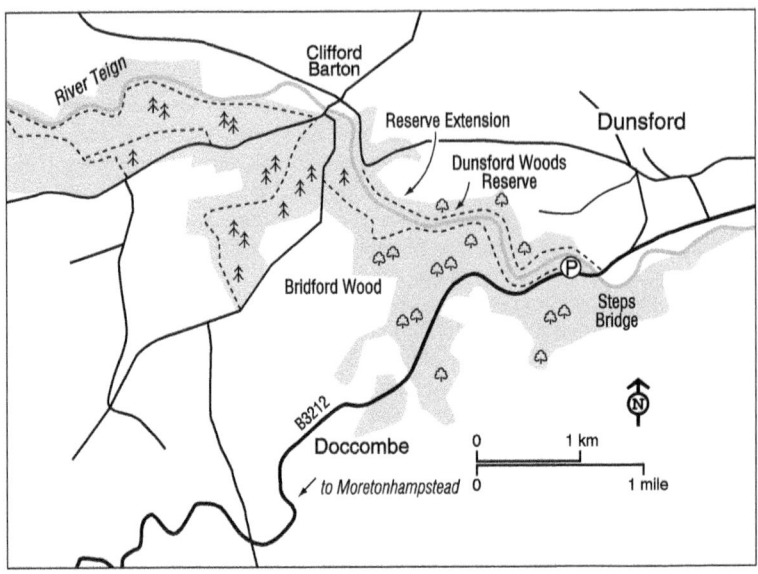

in summer in open areas. Steps Bridge itself lies at the lower end of the valley where it is crossed by the road. The section of woodland along the north bank adjacent to Steps Bridge is Dunsford Woods, a 56ha reserve managed by DWT and owned by the National Trust. West of the valley, Mardon Down is a 357m hilltop covered with gorse, bracken and rough grassland, giving extensive views over the east flank of the moors.

SPECIES

An attraction for visiting birdwatchers is the presence of some breeding species that are either specialised to moorland valleys or are localised and potentially hard to find elsewhere. A high resident population of woodpeckers is encouraged by retention of old and decaying timber. Dippers and Grey Wagtails are frequently encountered along the banks of the Teign, along with occasional Mandarin Duck and fishing Goosander. Kingfishers, which nest downstream, may visit the clear pools above the bridge to feed, especially after the breeding season.

From late spring into summer, as with most major Dartmoor valleys, the oakwoods are home to several migrant visitors, including Pied Flycatcher. Woodland edges hold Redstart and Tree Pipit. An Iberian Chiffchaff found one spring highlights the potential for rare migrants well inland.

Mardon Down is a vantage point that has produced occasional views of overflying raptors passing through the area, as well as the usual local breeding species. Passerine residents include Stonechat, Yellowhammer and Linnet.

TIMING

The best chance of seeing woodland residents is in late winter to early spring on fine days without too much wind, although luckily the steep-sided valley often shields the woods from most winds. On calmer days, woodpeckers are more likely to be active and visible moving through the treetops; later in spring, views will become complicated by leaf cover. Waterside species are present in most weather conditions. Walkers can be numerous on fine weekends along the valley paths but do not necessarily prevent sightings of woodland species; some disturbance of waterside birds may occur. Mornings will usually produce most song activity from breeding warblers and flycatchers in late spring and early summer. By late summer, when song ceases, the woods do not give up their birds so easily.

Mardon Down is exposed to most winds; fine windless days are best for seeing passerines perching on bushes and overflying raptors.

ACCESS

The area is easily reached along the B3212 east of Moretonhampstead, heading towards Exeter. From the bridge, signs point to the riverside walks; there is a car park with information boards 100m uphill west of the bridge. Bus services from Exeter and Moretonhampstead stop by the bridge. From the bridge, the signposted walks extend upriver for about 3 miles (5km) through the woods towards Clifford Bridge. Paths are generally even and wheelchair access is possible at Steps Bridge. Take the path that forks to the right to get closer views of the wood. The paths link again further on, and the return walk can be done by the waterside. At the far end, towards Clifford Bridge, just before the exit onto the minor lane, a steep-sided path on the right gives access to a high, open down area overlooking the valley, worth checking for a different range of bird species and butterflies in summer.

Other similar areas of valley woodland habitat, accessible by footpaths, are also found further up the Teign Valley, such as between Fingle Bridge and Chagford.

Mardon Down can be reached by leaving Steps Bridge westward on the B3212 and travelling about 3 miles (5km) past Doccombe hamlet, then following signs to the right up to the down, which is open land. Park at roadside pull-ins and explore hilltop paths on both sides.

CALENDAR

Resident: Mandarin Duck, Kingfisher, Dipper, Grey Wagtail, Marsh Tit, Nuthatch, Treecreeper, Yellowhammer.

December–February: Good chance of observing woodpeckers and other residents; Goosander.

March–May: Returning commoner passerine migrants, especially later in period.

June-July: Breeding species.

August–November: Quiet period as breeding migrant species depart and before winter thrushes arrive.

21K HEMBURY WOODS

OS LANDRANGER MAP 202
OS grid ref: SX7268
Postcode: TQ13 7RY
what3words: president.mermaids.dangerously

HABITAT
An extensive hillside of mature deciduous woodland owned by the National Trust, with Sessile Oaks predominating. The area faces south-east on the fringe of Dartmoor, with the River Dart flowing along its boundary. The river at this point alternates between fast stretches and clear, deep pools. At the top of the hill are the remains of a historic hill fort. The site is known for woodland flowers in spring.

SPECIES
The woodland and waterside habitat hosts a variety of species typical of Dartmoor valleys. In late spring, a variety of migrant passerines arriving at their territories includes small numbers of Pied Flycatchers and Nightjars. Occasionally on spring mornings, Golden Orioles have been heard giving their tropical-sounding fluty song.

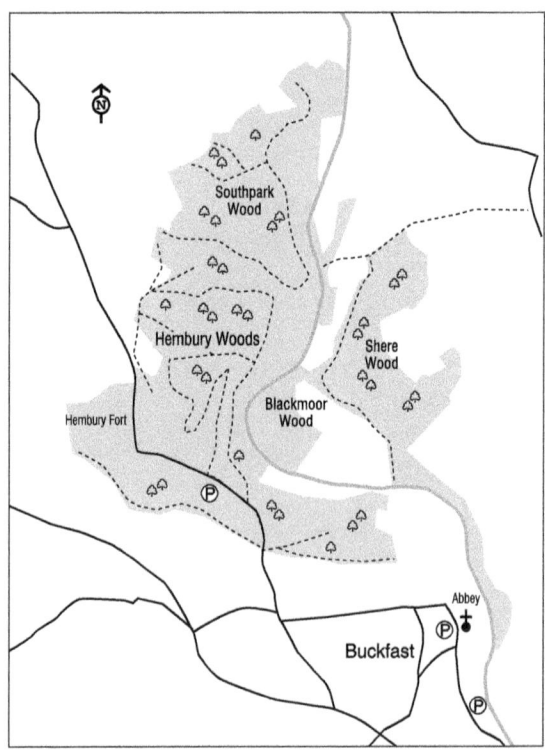

The River Dart often provides views of Dippers feeding along this stretch. Also to be expected are Mandarin Duck and Goosander, with families of chicks occasionally encountered in late spring after leaving a tree nest-hole.

TIMING

The area is popular with walkers at weekends so visiting early, or at other times of the week, gives a better opportunity to see waterside species. Woodpeckers and singing summer visitors are not really disturbed by visitors but are likely to be more active in the mornings. The site is partly sheltered from wind, but woodpeckers and other treetop feeders are likely to be more visible in calm conditions.

ACCESS

Take the A38 signposted to Buckfastleigh, turning off north from the dual carriageway at the main junction. At the first junction after leaving the main road, turn right towards Buckfast Abbey and Holne. After passing the abbey entrance, take the next turn right (Higher Mill Lane) into Buckfast village. Follow through the village (on Grange Road) and at the far end turn right, following minor roads towards Hembury Wood (signposted as 800m from the first crossroads). The wood is on the hillside ahead. After crossing a stream the road climbs, then an unmade track leads into car parking in the wood on the left. Check this area for woodpeckers. The main wood is across the road on the right; signposted footpaths give access throughout. Paths down to the right are signposted to the riverbank. To the left, other paths lead up to the fortification area at the top of the site.

CALENDAR

Resident: Mandarin Duck, Goosander, Grey Wagtail, Dipper, Marsh Tit, common woodland species, Raven.

December–February: Good chance to observe woodpeckers and other woodland species.

March– May: Breeding species include arriving warblers and flycatchers, maybe Nightjar later in period.

June–July: Breeding species.

August–November: Quiet period before winter thrushes arrive and woodland species start to form larger feeding flocks.

CORNWALL

22 ST JOHN'S AND MILLBROOK LAKES, LYNHER AND TAMAR ESTUARIES: GENERAL INTRODUCTION

HABITAT

This complex of tidal waterways is situated at the extreme south-east of Cornwall. All are interconnected by the wide, ill-defined Hamoaze channel, between Torpoint on the Cornish side and Devonport naval dockyards on the eastern bank. The Devon side of the Tamar–Tavy confluence is described under Plymouth, and the upper Tavy north of Plymouth forms a section of this chapter. All sites form mudflats at low tide, with St John's Lake nearest to the sea, directly linked to Plymouth Sound. Both St John's and the Lynher are wide and difficult to observe thoroughly.

All these sites are interesting for waders and waterfowl in autumn and, particularly, winter, with relatively little bird activity in summer. Together they form the region's most important estuary habitat after the Exe.

A particularly noticeable development in the 1990s was the concentrations of Little Egret occurring in this district; interestingly, both Cattle and Great White Egrets are now being reported across the complex. Little Egrets scatter throughout the confluence during the day and at low tide. Highest concentrations within this complex can only be attained by counting at the night-time roosts during optimum times and conditions, which are on spring tides during August and September. The actual roost sites can vary from year to year but are usually located within the lower reaches mainly around the Lynher, such as at Jupiter Point and near St Germans. Little Egret counts have at times exceeded 100 birds, once a UK record although since exceeded elsewhere, and are one of the reasons why the Tamar was designated a Special Protection Area. Little Egret has shown a slight decline in numbers since 2004.

22A ST JOHN'S LAKE AND MILLBROOK LAKE

> OS LANDRANGER MAP 201
> OS grid ref: SX4254
> Postcode: **St John's Lake** – PL9 2HT **Millbrook** – PL10 1DN
> what3words: **St John's Lake** – shaped.solved.lived
> **Millbrook Lake** – dripping.horseshoe.dancer

HABITAT

St John's Lake is a large area of open water and mudflats forming a semi-sheltered basin between Plymouth Sound and river estuaries upstream. Millbrook Lake is an estuary backwater providing further shelter from the wind, as does the adjacent tidal creek. All three sites are easily viewed from fringing roads, so are suitable for people with reduced mobility.

SPECIES

Because of the proximity of the sea, St John's Lake tends to harbour more marine species, perhaps when blown in by rough weather, while Millbrook is used more by estuarine and marsh birds. Divers are annual and regular, mostly Great Northern in ones and twos; single Black-throated may also occur, but Red-throated are very irregular. The most common grebe is Little, but small numbers of Slavonian, Black-necked and rather more Great Crested are also seen. Mute Swan numbers have fallen dramatically since 2008 and now there are fewer than 15 regular birds present on the whole complex, with only a pair or two breeding locally. Parties of both Pale-bellied and Dark-bellied Brent Geese are seen most winters but rarely exceed 50 in total. Shelduck are scattered across the mudflats, with 300–400 each winter. The most numerous dabbling duck is Wigeon, with rafts of up to 1,500; however, the flock may split and move to the Lynher if disturbed. Up to 750 Teal winter on the complex, and first-class views may be obtained of this small duck, along with other estuary birds, at Millbrook. Always check for Green-winged Teal and other scarce ducks such as Velvet Scoter, Scaup and Long-tailed Duck.

Outside the breeding season, Peregrine and Osprey are occasional visitors. Waders are well represented, with an interesting spread of species. Very small

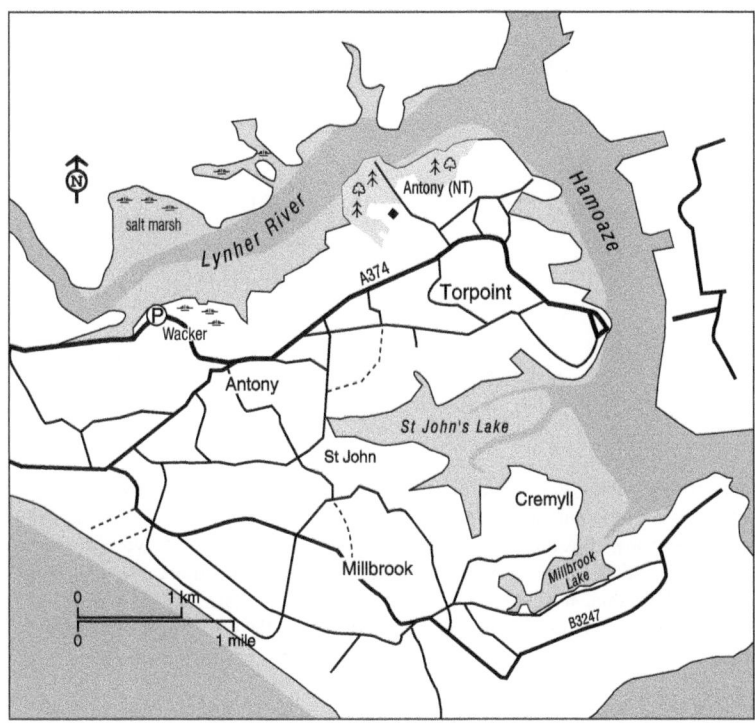

numbers of Little Stint and Curlew Sandpiper sometimes visit Millbrook and St John's Lake in autumn. Turnstone is usual, with groups sometimes totalling 50 or more – there are good views from the roads at Torpoint. Usually both species of godwit can be found, with Black-tailed being more numerous. Flocks of Redshank and small numbers of Knot and Avocet can also be expected. Whimbrel, passing northward in spring, may rest for a day or so; they are seen again in autumn on their return journey, numbers being highly variable but averaging 15; occasionally a couple will winter, favouring Millbrook. Very occasionally Spotted Redshank, which has declined drastically, can be seen. Greenshank and Green and Common Sandpipers use the area, chiefly in autumn, although in some years individuals elect to see the winter through here. Millbrook is popular with them, and in the last few years Avocets have also become regular winter visitors. Rarer wader visitors have included Black-winged Stilt and Semipalmated Sandpiper.

Among the Black-headed and Common Gulls, several Mediterranean Gulls may be present, although they can be hard to pick out, especially in immature plumage. Up to 150 at once are often recorded in July and August, when some are resplendent in summer plumage. Colour-ringed individuals prove most are of Dutch origin. Juvenile and first-winter birds have been reported, but most are adults. Even more difficult to identify are Ring-billed Gulls, which are occasionally reported here. Little Gulls are more obvious visitors in ones and twos, largely in autumn or early winter, juveniles being most usual. A very rare Bonaparte's Gull turned up one autumn at Millbrook. Terns frequently feed here. All the British sea terns have been noted in spring or autumn. Roseate and Little are seen the least, mostly in autumn. Higher tern numbers are expected in autumn, but not usually more than 10 of any single species; Sandwich and Common are most numerous, with a scattering of Arctic (mostly juveniles) and an occasional Black Tern. Auks drift in from the Sound, usually in late winter when they begin to come closer to shore, instinctively, at the start of their breeding cycle.

22B THE LYNHER

> OS LANDRANGER MAP 201
> OS grid ref: SX4056
> Postcode: PL11 3AH
> what3words: assume.skirting.cultivation

HABITAT

This estuary is wide at its mouth, where it joins the Hamoaze, narrowing sharply further upstream near Antony village. There is a small saltmarsh on the opposite bank to Antony, together with several narrow creeks. The main river, forming a long, narrow tidal creek above this point, itself splits into three: the first creek ends at Polbathic, the second at Tideford and the third near Trematon, just outside Saltash. All these creeks have saltmarsh, mostly towards their heads, little visited by birdwatchers because of access difficulties.

SPECIES

On the main estuary in winter, small numbers of divers and grebes may be seen, including an occasional Red-necked Grebe; possibly the same birds move up from St John's Lake. Ducks certainly move from site to site, notably Wigeon flocks, and at times of disturbance there may be wholesale interchange between sites. Pintail, once a Lynher speciality, are now rarely seen, reflecting a nationwide decline. A Spoonbill or two regularly favour this area, remaining throughout the winter. Migrating Redshank and Greenshank find the creeks ideal and may over-winter. Once a favoured place for wintering Spotted Redshank, this species is seldom recorded here now. Green and Common Sandpipers are also passage migrants that occasionally spend the winter in ones and twos. A Forster's Tern from America, which visited in 1982, was at the time only the second UK record.

Commoner species are the same as at adjoining St John's Lake, but generally in lower numbers. A substantial proportion of the district's Little Egret population, consisting largely of first-year birds, usually gathers to roost on the Lynher. Both Cattle and Great White Egrets are now being reported along stretches of the river regularly. Some winters, a large proportion of the Avocet flock may visit, but it is unclear whether this is due to weather conditions or food availability. Snipe are usually found on the saltmarsh around the Lynher, along with the occasional Jack Snipe.

22C THE TAMAR

> OS LANDRANGER MAP 201
> OS grid ref: SX4364
> Postcode: **Cargreen** – PL12 6PA **Kingsmill** – PL12 6LJ
> **Calstock Wetlands** – PL18 9QA
> what3words: **Cargreen** – buzz.bumps.keys
> **Kingsmill** – absorbing.watches.kickbacks
> **Calstock Wetlands** – custodial.wage.goodnight

HABITAT

This estuary forms the boundary between Devon and Cornwall. From the Tamar Road Bridge upstream to Kingsmill creek is a wide area of rather unproductive mudflats. Viewed from the Cornish side, the estuary becomes narrower but more productive as you travel upstream. It is mostly flanked by pasture farmland, and groups of trees meet near the water's edge. An up-and-coming area, always worth a look is The River Tamar Walkway and Wetland Project, usually referred to as Calstock Wetlands. On the west side of the upper Tamar, this area consists of scrapes, saltmarsh and reedbeds, approximately 11ha in extent.

SPECIES

Above all else, the mudflats of the Tamar are best known for that graceful wader the Avocet, adopted and made famous by the RSPB as its national emblem. Evidence exists linking at least some Tamar birds with those raised on RSPB reserves; some chicks marked with coloured plastic leg-rings have been seen

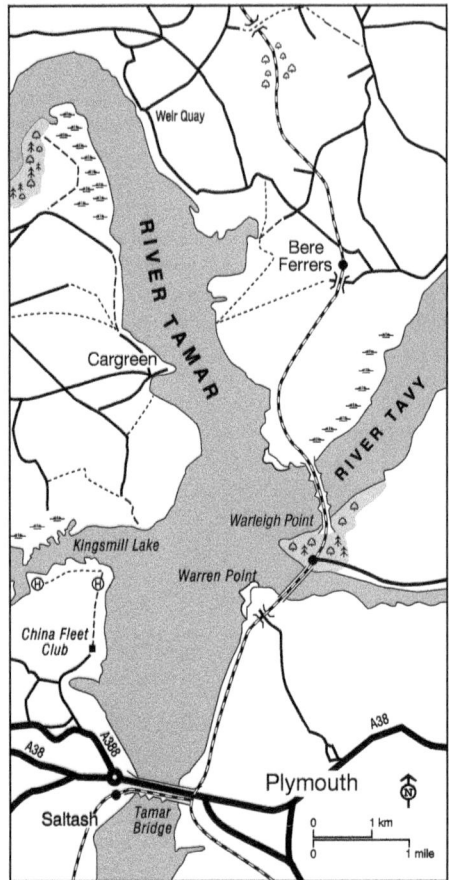

later as adults on the Tamar. Avocets begin to arrive from early winter, numbers generally peaking in mid-season with more than 150 present, but counts have exceeded 200. There is evidence that the wintering numbers have declined here over the last 10 years and that they are feeding in other areas of the estuary more regularly now.

During winter, other regular species include a few Little Grebes, small flocks of Mallard, Wigeon, Teal and the occasional Green-winged Teal. Pochard – once the most numerous diving duck, often exceeding 100 in some years – has almost disappeared from the estuary, along with Goldeneye; both species are down to low single figures now. From time to time small numbers of other diving ducks such as Tufted Duck or Scaup appear along with the occasional Ring-necked Duck. In severe weather all three 'sawbills' may be present.

From the first hide at Kingsmill Lake, the wide vista over the area gives a chance of watching wintering ducks and grebes, mainly Great Crested, and assembled gulls. Occasionally flocks of terns arrive on passage to fish, mostly comprising Sandwich and Common with the odd Arctic, but all the 'sea terns', along with Black, have been reported. Fishing Osprey can also be seen from here.

The second hide at Kingsmill Creek gives views over a high-tide roost site. Elegant Spotted Redshank occasionally winter, their two-syllable calls giving their presence away. Avocet is another annual winter visitor to the roost; 50 are not unusual. Black-tailed Godwit occurs in smaller numbers and a good range of other commoner waders are also present from early autumn through to spring, possibly including Little Stint and Curlew Sandpiper; Glossy Ibis and Cattle Egret may join them.

In the Tamar Valley Area of Outstanding Natural Beauty (AONB), the Calstock Wetlands, although still developing, has already attracted more than 60 species including Teal, which tend to draw in rarer species: Green-winged Teal, Garganey and Goosander. Ringed and Little Ringed Plovers, Green and Common Sandpipers, Curlew Sandpiper and (once) Pectoral Sandpiper have all been found here.

In early autumn (or more rarely, spring), the Tamar usually plays host to several Ospreys. These exciting raptors may establish temporary residence for a couple of weeks in autumn before setting off southwards. Outside the breeding season, a Peregrine might be watched flashing over the mud in pursuit of a luckless wader.

TIMING (SITES 22A–C)

The severity of winter weather will influence the variety and numbers of species; the harder the weather, the larger the numbers. Any daylight hours are suitable, but the state of the tide is important. For example, for watching waders across the mudflats the tide must be out as there are few easily checked roosting points. When the tide is out, major deepwater channels remain at all sites. These are used by divers, grebes and ducks. Incoming and neap tides allow assembling waders at the Kingsmill Creek roost to continue to feed and rest while mainly remaining in view. On high spring tides, many waders are lost to view in the salt-marshes, but as the tide drops they emerge again to feed on the newly exposed mud. Calstock Wetlands hold birds at all states of the tide, but high tides will push wading birds into the area.

Later winter afternoons are best for gulls using the lower estuary as a pre-roost stopover, while prolonged stormy weather encourages a few seaducks and divers to shelter in the lower estuary area off Kingsmill Creek.

Wader roosts at St John's Lake are also scattered and difficult to observe. Areas around Millbrook are utilised but suffer from disturbance by dogs and the public, so are not reliable.

Some shooting takes place on all sites. This disrupts normal flock behaviour, especially on the Lynher and St John's Lake.

Both Cattle and Little Egrets are scattered during the daytime, so are best watched going to night roost during the evening, when they fly in to congregate in favoured areas. Highest counts have been achieved when high spring tides force birds out from saltmarshes.

Late afternoon, on an incoming tide, is best for Mediterranean Gulls gathering at St Johns Lake before roosting; most then depart to roost elsewhere. At high tide a proportion roost on waterfront building rooftops.

ACCESS (SITES 22A–C)

From Saltash, **the Tamar** can be checked by taking the A388 and following signs for Cargreen, a favourite site for Avocets to feed. You are likely to see at least part of the flock, if not all. Views are reasonably close, and they can be seen from your car, as there are parking spaces near the waterfront; making it suitable for those who are less mobile.

Cornwall

For **Kingsmill Creek**, from the A38 take the road running parallel to the A38 road tunnel at Saltash (not through the town), turning onto the minor road signposted to Salt Mill and North Pill. Then follow the brown leisure signs to the China Fleet Club after less than 1 mile (1.6km), where there is ample free parking and toilets. The nature trail is located beside the golf range. This often muddy track follows the edges of the golf course and estuary. (The combination code for access to the hides can be obtained from the reception staff.) The first stepped hide allows views over the widest part of the Tamar Estuary. Continuing, the trail reaches the second hide towards the head of the narrowing Kingsmill Creek; the trail ends here. This hide is particularly well-sited to observe roosting waders, which assemble on higher tides. Waders utilise the saltmarsh and the higher muddy edges and are often watchable at close quarters. Looking northwards from the trail means the estuary is sunlit from behind you, at least from early afternoon. Other roost sites throughout the complex are few and usually difficult to watch, with the Kingsmill Creek roost being the single most easily accessed and most closely viewable.

Calstock Wetlands are reached from the A390 by taking the turning to Calstock and following the road for 3km (1.9 miles) until reaching the Village Hall car park, opposite the Tamar Inn. At present it is free to park, but fees may be payable in the future; there are also free toilets. There are two points of access to the circular route around the area from the car park; the most direct is the path beside the football pitch, to view the area from the river side via a gated entrance. This wetland venue forms part of the Tamara Way, a coast-to-coast footpath from Cremyll in south-east Cornwall to Morwenstow on the north coast of Cornwall. The path follows the River Tamar along the Devon/Cornwall border as closely as is possible.

The Lynher is reached from Torpoint via the A374 to about 1 mile (1.6km) past Antony; there is a well-signposted picnic area and parking place at Wacker Creek. Here you are opposite the saltmarsh and overlooking the best part of the estuary for birds. A telescope is essential, especially when checking birds on the opposite shore (where there are no public access points). Higher creeks are not easy to check; several roads pass near their edges at various points, where parking is very difficult and vision is restricted by trees.

St John's Lake is checked from Torpoint, where there are roads along the waterfront. Many birds congregate here, and excellent close views of Mediterranean Gull and Brent Geese can be gained from these roads. Most other species of interest occur in mid-channel or along the relatively undisturbed opposite shore, and a telescope will be necessary. Take the B3247 to Millbrook village (which has public toilets), with narrow waterside roads throughout its length and ample pull-in spots facilitating ease of viewing over part of the Tamar Estuary.

22D LOPWELL AND UPPER TAVY ESTUARY

> OS LANDRANGER MAP 201
> OS grid ref: SX4765
> Postcode: PL6 7BZ
> what3words: **Lopwell** – teaching.washable.darker
> **Upper Tavy** – flicks.passively.revamping

HABITAT
Located just beyond the northern outliers of Plymouth City, Lopwell Dam is a small, narrow, unused reservoir, leased by South West Water for angling. It, and woods adjacent, are designated conservation zones. Beds of bullrushes grow, especially at either end, and willows are profuse towards its very shallow head. Both steep banksides are heavily wooded, mainly with oak.

The River Tavy identifies itself on leaving the dam, but is narrow, tidal and soon lost to the estuary a few hundred metres downstream. At this higher reach, the estuary is mostly wide, broadest between Blaxton Marsh (not to be confused with Blaxton Meadow in Plymouth) and Bere Ferrers opposite. For much of its length it is tree lined.

SPECIES
This scenic spot is especially suitable for birdwatchers to see commoner species relatively easily. Most of the time the reservoir contains few especially interesting species; Mallard abounds, Little Grebe, Coot, Moorhen, Kingfisher and Grey Wagtail often breed, and Grey Heron nests in the vicinity. A few unusual species arrive occasionally: Grey Phalarope, Bittern, Ring-necked Duck and Green-winged Teal have all been recorded.

Winter on the estuary mainly offers smaller numbers of commoner waders, notably Redshank, Dunlin and Curlew, a few Greenshank and perhaps a Green Sandpiper, joined on occasion by parties of Avocet – often surprisingly reluctant to leave their most favoured haunt, the nearby Tamar Estuary. More rarely, the entire wintering flock may visit, for variable lengths of stay.

Common Sandpipers are frequent here at migration times and occasionally overwinter; the general habitat suits them well. Assessing their total migrant numbers is virtually impossible; some may linger, while others pass through rapidly to be replaced by yet more individuals, and inter-site movement further blurs the picture. A pure albino bird once caused a surprise! Two vagrant Spotted Sandpipers from the New World have also joined their Palearctic relatives to overwinter on widely separate occasions, allowing people time to compare the species side by side. Wintering ducks on this part of the estuary include relatively small numbers of Shelduck, Wigeon, Teal and Tufted Duck. Harder winters, especially further north or east, may cause visits by a few Scaup or Smew.

Gulls are largely unremarkable both in total number and species, chiefly Black-headed and Common, although there have been sporadic visits by some Plymouth-based rarities such as a Ross's Gull some years ago. The region's commoner raptors are regularly sighted. Ospreys are annual in autumn, some staying a day or two but others, especially immatures, may be present for up to a month. Less predictable are occasional spring visits, and rare summertime records have occurred; one such Osprey was watched chivvying a passing Black Stork!

Surrounding woodlands contain mainly expected common passerines and woodpeckers. Less usual is the recent addition of a couple of pairs of breeding Pied Flycatcher, using natural tree-holes.

TIMING

General public disturbance is less if the main summer months are avoided, especially at weekends; this is the least interesting time for birds anyway.

A rising tide will push waders nearer to the more easily watchable estuary head. Ospreys often favour the hour after low tide to fish, but older birds can be found fishing at any state of the tide. Cold spells may increase numbers and species of waders and waterbirds, including scarcer ducks.

ACCESS

Several roads leave the A386 towards Lopwell. That nearest Plymouth requires taking an exit left off a roundabout near Roborough, signposted to Bellever and Broadley industrial parks. Continue past the Broadley entrance (the road now narrows) until shortly reaching a bend. Here, take a sharp right turn onto a minor road signposted to Lopwell; continue along narrow lanes later signposted to Lopwell Dam.

Upon reaching the Tavy either turn right towards the dam car park (and toilets) or left for 150m to a smaller parking area, which gives views covering virtually the whole estuary as far down as the enclosing Tavy railway bridge. This is a good viewing spot for those restricted to viewing from the car.

For a closer look, walk left from this parking area for 100m then take the woodland path – beside the estuary – through Blaxton Wood, following this until meeting a narrow creek inlet at the wood edge, which prevents further access. At this widest point of the estuary, opposite Bere Ferrers village, there are good views of the main estuary.

For views of the main body of the reservoir, the only access is across a narrow stone causeway, which is covered by water at high tide, near the foot of the dam. On reaching the far side, part of the lower area can be viewed easily. For further views walk right, into a rough path along the wood edge. Owing to dense tree cover down to the water's edge, only intermittent views of the reservoir are possible. Follow this gradually deteriorating pathway until you are opposite a small narrow island with willows, and from here the remainder of the reservoir can be seen.

Note: From this point the path rapidly becomes almost non-existent – in fact positively dangerous. Following it further is both highly inadvisable and unproductive in terms of gaining any better views. Consideration needs to be given to the river crossing, as the causeway is fully tidal and covered completely on an incoming tide. In order to avoid a wait of several hours for the tide to fall, ensure enough time is allowed to recross.

Between both car parks an embanked footpath runs for a few hundred metres beside the very narrow Tavy outlet, flanked on one side by the steep, dense Lopwell Wood, and on the other mainly by bushes and small trees. Often this stretch is favoured by Common Sandpiper and Kingfisher.

CALENDAR (SITES 22A–D)

Resident: Cormorant, Grey Heron, Shelduck, Little Egret and Oystercatcher throughout the year.

December–February: Divers, particularly Great Northern; commoner grebes; possibly wintering Spoonbill, Dark and Pale-bellied Brent Geese, Wigeon, possibly Green-winged Teal with small numbers of dabbling ducks, and diving and sea ducks at times; Peregrine, Turnstone, Grey Plover, Knot, Dunlin, Greenshank, Green and Common Sandpipers, both godwits; Avocet peak in late December; Mediterranean Gull.

March–May: Most of above depart from early March; first migrants to arrive in April include a trickle of returning waders, notably Whimbrel; Sandwich and a few Common Terns; Possibly Osprey; by mid-March most Little Egret disperse to breed, and Mediterranean Gulls mostly depart by period end.

June–July: Very little other than a few late spring or early autumn passage migrants such as Ringed Plover; resident species; Little Egret numbers increase from late July, as do Mediterranean Gulls accompanying post-breeding Black-headed Gulls.

August–November: Osprey from early August through to late September; first returning common waders may be in summer plumage, joined by Little Stint, Green, Curlew and Wood Sandpipers, Greenshank; possibility of uncommon or rare waders; Avocet return from late October; terns pass through, mostly Sandwich and Common, in larger numbers, August–September, with Arctic from mid-September to mid-October; possibly Little and other uncommon or rare gulls; Mediterranean Gull peaks from mid-July-August; Cattle and Little Egrets reach peak numbers early in period.

23 RAME HEAD, WHITSAND BAY AND LOOE

> OS LANDRANGER MAP 201
> OS grid ref: SX4148 (Rame) SX2552 (Looe)
> Postcodes: PL10, PL11, PL13 (for more detail and what3words see Access section)

HABITAT

On the south-east coast of Cornwall, Rame faces south, the closest mainland point to Eddystone Lighthouse, 6 miles (9.6km) seaward. Rame peninsula includes Penlee Point, at the western entrance to Plymouth Sound. West of Rame is broad Whitsand Bay, terminating in the narrow, steep-sided Looe Estuary mouth. Along the steeply sloping coastline, gorse and bracken brakes are interspersed with Blackthorn, small clumps of trees and small, rough grazing fields. Flatter fields above are used for arable farming. The area around Rame Church and Farm affords more shelter, with groups of trees, mostly Sycamore, and a few gardens and hedgerows. A small road runs from the church to an old fortification above Penlee Point, overgrown with brambles and Ash trees. Habitat along this road is

Cornwall

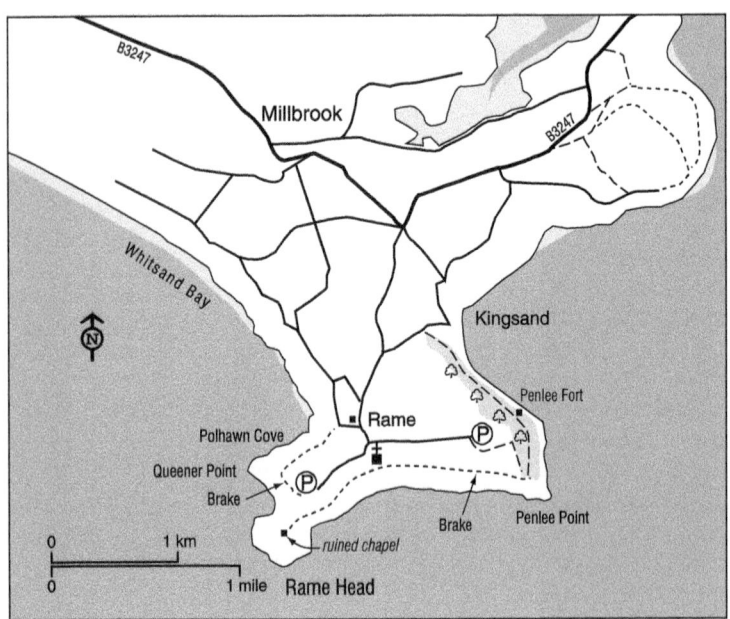

varied, with a wide, dense, mainly Blackthorn copse providing cover. Alongside this lie demolished buildings, colonised by various wildflowers. Adders are common in the area, and Fallow Deer from Mount Edgecumbe Park may be seen from the road between the church and Penlee Fort, especially in autumn and winter.

The coast road from Rame to Looe, following the escarpment edge overlooking the coastline, affords panoramic views. The air in spring can be heavily scented by countless gorse flowers. Europe's first American dragonfly, the Green Darner, was found here, part of an influx into the region. Another migrant American insect, the impressive Monarch Butterfly, has also arrived here on several occasions following suitable Atlantic storms.

SPECIES

The chief interest for birdwatchers visiting Rame will probably be spring and autumn migrants. These will mostly be hirundines, warblers and raptors, perhaps including a harrier or Honey Buzzard. Twice in spring, white Gyr Falcons have passed over.

Most passerine migrants do not linger on exposed heathland, but work quickly towards sheltered areas. Trees and hedgerows around the church and farm are favourite places, having produced scarcities such as Red-breasted Flycatcher and Yellow-browed and Pallas's Warblers. Also favoured are hedges and scattered groups of small trees around Polhawn Cove on the west side of the headland. Small fields among or near the brakes form yet another habitat. Resident Skylarks and Meadow Pipits in the fields are joined by passage flocks of the same species. Also sharing this habitat are migrants such as Tree Pipit, Yellow Wagtail and Wheatear. Cirl Buntings are resident, as are Linnets, whose numbers are boosted by migrants in autumn; a few Bramblings or Snow Buntings may join them, and maybe even an

Ortolan Bunting. Trees and bushes provide vital food and shelter, even if only for a few hours during early morning for overnight-arriving migrants. Species such as Blackcap, Whitethroat, Garden Warbler, Chiffchaff and Willow Warbler sometimes occur in good numbers. Goldcrest is most numerous in autumn and outnumbers the brighter Firecrest. Pied and Spotted Flycatchers can also visit in both seasons, as do Whinchat, Redstart and Black Redstart. North American vagrants have also occurred: the first European record of Wilson's Warbler was a brief visitor to Rame Head in October 1985, closely followed by a Northern Parula at Penlee. The region's first Red-flanked Bluetail, an Asiatic vagrant, once sheltered in Rame churchyard at the same time as a Chimney Swift from America commuted between there and Millbrook. Other notable European visitors to the area have included Roller, Little, Corn and Black-headed Buntings, Melodious Warbler and Spanish Sparrow. Dartford Warblers have at times maintained a small resident colony on the gorse slopes, but theirs is a tenuous foothold as hard winters greatly affect their populations.

When seawatching in spring, the most likely species of interest are Red-throated, Black-throated and Great Northern Divers, sometimes several hundred Manx Shearwaters and hundreds of Gannets. A few Pomarine and Arctic Skuas occasionally coast eastwards in spring, or westwards in autumn. Terns, particularly Sandwich, with some Common, pass east towards breeding grounds. Auks, particularly Razorbills, fly to and fro. Whimbrel and Bar-tailed Godwit also pass eastwards in flocks, the former often giving their diagnostic, seven-note contact call as they pass; one or two Whimbrel often winter along this coast. In autumn, some species can occur in larger numbers. Great Skuas should be more evident, with more seaducks such as Common Scoter. The chance of less common seabirds is greater in autumn; Balearic and Sooty Shearwaters may pass, and Cory's and Great Shearwaters have occurred. Yellow-legged and Mediterranean Gulls are regular.

Birds of special interest in Whitsand Bay, and particularly off Seaton, include Great Northern, Black-throated and Red-throated Divers, often in small, scattered groups totalling up to 10 at a time. From late winter into spring, numbers of all three diver species increase, with some late-staying birds even attaining summer plumage. Occasional Slavonian, Red-necked, Black-necked and Great Crested Grebes may visit in winter, usually in ones and twos. Seaducks such as Eider and Common Scoter sometimes visit in small groups, very occasionally attracting a Velvet Scoter to join them.

Off Looe beach in winter, you can expect to see the above waterbirds at various times, with good views of Eider. Search through rocky areas for Grey Plover,

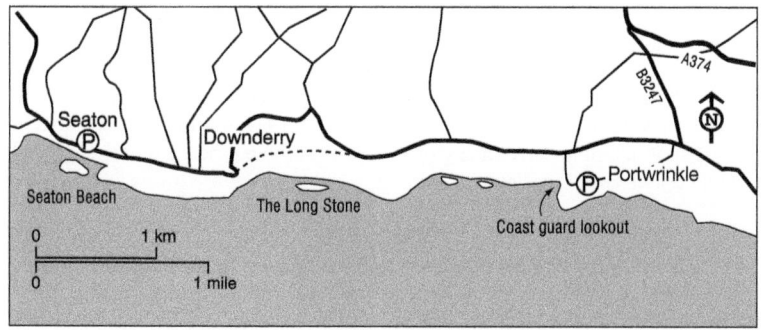

Cornwall

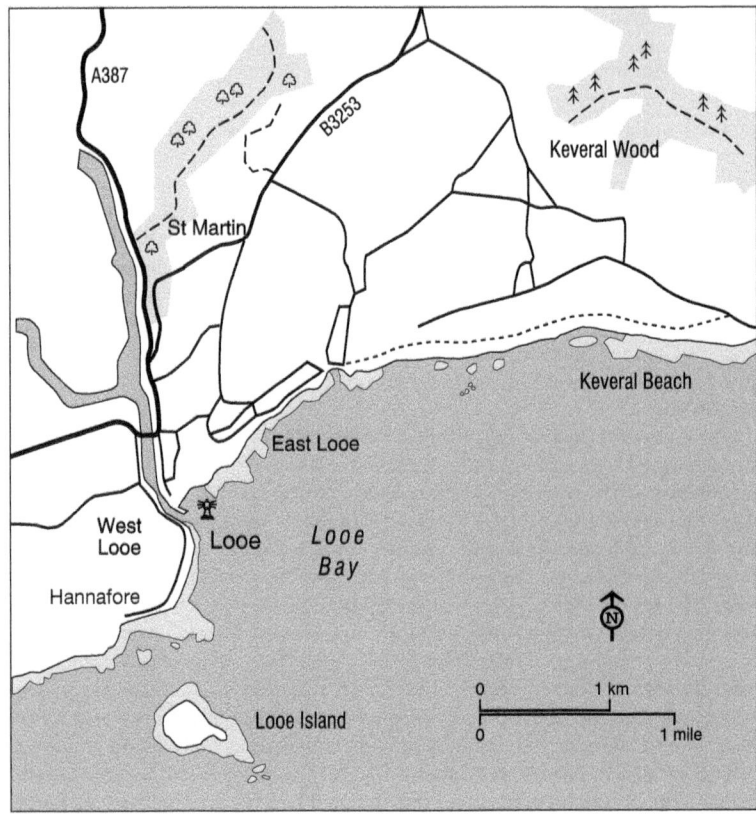

Turnstone and occasionally Purple Sandpiper, which gather in small, loose flocks, camouflaged among seaweed. The beach and trees at the far west end (Hannafore) are good for wintering Chiffchaff, Firecrest and Black Redstart, while the resident Rock Pipits are often joined by their Scandinavian cousins. In the narrow estuary, especially opposite Looe railway station, gulls assemble in large numbers, including Common Gull, particularly in late winter and early spring when they accompany passage Lesser Black-backeds; check among them for unusual gulls such as Glaucous and, less frequently, Iceland. As on many of the region's estuaries, Ring-billed Gull has previously been detected. Higher up the estuary, less common overwintering waders may be found along marshy fringes. These might include Greenshank as well as Green and Common Sandpipers. A Black-winged Stilt once visited. This area is also popular with wintering Kingfisher. In the hilltop trees, across the estuary from the railway station, is a heronry. Activity is visible from the station in early spring, before leaves fully clothe the trees. There is now a breeding colony of Little Egrets and Grey Herons.

TIMING

The whole area is heavily used by the public and tourists all year round, but weekdays are less busy. Morning visits to the Rame area in spring or autumn, especially in southerly or south-easterly winds during fall conditions, will almost certainly give you interesting species among commoner migrant birds, and at these times of year a visit at any time of day could produce a later-arriving raptor.

Seawatching in spring or autumn could be attempted in similar conditions to those for passerine fall arrivals, and in the same winds. Provided there is visibility of at least 1 mile (1.6km), winds from south and west also give good results; winds from these directions do not have to be strong to produce birds. Onshore winds induce birds to fly close to shore. As shelter is lacking, take waterproof clothing for seawatches.

From Hannafore at West Looe, opposite Looe Island, try seawatching from a car in strong to gale-force south-westerly winds, especially if it has been blowing overnight and and is accompanied by reduced visibility. From early autumn onwards, this appears to be one of the few places to produce a variety of seabirds close (often very close) in winds from this quarter. Skuas, storm petrels and shearwaters are often involved.

ACCESS

For Rame, take the A374 from Torpoint to Antony, then the B3247, signposted to Millbrook. Follow the road for 1.9km (1.2 miles) to the T-junction near Tregantle, turn left and follow the road for 800m, then turn right onto the coast road to Rame. Along this route, check Whitsand Bay and seaward brakes; there are frequent pull-ins. There is a car park at **Rame Head (PL10 1HL, vibe.footballers.nods)**. Public footpaths along the coastline, mainly of even terrain but often muddy, allow you to cover all the best bird spots around Rame. From the car park you can follow the coast path to Penlee or out to the headland. Another good route is to Polhawn, where bushes surrounding the private old fort can be viewed from the footpath. Following the above track will bring you back to Rame Farm and Church. The narrow road from the church towards Penlee and the overgrown fort should be checked for migrants. A path leads from the fort to connect with the coastal track at **Penlee**. To reach the seawatching folly at Penlee, park in the car park **(PL10 1LN, outfit.power.butternut)** and take the path down to meet the South West Coast Path towards Penlee Point. Seawatch from the folly, which is accessed by climbing down a steep but short path, taking great care not to slip; alternatively, use the seats on the path above the folly.

For seawatching from Rame there is a path down to the rocks but it is slippery and awkward, so care must be taken. Watch from near the bottom of the slope, directly in line with the old chapel at the tip of the headland. Small numbers of most seabirds can be seen from here in both spring and autumn.

From Tregantle, continue west along B3247 coast road to **Portwrinkle (PL11 3BP, assorted.broom.continues)**; you can detour down to the village waterfront, where divers or grebes may be offshore. The main road is high above the sea, and a telescope is essential for checking waterbirds.

Drive to adjoining **Seaton (PL11 3JQ, hexes.executive.bakers)**. Beside the beach is a car park, adjacent to which are Alder trees and willows by a stream; check these for wintering Blackcap, Chiffchaff, Firecrest or passing migrants. To check the sea, walk from the car park left onto the raised concrete walkway. Stop and check at intervals until the whole of the bay to Millendreath (to the right) is visible. Seabirds may pass close to shore. Divers often gather in groups, but may be further out in line with Looe Island. A telescope is essential.

From Seaton to Looe, take Looe Hill for a mile (1.6km) then turn right and follow the road for 9.5 miles (15km) to join the B3253 for **Looe (PL13 1HN, plants.**

Cornwall

business.ramps). Checking the estuary and gulls in Looe harbour then, if mud is exposed, proceed to the seafront at **Hannafore (PL13 2DJ, lend.spouse.nuns)**, where parking on the waterfront road is allowed. Check the whole seashore and bay along this road up to where it becomes a dead end. Divers and grebes often shelter from winds in the lee of Looe Island and can be seen from the road.

CALENDAR

Resident: Shelduck, Cormorant, Little Egret, Grey Heron, Sparrowhawk, Buzzard, Grey Wagtail, Stonechat, Linnet, Cirl Bunting, Skylark and Raven.

December–February: Mostly Red-throated, Black-throated and Great Northern Divers, Great Crested Grebe, with occasional Slavonian, Black-necked and Red-necked; all begin to increase towards end of period, more Red-throated Divers arrive in numbers from February; Little Grebe and Curlew on Looe estuary; Eider, Common Scoter, occasional Velvet Scoter, Grey Plover, Turnstone, Purple Sandpiper, possibly Redshank, Greenshank, Green and Common Sandpiper; possibly Glaucous, Iceland, Ring-billed or Mediterranean Gull.

March–May: Increased numbers of Red-throated and Great Northern Divers to April; many fewer of each late in period and declining chance of grebes after mid-April; Glaucous or Iceland Gull possible throughout period; terns, especially Sandwich, pass throughout, peaking in April when other terns coast by; shearwaters, mainly Manx, skuas, Whimbrel, godwit, from April on; Black Redstart, Chiffchaff, Wheatear, mid-late March; Hobby, hirundines, wagtails, pipits, warblers, flycatchers and Redstart, later spring; maybe Ring Ouzel or Hoopoe.

June–July: Large numbers of holidaymakers make birdwatching difficult and the roads can be congested. Mostly resident and breeding birds, including Blackcap, Whitethroat, Chiffchaff and Goldcrest.

August–November: Return passage of seabirds, birds of prey and passerines from early August; Fulmar, shearwaters, skuas, terns, late August–October; harriers and Merlin, mostly mid-September–October; passerine movement peaks same months.

SITE CLUSTER: BODMIN MOOR AND CENTRAL CORNWALL

24 Siblyback and Colliford Lakes
25 Upper Fowey Valley, Dozmary Pool and Moorland
26 Crowdy Reservoir and Davidstow Airfield
26A Goss Moor

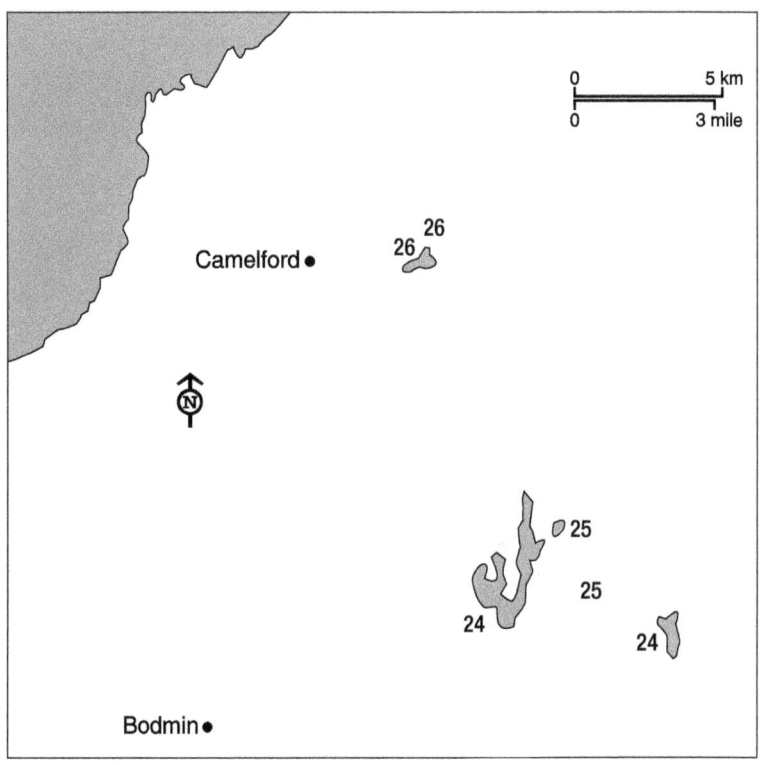

Cornwall

24 SIBLYBACK AND COLLIFORD LAKES

OS LANDRANGER MAP 201
OS grid ref: SX2371 (Siblyback); SX1772 (Colliford)
Postcode: **Siblyback** – PL14 6ER **Colliford** – PL30 4HE
what3words: **Siblyback** – slipping.topmost.midfield
Colliford – museum.flies.sprouting

HABITAT

Both of these reservoirs lie in wide, relatively shallow moorland valleys on the south-east edge of Bodmin Moor. At 360ha, Colliford Lake, which was filled in 1985, is one of the largest in the region. No water-based sports (other than angling) take place there, unlike at Siblyback Lake, thus leaving this large sheet of water undisturbed, an ideal place to create a nature reserve.

Known as Loveny, the reserve occupies the narrow northerly finger of water. This 136ha area contains willow carr at the bottom of a shallow valley; the valley sides are mostly rough pasture. Its most important role will be to provide breeding areas for a variety of birds, including waterfowl, waders and various passerines. Like Siblyback, Colliford's exposed location precludes the presence of tall broadleaved trees or lush bankside vegetation, making it suitable for birds requiring open habitat. The only tall trees are a group of conifers. Along the reservoir's western margin

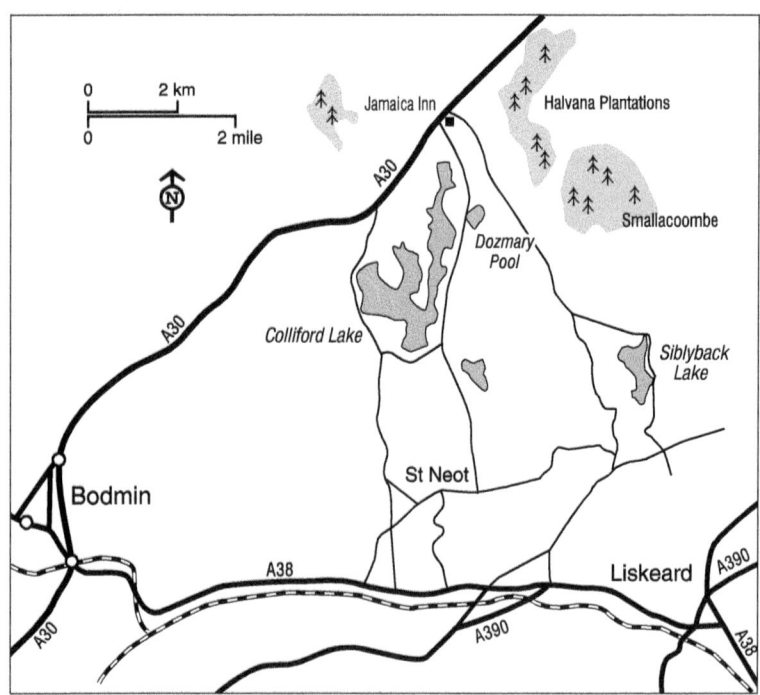

is one of Britain's largest colonies of Frog Orchids – at least 3,000. Among them are both Greater and Lesser Butterfly Orchids and the rare Moonwort Fern. About 10 species of dragonfly breed, unlike at the equally acidic Siblyback Lake, which has fewer of their habitat requirements.

Siblyback is a much smaller body of water, covering 57ha. The flooded valley in which it is set is surrounded by moorland and rough sheep pasture. The northern shore is shallow, with exposed mud becoming extensive in dry autumns as water levels drop. Along this perimeter are narrow areas of marshy vegetation, mostly rank grasses, bracken and bramble. As with all moorland reservoirs, the water is acidic, preventing a wide range of plants from growing. There are scattered willows, hawthorns and Rowans. Trout are the main fish stocked, the lake being extremely popular with anglers. Windsurfers, paddle-boarders and small sailing craft also use it.

SPECIES

Siblyback is noted chiefly for autumn waders and, to a lesser extent, winter wildfowl, including some scarcer species. During winter one of the most numerous birds is probably Mallard, usually 80 or so, with a few staying to breed. Coot numbers are low but there are always a few breeding pairs. Up to 30 Tufted Duck may winter, joined by Scaup, Goldeneye and Ring-necked Duck virtually every winter in recent years – and Lesser Scaup very occasionally. Three to five Smew, mostly red-heads, have been recorded at Siblyback in the past, and fellow sawbill Goosander is annual in twos and threes. Pochard, once regular here in winter, is now only occasionally seen. Dabbling ducks include small numbers of Teal and occasionally Wigeon. Little Grebe is present most of the year and occasionally a Red-necked Grebe will appear. Both Great Northern and Black-throated Divers have appeared here. Small parties of White-fronted Geese have visited, arrivals usually coinciding with hard weather elsewhere. Because there is no exposed mud in winter, when the water level is higher, most waders are then absent. A few Snipe frequent boggy margins and field edges, accompanied occasionally by the odd Jack Snipe or two. Flocks of Golden Plover and Lapwing also use the nearby fields, sometimes accompanied by Cattle Egret. Raptors wintering on the moor visit the area, no doubt attracted by the plover; Peregrine, Merlin and Hen Harrier are regular, and Red Kite is seen more regularly now.

As spring approaches, the avian population declines and changes. There are far fewer wildfowl, although Cormorant and Grey Heron still visit. Hirundines, especially Sand and House Martins, pause on passage, often in large feeding flocks, while Swift scream and fly over the water. A marsh tern, usually Black, could appear in summer plumage.

An ornithologically quiet summer gives way to a busier autumn as returning migrant waders are attracted to exposed mud. Wader numbers are never large, but apart from regular migrants, much less common waders such as Temminck's Stint, Red-necked Phalarope and an American vagrant Wilson's Phalarope have occurred. More routine annual visitors include both Ringed and Little Ringed Plovers, Little Stint, Pectoral Sandpiper, Dunlin, Curlew Sandpiper, Ruff, Redshank, Green, Wood and Common Sandpipers, and Curlew. Little Gulls, usually first-winter birds with blackish 'W' markings across the wings, pass through in ones and twos, as do Black Terns in dowdy grey-brown autumn plumage.

Colliford has shown potential for producing interesting birds, although some are the same individuals moving between this and other nearby waters. The same can

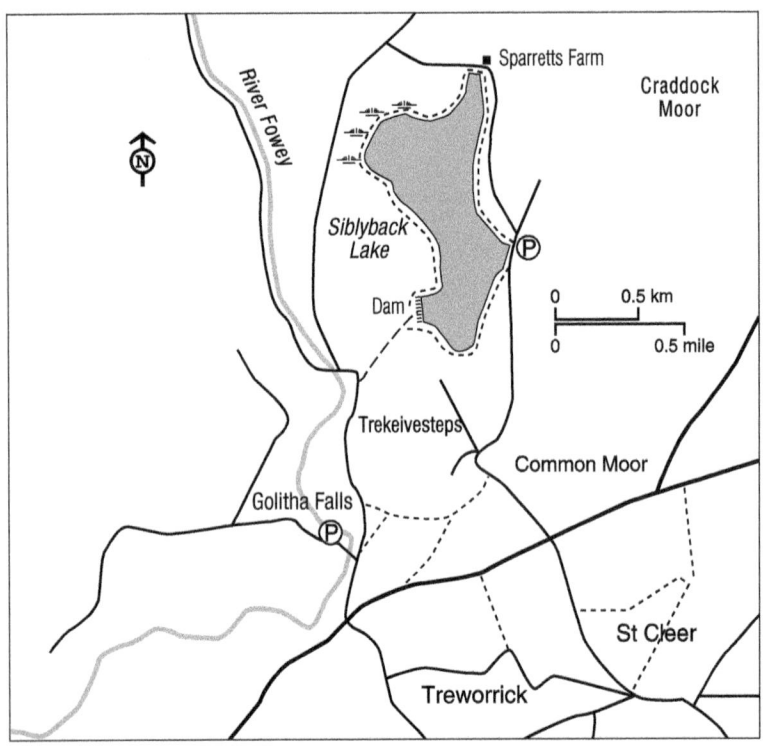

be said for birds flying across the lake's moorland surrounds, especially waders and raptors; thus, both reservoirs, historic Dozmary Pool, the Upper Fowey Valley and a huge tract of surrounding Bodmin moors now form a relatively easily accessible area where water and moorland birds may be encountered throughout.

Ducks used to visit Colliford in greater numbers than at Siblyback, and their decline is connected with a long series of mild winters. Major ongoing declines have been observed in duck numbers; Wigeon now average fewer than 20, Mallard around 30, while Pochard is a very rare visitor. Teal rarely reach 50 now, although the American form, Green-winged Teal – diagnosed by its vertical rather than horizontal white flank stripe – has also been seen here once. Rather surprisingly, there was also once a regular breeding pair of the usually coastal Shelduck. Diving Tufted Duck have also bred, albeit only a pair or two; they now number about a dozen in winter. Smew, Goosander and Goldeneye when present, which nowadays is only very occasionally, regularly move between sites. Coot are more static, but their numbers too have declined and breeding seems to have ceased. Unusually, Mute Swan has never occurred at Colliford.

As already stated, moorland waders such as Golden Plover and Lapwing roam the general area in winter, changing sites as circumstances dictate. Breeding waders once included a few pairs of Lapwing and Curlew, and probably Snipe, but breeding reports, if any, are now withheld. Raptors can include both Hen and Marsh Harriers as well as the occasional Short-eared Owl. Up to 20 pairs of Black-headed Gull once bred, although numbers were sporadic as was their success; this was one of only two colonies in our region, the other being at Crowdy Reservoir (site 26).

Unusual winter visits by Great Northern Diver occur, and Black-necked Grebe and Whooper Swan are possible.

Spring seems to have seen less coverage by birdwatchers; interesting birds noted have included Black Tern, Osprey, and three Spoonbill together. Surrounding cover has produced both Woodchat and Red-backed Shrikes and Wryneck.

Autumn waders have mostly been commoner species, including Greenshank, Green and Common Sandpipers, Little Stint and Curlew Sandpiper in small numbers. Stone-curlew and rarer species such as Dotterel and Pectoral and Buff-breasted Sandpipers have visited.

TIMING

The time of day is not critical, although mornings and evenings at Siblyback should have less human disturbance. This is usually minimal at Colliford. Hard winter weather may bring further interesting species. For autumn waders, dry conditions expose muddy margins which in very wet years may not exist. Winter afternoon gull roosts at Colliford can be interesting. Calm conditions allow easier viewing and birds are not driven to seek shelter.

ACCESS

From the A38 in Liskeard, to reach **Siblyback Lake** take the A390 from the town centre to the outer edge of town. Branch off onto the B3254 (where signposted to Siblyback Lake) for about 1 mile (1.6km). Leave the B road and take the road to St Cleer (also signposted for Siblyback). Just past the village turn right. At the road junction about 1 mile (1.6km) further on, take the minor road opposite which leads to the lake (again signposted). Birders can scan the lake from the large car park (fee required), where there are toilets (including disabled). The route around the lake is approximately 3 miles (4.8km); it is possible to walk or use a hired mobility scooter. Take the left path from the car park to reach the dam and continue on this path to the opposite shore. Alternatively, walk to the right, past dinghies on the lower edge of the car park, through a gate and continue around this side of the lake. Both routes lead to the shallower north end of the reservoir.

Windsurfers, paddle-boarders and boats are officially restricted from entry to the shallow end of Siblyback, but fishermen are not. Most birdwatchers approach this area from the car park side as ducks and waders mainly favour the shallower end.

Colliford Lake is most easily approached from the A30 Launceston to Bodmin road, where minor roads circle the reservoir. Entry is directly opposite the Jamaica Inn. This entrance is very close to that taken for the Upper Fowey Valley. Toilet facilities at the main Simonstone car park cater for the disabled. Three car parks along the western edge, and pull-in spots along the perimeter road, also allow some coverage by disabled birdwatchers. Waymarked moorland walks radiate from the main car park, although these can be muddy.

Much of Colliford can be viewed from various points on the surrounding roads. There are some rough footpaths, often used by anglers, but it is no longer possible to walk the entire perimeter of the reservoir.

For access between the two reservoirs, several minor roads can be taken from Siblyback signposted to St Neot, near which a minor road is signposted to Colliford. Probably the most direct and scenic route is to follow the road through the Upper Fowey Valley to Bolventor on the A30 (see site 25). Take the minor road from here to Dozmary Pool and the northern tip of Colliford Lake.

Cornwall

CALENDAR

Resident: Little Grebe, Coot, Mallard, Tufted Duck.

December–February: Geese, probably White-fronted and possibly Pink-footed, and wild swans are possible in hard weather; Teal, Wigeon, Tufted, possibly Lesser Scaup, Goldeneye, Smew, Goosander, possibly a 'sea grebe' or diver; maybe wintering raptors from the moors; Snipe and Jack Snipe; Golden Plover and Lapwing in surrounding fields; gulls, mainly Black-headed and Lesser Black-backed but Yellow-legged and Caspian are possible, and both Glaucous and Iceland Gulls have been reported in the evening roost near the dam.

March–May: Winter visitors mainly depart by end March; perhaps a stray passage diver, grebe or duck; perhaps a marsh tern, hirundines and Swift, late April and especially May.

June–July: Breeding species, including a few pairs of Whinchat and Sedge and Garden Warblers.

August–November: Waders arriving from early August, peaking late August and September, can include Pectoral and Wood Sandpipers, and both American Golden and Pacific Golden Plovers have been identified; Little Gull and Black Tern from late August; Golden Plover arrive from mid-September, waterfowl from mid-November.

25 UPPER FOWEY VALLEY, DOZMARY POOL AND MOORLAND

OS LANDRANGER MAP 201
OS grid ref: SX2174
Postcode: **Upper Fowey Valley** – PL14 6PD **Dozmary Pool** – PL14 6PY
what3words: **Upper Fowey Valley** – losses.alright.smuggled
Dozmary Pool – aside.polygraph.ruling

HABITAT

On the south-east fringe of Bodmin Moor, the Upper Fowey Valley (sometimes known as Lamelgate or Bolventor) is near the head of the long River Fowey. The valley is mostly shallow-sided and features several different habitats in miniature. Localised and uncommon wild flowers include Pale Butterwort, Lesser Bladderwort and Ivy-leaved Bellflower. The fast-flowing river is lined by Alder, willow and Blackthorn trees. There are large areas of peat bog, including some small, deep pools with sundews, including Long-leaved Sundew. Localised insects include Marsh Fritillary butterfly and Narrow-bordered Bee-hawkmoth. Drier areas support rank grasses, various heathers and patches of gorse. Lichen growth is varied and luxuriant in the moist, clean air. Surrounding farmland is mostly rough sheep pasture. Groups of large trees in the valley are mostly Beech. The huge Smallacombe forestry plantations can be seen above the hill crest.

Dozmary Pool, over the hilltop westwards, is naturally formed, circular, deep in the middle, with open perimeters. Higher moorland surrounding Dozmary has

Cornwall

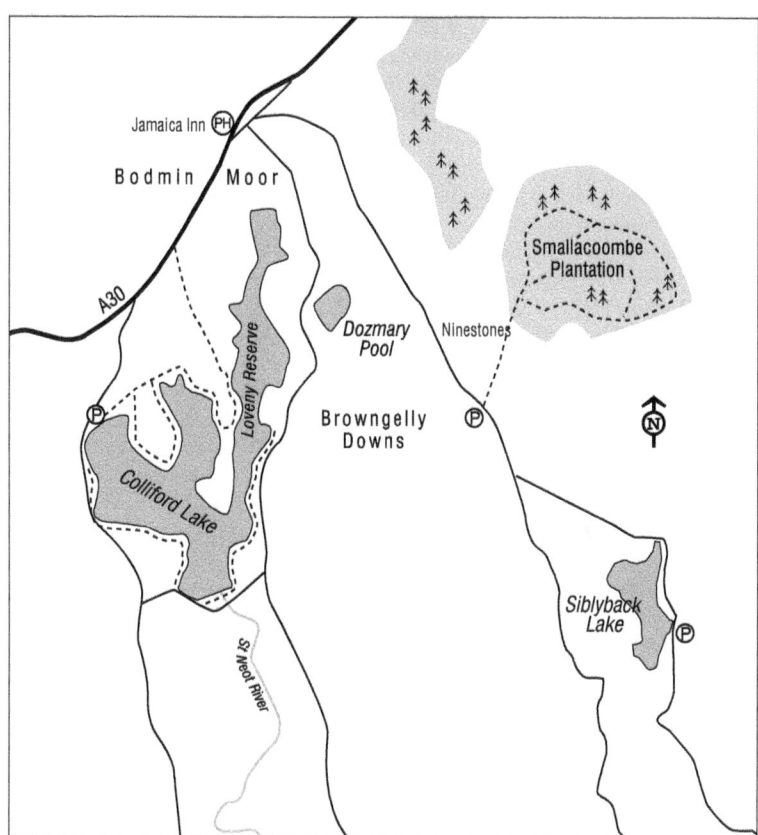

much the same vegetation as drier parts of the Fowey Valley. Lower-lying areas remain wetter, with patches of willow in the centre. The pool lies within sight of Brown Willy, at 423m the highest point on Bodmin Moor. A few hundred metres west of Dozmary Pool is the Loveny Reserve at the north-east tip of Colliford Lake.

SPECIES

There are no large flocks of birds, save for the hordes of wintering Starlings noisily searching for worms and leatherjackets on short sheep pasture. They are usually joined by winter thrushes, in particular several hundred Fieldfares. Resident specialities in the valley are Dipper and Willow Tit, while Raven can be seen in groups of 10 or more in winter. Kingfishers may breed; one or two remain through winter but may die off in severe weather. Many common lowland passerines such as Treecreeper can be found in this scenic moorland valley, alongside species such as summering Grasshopper Warbler. This mix enables you to see many kinds of birds in a small area.

In winter, fewer species inhabit the valley, but birds of prey (such as Hen Harrier or Merlin) might pass through on hunting trips. Moorland surrounding Dozmary Pool can also support interesting winter raptors, including Hen Harrier, Peregrine and Merlin, possibly Short-eared Owl and a Goshawk occasionally. Dozmary Pool is uninviting to most wildfowl, but small numbers of ducks come and go throughout the winter, and a dozen or so Tufted Duck are regular, as are Mallard. Goosander, Pochard, Goldeneye and Scaup visit very occasionally, as do small numbers of dabbling ducks, such as Wigeon and Teal. Scaup, Lesser Scaup and up to eight Ring-necked Duck have been recorded, and Smew and Long-tailed Duck have become regular visitors in recent years, almost certainly having moved off one of the nearby reservoirs. Coot are often present, but Bewick's and Whooper Swans are virtually never seen here now. Flocks of up to 5,000 Golden Plover occur during winter and have included both American and Pacific Golden. Snipe inhabit boggy margins and small numbers of commoner gulls usually roost; unusual for the region, there is a winter night roost of 50–100 Lesser Black-backed Gulls, arriving from late afternoon. In common with other species, they may also use other moorland waters, such as Siblyback and Colliford.

Spring in the valley echoes with the cascading notes of Willow Warbler song. Similar-looking Chiffchaffs are also present, their song enabling a ready distinction between the two, and both species breed. Blackcap and Garden and Grasshopper Warblers breed in very small numbers, as do a few pairs of Sedge Warbler, Wheatear and Redstart. Spotted Flycatcher and Whinchat have bred in the past but are somewhat sporadic now. A small number of Cuckoos parasitise nesting Meadow Pipits. Snipe are present throughout the year and possibly breed. A few Nightjars breed in scrubland and newly replanted forestry areas in Smallacombe and Halvana plantations. Good numbers of Lesser Redpoll have also bred in those plantations, ranging into the valley to feed, but their numbers fluctuate annually. Siskin, previously unrecorded as breeders in Cornwall, are now found annually in small numbers, and Crossbills are sometimes seen and have bred. Marshy areas and scrubby trees around Dozmary Pool are inhabited by Tree and Meadow Pipits, attended by Cuckoos, and Willow Warbler and Chiffchaff also nest there.

Late spring has produced one or two rare migrants, including Black-eared Wheatear and Red-footed Falcon. Increased watching throughout this under-watched and undervalued area would undoubtedly produce more scarce and rare species.

Summer becomes quieter, as birds settle into a more secretive breeding routine; lush marsh growth aids the naturally furtive behaviour of breeding waders. At the end of summer, families of young birds move around the area. Soon most summer visitors will move off and autumn may bring a few migrants, perhaps with an uncommon raptor such as Montagu's Harrier.

TIMING

For a general visit any time of day will suffice, although in late spring and summer the earlier the better to avoid disturbance from daytrippers. Birds have to be very active in the morning, ensuring for themselves and their mates or young a plentiful food supply to replace energy lost overnight, and they are more easily seen then. There is also a last flurry of activity before nightfall, when the crepuscular hunting Barn Owl and singing Grasshopper Warbler are more active.

Hard weather may produce more or different waterbirds on Dozmary Pool. Raptors are best seen an hour or two before dusk as they begin to congregate near roosting areas, becoming active again and attempting to kill and feed before nightfall.

ACCESS

From the A390 at Liskeard take the same route as for Siblyback Lake (site 24). At the crossroads to the lake, turn left onto the road signposted to Launceston. A few hundred metres down the road, take a sharp turn to the right signposted to Draynes and Bolventor. Follow this road until the hamlet of Lamelgate; on crossing the humpbacked bridge you have entered the valley, which is 3 miles (4.8km) long. A road runs the entire length, with several pull-ins. Most of the valley can be seen from, or near, a car.

Access to Smallacombe plantation is from the track at Nine Stones bridge in the valley; no vehicles are allowed up this road. The Bolventor road will also take you to Colliford Lake. Approach the valley from the A30 to Bolventor, directly opposite the Jamaica Inn public house. For Dozmary and the north-east end of Colliford Reservoir, turn off the A30 at Bolventor on the opposite side of the inn, along a minor road for about 1.5 miles (2.4km). The road skirts the pool; a rather rough track can be walked to the water's edge (this can be very wet). Any areas allowing a good view over moors either side of the pool are suitable to search for passing raptors. Halvana Plantation is open to the public and accessed by leaving the A30 at Five Lanes, taking the underpass below the A30 and following this road for 2 miles (3.2km). Limited parking is available, taking care not to block gateways.

CALENDAR

Resident: Sparrowhawk, Buzzard, Snipe, Barn Owl, Green and Great Spotted Woodpeckers, Grey Wagtail, Dipper, Marsh, Willow and Coal Tits, Raven, Reed Bunting, Siskin, Lesser Redpoll.

December–February: Teal, Wigeon, Tufted Duck; possibly Scaup, Lesser Scaup, Ring-necked Duck and Goosander; Hen Harrier, Peregrine, Merlin, possibly Short-eared Owl; winter thrushes.

March–May: A few raptors may linger into April; possibly Lapwing; Cuckoo, Sand Martin, Tree Pipit, Garden and Grasshopper Warblers, Blackcap, Willow Warbler, Chiffchaff, Wheatear, Redstart; Whinchat possible in small numbers; chance of an unusual migrant late in period.

June–July: Breeding species include Nightjar, Willow Tit and possibly Crossbill some years.

August–November: Breeding species flock early in the period; migrants begin to depart in August; Crossbill regular; passage migrants may occur; winter visitors start to return towards end of period.

26 CROWDY RESERVOIR AND DAVIDSTOW AIRFIELD

> OS LANDRANGER MAP 200
> OS grid ref: SX1483
> Postcode: **Crowdy Reservoir** – PL32 9XJ
> **Davidstow Airfield** – PL32 9YF
> **Rough Tor** – PL30 4PQ
> what3words: **Crowdy Reservoir** – grunt.mealtime.lime
> **Davidstow Airfield** – pioneered.spent.vouch
> **Rough Tor** – judge.manliness.refilled

HABITAT

Near Camelford town, these exposed moorland sites are close together, separated in part by maturing Forestry England conifers. The disused airfield consists of poorly drained short turf, grazed by livestock, with temporary surface water after rain. Remnants of the tarmac runways are still passable and the control tower, although ruined, still stands. The 47ha Crowdy Reservoir has a greater area of marginal bog than the other Cornish moorland reservoirs, even when water levels are high. Large areas of mud are exposed when levels are lower. There are several small islands near the shallow end (furthest from the dam) where English Sundew, Long-leaved Sundew and Pale Butterwort grow in profusion. The area, prone to high winds and thick mists, is often inhospitable in winter.

SPECIES

The main attraction for birdwatchers is the chance of good views of ducks, waders and raptors, including rarer species. During late autumn and winter, flocks of up to 5,000 Golden Plover occur regularly; Lapwing (usually totalling around 300) can also be seen, especially when hard weather persists elsewhere. Apart from high numbers of these plovers, there are few waders in winter. A wintering Woodcock may be flushed from the road near the reservoir and small numbers of Snipe are present at most times of year.

Little and Great Crested Grebes are resident in small numbers, only occasionally breeding. Other grebes and divers are very rare (fewer than Siblyback) and several years may elapse without any. Two or three Cormorants and Grey Herons are usual. Duck species and numbers are also quite restricted. Mallard and Teal both peak in autumn, a few pairs of Mallard once bred, but sadly numbers of both species have declined with only around a dozen Mallard and 40 Teal present in winter. Numbers of most other ducks are tiny. Gadwall, Wigeon and Pintail are now seldom seen, but Tufted Duck may reach 15 in late summer. Goosander may be present in winter but Smew, once regular, is now extremely rare. Other diving ducks are occasionally noted, including Scaup and the very scarce Ring-necked Duck from North America. 'Grey' geese, such as Pink-footed and White-fronted, have been recorded from time to time.

Unlike most reservoirs in the region, where spring sees the disappearance of most birds, several arrive to breed. A few pairs of Lapwing and Reed, Sedge and Grasshopper Warblers are summer residents. Black-headed Gull used to breed, fledging up to 50 young, but in recent years only a couple of pairs have bred. Other

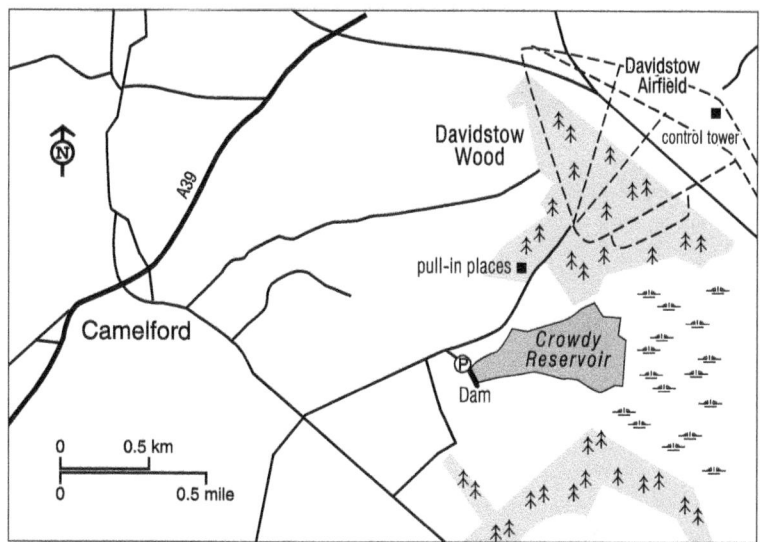

commoner gulls bathe and preen, with up to 100 Herring Gull being about normal in June and July, while Lesser Black-backed Gull can reach 800 in late autumn. A summer-plumaged Franklin's Gull was once seen. Small numbers of waders pass through in spring. Whimbrel are regular in small numbers and easily seen. Not so regular are mountain-nesting Dotterel, small parties of which have occasionally lingered on the airfield for a few days. They are more regular on return passage in autumn in ones and twos, often among Golden Plover. Montagu's Harrier has visited on spring passage.

Autumn draws the region's more active birdwatchers, often finding interesting migrants and rarities. One of the earliest flocks of Golden Plover in the region congregates here, attracting other related species. Rare, but recorded on several occasions, is American Golden Plover; difficult to identify unless you are fairly expert, it often resembles a miniature Grey Plover, which also occasionally turns up. Another American wader, the smaller Buff-breasted Sandpiper, is seen most years; when present, it often associates with plover flocks on the airfield. Unfortunately, Buff-breasted closely resembles a small female Ruff (called a reeve), which may also mingle with the Golden Plover. An Asiatic Sociable Plover has also been recorded on the airfield, as has a Black-winged Pratincole.

Small numbers of commoner migrant waders drop in on the reservoir's muddy margins, but also use Davidstow if disturbed. These can include up to 50 Ringed Plover, while Dunlin attain small flocks of around a dozen birds; Little Stint and Curlew Sandpiper are noted occasionally most autumns. The reservoir and airfield have had a fair share of American waders: Pectoral, White-rumped and Baird's Sandpipers, Wilson's Phalarope and Long-billed Dowitcher have all been recorded. (It should be noted that there is often interchange by many species between the two sites if there is disturbance at one or conditions become more favourable at the other; birds do not necessarily stick to their normal habitat.) Black Terns are occasional autumn visitors to the lake, often singly or in small numbers, and have passed through in spring.

Another group of species that ranges over both sites, as well as surrounding moorland, is birds of prey. Food supplies, in the form of flocking birds, are an obvious attraction. All three common resident raptors are here, with others particularly during autumn and winter. Several reliable records of the often misidentified Goshawk have come from here, with adults, immatures, males and females accurately described. Hen Harriers, present on nearby moorland, occasionally overfly the area, their wings held in a shallow 'V' as they glide; females and immatures (ringtails) are more common than adult males. Peregrines arrive in early autumn and may not depart until late spring. Dashing Merlins arrive later and normally depart earlier, ranging more widely. Hobbies have been seen in spring and autumn as irregular passage migrants. One or two Marsh Harriers pass through most years.

The woodland area between Davidstow and Crowdy can hold flocks of Crossbill, Siskin and Redpoll, especially in winter when Starling numbers can reach one million; Starling murmurations are spectacular and the noise incredible, and they attract raptors as well as human admirers!

Numbers of resident or breeding passerines are swollen in autumn by migrants, including Meadow Pipits and Skylarks. Other open-ground species such as Wheatears, which breed in small numbers nearby, become more numerous. Often, Pied (including White) and Yellow Wagtails assemble on the runways in autumn, allowing close comparison of the species. In late autumn, two uncommon open-ground buntings, Snow and Lapland, are occasional visitors to the outer margins of the airfield in ones and twos.

TIMING

On fine weekends, the airfield often suffers disturbance from model aircraft and gliders, so an early morning or late afternoon visit is preferable. The smaller American waders are unconcerned; neither of these activities scares them off. Other birds move to a quieter corner, while some leave the vicinity completely, a few alighting by the reservoir. Plovers usually leave completely. Towards evening in autumn, disturbed birds, including plovers, and those that have fed elsewhere, often return to roost. This can be a rewarding time, with raptors also more active. Barn Owls and other birds of prey are sometimes attracted to the vast Starling flocks. The murmurations can be seen throughout the winter but are particularly good in November and December.

Winds or thick mist may be localised here, or worse than elsewhere, and until your arrival you may have no real indication of the conditions. Hard weather elsewhere may increase species and numbers but, if conditions are really bad, almost certainly there will be a marked decrease. Fishermen sometimes disturb the birds but dog walkers have created more recent disturbances.

ACCESS

From the A39 at Camelford, well signposted minor roads lead to the site. A road runs lengthways through the airfield (with several places where you can pull off). From the A30 take the Altarnun turn, following minor roads after that village. From the A395, several minor roads will bring you to the road running the length of the airfield; the route from the A30 also leads to this same airfield road. The slightly raised road, along the flat airfield area (beware of wandering sheep), has pull-offs on either side which lead onto the old runways across the grass; you will need these to cover the whole area adequately.

Drive along both sides of all runways slowly, stopping every 100m or so to scan for birds; this allows close approach to species that would never permit such closeness on foot. On finding your quarry, it is essential to watch from the car. Very good views will then be obtained without disturbing it – or preventing others from seeing it. Areas near the old control tower appear favoured by many birds. Pools are attractive for some species. Raptors may be seen anywhere.

For the reservoir, from the airfield road follow the signpost to Crowdy Dam where the open water can be checked from the car park for waterfowl or birds flying over, all of which can be seen reasonably well especially if using a telescope. For closer access, walk from the car park to the water's edge and work your way along the northern shore; this is the best way of checking for waders.

The Starling murmuration can be watched from the roadside near Rough Tor car park; this is reached by turning left out of the Crowdy Dam car park and taking the first left turn onto Rough Tor Road to the car park at the end.

Davidstow, although bleak in winter, lends itself to visits by the elderly and disabled because of vehicular access to the airfield and the ease of overlooking Crowdy Reservoir from the dam car park.

CALENDAR

Resident: Little and Great Crested Grebes, Grey Heron, Sparrowhawk, Buzzard, Black-headed Gull, Great Spotted Woodpecker, Coal Tit, Raven.

December–February: Possibly wild swans; Teal, Tufted Duck, possible Goldeneye and Goosander; dabbling and other diving ducks in ones and twos, occasionally; Hen Harrier, Peregrine, Merlin, Golden Plover, Lapwing, possibly Ruff and Woodcock, Snipe; Fieldfare, Redwing, vast numbers of Starlings at roost.

March–May: Most winter visitors have departed by April; Wheatear arrives from mid-March, Whimbrel from mid-April, Dotterel (rarely) and Ruff in late April–May; chance of Montagu's Harrier, Hobby or Black Tern from end of April; Cuckoo, maybe Short-eared Owl.

June–July: Breeding species may include Wheatear, Reed, Sedge and Grasshopper Warblers, Spotted Flycatcher and Redstart; first returning waders, e.g. Redshank, towards end of period; a few pairs of Black-headed Gull.

August–November: Waders gradually increase in number and variety, with most seen on the reservoir early in period, e.g., shanks and sandpipers; a few hundred Golden Plover from early September; most other waders begin to peak through September; Black Tern; possibly Peregrine and Goshawk; gull roosts with Lesser Black-backed Gulls and occasional Yellow-legged Gull; Merlin arrive in early October, perhaps Snow and Lapland Buntings; Golden Plover, Lapwing and Snipe increase towards end of period; winter thrushes begin to arrive, as can Hen and Marsh Harriers and Short-eared Owl.

Cornwall

26A GOSS MOOR

> OS LANDRANGER MAP 200
> OS grid ref: SX9663
> Postcode: **Electric Sub-station End** – PL26 8BY
> **Tregoss Moor** – PL26 8NJ
> **Level Crossing End** – PL26 8NF
> what3words: **Electric Sub-station End** – crinkled.foot.romantics
> **Tregoss Moor** – dozen.partly.printout
> **Level Crossing End** – suggested.tunnel.flick

HABITAT

An area of rather high, poorly drained rough ground in central Cornwall. Small trees, especially willows, bushes and heather are interspersed with small fields. Goss Moor is a National Nature Reserve, a Site of Special Scientific Interest and a Special Area of Conservation because of the threatened habitat and its Willow Tit population. Cornish Moneywort, Yellow Centaury, Pillwort and Marsh Clubmoss are some of the rarer plants found at the site. Insects of note include Small Red Damselfly.

SPECIES

Among marshy pools and willows on Goss Moor, Willow Tit is resident, wintering Reed Bunting flocks may contain a rare Little Bunting, while Merlin, Short-eared Owl, Woodcock and Lesser Redpoll may occur. A Great Grey Shrike stayed

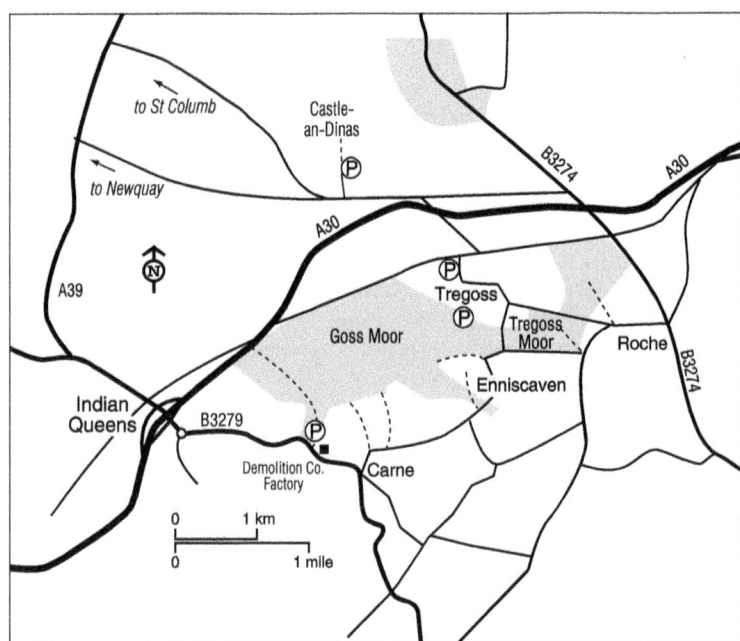

several weeks one spring. Willow Tit, Grasshopper and Garden Warblers, Nightjar and Cuckoo all still breed in the area. Rarer species have included Black Kite, Hoopoe and Bee-eater.

TIMING
Still days are best for visiting the Moor.

ACCESS
Approaching from Bodmin, travelling west, leave the new A30 dual carriageway at the Cornwall Services exit and take the B3274 off the roundabout. Continue through Victoria and follow the B3274 for 1.7 miles (2.7km) to Tregoss Moor car park. The level crossing car park is reached by continuing along the old A30 under the railway bridge. Alternatively, take the exit to St Dennis off the A30, the first exit off the slip road onto the B3279, then at the next roundabout take the first exit to follow the B3279 for 1.1 miles (1.8km) to the car park on the left. Goss Moor can be crossed by various footpaths, including a 7-mile (12km) circular route through the 480ha reserve, which can be accessed from any of the car parks suggested. Green and white Goss Moor Trail signs at most road junctions in the area help with access.

This site allows ease of viewing for the less physically mobile; many of the paths are now flat and surfaced to accommodate wheelchairs and/or mobility scooters.

CALENDAR
Resident: Willow Tit, Reed Bunting.

December–February: Chance of Cattle Egret, Glossy Ibis, Woodcock, Barn and Short-eared Owls, Merlin, Hen Harrier and winter thrushes and finches.

March–May: Garganey or Hobby occasionally arrive.

June–July: Breeding species may include Whitethroat, Grasshopper, Willow and Garden Warblers, Cuckoo, Nightjar and Willow Tit; Hoopoe and Bee-eater have occurred.

August–November: Towards end of period, returning winter thrushes, finches and buntings, possibly Merlin.

27 PAR BEACH AND POOL

OS LANDRANGER MAP 200
OS grid ref: SX0853
Postcode: PL24 2AS
what3words: punctual.synthetic.tripling

HABITAT
Par Sands Beach forms part of St Austell Bay on the mid-south Cornish coastline. It has a developed harbour waterfront on one side, the large industrial buildings

projecting incongruously into the scene. Par has three main centres of interest: a relatively small freshwater pool (set behind low sand dunes), a wide shallow sandy beach and the partly sheltered sea offshore.

Par Beach Pool is the single most important area of fresh water here, being about 1ha in extent. The pool has mostly open banks but with a fringe of reeds at the back and along one side. A caravan site is adjacent, with houses nearby. During summer the area is a busy tourist resort.

The sandy margins of the pool are one of only two known sites for Mossy Stonecrop in the region. The general area, including the dunes, is of great botanical interest. Owing to the brackish nature of the pool, the only odonate to breed here is Blue-tailed Damselfly. Eighteen species of butterfly breed here, including Dingy Skipper.

The dunes and pool are a Local Nature Reserve.

SPECIES

This site offers much of interest during winter and spring, and autumn also produces interesting birds at the pool, particularly elusive and rare reedbed

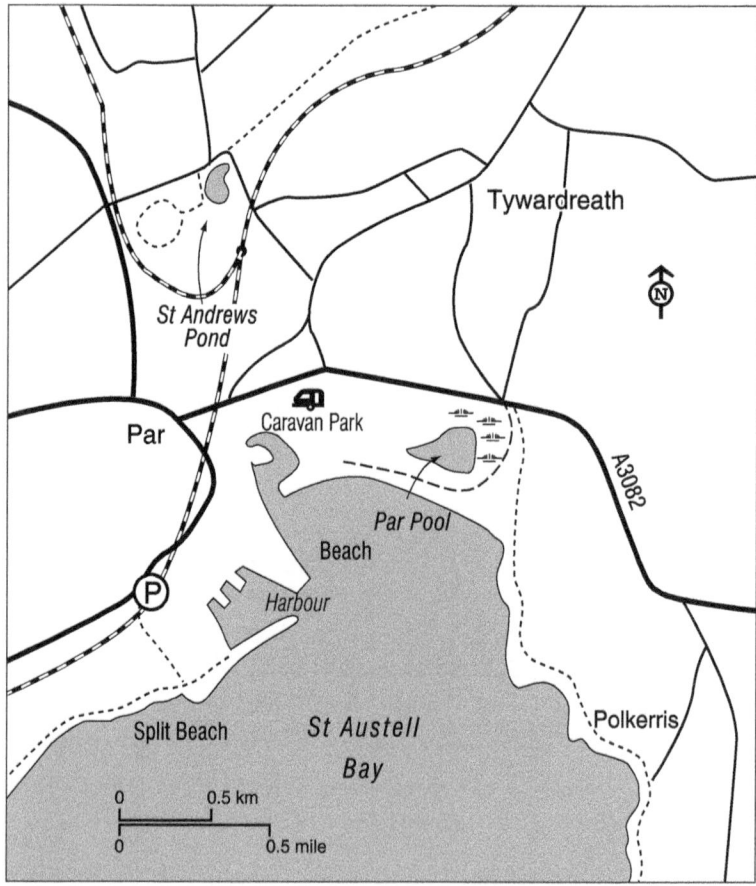

species (mainly discovered by ringers), such as the cryptically patterned Bittern, Spotted Crake and the plain-plumaged Savi's Warbler. Reedbeds, even small ones, are often invaluable as roost sites. Par is no exception, being well used by autumn's departing migrants. Swallows gather at dusk, along with Pied (including the attractive, grey-backed continental White form) and Yellow Wagtails in varying numbers. Pied Wagtails stay on with a few Reed Buntings, and noisy Starlings sometimes roost during winter.

Apart from resident Canada Geese, which can number up to 450 at times, with odd Mute Swans, Mallards and a bizarre mixture of feral ducks and Moorhens, a few pairs of Reed Warbler, a couple of pairs of Sedge Warbler and at least one pair of Cetti's Warbler breed in and around the reedbed. Three Night Herons once visited the poolside together.

As winter sets in, a variety of ducks arrive, mostly in small numbers. Diving Pochard, once common here, are now rare visitors along with small numbers of Tufted Duck. Mallard number about 100, and there is a handful of Coot. These species make up the bulk of waterfowl, with other ducks present only in very small numbers; perhaps Gadwall or Shoveler may arrive, or a few Scaup and Goldeneye. Little Grebe can be watched reappearing rapidly after a short dive; once up to 20 could be seen but they have become much scarcer.

Gulls inhabit the area in very large numbers, using the pool to bathe, drink and shelter, and taking advantage of a copious food supply laid on by residents – or birdwatchers trying to entice a Ring-billed Gull to feed from their hand! This American gull turned up here annually for many years in the past but only rarely in recent times. Black-headed and Herring Gulls are attracted to human environs generally; among them can be Common and Great Black-backed Gulls in varying numbers. Fewer Lesser Black-backed Gulls stay to winter, but by winter's end start arriving back from West African waters, assembling on the beach before moving off to their breeding grounds. Less usual gull species appear virtually annually, including Yellow-legged, Glaucous, Iceland, Mediterranean and Little, all mostly in immature plumages. They present a challenge when one or two of them may be settled among a tightly packed flock of similar commoner birds, sometimes a thousand strong.

Waders are few in winter. Surprisingly, numbers of Sanderling on this sandy beach hardly attain double figures, while Turnstone can number more than 30. The most common wader is Oystercatcher with more than 50 being regular (autumn passage may see more than 200 present). Purple Sandpiper is an occasional visitor in winter and on spring passage, as are Ringed Plover and Dunlin. A few Grey Plover may arrive, aptly named at this season. Unusual waders are few, although Curlew Sandpiper and Little Stint are possible; Wood and Green Sandpiper and Spotted Redshank may also stop over. Little Ringed Plover has visited, and so has the much rarer Kentish Plover (several times) during later spring. Once, this season also produced a group of four Black-winged Stilt flying in off the sea. Spring is also the season to expect flocks of migrating Whimbrel to drop in to rest. Terns also visit, pausing to fish, a bonus in a county not renowned for spring arrivals of this group. Scarcer species such as Little or maybe even Roseate Terns have occurred in small numbers, often with larger numbers of Sandwich Tern. Autumn return passage often brings similar numbers and species. A Forster's Tern from North America was an exceptional sighting.

The bay poses observation problems, being wide and not easily overlooked; however, the clifftop walk along the eastern edge offers your best chance of seeing over the further parts of the bay, with some species preferring this side. Numbers of other divers, grebes or seaducks are generally low, although Great Northern Diver can reach 25 and Black-throated up to 10; Red-throated Diver wanders into the bay only occasionally. Common Scoter can assemble in small flocks, sometimes containing a few Velvet Scoter. Eider appear in late July, but Slavonian and Red-necked Grebes are rare here.

TIMING

At such an exposed coastal site, calm conditions are obviously an advantage to watch passive gatherings. Strong westerly or southerly winds have no history of producing instant passage in this large bay, although they could encourage birds to seek relative shelter. In rough seas any divers, grebes or seaducks may be hard to see unless close inshore. During strong easterlies, the eastern (leeward) side of the bay is quite sheltered, providing refuge for waterbirds. Southerly winds in spring might encourage terns and some waders to track close to the English side of the Channel while migrating eastwards.

At Spit Beach there is a high-tide roost, particularly favoured by waders and terns at the appropriate seasons. Hard winter weather usually increases both numbers and species. Flat, overcast light is best; glare from a low winter sun can make viewing over the sea problematic.

ACCESS

The A3082 passes close by Par's beaches and pool; take the minor road sign-posted to Par Sands Holiday Park, the entrance of which is immediately west of the Ship Inn, leading to parking places beside the pool and overlooking the beach, while allowing unrestricted access for the disabled.

Note: Public access is allowed over this privately owned road (a charge is imposed during summer). There are accessible toilets for the disabled here.

For roosting waders and terns at high tide at Spit Beach, park in the free public car park behind the harbour (beside the A3082). A public footpath runs to Spit Beach. Birds also roost on the nearby harbour wall and can be viewed by walking towards it on the footpath, but there is no disabled person's access; there is also no public access into the busy, private dock.

A public footpath runs along low cliffs on the eastern shore, joined near the edge of the beach towards Kilmarth; the walk continues to Polkerris, about 1 mile (1.6km) away. In winter, this walk can produce finch flocks and allows uninterrupted viewing over the bay.

CALENDAR

Resident: Mute Swan, Mallard, Moorhen, Water Rail (has bred), Rock Pipit, Kingfisher, Grey Heron and Dipper.

December–February: wintering Little Grebe and Coot; Tufted Duck, occasional Pochard, Gadwall, Shoveler, single Scaup occasionally; Mediterranean Gull is regular and other gulls of interest could include Ring-billed, Glaucous or Iceland; a few Purple Sandpipers among commoner waders; Lesser Black-backed Gull increases towards the end of January; divers, grebes and seaducks in small numbers; small flocks of Siskin and Redpoll in trees behind pool, where wintering Yellow-browed Warbler has occurred.

March–May: Garganey is annual; wintering gull numbers decrease, but Lesser Black-backed may increase and Iceland and Little Gulls may arrive; Great Northern and Black-throated Divers usually increase, possibly in summer plumage; terns begin to arrive, April, with scarcer terns mostly May; Whimbrel and Purple Sandpiper can arrive throughout; chance of Kentish Plover; Reed and Sedge Warblers breed.

June–July: Tourist season, extremely busy, no special interest.

August–November: The reedbed may produce a rarity and hosts roosts of wagtails, Swallows and Starlings; early part of period sees terns passing through the bay; waders can include Curlew Sandpiper, Little Stint and Green Sandpiper; wintering species arrive in greater numbers towards end of period; Cattle Egret may be seen going to roost.

27A PORTHPEAN, ST AUSTELL BAY AND PENTEWAN

OS LANDRANGER MAP 204
OS grid ref: SX0350
Postcode: **Lower Porthpean** – PL26 6AX **Pentewan**– PL26 6BX
what3words: **Lower Porthpean** – stored.salutes.disposing
Pentewan – butterfly.overhear.payer

HABITAT

This southern section of St Austell Bay is wilder and more exposed to the elements, but also encompasses a small, easily viewable cove with an intermixed sandy and rocky foreshore. High footpath vantage points allow checking along a wide stretch of this part of the bay, not possible from the Par area. Pentewan is just a little further along the coast, and there the east-facing sandy beach can be viewed from sea level, allowing even greater coverage of the underwatched bay area.

SPECIES

Wintering water birds concentrate along the western coastal strip and may reach higher numbers than occur off Par; observation is also much easier here. The cove area has notably provided shelter for two long-staying Surf Scoter on separate occasions, adding extra interest to the range of regular divers and grebes that occurs here. Great Northern Diver can easily exceed 10 at a time throughout winter and spring, peaking at more than 20; Black-throated Diver can occur in groups of 10 or more from late winter into spring, but few are usually present through the whole winter period. Red-throated Diver remains typically scarce, in lower single figures. A White-billed Diver has also been sighted. Slavonian Grebe numbers probably equal Gerrans Bay for site fidelity, although it is sadly declining as elsewhere throughout the region. Red-necked Grebe is a not-infrequent visitor, though mostly as singles. Black-necked Grebe is infrequent, but Great Crested occurs more regularly. Common Scoter flocks can average 50; Velvets are sometimes present with them, while Eider and Long-tailed Duck turn up only irregularly in ones and twos.

An advantage in watching from St Austell Bay is that close views of all species are frequently possible, while the wide expanse of visible shoreline allows for high counts to be made. As the bay is such a favourable habitat for waterbirds it is perhaps unsurprising that a proportion of lingering winterers or new passage migrants can be admired in resplendent summer plumage – a definite bonus compared to the challenges of identifying divers and grebes in dull grey and brown winter plumage. In the right season, passing terns, Fulmars and Gannets are an expected part of the scene, along with other typical coastal species such as auks.

TIMING

Calm sea conditions allow checking at greater distance as birds are not obscured in wave troughs. Checking later in the day avoids looking directly into low winter sunlight; flat, overcast light conditions avoid such problems. As this is primarily a late autumn to early spring birdwatching venue, very busy holidaymaker activity is not usually a problem.

ACCESS

From the centre of St Austell town, continue along the A390 beyond Mount Charles roundabout, past which turn left onto a good minor road signposted to Porthpean after 1.25 miles (2km). Continue for approximately 1 mile (1.6km), then take a left turn signposted to Lower Porthpean; follow the road for half a mile (800m) to the car park (fee payable).

Check the nearby cove, easily scanned from the roadside wall located about 100m from the car park, or adjacent grass verge, which has seating. From here take the adjoining, ascending right-hand footpath. Check from limited vantage points between hedges for extensive views across the bay.

To reach Pentewan, turn right out of Porthpean car park and follow the road to a T-junction after approximately 600m and turn left. Follow the steep road down Pentewan Hill for 2.5 miles (4km) to the fee-paying car park opposite the pub. At the left-hand side of the car park is a path to a pond area leading to a footbridge and a promontory with a seat. It is possible to view the sea from here or further along the beach to the right towards Pentewan Sands, which allows better views towards Porthpean.

CALENDAR

Resident: No species of special interest, but common seabirds may pass year round.

December–February: All three diver species, mostly Great Northern, but increasing Black-throated later in period; Slavonian Grebe, chance of seaducks and good chance of other seabirds, including rarer species such as Surf Scoter.

March–May: All three diver species and grebes may be present earlier in period, maybe now in summer plumage; sea terns; auks might include a few Puffin, as this species naturally heads towards land early in the period.

June–July: Very busy with tourists and no species of special interest.

August–November: Returning sea terns earlier in the period; divers, grebes and seaducks towards the end.

SITE CLUSTER: LIZARD PENINSULA AND FAL ESTUARY

- **28** Gerrans Bay and Nare Head
- **29** Fal Estuary, Carrick Roads complex
- **29A** Boscawen Park, Truro
- **30** Falmouth, The Bay and Rosemullion
- **30A** Argal and College Reservoirs
- **31** Stithians Reservoir
- **32** The Lizard
- **32A** Loe Pool

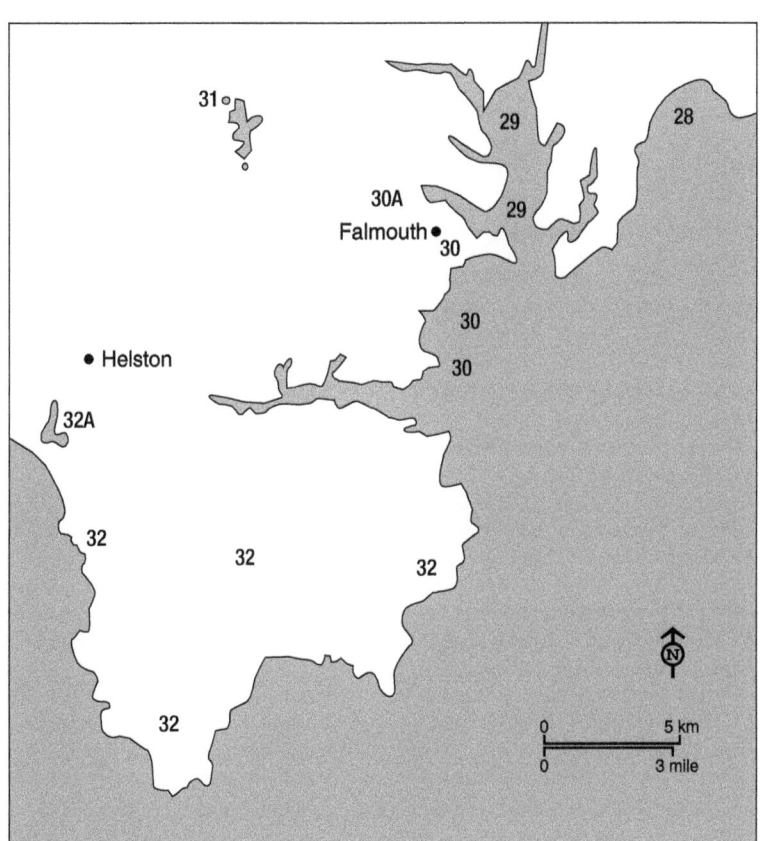

Cornwall

28 GERRANS BAY AND NARE HEAD

> OS LANDRANGER MAP 204
> OS grid ref: SW9038
> Postcodes: TR2 (for more detail and what3words see Access section)

HABITAT
A south-facing bay on the south coast of Cornwall, east from Carrick Roads ria system (near Falmouth). The bay has no apparent unique habitat features; a rocky coast extends its length, unprotected from heavy seas from most wind directions. Gerrans Bay runs from Nare Head at the east end west to Portscatho. The exposed but scenic Nare Head is a National Trust property with public footpaths. These paths run eastwards far beyond Nare and are continuous westwards to Portscatho and beyond.

Nare Head has a good range of commoner butterflies, including a strong colony of Green Hairstreaks near the mouth of the Nare Valley. A variety of habitats encompassing many wildlife requirements can be found in a fairly compact area, offering the chance of a good natural history walk combined with dramatic views. To ensure adequate coverage and certain identification of more distant seabirds, a telescope is essential here.

SPECIES
The bay's real claim to fame emanates from one species, Black-throated Diver. It once had one of the largest winter–early spring concentrations of the species in the UK, with up to 50 usual. Numbers have fallen since 2014 but the area still holds around 10 birds in winter. The population can fluctuate wildly throughout winter and spring months as some may move to another area (they frequently visit adjacent Veryan Bay). They are usually scattered across the area, but at times feed very close to shore, among rocky gullies densely covered in seaweed, searching out small crabs and fish. Later in April, a few may attain immaculate summer plumage; the white foreneck is lost, as are the white flanks, but as is common to all diver species they lack any trace of a tail, an important distinction from either Shag or Cormorant.

From 2017–2020 a Pacific Diver returned to the area each winter, but it no longer does. This species is similar to Black-throated but has a distinct black chin strap in winter plumage. It is slightly smaller and lacks the distinctive white flank patch of Black-throated but this can be difficult to ascertain in choppy water.

The most numerous diver is now Great Northern, averaging around 20 during the winter but often rising to 40 as spring passage gets underway. Red-throated Diver is a scarce, irregular visitor. Grebes are annual winter or early spring visitors; once the most numerous was Slavonian, but there are now only very small numbers here. Red-necked and Black-necked Grebes are found annually in ones and twos but are frequently further out in the bay so may be difficult to detect. Great Crested Grebe occurs irregularly. Seaducks are poorly represented, only small groups of Common Scoter visiting with any regularity. Other possibilities include an occasional Velvet Scoter, Long-tailed Duck or even Surf Scoter, possibly a few Eider (usually brown females or pied immature males). Most surprisingly, a female King Eider, a northern species that almost never reaches our region, has been recorded

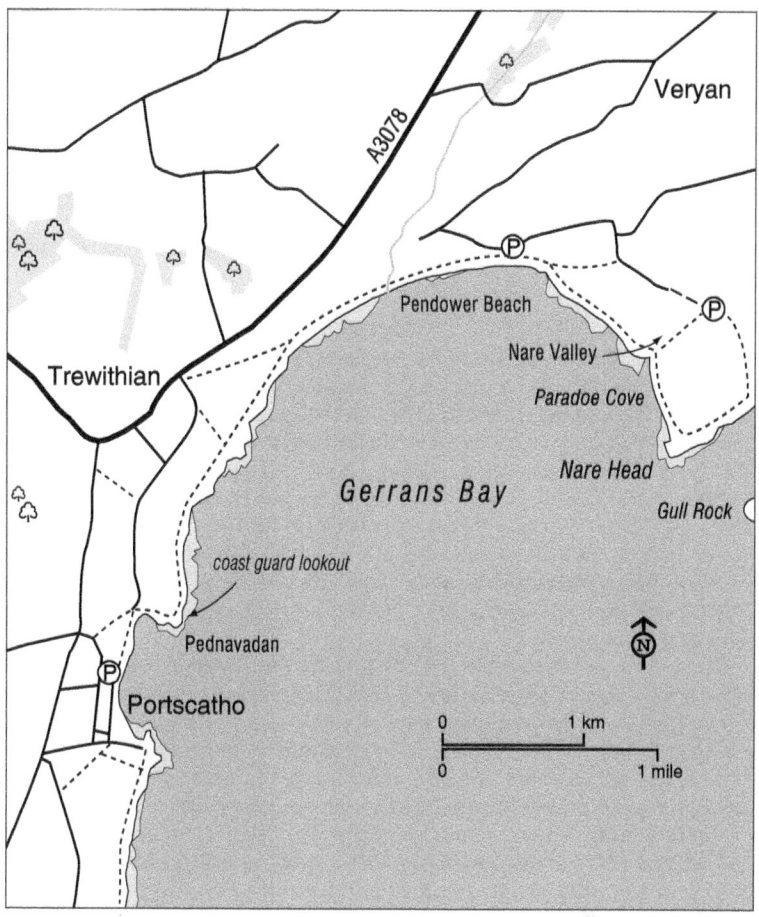

close inshore off Portscatho. Guillemot and Razorbill breed on Gull Rock (off Nare Head), although numbers of both fluctuate from year to year; a few individuals of both species are usually present throughout the year. Sandwich Tern can be watched heading eastwards from early spring or west in autumn. Other terns, such as Common or Arctic, are also seen, but less predictably. Whimbrels pass, usually in small flocks, and Fulmars may cruise by en route to nearby breeding ledges.

Nare Head remains underwatched and underrated with respect to a very wide range of migrants; the few watchers who do visit enthuse over its potential. Were it visited on a regular basis it would surely offer many avian rewards. Good numbers of all the commoner migrants are recorded, especially during spring, possibly less so in autumn. One notable rarity was a Red-rumped Swallow. Other unexpected visitors to the Gerrans Bay area have included Black Guillemot, Bonaparte's Gull, Least Sandpiper (a very rare midwinter record) and Lesser Grey Shrike. At Portscatho, Cirl Bunting can be seen all year round.

TIMING

Any daylight hour should suffice. Flatter light reduces glare and shadow caused by low winter sunlight. An incoming tide may induce birds to drift closer to shore. Calmer seas enhance the chance of picking out smaller birds such as grebes. Calm conditions are virtually assured with northerly biased winds. During westerlies, waterbirds often move to Portscatho. During the last hour or so of winter daylight, up to 300 Shags fly eastwards from the St Anthony Head area to roost at Gull Rock, at about which time divers cease feeding, remaining on the surface; the highest counts are often made then, whereas grebes continue diving almost until dark.

ACCESS

Leave the A3078 when signposted to **Pendower Beach**. The dead-end road runs adjacent to the cliff edge and there are roadside parking spaces for several cars **(TR2 5LW, warned.burst.breath)**. This is probably the best vantage point in the bay (also allowing ease of viewing for the less physically mobile), with at least a few divers and particularly grebes always present in winter; it is not unusual to find the largest flocks off here. From Pendower, rejoin the A3078 at the point where you left it. To check **Portscatho Lookout Station**, take the road signposted to Rosevine to Porthcurnick Beach from the A3078 and park carefully on the road **(flown.highbrow.certainly)**. Walk towards the beach, join the South West Coastal Path and head east to the lookout station, where there are good views of the sea.

To check around **Portscatho (TR2 5HT, fact.weep.chucked)**, from the A3078 take the road signposted to Portscatho, then the first left turn (again signposted to Portscatho). Divers, grebes and seaducks are recorded, especially during prolonged stronger westerlies when numbers often increase as birds seek shelter. Some rarer visitors have also occurred here. The bay here can be overlooked from the car, useful for the less physically mobile, but a telescope is essential.

For **Nare Head**, about 2 miles (3.2km) south of Tregony (just past the garage) turn left off the A3078. The distance from this turn-off to Nare Head is about 4 miles (6.4km). Follow signs straight on to Veryan; turn left at the signpost for Carne, straight over the crossroads, then follow the Carne and Pendower signs. After a few hundred metres turn left (still heading towards Carne), on a bend where a National Trust sign reads 'Nare Head'. Bearing right, pass over a cattle grid to the car park **(TR2 5PF, engulfing.building.cookie)**. The so-called circular walk around the Head comprises the high plateau clifftop some 100m above the sea, following a rough path down to within 10m of the sea, a steep incline. Our suggested route runs clockwise. From the car park follow a farm track southwards for half a mile (800m) in the direction of Lemoria Rock (with sea vistas and Gull Rock as a focal point). Turn northwards downhill (towards Pendower), to the mouth of the Nare Valley at Paradoe Cove. Turn north-eastwards up the valley amid bushes and some trees (good for migrants); the steep path then leads onto a field edge and back to the car park.

For **Veryan Bay** from **Portholland**, leaving the A3078 take the B3287 when signposted to Tregony for about 2 miles (3.2km). Then take the left turn signposted to Portholland, continue along the road signed to Caerhayes and take the right-hand turn to Portholland car park about 1 mile (1.6km) further on **(PL26, snake.football.withdraws)**. From the car park, walk the coastal footpath eastwards up an initially steep but good path for extensive views out over the bay and further eastwards.

CALENDAR

Resident: Cormorant, Shag, Guillemot, Razorbill, Cirl Bunting.

December–February: Up to early February, low numbers of Black-throated and Great Northern Divers, Slavonian Grebe; possible Red-throated Diver, Black and Red-necked Grebes; divers increase towards end; Common Scoter often present.

March–May: Black-throated and Great Northern Divers from March–early April but most divers and grebes have left by late April; Sandwich Tern from early April, Common Tern and Whimbrel from mid-April; possibly Arctic Tern, May.

June–July: Breeding species, including Guillemot, Razorbill, Fulmar and Stonechat.

August–November: First divers from late October, probably increasing in November, when grebes and seaducks begin to arrive.

29 FAL ESTUARY, CARRICK ROADS COMPLEX

OS LANDRANGER MAP 204
OS grid ref: SW8336
Postcodes: TR1, TR2, TR3, TR11 (for more detail and what3words see Access section)

HABITAT

The Truro and Fal Rivers, joining to form the Carrick Roads ria, enter the sea in Falmouth Bay, between the headlands of St Anthony on the east side and Pendennis on the west. Nearby is Falmouth town (see site 30). Carrick Roads is deep, tidal water, three quarters of a mile (1.2km) wide at its broadest; there are no sand- or mudbanks. On the east side of the Roads, a high steep bank forming a brake terminates in a low rocky cliff, shelving abruptly into deep water. On the west side, the land is more level with villages such as Mylor and individual houses scattered along its length.

Extensive creeks, sheltered from rough weather, lead off on both sides of Carrick Roads, the largest being Restronguet. Although Carrick Roads suffers from human disturbance along both banks, there is a quieter, very narrow area towards Devoran. Tresillian is a very narrow, tree-lined river with a small saltmarsh; it is very sheltered from high winds. Many of the trees lining the banks are alder. Ruan Lanihorne is the wide upper reaches of the Fal Estuary; here the surroundings are more open, and in the absence of human habitation there is much less disturbance.

SPECIES

The habitat and underwater diet preferences of diving ducks are reflected by their concentrations on the Roads; once regular Goldeneye are now intermittent, Red-breasted Merganser often exceed 25 and small numbers of Goosander are regular. All three divers visit, Great Northern being most frequent, with several present for much of the winter. Black-throated tend to appear later in the winter, and although recorded annually, the smaller Red-throated Diver is the least

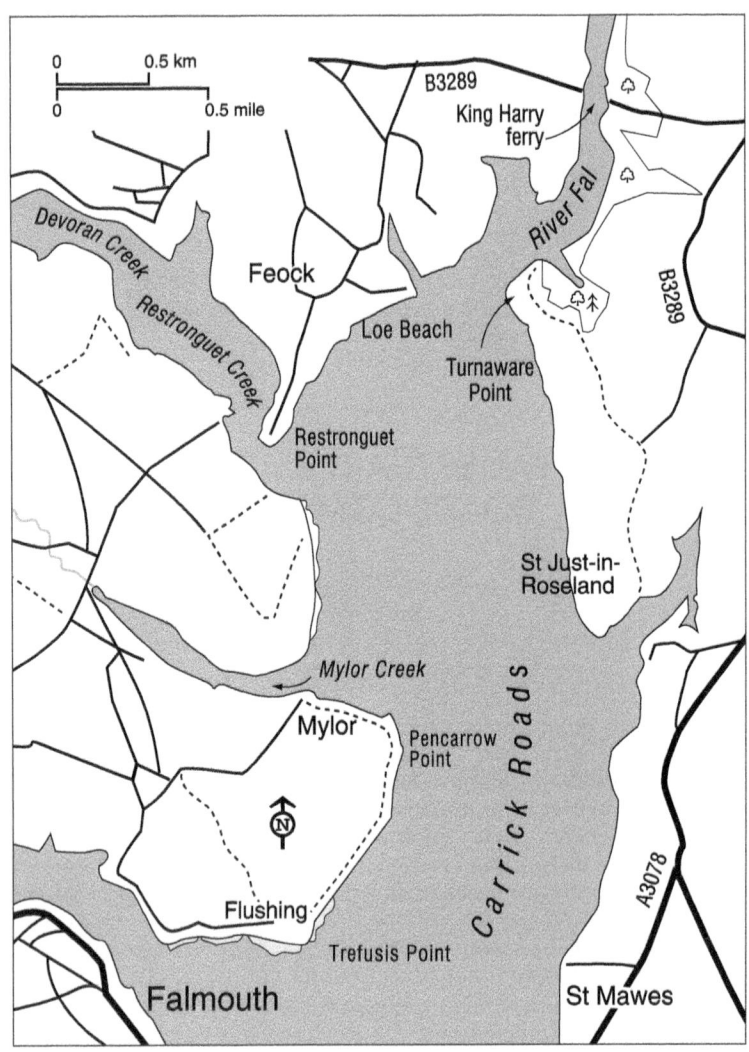

common. Grebes are regular visitors: Great Crested number a handful each winter; once regular Slavonian is now recorded in much lower numbers; Red-necked Grebe is annual but irregular, normally in ones and twos; and Black-necked Grebe was regular with the highest counts achieved in late afternoon/pre-dusk, but has been reduced to just single birds. Loe Beach and Turnaware Point are the best viewpoints. Eider and Common Scoter visit most winters, and single visits are occasionally made by Velvet Scoter and Long-tailed Duck. Among the few Razorbill and Guillemot seen in winter are now almost annual sightings of a single Black Guillemot; later sightings of this species may find it in full black and white summer plumage. Why this largely sedentary northern auk should turn up here is a mystery. Both Shag and Cormorant are common, their preferred habitats overlapping in the Roads.

Restronguet Creek seems to attract only unexceptional numbers of commoner waders, many of which feed along deepish freshwater channels flowing across the mudflats. When the channels are filled by the incoming tide, waders begin to fly to the Devoran roost, as the remaining mudflats are rapidly covered. Up to 200 Dunlin and 300 Redshank form the bulk of birds at the roost. A few Greenshank, Spotted Redshank, Little Stint and Curlew Sandpiper pass through in autumn. Two or three of both migrant shanks stay to winter. Little Grebes frequent the main stream, remaining in the creek even when the tide is out. Also, at Devoran on high tides, Common, Arctic and Sandwich Terns are regular early autumn migrants. Surrounding sheltered gardens and hedgerows provide habitat for overwintering Blackcap, Chiffchaff, Firecrest and Black Redstart.

Tresillian River, with dense bush and tree cover in places, provides winter quarters not only for the same passerines as found at Restronguet, but also for small flocks of Siskin, which find their favourite food, alder seeds, in the trees. Grey Herons are resident and several pairs breed, as do Shelduck. Probably two pairs of Kingfisher also nest. Autumn may bring a passage of Spotted Redshank and the larger Greenshank, some of these birds staying to overwinter. Greenshank have slow, graceful wingbeats, their dark upperwing contrasting with white underparts; their ringing *choo-choo* call also readily identifies them. Green and Common Sandpipers pass through in small numbers in autumn, but neither appears to stay regularly in winter. Bar-tailed and Black-tailed Godwits appear on passage.

On the ornithologically important mudflats at Ruan Lanihorne, waders attract the most attention. Apart from high numbers of common waders in autumn and winter, a small number of scarcer visitors to Cornwall are regularly noted, mostly in autumn. These include Wood Sandpiper, and rare American waders such as Baird's and Pectoral Sandpipers have been seen. Among the commoner waders, Dunlin, Whimbrel and Curlew can attain good numbers on both spring and autumn passage. Oystercatcher, Lapwing and Golden Plover will also be present, along with about 100 Black-tailed Godwit that overwinter. Ringed Plover often number 20 or so in autumn but, as usual in south-west England, only a few remain to winter. Spotted Redshank are very occasional passage and winter visitors; these elegant birds wade belly-deep while sweeping their long, straight bills sideways through the water. Greenshank can reach 20 in spring and up to 40 in autumn, several often staying to winter. Common and Green Sandpipers are annual in ones and twos, but Avocets are more unusual here. Gulls roost and loaf in the area, Mediterranean Gulls are often mixed in with Black-headed and Common Gulls, and larger gatherings of Lesser Black-backed Gull form from late winter. Ospreys are a regular feature of the district in early autumn.

On the Fal complex, dabbling ducks are generally restricted to the most common kinds. Average peak numbers around the Ruan area, where most are seen, are 250 Teal and Mallard, up to 300 Wigeon and about 100 Shelduck. Other ducks visit sporadically in ones and twos and include all the diving species.

Grey Heron, like Mallard and Shelduck, breeds near Ruan, as do one or two pairs of Kingfisher. Ospreys pass through in autumn, often staying several days, sometimes even weeks. Peregrines are frequent visitors, menacing and panicking Ruan's avian occupants through autumn and winter. A Spoonbill may arrive during autumn or early winter, possibly staying for a month or two. Little Egrets are now regularly present, as are Cattle and Great White Egrets – once-scarce visitors are becoming more and more regular.

TIMING

Incoming tides are required to see waders on mudflats such as those at Devoran Creek and Ruan; rising tides concentrate previously scattered birds, and those feeding in deep channels, into reasonably defined areas. There is no one consistent high-tide wader roost at any of the sites. Very high tides (over 5m) cover all the mud and saltmarsh, and waders are forced into fields or split up to roost until the water begins to ebb, exposing mud again. Higher tides are good for terns.

Near Ruan, waders are best seen an hour or so after the tide begins to rise, driving them out of the gullies and main channels (which fill first) across still-exposed mudflats. This enables you to watch waders for several hours, before high tide moves them off altogether. At high water in winter, diving ducks such as Red-breasted Merganser and the occasional Goldeneye may follow the tide up, swimming close to the shore.

It is pointless checking Devoran at low tide. As with Ruan, waders are forced out from deep channels and other hidden areas by rising tides. For about three hours before high tide, waders fly into Devoran Creek and close views are obtained. On very high tides (over 5m), roosting areas are flooded and the birds disperse. Greenshank and Spotted Redshank do not usually appear until almost high tide. At low tide on Carrick Roads, some birds drift downstream towards the mouth, returning when waters rise; many, however, stay around the wider middle reaches at all times. As with other similarly sheltered areas in the South West, hard weather brings a short-term increase in many species as they flee worse conditions elsewhere. Water sports activites on the Roads increase from April onwards and this, combined with a traditionally early departure by many waterfowl wintering in south-west England, means that few birds remain from that date.

ACCESS

To check **Carrick Roads**, leave the A39 Truro to Falmouth road at St Gluvias and drive to **Mylor village**, where there are parking facilities **(TR11 5UF, thighs.news.brass)**. Walk along the beach on the south side of the creek to Pencarrow Point overlooking the Roads. This widest area is usually one of the best for concentrations of most species. A telescope is essential for a complete check.

For the best area at **Tresillian**, mostly for close views of waders at low tide, leave the A39 where signposted to **St Clement**, where there is a car park next to the public footpath **(TR1 1SZ, civic.castle.parade)**. Take this good path, which follows the riverbank upstream towards Pencalenick. The track passes Tresemple Pool, which often provides first-class views of Kingfishers. This walk is about three quarters of a mile (1.2km).

South of Truro, from the A39 past Carnon Downs, access to **Devoran Creek** is gained by taking a right turn onto Greenbank Road, just before the A-road crosses the creek and before reaching a garage. After entering Quay Road, drive at least 50m past a very sharp bend (for safety) before parking beside the road **(TR3 6PW, triangles.town.tradition)**. Walk along this narrow road, adjacent to the creek. After about three quarters of a mile (1.2km), you can obtain close views of assembled waders, before and after high tides.

Black-necked Grebes use the northernmost sector of Carrick Roads. They are best viewed off **Turnaware Point** on the east bank or from **Loe beach** near Feock on the west bank. Turnaware Point is reached from the A3078 Truro to St Mawes road, turning north on the B3289 at St Just. After 2 miles (3.2km), turn left on a minor road, leading to farms; go past the farms to a road that ends at small car park

(TR2 5JJ, gulped.importing.stuffy). Walk down the track to Turnaware Point itself, for views up the River Fal. On the west bank, turn south from the A39 Truro to Falmouth road at Playing Place. Follow the B3289 for the first 2 miles (3.2km), then continue on to Feock village; at its end a small road leads down to Loe Beach, where there is a fee-paying car park **(TR3 6SH, nagging.icebergs.revolts)**.

The B3289 connects the east and west banks of Carrick Roads via the King Harry Ferry crossing, which operates all year round.

CALENDAR

Resident: Cormorant, Shag, Grey Heron, Sparrowhawk, Buzzard, Kingfisher, Raven.

December–February: divers of all three species; Little, Black-necked, Slavonian and Great Crested Grebes, and probably Red-necked Grebe; Cattle Egret (dependent on livestock presence), Little Egret; Teal, Wigeon and other dabbling or diving ducks visit irregularly; Eider, Common Scoter, possibly Velvet Scoter, Long-tailed Duck and Goosander; Goldeneye, Red-breasted Merganser, Dunlin, Redshank, Greenshank, Black-tailed and Bar-tailed Godwits, Curlew, Snipe, Avocet, possibly Spoonbill; Lesser Black-backed Gull numbers rise from February; Blackcap, Chiffchaff, Firecrest, Black Redstart, Siskin.

March–May: By mid-April, Most waders and waterbirds have departed by mid-April; Honey Buzzard, Gull-billed Tern and Black Guillemot are all possible from mid-April.

June–July: Breeding species. Waders such as Redshank, and Common and Green Sandpipers have returned by mid-July.

August–November: Cattle and Little Egret numbers build up from September. Most wader numbers and species increase through August and September, including Ringed Plover, Greenshank and Bar and Black-tailed Godwit; possible waders in October include Little Stint, Curlew and Wood Sandpipers and Ruff; Osprey and Peregrine; commoner sea terns in early part of period and returning divers, grebes and seaducks later.

29A BOSCAWEN PARK, TRURO

OS LANDRANGER MAP 204
OS grid ref: SW8343
Postcode: TR1 1SG
what3words: mull.visit.resort

HABITAT

Boscawen Park is situated on the outskirts of Truro and runs along the eastern side of the Truro River. It has formal gardens and ornamental trees, and more importantly a riverside walk, which is ideal for watching waders and gulls on the mudflats. This short walk enables less able-bodied individuals a chance to view a variety of species; it is wheelchair/mobility scooter friendly and there are plenty of seats. It also gives entry-level birders, including children, the chance to familiarise themselves with a variety of commoner and scarcer species.

SPECIES

The level walk from the car park downstream to Sunny Corner is about half a mile (800m), affording good views across the mudflats and a chance to learn and study many of the commoner waders such as Dunlin, Redshank, Curlew and Black-tailed Godwit (numbers of which can reach 150), as well as the ubiquitous Oystercatcher. All these can be seen easily during the winter months. Shelduck are present for much of the year on the river, Wigeon and Teal are regular winter visitors and may be joined by the occasional Shoveler. Goosander and Red-breasted Merganser are both possible on the river and are often seen from Sunny Corner around the mouth of the Calenick River. Little Egret and Grey Heron are regular, and Spoonbill has been recorded on several occasions. Greenshank and Avocet are regular wintering species in small numbers, but Spotted Redshank is seen less frequently, and the mudflats may produce migrating Whimbrel.

Through spring and summer, commoner woodland species that can be found include Nuthatch and Great Spotted Woodpecker. Both Grey and Pied Wagtails nest in the general area. The duck pond across the road may also be worth checking as is the surrounding woodland during winter.

Autumn sees the return of wildfowl and waders, with possible Mediterranean Gull and fishing Osprey. Cattle Egret is increasingly recorded, and an intermittent roost has been noted in recent years containing around 50 Little and Cattle Egrets. Mediterranean Gull and Osprey are most likely to be seen downstream towards Malpas, but they can be present anywhere on the estuary depending on the state of the tide.

TIMING

The park is busy, more so at weekends, so midweek visits are more productive. Low or preferably rising or falling tides are essential for watching waders on the mudflats. The summer months are less productive on the river and the park becomes very busy.

ACCESS

From the A390 in Truro take Malpas Road off the Trafalgar roundabout, which is signposted to Boscawen Park, 1 mile (1.6km) away. At the mini-roundabout take the third exit into Boscawen Park where there is ample parking and plenty of seats; the toilets and café are open year round.

There are train services to Truro and bus services pass the park; see the Traveline South West website for further details: travelinesw.com.

CALENDAR

Resident: Nuthatch and Great Spotted Woodpecker among other common woodland species.

December–February: Shelduck, Wigeon, Teal, Goosander, Red-breasted Merganser, Spoonbill, Little Egret, Oystercatcher, Avocet, Curlew, Dunlin, Redshank, Black-tailed Godwit, Kingfisher.

March–May: Whimbrel possible from April, and maybe other migrant waders.

June–July: Returning and passage waders such as Common Sandpiper.

August–November: Greenshank, possibly Cattle Egret, occasional Spotted Redshank, Osprey in late August and September; above wintering species return end of period.

30 FALMOUTH, THE BAY AND ROSEMULLION

> OS LANDRANGER MAP 204
> OS grid ref: SW8031
> Postcode: **Swanpool** – TR11 5BG
> **Maenporth** – TR11 5HN
> **Mawnan** – TR11 5HY
> what3words: **Swanpool** – chip.crass.margin
> **Maenporth** – dent.blunt.thing
> **Mawnan** – regress.oldest.august

HABITAT

On the west side of the large Carrick Roads–Fal Estuary complex, at its mouth, lies the town of Falmouth. Eastwards, docks face back towards Carrick Roads (see site 29); southwards, the town looks on to a deep but sheltered bay. A mile (1.6km) of mainly rocky shoreline with small shingle beaches extends between Pendennis Castle promontory by the estuary mouth, and wooded Pennance Point to the west. A marshy wooded valley runs down the west side of the town, culminating in Swanpool, a 400m-long saline park lake with reedy fringes and sheltering Alder trees immediately behind the beach. The town has large gardens with mature trees and bushes, including palms and other exotics.

West of Pennance Point, the high rocky coast of Falmouth Bay curves south towards the Lizard peninsula, interrupted by the deep mouth of Helford River (known as the Passage). Overlooking the Passage is the open downland National Trust property of Rosemullion Head, with wide coastal views, projecting eastwards into the bay. The only gap in the cliffs between Falmouth and Helford Passage is at Maenporth, a deep, sheltered cove and stream valley 1 mile (1.6km) south of Pennance Point.

Water Voles lived at Swanpool (which is a Local Nature Reserve and Site of Special Scientific Interest) until released American Mink caused their demise. It is also the only known UK site for Trembling Sea-mat, a rare saltwater bryozoan.

SPECIES

Falmouth has gained a reputation, in winter, as a feeding area for large numbers of gulls, including regular occurrences of scarcer species such as Little and Glaucous Gulls. The sheltered valley behind Swanpool hosts overwintering Chiffchaff, Siberian Chiffchaff and Yellow-browed Warbler.

The previous sharp rise in gull sightings off Falmouth was probably due partly to

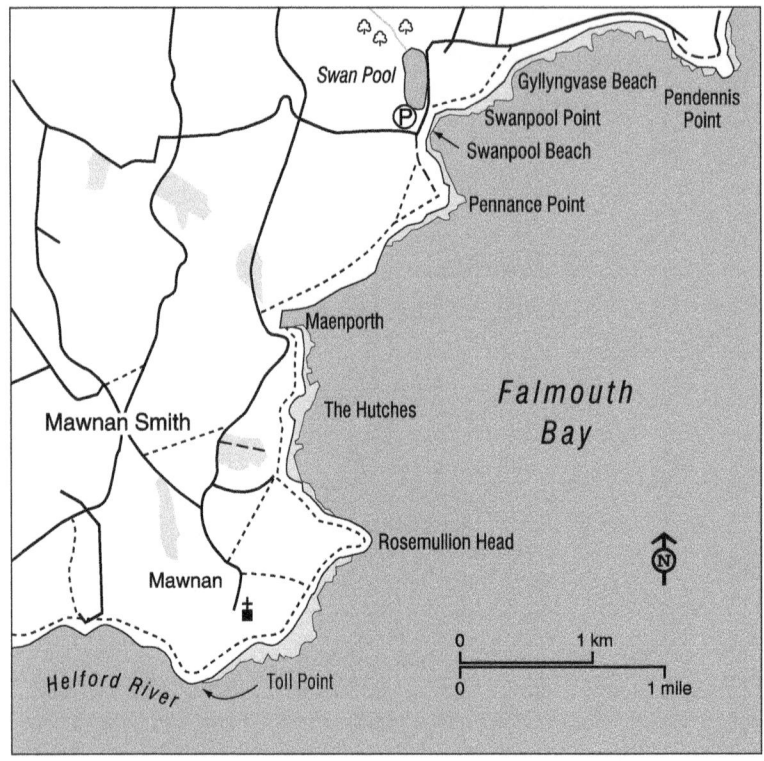

an increase in careful watching, and partly due to the large trawlers and fish-factory ships that sometimes base themselves in the bay for periods during the winter. Gulls wheel screaming over the ships, often too distant to watch, or rest in large numbers along seafront rocks, where they can be checked. Swanpool Lake and Maenporth Cove serve as drinking, bathing and preening areas, with a steady stream of gulls commuting to and from the boats. The majority of birds following trawlers are Herring Gulls, with the brown immatures being most numerous. The more slender Iceland Gull, with long white wingtips, might be picked out among a resting flock; often they sit on flat rocks just east of Swanpool Beach. However, care should be taken in distinguishing them from the other northern gull, the burly, thick-billed Glaucous, also a regular visitor. The latter can often be seen resting on Maenporth Beach, where many larger gulls, including Great Black-backed, gather. Wind and tide drift fish scraps onto the seashore, giving agile Black-headed Gulls a chance to feed over the tideline; they are sometimes joined by a Little Gull. Mediterranean Gulls are present all year in varying numbers and Common Gulls move through in flocks towards spring. Kittiwakes, normally oceanic feeders in winter, often gather in good numbers to feed on easy food sources here when the fishing fleet is present.

In early spring, most of the large gulls move off, but the odd Glaucous or Iceland Gull may linger late, fresh individuals appearing with groups of other gulls on passage up the coast. Black-headed and Common Gulls move through, with the chance of a rare transatlantic visitor such as a Bonaparte's or Ring-billed Gull among them. Identification of the varying plumages of the many gulls present requires patient, skilful and meticulous watching.

Although most birdwatching visitors expect to see gulls, other species of interest may be found. Small numbers of Great Northern and Black-throated Divers, and the occasional Slavonian Grebe may be seen offshore. Small groups of Eider are irregular off the rocks, where Turnstone and Purple Sandpiper forage busily; a Black Redstart is likely in a sheltered corner of the shoreline or around seafront buildings. Auks are scattered on the sea in small numbers, and Black Guillemot has been reported in the bay several times. The deep waters off Rosemullion and Helford Passage may also be used by feeding divers, seaducks (often with a Velvet Scoter or two) and auks. Red-necked Grebe, if present, favours the deep, rocky bays more than other grebes; this species and Velvet Scoter are also seen intermittently off Falmouth seafront, presumably the same individuals moving along the coast. Sometimes seaducks such as a single Long-tailed take up residence along with 20 or so Tufted Duck on Swanpool, where close views are possible; Water Rails lurk in the margins there.

Moving inland, sheltered trees near the stream behind Swanpool often hold wintering Blackcap, Firecrest, Yellow-browed Warbler and Chiffchaff, all of which can be seen in the well-vegetated gardens around the town. Chiffchaff can be quite numerous, with more than 40 wintering birds having been counted in the district. Small numbers of Siskin feed in the waterside Alders.

In early spring, warblers and hirundines appear in sheltered coves. Groups of up to half a dozen Black-throated Divers pass through the bay, where the odd Slavonian Grebe may linger and acquire breeding attire, and Sandwich Terns are seen in small numbers. A variety of passerine species may be seen around Swanpool, including one or two Sedge and Reed Warblers later in spring; they may stay to breed, as does Little Grebe most years. Other wetland species have included overshooting rarities such as Little Bittern, surprisingly hard to see when not flying, even in this thin fringe of reeds.

In later spring and through to early autumn, seawatching off Rosemullion promontory can be worthwhile, with a good chance of Manx and Balearic Shearwaters, skuas and terns passing south offshore after being pushed into Falmouth Bay in poor weather. Although numbers have not been high, three or four individual skuas in a watch is possible, along with the possibility of Cory's and Great Shearwaters in more recent years. Interesting observations have included feeding parties of tiny European Storm Petrels and a non-breeding summer flock of Pomarine Skuas. Falmouth is busy with tourists throughout summer and relatively little visited by birders until late in the year, when gull numbers start to build again. One winter, Britain's first Forster's Tern, from the Americas, spent several weeks fishing off the seafront. Late autumn gales may blow a tired Grey Phalarope or Little Auk into the bay or force it to rest on Swanpool Lake. Warblers around the lakeside at this season have included Yellow-browed and Pallas's.

Near Rosemullion in 2006, the RSPB instigated a Cirl Bunting reintroduction scheme. Breeding has been slow but steady and the success of the scheme continues to depend on a farming system that puts wildlife at its heart.

TIMING

In peak winter periods, gulls are constantly moving in and out from the beaches to ships when present, so give yourself time to wait (two or three hours at least) at strategic points such as Swanpool and Maenporth for incoming birds. For resting gulls on shoreline rocks and beaches, a falling tide leaving more exposed landing space is best. Time of day is not critical; afternoon is usually best at Swanpool Lake for gulls but avoid very late afternoon when fading light will not permit detailed watching. Easterly and south-easterly winds bring the most fish debris onto the beaches.

Swanpool Valley is most likely to hold interesting spring migrants and overshoot species when they funnel in on southerly and south-westerly winds. Wintering passerines are most numerous in years without heavy frost. Seawatching at Rosemullion seems best in winds between the south and east in early morning, tending to drift seabirds nearer shore, and in poor visibility or drizzle, especially after anticyclonic spells. Strong depressional south-westerlies do not seem to produce much here but may force individuals to shelter on Swanpool in late autumn.

ACCESS

Falmouth lies at the south end of the A39 from Truro. For **the Swanpool district**, follow signs to Swanpool and Gyllyngvase beaches along a right fork as you enter Falmouth. (There is only a short gap between Penryn and Falmouth towns along the main road.) Continue along a suburban B-class road for 1.5 miles (2.4km), at the roundabout take the third exit, then take a signposted right turn downhill past the cemetery. Arriving at the top end of the pool, stop to check marginal vegetation and trees behind the pool.

Note: Do not trample down reeds as some irresponsible birdwatchers have done in the past.

Drive down to the fee-paying seafront car park, from which gulls are clearly visible flying in to bathe. Spend time here but also try walking east (to your left) along the tarmac footpath overlooking the shore rocks, round to Gyllyngvase beach (half a mile/800m), or further if large groups of gulls are visible ahead. Most scarcer species, however, are seen near the Swanpool end of the bay. Also try walking up past the café from Swanpool and along the muddy half-mile (800m) track to Pennance Point for gulls and seawatching. The pool and much of the bay can be viewed from adjacent roadsides, vital for the less physically mobile.

Maenporth is reached by following Swanpool beach road over the hilltop past the café then forking left along the minor road, or by the coast footpath beyond Pennance.

For **Rosemullion and Helford Passage**, continue beyond Maenporth for 2 miles (3.2km) to Mawnan village, parking near the old church. On the coast path, turn left for half a mile (800m) out to Rosemullion for passing seabirds, or right for a few hundred metres to view the bay for divers, grebes and seaducks in winter.

CALENDAR

Resident: Little of note, apart from Little Grebe, Shag, Cirl Bunting.

December–February: Great Northern and Black-throated Divers, Red-necked and Slavonian Grebes, Tufted Duck, seaducks, Water Rail, Turnstone, Purple Sandpiper; gull flocks peak in February, including Glaucous, Mediterranean and Little among commoner species; auks; Blackcap, Chiffchaff, Firecrest, Black Redstart.

March–May: Wintering divers, grebes and gulls present to early April, with further migrant groups arriving, but total numbers drop from mid-March; possibly a rare gull March–April; Sandwich Tern, early hirundines and singing warblers, late March; summer migrants and maybe an overshooting rarity from mid-April; Manx and Balearic Shearwaters, Arctic, Pomarine and maybe Great Skuas, Sandwich, Common and Arctic Terns all possible off Pennance and Rosemullion, especially May.

June–July: Breeding Reed and Sedge Warblers; off Rosemullion, possible seabirds include Manx and Balearic Shearwaters and, later in the period, Cory's and Great Shearwaters, European Storm Petrel, skuas, auks; Fulmar breed.

August–November: Quiet period. Maybe skuas or terns off Rosemullion and Pennance August–September; possibility of shearwaters and 'sea grebes'; Grey Phalarope or Little Auk possible in the bay or on Swanpool Lake in November.

30A ARGAL AND COLLEGE RESERVOIRS

OS LANDRANGER MAP 204
OS grid ref: SW7633
Postcode: **Argal** – TR11 5PE **College** – TR11 5PD
what3words: **Argal** – straw.indoors.warthog
College – crispier.yummy.circus

HABITAT
In the hills immediately west of Falmouth lie these two adjacent reservoirs. Argal (26ha) and College (14ha) lie on a north-south line, College being the more northerly. Argal has mostly open banks, but College has surrounding woodland. Both sites are steep-banked, lacking marsh or adjacent wetland. They are heavily used by anglers.

SPECIES
The main interest is a variety of ducks, mostly diving species, and occasional interesting migrant waders. Waterbirds are likely to interchange with the Stithians Reservoir population (see site 31), especially when human disturbance drives them from here. Duck numbers are perhaps higher on Argal than on College, with up to 50 Tufted being regular. Other sporadic diving visitors have included Goosander, Scaup and the occasional Goldeneye. Rarer visitors have included a Ferruginous Duck on College Reservoir. Dabbling ducks are not particularly attracted to these reservoirs, apart from the expected Mallard, 50 or so Wigeon during winter and up to dozen Shoveler on College. Both Green-winged and Blue-winged Teal have been recorded here. Winter visitors to the reservoirs might see groups of bathing and roosting gulls; while they are less important gull sites than the nearby coast, there have been records of Mediterranean and Ring-billed Gulls, so it is worth checking. A Kingfisher may be present along the banks, and College Wood holds a cross-section of common woodland passerines and woodpeckers, often easier to see on leafless trees.

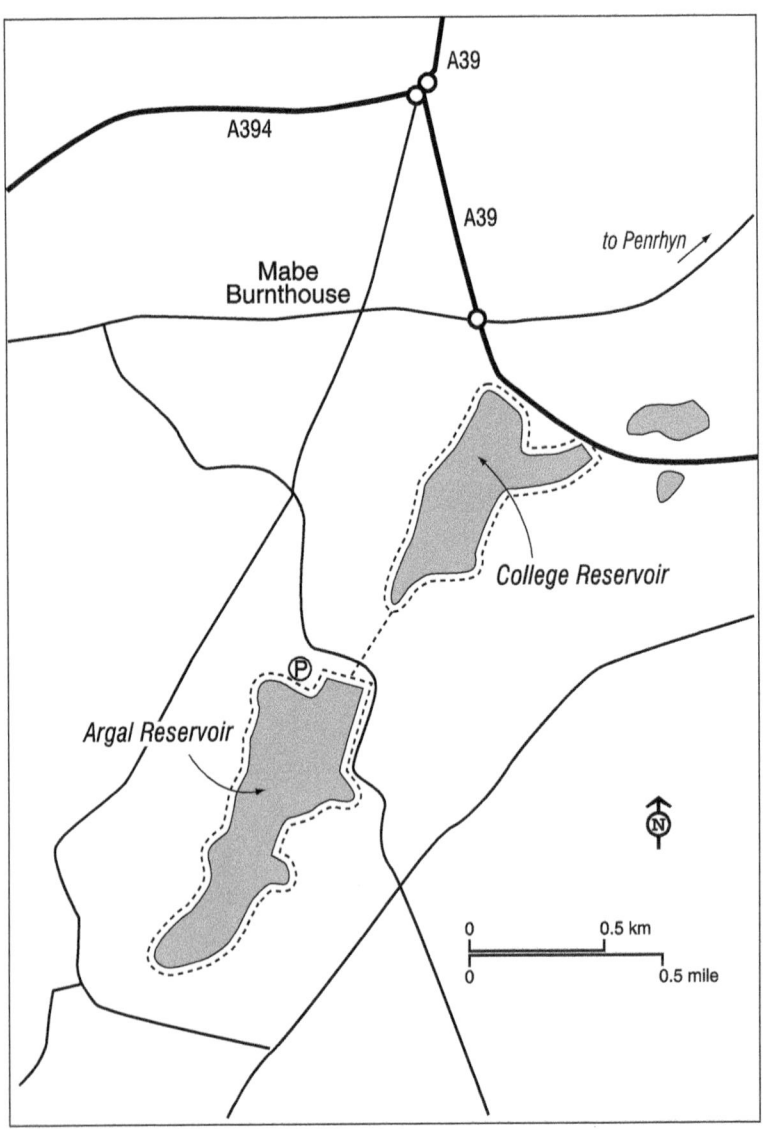

There is usually little of note after spring passage, during which Night Heron and Purple Heron have been found on several occasions. Coot, Moorhen and Great Crested Grebe breed on both reservoirs. Neither reservoir is noted for wader passage, but if the water levels drop in late summer Green and Common Sandpipers are possible, as is the odd Wood Sandpiper or Ruff. As with most Cornish lakes, there have been a few sightings of American wader vagrants, including Pectoral and Least Sandpipers. Black Tern is noted occasionally.

TIMING

The major factor to consider is human disturbance, so early morning or weekday visits are advised. Cold winter weather will boost duck numbers and dry autumns will increase the mud available for waders, which might include American species after westerly gales.

ACCESS

From Falmouth take the A39 to Penryn, turning left on the B3291 towards Gweek and Helston. After 2 miles (3.2km) turn right onto a minor road, which takes you between the two lakes. A good footpath, with a marked nature trail, leads around College Reservoir, which has open access; at Argal there is a 1.3-mile (2km) walk around the water; the path is generally good but can be muddy at times. Argal can be viewed from the car park (charges apply) and picnic area.

CALENDAR

Resident: No species of special interest.

December–February: Flocks of common dabbling and diving ducks and gulls may contain scarcer species.

March–May: Common spring migrants in low numbers; rarer herons, such as Purple, have occurred.

June–July: Breeding species.

August–November: Chance of marsh terns early in the period; duck and gull numbers build towards end of period.

31 STITHIANS RESERVOIR

OS LANDRANGER MAP 203
OS grid ref: SW7135
Postcode: **Golden Lion End** – TR16 6NW **Southern Cut-off** – TR16 6PB
what3words: **Golden Lion End** – edgy.ranged.marine
Southern Cut-off – puppy.crowns.snuck

HABITAT

At 111ha, this reservoir, south of Redruth, is the largest in western Cornwall. It lies within a large area of high, rough ground, much of it semi-moorland covered by bracken and heather, reaching an altitude of 250m. This setting produces weather conditions far removed from those on the sheltered south coast. Even on otherwise warm days, a chill wind often blows across this exposed water.

The reservoir is quite shallow over large areas, having steeper sides only towards the dam, and a margin of mud is quickly exposed at its furthest perimeters when water levels drop. No islands break the lake's expanse. There is only minimal human habitation immediately surrounding the reservoir.

SPECIES

This is one of Cornwall's most important reservoirs for birds. As ducks and waders are its main groups of species, most interest centres on autumn and winter. The surrounding rough, open terrain is attractive to small numbers of birds of prey, which also hunt near and over the reservoir, providing added value for birdwatchers. Winter is particularly bleak here, so few of the waders that typically winter on the region's sheltered estuaries remain at Stithians throughout. Conversely, autumn wader counts for some species are the highest in Devon and Cornwall, and rarities are found annually.

There are three accessible hides around the reservoir. The Golden Lion Hide, owned and managed by South West Lakes Trust, overlooks the cut-off at the northern end and can be good for waders such as Green and Common Sandpipers and occasionally Wood or Pectoral Sandpipers during autumn migration. The other two hides can be found at the southern end of the reservoir. The Stuart Hutchings Hide overlooks the reservoir and is particularly useful during the migration periods for viewing waders and visiting waterbirds, including scarcer ducks such as Goldeneye and Pochard. The Feeder Hide, like the previous, is owned and maintained by CBWPS and looks eastwards over the southern cut-off. During winter, the maintained feeders attract the resident Reed Bunting, Marsh Tit and occasionally Great Spotted Woodpecker.

There are more dabbling ducks than diving species, possibly owing to the shallow grassy margins which they favour. Numbers, however, are not that large, and variety is limited. Teal and Wigeon are usually present, averaging 60–100 of each, while Mallard total only about 30. A few other species such as Shoveler and Gadwall occur regularly, but only in small numbers. The most numerous diving duck is Tufted, with 10–25 usually present; Pochard is now a very rare visitor, and counts of four or five Goldeneye are regular. Scaup are almost annual, visiting from late autumn on, often in twos and threes, and may include grey-backed males. Two rare American visitors have also appeared: Lesser Scaup and (once) a Bufflehead. Goosander do not arrive annually, but two or three might be present. Probably because of the reservoir's expanse and relative solitude, various wandering 'grey' geese sometimes visit. The region as a whole is poorly served for the latter, so any occurrences are noteworthy. White-fronted Geese predominate, and once a group of the Greenland form, which winters in large numbers in Ireland, was identified; Pink-footed and Greylag Geese have also been seen.

Two or three pairs of Little Grebes breed, and in winter up to 20 are seen. Great Crested Grebes are present all year and breed in small numbers, but other grebe species are almost non-existent. Divers, although only ever accidental on our inland waters, also shun this locality, but a few single Black-throated or Great Northern Divers have been reported. Cormorants fly far inland to feed, and around a dozen are not unusual. Coot can muster over half a dozen from late autumn onwards and have bred. Moorhen are present in small numbers and breed most years. A few uncommon species of gull are seen, such as Yellow-legged Gull, and up to 30 Mediterranean Gulls have been identified among the Black-headed Gulls in more recent years.

As spring approaches, wintering ducks and other species are quick to depart. A combination of high water levels and generally poor spring wader passage in Cornwall means that very few pass through here at this season. If Stithians does not stand out as a hotspot for spring waders, the same certainly cannot be said in autumn; indeed, waders pass in reasonable numbers from late summer. Most of those early high numbers are created by Green, Wood and Common Sandpipers. This reservoir is a good venue for these three birds. Green Sandpipers tend to disappear into narrow gullies and hug the grassy margins. Wood Sandpipers are much less common, but here 10 or more have been seen together, although one or two is more normal. More elegant in stature, they regularly feed in the open.

Soon a wide range of other waders appears, the plover family being well represented. Ringed Plover, sometimes reaching more than 30, are regular passage visitors while Little Ringed only occur occasionally and may be watched among their similarly marked, chubbier cousins. Lapwing congregate early, but only around 100 now spend winter in the general area. Golden Plover, too, return early, this being one of the few places where they do so; they may number fewer than 50 at first but reach 200 later. The small early flock is often enough to lure one of Stithians' specialities, American Golden Plover. This species was previously almost annual, with two or three in some autumns. In flight, its underwings are dusky grey, as opposed to the commoner bird's white. Pacific Golden Plover and Dotterel have also been recorded.

Greenshank, Redshank and Spotted Redshank occur occasionally on passage. Dunlin numbers average 20, and Ruff can number three or four, although 10–20 was once more usual and the species would occasionally overwinter. As autumn advances, more species arrive, including Little Stint and Curlew Sandpiper from Russia. In years when numbers were generally good, 15 or more of each would have been seen together; now singles of both species are the norm.

One of the more regular scarce waders is Pectoral Sandpiper, which is almost an annual visitor; exceptionally, seven were once seen together. A rarer American visitor, Long-billed Dowitcher is nevertheless fairly regular and has been known to stay the winter. Lesser Yellowlegs, which resembles Redshank but has long, slender, yellow legs and lacks white on the wings, has turned up several times. Other rare American waders recorded at Stithians are Baird's, Solitary and Semipalmated Sandpipers, and Wilson's Phalarope. Snipe usually number around 30 in late autumn and winter, possibly accompanied by a Jack Snipe or two.

Teal arrive back early and attract other closely related species. Garganey have visited here in spring, but this is one of the very few places in South West England where they are seen more often in autumn, a careful search revealing one or two in most years. Two American teal species have also been found among their European relatives: Cornwall's first record of Blue-winged Teal was at Stithians, and Green-winged Teal has stayed. Probably the same Black Duck – another 'Yank' – has been seen in the area a number of times.

One or two Little Gulls, often immatures, and similar numbers of Black Tern pass through. The much-hoped-for White-winged Black Tern has also been seen.

Great White Egret is seen increasingly regularly, and birds of prey other than the residents are seen quite often; probably most regular is Peregrine.

The moorland attracts small numbers of Skylarks and Meadow Pipits. Merlins have adapted their feeding technique to become adept at chasing small passerines over open ground; these tiny falcons have on occasion been watched hurtling and twisting among panic-stricken flocks. There have also been sightings of the opportunist Hen Harrier, dropping into bracken after prey. The plentiful moorland rodents are probably of most interest to the one or two Short-eared Owls that are seen most winters and often stay through to spring. Dead sheep are more to the liking of the few Red Kites that have drifted over. Passing Ospreys and Hobbies have also been seen. Hirundines feed over the water in summer and were once joined briefly by Britain's first Crag Martin. A Baillon's Crake has also obliged a few very lucky observers.

TIMING
If winds are high elsewhere, from whatever direction, they will be stronger here. This makes observation difficult and encourages birds to huddle together or seek whatever shelter is available. Anglers and practitioners of water sports use the water, and disturbance is usually worst on weekend afternoons; the waders are not usually disturbed, but waterfowl are sometimes moved around.

ACCESS
The nearest major road is the A394 from Helston to Penryn, from which you follow the Stithians sign north. The reservoir is reached by a minor road signposted to Carnkie. Roads run beside the lake at several points. Most people get good views from these points, which happen to be the most important wader spots, assisting the disabled birdwatcher.

A road cuts off a small marshy part of the reservoir's southern tip and there are two hides, one either side of the road. From the road, views can be gained of large stretches of open water, often used by ducks. Access to the Stuart Hutchings Hide is directly off the road through a galvanised gate at the west end of the reservoir; there is a short, often very muddy path to the hide. The feeder hide can be found by accessing the galvanised gate on the southern side of the road and walking 50m alongside the fence.

At the northern boundary of the reservoir, near the roadside Golden Lion Inn, a road divides a small marshy area from the main lake. Part of the main body of water can be viewed from the road. Access to the Golden Lion Hide is via a wooden gate opposite the pub; follow the path towards the pumping station then take the wooden boardwalk to the right towards the hide.

There is a 4.8-mile (7.8km) walk around the reservoir, but be aware that some of the path is along roads – which can at times be busy. The off-road paths can be very muddy after rain, so boots are recommended.

CALENDAR
Resident: Little and Great Crested Grebes, Coot, Reed Bunting, Marsh Tit.

December–February: Possibly Bewick's Swan or 'grey' geese such as White-fronted; Teal, Gadwall, Wigeon, Tufted Duck, possibly Scaup or Goosander, Goldeneye; possibly Hen Harrier, Merlin or Short-eared Owl; Golden Plover, Lapwing, Ruff, Snipe, possibly Jack Snipe, Mediterranean Gull.

March–May: Most waterfowl leave by end of March; light wader passage possible, including Ruff; Short-eared Owl possible, March–early April.

June–July: Breeding species; first returning waders, especially Green, Wood and Common Sandpipers by early July.

August–November: From early August, Golden Plover, Lapwing, Ringed Plover, Dunlin, possibly American Golden Plover and Pectoral Sandpiper; from late August through September, Teal, maybe Garganey, Peregrine; in September and October, Little Ringed Plover, Little Stint, Curlew Sandpiper, Ruff and Greenshank possible, chance of American rarity; Little Gull, Black Tern; most waders leave by the end of

October, but Lapwing, Golden Plover and Snipe increase; most waterfowl begin to return in November.

32 THE LIZARD

OS LANDRANGER MAP 203/204
OS grid ref: 7012
Postcodes: TR12 (for more detail and what3words see Access section)

HABITAT

On Cornwall's south coast, this is the most southerly peninsula in England. It is flat-topped, with few trees, and large areas inland are not particularly scenic. However, with high cliffs (of serpentine rock in places), the coastline is spectacular, wave-lashed and rugged. Coves such as Kynance have superb scenery; their valleys often contain little dense cover, as soil is sparse, with a few wind-blown bushes, bramble and bracken. Church Cove offers more shelter than Kynance. Cottage gardens scattered through the valley provide further shelter. Towards the cove's mouth, the bushes peter out to bracken and bramble. A brook runs through the valley. Another small bushy valley runs parallel about 100m to the north, linked by a footpath. Gunwalloe Valley has trees towards its head, but the valley bottom consists of a reedbed and marsh, lacking open water; a golf course flanks the south bank.

Towards the tip of The Lizard are very large tracts of wet maritime heathland, a habitat of European conservation importance. Most is owned by the National Trust. A large, especially interesting stretch lies above Kynance Cove: Predannack Downs Nature Reserve, renowned for its specialised habitat. Here, lilac-coloured flowers of the rare Cornish Heath are abundant. A wide variety of heathers mingle with the bright yellow flowers of Western Gorse. Open heathland also predominates on the

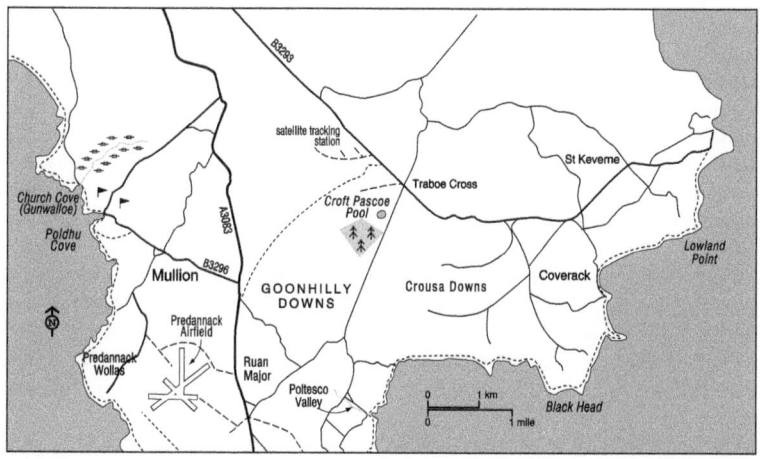

west side of Lizard Point, the nearest sheltered area from the tip being the small Caerthillian Cove.

In a joint venture between CWT and CBWPS, the small Windmill Farm and Ruan Pool area adjacent to Lizard Downs has been acquired and managed solely for conservation benefit. During its relatively short history, this 83ha farm has been transformed to include the creation of several shallow pools and a boardwalk through otherwise wet and impenetrable areas, with cattle grazing on other heathland patches.

The windmill itself has a viewing platform at the top, accessed by a steep metal spiral staircase, from where good views of the surrounding area can be obtained. Hunting raptors, if present, can be seen more easily, and in the right season harriers sometimes hunt close to the building. Trail maps are available at the windmill. Wellingtons are recommended all year round for walking.

Restored and enlarged, Ruan Pool is more suited to attracting ducks and waders.

Among other interesting plants on The Lizard are Lesser Quaking Grass, both Dwarf and Pygmy Rushes, Three-lobed Water-crowfoot and several unusual clovers, including Upright and Twin-flowered. Large populations of Adder and Common Lizard are found on the heaths and farm. Among a variety of butterflies are Dark Green, Small Pearl-bordered and Marsh Fritillaries and Grayling. Migrant insects include many unusual or rare moths. Dragonflies such as Red-veined Darter, Britain's first record of Scarlet Darter and several Vagrant Emperors and Southern Migrant Hawkers have been recorded here.

SPECIES

There is just a handful of skilled and dedicated birdwatchers working the huge Lizard Peninsula. Some parts are difficult to access, requiring long walks over rough or steep terrain, and landowners deny access to other places that are good for birds. This book therefore concentrates on relatively accessible southerly coastal sites. These include the regular Chough breeding site, which attracts many birdwatchers to the area. Habitat management and creation at the Windmill Farm reserve has resulted in a quite different spread of species visiting this part of The Lizard, such as wintering dabbling ducks, herons and waders.

Winter is the quietest time of the year on the sea, but at Lizard Point Gannet can be watched fishing or passing in hundreds, along with Kittiwake, Razorbill and Guillemot. On calm days it is also possible to pick out three species of divers, and commoner gulls and Shag should be expected too. Purple Sandpiper and Turnstone feed in small groups among seaweed-covered rocks.

On land, too, interesting birds are few, with little suitable shelter from winter storms, though Chough and Jackdaw can be seen regularly. Most common woodland species are very scarce in this relatively treeless landscape. Birds of prey hunt over open expanses, with Peregrine, Merlin and Hen Harrier all present every year outside the breeding season. The fast, agile Merlin hunts largely over heaths, as does the larger Hen Harrier. Two or more of each raptor usually overwinter. Sometimes there is a light spring passage of Merlin, and a small autumn passage of all three species. During spring, further migrant raptors occur, including a few Hobbies, and on some anticyclonic days a couple of hundred immature Red Kites will drift around. Increasingly rare in Cornwall, Montagu's Harrier is still noted some springs but now only singly. Two or three Short-eared Owls arrive in spring and often stay, and a few regularly overwinter. There are spring records of the lovely little insectivorous Red-footed Falcon, a true rarity.

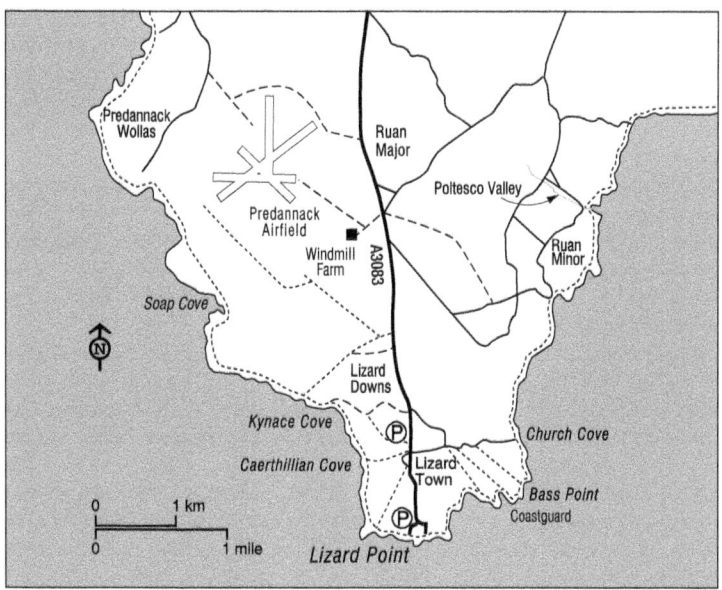

Early spring brings the first passerine migrants, a group of chestnut-tailed Black Redstarts, a Wheatear or two, and less often, but equally early, a Ring Ouzel or a few Firecrests. In general, high numbers of migrant passerines are not the order of the day. Throughout spring, a scattering of short-staying migrants passes through in small groups; Chiffchaff, and rather more of the later Willow Warbler, arrive in parties of 10 or more. Later still, Whitethroats come and Wheatear numbers increase; some Wheatears breed but numbers have declined since 1999. Whinchats pass in groups of two or three throughout later spring. Far more Hoopoes are usually reported by the public than found by birdwatchers, and a few are seen annually in this area, including one or two autumn sightings when they are less expected. Other exotic overshooting migrants in spring have included, for instance, Collared Pratincole, Eastern, Western and (probable) Moltoni's Warblers, Woodchat Shrike (annual), Marsh and Dusky Warblers, Golden Oriole, Serin, Bee-eaters and the white-bellied Alpine Swift. Other commoner migrants are regular in spring, but normally in tiny numbers, with just two or three Redstarts or Spotted Flycatchers at a time.

Seawatching in spring may provide a few coasting skuas, including perhaps a Pomarine. The passage of most seabird species, including Sandwich Tern, is generally light, however, although auks and Gannets can pass in hundreds. Rarer species have included Black-browed Albatross. March is the best month for Puffin passage at Lizard Point. Fulmar and Kittiwake breed in very small numbers. Spring sees Manx Shearwaters pass by in their thousands. Common Scoter numbers peak here in summer, with up to 60 or so passing in a day. Rather more skuas are seen from July to August than in spring, and Sooty and Balearic Shearwaters are annual in small numbers. Both Great and Cory's Shearwaters occur regularly from July to October, with the latter peaking in September when, exceptionally, up to 5,000 have been seen along with up to 1,500 Greats. Rarer seabirds such as Wilson's Storm Petrel and Desertas-type petrel may occur.

During late autumn 2001, a small group of Chough arrived on The Lizard. DNA later established that these were Irish birds; a year later a pair bred successfully at Lizard Point and have done so every year since. Slowly, they have increased in numbers and can now be found in many Cornish coastal areas. This has been a most unexpected and welcome return for a species extinct as a resident in Cornwall for over 30 years, having last bred in the mid-20th century.

As September approaches, passerine migrants such as Wheatear, Whinchat, Tree Pipit and Spotted and Pied Flycatchers begin to pass through in small numbers, on their way south. Small groups of both Yellow and White Wagtails can be found along with Grey Wagtail, sometimes a steady trickle of ones and twos through the day for several weeks. Buff-bellied, Tawny and Richard's Pipits have all been found among wagtail and pipit flocks.

Scarce migrants that appear almost annually, often in early autumn, are Wryneck and Icterine and Melodious Warblers. Although the first is a woodpecker, it often creeps along low stone walls in search of food. The two stout warblers, both possessing a long dagger-like bill, require experience to tell apart. Swifts, late arriving and early departing, pass through in hundreds per day in both seasons. During the early autumn period, Red-backed and Woodchat Shrikes sometimes arrive. All shrikes are uncommon, and colourful adult males are a lucky find, but grey-brown immatures are more likely. Among major autumn rarities have been an Upland Sandpiper, an American wader of grassland, and an elusive Little Bustard, which was searched for by many birdwatchers. An Isabelline Wheatear was the first for mainland Cornwall and an American Northern Harrier once frequented the open moorland.

From late autumn, a few Ring Ouzels, Black Redstarts and Firecrests replace the early migrants; occasionally Yellow-browed or Pallas's Warblers are recorded. One or two Lapland or Snow Buntings may appear on open ground towards the close of autumn. Finches and buntings are always among the last passerine arrivals. Chaffinches form the bulk, but among them may be the similar but distinctively white-rumped Brambling, often picked out by nasal *tchaek* calls overhead.

At the Windmill Farm CBWPS reserve, following substantial habitat and access improvements, a range of noteworthy and rare species have occurred, including Cattle and Great White Egrets, a flock of Glossy Ibis, Pectoral Sandpiper, Lesser Yellowlegs and Citrine Wagtail. Cuckoo and Willow and Grasshopper Warblers nest, and Lesser Whitethroat is thought to breed.

MAIN BIRDWATCHING ZONES

Because of the size and complexity of the area we have split the following text into zones, concentrating on those areas less frequently visited by birdwatchers with the easiest public access and with a high potential for attracting interesting birds. Some suggested localities are as follows.

Lizard Village and Headland area. Radiating from Lizard village are a number of public footpaths, encompassing the entire area (and well beyond). Even within the immediate village precincts, among areas with small trees, bushes, hedgerows, fields and sheltering gardens, interesting passerine migrants are often found, especially in fall conditions when human activity is of little importance to freshly arrived migrants urgently seeking food and shelter. At such times, in poor visibility when the foghorn blasts, the scene can be set for some very rewarding birding in spring or autumn. Even when such ideal conditions do not exist, it is still worth checking the same spots together with those slightly further afield. Scan hedgerows for a shrike perhaps, or weedy crop fields for finches and buntings, pipits favouring grassy fields, or bushy plots for warblers, chats and flycatchers. Many birds of major interest, such as Woodchat Shrike, Subalpine Warbler species and Serin, have been located within half a mile (800m) or so of the village.

The track leading from the lighthouse road across to Housel Bay, passing a small farm pool (once favoured by a Bee-eater), bushy gardens, small fields and hedges, may be especially rewarding. Then continue west on the coast path, beyond Southerly Point. A small colony of cliff-nesting House Martins could once be found here. At Pistil Meadow a path leads back to the village, passing good birding spots around fields and hedges. Alternatively, continue along the coast path until reaching the often excellent Caerthillian Cove, or walk other routes before reaching the cove; all tracks will return you to the village.

Church Cove is another short walk from the village. The sycamores, which are overlooked from the small car park behind the church, have produced some of The Lizard's best finds: Red-breasted Flycatcher, Bonelli's, Pallas's and Paddyfield Warblers, Subalpine Warbler species, and Red-eyed Vireo, for instance. Various footpaths, often rough and muddy, can be taken from the village to form circular walks; all have the potential for providing very interesting birds.

Lizard Downs–Kynance to Predannack Wollas. The entire walk covers up to 2.5 miles (4km) over mainly high open terrain, encapsulating much of the dramatic scenery for which The Lizard is famed: vast sea vistas, where Britain's third Brown Booby was found, sheer cliffs and heathy moorland, often wet and windswept. On calmer days along the way, bushy outcrops as well as the sparsely vegetated Kynance Valley are attractive to migrants seeking cover, once including an Arctic Warbler. The northward route from Kynance National Trust car park also passes beside the western boundaries of Windmill Farm and Predannack airfield. Here the open moorland gives way to bushes and small rough grazing pastures. These differing habitats fringing the airfield have public access (unlike the airfield) but are seldom walked. Along this route lies a tiny narrow-sided valley leading to Soap Cove, where there is a possibility of Ring Ouzel or Firecrest especially in late autumn. With more coverage over recent years, **Soap Cove** has regularly produced less common migrants, such as a rare Brown Shrike. Prior to reaching Predannack Wollas National Trust car park, check around areas of scrubby Blackthorn and willows in the little wet valley just before farm buildings, a favourite spot for warblers.

On retracing your steps, it is possible to vary your journey, following other tracks and enabling more comprehensive coverage. An unusual raptor might be encountered, occasional Montagu's and Marsh Harriers pass through, and Black Kite has occurred more than once. Often routes may be over uneven terrain and be wet.

Windmill Farm. Since this otherwise virtually unwatched location has become a successful nature reserve, the number of notable species seen here has soared, which is hardly surprising given its favourable location and new, improved habitat. Many of the scarcer species seen here are those that might be found throughout The Lizard. Since the improvements to the farm have been undertaken, more of these scarcer birds, both passage migrants and breeders, have been recorded and in greater numbers. It is possible to spend an entire day exploring the whole farm area and nature trail; the unlocked information centre contains an account of the general and historical interest of the area, as well as a logbook to check or enter sightings.

Goonhilly Downs–Traboe Cross. At Traboe Crossroads and along adjacent slightly higher ground beside the road, there are extensive views across moorland areas, ideal for searching for passing raptors. From Traboe Cross, a good footpath can be taken across the downs, allowing a closer search for passerines, especially open-country species such as Whinchat. Nondescript pools have hosted unlikely waders, including Black-winged Stilt, but are more usually the haunt of Snipe or Curlew. The good-quality, raised stony path reaches a group of trees and paddocks, all worth checking.

Note: If choosing paths to venture further from here, or to take another return route, be warned that they are likely to be wet and muddy for much of the year.

Croft Pascoe pool is usually checked from the roadside pull-in. Insect-hunting Red-footed Falcon is among several rarities noted here.

Crousa Downs and Coverack area. Situated on the eastern flank of the peninsula, above and behind Coverack, lie Crousa Downs with various underwatched habitat types. This area has produced many interesting birds in recent years, including a singing Iberian Chiffchaff, Common Crane, Purple Heron, Ortolan Bunting, Yellow-browed Warbler, several Hoopoes and a couple of Bee-eaters. A Pallas's Warbler has overwintered at Coverack along with several other warblers and crests.

Coverack is a very popular, picturesque tourist village. The surrounding coastal belt is therefore less visited by birdwatchers, and access to some parts is difficult due to the terrain and poor condition of footpaths. The eastward footpath from the north end of the village to Lowland Point offers views of bushy, rock-strewn outcrops, rough pastures, hedges and denser brakes. Lowland Point is a grassy plateau a few metres above sea level. Walking south from Coverack along the coast path, almost immediately the various footpaths begin to rise; scattered trees and bushes in more sheltered gardens and other areas on the outer fringe of the village could all be checked.

Steep, rough tracks pass Chynhalls Point, eventually merging when approaching the high, exposed, gorse-clad clifftop of Black Head. This route passes a few arable fields – all worth a look – especially as a Rufous-tailed Scrub Robin was found there in late August 2021.

Coverack Bay has a mainly rocky foreshore, which is not very productive in terms of interesting birds, though Black Redstart uses it in winter. However, the bay is naturally sheltered from northerly winds, and careful checking has shown a variety of species can be found. Black-throated Divers like the bay during winter, and passing Cory's Shearwater and Sabine's Gull have been recorded.

Poltesco Valley. The habitat here is unlike much of the coastal Lizard area, with a fairly narrow valley well grown with large trees. Part of the valley floor is given over to grazing meadows with bushy surrounds. During late spring or early autumn, tree density may hide birds from easy view, but various more open sunny spots can be checked. Earlier and later migration seasons can be productive, particularly when parts of The Lizard area are exposed to strong winds but this valley remains sheltered.

The few records emanating from here only reflect the unfortunate fact that not many birders visit. Britain's most southerly breeding Grey Wagtails are present, and various warblers and flycatchers visit – as has Golden Oriole.

Gunwalloe. The reed-filled shallow valley of Gunwalloe is also known as Church Cove, but referred to by its former name here to avoid confusion with the Church Cove near Lizard village. Public access restrictions mean that close checks of the reedbed cannot be undertaken, but the whole valley is easily scanned and larger birds such as an occasional visiting Marsh Harrier can be watched from the National

Trust car park. Reed and Sedge Warblers can be found in the bankside vegetation, Savi's and Great Reed Warblers have been noted in the reeds on rare occasions in spring, and Purple Heron and Aquatic Warbler have also been recorded. The squeals of Water Rail are heard all year round, suggesting breeding, though that is not proven. There is a Sand Martin colony in the sandy cliffs near the church, and the area around the church is excellent for Black Redstart and perhaps Yellow-browed Warbler in autumn.

Poldhu Marsh. Part of this habitat has been infilled to provide a large car park. The marshy reedbed here is small, but its position on the coast means it is capable of producing occasional interesting species such as Purple Heron, and in late autumn and winter a spectacular Starling murmuration. The sandy beach was once graced by a Ross's Gull and occasionally holds an Iceland or Glaucous Gull. A short, attractive clifftop walk separates this valley from Gunwalloe; its species range is similar.

TIMING

Even with the right weather conditions, spring passerine migration is generally light. Winds off the Continent, particularly southerly or south-easterly winds, will bring birds across the Channel, and a small proportion of those passing over will land before travelling on. However, they often stay for only a couple of hours after dawn if they have arrived overnight, especially in later spring. So by mid-morning, an area which held a scattering of interesting migrants at dawn can be almost empty. Exceptions are day-flying migrants such as Swift, Swallows and pipits, which leave the French coast at first light, arriving here four or five hours later; in mid-spring they begin to arrive about mid-morning. Calm weather increases chances of sightings in the reedbed habitats; in windy weather, sheltered valleys may be the most productive. Open coastal downland is exposed to high winds.

During autumn, movements are much more protracted and, although quiet mornings are still often best, many birds remain throughout the day, perhaps for several days.

Although Lizard Point is a very good seawatch headland, it is useless unless winds are in the southern half of the compass; even if winds are only light from southerly quarters, passage occurs. In spring, a seawatch between dawn and mid-morning is best; after this time migration usually slows. The same applies in autumn unless winds are gale force, when heavy passage can last all day. Sea mist and poor visibility, causing birds to hug the coastline, can also bring results.

For winter landbirds, choose a fine day without high winds, when birds will not shelter and raptors can hunt over moors.

ACCESS

The A3083 runs south along the peninsula from Helston. The first cove off this road is **Gunwalloe** (or Church Cove). Follow a good road taken opposite the southern end of Culdrose Airfield, through Gunwalloe village, following signs to Church Cove where there is a large National Trust car park **(TR12 7QE, employers.print.bikers)**. Check the tamarisk bushes in the car park hedges and around adjacent farm buildings for migrants. Among reeds and marsh are breeding populations of Sedge Warbler and Reed Bunting. Cetti's Warbler almost certainly breeds but is far more often heard than seen. Public footpaths follow the coastline left and right of the cove. Sand Martins breed among the cove's sandy-topped cliffs.

For **Windmill Farm**, follow the A3083 south from Helston on the Lizard road.

About 2 miles (3km) after passing the B3296 junction signposted to Mullion Cove, and just prior to the second Ruan Minor sign, take a narrow (partly concealed) lane on the right-hand side and continue along its length until reaching the farm gate. Parking is available in the old farmyard area **(TR12 7LH, guideline.economies. hobbyists)**. Please close all gates as you go, even if the gates are open when you drive through them. Ruan Pool is accessed from Windmill Farm by following the designated footpath. Various footpaths traverse the reserve, and a hide has been constructed overlooking Ruan Pool.

Note: There is no public access onto the farm reserve, which is restricted to members of CBWPS and CWT, or others by prior arrangement. The footpaths are often very rough and uneven, and substantial sections are wet for much of the year, probably only drying out in summer. Wear appropriate footwear.

Further south still, **Kynance Cove** is reached via a private National Trust-owned road off the A3083; at the bottom is a car park **(TR12 7PJ, frizz.protrude.mavericks)**. Walk right for a few hundred metres to the steep but rather small valley. For **Predannack Downs**, continue up the short steep valley slope also taken for Soap Cove further along the coastal path. Alternatively, park in the small car park just before the bungalow on the National Trust road and take the waymarked path to view the Predannack area. A map is usually necessary and the paths are often muddy. Small grassy fields on the perimeter of Predannack airfield are favoured by pipits, while more open areas are used by raptors.

For **Church Cove** near Lizard village, take the road forking left just before the village, immediately past the private Kynance road. Follow signs until the church, where there are limited parking spaces **(TR12 7PH, lawfully.bordering.flaunting)**. Walk down through the village after searching through the adjacent churchyard area. The tarmac road becomes a rough track near the cove. A National Trust footpath can be taken on the left, and another small, bushy valley leads back to the church. A right-hand track leads to Bass Point to the south of Church Cove; it is possible to walk past the lifeboat station to Lizard Point.

Lizard Point can also be reached through Lizard village on foot or by car. A car park adjacent to the café overlooks the sea **(TR12 7NT, bulk.clearcut.boldest)**. Choughs nest along the cliffs on either side and views can be obtained from the coastal paths as the adults forage in pasture, joined by their offspring as the year progresses.

Caerthillian Cove is signposted from Lizard village. Park in the village square, where there are public toilets, then follow the public footpath beside it, signposted to Caerthillian Cove, Kynance Cove and Pentreath Beach. Walk for about three-quarters of a mile (1.2km) along a wide track beside a row of houses; the last house overlooks the small, shallow, treeless valley. Blackthorn, bramble and gorse, especially towards the head of the valley, provides cover for small migrants. Although sparse, this is the only cover within 2 miles (3.2km) of the Point.

The flat **Goonhilly Downs (TR12 6SN, kidney.intruding.lime)** are reached on the B3293, a turning to the left off the A3083. Scan the moorland around the satellite-tracking dishes. Minor roads can be explored to the left and right. Raptors use this area, and it is best to use your car as a hide. The B3293 continues to Coverack Cove.

There is a car park at Traboe Cross.

For **Crousa–Coverack**, continue along the B3293 into Coverack **(TR12 6TF, published.suffer.commenced)**. A footpath towards Lowland Point is now much improved, although it can be muddy. Crousa Downs are reached from a minor road off the B3293 at Zoar (which could also be worth a look); there are no car parks, but roadside parking places and pull-ins which allow relative ease of checking around the area.

Poltesco lies only a short distance from Ruan Minor and may be walked or driven to via a narrow road beside the church there. The coastal footpath connects with it. From the A3083, turn left where signposted to Ruan Minor and Kennack Sands. In Ruan Minor take the left-hand turn into Poltesco Lane (not signposted) and follow the lane through the valley to the National Trust car park at the end of the road **(TR12 7LT, september.mission.upward)**. Footpaths can be used to explore the whole valley.

Gunwalloe and **Poldhu** lie to the north-west of Mullion village, halfway down the Lizard Peninsula. Poldhu, which is reached first (after about 1 mile/1.6km), is signposted from the middle of Mullion village off the B3296. For Gunwalloe, from the previously mentioned National Trust car park, follow the road on foot towards the beach. Turn left onto a wide public track over a stone bridge at the mouth of valley. Continue uphill across a golf course on same public track, which allows good views of the reedbed. Continuing on this path brings you to the road (near the golf clubhouse). Walking right, the road brings you to Poldhu.

At Poldhu, much of the reedbed can be viewed from the car park near the beach **(TR12 7JB, degree.noble.headstone)**. There is no other access. The only other reasonable view of this valley is from a roadside gateway halfway up the hill on the Mullion side. Walking the coastal footpath northward from here for half a mile (800m) brings you to Gunwalloe, enabling a circular route.

CALENDAR

Resident: Shag, Sparrowhawk, Buzzard, Cetti's Warbler, Stonechat, Raven, Chough; Gannet and Kittiwake offshore all year.

December–February: Seabirds including Black-throated or Great Northern Divers, Guillemot and Razorbill; Hen Harrier, Peregrine, Merlin, Purple Sandpiper, Turnstone, possibly Short-eared Owl, winter thrushes.

March–May: Firecrest and Black Redstart by early March; Chiffchaff and Wheatear, possibly Ring Ouzel, by mid–end March; Willow Warbler, possibly Hoopoe, by early April; possibly Merlin, Short-eared Owl, Whitethroat, hirundines, perhaps rarer southern overshoots, mid-April; Swift, other common warblers, Whinchat, Redstart, Spotted Flycatcher, possibly Hobby, Cuckoo, end April–early May; Puffin, Manx and Balearic Shearwaters and possibly Arctic and Pomarine Skuas.

June–July: Breeding species, including Wheatear, Whitethroat, Sedge Warbler, Sand Martin; seawatching from July, when Manx Shearwater and Common Scoter are usual, Cory's Shearwater generally pass through earlier than Great Shearwater.

August–November: Seabirds, including a few Arctic, Great or Pomarine Skuas; Great Shearwater later than Cory's and Sooty at any suitable time; commoner passage migrants, especially Wheatear, Whinchat, Tree Pipit, Yellow Wagtail, coasting Grey Wagtail, possible Woodchat and Red-backed Shrikes through September; Firecrest, Black Redstart, Ring Ouzel, possibly Snow or Lapland Buntings, Chaffinch flocks with Brambling, winter thrushes, from mid-October through November; Starling murmurations from late November.

Cornwall

32A LOE POOL

OS LANDRANGER MAP 203
OS grid ref: SW6424
Postcode: TR13 8WN
what3words: **Boating Lake** – boat.scoping.crackles

HABITAT
At 51ha and only 1 mile (1.6km) long, this relatively small lake is nonetheless the largest area of naturally occurring fresh water in Cornwall. Situated near the town of Helston, it is separated from the sea at Mount's Bay by a massive shingle bank, known as Loe Bar. Towards the further end from the sea is Loe Marsh. Small woods on either side give shelter from onshore winds. Loe Pool lies amid the National Trust-owned Penrose Estate; there is no shooting permitted and bank fishing is limited. It has been designated a Site of Special Scientific Interest because of its importance for wintering Shoveler. Helston Boating Lake Is a recreational pool on the west side of Helston town.

SPECIES
Some interest may be sustained throughout the estate all year if watching the many kinds of common woodland passerines, although autumn through to spring

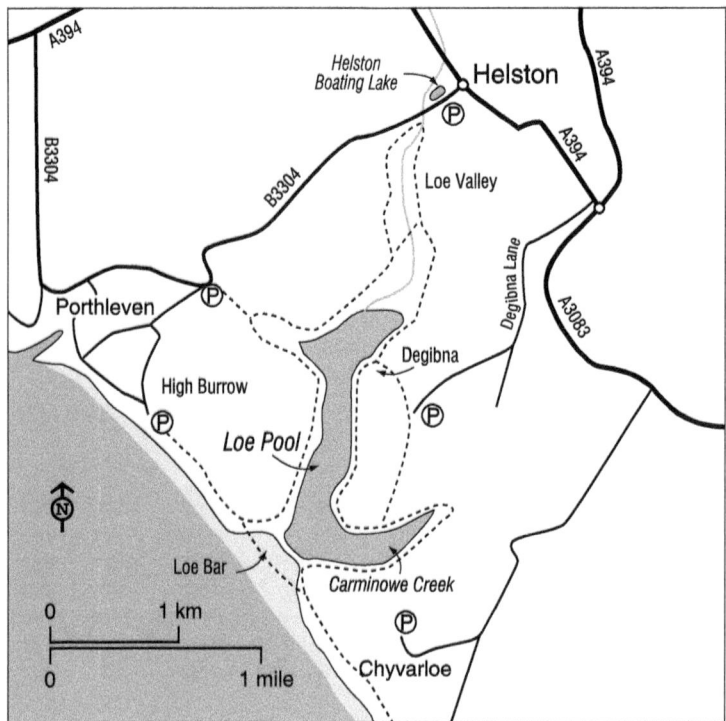

provides the opportunities of greatest interest on and around the pool. Autumn's muddy margins produce only small numbers of commoner waders, including Common and Green Sandpipers, with one or two regularly wintering. Little Stint, Greenshank or Wood Sandpiper may pass through, and Wilson's Phalarope and Lesser Yellowlegs have been reported. Prior to the construction of several large reservoirs in the county, this site was regarded as one of the better places for wintering ducks, particularly diving species (albeit in small numbers). Tufted Duck counts average 50 but more than 100 can sometimes be found on Helston Boating Lake. Pochard, although declining, can reach 40 but only occasional Goldeneye are recorded now. Both Long-tailed Duck and Scaup are less common, but regularly turn up in ones and twos. The rare Ring-necked Duck has appeared several times and a Surf Scoter put in an appearance in October 2023. Dabbling ducks chiefly comprise Mallard, of which about 150–200 regularly winter with several pairs staying to breed. Small numbers of Teal, occasional Gadwall and around 20 Shoveler are regular, while Wigeon flocks increase in hard weather. Other species of duck are attracted irregularly in small numbers. The pool shelters an occasional diver or unusual grebe such as Red-necked. Great Crested Grebes number around 30 in winter and occasionally stay to breed, along with a pair or two of Little Grebes; other species of grebe are very rare visitors, although Pied-billed, a rare transatlantic vagrant, has occurred. Coot vary between 10 and 80 depending on winter severity, and occasionally attempt breeding. Moorhens are well represented, joined by furtive Water Rails in winter, when you may chance upon a Bittern.

Wintering Common Gulls are often present, averaging around 100 birds, but numbers rise in February as passage begins. Great Black-backed Gulls form flocks of 50–200, transient Lesser Black-backed Gulls may reach 50 or so in spring and autumn, and there may be a Glaucous, Iceland, Kumlein's or Ring-billed among them. Mediterranean Gull is increasingly seen here. The gulls often commute between Loe Pool and the boating lake.

Breeding species are curiously few, but there are small numbers of Reed Warblers, and Cetti's Warblers are increasing. Unexpected scarcities or rarities might turn up; these have included Hoopoe, Green-winged and Blue-winged Teal, American Wigeon, Lesser Scaup and Glossy Ibis. Cattle and Great White Egrets are more regularly being reported in recent years.

The sea off the Bar is not very productive, with most birds preferring more sheltered and probably shallower areas of Mount's Bay. However, small numbers of divers, including Black-throated, grebes and seaducks are occasionally recorded, particularly at the western end of the Bar towards Porthlevan, where the rare sea-going Surf Scoter has occurred several times.

TIMING

Considerations are few, although harder winters increase numbers and species. Calmer conditions will allow easier viewing over Loe Pool, when birds are not attempting to seek shelter. Time of day can decide which side of Loe Pool you walk, because looking into the sun can be a problem, especially with low winter light. The boating lake is best viewed when less disturbed.

ACCESS

From the A394, take the B3304 on the outskirts of Helston. Park in the council car park opposite the boating lake (which has attracted Lesser Scaup and Bonaparte's,

Cornwall

Franklin's and Ring-billed Gulls). Cross the road bridge over the stream and go through the right-hand gate and along the rough drive to eventually reach Loe Pool. It is now possible to walk the entire 7-mile (11km) perimeter of the pool and marsh. Access is unrestricted, year round. Stretches of unsurfaced path on the eastern side of the water can be very muddy in winter, and after prolonged heavy rain some parts flood and become unpassable; walking boots are recommended.

CALENDAR

Resident: Wide selection of typical woodland passerines.

December–February: Bittern possible, small numbers of diving ducks, fewer dabbling species include Shoveler and Gadwall; rare ducks or gulls possible; few divers and grebes offshore due to unsheltered position.

March–May: A wide range of migrants, including rarities.

June–July: Breeding species. Early-returning waders such as Common and Green Sandpipers.

August–November: Waders, including less common species, earlier in period; ducks arrive later.

SITE CLUSTER: WEST CORNWALL

- **33** Marazion Marsh, Mount's Bay and Waterfront to Newlyn and Mousehole
- **33A** Drift Reservoir
- **34** Porthgwarra and Land's End area
- **34A** Sennen area
- **35** The Isles of Scilly
- **35A** Pelagic seabird trips (other than those launched from Scilly)
- **36** St Ives Island and Bay
- **37** Pendeen Watch
- **38** Hayle Estuary (Including Carnsew Pool and Copperhouse Creek)

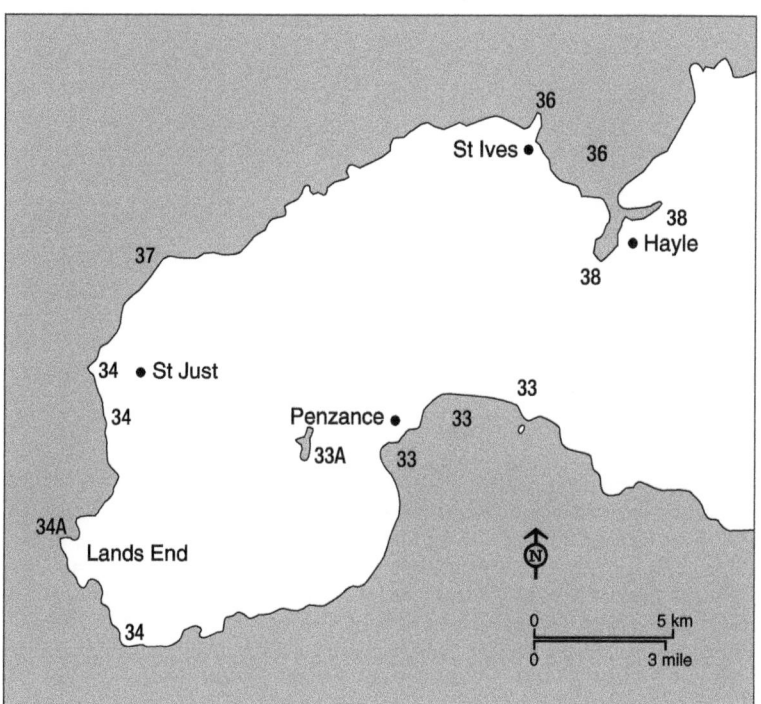

33 MARAZION MARSH, MOUNT'S BAY AND WATERFRONT TO NEWLYN AND MOUSEHOLE

OS LANDRANGER MAP 203
Postcodes: TR17–19 (for more detail and what3words see Access section)

HABITAT

Penzance is probably the best-known locality in the area and the most westerly large town on the south coast of Cornwall. The harbour entrance leads out into Mount's Bay, at the eastern side of which lies St Michael's Mount, a steep, rocky, privately owned island. Marazion Marsh is opposite the island, just inland from the sandy beach.

Penzance harbour and adjoining Newlyn contain most of west Cornwall's fishing fleet, mainly small inshore trawlers, although larger trawlers operate far offshore. Passing through Newlyn towards Mousehole affords views of St Clement's Isle, where many gulls roost. Mount's Bay's seabed is largely sandy, with the greatest area of rocks being around St Michael's Mount. Several freshwater streams drain across the broad beaches. As the bay faces south, it is sheltered from northerly winds.

Marazion Marsh is not large, covering only some 35ha, but it is the largest reed-bed in Cornwall, and is a Site of Special Scientific Interest and a Special Protection Area. A main road runs along the seaward side, a major railway line crosses the marsh and houses are adjacent on one side. The marsh comprises an expanse of dense *Phragmites* reeds, relatively small areas of open water and an area of low sedges and flag iris, in which clumps of willow grow. There is a small stand of pines at the rear. The marsh is leased to the RSPB to manage as a reserve.

SPECIES

Their geographical position makes the marsh and bay one of Cornwall's most important sites for birds. Winter is very interesting in each habitat within this area. The bay regularly attracts low numbers of divers, grebes and a few seaducks, while unusual gulls and several wader species are found along the shoreline. Great Northern Divers appear from early winter and decrease by early spring. In good years up to 15 might be present at a time, often cruising close to shore in search of small crabs, which they find on almost every dive. Black-throated and Red-throated Divers may occur through the same period, generally increasing from late winter as passage migrants gather; numbers are low, but up to 30 in total may be present when passage begins. The largest numbers of these divers are usually to be found at Little London, east of St Michael's Mount. In early 2018, Mount's Bay hosted all five of the world's diver species, including a rare White-billed and a Pacific Diver which had been returning to the bay each winter for about 12 years. Slavonian Grebes may be present, and late-departing divers and grebes sometimes attain summer plumage before they leave. Black-necked and Red-necked Grebes are only rare visitors. Seaducks are irregular in occurrence, and only commoner species are generally seen – two or three Eider perhaps, or a small flock of Common Scoter, which may contain a Velvet Scoter, its

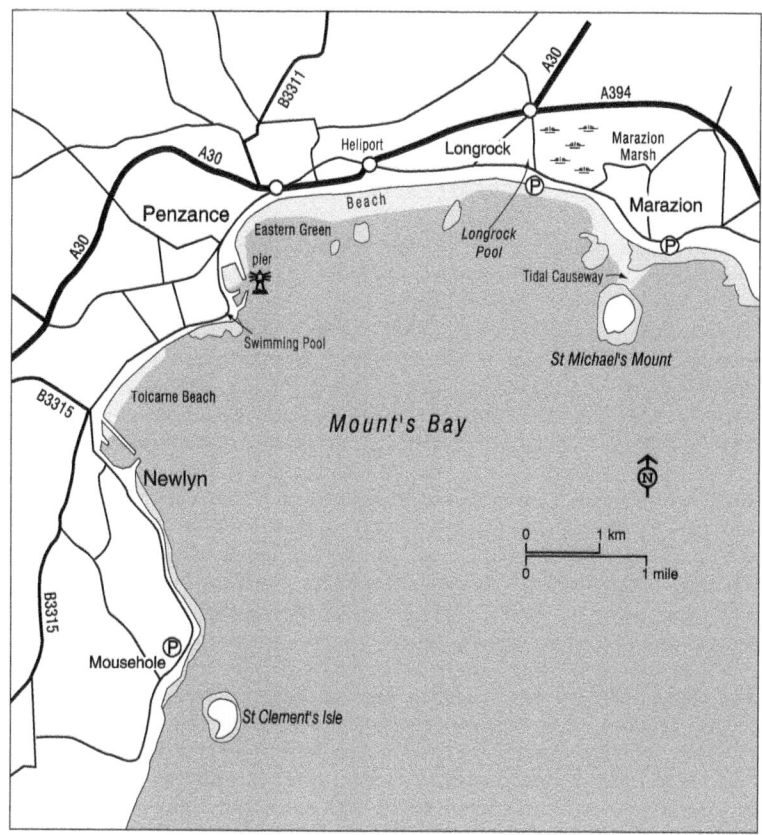

wedge-shaped head profile more reminiscent of an Eider. Dowdy immature or female Long-tailed Ducks have visited, usually singly. The area has hosted a wintering female King Eider, only Cornwall's second.

Large numbers of gulls are found throughout the district. Gull flocks use freshwater outlets running across beaches at low tide to bathe, preen and drink. From semi-concealed positions behind rocks nearby, it is possible to get extremely good views of assembled birds. Unusual gulls occur here regularly, the standard quartet being Little, Mediterranean, Iceland and Glaucous, although in recent years only Mediterranean has been reliable. Occurrences of Ring-billed Gull, once considered an extremely rare vagrant, increased so that it became at least as frequent as Iceland Gull, but in recent years it has become a rarity once more. Mediterranean Gulls of all ages appear in good numbers, with a late winter or early spring peak as different birds stop here briefly on passage. A similar pattern of occurrences exists for Iceland Gull, but these are mostly pale-fawn-speckled immatures. Glaucous Gulls, often similarly marked and coloured immatures, arrive less predictably. Little Gulls tend to appear towards spring. Common Gulls are found in good numbers when late-winter migrants arrive. Gull flocks are further increased by the passage of Lesser Black-backed Gulls (in similar numbers to Common), while a few Kittiwakes may also be present. Other gull species reported have included several more

American vagrants, stopping off at this, the first resting and feeding area they reach on the British mainland. Bonaparte's Gull has become almost a regularly occurring rarity in winter, with two seen together on several occasions and three together once! A Laughing Gull has stayed to winter. The particularly rare, dark-backed Franklin's Gull has strayed here, and the high-Arctic Ross's Gull has also been recorded, as has American Herring Gull. Caspian and Yellow-legged Gulls are frequently recorded at the St Clement's Isle roost, which can be viewed from the road, but a telescope is essential.

Other irregular visitors to the bay might include storm-driven Little Auks, petrels, Grey Phalarope or skuas. The western side of the bay around Newlyn and Tolcarne beach seems to attract more of these sightings in very rough weather. There is no skua passage as such, although that traditional harbinger of spring, Sandwich Tern, is usually a particularly early arrival, and a small but steady passage ensues. Later, small numbers of Common and a handful of Arctic Terns pass by, with maybe one or two Roseate and Little Terns. In autumn, especially earlier, terns are the only seabirds of interest seen regularly, although, as in spring, numbers are small.

Waders are generally low in number, the sandy beach habitat being responsible for several omissions. One species specialising in sandy conditions is the pale grey and white Sanderling, uncommon in many parts of Cornwall. Over 100 may gather in Mount's Bay, its stronghold on the Cornish mainland. Sprinting along the tide-line, they follow receding waves down the beach. There are never fewer than 50 winter, but counts at migration times are erratic, with peaks occurring in spring in some years and autumn in others; some stay to early summer at least, moulting into bright, brown-spangled summer plumage. Ringed Plover also like this habitat and are scattered throughout. In spring, the rare Kentish Plover might be seen. Bar-tailed Godwit and Grey Plover share the beaches, usually only in small numbers. Turnstone will turn seaweed and even tin cans when searching for food, and are found all along the shore, more than 50 being usual. At high tide they often sleep on moored trawlers. Purple Sandpiper flocks, on the other hand, remain loyal to rocky outcrops, especially around Jubilee Pool at Penzance; 20 or more is not unusual, but at times more than 50 may occur. Black Redstarts usually winter somewhere around Penzance and Newlyn, favouring walls and rocky shores, but they are often seen on Little London beach to the east of St Michael's Mount.

Marazion Marsh has an interesting and regular wintering avifauna, annually supplemented with unusual visitors. No bird species is present in very large numbers, although gulls may visit in higher numbers for short periods to bathe and preen, and may include individuals of scarcer species. Mallard and Teal often total 30 apiece, and a handful of Shoveler may occur. Other dabbling ducks turn up occasionally, mostly in ones and twos, and regularly include Gadwall. A small number of Tufted Duck and the occasional Scaup are possible on Long Rock Pool. Several Little Grebe and both Coot and Moorhen are present, but only the last breeds. Water Rail are also present at this season, but are too secretive for their numbers to be estimated accurately (probably less than 10). In some winters, particularly in hard weather, a Bittern or two may briefly take up territory, although views are likely to be brief. Snipe often remain unseen until they fly, and Jack Snipe are scarce. Completing a group of hard-to-see species is Cetti's Warbler; this vocal bird is a breeding resident, though probably no more than a dozen pairs nest.

Grey Herons are far more obliging residents, and 10 or more may be seen at once. Five or six pairs breed, some in traditional habitat high among the topmost branches of nearby pines; each year, however, two or three pairs nest on the ground among reeds, unusual behaviour for this species in Britain. Glossy Ibis, Purple Heron, Spoonbill, and Great White, Little and Cattle Egrets all now regularly use the area in small numbers. During irruption years, when Bearded Tits have had a successful breeding season in East Anglia or the Netherlands (each pair can produce as many as three broods, each with five or six young), the species visits reedbeds far outside its normal range in search of food; Marazion is no exception, though numbers have declined in recent years. Every autumn and winter, many thousands of Starlings use the reeds as a night roost.

On average each year, the marsh probably produces some of the earliest returning hirundines in Britain. Sand Martins are by tradition early, but at Marazion a few Swallows and sometimes a House Martin may equal them; later, numbers of all three species increase substantially. Other migrants well known for making early landfalls also visit, including Wheatear, shy Garganey swimming close to reeds fringing the pools, and perhaps a Hoopoe. Further exciting visitors usually occur later in spring. Common waders passing through early, such as Dunlin, are supplemented by a few Ruff. There may also be Little Ringed Plover, and Whimbrel are annual passage migrants, often counted in hundreds through a season. Sparrowhawk and Buzzard regularly hunt the marsh, sometimes joined by a Marsh Harrier quartering the reeds. A White-winged Black Tern in full summer plumage also hawked over the reeds one spring. Yellow Wagtails pass through in small numbers in spring and autumn, and a pair or two have bred in past seasons. Among their number, more exotic subspecies sometimes appear, 'Blue-headed' being the most frequent. Migrant parties are joined by a few White Wagtails, and at the same period, or perhaps earlier, the uncommon Water Pipit may be seen by freshwater margins. Sedge and Reed Warblers arrive to breed in the marsh; in autumn juveniles of the former can be mistaken for the more brightly marked Aquatic Warbler. This early autumn rarity was once regular but now seldom appears, its population decline in Eastern Europe rendering it a globally threatened species.

During autumn it is possible to see many species noted in spring, but others are restricted to autumn. Difficult, but not impossible, to see is the intricately marked Spotted Crake; patience and silence pay off when one steps nervously from deep cover, warily picking insects from a muddy pool. Some years, three or four have been present together. Once, an unusually obliging Little Crake stayed into late autumn. Another major rarity, Paddyfield Warbler, once tantalised hundreds of patient watchers with brief views at the edge of Long Rock reedbed. Citrine Wagtail has occurred several times during the autumn. Interesting waders may include a Little Stint or Curlew Sandpiper, and American scarcities and rarities are expected, though not necessarily annually. The most regular of these is Pectoral Sandpiper, and both Long-billed Dowitcher and Baird's Sandpiper have been seen several times. The beach is always worth checking for unusual waders.

Hirundines once again begin to mass, joining large groups of Swifts feeding before departure. Swallows roost at night in the reeds, where over 1,000 may assemble. This late activity attracts another migrant, Hobby, preying on hirundines at this time of year. Among the Swallows and martins feeding on the myriad insects, especially flying ants, over the marsh, there may be a Little Gull or Black Tern.

For seawatching at Mousehole, ideally the wind should be southerly or south-southwesterly, but for checking St Clement's Isle and the gull roost the wind is irrelevant. This venue enables less mobile birdwatchers to scan from the car park, from where it is possible to see a selection of quality seabirds. A telescope is essential, as passing species, such as large shearwaters, terns, petrels and skuas, can be

500m offshore and often lost to view between wave troughs. Wintering seabirds may also occur.

TIMING

Gulls gather at freshwater outflows on the beach when the tide is out and also along the tideline, with waders. During rough weather, especially from late autumn through to spring, a wide variety of species may seek the bay's comparative shelter, particularly if winds are from northerly quarters. The beaches are popular with local people as well as tourists, so if possible early morning or midweek visits are advised, on ebbing tides in good weather. When trawlers unload in the harbour, gulls are drawn from widely scattered areas and this greater concentration may contain unusual species. Check the rooftops at Newlyn Harbour for roosting gulls, as well as the water inside the harbour at high tide, when close views of divers and auks can be obtained.

Even very early in spring, a spell of settled weather with winds from southerly quarters off the Continent may produce a wide range of early migrants, including passerines, waterbirds and waders. The marsh is far less disturbed than the beach, and most species adapt to the presence of trains and cars. Lower water levels encourage waders to visit and stay, while hard weather may increase numbers of more common birds and produce a rarity. Westerly winds from the Atlantic are mostly responsible for the arrival of American ducks and waders. Calm winter days are best for views of egrets or Bittern and other reed-dwelling birds.

There is a good deal of interchange, with birds commuting between here and the Hayle Estuary complex to the north. If conditions are rough at one site, they are often sheltered at the other. Although the two localities are quite close, they are on opposite coasts and their tide times are slightly different; many birds, especially gulls, take full advantage of this. Also note that some gulls fly inland to bathe at Drift Reservoir (see site 33A).

For Mousehole, southerly to south-south-westerly winds produce ideal seawatching conditions, especially during earlier mornings, but late afternoons are best for the gull roost on St Clement's Isle. Calm seas are needed for wintering seabirds.

ACCESS

The A30 runs alongside Mount's Bay and through Penzance, beside the waterfront. From Marazion Marsh to Newlyn is about 3 miles (4.8km). There are fee-paying car parks throughout the area. Public roads fringe harbours and fish quays, where public access on foot is allowed. The full length of the beaches can be walked, from Marazion to Penzance. Alternatively, the beach named Eastern Green, immediately east of Penzance, may be reached on foot via a footbridge over the railway line; this area is favoured by gulls.

Marazion Marsh can be viewed easily from the roadside pavement. Arriving on the A30 from the Hayle direction, turn left at Long Rock, before Penzance, and drive east along the front to the marsh. There is a large pay-and-display car park opposite Long Rock Pool **(TR17 0EP, breed.abstracts.dame)**. To access the marsh, take the path opposite the small grassed area at the east end. Please do not enter the marsh carelessly and disturb birds. The concealment provided by low clumps of bushes makes it easier to approach carefully. The narrow, sometimes muddy streamside path leads to a small, often unproductive pool 600m inland at the east side of the marsh. Do not wander off any of the footpaths. Long Rock Pool and surrounding reeds can also be viewed from the roadside; it is possible to pull in here and watch from car windows for a short period.

For the less mobile birdwatcher, it is possible to view the bay and its beaches at conveniently sited car parks and roadside pull-ins, such as that at **Long Rock**. There is a seafront car park on Long Rock Road, past the supermarket when leaving Penzance and travelling eastwards **(TR17 0DA, testy.position.boating)**. It is just before the industrial estate, crossing the railway line via a level crossing. In **Penzance** itself, the main quayside car park for the town (doubling as a boat park) allows close checking of the far western end of the bay **(TR18 2GB, another. brings.blotches)**. A slipway also allows beach access and unrestricted viewing, including easy access for those less mobile. To check **Newlyn Harbour** and the far western end of the bay (Tolcarne Beach), take the road passing the harbour; a car park is on the left just after the fish market on the dockside **(TR18 5HW, mango. group.dote)**.

Purple Sandpipers gather to roost at high tide on the rocks around the outdoor swimming pool (Jubilee Pool) on the Newlyn side of Penzance.

For **Mousehole**, from the A30 take the B3315 for 0.6 miles (1km) to Newlyn. At the crossroads by the bridge, continue straight over and follow the road to Mousehole, about 1.5 miles (2.4km) further on. There are parking places on The Parade, from where St Clement's Isle can be viewed for roosting gulls; alternatively, use the fee-paying car park on The Parade for seawatching **(TR19 6QE, magnitude.relief.ramps)**.

CALENDAR

Resident: Cormorant, Shag, Grey Heron, Stonechat, Cetti's Warbler, Reed Bunting.

December–February: Divers, especially Great Northern, with Black-throated and Red-throated mostly towards end of period, grebes; unusual gulls, including Glaucous (early in period), Little, Mediterranean, Caspian, Yellow-legged and Iceland (mostly towards end, when Common and Lesser Black-backed Gulls and Kittiwake arrive); Eider, Common Scoter and Long-tailed Duck possible; Sanderling, Purple Sandpiper, Turnstone, Grey Plover, Ringed Plover, Snipe, Teal, Shoveler, probable Gadwall and Tufted Duck; Water Rail; Bittern possible.

March–May: Seawatching in suitable weather; unusual gulls possible throughout, mostly March, when Ring-billed possible; divers often peak in early April; first Sandwich Tern, Garganey, Ruff, Swallow, Sand Martin, Wheatear, maybe Water Pipit and Hoopoe, from mid-March; Whimbrel, Common and Arctic Terns, and possibly Roseate or Little Terns from mid-April; Little Ringed and Kentish Plovers, Spoonbill and other southern overshoots possible.

June–July: Breeding species, including Cetti's, Reed and Sedge Warblers.

August–November: Seawatching throughout in suitable weather; return tern passage from mid-August to late September; light passage of common waders, including Sanderling; more unusual waders, including Little Stint, Curlew Sandpiper, possibly Green and Wood Sandpipers, maybe American species; from mid-August through October, possible Spotted Crake, Black Tern, Little Gull, Swallow roost to end of September, possible Hobby; shearwaters, petrels and other passage seabirds; Starling roost from early September; divers, grebes and seaducks begin to return in November.

33A DRIFT RESERVOIR

OS LANDRANGER MAP 203
OS grid ref: SW4329
Postcode: TR19 6AE
what3words: coil.condensed.pave

HABITAT
This most westerly English reservoir, set in the hills between Mount's Bay and Land's End, is 26ha in extent. Its waters are shallow, with broad muddy margins at summer's end, which are exposed to a greater extent and for longer periods than those of a deep-sided reservoir. This makes it attractive to both waders and diving ducks (which prefer not to dive too deeply for prey). Wooded at its north end, it is mostly surrounded by open farmland. Although used by many anglers, it has no water sports.

SPECIES
This reservoir's proximity to Penzance and Newlyn encourages some species to move between sites freely. For example, gulls consistently fly in from Mount's Bay, especially at high tides or during stormy weather. Some gulls roost and preen here. Scarcer gulls are frequent; if missed at the coast, an errant bird may well turn up here. Of these, Mediterranean Gull is seen most often, but Glaucous, Yellow-legged, Caspian, Iceland and Ring-billed Gulls have all been attracted, and even Bonaparte's and Laughing Gulls have been seen.

During autumn, this reservoir has a reputation for producing rarer waders. Wader passage in west Cornwall is poor compared with other areas of the region, but among small numbers of commoner waders, scarcer species such as Ruff, Little Stint, Curlew Sandpiper and Wood and Green Sandpipers may occur. Virtually annually it produces an American wader, often a Pectoral Sandpiper. Lesser Yellowlegs, Long-billed Dowitcher, and Semipalmated and Spotted Sandpipers have also been found. A Sharp-tailed Sandpiper was an extremely rare Asiatic visitor in August 2004. Osprey is a regular passage migrant in August and September.

During winter, Drift may host a sheltering diver or two, while grebes are a more frequent sight. Little Grebe numbers reach only about 10, and Great Crested have attempted to breed in recent years. Duck numbers are unremarkable. Mallard, Teal and Wigeon are typical dabbling ducks, though never numerous. Goldeneye, Ring-necked Duck, Scaup and Goosander may arrive occasionally in ones and twos, and Britain's first female Lesser Scaup was identified here. The last species has occurred on several occasions since, and in October 2023 there was a party of 10 at the reservoir, the highest number ever recorded in Britain; the flock consisted of four drakes and six females. In December 2023, a Dusky Warbler visited the reservoir bushes.

Breeding species are few but include Willow and Sedge Warblers.

TIMING
Gales may induce birds to shelter, and high tides can cause gulls to arrive. Hard winters increase numbers and species. Strong westerly winds are responsible for autumn arrivals of American waders. Calm conditions allow easier viewing.

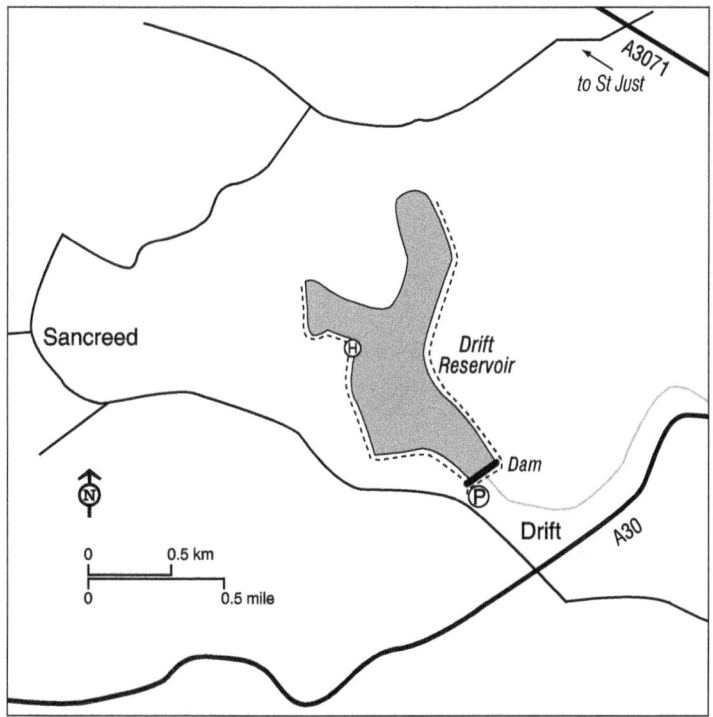

ACCESS

The A30 passes through the village of Lower Drift. If heading west towards Land's End, take the minor road on your right in the village, which is signposted to Sancreed. Opposite the dam is a car park, just off the road. Elevated above the reservoir, it offers extensive views and is thus useful for less mobile watchers, although a telescope is essential. From the car park, check nearby fields for gulls, geese or egrets. There is no close circular route around the reservoir.

From the car park, a path leads past buildings to the water's edge. Turn left through a gate marked 'permit holders only', where access is restricted to CBWPS members. After about 300m, you reach a vantage point overlooking most of the reservoir; from here it is possible to scan through the flocks of gulls and ducks. Continuing to the end of the boardwalk, follow the path to the hide; this can be very muddy and uneven. Walking from the car park across the dam and down the eastern side (again, access is restricted to society members) can give close views of waders when the mud is exposed.

CALENDAR

Resident: No species of special interest.

December–February: Small numbers of ducks, loafing commoner gulls have attracted rarities; Great White, Little and Cattle Egrets.

March–May: Returning common migrants and occasional scarcer species.

June–July: No species of special interest.

August–November: Returning waders in small numbers earlier in period have included American vagrants; Osprey is now annual here; duck and gull numbers build towards end of period.

34 PORTHGWARRA AND LAND'S END AREA

OS LANDRANGER MAP 203
OS grid ref: SW3722
Postcodes: TR19–20 (for more detail and what3words see Access section)

HABITAT

Porthgwarra Valley and the adjacent south-projecting Gwennap Head lie only about 3 miles (4.8km) from Land's End. Birdwatchers consider the area to include everything south of a line from Carn-les-Boel cliffs in the west to St Levan Church to the east. Except for the lower valley and areas around St Levan Church, this coastal site is exposed to winds from most directions, and in stronger winds even gardens and more sheltered areas are affected. At the head of the valley is a small bush-fringed pond, shallow and usually dry from late spring to late autumn. There are small fields of rough pasture and arable land on the landward side of the valley. Above the more luxuriant growth in the valley lies an expanse of more exposed heathland. Gorse and heather, including Western Gorse and Cross-leaved Heather, grow in profusion. The 'moors' in late summer are a mixture of blazing purple and gold. In the stream valley, groups of trees, mostly willows, are kept low by salt-laden winds. Stands of Cornish Elm are affected to various degrees from time to time by the ravages of Dutch Elm Disease. Royal Fern grows in boggy patches near the stream. Dense areas of bracken, bramble and Blackthorn also occur. The magnificent cliffs contain huge, rounded granite boulders, the heath extending to cliff-edge turf. Among this fine, short grass grow blue carpets of Autumn and Spring Squill, Rock Sea Lavender and Golden Samphire. Around St Levan church are sheltered groups of trees, gardens and hedgerows. A brook runs through the centre. Looking seaward on a fine clear day, the outline of the Isles of Scilly can be seen 28 miles (45km) to the south-west. About 1 mile (1.6km) offshore from Gwennap Coastguard lookout lies the Runnel Stone Reef, marked by a bell-buoy which sounds with the movement of the waves. A powerful tide race flows past the headland.

Porthgwarra is a good spot for migrant butterflies including Monarchs and Clouded Yellows. Some years in early autumn, thousands of migrant day-flying Silver-Y moths drink from heather flowers. Adders and Grey Seals are common in the area, while dolphins, Basking Sharks and Blue-fin Tuna can sometimes be seen offshore.

North of Porthgwarra are other, often sheltered, coastal valleys close to Land's End. A stream lined with bushes and hedges flows through the Nanquidno Valley, near St Just. The small Cot Valley regularly attracts interesting or uncommon

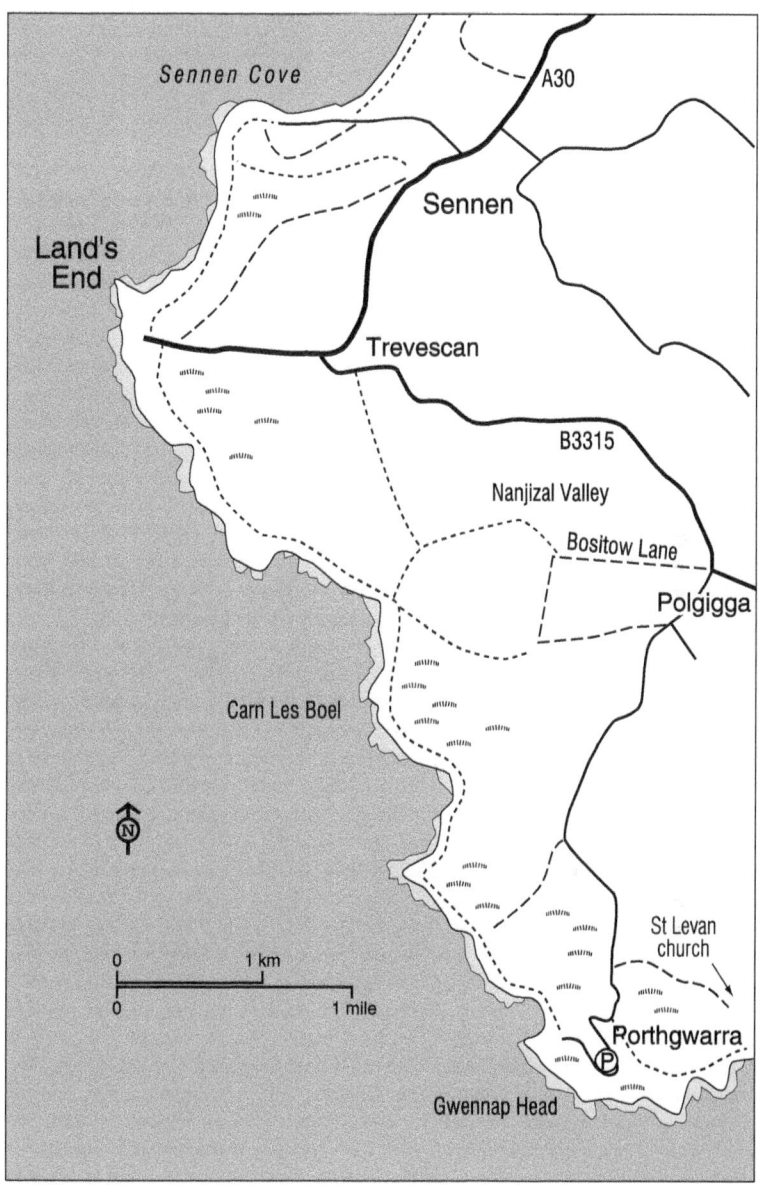

migrants in spring and autumn; this picturesque valley, steep sided and gorse covered, with rubble from disused mine workings spread over its sides, has the most cover, including trees and cottage gardens towards its head. Some willow and Elder bushes grow beside its stream. Sea views are panoramic, facing The Brisons rocks, 1 mile (1.6km) distant. Kenidjack, just north of Cape Cornwall, is another quite sheltered valley. On flat land overlooking the bend of the valley is St Just Airfield, an open area of short turf. Further inland, east and north along Land's End peninsula, an exposed band of moorland and hills with heather, brambles and rough pasture rises to 200–300m, overlooking the cultivated coastal plain and extending some 12 miles (19km) to St Ives.

SPECIES

Porthgwarra is visited by birdwatchers seeking migrants – preferably rare! – for which this beautiful area is nationally known. Because of the exposed habitat, residents are few, but occasionally woodland birds wander into the area, when in autumn or winter foraging birds extend their travels. Lengthening spring days herald traditionally early migrants: a scatter of Wheatears, Chiffchaffs and Willow Warblers, often backed by an arrival of Black Redstarts from early March. Goldcrests, calling almost incessantly, may be present in high numbers, perhaps with a Firecrest among them, calling more deeply and less often. The outside chance of a Hoopoe increases slightly a month later when more migrants arrive. Porthgwarra does not seem usually to attract large spring falls; small arrivals of up to 10 birds are more likely, often a handful of breeding-plumaged birds, including Blackcap, Whinchat, Redstart and Ring Ouzel. Later in spring, commoner species such as Whitethroat and hirundines pass through in groups of 10 or so of each at a time. Sedge Warblers appear as migrants and may stay to breed in the valleys, as do a few pairs of the secretive Grasshopper Warbler on the moors and hills. This latter also appears as a coastal migrant, together with Spotted and Pied Flycatchers, Cuckoo and, decreasingly, an occasional Turtle Dove.

Rarer migrants are mostly expected later in spring. Every year, two or three at least are found in the Porthgwarra district. Woodchat Shrike has turned up on many occasions, although it is not annual; it has also been seen in early autumn and is more frequent here than the declining Red-backed Shrike. An exciting bird may be a raptor, drifting overhead; Honey Buzzard, and Montagu's and Hen Harriers have all been seen on several occasions, with Hobby much more frequent. In more recent years, an annual spring influx of hundreds of Red Kites has occurred during settled anticyclonic periods. These are non-breeding immatures from breeding areas 'up country'. On reaching Land's End, they decide not to venture out into the Atlantic and instead roam through western Cornwall in particular, prior to returning to their natal areas, usually when the weather deteriorates. Migrant Black Kites have occurred here; they are now annual in Cornwall, probably lured by the numbers of their cousins that occur from April to June in the right weather conditions. Both Eastern and Western Subalpine Warblers have been found among commoner warblers.

Off the headland, small groups of Whimbrel pass eastwards close to shore. The casual watcher will almost certainly see Gannets and Fulmars just a few metres offshore, but a more sustained watch is required to see more interesting seabirds. The best months to see divers passing are April and May, but there will probably be only two or three in a morning. Most commonly seen is the large Great Northern, with its slow wingbeats; next most numerous is the slightly smaller Black-throated with faster wingbeats, showing strongly contrasting black upperparts and white underparts; least numerous, as always in south Cornwall, is the smaller, browner, fast-beating Red-throated. A few Common Scoter flying past close to the sea in single file are the only regular ducks. There is very light skua passage; Arctics travel singly, perhaps numbering two or three a day, but rarely a pack of skuas is seen, most likely Pomarine. Tern passage is also light, mostly Sandwich, often in small groups of up to 10; a few Common Terns pass, but Arctic or Roseates are less likely.

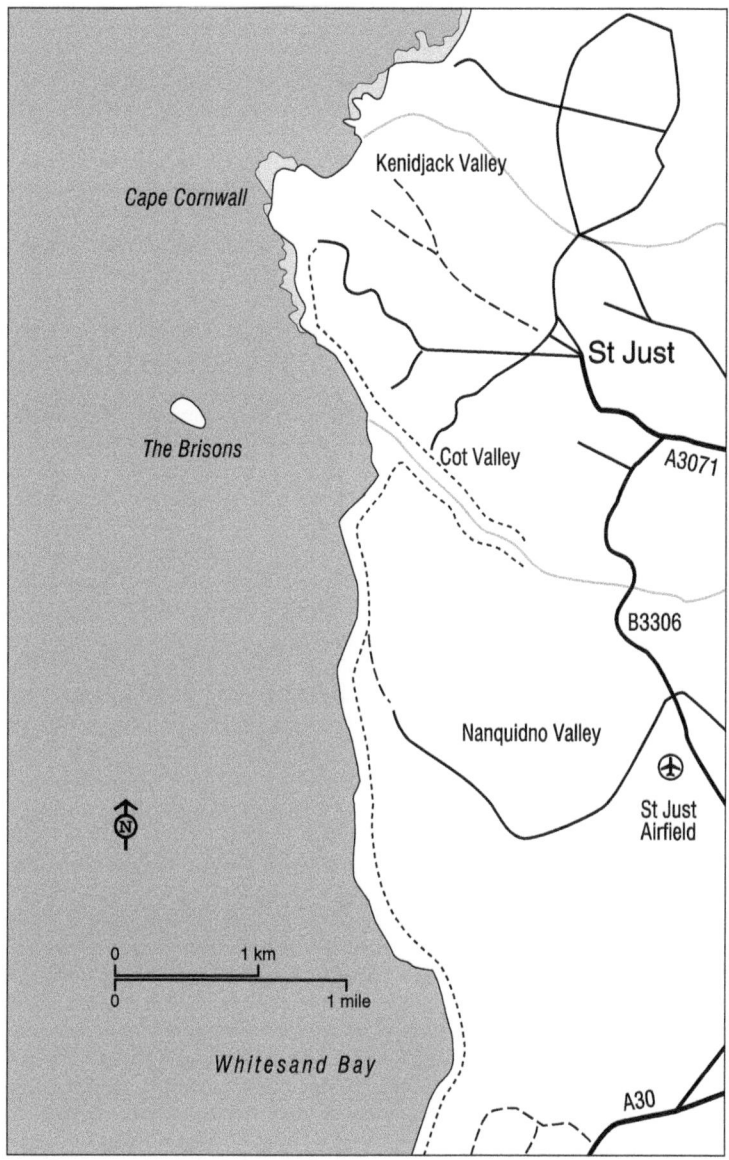

Skua and tern passage is eastward, usually within 1 mile (1.6km) of the coastline. Seawatching in summer can be rewarding, with ocean-going Kittiwakes always present. Manx Shearwaters pass by during most of the year, sometimes in their thousands and often strung out in straggling groups. Auks constantly pass to and fro and will often include at least a few Puffins. Harder to observe are European Storm Petrels, which are often seen singly, but groups of three or four may 'dance' over the water together and it is possible to see more than 100 on a good day. From July, Cory's Shearwaters can be watched for; unlike Manx, which they dwarf, they do not continually bank from side to side, but glide, often on bowed wings, giving a few languid flaps before another extended glide. Their numbers vary dramatically from year to year, from very few to several thousand a day.

In midsummer, commoner seabird migrants begin to pass westwards. Sooty, Cory's and Great Shearwaters tend to appear later in the season, and records of Balearic Shearwater also increase. Through early autumn, seabird numbers and variety improve. Skua numbers are higher, although only three or four Arctic or Great per day pass, and Pomarine are even less frequent. Lesser Black-backed Gulls, including many first-year birds, may pass westwards in their hundreds. Offshore, it is certainly possible to see unusual or rare birds; apart from those already mentioned, Desertas-type petrel (often detected in Manx Shearwater flocks) and Black-browed Albatross have been reported more than once. Possibly influenced by warming waters, Wilson's Storm Petrels are now occurring far more regularly as they follow their food sources.

Passerine migrants return from early autumn; average numbers are higher than in spring and birds often stay longer. Expected early birds are Spotted and Pied Flycatchers, *Phylloscopus* warblers such as Willow Warbler, and Whinchat. Among the first unusual warblers may be Melodious; although virtually annual, only one is likely in a season. The similar Icterine Warbler is less regular. Open-ground species favour the heath and pasture: 20–30 Wheatears, White and Yellow Wagtails and Meadow Pipits gather, and a few Tree Pipits are often heard calling among them. The larger, long-tailed Tawny Pipit may visit from the Continent; looking like a very pale juvenile Yellow Wagtail, but larger, it has a similar call, plus a sparrow-like *chir-rup*. The Asiatic Richard's Pipit, with richer brown coloration, is similar, but its *shreep* flight call is distinctive. Sharing the moorland habitat with the pipits and wagtails may be a Dotterel, occasionally two or three, although not every autumn. Whimbrel also stop to feed among the heather, where the *quip* call of Ortolan Bunting has often been heard. Single Corncrakes, now very rare migrants, are occasionally flushed from the same habitat.

Grassland-loving species are attracted to St Just Airfield, where Dotterel and the rare larger pipits have been recorded on a number of occasions; other plovers, and waders such as Buff-breasted Sandpiper, have also visited here in autumn. On the short grass, any birds present may be easier to see than at Porthgwarra, although slight undulations in the ground can conceal even Dotterel when sitting. However, when there are a lot of flights, the birds desert the airfield. Other open grassy areas in the general vicinity have provided records of difficult-to-identify pipits such as Red-throated, Blyth's and even Pechora. Raptors are regular autumn visitors to the area, with one or two Peregrines, Merlins and Hobbies passing over the coastal valleys; other less frequent birds of prey include Osprey, Black Kite, Honey Buzzard, and Montagu's and Pallid Harriers; one mega-rare find was an Amur Falcon in July 2017.

As the season progresses, numbers and species of birds begin to dwindle. Replacements are likely to be more unusual or rare species. Regular, though only in ones and twos each autumn, are exquisite, intricately marked Wrynecks. Barred Warbler, large, grey and white with few markings, is also found in some years. Migrants that traditionally arrive late and in larger numbers include Robin, of which 40 or more may be present, and Goldcrest, perhaps in similar numbers. Firecrest have peaked at about 10 at Porthgwarra, but three or four is more likely. Five or so Black Redstart may be seen at a time, but sometimes there are more in late autumn. Other later migrants include Short-eared Owl, Hen Harrier and Ring Ouzel. Lapland

and Snow Buntings, feeding on heather seeds on the heath above the valley, are difficult to see on the ground; they may also turn up on the airfield. Red-breasted Flycatchers and tiny, hyperactive Yellow-browed Warblers both prefer valley trees. Arctic and Greenish Warblers have also been seen on several occasions in various locations. All the above species may also turn up in the other valleys.

If conditions are right, large movements of finches pass over the valleys. Large numbers of Chaffinches often arrive, with Bramblings and dozens of Siskins typically involved. When such movements take place, with hundreds of Skylarks and flocks of Woodpigeons and Stock Doves passing overhead, a Twite or Serin just might be recorded. Rustic Bunting, very rare on the region's mainland, has also been seen late in the season.

By the end of autumn, most migrants have departed, but a few individuals linger into early winter. Some may even stay, such as Water Rail, Firecrest, Black Redstart, Snipe, and perhaps Jack Snipe and Woodcock. Short-eared Owls and other predators may also be encountered; two or three of these day-flying owls, plus one or two Merlins and often four or five Hen Harriers – west Cornwall's largest concentration – arrive to winter on the peninsula's higher moorland slopes, which have also been graced by the ghostly white Gyr Falcon and Snowy Owl. By the start of winter, Porthgwarra or another nearby venue may have produced another major rarity for Cornwall, maybe an American thrush or perhaps a Tree Sparrow! Like the Isles of Scilly, this area has an enviable record for producing American vagrants. Three notables seen here have been American Redstart, Veery and two Chimney Swifts together. A Blackpoll Warbler and a Radde's Warbler were both first records for the Cornish mainland, too. Other neighbouring valleys share in these surprise arrivals: among a plethora of rare and very rare birds have been Europe's first Varied Thrush, a bird of Pacific coast woodlands, found at Nanquidno (November 1982). Kenidjack has scored with an American Redstart and a Yellow-throated Vireo, while Cot Valley has produced Swainson's Thrush and Upland Sandpiper, and St Levan Pechora Pipit and Baillon's Crake. A Bay-breasted Warbler near Land's End was Britain's first. Red-eyed Vireo has occurred several times in the district.

Around Land's End, essentially the same species occur as in the neighbouring locations, both as residents and migrants. However, several extreme rarities have also been located here, including Grey Catbird, Pechora, Buff-bellied and Blyth's Pipits and several Penduline Tits. Wryneck seem to favour these surroundings, and the small meadows adjoining the site regularly turn up Richard's and (less frequently) Tawny Pipits, as well as Ortolan Bunting. Since the successful natural breeding by Chough on The Lizard, ever-increasing numbers of their offspring have taken up residence along the extensive coastlines of the Land's End peninsula (and beyond) and can be seen anywhere along the clifftops.

TIMING

For seawatching off Porthgwarra or other nearby sites, light to moderate south-easterly to south-south-westerly winds are best. Mist at sea can be an advantage, as long as you can see 1 mile (1.6km) or so out. Strong or gale-force south-westerlies or strong offshore winds are the least productive, but birds may appear soon after these have abated or pass before the advance of a front. Very early mornings, late afternoons and evenings through spring and summer and very early autumn have all been good. During autumn migration, seawatching at any time of day will probably be rewarding in the right conditions. Strong sunlight causes issues, as everything is in silhouette and eyestrain can be a problem.

When the sun has moved around, later in the day, conditions improve a little. It is best when there is no direct sunlight on the water.

For land birds in spring, any light to moderate wind from a southerly quarter can produce a few migrants; the valleys are adversely affected by high winds. If conditions are clear, most soon depart. Mist or drizzle, of the type associated with wet southerlies or south-easterlies, may delay them and produce more birds. The same conditions in autumn are responsible for some of the best bird days. In autumn, light easterlies are also excellent, especially if cloud or rain causes birds to land. Usually, birds are slower to move off in autumn, but not always. Strong winds from any direction, funnelling through valley bushes, make the area inhospitable; few migrants are seen on such days, but St Levan may be more sheltered and could be worth checking. Strong northerly winds make visits largely a waste of time. Watch St Just Airfield when it is quieter or not in use; early mornings and evenings are often best.

Fine days are good for moorland raptors in winter; late afternoon, when Short-eared Owls start hunting and harriers or Merlin strive to make a last kill before nightfall, can be interesting. Two or three hours' watch is needed, ideally over an open stretch, to see raptors coming and going, since they range widely.

Ideally, Land's End should be checked during early morning before the area is substantially disturbed by tourists. This higher site is particularly exposed to adverse weather conditions.

ACCESS

For **Porthgwarra**, after leaving Penzance towards Land's End on the A30, take the B3283 through St Buryan. Follow this road to the B3315 and continue until a left turn onto a minor road signposted to Porthgwarra village, where there is a car park (fee payable) **(TR19 6JP, pasting.spruced.bathtubs)**.

Check for passerines among trees and sheltered gardens, especially tamarisk bushes, at the base of Porthgwarra Valley. Follow a steep path from the cove or walk up the road to the coastguard cottages and heathland. There are good paths from here to the cliffs or across the heath. From these paths, search carefully through bushes and trees in the valley and the moorland beyond.

For seawatching, either sit left of the coastguard lookout, more or less opposite the Runnel Stone Reef marker buoy, or walk back out of the car park to the small cove where there are a few seats, though the views here are more restricted. Seabirds often feed around the reef and over the tide race. It is possible to walk to St Levan Church via a highly scenic coast path. Check among the trees and bushes for small birds, and the fields for pipits. The South West Coastal Path runs from Mousehole around the entire Land's End peninsula to Hayle.

From the B3315 past Porthgwarra, to reach **Nanquidno** and **St Just**, continue west towards Land's End, turning north on the A30 then left on the B3306 towards St Just. Before reaching the village, turn left immediately after the airfield along a minor road skirting the airfield's northern boundary towards Nanquidno. Good views of the airfield are possible from this roadside **(TR19 7NU, masterful.deleting.ruffle)**. There are several verge-side pull-offs for cars further down the valley, but it is better to park and cover the whole valley on foot.

The higher ground between Porthgwarra, St Levan and Land's End has many footpaths where migrants – including scarcer species – regularly occur.

At **Land's End**, continuing from the Sennen road, follow signs to the tourist complex and park in the fee-paying car park **(TR19 7AA, loudness.found.**

fighters). Low, scrubby, windswept willows, patches of heath and small fields provide cover for migrants seeking shelter; all these habitats can be adequately covered by numerous footpaths, including beside dramatic cliff edges and through fields. One of the best tracks is also used by cyclists and horse riders, and starts immediately before the Land's End Visitor Centre, to the right of the entrance road. It runs northwards, either to further cliffside paths or into Sennen village, and passes all the area's typical habitats; this area is particularly favoured by Wrynecks.

To reach the **Cot Valley**, take the road signposted to Cape Cornwall from the middle of St Just village; within 200m, take a minor road on the left, signposted to Cot Valley. There is limited car parking beside a narrow road at the head of the valley (this road runs the whole length of the valley, with further limited parking) **(TR19 7NS, interests.player.event)**. On sunny weekend afternoons, you may have to park in St Just, as this is a popular tourist spot, but few birds will be seen at these times anyway. Follow the often muddy but reasonable public footpaths around gardens at the valley head (good for flycatchers and warblers). An elevated path on the left (facing the sea) runs the length of the valley. Check the lower rocky areas for such species as Wheatear and Black Redstart. Seawatching can prove very productive here.

Note: There is a youth hostel in the valley.

For **Kenidjack**, after leaving St Just northwards towards St Ives, take the first left-hand turn at the bottom of the hill. Limited parking is available **(TR19 7QW, baker.caves.hotspots)**. Walk the length of the valley over often rough tracks.

Several good minor roads intersect the high moorlands and all can produce interesting raptors. A particularly high vantage point with the widest possible vista is required to enable sightings of more distant birds of prey. One of the better places is near **Trewey Hill**. Heading from St Just to St Ives, turn right off the B3306 along the minor road signposted to Newmill and Penzance; this rather steep road begins to level out, with views over a wide area of moor **(TR20 8UY, thirsty.fancied.remainder)**. Pull off on to the verge and scan the area. Also try other minor roads near Trewey.

CALENDAR

Resident: Shag, Cormorant, Razorbill, Guillemot, Sparrowhawk, Buzzard, Green Woodpecker, Rock Pipit, Stonechat, Reed Bunting, Raven, Chough.

December–February: Few interesting birds winter regularly on the coast but Black Redstart possible. Inland, on the hills, possible Peregrine, Hen Harrier, Merlin, Short-eared Owl.

March–May: Seawatching opportunities can arise throughout. Auks, including Puffin, Fulmar, Kittiwake, Black Redstart, from early to mid-March; Chiffchaff and Wheatear by end of March; Willow Warbler and Goldcrest by early April; hirundines, Whinchat, Redstart, Ring Ouzel, possibly Hoopoe from mid-April onwards; Whitethroat, Grasshopper Warbler, flycatchers, Cuckoo, Turtle Dove, Whimbrel by end of April–May; all three divers, Manx Shearwater, Sandwich and Common Terns, possibly Arctic Tern and Pomarine Skua offshore in April–May.

June–July: Breeding species and late-arriving migrants, possibly including southern European overshoots; Manx and Cory's Shearwaters, European Storm Petrel, Common Scoter, Puffin.

Cornwall

August–November: Cory's, Great, Sooty and Balearic Shearwaters, Pomarine, Arctic and Great Skuas, Sandwich and Common Terns, August–September; Willow Warbler, Whitethroat, Wheatear, Whinchat and Redstart, Spotted Flycatcher, possibly Melodious Warbler or Woodchat Shrike, from early August; Whimbrel, Tree and Meadow Pipits, possibly Osprey, Dotterel, Wryneck, Barred Warbler, possibly Tawny Pipit, White, Grey and Yellow Wagtails, scarce or rare species, September; Hen Harrier, Peregrine, Merlin, Short-eared Owl, crests, Ring Ouzel, chance of Richard's Pipit from early October; Black Redstart, finch flocks, Skylark, Woodpigeon and Stock Dove, Water Rail, Woodcock, Snipe, Jack Snipe, Lapland and Snow Buntings and Red-breasted Flycatcher later in the month; eastern vagrants, including Yellow-browed, Radde's, Pallas's and Dusky Warblers; North American wader and passerine vagrants.

Website: The Sennen Cove website gives daily bird sightings from around the district. (sennen-cove.com)

34A SENNEN AREA

OS Map 203
OS grid ref: SW3526
Postcode: **Sennen Cove** – TR19 7DG **Sennen** – TR19 7AD
what3words: **Sennen Cove** – computer.scribbled.reserve
Sennen – loudness.deed.risk

HABITAT

There is a wide, deep, sandy bay, usually identified on maps as Whitesand Bay, between Land's End and Cape Cornwall. It is flanked by high cliffs on either side. On the southern edge, a flat-topped rocky outcrop known as the Cowloe stands just offshore. Facing westwards, the bay is exposed to all westerly and south-westerly winds, which here are frequently strong. It is, however, sheltered from any easterly winds.

A major tourist area, the beach is also popular with surfers.

The fields, visible from footpaths around Sennen, often produce rare migrants in spring and autumn.

SPECIES

The bay is interesting for occasional wintering Common Scoter (Surf Scoter has visited) or Long-tailed Duck. Divers and grebes visit occasionally. Gulls are mainly the local Kittiwakes and Herring Gulls, but they are often joined by single Glaucous or Iceland Gulls in winter. Good numbers of Mediterranean Gulls are present for most of the year now. After autumn gales the bay may harbour a Sabine's or Little Gull. Terns, mostly Sandwich, pass through in small flocks, with some Common in both seasons, and scarcer species are seen occasionally. Few waders visit, but Grey Plover, Purple Sandpiper, Turnstone and Oystercatcher are all likely in small numbers. All gulls, terns and waders may use the Cowloe to perch or shelter on.

In late autumn, the crop fields around Sennen and Sennen Cove are worth checking for Snow and Lapland Buntings, and sometimes rarer pipits such as Richard's, which frequent rough grazing fields. Black-winged Pratincole, American Golden Plover, Dotterel, Azores Gull (the *atlantis* form of Yellow-legged Gull), Wryneck and shrikes have all occurred. Spring migrants reported around Sennen include a fine male sub-adult Pallid Harrier, Black Redstarts, shrikes and Golden Orioles.

TIMING
Visit on calmer days for waterbirds or during sheltering easterly winds. Westerlies may induce a few passing seabirds to fly closer or attempt to find some shelter, but no sustained passage occurs regularly.

ACCESS
The A30 passes through Sennen village, and the minor road marked to Sennen Cove leads down a very steep hill. The bay is overlooked from two low-set car parks, one of which directly overlooks the Cowloe rock outcrop.

Checking the often productive sea area around Aire Point (at the northern end of the bay) is almost impossible without a telescope. On leaving the cove, turn south for a quarter of a mile (400m) on the A30 and park near the post office to check nearby fields. Other fields in the area, such as at Trevorrian by the A30 and Bosvine Corner, are regularly checked by birdwatchers at migration periods to good effect.

CALENDAR
Resident: No species of special interest, but Fulmar and Gannet present offshore all year; Mediterranean Gull.

December–February: Small numbers of divers, grebes and seaducks; Purple Sandpiper, Glaucous or Iceland Gulls possible.

March–May: Passage migrants can include thousands of Manx Shearwater offshore, and terns.

June–July: No species of special interest; extremely busy with tourists.

August–November: Still busy with tourists in August and early September. Returning migrants can include interesting gulls, skuas and terns; fields and hedges may hold rarer migrants; storm-blown seabirds such as phalaropes; wintering species later in period.

Cornwall

35 THE ISLES OF SCILLY

> OS LANDRANGER MAP 203
> OS grid ref: SV9011
> Postcode: **Hugh Town, St Mary's** – TR21 0HU
> what3words: **Hugh Town, St Mary's** – waltzes.forces.travels

HABITAT

About 28 miles (45km) beyond Land's End, and visible from Cornwall on a clear day, the Isles of Scilly are a world apart from the rest of the region. This highly scenic archipelago of 140 or so rocks and islands covers no more than 10 miles (16km) from corner to corner, with a variety of habitats including rocky and sandy shores, cliffs, farmland, heathland, sea turf, marshes, lakes and woods. The land is characterised by lush vegetation in sheltered areas, responding to the mild oceanic climate and lack of sustained frosts. Tall, wind-resistant hedges of salt-resistant *Pittosporum* and other frost-tolerant exotics shelter small, flower-growing

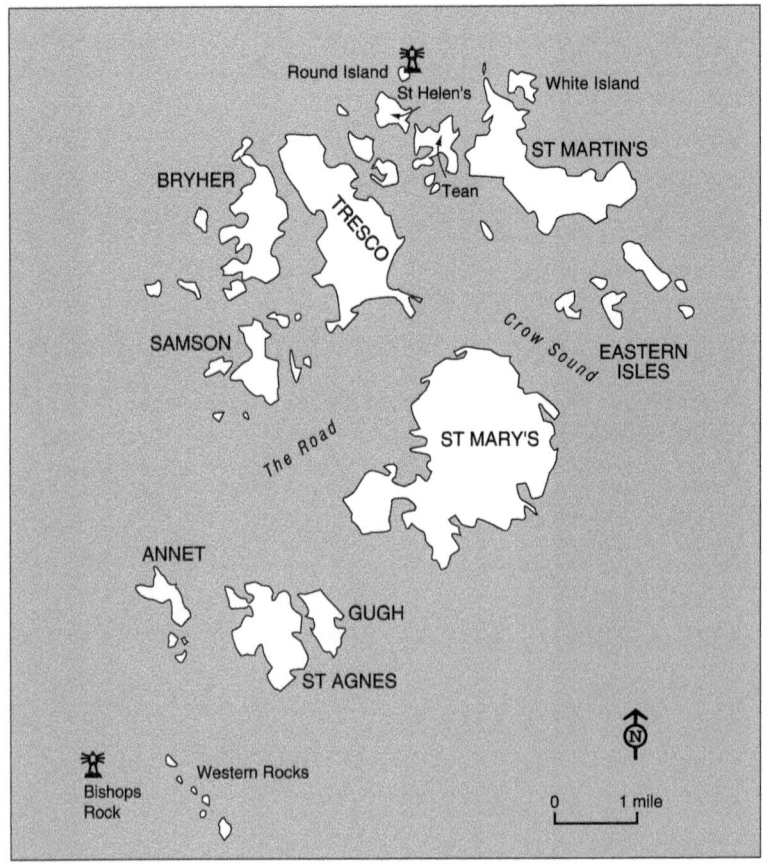

fields and are a characteristic landscape feature on the five inhabited islands. Other introduced subtropical plants such as tamarisks and palms form a substantial addition to the native flora of the main islands. Island wildlife includes the Lesser White-toothed Shrew, found nowhere else in the UK. Common, Bottle-nosed and Risso's Dolphins may be present between Scilly and Land's End, with Humpback and Fin Whales around the islands in recent winters. Resident Grey Seals are often seen basking on rocks in fine weather; they breed on quieter outer isles. Many rare wild flowers are found, alongside exotic species thriving in the mild climate. Autumn winds have brought Monarch butterflies from America and Clouded Yellows from southern Europe. Although Rabbits are widespread, many mainland animals are unknown here; snakes, Fox, Badger, Stoat and Weasel are entirely absent, but Hedgehog (St Mary's) and Red Squirrel (Tresco) have been introduced.

These are the main islands and islets:

St Mary's is the largest, 2.5 miles (4km) long and home to most of the islands' people, especially in Hugh Town, the port and main centre for the archipelago. Chiefly agricultural, the island has two major boggy, south-facing valleys, Lower Moors and Holy Vale–Porth Hellick, with water and sheltered bushes and

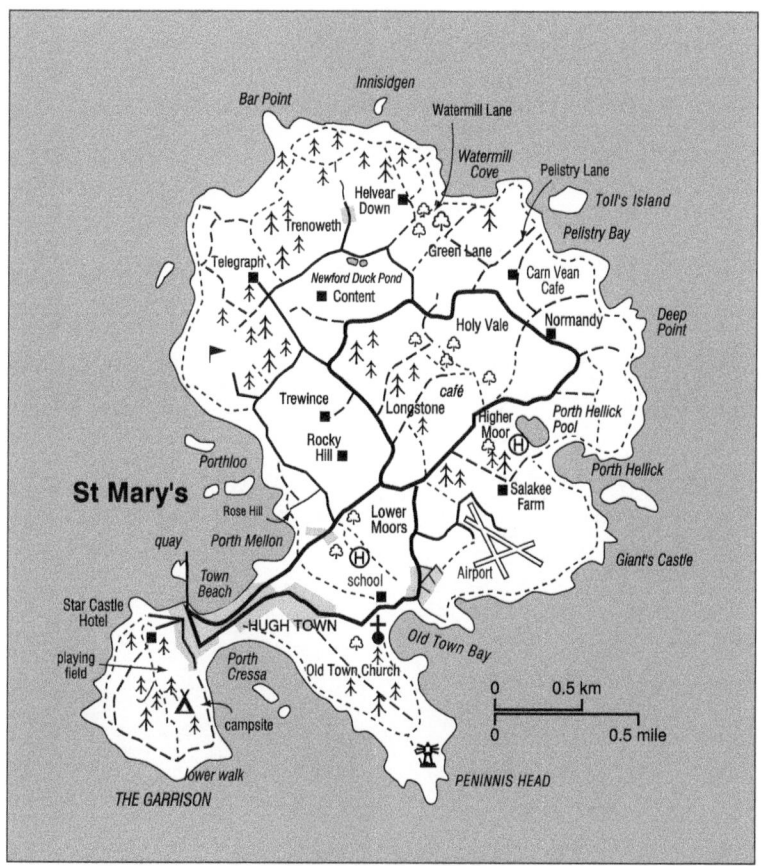

woodland. Areas of open heathland and granite boulders face the coast. The turf expanses of the airfield and golf course occupy prominent positions on the higher slopes of the island. West of Hugh Town is The Garrison headland, with mature trees and bracken, from which wide scenic views can be gained across to all the other main islands.

St Agnes, to the west, is separated from the others by a deep and sometimes rough channel. This island, little over 1 mile (1.6km) long, is the last inhabited outpost of Britain. The windswept south (Wingletang Down) and west of St Agnes are open, rocky heathland with bracken, but the centre and east contain tiny hedged fields. The heath and bracken-covered islet of Gugh is connected to the east flank of the island at low tide by a sand bar. Parsonage Wood near the old lighthouse is a small, sheltered area of Elm trees. Beyond this lies a small marshy pool and beaches near the north end of the island, looking out towards Annet, an uninhabited 800m island of rocks and turf. Annet, an important seabird sanctuary, faces onto open ocean westwards, with Bishop Rock lighthouse standing 4 miles (6.4km) to the west.

Tresco, which is privately owned, lies across the shallow, sandy sound north of St Mary's. It has an abbey, subtropical ornamental gardens, lakes and sand dunes. The northern part of the 2-mile (3.2-km) island is mostly open heathland. Castle Down, at the extreme north, has a series of shallow turfy depressions attractive to open-ground species. Pine plantations and dense rhododendrons grow on the sheltered east side. Lush subtropical gardens surrounding the abbey are bordered by tall mixed woodland. This overlooks the shallow, 800m-long Great Pool, which is fringed by reeds and willows and runs across the southern half of Tresco. In front of the abbey, separated from the Great Pool by a narrow twisting isthmus of bracken, is sandy Abbey Pool. West of Tresco lie the twin bracken-clad hills of Samson (uninhabited) and Bryher.

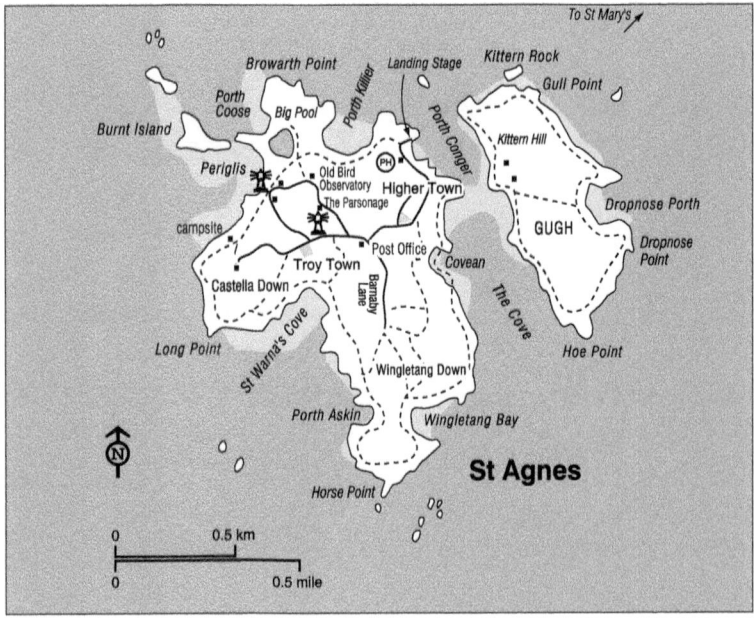

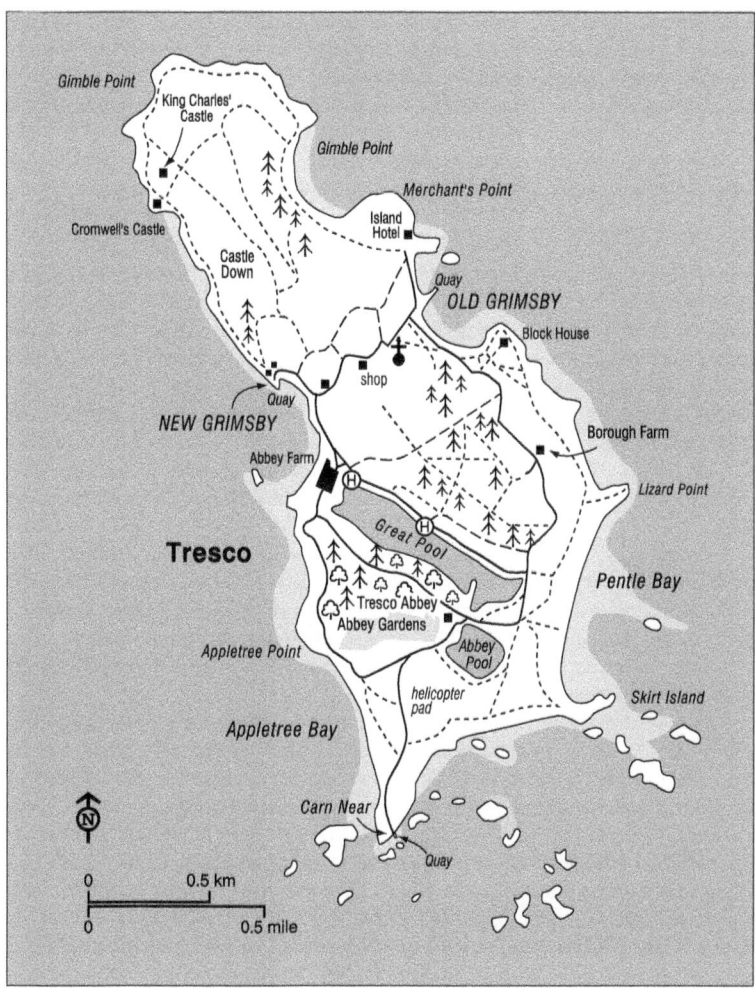

Bryher, just 1.3 miles (2km) in length and 0.6 miles (1km) across at its widest point, can be reached from Tresco on foot at extreme low tides. It consists of a series of scrub-clad hills, open beaches, small field systems and many sheltered areas. There is also a small open-sided pool. The headland at the north end gives spectacular views and is good for open-ground birds. Access remains more open than elsewhere. Despite having produced some spectacular birds, this island is often overlooked.

St Martin's, to the east of Tresco, has a 2-mile (3.2-km) long ridge that overlooks extensive white, shell-sand beaches facing across the sound towards St Mary's. Although mainly agricultural on its southern slopes, the top of the island, The Plains, is mainly heathland, lacking deep cover, as is the open ground at the east end near the Daymark beacon. Most of the sheltered fields are along the south side of the island, above the beach. To the north-west lie Round Island, St Helen's, Tean and Men-a-vaur.

There are three other main groups of uninhabited rocks and islets: Western Rocks, a series of jagged reefs and stacks in deep water 4.8km west of St Agnes; Northern Rocks, jagged rocks west of Bryher; and the Eastern Isles, between St Martin's and St Mary's. The more sheltered isles are covered with grass, Tree Mallow and gorse, with sandy bays between them.

The islands, visited by thousands of tourists in summer, can play host to hundreds of birdwatchers, especially in October, traditionally the peak rarity season.

SPECIES

The Isles of Scilly have a reputation as probably the best place in Britain to see stray migrants from all over Europe, Asia and North America. This is due to their position on the outer fringe of the European landmass, acting both as a last resort for birds blown across from the east, and as a first landfall for birds that have made accidental crossings from North America. Some of these intercontinental wanderers, although very rare on the British mainland, have become 'regulars' on Scilly at certain seasons.

Late summer specialist boat trips in search of pelagic seabirds give a significant opportunity to encounter rarer species among the thousands of locally breeding birds.

Resident species on the islands are relatively few, including Song Thrush, Blue and Great Tits, Wren, Starling, Robin, House Sparrow and Dunnock. Many familiar mainland birds, especially those of woodland, such as woodpeckers, Coal and Long-tailed Tits, Nuthatch and Treecreeper, are absent. Apart from Carrion Crow and Raven, even corvids are rare. The bird population is augmented by important seabird colonies in summer.

Few birdwatchers visit Scilly in winter, when flocks of dozens of silver Sanderling scurry along windy beaches with Turnstone and Purple Sandpiper among seaweed-covered rocks, and an occasional Merlin wanders between islands in search of small passerines. In recent years, a few Spoonbill have remained, often between Tesco and Bryher. Great Northern Divers are seen in the sounds between the islands, where Gannets and Kittiwakes shelter from gales. Tufted Duck and Pochard gather on Tresco's pools, where, over the years, several American Black Duck have taken up long residences. Water Rails can be confiding, and Firecrests winter. A few Black Redstarts are present in sheltered coves, where dead seaweed encourages insect life. There is always a chance of a rarity 'left over' from the previous autumn, particularly a wader. The orange-rumped Killdeer from North America has turned up several times in late autumn and winter on open, damp grassland. At this season some species not usually found on Scilly, such as seaducks or grebes, may arrive. Gull occurrences may include occasional white-winged gulls, and rarely Ring-billed. Rarities are too numerous to list, but have included Great Blue Heron, American Herring and Laughing Gulls and, one Christmas, an American Royal Tern.

Spring is the less visited of the migration seasons on the islands, with considerable scope for further discovery, although many overshooting Mediterranean herons and warblers often move on within a few days. As with other coastal areas in the region, characteristic early spring arrivals include Firecrest, Wheatear and Black Redstart. Hoopoe is annual on coastal grassland. Later in spring large falls of warblers, especially Willow, can occur, as well as smaller numbers of all common migrants. Exotic overshoots may well include a Woodchat Shrike or Short-toed Lark, both of which are annual. No spring passes without the liquid warbling of Golden Oriole, although even the brilliant yellow and black males can be hard to spot in thick cover. Sometimes loose parties of several birds arrive in warm weather and stay for weeks. Other notable species at this season have included Caspian Plover, Egyptian Vulture, Belted Kingfisher, two Lesser Kestrels and, just from Bryher, two Rock Thrushes, Squacco and Great Blue Herons, Crag Martin and a singing Arctic Redpoll.

Among the seabirds, Fulmars and auks tend to arrive early in spring, while the terns do not arrive until up to two months later. Although the seabird colonies are small in comparison with some on the Scottish and Irish coasts, 500 or so pairs of Razorbill and over 180 pairs of Puffin (the latter mostly on Annet) are greater than those remaining on the mainland coast of our region. Common Tern, which once bred regularly, is now mostly only a visitor, and Arctic and Roseate Terns make occasional appearances. A few Sandwich Terns may also be seen. Out in the sounds, dozens of Shag are usually fishing, and at times 200–300 gather to attack fish shoals.

In contrast to the Eastern Isles, the rockier northern and western sides of the archipelago support deep-water feeders, with most Fulmars and auks in the Men-a-vaur, St Helen's and Round Island area north of Tresco and St Martin's. The most dramatic seabirds are on Annet (where landing is not permitted), on the outer western edge of Scilly, which supports important breeding populations of Manx Shearwater and European Storm Petrel. These elusive breeders avoid gull attacks by approaching their colonies only after nightfall, spending daylight either well out to sea or nesting in burrows and crevices. These species are increasing, with surveys revealing more than 1,600 pairs of European Storm Petrels and over 1,000 pairs of Manx Shearwater. The removal of Brown Rats from St Agnes and Gugh has boosted the numbers and success of both species. Breeding gulls are doing less well, with Kittiwake effectively extinct, but more than 1,000 pairs of Lesser Black-backed and 600 pairs of Great Black-backed Gulls constitute the largest populations in the region.

Breeding landbirds are limited, although the abundance, and tameness, of Song Thrushes and House Sparrows is noticeable. Linnets, Rock Pipits and a few Stonechats are found around the coastal fringes, while reedbeds and damp areas of cover host a few Reed and Sedge Warblers. Little Egret, Coot and Gadwall are commonest on Tresco, where Pochard, Shoveler and Teal have also raised broods. The absence of many of the breeding summer visitors found on the mainland means the arrival of new migrants is easily noticed. A strange feature of migration on Scilly is that the counts of rarer arrivals can be greater than those of 'common' species!

Early autumn is not traditionally the peak period for rarer migrants on Scilly but produces a good number and variety of common and scarcer species, always with a chance of a major rarity. This is the best period for wader variety; low water levels on pool margins leave mud, which attracts migrant waders such as Curlew Sandpiper, Dunlin, Little Stint and Greenshank in small numbers. Likely American species include Pectoral Sandpiper, sometimes in twos and threes. Other rarer visitors, such as Short-billed Dowitcher and Wilson's Phalarope, have turned up, and the very rare, dark-winged Solitary Sandpiper has been seen on several occasions. Along rocky bays, any Common Sandpiper should be checked carefully for its similar transatlantic cousin, Spotted Sandpiper. At the same time the autumn's first Dotterel, from the mountaintops of northern Europe, may stop off. Early passerine migrants include a chance of Melodious or Barred Warblers among commoner species, perhaps an Ortolan Bunting, and very often a Red-backed Shrike hawking bees from a prominent bramble perch.

Cornwall

In late summer and early autumn, special pelagic boat trips are run for birdwatchers from St Mary's towards the seabird feeding areas of the Western Approaches. These have found a number of rarer pelagic species, with Wilson's Storm Petrel nowadays expected. Some trips have found dozens of the latter among many European Storm Petrels and other commoner species. Swinhoe's Storm Petrel and Zino's Petrel have been seen, with several Scopoli's Shearwaters picked out among increasing numbers of Cory's and Great Shearwaters. Use of 'chum' – a pungent mix of fish offal – attracts seabirds to feed very close to the boat at times. The same boats helped many to see Britain's second Red-footed Booby roosting on Bishop's Rock lighthouse, one afternoon, alongside a Brown Booby. Whilst pelagics give the best chance, Great and Cory's Shearwaters and other scarce seabirds have also been seen from land, particularly off south-facing headlands.

The pace quickens from mid-autumn as birdwatchers arrive from all over Britain. On St Mary's, an evening bird log takes place during October at an advertised venue. Those crossing by ferry from the mainland often report Sooty Shearwaters and skuas passing close by the boat, or occasionally a raft of dark-capped Great Shearwaters on the sea. In October, rare birds are the focus, with observers hurrying from island to island to see the latest arrivals, and others searching to find their own. Birds become more varied and numerous through mid- and late autumn, with summer visitors continuing to pass through the islands when nearly all have left mainland Britain. Buff-breasted Sandpiper is a local speciality, being seen annually on areas of open grassland, with double figures sprinting around the airfield on occasion. These same areas may hold one or two Dotterel, perhaps at point-blank range, and an American Golden Plover might drop in with a group of Golden Plover. The same habitat may hold a Richard's or Tawny Pipit or an inconspicuous Lapland Bunting, although this regular visitor is more likely on coastal heath. The extra birds arriving attract a few predatory Merlin, while larger raptors such as Osprey, Black Kite, Honey Buzzard, and harriers may spend two or three weeks wandering from island to island. One of Scilly's most prized rarities was a Short-toed Eagle, which spent several days ranging over the islands one October.

Facing the Atlantic, the Scillies are at risk of October gales, so high winds, rain and sea spray can disrupt birding. Some try to seawatch, although numbers of birds passing are usually low compared to mainland headlands. However, Great or Sooty Shearwaters, Leach's Storm Petrel or skuas may be noted. Passengers on RMV *Scillonian III* may have better luck, with a chance of a Sabine's Gull following the boat and sometimes even a flock of Grey Phalarope's sitting on the sea. Such storms build anticipation for spotting American landbirds when the weather abates; the islands are one of Europe's centres for encountering these lost wanderers. Although sightings are irregular, depending on the strength and timing of gales, a few are brought across every year. Watching a Common Nighthawk hawking around St Agnes lighthouse at dusk, or a tiny, striped Black-and-white Warbler scrambling head-first down a tree trunk will create a lifetime's memory for many keen watchers. Many firsts for Britain have been found at this period, with multiple arrivals of Grey-cheeked Thrush, Blackpoll Warbler and Red-eyed Vireo. Other New World species have included Swainson's, Wood and Hermit Thrushes, 11 species of New World warblers, Cliff Swallow, Cedar Waxwing and over a dozen Rose-breasted Grosbeaks.

In favourable conditions, a wide variety of interesting Eurasian migrants may be encountered. Spotted Crakes are glimpsed regularly in marshy valleys and pool sides. Firecrests are frequently seen, and there will usually be several Yellow-browed Warblers, sometimes dozens across the islands, often lingering where insects are plentiful. Icterine Warbler is still seen, and Red-breasted Flycatcher is another regular, often seen flicking white tail-patches in wooded areas. Towards late autumn almost anything from the Northern Hemisphere might be found, setting identification puzzles, especially when Booted, Blyth's Reed, Paddyfield or Sykes's Warblers are reported. Green and Two-barred Greenish Warblers are examples of UK 'firsts' detected by close observation on these islands. Asiatic thrushes can produce some surprises to match their New World counterparts and Siberian, White's, Black-throated, Dusky and Eye-browed Thrushes have all been seen. The few remaining weedy fields prove attractive to elusive buntings, including Little, Rustic and – once – Yellow-browed, and perhaps rare pipits such as Olive-backed or Red-throated from the Far East; the wonderfully streaky Pechora Pipit has also been seen three times. Most autumns, a pallid young Rose-coloured Starling is found, along with Ring Ouzel and the increasingly rare Turtle Dove; the islands are now the best place in the region to see this once widespread summer visitor. Black Redstart can be surprisingly numerous around coves and buildings at this season, with falls sometimes estimated at several hundred across the island group. A Woodcock or Short-eared Owl may be flushed from coastal bracken, and one or two scarce Pink-footed Geese or Whooper Swans appear some years, usually not staying for long.

Birds can continue to arrive right through to the end of autumn, while mild weather encourages some vagrants that arrived earlier in autumn to stay on. Very late arrivals often include a Dusky or Pallas's Warbler, with Eastern Yellow Wagtail, Masked Shrike and – from America – Hermit Thrush, all arriving after visiting birdwatchers have returned to the mainland.

TIMING

Most people on pre-arranged visits will be unable to alter timing according to weather conditions. Warm southerly winds are most likely to produce spring exotic overshoots and falls of commoner summer migrants. In autumn, deep transatlantic depressions, especially those that originated as hurricanes off the coasts of Florida and the Gulf of Mexico, often affect the Scillies. Look for American vagrants on the first bright day after such gales, as they come out to feed. In windy weather, sheltered areas such as Broome Platform on St Mary's, the eastern side of St Agnes or perhaps Tresco, may be productive. In southerly or south-westerly gales, try seawatching off southern points such as Porth Hellick or Peninnis on St Mary's, or Horse Point on St Agnes. Porth Hellick Point should be the first landfall for birds moving past the islands. Results are probably best in bad visibility rather than in gales, which push birds towards the Cornish mainland. In strong north-westerlies, shearwaters and skuas have been seen from Tresco's north cliffs. For breeding shearwaters and petrels coming to Annet, a dusk visit by boat will give a chance of seeing birds gathering nearby. Late summer is best for pelagics for Wilson's Storm Petrels and other notable species. For European and Asiatic migrants, a south-east wind, even if light, usually brings good watching in autumn. Surprisingly, however, the passing of a deep depression can funnel in birds from both east and west, bringing a complete mix of rarities.

ACCESS

By boat on RMV *Scillonian III* from Penzance to St Mary's, a two-and-a-half hour journey and sometimes very rough, although interesting for seabirds.

Details of sailings from islesofscilly-travel.co.uk/scillonian-iii or 01736 334220. Day trips to St Mary's (four hours ashore) are possible.

By aircraft from Land's End, St Just; more information at islesofscilly-travel.co.uk/skybus or 01736 334220. Flights also depart from Exeter and Newquay from March to September.

By helicopter from Penzance; more details from penzancehelicopters.co.uk or 01736 780828.

Note: The boat may be unable to sail in exceptionally severe gales, and all flights may be suspended in fog. All services cater for disabled and less mobile visitors, but the use of inter-island boats is more challenging.

Most birdwatchers base themselves on St Mary's. Inter-island boats leave Hugh Town quay at 10.15 a.m. most mornings; details are chalked on the noticeboard outside the shipping office in the main street. You can usually return in mid- or late afternoon. Groups often arrange by request to charter boats for special outings. Some visitors may prefer to keep out of the 'ornithological rat-race' and conduct their birdwatching at a quieter, more leisurely pace. Those more attracted by this idea could consider visiting in spring or basing themselves on St Martin's or Bryher, which provide plenty of scope for finding birds but are less visited.

Local resident birder and naturalist Will Wagstaff runs guided trips between spring and autumn. Contact Will at islandwildlifetours.co.uk or 01720 422 212.

For details of pelagic trips see scillypelagics.com.

Note: On all the islands, there are lanes, public paths, nature trails and coast walks, which enable birdwatchers to search the ground thoroughly. There is no reason to enter fields without the farmer's permission. Boardwalks are located at Higher Moors and Porthellick, extending access into marshy ground. Most fields are small and can be scanned easily from the edge. If a bird fails to appear, wait until it does because dry stone walls may collapse if leant on! Please keep to paths; boots can bring soil parasites such as nematodes from an infected area into a healthy field, ruining crops and putting livelihoods at risk.

Migrants, including unusual birds, can turn up anywhere but some of the best-known areas to watch are:

St Mary's: Trees around The Garrison for warblers; Lower Moors (two hides) for raptors, crakes, waders or warblers; Peninnis Point for larks, pipits, Lapland Bunting and possibly passing seabirds; Porth Hellick Pool (two hides) for herons, ducks and waders; Holy Vale for warblers, flycatchers and other passerines; the airfield for Dotterel and other waders, pipits and Lapland Bunting; Salakee Farm area between the airfield and Porth Hellick for small passerine migrants; fields east of Telegraph Hill for rarer buntings and pipits. Newford Duck Pond and Watermill Cove on the north-east side of the island for passerines.

St Agnes: The Parsonage for warblers and flycatchers; the pool and surrounding beaches for waders; Troytown fields for warblers, pipits and buntings; Barnaby Lane and Covean for warblers; Chapel Fields area especially good for warblers; Wingletang Down and Gugh for Merlin, Short-eared Owl, pipits and Lapland Bunting; Horse Point for seabirds passing.

Tresco: Great and Abbey Pools (two hides by Great Pool) and surrounding vegetation for ducks, raptors, waders and warblers; Borough Farm for pipits and buntings; north cliffs for passing seabirds; Castle Down for open-ground species including Dotterel and Wheatear; south-facing beaches for waders and terns.

Bryher: Weedy fields and sheltered scrub in the south and centre, and near the pool, for warblers and buntings; Hangman Down for open-ground species, including Buff-breasted Sandpiper.

St Martin's: Fields and hedges on the southern slope for warblers; The Plains and fields across the central spine of the island for pipits, buntings and plovers; also sheltered fields around the cricket pitch for passerines.

Annet: This closed island is fragile, with seabirds and seals highly vulnerable to disturbance. Please admire the island from a wildlife safari boat instead.

The Isles of Scilly Wildlife Trust manages around 700ha of land as well as maintaining 52 miles (85km) of paths around the islands. The Trust can be found at Trenoweth, St Mary's, Isles of Scilly TR21 ONS (Tel: 01720 422 153).

CALENDAR

Resident: Little Egret, Cormorant, Shag, Gadwall, Kestrel, Peregrine, Moorhen, Oystercatcher, Ringed Plover, Great Black-backed Gull, Stock Dove, Raven, Cetti's Warbler, Rock Pipit, Stonechat. Gannet and Kittiwake offshore all year.

December–February: Great Northern Diver, Wigeon, Teal, Shoveler, Tufted Duck, Pochard, possibly Goldeneye, Long-tailed Duck, Merlin, Water Rail, Golden Plover, Turnstone, Sanderling, Purple Sandpiper, Woodcock, Jack Snipe, Grey Wagtail, Blackcap, Firecrest, Black Redstart; possible wild geese.

March–May: Fulmar and auks arrive back (Puffin from third week of March), Hoopoe, Chiffchaff, Firecrest, Wheatear, Black Redstart passing through from mid-March; Manx Shearwater, European Storm Petrel, terns arrive April; commoner passerine migrants peak late April; overshooting southern species mostly May, the best month for Golden Oriole.

June–July: Breeding seabirds, Gadwall, Oystercatcher and Ringed Plover, Reed and Sedge Warblers; occasional late migrants and overshoots remain from spring; occasional terns; migrant seabirds, including Wilson's Storm Petrel, possible from pelagics (July).

August–November: Seabirds on *Scillonian* crossing, including Sooty, Cory's and Great Shearwaters (August-September), Grey Phalarope, skuas, occasional Sabine's Gull; possibility of rarer seabirds from pelagics early in period; on islands, wader movement may include American species such as Buff-breasted Sandpiper and peaks mid-September; European plovers, including Dotterel (late August–mid-October); raptors from early September. Passerine movement begins in mid-August with a chance of Icterine or Melodious Warblers and Ortolan Bunting; warblers, flycatchers, chats and pipits, with chance of Richard's and Tawny Pipits, from mid-September; Wryneck, Barred Warbler, Red-backed Shrike, Red-breasted Flycatcher and Lapland Bunting; Short-eared Owls arrive mid– late October, Black Redstarts often abundant end October–early November, and late summer visitors and some vagrants stay into November, when Pallas's Warbler possible. Peak periods for rarer species: American landbirds, late September–end October; European and Asiatic rare pipits, warblers and buntings, early October–early November.

The Isles of Scilly Bird Group includes latest sightings and boat trip schedules on their website (scilly-birding.co.uk). There are also maps of the islands, species lists and photographs.

35A PELAGIC SEABIRD TRIPS (OTHER THAN THOSE LAUNCHED FROM SCILLY)

HABITAT
In the Western Approaches to the English Channel, approximately 70 miles (112km) west-south-west of the Isles of Scilly, lies an area of rich fishing waters at the outer edge of the Continental Shelf.

SPECIES
In late summer and early autumn, charter boat trips have taken birdwatchers out to deepwater fishing grounds near the edge of the Continental Shelf. Here, several hours' voyage out of sight of land, many seabird species, including some rarely glimpsed from mainland watchpoints, can be viewed in quantities following fishing trawlers. 'Chum', a smelly fish oil mixture thrown overboard, lures birds close to vessels, allowing spectacular views of skuas, numerous storm petrels, Great, Sooty and Cory's Shearwaters within photographic range – at times just a few metres from the boat. Wilson's Storm Petrels, formerly almost unknown off British coasts, are identified on most trips with European Storm Petrels. Other extremely rare petrels and shearwaters, plus Black-browed Albatross, have also been reported and photographed. One or two Sabine's Gulls are likely to be seen with feeding petrels. Dolphins and porpoises may follow the boat, and occasional whale sightings (increasingly, Humpbacks) can be an additional attraction. When easterly winds carry small migrating landbirds out to sea, they may choose to rest on a passing ship; a number of unexpected species, including warblers and flycatchers, have been sighted during pelagic trips.

TIMING
Trips have traditionally been between one and three days; there is little point in going without adequate time to search the trawler area thoroughly. Fares can be expensive, and seasickness is common; conditions can quickly become very rough. More recently, shorter trips from Falmouth and Penzance have become popular and often produce good views of most species if conditions are right.

ACCESS
Look for advertisements in bird magazines to find out if anyone is planning to run them. These usually require pre-booking, sometimes some months in advance. Trips from Penzance or Falmouth run between the end of July and mid-September. AK Wildlife Cruises operate out of Falmouth and can be contacted through their website or by phoning 07553 606838; this company offers a variety of cruises and it is also possible to hire the whole boat. Mermaid operates from Penzance and again offers a variety of trips and the opportunity to hire the entire boat; phone 07901 731 201. In the east of the region, occasional longer boat trips head out into Lyme Bay from Brixham Harbour.

Those wishing to extend their pelagic birding further afield may consider watching from the large Brittany Ferries ships that sail from Plymouth past the tip of Brittany to Santander in Spain, crossing the Bay of Biscay en route. Some seabirds are likely to be seen a few miles off Plymouth, when passing Eddystone Reef and lighthouse; these will usually be species one might expect to see from south-west coastal points. From the tip of Brittany southward into Biscay, numbers of Great and Cory's Shearwaters might be feeding around the edge of Continental Shelf waters. Flocks of hundreds of both species have been encountered regularly, together with groups of Sabine's Gulls and Wilson's Storm Petrels, and small numbers of Little Shearwaters on several occasions. Cetaceans are another potential attraction of a Biscay crossing; late summer/early autumn records include scores of dolphins, a wide range of whales, including some species only ever rarely observed. Turtles, tuna, Ocean Sunfish and sharks are also possible.

To book a Biscay ferry journey (24 hours each way), contact Brittany Ferries, but note that faster passenger vessels have now started to make observations extremely difficult.

Websites:
Pelagic birdwatching and wildlife boat trips: cornwallboattrips.co.uk
Wildlife cruises and Falmouth boat trips: akwildlifecruises.co.uk
Trips from Brixham Harbour: mikelangman.co.uk/guided-cruises
brittany-ferries.co.uk

CALENDAR

Resident: Generally only common species such as Gannet, Kittiwake and Fulmar.

December–February: Not applicable as no trips are undertaken at this period.

March–May: No trips generally undertaken.

June–July: Increasing chance of rarer petrels and large shearwaters as the period progresses, along with a range of commoner seabirds.

August–November: Good chance of encounters with a range of shearwaters, petrels and Sabine's Gull in August; fewer species in September but shearwaters can still be numerous, with Sabine's Gull and phalaropes; usually fewer seabirds after late September.

36 ST IVES ISLAND AND BAY

OS LANDRANGER MAP 203
OS grid ref: SW5241
Postcode: **St Ives Island** – TR26 1SY **Carbis Bay** – TR26 2NN
what3words: **St Ives Island** – contacts.ruling.unfolds
Carbis Bay – organs.patch.mainly

HABITAT

St Ives is in far west Cornwall, on its north coast. The Island (St Ives Head) is a 20m-high rocky headland with a coastguard station on top, from which you can

Cornwall

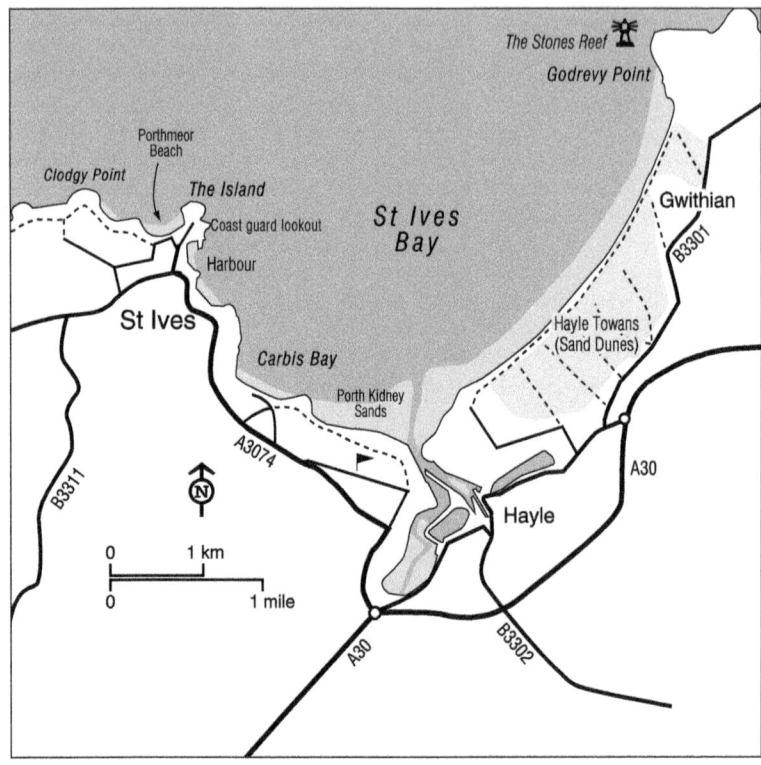

look across the bay to Hayle Sands and Godrevy Point lighthouse, 2.5 miles (4km) away. Directly seawards off Godrevy Point is a long, narrow reef called the Stones. Running in a semi-circle from the edge of St Ives town, Carbis Bay is a particularly sheltered section of the larger St Ives area, the whole of which remains protected from most easterly and all southerly winds, including prevailing south-westerlies. Overall, it has a sandy bottom, with long stretches of wide sandy beaches, backed towards Hayle Towans by high sand dunes. Some parts have a rockier shoreline, like that found near The Island.

As the bay and headland face north, strong opposing sunlight is not such a problem as at many coastal points, except perhaps in early mornings. The high light values in the far west produce perfect colour and detail.

In late summer and autumn, Harbour Porpoises and dolphins are often seen, and there is the occasional Humpback Whale sighting; exotic-looking Ocean Sunfish and impressive Basking Sharks may swim close offshore.

SPECIES

In the past, this area has been famous for spectacular passages of seabirds off The Island, especially in autumn gales when birdwatchers from many parts of Britain came to see pelagic birds rarely seen from land. However, The Island is less well used for seawatching now and Pendeen has taken over as the prime site.

In winter and early spring, St Ives Bay is noted mainly for diving birds, especially when sheltered from rough seas. Most numerous of the interesting species are divers and grebes. Two or three Great Northern Divers are almost always present, and sometimes there may be 15 or more. Smaller and more snake-necked, Black-throated Divers often occur singly, but there can be five or more; numbers tend to rise from late winter and by early spring 10 may be present. Red-throated Divers are often present in winter, with up to 20 possible. Nowadays, grebes are unusual visitors to the bay, which once always hosted Slavonian and Red-necked during the winter months. A very light scattering of seaducks may come and go through winter; Common Scoter may reach 40 some winters, the odd Long-tailed Duck occurs and once there was an American Surf Scoter. None of the above diving species competes for food with the 50 or more Shag and the dozen or so Cormorant regularly seen in the bay. Small groups of Purple Sandpiper forage with Turnstone along rocky foreshores, often below seafront houses in the town.

When spring arrives, ducks leave quite soon as a rule, as do most Great Northern Divers and grebes; as is usual in Cornwall, however, Black-throated Divers often increase in spring. Lingering individuals may attain summer plumage. Sometimes a Glaucous Gull frequents the harbour and fishing boats, irregularly joined by a smaller, slimmer Iceland Gull. The biggest male Glaucous Gulls can be larger than the largest Great Black-backed Gull, while small females may be only a little bigger than a Herring Gull. Very early spring is a good time for unusual gulls, with Little Gulls appearing in groups of two or three; Mediterranean Gulls, like Little, tend to hover over wave crests, picking scraps from the surface. Rarities such as Laughing Gull have been found at this season.

Soon, the first migrant terns appear in the shape of excited Sandwich Terns, loudly proclaiming their arrival while diving for fish; this is the most common tern in spring. Later, small flocks of 10 or more, moving through the bay, may be joined by two or three Common or Arctic Terns.

Seawatching from The Island is possibly worth a try year-round in any conditions, on the off chance that something interesting may fly past. Numbers and variety of species vary greatly from year to year depending on how many observers there are and whether or not they report their findings; the figures given impart merely a flavour of what is possible.

From March, prospects become more certain, and if conditions are favourable a light or even sustained passage may occur. True seabird movement is usually east-wards, up the coast, as opposed to milling around the general area, which is the typical behaviour of some Gannets. Fulmars are present in the region, but hundreds streaming past the headland indicates real movement. Manx Shearwater and Kittiwake are also involved in the passage, often several thousand of each heading towards breeding colonies. Among the Manx, there may be a few browner Balearic Shearwaters. If divers are passing (usually only in twos and threes), they are now most likely to be Black-throated. A few Bar-tailed Godwit or Whimbrel may pass later in the season, and there is always the chance of a skua or two, or even a few European Storm Petrels. Sightings of the latter are on the cards throughout late spring and summer, and small feeding parties occasionally wander close to shore. If winds blow strongly from the right direction, even in high summer, especially in early mornings, odd non-breeding birds of several interesting species may be seen; these may include a stray from the southern oceans, possibly even an albatross!

As midsummer approaches and Atlantic depressions with their associated gales become likely, the chance arises for the first major seawatch. Really high numbers of seabirds do not occur early on, but some will already have left their natal colonies to begin their westward journey. All true passage will now be westward.

Cornwall

Note: All numbers quoted below are on a per-day basis.

St Ives Island has, in the past, produced some of Britain's highest totals of migrating seabirds, as well as some of its rarest species.

Shearwaters, skuas and terns make up the bulk of early passages, if conditions cause them to occur, Common and Sandwich Terns pass, perhaps accompanied by Little or Black Terns; terns use the bay regardless of winds, small groups fishing or gathering along quieter sandy beaches. Skuas may be present in ones and twos, skilfully harrying feeding terns; early ones will be predominantly Arctic, with a few stocky Great Skuas (frequently called by their Scottish name, 'Bonxie'). Manx Shearwaters can pass in good numbers early on; the more usual counts of 10,000 have occasionally risen to well over 15,000, among which may be 15 to 20 Balearic Shearwaters. Sooty Shearwaters speed through, attaining peak numbers of around 15; smaller numbers are also seen outside their main season. European Storm Petrels appear off the headland in variable numbers, passing throughout autumn; they may be absent on some days, or up to 100 may be counted flitting low over the waves. One year, a Brown Booby put in an appearance for a few days in late August, visiting both Carbis Bay and St Ives.

From mid-autumn, earlier and later migrants merge, numbers changing on a daily basis. It is now that St Ives' speciality is most likely to be recorded: the dainty, fork-tailed Sabine's Gull, which has been recorded here more frequently than anywhere else in Britain. Even so, only occasional birds pass in some years, sometimes amid throngs of similarly marked first-winter Kittiwakes. Little Gulls are recorded most years in small numbers. Few Leach's Storm Petrel are seen early in the season, and in some unfavourable autumns they are absent; rather like European Storm Petrel occurrences, some apparently good days produce none, while on other days 50 or more may move past. Gannets are always visible in hundreds, even on quieter days.

As the season moves on, and tern and shearwater numbers decline, other birds come to the fore. Replacing black-and-white hordes of Manx Shearwater are auks, in even greater number. They appear to be mainly Razorbills, but distance often precludes accurate identification. The flocks passing on whirring wings act as a backdrop to more exciting species. Puffins, strangely, are almost non-existent, while Little Auks appear only at the very end of autumn. The latter, too, have good and bad years, in some barely seen, while in others 50 can pass in a day. Another later species is a sea-going wader, the small greyish-white Grey Phalarope, often stopping to rest on the waves.

Divers come through in higher numbers later in the season as do a few other ducks that may attach themselves to small parties of passing Common Scoter; there may be a larger Velvet Scoter, showing distinctive white wing-patches, or even a rare Surf Scoter. Geese, uncommon in the far west, have been seen in small flocks, usually 'black' geese (Brent or Barnacle). A thin scattering of northern white-winged gulls, such as Glaucous, occurs. Herring Gulls can pass in hundreds still, whereas Lesser Black-backed Gulls, which move in autumn and early winter, have now slowed down dramatically.

The most notable omissions from the species list are Cory's and Great Shearwaters, which regularly gather in thousands to feed at the entrance to the Western Approaches, off Ushant, Brittany. They are noted passing St Ives in very small numbers in the right conditions but are more regularly noted at Pendeen, in some years in triple digits.

TIMING

More or less any time could justify checking the headland or bay if you are in the area. Conditions conducive to heavy passage past The Island are highly critical, although birds such as terns pausing to feed in the bay or semi-resident winter divers and grebes may be seen in varying conditions. In the wrong weather, however, there will be little or no actual passage off The Island.

To experience substantial seabird movement, winds should be between west-north-west and north. Ideally, an Atlantic depression from the south-west will have just passed through, the closer the better but preferably with its centre not much further north than Northern Ireland. As it passes, the wind veers from south-west to northerly; at this point seabirds begin to pass. The larger, more vigorous, faster-travelling and more rain-bearing the depression is, the greater will be the resulting seabird passage.

There are many variations but results then become more uncertain. Sometimes a strong front of northerly air alone will produce good results. At other times, days of south-west gales which fail to veer finally do so but quickly abate to a breeze; either few birds then pass, although they may include a rarity, or a good passage may take place as tired birds merely track with the wind. On the day of a major gale, those species able to cope pass through. The next day, provided winds are still from the right direction, smaller species such as terns, small gulls or Long-tailed Skua come through when the strong winds have decreased. Strong winds from due west usually produce little or no close passage; the moment they flick north of west, especially if the weather system contains frequent squalls, the bay can be seething with birds, all of which were passing by, unseen, further out! Sometimes ideal conditions start early in the morning; heavy passage takes place, the wind then dies or backs to south-west, and passage ceases, perhaps by midday. Conversely, passage may not start until late afternoon, frustrating if you have been watching an empty sea for five hours, knowing what you are missing. Very occasionally, correct winds will blow for two or three days, during which passage will be sustained. Until these critical conditions arrive, some years for only three or four days, major passage is non-existent.

Although most passage occurs within 1 mile (1.6km) – and often very close – it should be remembered that perhaps less than five minutes may elapse between the initial sighting and brief views before a moving seabird is lost to view around the headland; the sheer numbers can also cause bewilderment. It is better to learn basic seabird identification elsewhere if possible, or visit on a quieter day, if you are inexperienced.

ACCESS

St Ives is reached by the A3074 from Hayle. For The Island, head to the northern tip of the town, following signs to the car park. This car park lies immediately below the steeply rising headland; a tarmac path leads to the top. However, one of the reasons for this once pioneering venue's demise is that the adjacent car park is often full and the narrow roads in the town are often congested. Watch from areas sheltered from the wind (if possible) around the coastguard lookout. The outer part of the bay can also be checked from this car park or from the harbour walls, as well as from roads next to the bay. Check the harbour for unusual gulls. Public footpaths lead from the town, remaining close to shore and extending to the mouth of the Hayle Estuary at Porthkidney beach (part of Carbis Bay), where terns often rest. The footpath to the left of The Island leads towards

Cornwall

Clodgy Point and gives another chance for interesting birds to be seen. A branch railway line from the London to Penzance main line runs from St Erth to St Ives all year round, giving panoramic views en route.

CALENDAR

Resident: Gannet and Oystercatcher; Cormorant, Shag, Razorbill, Guillemot and Rock Pipit breed nearby.

December–February: Black-throated and Great Northern Divers with Red-throated mostly passing The Island; Occasional grebes, possible Eider, Common Scoter, other seaducks; Turnstone, Purple Sandpiper; Grey Phalarope, Great Skua, Little, Mediterranean, Glaucous and Iceland Gulls and Little Auk are all possible.

March–May: Apart from Black-throated Diver and uncommon gulls, all the above species gradually decline; Fulmar, Manx Shearwater, possible European Storm Petrel, especially towards May; Bar-tailed Godwit and Whimbrel pass from mid-April; skuas possible throughout; Sandwich Tern from mid-March, and a few 'commic' terns from April.

June–July: Breeding species, including Kittiwake nearby; chance of seabird movement, particularly Manx Shearwater or European Storm Petrel; terns reappear in bay at the end of the period.

August–early September: Fulmar, Sooty, Manx and Balearic Shearwaters; Black, Sandwich and Common Terns often peak; Whimbrel, skuas (mainly Arctic), Little, Lesser Black-backed and possibly Sabine's Gulls.

Mid-September–mid-October: All the above, with Arctic Skua peaking; Leach's Storm Petrel, Common Scoter, Great, Pomarine Skuas and possible Long-tailed Skuas, Mediterranean Gull, Arctic Tern, Grey Phalarope.

Late October–November: three species of diver; Grey Phalarope and Great Skua may peak now; Glaucous Gull; Kittiwake and auk passage increases greatly, the latter perhaps including Little Auk; Black Redstart and Snow Bunting possible around The Island and Clodgy Point.

37 PENDEEN WATCH

OS LANDRANGER MAP 203
OS grid ref: SW3836
Postcode: TR19 7ED
what3words: **Lighthouse car park** – shipyards.rags.scored

HABITAT

Pendeen Watch lies at the far north-western tip of the exposed Land's End peninsula, some 12 miles (19km) west by road from St Ives. It is the last north-facing point on the coastline. The viewing area is an open, grassy clifftop beside and below the lighthouse, where there are a few seats. It is also possible to watch from the area to the right (east) of the lighthouse at the bottom of the hill. In the last two decades, Pendeen has overtaken St Ives as one of the premier sites for seawatching in Cornwall.

Differences between the sites are perhaps ill-defined, but while the seabirds tend to be a little further out at Pendeen and they linger less often compared with St Ives Bay, feeding flocks of Manx and other shearwaters are sometimes present. Unlike St Ives, winds from more westerly quarters can produce an excellent passage, especially earlier in the morning, but this may decrease or cease if the wind direction is not sustained. Attributes shared with St Ives include wide, uninterrupted vistas and superb light. At Pendeen, a nearby reef helps as a focal point, with much movement on a good day taking place about halfway between the land and the reef.

The surrounding areas consist mainly of rough pasture with low stone walls or sparce hedges of hawthorn, gorse and bracken. There are a few stunted trees and bushes (mostly willows) but these are mainly in the gardens of the properties along the road. These areas can be especially productive in spring and autumn for passerine migrants, and are visible from the tarmac road leading to the lighthouse and public footpaths around the area.

SPECIES

Pendeen is a great seabird migration watchpoint, and all aspects affecting passage at this site are similar to those at St Ives. The range of species passing at sea is much as it is for St Ives throughout the year, and individual birds may be seen passing at both sites. Due to increasing sea temperatures, predicting good seawatching days has become more difficult and the list of potential seabird species wider; it is an exciting time to be a keen seawatcher! In 2023, coinciding with record numbers of Cory's Shearwaters, individuals resembling the extremely rare and closely related Scopoli's Shearwater were claimed in July and August.

Great, Cory's and Sooty Shearwaters are regularly recorded off Pendeen, and on exceptional days all three species have occurred in hundreds, when few or none are seen at St Ives. It is also a good site from August to November for the three most regular skua species (Great, Arctic and Pomarine), but Long-tailed is rare, as it is at St Ives.

Chough is expected here, either flying over the car park or feeding a few feet from the coast path, which runs around both sides of the lighthouse. The area also attracts good numbers of open-ground migrants in spring and autumn such as pipits, wagtails and buntings. However, since the area currently lacks arable crops to attract and hold birds, many pass through quickly. From late autumn until early spring, Black Redstarts are often seen around the lighthouse but are typically elusive and easily overlooked. Scarce but regular species in autumn include Wryneck, Richard's Pipit, Yellow-browed Warbler and both Snow and Lapland Buntings, though numbers recorded vary between years and are dependent on weather conditions. Rare landbirds such as Brown Shrike occasionally visit.

ACCESS

From St Ives, take the B3306, which passes through the village of Pendeen some 10 miles (16km) to the south-west. Then follow a minor road signposted to the lighthouse for about 1 mile (1.6km). There is parking where the road ends above the light. Steps lead down the right-hand side of the lighthouse. A position near the base of the eastward-facing wall affords some shelter from north-westerly winds and gives good views over the sea.

Following the footpath to the right of the lighthouse gives access to the area at the bottom of the track; here, watching gives more restricted views and a greater distance between you and the birds, but being closer to the sea makes it easier to pick them out.

The South West Coast Path website suggests a variety of routes to walk from Pendeen lighthouse, depending on ability and fitness. The easiest, with the best chance of migrants, is to wander up the lane from the lighthouse car park back to the B3306, which gives good views over the surrounding areas.

Website:
southwestcoastpath.org.uk

CALENDAR

Resident: Shag, Fulmar and Gannet usually present offshore; Chough, Stonechat and Rock Pipit on cliffs and paths.

December–February: Fulmar regular (400 per day have been recorded in late winter), Manx Shearwater; divers, skuas (mostly Great, occasionally Pomarine), possible Glaucous and Iceland Gulls; passage of auks and Kittiwake sometimes breathtaking; Purple Sandpiper; Siberian Chiffchaff sometimes in willows; rarities have included White-billed Diver and Black-browed Albatross.

March-May: Manx Shearwater become more regular and build up to mesmerising numbers in May. Balearic Shearwater is rare in this period, but European Storm Petrel likely in May. Sandwich Terns occur regularly in small numbers; other terns are scarce. A White-billed Diver was recorded on an April seawatch. Ring Ouzel possible on surrounding heathland. Among commoner migrants, on good days Wheatear have occurred in large numbers and nest in the area. Occasional Yellow Wagtail and Tree Pipit, mostly flying over.

June–July: Range of seabirds, depending on sea and weather conditions, begins to increase from late June. These can include European Storm Petrel, Cory's, Great, Sooty and Balearic Shearwaters, numbers and species mix vary between years. Rare seabirds have included Desertas-type petrel and increasingly Wilson's Storm Petrel. July sees beginnings of wader passage, for example Whimbrel and Dunlin, and Common Scoter start to appear.

August–November: During good seawatching weather all main seabird groups can pass by, often in large numbers, and have included scarce to very rare species among them. Wilson's Storm Petrel, Sabine's Gull and Grey Phalarope are all annual in varying numbers. Variety and numbers of ducks and waders passing peak in this period. In addition to those landbirds mentioned earlier, surrounding bushes and fields regularly produce a few Pied Flycatcher and Firecrest, with scarcer migrants such as shrikes (Red-backed and Woodchat in recent years). Lately, Rose-coloured Starling noted annually in Pendeen village. Purple Sandpiper return in October.

38 HAYLE ESTUARY (INCLUDING CARNSEW POOL AND COPPER HOUSE CREEK)

OS LANDRANGER MAP 203
OS grid ref: SW5436
Postcodes: TR27 (for more detail and what3words see Access section)

HABITAT

Hayle Estuary and neighbouring areas are adjacent to Hayle on the north coast of west Cornwall. The area is important as it is the only estuary in the far west and very sheltered from the sea. The mouth lies at a different angle from the main basin, separated by a long, curving channel cutting through a barrier of dunes. The lower estuary is predominantly sandy, becoming muddy higher up. A freshwater channel flows at low tides. At the bottom of the estuary, an embankment encloses an artificial tidal area known as Carnsew Pool, where a large area of water is retained, even at low tides when soft mud is exposed elsewhere. Running alongside the town centre is another muddy tidal area, Copperhouse Creek, less than half the size of the main estuary.

Winter temperatures in low, sheltered areas of the far west at times bear little resemblance to those even as close as eastern Devon. Apart from exceptionally cold years, far fewer days are below freezing and snowfall is not annual.

This ecologically important estuary is relatively small at 90ha and is a Site of Special Scientific Interest.

Among other interesting fauna is a centipede that inhabits the shore edge

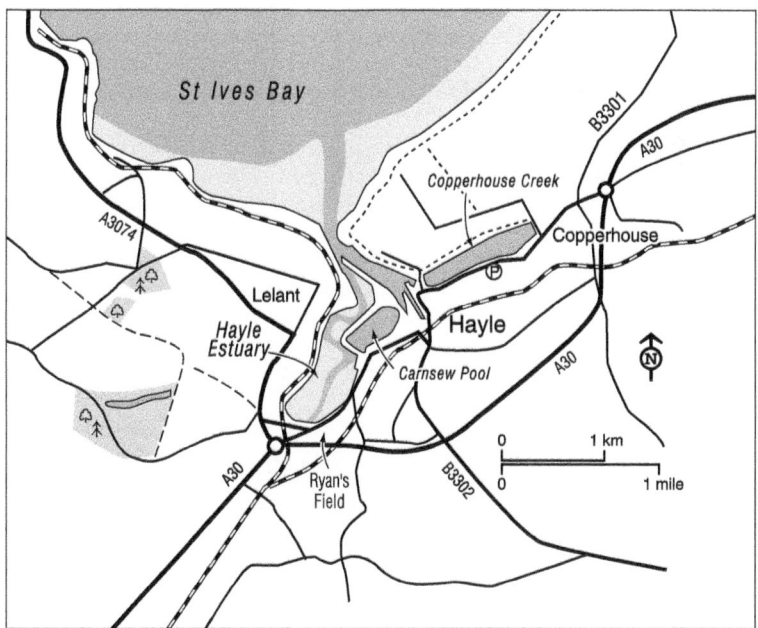

around Lelant; it occurs nowhere else in England. Several locally rare plants grow, including Sea Aster, while four species deemed nationally rare are found there: Ivy Broomrape, Wild Cabbage, Purple Ramping Fumitory and Round-fruited Rush, the latter growing near the reeds at Copperhouse.

It remains to be seen how extensive developments planned for the estuary area will affect the complex. The main basin has become an RSPB reserve. Ryan's Field, across the main road from the estuary, has also been secured by the RSPB, which has created an extensive scrape overlooked by a large hide.

SPECIES

Although well known to most birdwatchers for its migrant waders and wintering ducks, the first sight as you glance over the estuary in winter will probably be of flocks of gulls. They congregate mainly towards the middle and upper sections. This estuary does not attract extremely high numbers, with perhaps no more than 1,500 Herring Gulls at its peak. Black-headed Gulls, which feed in nearby fields, often number fewer than 500 on the mudflats. Mediterranean Gulls are usually present year round, with numbers reaching up to 200 towards winter. Usually, about 200 Great Black-backs gather. The two most numerous migrant gulls, Lesser Black-backed and Common, achieve their highest numbers in late winter and early spring. Common Gulls are not at all numerous in Cornwall until fresh migrants (mostly adults) appear, swelling the small winter population; flocks of 100 or more then become more commonplace. The build-up of Lesser Black-backed Gulls is even more noticeable, as many fewer remain through early winter; concentrations of more than 500 appear in late winter, maybe reaching 1,250 or so in February; autumn passage peaks at around 100.

Uncommon gulls are relatively frequent visitors at any time outside the breeding season, but more occur from late winter through spring. Usually present as single birds, species such as Glaucous, Yellow-legged and Little Gulls may then be present in better numbers; Iceland is less frequent, with normally one or two a year. Rarer gulls such as Kumlein's, Caspian, Bonaparte's and Franklin's have appeared. Ring-billed Gull has been identified, but with decreasing regularity, mostly in winter and early spring.

When conditions are severe elsewhere, weather movements bring higher numbers of ducks and waders to the milder far west of Cornwall. Groups of up to 10 Brent Geese may arrive. Average winter populations are neither large nor particularly varied. Wigeon is the most numerous duck, peaking at about 800, and American Wigeon occurs quite regularly, occasionally more than one. Teal peak at a little over 300, and sometimes their American cousin, Green-winged Teal, visits. Mallard and Shelduck reach about 50 and 30 respectively; one or two pairs of each breed. Other common dabbling ducks occur annually at irregular intervals. Goosander visit most winters, but the closely related Red-breasted Merganser is now an irregular visitor.

Wintering flocks of waders are rather low. Dunlin numbers fluctuate widely, averaging more than 100. Curlew numbers can exceed 150 in winter and more than 200 are often counted in autumn. Lapwing use the estuary as a temporary roost, several hundred sharing local fields with Black-headed Gulls, but only a few visit the estuary at any one time. Grey Plover keep to the estuary, peaking at about 50 birds. Knot occasionally winter, but in autumn a dozen or more may be seen. Bar-tailed Godwit arrives in autumn and a few stay throughout winter. Black-tailed Godwit visits in low numbers in autumn and a few winter, while Oystercatchers gather in almost static numbers of up to 50 for much of the later year. During autumn, a passage of Ringed Plover peaks at more than 100 and as many as 25 may overwinter. Whimbrel, often heard before being seen, stop off briefly in spring in groups of up to 60; there are many fewer in autumn but one or two may overwinter. Redshank, known as the 'sentinel of the marshes' for their loud ringing calls and wary nature, are present in most months of the year; autumn flocks build and around 100 usually winter. Turnstone can gather in groups of up to 25 in autumn, also staying to winter.

Small numbers of less common waders regularly occur on autumn passage. Both Little Stint and Curlew Sandpiper are more or less annual. Ruff visit on passage in ones and twos most years. Greenshank and Common Sandpiper appear on passage, maybe 15–20 of each, and some winter, while Spotted Redshank are less numerous, often with only singles visiting mainly in autumn. Little Ringed Plover, once more or less annual, are now rarely seen in either migration season.

Rarities turn up annually. Pectoral, White-rumped, Baird's and Least Sandpipers, Lesser Yellowlegs and Long-billed Dowitcher have all been seen over the years, some of them several times; one of these can be expected annually. This is probably due largely to its geographical position, being both the first and last estuary most migrants will see in Britain. One spring, Cornwall's first Broad-billed Sandpiper, a rare European wader, was identified. Spoonbill visit and have lingered for long periods and Black-winged Stilt has been recorded; Gull-billed and Whiskered Terns and Wilson's Phalarope are among other very rare sightings. Ryan's Field has held several Lesser Yellowlegs and a Citrine Wagtail.

Grey Heron and Buzzard are resident and, whenever either flies over, gulls and waders take flight in alarm. Peregrine has the same effect, with better reason; they often visit through autumn and winter. Ospreys are regular autumn migrants, sometimes staying several days. One or two Kingfishers are present throughout the same period. Great White Egrets visit sporadically, but Little Egrets are resident.

A small passage of terns occurs at the estuary. Having followed the main channel up from the sea, they find shelter especially in rough weather. Sandwich Tern is the most common of these and among the first spring migrants to reach us; later groups of 20 or more may gather and higher numbers are usual in autumn. Arctic and Little Terns occur sporadically in flocks of fewer than five in spring and autumn. Ten or more Common Terns at a time come through in spring, often with many more in autumn. The rare White-winged Black Tern has occurred on several occasions.

An exhausted diver may shelter in the quiet winter waters of Carnsew Pool; single Black-throated and Great Northern Divers are not uncommon. An extraordinary arrival was a rare White-billed Diver that remained in the area, visiting the pool and adjacent sheltered estuary channels for several weeks and giving unprecedented close views of a species almost unknown in our region. Occasionally, Slavonian Grebes appear but Little Grebes are more usual; all other grebes are rarer visitors, as are Long-tailed Duck. Many birds that use the main estuary, including most smaller waders, also habitually visit Carnsew.

Copperhouse Creek is quite narrow and more open to disturbance, so it is less attractive to wary species. The gull flocks that congregate should be checked for uncommon species, which regularly occur. Canada Geese use Copperhouse and Hayle and can reach 500; the flock is always worth checking for rarer 'grey' geese. A few Mute Swan may appear here in autumn and winter. Some waders seem to prefer this area: Wood and Green Sandpipers in spring and autumn, for example, are less often seen on the main estuary. Pectoral Sandpipers tend to frequent this spot. In an area of grassy wasteland in hard weather, up to a dozen Snipe may flock;

among them a Jack Snipe may be flushed. The same area in autumn may have standing pools which have attracted interesting waders, including rare Temminck's Stint and Least Sandpiper. Behind this small grassy area is an equally small stand of *Phragmites* reeds, probably most important as an autumn roost for Pied and White Wagtails and Swallows.

TIMING

A visit at any time of day, in any season, could prove worthwhile, with the chance of occasional late passage or non-breeding birds and strays moving through. Low winter sunlight is not much of a problem at Hayle, as you can face away from the sun most of the time. For waders, the tide must be at least partially out. A rising tide, or one just starting to fall, forces many waders to alight on relatively small areas of mud at the head of the estuary, when close views are obtainable; there is no central high-tide roost. Hard winter weather may increase numbers and species, while rough seas will induce some terns or divers to shelter. Strong westerly airstreams in autumn are responsible for American vagrants.

ACCESS

The main estuary is just west of **Hayle** town. The main road through Hayle runs beside the sites. There is convenient car parking in the town **(TR27 4DH, restrict.upsetting.either)**. The estuary is flanked on the north side by a branch railway line, but the main road along the opposite shore allows checking along its length.

Across the road to the south side of the estuary lies **Ryan's Field**, which can be viewed from the roadside path. To access the hide on foot, you can take a small path from the roadside past the field. Alternatively, drive to the St Erth turning on the south estuary bank, then after 100m take a signposted RSPB track to the right just before the railway bridge. This track is driveable for about 200m beside the scrape; you can park at the far end near the hide **(TR27 6JF, stupidly.lentil.alone)**. Disabled access is available for entry into the hide.

Access to **Carnsew Pool** is by a public footpath located from the road leading to the supermarket car park (do not park in this car park as it is time restricted). From the viaduct car park **(TR27 4AE, shapeless.taken.dads)** walk towards the supermarket, cross Carnsew Road and, at the traffic lights, walk down the left-hand side of the building. Access to the pool is on the left; extremely good views are possible but the paths are uneven.

In addition to the main road through Hayle, public paths run along the remaining three sides of **Copperhouse Creek (TR27 5AA, reworked.ages.fame)**, including alongside the grassy areas at its head (which is on the right as you enter Hayle town from the east off the A30).

CALENDAR

Resident: Grey Heron, Little Egret, Oystercatcher, Shelduck, Buzzard.

December–February: Black-throated and Great Northern Divers probable; Little Grebe, possibly other grebes; Brent Goose possible; Teal, Wigeon, Long-tailed Duck possible, Red-breasted Merganser, Goosander, Peregrine possible; Ringed and Grey Plovers, Lapwing, Turnstone, Dunlin, Knot, Redshank, Spotted Redshank possible, Greenshank, Common Sandpiper, Bar-tailed Godwit, Curlew, Snipe, Jack

Snipe possible; Mediterranean, possible Ring-billed, Little, Iceland, Yellow-legged, Caspian and Glaucous Gulls, particularly towards end of period; Lesser Black-backed Gull passage from late December, may peak at end of period; Common Gull arrives from mid-February; Kingfisher; chance of storm-driven seabirds.

March–May: Most grebes, ducks and waders begin departure from early March; Sandwich Terns arrive from second week of March; uncommon gulls; Whimbrel arrive mid-April; Common, Arctic and possibly Little Terns, late April and May; Ruff, Wood Sandpiper and Black Tern possible.

June–July: Shelduck and Mallard breed; first returning waders, including Green Sandpiper, late July.

August–November: Most common waders gradually increase throughout period. Whimbrel pass through early in period; Ringed Plover peak in September; Little Stint and Curlew Sandpiper can arrive from early September (leaving by early November); Ruff, Spotted Redshank, Greenshank and Common Sandpiper peak early September; Little Gull possible, and Lesser Black-backed Gull peak September; Black, Sandwich, Common, Arctic and Little Terns, August to October; Wigeon and Teal begin to return from mid-September.

Cornwall

SITE CLUSTER: NORTH CORNWALL COAST

39 Newquay district
39A Trevose Head
40 Camel Estuary, Treraven meadow, Clapper and Amble Marshes

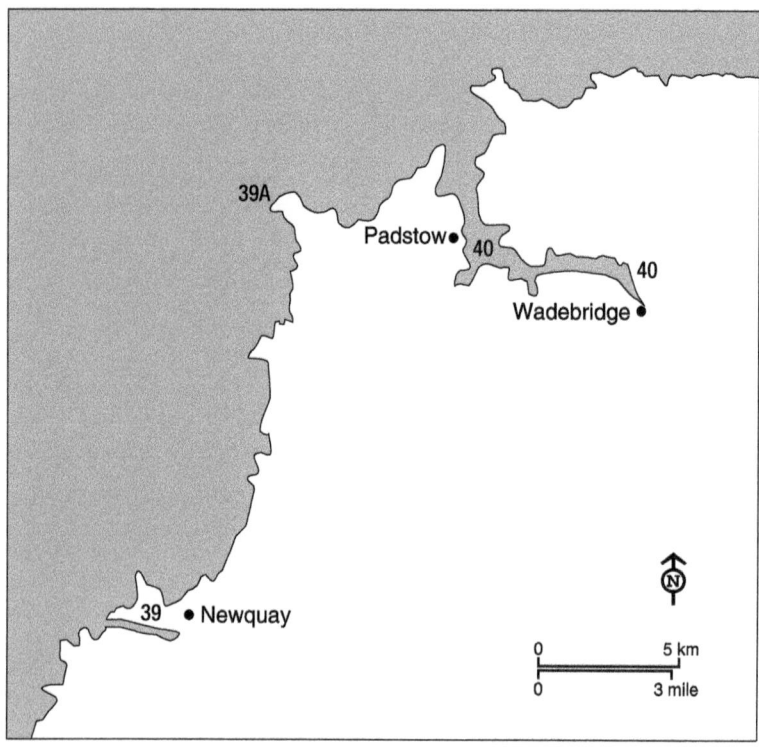

39 NEWQUAY DISTRICT

> OS LANDRANGER MAP 200
> OS grid ref: SW8063
> Postcodes: TR7–8 (for more detail and what3words see Access section)

HABITAT

Halfway along Cornwall's exposed north coast, the tourist resort of Newquay stands on open clifftops, with high, exposed turf and rocky headlands on either side. Sandy beaches intermingle with cliffs. At the north-west side, Towan Head projects seaward. The bay east of the headland, known as The Gazzle, forms a slightly sheltered area of sea even in rough weather. The south side of the town is bordered by the sandy Gannel Estuary, which has a small area of saltmarsh on its upper reaches but is subject to human disturbance. Beyond this, to the south, lie extensive National Trust areas around West Pentire and Kelsey Heads, separated by the sheltered valley of the Porth Joke stream. Behind the clifftops lies open arable land, left as stubble in autumn. Immediately west of Porth Joke lies rolling Cubert Common, which is owned by the National Trust. This area of botanical interest is covered with cowslips in spring. The Porth Joke stream is lined with irises in summer, then tends to flood in autumn, forming small pools in the hollow between the upper stream and Cubert Common.

About 2 miles (3.2km) inland, to the east of Newquay, and set in a steep-sided farmland valley, lies the 16ha Porth Reservoir (formerly known as Melancoose). South West Lakes Trust maintains the area furthest away from the dam as a bird sanctuary. Copses border the lake and there is a small area of marsh and damp woodland at the top end.

Coastal areas around Newquay are heavily used by holidaymakers throughout the summer.

SPECIES

The Newquay district's varied habitats provide a good list of migrants and seabirds, plus one or two localised breeding species. It is, in particular, one of the

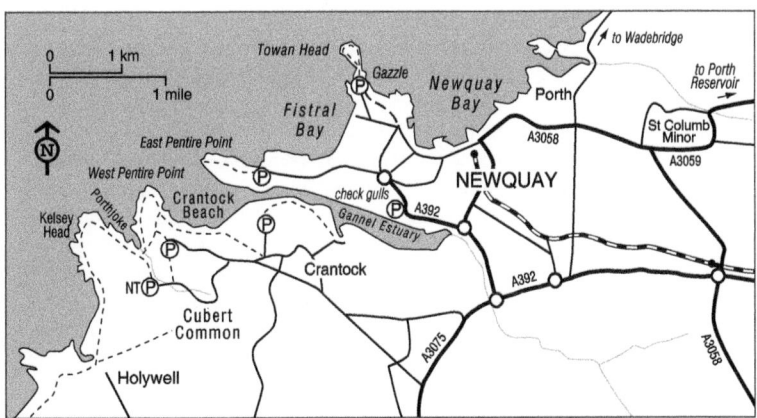

region's best seawatching stations away from Pendeen, although for most species it only receives 25–30 per cent of the overall passage numbers recorded at that more famous site.

In winter, strong gales blowing in off the Atlantic may bring very large westward movements of seabirds off Towan Head, the point from which most observation is carried out. This passage can include thousands of Gannets, auks and Kittiwakes. Occasionally a Grey Phalarope, Little Auk or even a Puffin may accompany them. A Wilson's Storm Petrel has been identified here, as well as a King Eider. Small parties of Purple Sandpiper and Turnstone, probably no more than single figures of each, scurry about the rocks below the headland. Two or three Eider or Common Scoter are often driven into The Gazzle by rough conditions. Small numbers of all three diver species are seen off Towan Head in winter; Black-throated are scarcest, perhaps only seen as late autumn migrants. Shags feed commonly on the sea across the whole district, with 200–300 congregating off headlands, especially at Godrevy.

The Gannel Estuary does not attract any regular or substantial wader numbers, owing to its disturbed position and open sandy bed with little food content. A few Oystercatchers are most likely to be present in daytime, accompanied by scattered Curlew. More prominent on the estuary are flocks of resting and bathing gulls. In the bay, an excellent pre-roost congregation of smaller gull species is worth checking. Some 1,000 Black-headed Gulls form the bulk, although Mediterranean Gulls are regular and Little Gull is annual. A contingent of American rarities identified here has included Franklin's, Laughing, Bonaparte's and Ring-billed Gulls. Larger gulls on the estuary consist mainly of up to 1,500 Herring, with a few dozen Great Black-backed. In late winter, as gull passage commences, up to 100 Lesser Black-backed and a few Common Gulls may join them.

The saltings harbour Snipe, and Rock Pipit may be joined by one or two pale Water Pipits. A Dusky Warbler once wintered in adjacent gardens. Ducks are not numerous, but usually include 20–30 Wigeon, together with ones and twos of other dabbling ducks at times. The upper estuary may attract one or two Little Grebes and perhaps a Goosander. One or two Grey Heron fishing here are joined by conspicuous Little and occasional Cattle Egrets.

At the edge of the town near the estuary is open-banked Trenance Park lake, inhabited by ornamental ducks; in winter, wild Tufted Duck join them. Gulls fly in to bathe in the fresh water, and at this closer range identification of more difficult species has sometimes been possible.

Sandy Crantock Bay, off the mouth of the Gannel Estuary and flanked by East and West Pentire heads, holds a regular flock of Red-throated Diver in the winter months. Single figures of Great Northern may also be seen. The open downland overlooking either side of the bay may hold one or two wintering Snow Buntings, shuffling along low in search of seeds. Other passerines which might be seen along the coast, besides the ubiquitous Rock Pipit, are Stonechat and occasionally a Black Redstart. The stubble fields towards Kelsey Head hold flocks of Skylark and Meadow Pipit. Unfortunately, Corn Bunting no longer occurs in this former haunt. The flocks form a target for one or two wide-ranging Merlins; Peregrines overfly the entire area and can even be seen over the main seafront at times. The small Porth Joke cove beach acts as a refuge for gull flocks disturbed off the main beach, and Mediterranean Gulls are often found here.

Porth Reservoir is not a major duck habitat, but up to 10 Tufted may gather, joined by up to 100 Mallard and perhaps a few Teal; ones and twos of other dabbling ducks visit, and occasionally very small numbers of Goldeneye, Goosander or Scaup, hard-weather specialities. Several Ring-necked Duck have wintered. Occasionally in a cold spell, a Bittern may occupy the tiny marsh at the top end of the reservoir, where Purple Heron has also been recorded. Singles of various grebes have occurred; about 15 Great Crested are present all year and the species breeds regularly. A Kingfisher may flash past low over the water. Dipper have been found just below the dam in winter, where small groups of Siskin may gather to feed on lakeside trees, which have Great Spotted and Green Woodpecker.

Up to 350 pairs of Kittiwake return each spring to breed on the cliffs at Porthmissen. Shag and Herring Gull breed more widely along the coast. Spring migration of small passerines can be noticeable around Porth Joke, with varied falls in the streamside bushes; a Hoopoe or Quail might be reported in the valley. Singing Sedge Warblers and one or two Grasshopper Warblers may stay to nest. Passing flocks of Whimbrel drop in to feed in clifftop fields and occasionally a noteworthy wader stops off at the Gannel Estuary; Black-winged Stilt has been recorded. Wader numbers, however, remain low in spring. Hirundines gather over Porth Reservoir and commoner warblers sing in the surrounding trees, but no major passage occurs; intermittent scarcities have included Osprey and White-winged Black Tern. The flat, rattling song of one or two Lesser Whitethroats might be heard in hedgerows near Porth and the Gannel river. The sea may be quiet, although gulls, which start to pass through early, may still provide a scarcer species. A few Sandwich Terns pass north-east at sea, and with the onset of the breeding season, seabird flocks from Britain's west coast colonies start to file through on a daily basis en route to feeding grounds. Manx Shearwaters are seen commonly, with up to 10,000 having been recorded on some days. Gannets and auks, which may later include a few Puffins, pass by in large parties. The summer season, when Newquay is full of tourists, used to see the occurrence of one of Newquay's specialities: the tiny, ocean-going European Storm Petrel; although once frequent, it is now seen only occasionally. Rough weather may still drive them in, or a passing flock may be attracted into the bay to feed around a fishing boat, coming close to shore at times; birds may remain, fluttering over the water for hours.

After strong autumn gales a Grey Phalarope might be blown in; one or two terns may also occur here or on the Gannel in similar conditions, Common, Arctic and Black Terns have all been recorded. A few waders occur on the Gannel and have included American vagrants such as Lesser Yellowlegs and Baird's Sandpiper. The pools between Porth Joke and Cubert have also attracted varied waders, on occasion including American species such as Pectoral Sandpiper, but they are not a reliable site for waders. Previously, Porth Reservoir hosted small numbers of autumn passage waders along muddy margins. Unfortunately, a change in South West Water capacity strategy means it is now kept full, making it uninhabitable for waders. However, a long-staying Purple Heron and a Great White Egret prove it is still capable of attracting interesting birds. The headlands have very occasionally produced typical waders of such short grassy habitats including Dotterel and Buff-breasted Sandpiper. This habitat is also attractive to Yellow Wagtail.

Passerine migration, apart from Wheatears on clifftops, can include reasonable falls in valleys such as Porth Joke, although numbers do not match those further east in Britain; even on the best days, warblers, for instance, are counted in dozens rather than hundreds. Firecrest is expected in later autumn, and scarcer species have included Red-backed Shrike, Red-breasted Flycatcher and Yellow-browed Warbler. Greater coverage by watchers at Porth Joke in particular has resulted in several autumn records of less common migrant species. In late season, visible migration overhead can be interesting. Fly-over raptors have included Marsh and Montagu's Harriers and Osprey. Winter thrushes and pipits drop in to rest in the valley and Richard's Pipit has also been seen. Five Stone-curlews, rarely seen anywhere on passage, were once found in a nearby field. Large flocks of larks, finches and pipits may accumulate at Kelsey Head. Fields at West Pentire on the east side of the valley can also be productive for these species, including one or two Snow and Lapland Buntings. These flocks may attract passing raptors, including a Hen Harrier or Short-eared Owl; Merlin often stays to the year's end.

At sea, Sandwich Terns, which start to pass at the end of summer and early autumn, may be pursued by a few Arctic Skuas. Numbers of both predator and prey build up as autumn continues; all four skua species have been recorded during autumn. Gales have produced Arctic and Great Skuas, and occasionally Pomarine and Long-tailed. Terns also pass, mostly Sandwich and Common, with a few Arctic. Roseate, Little and Black Terns are very scarce. Terns often congregate in flocks in The Gazzle. Terns, in common with waders and sometimes skuas, tend to fly across the isthmus by the lifeboat slip behind Towan Head rather than around the headland itself, especially in high winds.

Little Gulls might pass in small numbers through autumn. The strikingly marked Sabine's Gull, a Cornish autumn speciality, is seen mostly passing in ones and twos. European Storm Petrels continue to be recorded through autumn, sometimes accompanied by a few larger, browner Leach's Storm Petrels, often passing close enough to be able to see their forked tails. Fulmar is an abundant migrant, reaching counts of more than 200 in a day. Manx Shearwaters are joined by a few Balearic from late summer; Sooty Shearwater, flying swiftly without lingering in the bay, has an extended passage period, with ones and twos being routine most autumn days. Cory's Shearwater is much rarer, with no regular passage, although a few storm-driven birds do move through. Gannet is a familiar and common migrant. Late autumn and early winter can produce maximum passage of Kittiwake, reaching more than 500 a day. This period brings some passage of divers and ducks; all three diver species may fly past in small numbers. Seaducks such as Common Scoter may be joined by scarcer species such as Velvet Scoter (once even a Surf Scoter) and a few dabbling ducks may also pass through. Grey Phalarope is a storm-blown later-autumn migrant, and as many as 15 have been seen together. Little Auks may pass at similar times, although they are unusual visitors. At this season, watchers often see a few Black Redstarts flitting around seafront rocks.

TIMING

Seawatch conditions for maximum passage off Towan Head are similar to those at St Ives, with peak passages being recorded on much the same dates, although westerly winds are better than north-westerlies. Birds may shelter The Gazzle in west or even south-west winds, especially in drizzle and poorer visibility. Such conditions can also blow a stray tern or phalarope to Porth Reservoir, and possibly transatlantic vagrant waders to freshwater margins. European Storm Petrel may pass with little wind in summer, especially if there are fishing boats close offshore, although gale days can bring good numbers. Summer feeding parties of Manx Shearwater are seen mostly in early mornings and evenings. Black Terns in autumn are seen mostly in southerly to south-easterly winds, particularly with rain. Passerine migrants are, as usual, seen mostly in east, south and south-east winds, when many birds seem to pass straight across from south to north Cornish coasts, especially in fine anticyclonic conditions. Light north-easterlies can still be productive.

Gulls are best checked on the Gannel from late afternoon, especially if there are onshore winds blowing. For waders and other species on the estuary, early mornings and weekdays on incoming tides are best, prior to dog walkers arriving. Human disturbance can be considerable.

If watching westward off Towan Head, later afternoon light can be poor against the sun, although most observations will be of birds coming in from north.

ACCESS

Newquay, a major coastal resort, is well signposted on A-roads. Leaving the town eastwards on the A392 towards Bodmin, after 2 miles (3.2km) turn right (south) on a minor road signposted to **Porth Reservoir**. After 1 mile (1.6km), turn left into the reservoir car park **(TR8 4XE, hunk.easily.yawned)**. Footpaths lead along both north and south banks. A permit is not required. There are two hides; the first, near the entrance, has access for the disabled; the second, at the top end, overlooks reeds.

In Newquay itself, follow signs north past the harbour towards Fistral beach for **Towan Head**. Turn right, down to the small car park at the end, on the narrow neck of land just behind the headland **(TR7 1HN, ratty.instincts.recovery)**. You can watch from here, or even from the car window in bad weather, parking before the bottom car park to gain height. This vantage point is suitable for disabled birdwatchers. Some seabirds fly south directly over the car park in bad weather, and birds circle the bay in front. A footpath also leads all around the headland; for best views in bad weather, you can shelter behind rocks on the north-east corner. For species such as shearwaters, this may be a better watchpoint.

To check the gull flocks on the **Gannel Estuary**, follow the signs for the A3075 towards Redruth and Truro south from the town centre, passing Trenance Park lake on the right. At a roundabout turn right, taking Pentire Road; follow it until reaching the Fistral Bay Hotel. Turn left here, then take the second left into Penmere Drive, then right again into Trevean Way until reaching a wide grassed area. Beside this road there is roadside parking **(TR7 1QU, rebounder.flush.overjoyed)** and uninterrupted viewing over this wide section of the estuary, where most gulls gather. From here, drive on through Pentire, parking in the car park at the end of Pentire Avenue **(TR7 1HN, merely.aced.neutron)** to scan across Crantock Bay for divers in winter; walk on across the open down headland to East Pentire Point.

To check **Porth Joke** and **Kelsey Head**, continue from the mini-roundabout for 1 mile (1.6km) further on the A3075, turning right towards Crantock. Follow signs to West Pentire, then turn left on a minor road past Treago Farm. Pass the farm and through the gateway past the National Trust sign for **Cubert Common**. Remember to shut the gate after entry. The stream to the left widens 200m upstream; if flooded, this is the area where waders may occur. Downstream lies the first section of streamside bushes used by migrants. Drive on down the sandy track. The point where the track branches right to a group of buildings has a particularly sheltered area of bushes, which are ideal for migrants. Keep left on the track to the National Trust car park **(TR8 5HW, kick.polishing.student)**. From this car park turn right to check stubble fields and the headland at **West Pentire Point (TR8 5SE, squeaking.prestige.frogs)**; a circular walk brings you back into the valley. Alternatively, walk on down the valley from the car park; on reaching the cove, walk left onto the coast path for Kelsey Head to scan the sea.

Cornwall

CALENDAR

Resident: Little Egret, Shag, common raptors, Great Black-backed Gull, Rock Pipit, Stonechat, Raven.

December–February: Divers, chiefly Red-throated, which peaks end January–February; occasional Slavonian Grebe; Cormorant, Eider, Common Scoter; passage of commoner seabirds in gales, with Grey Phalarope, Little Auk or Puffin possible; Merlin, Peregrine, coastal flocks of larks and pipits, possible Black Redstart, Snow Bunting. Tufted Duck, Wigeon and Teal, occasional rarer ducks on freshwater areas; Kingfisher, Dipper, Siskin likely at Porth. Gull flocks in coastal areas include Mediterranean, Little, possibly Iceland. Curlew on Gannel Estuary, Water Pipit possible, Grey Heron, Purple Sandpiper, Turnstone.

March–May: Residents breed. Kittiwake at colony; Manx Shearwater feeding passages from April; gull passage peaks early, Mediterranean or Little possible throughout, Lesser Black-backed and Common Gull build into March; Sandwich Tern from end March; some early passerine migrants from early March but peak from mid-April, especially at Porth Joke; Whimbrel, Sedge and Grasshopper Warblers, possible Lesser Whitethroat and scarcer migrants.

June–July: Manx Shearwater feed, Puffin possible with passing auks, European Storm Petrel possible; towards end of period, Sandwich Tern and possible Arctic Skua, Balearic Shearwater and Sooty Shearwaters; Common and Green Sandpipers, Greenshank, Whimbrel, Curlew.

August–November: Freshwater margins attract waders mostly August–September, with chance of Pectoral Sandpiper or other rarer species in September; seabird passage increases in volume and variety, with greatest variety probably in September, when Leach's Storm Petrel, Sabine's Gull and phalaropes start passing; after mid-October, less variety but great numbers of Gannet, Kittiwake, auks, possible phalaropes and Little Auk; divers and seaducks pass mostly from late October; passerine movement may include occasional rarer species in September–October, with finches, larks and pipits mostly October, along with attendant raptors and chance of Snow and Lapland Buntings.

39A TREVOSE HEAD

OS LANDRANGER MAP 200
OS grid ref: SW8576
Postcode: **Lighthouse car park** – PL28 8SH
what3words: **Lighthouse car park** – undertook.handfuls.bunny

HABITAT

This exposed, rocky headland sits between the seaward entrance to the Camel Estuary and Towan Head further south-west, and is owned by the National Trust. A lighthouse stands on the cliff edge. High ground behind the headland car park is partly agricultural and partly covered in sparse gorse and rough turf. Sloping westwards are more fields, often growing cereals, their dividing hedges mostly formed from salt-resistant tamarisks. The offset tip of the Trevose peninsula, Dinas Head, points west into Constantine Bay, which is mainly sandy with a rocky foreshore. On the east side of the peninsula, Mother Ivey's Bay is sheltered from most westerly winds. Here, a few scattered houses and a lifeboat station are located amid the dramatic seascapes adjoining Harlyn Bay.

In windy conditions, there is very little shelter at any of these locations. Trevose is excellent for seawatching because it is such a prominent headland; visitors can expect some seabird passage in any wind direction or conditions. Some of the best seawatching has been in flat calm conditions with offshore winds.

SPECIES

Because of the limited habitat range and mainly exposed terrain, this is not a premier birdwatching site in comparison with some of the region's best headlands. Principally it is a migrant watchpoint where species typical of the county occur regularly (albeit often only briefly), though there is always a chance of something more special among them.

During winter months, and in particular in the very early spring, there is a concentration of Red-throated Divers, mainly centred around Mother Ivey's Bay and Harlyn Bay. Gatherings of this species are not predictable around Cornish coasts. They may be joined by a few Great Northern Divers and occasional Common Scoter, Eider, Velvet Scoter or Long-tailed Duck. Nearby, the shore of Constantine Bay hosts small numbers of Turnstone and the occasional Purple Sandpiper and Grey Plover, but Oystercatcher is more numerous and Mediterranean Gull occurs in double digits.

Those passerine harbingers of spring, Wheatears, gather increasingly from early spring, flashing their distinctive white rumps. Mainly smaller numbers of commoner passage migrants follow in their wake. Easily seen are groups of Whimbrel, often settling in surrounding fields. Occasional Merlin, Hobby or Short-eared Owl have occurred in spring as well as autumn, the first also having wintered in the general

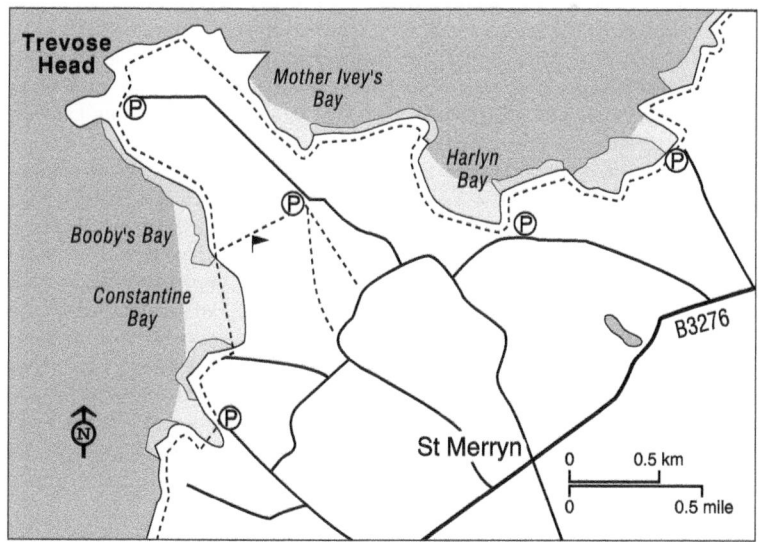

area, and a Gyr Falcon once stayed for several days. Other scarce or rare spring migrants have included Dotterel, Golden Oriole, Tawny Pipit and Sardinian Warbler. Woodchat Shrike has occurred on several occasions.

The quieter breeding season months here are enlivened somewhat by a local speciality: Corn Bunting. An ongoing National Trust initiative on the headland means bird-friendly seed crops – so-called sacrificial crops – have been grown specifically for it and other seed-eaters such as Skylark. Throughout the Corn Bunting breeding season (mid-March–October) males are easily detected as they deliver their monotonous jangling song throughout most of the day from a prominent perch, hedge-top or farm building. Areas around the farmstead are particularly good spots to watch them. During winter, they form discreet wandering flocks and may be very difficult to locate. However, despite these targeted efforts to provide supplementary foods their numbers remain low and vulnerable.

Breeding seabirds are represented only by low numbers of Shag, Razorbill, Guillemot and Herring Gull, but more pairs of Fulmar and Kittiwake breed in the general coastal vicinity. Rock Pipits search unobtrusively amid a habitat that suits them well, while Kestrel, Stonechat and Raven are more readily viewed.

Autumn's onset brings gradually increasing numbers of traditionally early departing species. Once again Wheatears are to the fore: by now, once-bright males are attired in drab female-like tones and fewer gather than in spring. Meadow Pipits, in contrast, build up into flocks of several hundred, as do Goldfinches prior to migrating. During this early autumn period be aware of the possibility of finding an Ortolan Bunting, several of which have occurred in adjacent fields.

As autumn passes, the range and quality of species at Trevose usually improves. On suitable visible migration days, flocks of emigrating birds fill the early morning sky. Hundreds, at times thousands, of Chaffinches pass over, accompanied by lesser numbers of other passerines such as Siskins, sharing airspace with Skylarks and Linnets. Checking hedges could reveal a few Firecrests among more plentiful Goldcrests, and once a Red-breasted Flycatcher. Open areas typically yield Black Redstart. Searching among flocks of common birds could well reveal those less common, such as Dotterel. Richard's Pipit is fairly regular; Snow Bunting, mainly noted in low single figures, is annual, as is Lapland Bunting. Exceptionally a flock of more than 20 Snow Buntings has been sighted: more often both these bunting species are discovered creeping through stubble fields in ones and twos. Occasionally, Lapland Bunting overwinters. Very rare in Cornwall, Shore Lark has been found here more than once, as was a rare Coues's Arctic Redpoll.

Probably because of geographical factors, seabird passage is generally not very close to the shore. Seawatching is usually undertaken from the quarry below the car park, as there is no really good, sheltered vantage point available, although it is possible to watch from the car park in calm weather. Manx Shearwaters may pass in thousands without too much wind inducement during springtime feeding movements; similarly Fulmar and Kittiwake can be numerous, but Gannet less so. All such observations may be repeated in autumn. From August onwards with westerly winds, Balearic, Sooty, Cory's and Great Shearwaters may be recorded. September is best for seeing the widest range of species; then, skuas, terns, Sabine's Gull and petrels pass through, as well as shearwaters. Passage continues into October and November when auk and Kittiwake numbers increase; Little Auk, Grey Phalarope and Little Gull are all possible during this period.

TIMING

Because the site is particularly open, calmer conditions are essential for seeing most species. Typical 'fall' conditions in either migration season will produce more birds, while quiet, clear early mornings in autumn are probably best for witnessing visible migration. Calmer seas aid checking for waterborne seabirds such as divers. Westerly gales may induce seabirds to pass closer to shore.

Avoid times of day or year when the general area is heavily populated with tourists (throughout summer), or when public activities are busiest. When surf is running, there may be some disturbance in the bays from surfers who frequent the area all year in suitable conditions.

ACCESS

From the A389, take the B3276 to St Merryn, where a minor turn from a crossroads in the village is signposted prominently to Trevose Head. Free but limited roadside parking is available near the entrance to Mother Ivey's Bay Holiday Park, facilitating inspection of the lower bushy areas, hedges and farm area for passerines. Alternatively, a narrow road leads beside a farm to the National Trust car park at the headland. From the car park, walk the entire area. Walking westwards, the coast path allows easier checking of open crop fields (which may contain buntings, pipits or waders). The path leads on to Constantine Bay and the golf course–sand dune perimeter. Check around the often productive and rather more sheltered farm area, and also in the bushes fringing fields and part of the golf course. Walk down a private road leading off the headland road, signposted to Trevose House and Polventon, as this road also forms part of the public footpath. On reaching houses, either take a good left-hand path leading to high ground, returning to the headland and passing bushy gardens en route, or take the often-muddy right-hand track running along the clifftops overlooking Mother Ivey's Bay. The latter can be followed to the promontory overlooking Harlyn Bay, especially if looking for wintering seabirds.

CALENDAR

Resident: Corn Bunting, Skylark, Stonechat, Rock Pipit, Kestrel, Raven.

December–February: Red-throated and Great Northern Divers, Fulmar, possibly less common seabirds, including seaducks, Purple Sandpiper, Turnstone, Oystercatcher.

March–May: Wide range of migrant passerines and other species; Manx Shearwater feeding parties can pass in thousands; chance of rarer species on land or at sea; Whimbrel flocks later in season.

June–July: Breeding species.

August–November: Returning passerine and other migrants, including raptors, with a good chance of rarer species; later in period, Black Redstart and Snow and Lapland Buntings; seabird passage includes Balearic, Sooty, Cory's and Great Shearwaters from August, and skuas, terns, Sabine's Gull and petrels from September through October; Little Auk, Grey Phalarope and Little Gull possible during October and November.

Cornwall

40 CAMEL ESTUARY, TRERAVEN MEADOW, CLAPPER AND AMBLE MARSHES

OS LANDRANGER MAP 200
OS grid ref: SW9874/SW9971
Postcodes: PL27–28 (for more detail and what3words see Access section)

HABITAT

On Cornwall's north coast, near the town of Wadebridge, this very interesting area of diverse habitats combines marshy meadows, mudflats on the upper Camel estuary, and a sandy lower estuary around Padstow and Rock towards the sea. Near the river mouth are extensive, high sand dunes along the north shore. At low tide, two very large sandbanks and several smaller ones are exposed.

Along these lower estuary shores few trees grow, unable to survive salt-laden Atlantic winds. Further up the estuary, sand gives way to mud, trees grow on the more sheltered margins, and the estuary forms a much wider basin towards the head. The River Camel meets the smaller River Amble at the head of the flats. The Amble flows through the marshy ground around Chapel Amble, where an area known as Middle Amble has been acquired by CWT and CBWPS jointly and provides an extension to Walmsley Sanctuary. There is little human habitation over much of this area, which therefore remains relatively undisturbed. Amble Marsh is a Site of Special Scientific Interest.

Between Sladesbridge and Wadebridge town lies a floodplain adjoining the River Camel. Here a flood defence system constructed throughout its length has linked various marshy areas now collectively known as Clapper Marshes and Treraven Meadow. Birds quickly began to use the resulting pools, ditches and wetter grazing land. Prominent bushy patches attract a further range of species.

Treworder Valley is a more sheltered area. It has a wet valley floor containing a stream, a small reedbed with intermingling willows and alder, and surrounding mature woodland.

Among interesting plants on the sand dunes is Musk Storksbill, which attracts Brown Argus butterflies. Marbled White and Large and Small Skippers are all found on the north side near Rock and Daymer Bay. Walmsley Sanctuary has less common breeding dragonflies: Migrant Hawker, Scarce Blue-tailed Damselfly and Black-tailed Skimmer, among more common species. Walmsley and Amble have rightly earned their reputation as flagship reserves for CBWPS and are a tribute to the small, indefatigable group of committed volunteers.

SPECIES

The varied habitat results in a good selection of species, the area being particularly important for waders and wildfowl. During winter, Amble marshes attract a couple of hundred Snipe, often difficult to see as they crouch among rough grass; one or two smaller Jack Snipe may associate with them. Walmsley Sanctuary was originally created primarily to protect a regular wintering flock of White-fronted Geese, which formerly attained 100 or so individuals each year. Nowadays, the flock no longer comes. Unusual species have included other geese, and the orange-billed Greenland White-front has been recorded on several occasions. Whooper Swans turn up in small groups from time to time, but they are not

Cornwall

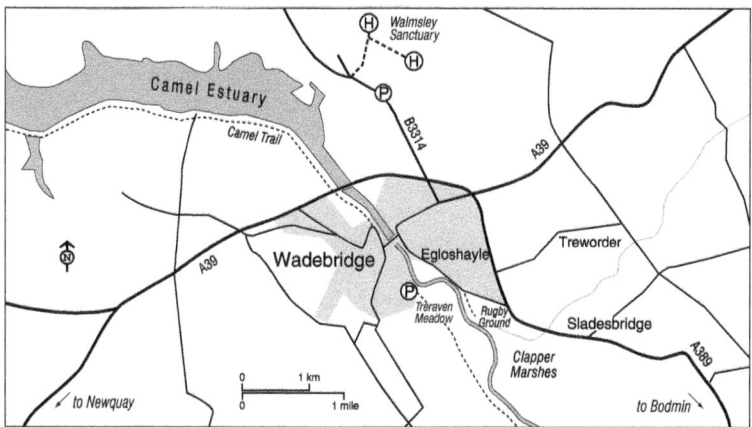

annual. The marshes here support huge concentrations of Lapwing and Golden Plover; in normal winter periods they may exceed 1,000 apiece, but with prolonged hard weather numbers of both species could increase. Dabbling ducks, mostly Gadwall (a few pairs breed), Wigeon and Teal, use both estuary and marshes, flying to and fro, with Wigeon giving their high-pitched, whistling *wheeoo* calls; more than 200 of each species may gather. Among these regular visitors, Shoveler occurs in double digits. Among many other notable birds found on these pools have been American Bittern, Black Stork, Common Crane, a wintering Temminck's Stint, Long-billed Dowitcher, Wilson's Phalarope, Gull-billed Tern and Citrine Wagtail. A flock of six Black-winged Stilt one recent spring added beauty and grace.

Other unusual birds seen in the Walmsley area have regularly included Bittern and Spoonbill, while Green and Common Sandpipers often overwinter and several Ruff can visit for extended periods.

Nowadays, as elsewhere, large numbers of opportunistic Cattle Egret are regular, and both Great White Egret and Glossy Ibis visit on occasions. During spring and later summer into autumn, high numbers of hirundines congregate over the marshes. These, along with numerous dragonflies, lure in an aerobatic Hobby or two. Several pairs of Sedge Warbler breed.

On the higher estuary diving ducks are few; Tufted Duck may occur, but in harder weather very small numbers of other ducks may visit, including Goosander.

Through winter, interesting waterfowl are expected on the lower estuary and around the mouth where it meets the sea at low tide. Three or four Great Northern Divers are often seen, with both Black-throated and Red-throated in ones and twos. Slavonian, Red-necked and Black-necked Grebes occur very occasionally, along with a few Great Crested. Seaducks may be present but only in small numbers. Common Scoter and Eider visit less than annually, mostly in the form of brown females or patchy black-and-white immature males. Three or four Red-breasted Mergansers may be seen intermittently. Shag is common in the lower estuary but usually fails to penetrate further upriver, a niche occupied by Cormorant; the habitat division between the two is clearly marked here.

Further upriver, waders mass. The small grey-brown Dunlin is the most common, with as many as 900 probing the soft mud. More than 200 Curlew winter and their numbers may peak at 500 in early autumn. Oystercatcher averages about 300.

Ringed Plover tends not to winter in large numbers in the South West, but 30 or so have been counted on the estuary, often favouring sandy lower reaches. In its winter plumage, Grey Plover is well named, having only a jet-black patch at the base of the off-white underwing as a noticeable diagnostic field mark; 30 can sometimes be seen. As many as 300 Black-tailed Godwit can be found on the estuary in winter and half-a-dozen Bar-tailed may be mixed in with them; both species fly into the Walmsley Sanctuary at high tide.

Quite high numbers of gulls use the estuary in winter, with more than 1,000 Black-headed being the most numerous; Herring Gull averages 700, often with 100 Great Black-backed. Some 200 Common Gulls winter; by late in the season northbound migrants can increase their numbers greatly, and 1,000 have been counted. Lesser Black-backed Gulls arrive at about the same time, and more than 100 may assemble for a week or two before moving on. Gull sightings around Padstow Harbour have also included Glaucous, Iceland and Ring-billed. Over 600 visiting Mediterranean Gulls can gather on sandbanks on the lower estuary at peak periods, with a few wintering. These are the highest totals in Cornwall for this nationally increasing breeding species.

The Camel is well known for terns, seen from the estuary mouth and flying up to the highest reaches to feed. High numbers are recorded in spring as well as autumn. As always, Sandwich Terns are first to arrive and most numerous, with up to 50 in both seasons. In spring, only two or three each of most other tern species are seen, although Common may reach 10 or more occasionally. Arctic is also seen, and very occasionally the rosy-breasted Roseate, whose long tail-streamers and graceful flight make this now uncommon bird perhaps the loveliest of sea terns. Little Tern is a declining species in Britain, and occurs only infrequently in low single figures. Black Tern is rarely seen but singles may appear on passage. Terns settle on sandbanks that become exposed at low tide and dive for sand-eels among the shallows; as incoming tides submerge the sandbanks, they follow the rising tide up the estuary. A Whiskered Tern visited one spring.

Whimbrel constitute by far the strongest spring wader migration, with flocks of more than 30 sometimes passing overhead, giving their distinctive multiple whistling calls or resting for short periods; there is also a strong autumn passage. As autumn approaches, waders begin to gather. Among the first to arrive is Greenshank; high numbers pass through in some years, in excess of 50 in loose flocks, with up to 10 staying to winter. Up to 15 Common Sandpipers may be noted, again wintering on sheltered stretches of the river running through Wadebridge. Each autumn, one or two Wood Sandpipers pass through. A Spotted Redshank may sometimes join the 200 or so shorter-billed Redshank and may stay on with them. Up to five Ruff can be seen and a couple may stay through winter, while two or three at a time may also pass in spring. Only about four or five Curlew Sandpipers are usual, but Little Stints are much rarer; the latter, now undergoing a population decline, has a history of one or two birds occasionally wintering here. When all the other waders that sometimes winter on this estuary are present together, there may be more unusual species here than on any other estuary in south-west England. Rarer waders visiting on migration have included Collared Pratincole, American Golden Plover and Semipalmated Sandpiper.

In addition to the commoner breeding raptors, Marsh Harrier successfully bred for the first time in Cornwall in 2023 and fledged three young. Two other regular raptors hunt through the non-breeding seasons, a third less regularly. Peregrines, often inexperienced juveniles, chase the estuary's waders, which demonstrate spectacular displays of aerial skill as they attempt to outmanoeuvre the hunter. These raptors are seen from late summer, with two or three different birds during autumn and winter. Merlin is much less regular but favours this area, appearing from late autumn, and one or two prey on small waders and passerines through winter. One or two Ospreys fish the estuary each autumn, possibly staying several weeks.

One of the largest heronries in Cornwall is situated among the estuary's bankside trees; about a dozen nests are occupied each year. A few pairs of Little Egret now breed; they are present year-round on the estuary and reach 80 or more at peak periods. Kingfishers are resident and one or two pairs breed, along with two or three pairs of Mute Swan. A few Mallard also breed, but their numbers here are rather low. Perhaps six or more pairs of Shelduck breed, and in winter their numbers may rise to over 200.

Both Clapper Marshes and Treraven Meadow have attracted reasonable numbers of ducks and waders, regularly hosting a few Garganey. Wintering Wigeon and Mallard reach up to 100 each, while Shoveler reaches lower double figures, as does Teal. Rare North American birds have joined them: male and female American Wigeon, several Pectoral Sandpipers and Cornwall's only Greater Yellowlegs.

Fifty or so Curlew gather, with lower numbers of Black-tailed Godwit. The marshes' speciality, however, is Green Sandpiper, with up to five seen each winter. Common Sandpiper is present in similar wintering numbers. Both species are also regular as late summer and autumn migrants, attaining double figures. The wet meadows and surrounding woods are favoured by flocks of winter thrushes, Water Pipits regularly visit, mostly from later autumn and often throughout winter, while bushy habitats host a small wintering population of Chiffchaff. Bathing gulls mostly favour the brackish pools at Treraven and to date have included two Ring-billed along with Mediterranean and Little Gulls.

Treworder Valley has breeding Reed and Sedge Warblers among other common breeding birds of such habitats. During winter, this is a good spot for Blackcap, Firecrest and Siskin, and once hosted a wintering Pallas's Warbler. Two Night Herons were rare spring visitors.

TIMING

On fine weekends and throughout summer Padstow and Rock can both be crowded with visitors. Low tides are essential to see waders on the estuary mud, and for terns gathering on sandbanks or feeding in shallows near the river mouth. High or rising tides encourage terns to fly upriver. A rising or just ebbing tide is best for watching waders from the CBWPS Burniere Hide at the Amble Dam outflow overlooking the head of the estuary, and at Tregunna, also near Wadebridge. From midwinter, especially if there is a hard spell, geese and wild swans can occur on the marshes. Numbers of other species also rise, both there and on the estuary. High tides encourage waders to roost at Walmsley.

For Clapper Marshes, Treraven Meadow and Treworder Valley, tides are a less important consideration. The pools and stretch of river nearest to the rugby ground will be disturbed at match times, when birds either move to Treraven or fly to Walmsley or the estuary. Spring tides increase the area of water in the pools at Treraven Meadow.

ACCESS

The B3314 north out of Wadebridge crosses **Trewornan Bridge** over the River Amble. There is limited roadside parking near the bridge **(PL27 6EW,**

newlywed.guru.sonic). To access the **Burniere Hide**, pass through the gate leading into a field on the left just before crossing the bridge. Follow a footpath, keeping close to the hedgerow so as not to damage farm crops, then continue through another field to the CBWPS hide. Access is often wet and muddy. Views from the hide are very good, covering the head of the mudflats where many ducks and waders assemble on incoming tides. Gaps in the hedge near the hide also allow good views. Use the same very limited lay-by car parking to access the **Walmsley Sanctuary** reserve, where the hide on stilts gives good views over the site. Access for both Walmsley Sanctuary hides entails walking over Trewornan bridge, taking extreme care, and entering a narrow pedestrian gate on the right of the grass verge just past the bridge. Follow an ill-defined public footpath diagonally across this first field to a stile set in the hedgerow into the next field and follow the level public footpath, remaining close to the hedgerow, to a second stile leading to a small hide. For the stepped stilt hide do not cross the second stile, but closely follow that hedgerow right to the gated entrance of the hide. Keys can be obtained from the CBWPS as it is a members-only hide (see CBWPS website for details). The grass is often very wet and this is not suitable for disabled visitors.

For the **Middle Amble** hide, park in Chapel Amble **(PL27 6EU, districts.roadways.allergy)** (in the main village car park, not the cemetery) and walk for 150m, past the pub and the post office on your right, before taking the left turn to Lower Amble. Pass the bungalows and cemetery and after 420m you'll reach a footpath on the left just before a cottage. At the bottom of the track go through the gate marked 'Middle Amble Marsh' and follow the track to the right. The members-only hide is around 75m further; this bit of the track is often muddy and wellingtons may be needed. The code for the hide is on the members' page of the CBWPS.

Please be aware that wildfowlers shoot on the open estuary on Tuesdays, Thursdays and Saturdays between September and February.

For the hide at **Tregunna**, from the A39 at Wadebridge take a minor road to Edmonton (to the right, on a sharp left-hand bend). Take the right-hand turn to Tregunna, down narrow lanes, where there is limited roadside parking near the farm **(PL27 6HF, peroxide.digs.unit)**. Follow a lane for about 400m to the estuary and hide. Alternatively, follow the public path/cycle track along the now-disused railway from Wadebridge; the track runs beside the hide. This track (known as the Camel Trail) continues along the whole length of the estuary to Padstow, giving excellent views throughout. The Camel Trail is level throughout, surfaced with fine gravel, so access from either Wadebridge or Padstow is possible for less able-bodied vistiors and those using mobility scooters. The substantial gull roost is best viewed from Padstow Station car park.

To reach the lower estuary, continue from Trewornan Bridge to St Minver and take a narrow but good road signposted to **Rock**, where there is a car park **(PL27 6LD, maternal.films.feuds)**. Good views of this part of the estuary – including the sandbanks when the tide is out – are possible from the road. A main channel continues to flow and often contains the same birds, such as divers and grebes, as when the area is inundated by the tide. At low tide you can walk to the mouth where there are other waterbirds, especially terns. Access onto the dunes is from the car park. From Amble marshes to the river mouth is about 4.5 miles (7km). For **Padstow**, take the A389 for good views of terns, divers, grebes and gulls off the harbour, opposite Rock **(PL28 8BY, victory.observes.trappings)**.

Clapper Marshes can only be viewed from the grassy road verge running parallel to them. For much of its length this raised verge allows safe, mostly open and easy viewing. From Bodmin on the A389, park at Sladesbridge in a lay-by running directly in front of the garden centre **(PL27 6JA, policy.mastering.cattle)**. Take care when crossing the very busy road to view the marshes. From here, the entire length of the marshes can be walked easily, including both sides of the river via Wadebridge. Alternatively, roadside parking is available along **Egloshayle** Road or in the town car parks **(PL27 6HY, tadpole.wrenching.pirate)**. At Egloshayle Road, from the Bodmin direction, at the point where the low roadside wall begins is a riverside footpath which also skirts the edge of the rugby field. Several pools can be more closely viewed by following this path. Further roadside parking at **Guineaport (PL27 7BP, posts.unhappily.bedrooms)** (in Wadebridge beside the river) allows the Treraven Meadow tidal pools to be checked; these are out of sight from the Egloshayle Road section. The tidal grazing marsh is located about 100m after the entrance to the Wadebridge to Bodmin section of the Camel Trail, which can be followed until it enters woodland. Since this path has a hard surface, it is suitable for the less mobile visitor and for those using mobility scooters.

For **Treworder Valley**, park in the same lay-by at the garden centre. This site lies on the eastern boundary of the garden centre. The public footpath, often muddy, is joined via a stile near the road bridge. Most birdwatchers cover only the lower valley area, but this quiet, wooded footpath can be walked to Higham Mill, with common woodland species en route. From Wadebridge bus station, pedestrians can cover this entire area in reverse.

CALENDAR

Resident: Cormorant, Shag (breeds nearby), Grey Heron, Little Egret, Mute Swan, Shelduck, Gadwall, Mallard, Oystercatcher, Lapwing, Kingfisher, probable Marsh Harrier.

December–February: Great Northern and other divers and various grebes likely; Teal, Wigeon, Eider, Common Scoter, possible Velvet Scoter and Long-tailed Duck, Red-breasted Merganser, Peregrine, Merlin, Ringed Plover, Lapwing, Grey and Golden Plovers, Dunlin, Knot, Sanderling, probably Ruff and Spotted Redshank, Redshank, Greenshank, Common and Green Sandpipers, Black-tailed and Bar-tailed Godwits, Curlew, Snipe, possible Jack Snipe, commoner gulls, Mediterranean Gull (migrant Lesser Black-backed and Common arrive from February), possible Bittern, Cattle and Great White Egrets, Spoonbill, Glossy Ibis.

March–May: Most of the above-mentioned waders and waterfowl begin to leave by early March. First Sandwich Tern from end of March, Whimbrel and other tern species from mid-April onwards, hirundines, probable Garganey, Hobby, rarer species.

June–July: Commoner waders, including Green Sandpiper, start returning from mid-July, Sedge Warbler breeds.

August–November: Mediterranean Gull peaks earlier in period; wader numbers and variety increase through early autumn; hirundines late August to October; possible Little Stint, Curlew Sandpiper, probable Wood Sandpiper, Whimbrel; terns, Peregrine, Hobby, Osprey; Merlin likely from end of September; waterfowl return from end of period; rarer migrants.

Cornwall

SITE CLUSTER: BUDE AND NORTH-WEST DEVON

41 Bude district
42 Tamar Lakes
44 Hartland Point and district

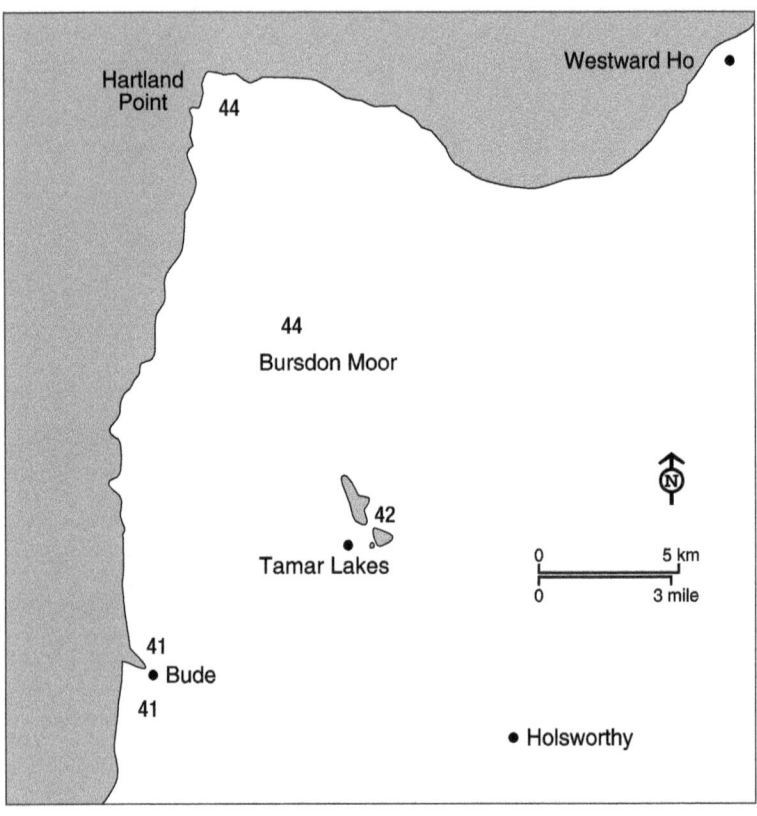

41 BUDE DISTRICT

> OS LANDRANGER MAP 190
> OS grid ref: 2106
> Postcodes: EX23 (for more detail and what3words see Access section)

HABITAT

The small tourist town of Bude faces west towards the Atlantic in the centre of a long line of jagged cliffs and high coastal downs leading towards north Cornwall's border with Devon. Maer Downs are the open clifftop areas just north of the town. The small Neet River drains down into sandy Bude Haven bay; the river valley just east of the town centre has damp meadows and pools at Petherick's Mill, and a small area of reedbed (Bude Marshes), which are both Local Nature Reserves. A disused canal runs inland adjacent to the reeds and continues for another 2 miles (3.2km). Immediately north of the town, within a few metres of housing in the Flexbury district, is low-lying Maer Lake. This semi-permanent area of inundated meadow, with muddy freshwater pools and ditches, extends in the wet season into a shallow lagoon of several acres; in midsummer it almost dries out. It is now a joint CWT/CBWPS reserve. Migrant Hawker and Black-tailed Skimmer dragonflies occur in good numbers. Maer is cattle-grazed throughout the summer.

About 5 miles (8km) north of Bude is Cleave Camp, an area of high coastal downland occupied by prominent satellite-tracking radar dishes; coastal footpaths lead across the slopes of the downs, which have extensive gorse thickets, and down into sheltered hollows leading towards Coombe Valley on the south side. About 1 mile (1.6km) to the south, back towards Bude, high farmland overlooks tiny Sandy Mouth inlet; the fields above are often left as stubble in autumn. Five miles (8km) south of Bude, along a straight, open stretch of coast fully exposed to wind and surf, lie Widemouth Bay sands; at the south end, the rocky Millook Haven bay is more sheltered.

SPECIES

Although it has no species unique in the region, the Bude district has a combination of habitats which can produce a good variety of birds for most of the year.

Winter brings more floodwater to Maer Lake, with the likelihood of around 100 Teal and a few Wigeon; other ducks are relatively scarce in the area, except for tame Mallard hybrids along the canal banks. Teal, and occasionally other ducks such as Shoveler, also visit Bude Marsh, where a very rare Sociable Plover was identified among a flock of Lapwing in December 2020; the bird stayed until February 2021. A Goosander or seaduck might arrive on the sheltered waters of the canal, while an Eider or two spend periods off the harbour mouth in some winters. In the reedbed, Cetti's Warblers occasionally burst into song and Water Rails squeal; one or two Chiffchaffs often winter here, once accompanied by a Dusky Warbler. In sustained cold, a Bittern or a group of agile Bearded Tits may arrive in the reeds. Snipe can occur in the reedbed but are more likely (and in larger numbers) at Maer Lake. Curlew can be seen feeding on lakeside fields, which are also visited intermittently by large flocks of Lapwing and Golden Plover, which also visit the lake. The windswept beach can only boast a few Oystercatchers and Purple Sandpipers, while small numbers of Dunlin winter at Maer Lake.

Cornwall

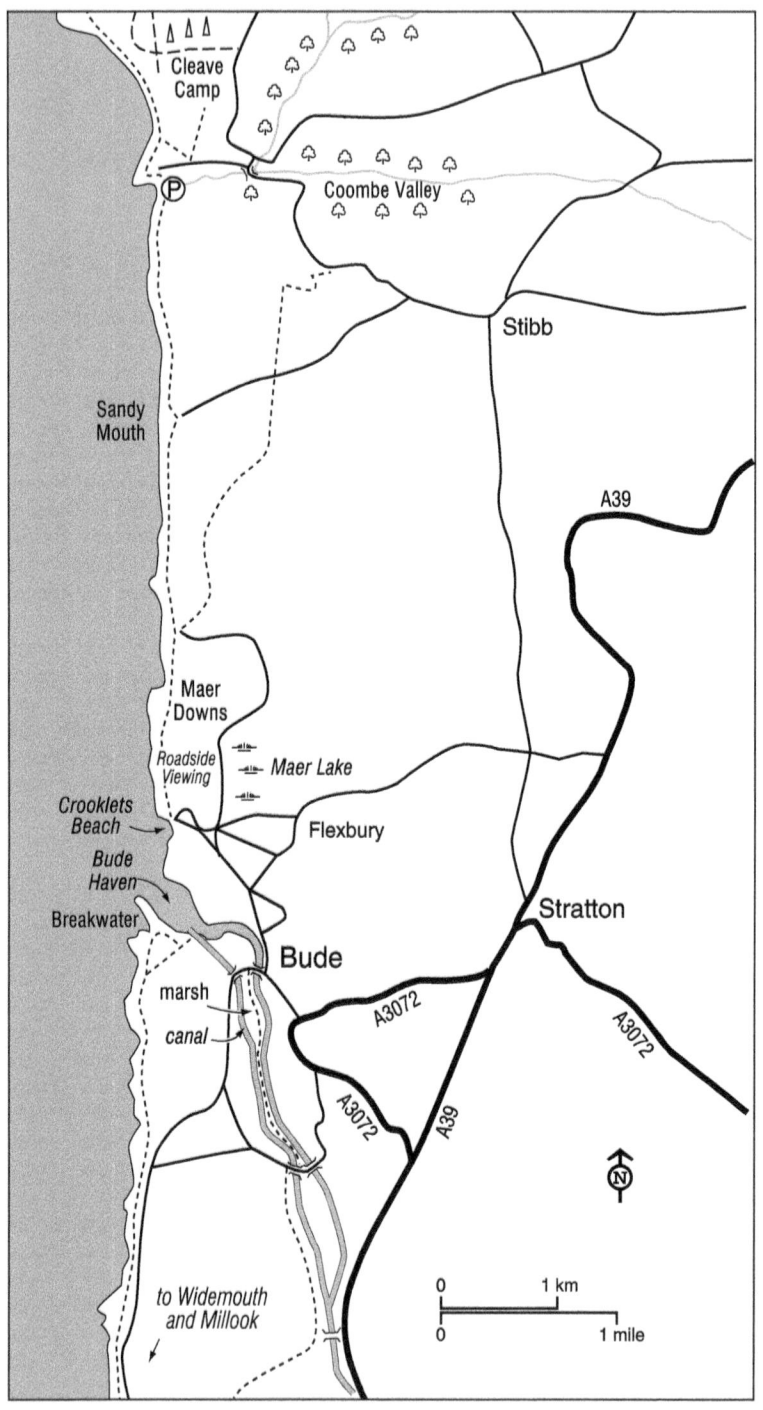

Gulls are present, generally not in very large numbers though gales offshore may drive thousands to fly in to roost at Maer Lake. There, scarcer species such as Iceland Gull might be picked out by thorough searching among Black-headed and Herring Gulls, while Mediterranean Gull can reach lower double digits; a few Lesser Black-backed and Common Gulls are also expected. Some gulls, particularly larger species, also bathe in the river mouth; these have included Glaucous. Other seabirds offshore may include passages of Gannet and Fulmar down the coast in gales; Kittiwake is relatively scarce in winter except for storm-blown individuals, which may fly in to Maer Lake to shelter. Divers, however, may be seen offshore most days; as at Hartland to the north, most are identified as Red-throated. Up to 30 are seen at times in the southern half of Widemouth Bay and Millook Haven; they seem to fly north along the coast past Bude, presumably to join the large concentrations reported off Hartland Point's tide race, then fly back south after feeding.

Passerines on land in winter are variable in interest. Some winters when stubble fields on high coastal downs are left unploughed, large flocks of Skylark gather, perhaps accompanied by a few Snow or Lapland Buntings, which are often picked out by their calls when a flock takes to the air. The rattling *tick-tick-tue* calls of Lapland are distinctive once heard, but take care when separating from Reed Bunting, which may also fly to stubble to feed in winter. Fields above Sandy Mouth are a possible location for these flocks, which may attract a wide-foraging Merlin, also hunting occasionally at Maer Lake. A Black Redstart may stay in seafront gardens in Bude, where Stonechats come down from the clifftops to shelter and Grey Wagtails feed with many Rock Pipits. The pale-fronted continental Water Pipit can sometimes be detected around the edges of Maer Lake, and one or two might stay through some winters.

Spring can bring some large flocks of Whimbrel moving north along the coast, or occasionally resting by Maer Lake, along with Black-tailed Godwit and other common waders. Occasionally, a flock of Arctic Terns is blown into the bay; Black and Little Terns have also been recorded several times in more recent springs, although Sandwich is the most regular. Auks pass offshore on feeding movements from colonies, and very soon the mass southward movements of Manx Shearwater commence; as at Hartland, these are chiefly an early morning phenomenon, with thousands passing in a few hours. Views off Bude itself are not very close and a telescope may be needed to obtain good views; headlands to the north of Bude may give better results, although perhaps not as good as at Hartland.

Passerine migration is not particularly known in this area, but high headlands such as Cleave Camp may attract resting parties of north-bound migrants such as Wheatear, with commoner warblers in the surrounding gorse and scrub. The nearby valleys such as Coombe may be productive, but few birdwatchers visit them. Birds of prey, including the occasional harrier, may circle over, and Raven breeds on nearby cliffs. At the reedbed, Sedge and Reed Warblers arrive in good numbers, this being one of very few north Cornish breeding sites for Reed; singing birds may extend inland along overgrown canal fringes. Once, a Squacco Heron was seen in a flooded water meadow nearby, Garganey may drop in on Maer Lake and Little Ringed Plover are almost annual. Vagrants at the lakeside have included Purple Heron and male Citrine and Black-headed Wagtails. Yellow Wagtails arrive in small numbers and have included the Blue-headed form. Other spring migrants seen in the general area have included vagrant Alpine Swift, Red-rumped Swallow, Sardinian Warbler and Scops Owl.

Cornwall

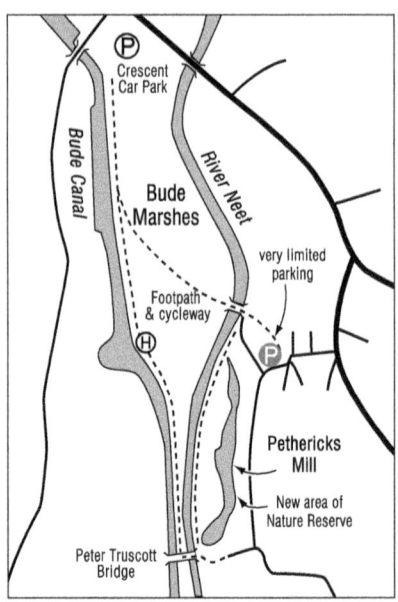

Summer is not a particularly good time of year for birdwatching here, with large numbers of tourists using the coastline. Offshore, however, feeding movements of Manx Shearwater and other commoner seabirds continue on a daily basis. In late summer–early autumn, the movements start to contain more variety, with a skua or Balearic or Sooty Shearwater. When autumn gales start, seabird species passing may reflect those recorded off Newquay and St Ives, although numbers are much smaller with less chance of a major rarity. Wader migration at Maer Lake can be interesting at this time, with a chance of less common species; European migrants such as Little Stint and Wood Sandpiper are recorded, and the stint-like Semipalmated Sandpiper from America has been seen twice. Other transatlantic vagrants have included Green-winged Teal, Laughing Gull, Upland, Buff-breasted and Pectoral Sandpipers, and Wilson's Phalarope. American Golden Plover has been found on several occasions, and both Grey and the rarer Red-necked Phalarope have been recorded here, as have Black-winged Stilt and Temminck's Stint. As elsewhere in the region, visits by both Cattle and Great White Egrets can occur at Maer, joining the Little Egrets. Another larger wading bird, Glossy Ibis, also visits. The small reedbed, as with all similar habitat, can attract hundreds of Swallows and Starlings, roosting from early autumn.

From mid-autumn, the downs and sheltered valleys around Cleave Camp and Coombe Valley are watched for passerine migrants; these areas have had a good share of passing species, such as Ring Ouzel (perhaps attracted at night by the bright illumination around the radar station). Scarcer continental migrants such as Red-breasted Flycatcher, Icterine and Barred Warblers, Wryneck and Red-backed Shrike have been recorded in nearby thickets, and once there was a Red-eyed Vireo from North America. Later in the season, large-scale finch and pipit movements take place early each morning, with birds coasting southwards low along the edge of the downs. This is a good time to check for oddities, Richard's Pipit having been reported, while Snow and Lapland Bunting pass through quite regularly. Coombe

Valley and areas near the camp are worth checking into late autumn, with a chance of scarcer warblers such as Yellow-browed and – outstandingly – once a Dusky Thrush. More attention to this site would certainly repay the effort.

TIMING

Activity at Maer Lake is largely governed by water levels. In summer, it may be too dry to support birds, while winter floods attract ducks and force waders out onto the edges to feed. Onshore gales bring in sheltering gull flocks. East and south-east winds in spring also bring terns and godwits, among other species. Westerly gales in autumn might bring a vagrant American wader. The small reedbed and nature reserve is likely to be most productive in early morning or at dusk when roosting species are gathering. The tracks around the reserve are popular with weekend walkers so there may be disturbance.

The regular feeding movements of shearwaters and other seabirds offshore are chiefly in the first three hours or so of daylight. Autumn gale seawatching requires sustained rough weather to force oceanic birds this far towards the mouth of the Bristol Channel before they pass back southwards. The second day of a gale may be more productive than the first. The winds required are much as at St Ives, with depression-related south-westerlies and rain followed by clearing weather from the west and north-west.

Passerine migration at Cleave Camp is similar to other coastal migration points, winds with an easterly or southerly component bringing scarcer night migrants, while the 'coasting ' movements on late autumn mornings are chiefly into light–moderate west or south-west winds.

ACCESS

Bude is reached by turning west off the main A39 north Cornwall–north Devon coast road at Stratton. On entering the town, turn left at a mini roundabout into the large car park by the Tourist Information Office **(EX23 8LE, airliners.empty. prickly)** to view the adjacent canal and reedbed; a track runs around the marsh and a hide overlooks the reeds from the canal bank. This is a flat area that would suit those unable to walk too far. A footbridge (50m past the hide) crosses the River Neet, linking the canal towpath to an extended area of the Local Nature Reserve at Petherick's Mill. The whole site is now covered by a good-quality, level footpath, creating a circular walk offering excellent views of Kingfishers outside the breeding season.

For the seafront and breakwater, walk to the right from the car park along the canal towpath, crossing over at a lock gate and walking down the west side. At the end, a footpath leads to the left overlooking the shore and river mouth. At the breakwater, walk left until you come to a series of brick shelters inset into the rock face, a convenient sheltered spot for seawatching in bad weather (a telescope may be needed).

Maer Lake (also known as Maer Marsh) can be reached by continuing from the first roundabout through the town centre and left at the top across the golf course to Crooklets Beach car park **(EX23 8NE, zoned.elephant.tentacles)**. Turn inland on foot for 100m; a sign points up a lane northwards towards Bude Holiday Resort. From this lane, after 100m Maer Lake is obvious on the right (whether it is actually a lake or just a muddy expanse depends on season and rainfall). It is best to watch from the verges since there is no access to the marsh, the perimeters being private farmland; closer approach would only frighten off birds using the area. Closest views are probably from the town end near the start of Maer Lane, from which Jack Snipe might be seen.

Cleave Camp is not actually marked as such on current OS Landranger maps; it is the area between Morwenstow village and the Coombe Valley; however, the radar dishes are marked. Drive north on the A39 from Stratton for about 4 miles (6.4km) then turn west down a minor road to **Coombe**. Park in the car park at the end of this road **(EX23 9HW, outnumber.shrub.pardon)**; check streamside vegetation for warblers and walk north along coastal footpaths, which are steep and muddy in places, exploring thickets. The public footpath leading into a sheltered hollow on the south side of the radar station boundary (towards the middle radar and adjacent buildings) is also worth checking for migrants. **Sandy Mouth** can be reached by turning off left halfway along the minor road to Coombe; it is also signposted from other junctions along the main road. Park at the sea-edge car park **(EX23 0AW, basket.script.forkful)** and walk back up to the hill crest; public paths run across fields to the north and south. Look for stubble fields to find lark flocks with attendant species.

From Bude car park, turn left to reach **Widemouth Bay** by a minor coastal road with viewing points; at the south end towards Millook, about 5 miles (8km) from Bude, the road becomes narrow and winding with steep inclines. A high car park overlooks the rocky Millook Cove **(EX23 0DF, quicksand.sweep.rang)**.

CALENDAR

Resident: Shag, common raptors, Raven, Rock Pipit, Stonechat, Cetti's Warbler, Reed Bunting.

December–February: Divers (mostly Red-throated), Fulmar, Gannet, Teal, Wigeon, occasional Eider, possible Peregrine, Merlin, Water Rail, Oystercatcher, Curlew, Snipe, possible Jack Snipe, Golden Plover, gulls (including scarcer species), Kingfisher, Black Redstart, Grey Wagtail, Water Pipit, Skylark, possible Snow or Lapland Bunting.

March–May: Gulls pass from early in period, with scarce species possible; Wheatear on downs from late March, chance of Garganey on marsh; warbler migration from early April with Sedge and Reed from mid-month; occasional Little Ringed Plover; possible raptor over downs April to May, when Manx Shearwater and other seabirds pass; terns and waders move north from mid-April; Whimbrel, godwits, and various sandpipers may drop in at Maer Lake.

June–July: Least interest. Cattle and Great White Egrets, Glossy Ibis, seabirds (mostly common species) pass offshore, occasional Balearic or Sooty Shearwater late July; Snipe and Teal return later in period; breeding species include Reed Warbler.

August–November: Unusual waders possible with common species at Maer Lake (mostly August–September); Cattle and Great White Egrets, Glossy Ibis, seabirds include some less common species (mostly August–October); reedbed roost; warblers and other passerines on downs (September–October), pipits, finches and buntings moving south October–November with occasional rarer species; at end of period Water Rail and Jack Snipe more easily viewed, and late-arriving migrants may include uncommon and rare birds.

CORNWALL/DEVON BORDER

42 TAMAR LAKES

OS LANDRANGER MAP 190
OS grid ref: SS2911
Postcode: **Upper Lake** – EX23 9SB **Lower Lake** – EX22 7LB
what3words: **Upper Lake** – chain.requiring.expansion
Lower Lake – stung.impaled.agenda

HABITAT

Straddling the north Cornwall/Devon border, these two neighbouring artificial reservoirs with natural banks lie among high, rolling farmland in a sparsely populated district. The 16ha Lower Lake, tree-fringed with shallow marshy areas and rushes at the top end, is predominantly managed as a nature reserve and not used for sailing or paddle-boarding since completion of the 33ha replacement Upper Lake, with its more open banks. Both lakes are stocked with trout and used extensively for fishing, while sailing is regular on the Upper Lake. Wildlife includes occasional Otters glimpsed on the banks on quiet mornings.

SPECIES

Although these two reservoirs are under-watched, more than 200 species have been reported. Unfortunately, because the lakes cover two counties, people often do not report their sightings at all! Scarcer migrants, particularly waders and ducks, have been noted in the past, and the lakes, although comparatively small, attract a good variety of these and other waterside species. The main

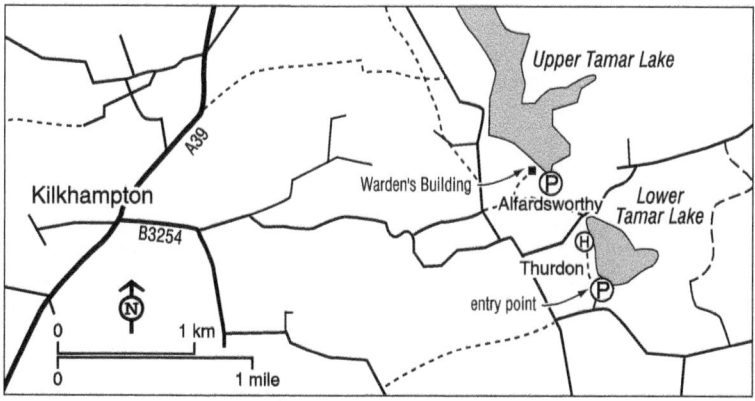

reason for this is that there was no comparable habitat in this corner of the region until Roadford Reservoir was constructed.

An attraction at the beginning and end of the year is the very occasional occurrence of small parties of Whooper Swan and 'grey' geese, both quite scarce and irregular visitors to most of the region. The swans may be found on either lake, but the grassy banks of the Upper Lake and surrounding fields are more attractive for grazing geese, which usually comprise around 100 Canada Geese. The grey-brown Little Grebe is a much smaller winter visitor, regularly found in twos and threes. Great Crested, the only other grebe at all likely, was formerly a passage migrant but can now be found year-round, with numbers increasing to around 15 in the winter months. Cormorants usually fish on the lakes. Dabbling ducks, although not found in huge numbers, are attracted by the relatively shallow, muddy banks and often include more than 50 Mallard and varying numbers of Teal, often concealed among marshy vegetation. With careful observation, both Green-winged and Blue-winged Teal from the Americas have been found among their commoner cousins. Wigeon numbers have fallen in recent years but still occur here, often grazing on the grassy banks, the male's yellow crown-stripe conspicuous. Shoveler are regular, but counts are usually in single figures; bright chestnut-and-white-sided drakes usually form the majority. Gadwall, the females easily mistaken for slim Mallard but for the white speculum-patch, are usually present in small numbers in winter. Diving ducks occur in winter; counts of 15 or so Tufted Duck are usual, with perhaps a single brown-headed female or juvenile Goldeneye feeding in the deeper stretches. Ring-necked Duck has been seen several times, with four once wintering on the Upper Lake, and unprecedented were five Lesser Scaup, including three drakes, on the Lower Lake for several weeks. Up to 60 Goosander may roost in the winter months, while singles of 'coastal' species such as Scaup and Long-tailed Duck have spent long periods here through winter, especially on Upper Lake, sometimes remaining into spring.

Waders tend not to winter in numbers on the reservoirs, where water levels are too high for edge feeding, but Green and Common Sandpipers have been flushed from quiet bays, where up to 25 Snipe and occasionally a Jack Snipe can be found. In colder winters flocks of Lapwing, often accompanied by Golden Plover, gather on nearby farmland. These, and reservoir ducks, may attract a passing Peregrine to try its luck, but the hundreds of Fieldfare and Redwing feeding in the vicinity may be more to the taste of Merlin, seen dashing overhead at irregular intervals some winters; these raptors may be the same as those seen at other sites in north Cornwall and north-west Devon. Another smaller but no less fierce predator, Great Grey Shrike, has been seen at times among bushes on open land near the reservoir banks. Gull flocks often bathe and preen, but totals of 150 or so Black-headed and Herring Gulls are unexceptional and, apart from a few Common Gulls, occurrences of this family are not usually noteworthy.

Warmer weather brings activity among residents. Hissing cob (male) Mute Swans defend territories vigorously, while a pair or two of Coot and Moorhen nest. A pair of Kingfishers usually breeds in the area and singles may be disturbed from waterside trees, darting off low and straight across the lake. The nasal 'buzzing' calls of nesting Willow Tit can usually be heard in trees by the Lower Lake. Up above, Rooks are also busy nesting, and several pairs of Grey Heron build bulky treetop nests nearby. Spring migrants, although less varied than those of autumn, can be numerous, with hundreds of hirundines and Swifts massing to feed low over the water on their way north. Sometimes in late spring they are joined briefly by a breeding-plumaged Black Tern or two, scarce in the region at this season. At the same time, a few pairs of Reed and Sedge Warblers join smart, black-headed male Reed Buntings singing in the fringe vegetation of the Lower Lake. Wader migrants usually include Ruff, Green and Common Sandpipers (once a Spotted Sandpiper), and one or two noisy Greenshank. Ringed Plovers are regular inland passage migrants with as many as 25 in autumn, and the flat *peeo* calls of a slimmer-winged Little Ringed Plover have been heard.

In autumn, when water levels have dropped, waders can be present for longer periods. The marshy end of Lower Tamar Lake is favoured. Green Sandpiper is regular, joined by varying numbers of Wood Sandpiper with its pale-spangled upperparts. Similar numbers of Little Stint peck at titbits on open mud and may stay for several days with groups of Dunlin and often a Curlew Sandpiper. Usually, one or two Greenshank and Ruff can be found, and the first few Teal are often seen in the shallows. Black Terns may appear, being seen through early and mid-autumn, with one or two pale winter-plumaged and juvenile birds. A White-winged Black Tern has been reported; other scarce or rare migrants have included Spotted Crake, Pectoral Sandpiper and Long-billed Dowitcher, the last looking somewhat like a large, greyish Snipe. A very confiding Wilson's Phalarope has also been seen.

TIMING

This type of habitat repays regular visiting rather than one-off visits, as birds filter through over a period. Black Tern and large hirundine flocks are most likely on humid, cloudy days, possibly with drizzle, especially with winds from southerly or easterly quarters. Dry autumn periods with falling water levels leaving muddy margins are best for feeding waders. American species are, as usual, most likely after strong westerly winds. Disturbance from fishing and sailing is normally less on weekdays or early mornings. Wild swans or geese are seen mostly in cold weather, but geese may soon depart because of disturbance.

ACCESS

Although the A39 Bude to Bideford road lies only 4 miles (6.4km) to the west, the reservoirs might easily be missed; look for brown tourist signs advertising them. From the Bideford direction, turn left (east) off the A39 at Kilkhampton on the B3254 towards Launceston, turning left after half a mile (800m) on minor roads towards Bradworthy and Holsworthy. For the Upper Lake, turn first left after 1 mile (1.6km), then take a left turn signposted to the reservoir car park. For the Lower Lake, continue towards Holsworthy, turning second left after leaving the B3254, then pulling into the lower car park. A footpath connects the two. The marshy end of the Lower Lake is overlooked by a bird hide. There is open access to the lake via level footpaths, but these can be muddy at times. Visitors to the Upper Lake banks can walk the entire perimeter of the water, but again the paths can be uneven and muddy. There is another hide at the far end of the Upper Lake.

CALENDAR

Resident: Grey Heron, Sparrowhawk, Buzzard, Coot, Barn Owl, Kingfisher, Marsh and Willow Tit, Reed Bunting.

December–February: Little Grebe, Cormorant, possible wild swans or geese, Teal, Wigeon, Gadwall, Shoveler, Tufted Duck, Goldeneye, maybe Scaup or Long-tailed Duck, Goosander roost, irregular Peregrine and Merlin, possibly Green or

Common Sandpipers, Snipe, maybe Jack Snipe, commoner gulls, very occasionally Great Grey Shrike, winter thrushes.

March–May: A few ducks, especially diving ducks, such as Tufted or Long-tailed, may stay through to April; early migrants, including Sand Martin, from mid-March; others from mid-April, including Reed and Sedge; hirundine flocks, migrating waders, possible Black Tern late April–May.

June–July: Breeding species, including Willow Tit, Sedge Warbler; migrant waders, including Ringed Plover, Dunlin, Ruff, Green Sandpiper, from late July.

August–November: Protracted wader migration peaks end August–September, with Ringed Plover, Ruff, Greenshank, Dunlin, Little Stint, Curlew Sandpiper, Common, Green and Wood Sandpipers, maybe scarcer species, but most leave by late October; possible Black Tern August to early October; winter visitors mostly arrive in November.

DEVON (NORTH COAST AND INLAND)

43 ROADFORD RESERVOIR

OS LANDRANGER MAP 190
OS grid ref: SX4290
Postcode: **Roadford Reservoir** – PL16 0SW **Southweek Viaduct** – EX21 5BB
what3words: **Roadford Reservoir** – struck.adverbs.speaking
Southweek Viaduct – bless.stormed.testy

HABITAT

In mid-west rural Devon, in sparsely populated farmland underlain by the Culm Measures (a Carboniferous rock formation), the region's largest and most recent reservoir started to fill during the early 1990s. The 299ha, Y-shaped lake is 120m above sea level and is up to 35m deep in places. It is the only non-acidic 'mud-bottomed' Devon reservoir; most others are in acidic moorland areas, providing a lower natural food supply.

The shallower upper arms of the 'Y', away from the dam, are kept as nature reserves, with a boom across the upper lake to prevent sailing boat disturbance. This relatively undisturbed area still has occasional visits from Otters, with Brown Hairstreak butterflies in suitable margin habitat.

SPECIES

Roadford brought a large area of new habitat to mid-Devon, becoming best known for wildfowl, mostly diving ducks, and breeding residents. Few observers cover it regularly, although its proximity to the A30 trunk road facilitates casual visits. A reasonable variety of winter ducks visit, with occasional counts of up to 200 Wigeon, more than 200 Teal and Mallard, and small numbers of other dabbling ducks, including Gadwall and Shoveler. These species are naturally more attracted to the shallower northern arms of the lake. A Green-winged Teal from America has been seen with its European counterparts, as have Blue-winged Teal and American Wigeon. Diving duck populations at this rather steep-banked lake have proved to be some of the largest in the region, with a wide representation of species. Tufted Duck regularly exceed 60, while more unexpectedly, Goldeneye often now outnumbers Pochard, with up to a dozen of either at peak periods. Flocks are usually distributed all over the lake. Another expected species is Goosander, two or three of which are often present. Other diving species on the lake in winter have included Scaup, Long-tailed Duck and occasional rarer species, including Lesser Scaup and Ring-necked Duck. A smart drake Bufflehead, Devon's only record, once wintered, attracting many visitors. Other waterfowl seen on the banks include assorted geese of feral or escaped origin, including Barnacle and Snow Geese. These, and the occasional

Devon (north coast and inland)

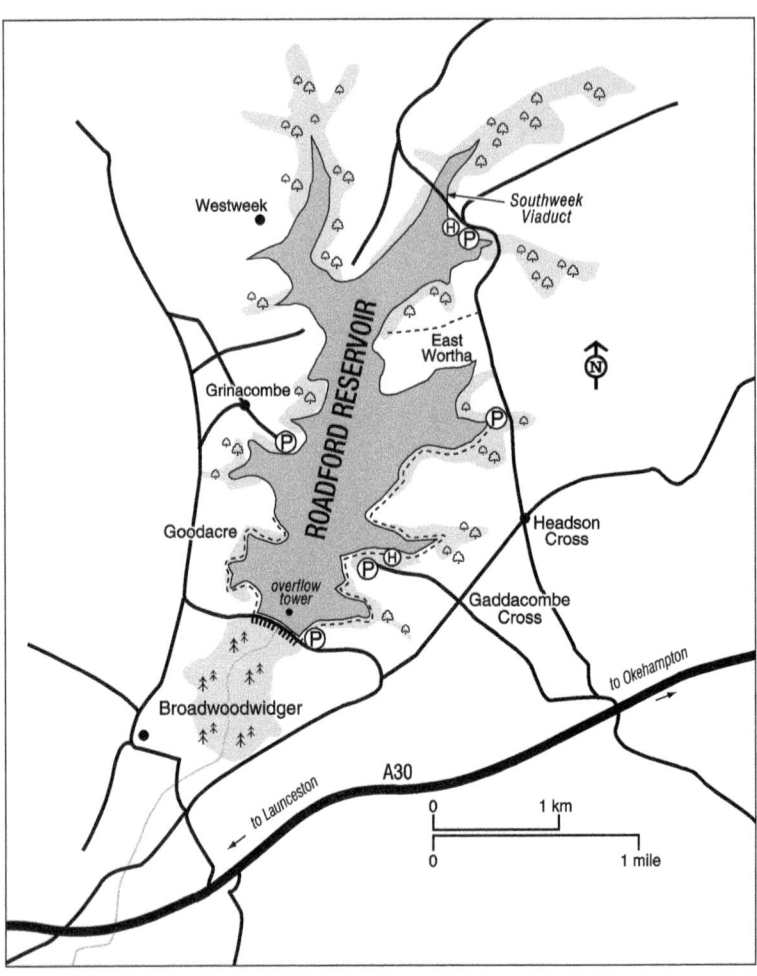

wintertime 'grey' goose, join a substantial flock of Canada Geese which often exceeds 600.

Other wintering waterbirds include Great Crested Grebe, usually in low double figures, Coot, which has reached 100 at times, and a semi-resident population of Cormorants, including white-breasted immatures. Great Northern and Red-throated Divers, along with Slavonian, Black and Red-necked Grebes, have all been recorded, despite the site's distance from the coast.

Gulls are perhaps surprisingly present in large numbers at times, with dozens of Herring Gulls roosting even in midsummer and a few Great Black-backed visiting. Substantial numbers of Lesser Black-backed gather at times in winter and on passage, a record of 7,500 in late autumn being exceptional.

As with any area of open water and land in winter, other species are attracted, particularly predators lured by enhanced wintering bird populations. Occasionally a Peregrine, Merlin, Short-eared Owl or Hen Harrier hunts along the reservoir banks, although none is regular. Other wintering species include one or two

Kingfishers and a few Stonechats. Small numbers of Grey Heron are regular, now joined by Little Egret.

Roadford, due to its steep banks and perhaps its size, is not significant for a variety of waders, although Common Sandpiper winter some years, Snipe gather around the shoreline and a trickle of regular species pass through on migration, including small groups of Whimbrel and inland oddities such as Avocet, Grey Plover and Turnstone.

Other possible spring migrants include Garganey, Common Scoter, Black Tern and Osprey. Autumn brings a few Green Sandpipers in the viaduct area; occasionally a Wood Sandpiper joins them for a few days, and there was once a Lesser Yellowlegs from America. Other autumn passage is not very marked, but may include Osprey.

Roadford is significant for its breeding bird populations, including some local and interesting species, both waterfowl and landbirds. Tufted Duck has bred and is generally present in summer, as is Great Crested Grebe, although fluctuating water levels and lack of secure islands or artificial nest-rafts have so far prevented stable breeding populations from developing. The small island at the north end was occupied for some years by Devon's only breeding Black-headed Gulls, although breeding occurs more regularly on Bodmin Moor, in Cornwall, only a short flight away. Occasional inland breeding by Great Black-backed Gull here is also notable. One or two Goosander have stayed into late spring–summer, hinting at possible future breeding in nearby woodlands. Lesser Redpolls, often heard trilling overhead, breed in plantations near the lake and fly down to feed in waterside bushes. Willow Tits, often detected by harsh 'buzzing' calls, are thinly distributed in the area and might be found anywhere in the nearby Culm Measures farmland and copses.

A particularly welcome sight is the gold, cream and white Barn Owl, which resides near the lake. The wide areas of rough grassland and weeds that encircle the lake perimeter at times of low water levels provide additional feeding ground for them to hunt low across in the evenings. A few Grasshopper Warblers may 'reel' from bushes around the reservoir perimeter, together with larger numbers of Willow Warblers and a scattering of Tree Pipits and Reed Buntings. Hobbies sometimes hunt the reservoir on summer days, targeting hirundine flocks.

TIMING

Sailing and angling can cause disturbance on the main body of the reservoir, especially at weekends, and this may cause waterfowl to use the quieter northern areas or fly elsewhere.

This is a large, quite exposed area of water so viewing conditions can be difficult in windy weather, with rough water pushing ducks into bays to shelter. As with any water body in the South West, more severe icy conditions further north or on the Continent can cause influxes of sheltering wildfowl here.

Late afternoon to dusk in winter gives the best chances of seeing Goosanders. Barn Owls will fly in daylight at any time of year after wet weather, although late afternoon and evenings are probably best.

ACCESS

From the A30 between Okehampton and Launceston, turn left on a minor road signposted, among other places, to Broadwoodwidger and Roadford. The lake is also signposted. Follow this minor road for about 2 miles (3.2km), turning right into the South West Lakes Trust (SWLT) car park just before the dam for a view of the main lake area. There is a fee-paying car park here, which gives open views. A café, shop (open Easter–October, 11.00 a.m. – 5.00 p.m.) and separate toilets, including disabled access, adjoin the car park. From here it is possible to walk across the dam, take a footpath right into sheltered Goodacre inlet and look at nearby Goodacre Wood copse, which contains nest-boxes; this 500m walk is the only signposted one on the west bank of the lake. From beyond the café on the east bank there is a network of level, graded paths suitable for wheelchair users. These lead around inlets and bays to Gaddacombe Hide and beyond. From the car park to Gaddacombe is 750m.

Further tracks lead up the east bank to Wortha inlet. Details of these and a map leaflet can be obtained from the café when open, or via SWLT. Alternatively, points on the east and north-east of the lake can be reached by road. Take a left turn out of the dam car park and continue for half a mile (800m), then turn left along a road signposted towards Bratton Clovelly; after another half a mile take a left turn marked 'road closed' and drive down to the car park at the end of the lane on the right. Gaddacombe Hide is nearby. Return to the road, turning left to continue along the lake perimeter (rarely in open view from the road). At the next fork, keep left towards Germansweek. The next access is to Wortha inlet, parking in a small partly concealed car park on the left about a mile (1.6km) after the fork. From here, a narrow path brings you to the lake after about 200m.

The most frequently watched point for birdwatchers, and probably the best section of the lakeside, is the shallow inlet and stream mouth at Southweek viaduct at the north-east tip of the lake. This is about 2 miles (3.2km) from the previous halt. There is a clearly marked parking bay on the left just before the road viaduct. From here, walk a few metres down to the left and through a gateway signposted to the bird hide. This looks out on the bay where ducks and waders often congregate; it has open access. It is worth spending some time in this area. The stream mouth is partly concealed from the hide, and it is worth walking along the viaduct to check more thoroughly. A small, rather overgrown public footpath starts on the right just beyond the viaduct, giving access to the perimeter of the cut-off lake arm and surrounding bushes. In poor weather, some views may be obtainable from the car parking bay, especially using a telescope.

Shortly after the viaduct, a small lane on the left marked as a 'no through road' leads to a car pull-in nearer to the north-west (Westweek) arm of the lake. Car parking is, however, very restricted, so it is better to walk from the previous stopping point by the viaduct. The inlet is to the right; an island in the middle may prove attractive to resting ducks or waders, perhaps even breeding species eventually.

In order to complete coverage of the lake it may be worth checking the water from the west side (cross the main dam and turn right) at the sailing centre and nearby Grinacombe, although no paths are available along these sections of shoreline. With such a large expanse of water, birds may be a long way from convenient access points, making a telescope essential for adequate coverage. The various car parks and roads circling the lake enable some views for those confined to a vehicle.

CALENDAR

Resident: Grey Heron, Tufted Duck, Great Crested Grebe, Barn Owl, Willow Tit, Lesser Redpoll, Reed Bunting.

December–February: Possible Great Northern Diver, Pochard, Goldeneye, occasional Scaup, Wigeon, Teal, occasional rarer ducks, Snipe, maybe Peregrine or other raptors, winter thrushes.

March–May: Goldeneye, Goosander and possibly rarer ducks into March. During April–May, a few waterfowl linger, possibly migrants including Garganey, waders including Whimbrel, Ringed Plover, Dunlin, Little Ringed Plover, spring passerines including Willow Warbler, Tree Pipit.

June–July: A few summering ducks, breeding passerines and other residents, possible Hobby.

August–November: Waders including Green and perhaps Wood Sandpipers, possible Black Tern or Little Gull, August–September; duck numbers build up by November.

44 HARTLAND POINT AND DISTRICT

OS LANDRANGER MAP 190
OS grid ref: SS2327
Postcode: **Hartland Point** – EX39 6DU **Bursdon Moor** – EX39 6HA
what3words: **Hartland Point** – scooters.punchy.callers
Bursdon Moor – consoles.elevate.liner

HABITAT

On the corner where the north Devon coastline turns sharply south towards Cornwall, the high jagged cliffs of Hartland face across deep water towards Lundy island, 12 miles (19km) away. On a ledge below the cliffs stands a lighthouse, overlooking strong currents offshore. Grey Seals might be seen and Harbour Porpoises frequent the tide race. The surrounding gorse-clad coastline, backed by high farmland, includes many small coves and rocky promontories. A sheltered, scrubby valley lies just west of the Point. Eastwards towards the village of Clovelly, about 6 miles (9.6km) away, the cliffs are heavily wooded. Inland, 4 miles (6.4km) south of Hartland village, lie the dense conifer plantations of Hartland Forest, and nearby Bursdon Moor represents one of the largest remnant blocks of culm grassland in the area – a rare, species-rich habitat formed above the Culm Measures. Other forestry plantations lie further inland. Parts of northwest Devon remain a patchwork of fields and damp, rushy hollows lying on the poorly drained Measures. Other areas are overgrown with willow scrub or small patches of uncultivated heath.

SPECIES

The Point is well placed for seeing birds moving across from Wales and the Bristol Channel coastline. The powerful lighthouse can also act as a magnet for nocturnal migrants. Early in the year the area is very windswept, and the most obvious birds are parties of Ravens foraging along clifftops. Flocks of over 100 Red-throated Divers at times gather inshore, but numbers vary, with birds doubtless often feeding further offshore; these are by far the largest concentrations of

Devon (north coast and inland)

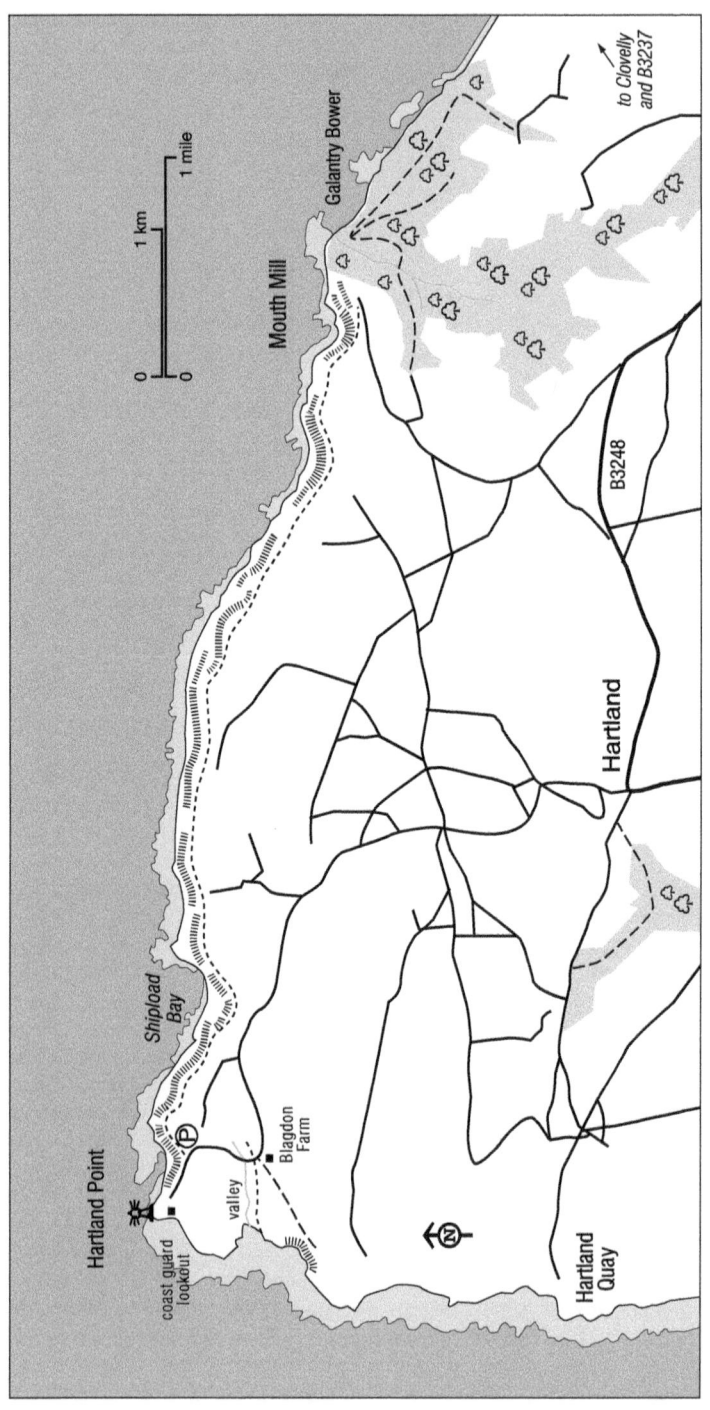

divers in the region, dwarfing most other regular wintering groups. The divers appear to commute in to feed from various parts of the north Cornwall and north Devon coast. They may also be connected with substantial wintering numbers reported feeding off south Wales. Divers feeding in the tide race may fly in at the top end of the race, let themselves be drifted through as they dive repeatedly for fish, then fly back across to the start when they have drifted too far past. This intense activity, presumably because of an outstanding food supply in a small area, can make watching individual birds difficult. A telescope is recommended, as birds may be scattered well out to sea. The area between the lighthouse and Shipload Bay to the east is often the most productive. A few auks also feed in the area, while Fulmar are rarely absent and Gannet pass offshore.

The rough farmland and heaths inland are hunted over by raptors in winter, although the numbers of individual birds involved are small and they cover large areas. Hen Harrier and Merlin are the main winter specialities, although Peregrine is also seen; the best ways to see raptors are at concentrations of food prey or as the hunters themselves go to roost. Starlings mass in winter roosts of hundreds of thousands (exceeding a million at times), a spectacular sight as they gather. Large flocks can be seen heading direct and low to the roost over much of the area. Roost sites change every few years, but large gatherings have been seen at Trew Plantation, a forestry area about 10 miles (16km) south-east of Hartland village; any gathering may attract raptors, including resident Buzzard, Sparrowhawk and sometimes a Peregrine or Goshawk. Lesser Redpoll and Siskin are resident in the plantations, where Woodcock can be seen flying out to feed on a winter evening. Hen Harrier and Merlin, which hunt the inland areas, have been seen returning to roost at Bursdon Moor for many years; both species are often seen, but disturbance and fires have reduced the site's suitability and numbers. A Barn Owl may still be seen patrolling silently over the heaths, sometimes joined by a Short-eared.

Small passerine migrants arrive early in spring at Hartland Point if the weather is fine with high barometric pressure, first dates being even earlier in some cases than on the south coast. The birds have flown over Devon without stopping, coming to rest on the north coast before making another sea crossing towards Wales. Wheatears are often the first arrivals, and passerine migrants later in the season include all the commoner warblers. Among these may be several Grasshopper Warblers, the males detected by their high 'reeling' song; some stay to breed in coastal scrub. Most other transient species, including Lesser Whitethroat (scarce this far west), occur in thick bushes along the stream valley on the west side, where they can be hard to watch. Sedge Warblers stay to nest in the damp undergrowth. Visible migration overhead can be particularly noticeable; a constant passage of Swallows and House and Sand Martins follows the coast northward, passing in thousands on good days. Other small diurnal migrants such as pipits, wagtails and finches may also pass over. Generally they circle up and depart north towards Lundy, which is visible in clear conditions, and the more distant Welsh coast. Larger species may also pass through. Raptors such as Hen and Marsh Harriers, Osprey and Merlin have been seen departing from here. Rarer species are a possibility: Red-footed Falcon, Bee-eater and Alpine Swift have passed over with Rose-coloured Starlings dropping in. One spring brought a tiny Scops Owl to Morwenstow Cove a few miles south of here. Few birdwatchers live close enough to Hartland to watch the passage regularly, and further attention would surely prove worthwhile.

On early mornings in summer, Manx Shearwaters pass westwards in long strings, flashing black and white as they bank low over the waves. Numbers often run into

Devon (north coast and inland)

thousands (25,000 have been counted in a day); formerly, these were mostly breeding adults from Skokholm and Skomer islands in Pembrokeshire, en route from their colonies on regular journeys to feeding grounds. Increasing numbers now visit from Lundy, where the eradication of rats has enabled a recovery. At times, feeding frenzies of large numbers of shearwaters can be seen out towards the island. Some, often young, birds may be confused by the lighthouse beam on dull nights and land among the buildings. European Storm Petrels have been recorded fluttering in the lighthouse beams but are hardly ever seen in daylight. Other seabirds flying past on summer days include feeding parties of Balearic Shearwater, Gannet, Kittiwake and auks. Fulmars are common breeders, heckling each other noisily on cliff ledges, together with Herring Gulls. Great Black-backed Gulls nest in small numbers on isolated rocks, while several pairs of Oystercatcher raise young in quiet coves. Coastal passerines include Stonechat and Whitethroat in thickets and Rock Pipit around the cliffs.

For those wishing to see woodland species, there are breeding season records of a variety of birds in Hobby Drive woods above Clovelly. Singing Pied Flycatcher occurs in small numbers and Wood Warbler may be heard on migration, while Grey Wagtails flit along the damp woodland tracks. Breeding birds of the inland area include Grasshopper Warbler on open heathland, and Willow Tit is a thinly scattered local resident. Both species may also be found in young plantations, where churring Nightjars are increasingly found.

In autumn, westward movement of seabirds off the Point can be good, especially following an Atlantic depression, although both variety and numbers of species seen tend to be lower than those seen further south-west along the north Cornwall coast. Shearwater species have been particularly prevalent among autumn seabird records. Regular watching has demonstrated that Balearic and Sooty Shearwaters occur annually, although numbers vary greatly from year to year. The scope for observation here was highlighted by a September watch in which a then county record of 301 Cory's and 140 Great Shearwater passed westwards in a few hours, accompanied by numbers of common seabirds. During another autumn period, abundant food supplies produced a feeding frenzy of shearwaters visible off the Point on most days for two weeks; most were Manx, but Balearic and up to 45 Great Shearwaters stayed in the area. There are annual records of Arctic and Great Skuas, usually no more than half a dozen of either in a day. There is always the possibility of a scarcer species in the right conditions; Pomarine and Long-tailed Skuas, Little Auk, Leach's Storm Petrel and Sabine's Gull have been recorded but remain rare, as elsewhere in the region. An exceptional December gale displacement once produced another county record count: 158 Leach's Storm Petrels moving west out of the Bristol Channel.

Morning coasting movements of landbirds may be interesting, with flocks of thousands of Chaffinches and Meadow Pipits in later autumn, perhaps pursued by a Merlin or Peregrine. Merlins moving down the west coast appear to cross into Devon and Cornwall in this area and sometimes several fly through in a day. Brambling, Siskin and Lesser Redpoll may also pass over in good numbers; exceptionally up to 2,000 Siskins in a day have been counted. Scarcer migrants such as Richard's Pipit or Snow or Lapland Buntings might be found among the passing flocks. Birds recorded heading south over Lundy have even been tracked continuing over Hartland Point. Lapland Bunting may drop into any stubble field and has overwintered. As warbler movement slackens after mid-autumn, a few Firecrests arrive, often two or three giving hoarse *zip* calls from sheltered bushes. Large movements involving thousands of Fieldfare, Blackbird and other thrushes have been seen, with the chance of scarcer warbler species during these falls. Red-breasted Flycatcher and Yellow-browed Warbler have been noted, but so far not the major rarities recorded on nearby Lundy; again, there is scope for future discovery. A Black Redstart is often present around rocks and buildings at the start of winter, while Purple Sandpiper pick over the tideline rocks.

TIMING

To see wintering diver flocks, calm seas are helpful; greater numbers also seem to occur then. Birds may move up the coast to gather off Hartland Point at high tides. Terns and Arctic Skua have been seen in early autumn during anticyclonic easterlies with haze. The most likely conditions for numbers of other seabirds would be a strong westerly or north-westerly gale, after a period of south-westerly winds has driven birds up towards the Bristol Channel. Summer feeding movements of Manx Shearwater take place early morning, but further out in calm weather.

Spring visible migration passage northwards over the Point may not peak until some hours after daybreak, as birds move up the coast from other parts of Devon and Cornwall. Larger species such as an Osprey or harrier might not pass until after mid-morning. The largest arrivals of thrushes and warblers take place in typical fall conditions, overcast with east winds, but clear mornings (during the first three or four hours of daylight) with an opposing breeze are best for diurnal passage, especially finches.

On the heaths and plantations fine weather is needed to see raptors. They may be encountered hunting at any time of day but in the last hour of light they will be seen approaching their roosting areas. Fine summer evenings are necessary for crepuscular species such as Nightjar and Grasshopper Warbler, and in late summer, with hungry broods to feed, Barn Owl might be active before nightfall.

ACCESS

The area is reached from the A39 between Bideford and Bude. For Hartland Point and lighthouse, follow signs towards Hartland, bypass the village and follow separate signs down lanes to the Point. The road bends down past a farm entrance and terminates in a clifftop car park (fee paying). Unfortunately, subsidence of the tarmac lighthouse track and stonefalls from unstable cliffs mean the lighthouse approach is now closed to public access. The coastal footpath runs across the clifftops westward above the lighthouse, where a lookout area is situated next to the fenced coastguard station building. This provides an extensive view across the top of the Point and down towards the lighthouse below. Visible migration generally passes over this viewpoint, and in spring departing birds often circle over here, or over the high pinnacle of rocks situated just ahead. Westwards beyond the top of the Point, the path runs across the mouth of the sheltered stream valley, which is worth a look for migrants. Alternatively, walk down the track (a signposted public footpath) into the valley past the farm buildings at Blagdon Farm on the corner of the road.

The coast path in the other direction runs eastwards from the car park, past the radar station to Shipload Bay.

For Clovelly woods, take the signposted turn off the A39 4 miles (6.4km) east of Hartland. Drive to the main tourist car parks. Walk right along wooded Hobby Drive, which can be followed for 2 miles (3.2km) until it rejoins the main road.

Devon (north coast and inland)

For the plantations and Bursdon Moor, continue west towards Bude on the A39 past the Hartland turn. From the Forest Office on the left (east) side of the main road as you reach the plantation, take signposted woodland walks. Over the next 2–3 miles (3–5km) southward, heaths can be seen to the right of the main road; Bursdon, one of the largest, is opposite the south end of the plantation. Pull over by the entry to the wood and scan across the road for raptors; do not cause disturbance by walking on the heath. The woodland walks leading from the adjoining plantation edge may produce Nightjar in summer. At the south end of Bursdon Moor, a small, poorly signed turning on the right takes you north-west towards Tosberry Moor, giving another chance to scan for raptors. Park at a central open viewing point such as the small road junction at the centre of the Moor, taking care to stay in your vehicle and not to block traffic. Alternatively, Starling roosts and attendant predators could be watched at Brimford Bridge Plantation, reached by turning off the A39 on a minor road to the east 2 miles (3.2km) further south down, then following signs towards Bradworthy; after another 2 miles (3.2km) turn left towards Northmoor and the plantation is on the left. Other nearby plantations and high open ground, e.g. around Trew Plantation, just east of Hartland Forest, can also be worth checking from roadsides and vantage points but there are few public footpaths in this area.

CALENDAR

Resident: Shag, common resident raptors, Oystercatcher, Great Black-backed Gull, Barn Owl, Raven, Willow Tit, Stonechat, Rock Pipit, Grey Wagtail, Lesser Redpoll.

December–February: Red-throated (flocks) and Great Northern Divers, peak late January–February; Fulmar, Gannet, auks; Hen Harrier and Merlin over heaths (may leave by mid-February if weather mild); Woodcock, Purple Sandpiper, Starling flocks, winter thrushes, maybe Black Redstart, possible Great Grey Shrike.

March–May: Fulmar, Manx Shearwater from end of March; Wheatear and Chiffchaff from mid-March; other warblers, including Whitethroat, Sedge and Grasshopper, mostly from late April; common summer visitors from April.

June–July: Offshore, Manx Shearwater, possible European Storm Petrel, Fulmar, Gannet, Kittiwake, auks; breeding species including Whitethroat, Sedge and Grasshopper Warblers flycatchers, Nightjar (from late May), common woodland passerines at Clovelly.

August–November: Arctic and Great Skuas; potential for scarce seabirds including larger shearwaters, warblers, chats and flycatchers, end of August–September; Firecrest (mainly October), Black Redstart (late October–November), winter thrushes (late October–November), finches, pipits, raptors (mainly October–November); considerable potential for rarer migrants throughout period.

Devon (north coast and inland)

45 LUNDY

> OS LANDRANGER MAP 180
> OS grid ref: SS1444
> Postcode: EX39 2LY
> what3words: bystander.retina.splice

HABITAT

About 12 miles (19km) north of Hartland Point, between the north-west corner of Devon and the Welsh coast, lies the rugged granite mass of Lundy. The island, 3.5 miles (5.6km) long from north to south and half a mile (800m) wide, has a near-level plateau which sits approximately 100m above sea level. Much of the top is boggy and stony moorland, except in the southern quarter where there are a few rough or improved pasture fields. Stone walls cross the island to mark quarter, half and three-quarter points northward from the south end. Permanent standing water is found at Pondsbury, almost halfway up, and at small pools near Quarter Wall, on Ackland's Moor and near the Rocket Pole in the south-west corner.

The north and west of the island are flanked by deep gullies, spectacular cliffs and rock buttresses, but the east side is a little more sheltered, with steep slopes clothed in bracken and patches of scrub and a copse. At the south end is the partly detached block of Lametor, with a lighthouse. There is also a working lighthouse at the north end. The old light-tower, a prominent landmark across the top of the island, accommodated the bird observatory from 1947 to 1968 but is now a Landmark Trust property. Nearby, at the south-east corner of the plateau, stands a small collection of houses, farm buildings and the Marisco Tavern. East of the village towards the sea lies Millcombe, a valley offering sheltered walled gardens, a pond and stream, mixed woodland and Blackthorn thickets; at the foot is the stony Landing Beach and jetty. Off the beach, The Roads form a calmer, sheltered expanse of sea in prevailing and often strong westerly winds. Strong tide races occur off both ends of the island.

Away from the grazed fields in the south, largely surrounded by stone walls, much of the top of the island is more exposed, with heathland increasing as you head north. Feral Goats and Soay Sheep, small brown goat-like animals originating from St Kilda, spend a hardy existence feeding on steep slopes and crags. Offshore, Grey Seals are a frequent sight, and their moaning breeding calls can be heard from sea caves at several points around the coastline. Botanical interest includes the unique Lundy Cabbage, much boosted by the removal of invasive species. Other than bats, Pygmy Shrew is the only native land mammal, and following the successful eradication of Brown and Black Rats in the early 2000s, other species are limited to Sika Deer and a fluctuating population of Rabbits. The island is owned by the National Trust and is managed by the Landmark Trust; the waters around the island are a Marine Nature Reserve and hold a wide range of scarce species.

SPECIES

Lundy has a long tradition of bird observations, encompassing accounts both of its seabird colonies and of many rare and exotic migrants noted over the decades. No fewer than 10 'first records' for Britain have been recorded here, and it must be regarded as one of the region's premier bird migration sites.

Devon (north coast and inland)

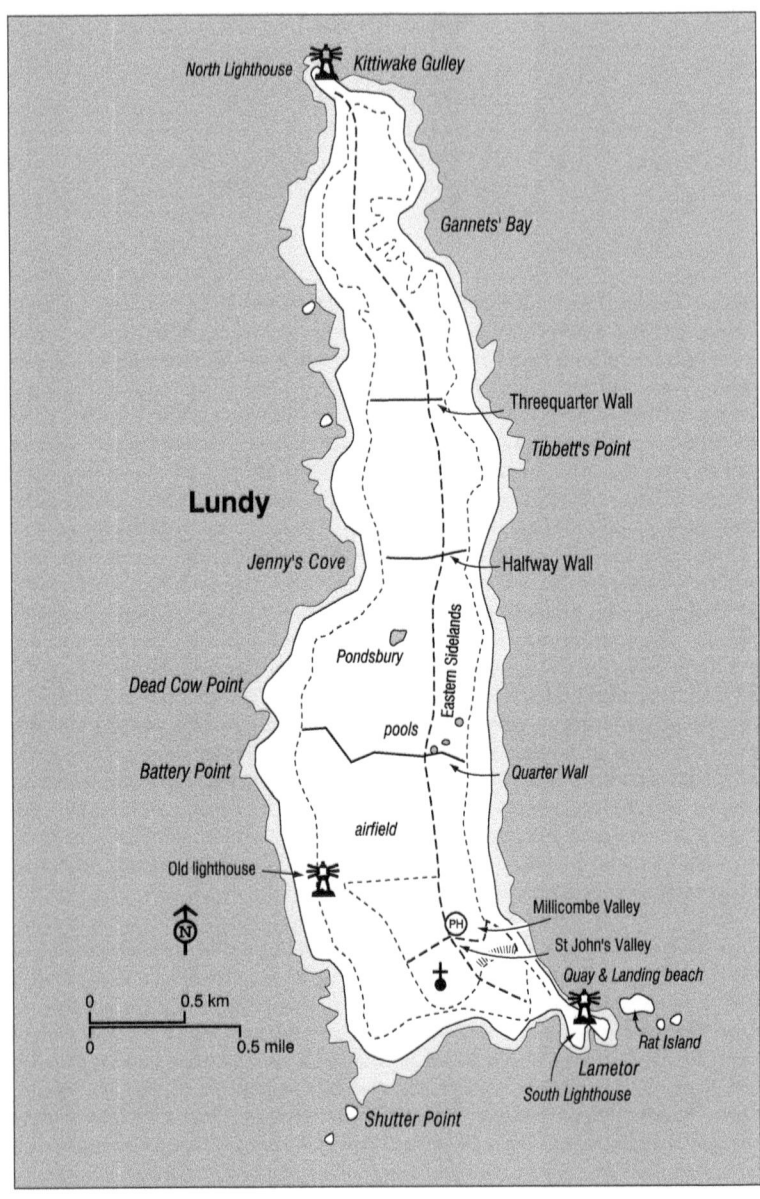

From 1947 to the end of 2022, bird recording on Lundy was coordinated by the Lundy Field Society, which published the annual *Lundy Bird Report* during this period. Early in 2023, the Bird Observatories Council accredited Lundy as part of the network of British and Irish Bird Observatories following a concerted effort involving many individuals and organisations. This was technically a re-accreditation since Lundy previously held Bird Observatory status until the early 1970s.

Those who wish to search for a variety of migrants, including the chance of unusual finds, but do not wish to join the throngs on Shetland or the Isles of Scilly in autumn, may find Lundy an ideal alternative; like all islands, however, in unfavourable winds it can have quiet weeks, when few birds are present.

The open, windswept nature of much of the island prevents many species from remaining all year, although Ravens are often in view as resident pairs and a non-breeding flock soar over the steep sidelands. Shag, common breeders, can still be seen in small numbers in other months, although the less marine Cormorant is only a passing migrant. In stony coves, Oystercatchers are present in small numbers, with several pairs staying to nest, while Turnstones and Purple Sandpipers can be seen on weedy rocks in winter. Snipe are commonly met on the rough grassland; winter influxes of Lapwing may occur, joining dozens of Golden Plover feeding with Starlings and winter thrushes on the pasture. Short-eared Owl and Merlin may occur. Even Skylark and Meadow Pipit, typical summer residents of open terrain, move away in winter, although numbers may be boosted in cold weather. The population of common woodland passerines is very limited; Nuthatch is unknown and tits are rare migrants.

Some breeding seabirds return early to the island. Auks, Fulmar and Kittiwake loiter in the area from late winter, coming ashore intermittently, although not fully occupying ledges until late spring. Manx Shearwaters return to burrows on the slopes; since the removal of rats the population has soared, with over 12,500 pairs around the island. This species is seen at sea in daytime around the island in late spring and summer, often zigzagging low over the tide races or flying south in lines past the west cliffs. Flocks of thousands seen from the boat, resting in masses on the sea between Lundy and the Devon mainland on calm summer days, are also thought to include birds from the many thousands breeding on Skokholm and Skomer islands off Pembrokeshire. The wailing cries of incoming birds circling low over the island at night is an aural experience available only to those who stay on the island. European Storm Petrel now also breeds in good numbers, with more than 160 pairs and increasing, mostly along the wildest rocky west cliffs, but it is rarely seen in daylight except when gales drive small flocks in to patter over The Roads or when one is glimpsed from the boat crossing. Gannets are frequently seen feeding offshore, although counts of more than a few dozen are unusual. Most of the seabird breeding populations are concentrated on the higher cliff slopes of the west and north. The Lesser Black-backed Gull summer breeding population fluctuates, dropping to under 100 pairs in recent years. Herring Gulls are widespread, with more than 200 pairs. Great Black-backed Gulls also breed, with about 30 pairs on the island. The island's Kittiwake population continues to bounce back following the rat eradication; it is most conspicuous around the north-west, with over 300 pairs now present.

Many visitors to Lundy's cliffs seek out the island emblem, the ever-popular Puffin; the island's name comes from the Norse word for the species: *lund*. Numbers of this very localised seabird sadly decreased almost to the point of extinction on the island in the early 2000s, but they are now recovering, with more than 1,300 individuals logged in 2023. Numbers are commonly seen around Battery Point and Jenny's Cove on the west coast. An astonishing discovery was an Ancient Murrelet, a small North Pacific auk, summering at the latter in 1990–92. Other auks are scattered around the island, Razorbill taking advantage of crevices and fissures between granite rocks to support a population of more than 3,700 individuals (the region's largest). Guillemot, previously restricted to the sheerer cliff faces, now numbers nearly 10,000 individuals. All the auks disappear swiftly to sea once chicks have fledged in late June, with a mass clear-out by the end of July.

Spring migration can be heavy and concentrated, with Millcombe hopping with scores of fluttering *Phylloscopus* warblers in early mornings, animated by constant *hooeet* calls from all directions. As spring progresses, many warblers and other small passerines such as chats, flycatchers and a few Redstarts feed on the East Sidelands as they work their way northward. Other sheltered areas such as St Helen's Copse and, further up the east slopes, the disused quarries and the Terrace, with water and bushes, can also concentrate small migrants. As at the region's other migration points, the main passage is often preceded by good numbers of Wheatear, Chiffchaff and Goldcrest, with a couple of Firecrest in the bushes or Black Redstart on the rocks. The shorter turf towards the south of the island is ideal for a probing Hoopoe, likely to turn up most years. The most noticeable bulk of spring passerine movement consists of commoner warblers, which may be present in mixed aggregations of several hundred on fall mornings, Willow Warbler being most abundant, and hirundines, which pour northward overhead from mid-spring. A very wide range of small birds passes through annually, with always the chance of a really rare sighting, especially towards the end of spring or in early summer. The unfamiliar song of Britain's only Sulphur-bellied Warbler was heard in Millcombe one June morning, while a superb, black-hooded male Rüppell's Warbler (Britain's second) once spent several weeks on the East Sidelands. Lundy shares with the Isles of Scilly the distinction of late spring visits by the beautiful but elusive Golden Oriole, sometimes two or three together, and its fluting 'weela-weeoo' song is heard annually in Millcombe. Some late arrivals stay for long periods in thick cover; Common Rosefinch is suspected to have bred and both Eastern and Western Subalpine Warbler are regular, despite their rarity elsewhere in the region.

Up on the plateau there is a steady spring passage of open-ground species, including departing groups of winter thrushes and Starling, along with Pied and White Wagtails and Meadow Pipit, with maybe a Merlin in pursuit or a passage Short-eared Owl. A Killdeer once appeared, Golden Plover often pass through in small flocks, and the once-frequent Dotterel, boasting smart breeding-plumage finery in the spring, is less reliable by the year. Walls near the village, or up on the east side, may attract a perching migrant shrike, occasionally a Red-backed, or a Woodchat. Linnet often frequent open areas around the tracks, with Short-toed Lark and once a pink-flushed Trumpeter Finch also recorded. Occasionally, a raptor such as an Osprey or maybe even a Montagu's Harrier or Black Kite drifts over.

In summer, an occasional pair of migrant warblers, perhaps Whitethroat or Willow Warbler, stays to breed. A surprise southern vagrant could still turn up at any stage. Wheatear is another species to have greatly benefited from the absence of rats, with over 100 pairs now nesting. As with shearwaters, ringing studies have shown a link with Pembrokeshire islands. In some years, late summer may bring an influx of Crossbills, these stout pine-feeding birds looking strangely out of place on Lundy, where they may glean a temporary living from eating seeds at ground level before finding the few conifers in Millcombe; such arrivals, however, are irregular and unpredictable.

Waders are among the first migrants to indicate the end of summer; a small party of Dunlin or a Green Sandpiper may drop in beside Pondsbury, or at tiny pools in the south of the island. As autumn progresses, these miniature habitats are worth watching for waders, and although there are usually no more than a handful of birds, there is often variety. A Knot once favoured the lawn outside the Tavern for several days, so birds can turn up anywhere! Towards mid-autumn, Buff-breasted and Pectoral Sandpipers have been recorded, and any waders should be carefully inspected, as other transatlantic visitors such as Least, White-rumped and Semipalmated Sandpipers have all been found here. Mid-autumn usually brings another chance to see the scarce but often tame Dotterel on open spaces such as the Airfield.

Autumn passage falls are often less concentrated than in spring as far as small night migrants such as warblers and flycatchers are concerned, although very large arrivals (over 1,000 birds coming in overnight) are on record. The daily trickle of migrants may include a heavier-built Melodious Warbler among Willow Warblers and Chiffchaffs. Lundy is one of the region's few localities where skulking East European breeding birds such as the grey Barred Warbler have been found regularly; mist-netting by ringers has helped to reveal this and other unobtrusive species, such as White's Thrush, Red-flanked Bluetail and Devon's only Thrush Nightingale and Paddyfield Warbler. Intensive watching of the East Sidelands bushes and Millcombe is needed to discover warblers and flycatchers, often busy feeding under cover; unless there has been a big fall, the casual observer may see little without searching or waiting awhile.

Lundy's high top attracts large numbers of passing pipits, larks and buntings to stop off in autumn. Numbers of early migrants such as Yellow Wagtail and Tree Pipit may trickle through, but Meadow Pipits pass in many hundreds, and occasionally a rarer pipit such as the heavily streaked Red-throated or larger Richard's is seen. Seed-eating species include near-annual occurrences of Ortolan Bunting, a very scarce migrant in our region. There have been a number of occurrences of Little and Rustic Buntings from the sub-Arctic, with Yellow-breasted and Black-faced Buntings from further east. Often a few Lapland Buntings are seen in moorland habitats, recognised by the hard *tick-tick-teu* call as they fly up, and Snow Bunting may also be encountered. Other migrants on top may include a dull immature Rose-coloured Starling or Woodchat Shrike, with a passing raptor such as Hen Harrier or Merlin sometimes staying for longer to take advantage of migrant passerines. Rough-legged Buzzards, which arrive in autumn, have wintered on two occasions – unusual this far west. Wildfowl may include a party of Pink-footed Geese or Whooper Swan from Iceland, while aside from Teal and the ubiquitous Mallard, other duck species are scarce visitors. Snipe are regularly encountered on wet ground, with Woodcock and Jack Snipe both a distinct possibility. Late in autumn, flocks of finches coast high overhead; Chaffinches, sometimes thousands a day, form the bulk, but Siskin, Lesser Redpoll and Brambling are also heard calling as they pass over, with scarcer migrants including Hawfinch and Common Rosefinch sometimes also dropping in. There may still be a surprise in store, such as an American Robin joining Fieldfare and Redwing flocks, although one or two Ring Ouzels are more likely. Lundy has a long list of American rarities, including Black-billed and Yellow-billed Cuckoos, Northern Oriole, Myrtle Warbler, more than a dozen Red-eyed Vireos, and the small, thrush-like Veery (the second and third records for Europe).

TIMING

As with all islands, most watchers find themselves constrained by access, which makes timing a visit for special conditions difficult. Birds may 'filter through' Lundy, between the landmasses of Wales and Devon, so it cannot always be assumed that birds will tie in exactly with expected arrival weather. Nevertheless, larger numbers of warblers, flycatchers, thrushes and other insect-eating passerines are seen in classic overnight fall conditions after high pressure, and east or south-east winds are, as at all migration points, the most interesting, especially in autumn. Most finch and pipit movements in autumn are against light headwinds. Open-ground species such as wagtails, wheatears and Whimbrel may be 'held up' on the bare north end in spring if weather conditions prevent them from continuing their northward journey. Hirundines and other diurnal migrants arrive early morning in spring, having roosted on the nearby Devon mainland, in contrast to arrivals on the south coast of the region where arrivals of diurnal migrants take place 4–5 hours after a dawn departure from France. Larger species such as raptors take time to soar up and may not arrive on the island until later in the day. Fine spells of weather with light southerlies have brought many scarcer birds, including spring exotics. Most American rarities have occurred after strong Atlantic depressions with westerly gales. Even in such winds the island has not proved very good for seawatching, except for common species and the odd sheltering European Storm Petrel or Grey Phalarope. Few seabirds seem to pass here on migration, but poor visibility may bring those that do closer (such as occasional skuas).

Gales from any direction may cause sailings to the island to be cancelled.

ACCESS

By ship from Bideford or Ilfracombe in north Devon (depending on tides) by MS *Oldenburg*. Tickets from the Lundy Shore Office, The Quay, Bideford EX39 2EY (Tel: 01237 470074). Additionally, steamer excursions may be arranged for tourists, although time ashore on Lundy is limited. Devon Birds run an annual excursion, usually in May, advertised through their membership.

For details of regular transport to Lundy and accommodation in the island's 24 rental properties or the camping field, contact The Landmark Trust, Shottesbrooke, Maidenhead, Berks, SL6 3SW (Tel: 01628 825925).

Most bird news is exchanged in the Marisco Tavern, where a bird log is held each evening, usually at 8.00 p.m., and a logbook is kept for sightings.

On a day trip, time ashore is limited. Most visitors usually concentrate on Millcombe and St John's Valley, the Terrace and East Sidelands, or the main seabird colonies such as in Jenny's Cove or at Battery Point along the west coast – the best options for seeing Puffin. If visiting the north end, Long Roost offers the best seabird location. The main track from the jetty winds steeply up along the cliffside and through Millcombe or up St John's Valley to the village. The main track north from the village passes the airfield just short of Quarter Wall, then onwards past Pondsbury up to Halfway Wall, across Middle Park to Threequarter Wall and onwards to the North Lighthouse. From the village to North Light is about an hour's walk, if you don't stop and look at birds …

CALENDAR

Year Round: Resident passerines such as Wren, Dunnock, Blackbird, Starling, House Sparrow (studied for over 20 years) and Chaffinch frequent the sheltered south-eastern valleys and copses, while Rock Pipits occupy the rocky beaches, cliffs and sidelands; Water Rail can be encountered in any given month, along with Raven, Mallard, and Herring and Great Black-backed Gulls.

December–February: Reduced winter numbers of common residents. A few Lapwing, Golden Plover, Snipe and Jack Snipe, Woodcock; possible weather influxes of other open-ground species such as larks or winter thrushes; Fulmar,

Kittiwake, Guillemot, Razorbill start to return at end of period; Purple Sandpiper and Turnstone, especially at Brazen Ward.

March–May: Wheatear, Black Redstart, Chiffchaff, Firecrest, maybe Merlin or Short-eared Owl from mid-March; most departing winter species have passed by late April; chance of Hoopoe from mid-March, Manx Shearwaters from end of March; main passage of small migrants from mid-April, including hirundines, pipits, Yellow Wagtail, commoner warblers, a few Pied Flycatcher, Redstart, Whinchat, Ring Ouzel; possible Dotterel and southern rarities, e.g. Woodchat Shrike, or vagrant warblers, late April–May; Golden Oriole virtually annual mid-late May; steady Whimbrel passage April–May; all cliff-nesting seabirds present by May.

June–July: Chance of late commoner migrants, maybe a vagrant; breeding seabirds including Manx Shearwater and European Storm Petrel, possible on crossing; breeding Wheatear and Rock Pipit; chance of wader passage and first warblers by end of July, when auks have left.

August–November: Warblers, flycatchers and other small migrants increase through August, peaking usually early–mid-September; maybe Melodious Warbler, Wryneck or a shrike, August–September; thin wader passage, e.g. Dunlin, Whimbrel, Common and Green Sandpipers, with American species possible, especially September; chance of Dotterel mostly late August–early October; Ortolan Bunting possible late August–September; Merlin, Lapland Bunting, maybe Snow Bunting from October; scarcer eastern migrants mostly from late September; pipit passage peaks late September–October; coasting finches peak end of October, winter thrushes arriving, maybe a rarity October–early November, when Firecrest and Black Redstart arrive (American passerine vagrants still possible); Hen Harrier, Short-eared Owl and Merlin probable in November.

Useful websites:
Lundy Bird Observatory: lundybirdobs.org.uk
The Landmark Trust: landmarktrust.org.uk/lundyisland
Lundy Field Society: lundy.org.uk
The Birds of Lundy: birdsoflundy.org.uk

SITE CLUSTER: NORTH DEVON

46 Taw – Torridge Estuary
47 North Devon Coast (Morte Point – Lynton)

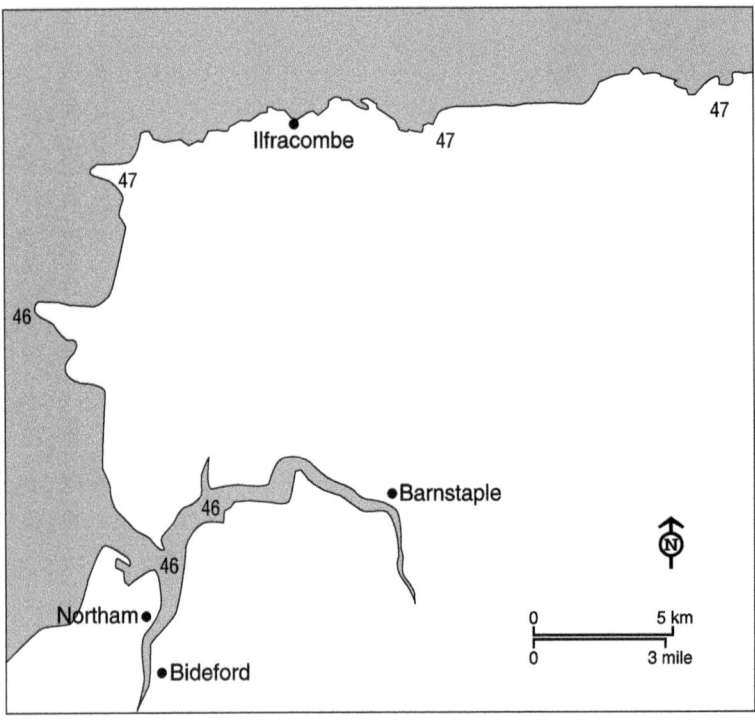

Devon (north coast and inland)

46 TAW–TORRIDGE ESTUARY

> OS LANDRANGER MAP 180
> OS grid ref: SS4732
> Postcodes: EX31, EX33, EX39 (for more detail
> and what3words see Access section)

HABITAT

The exposed, rocky coastline of north Devon is interrupted by only one substantial river mouth, the wide double estuary of the Taw and Torridge. This wide, sandy basin is fringed by high sand dunes and low-lying rough grazing marshes. On the north side of the estuary lies the 1,350ha expanse of Braunton Burrows, a UNESCO Biosphere Reserve with dunes up to 29m high. On the south side of the estuary mouth is the smaller Northam Burrows area, a country park with a high pebble ridge along its seashore. Skern saltmarsh lies on the upriver side of Northam Burrows. Between these two peninsulas is the relatively shallow river mouth into Bideford Bay. The estuary's sandy nature creates a less rich intertidal fauna than is found on some of the region's muddy estuaries, but its value is enhanced by the large area of thinly populated bordering marshland, especially alongside the Taw. Larger areas of saltmarsh occur on the Taw's south bank at Penhill Point and Isley Marsh; the latter, which has deep, sheltered, muddy channels, is an RSPB reserve covering 34ha. Fremington Pill and the nearby Gaia Trust reserve host similar habitats.

Just north of Braunton Burrows lies the headland of Downend, with a rocky foreshore. The sweep of Croyde Bay sands separates this from Baggy Point, projecting into Bideford Bay, to the north. The main centres of human population are Bideford on the Torridge and Barnstaple on the Taw, both at the head of the rivers concerned. On the north-west side of Bideford is the small area of pools and bushes at Kenwith Valley, a 8ha nature reserve. A small freshwater marsh and surrounding flood meadows at Bradiford Water, just west of Barnstaple, are also managed by Devon Birds.

Wildlife on the marshland includes elusive Otters, and Atlantic Salmon pass up the estuaries. Braunton Burrows is of exceptional botanical interest; rarer plants include Water Germander and Round-headed Club-rush. Other flora of interest include Sea Stock and Sea Holly, and orchids such Early Marsh and Marsh Fragrant among an abundance of Marsh Helleborines. In early summer, the dunes can be a mass of flowers. Water Germander is also found at Northam, together with Sea Stock and yellow Dune Pansies. Small Blue and Grayling butterflies are to be found at Braunton Burrows.

The beaches at Northam Burrows and neighbouring Westward Ho!, as at Saunton Sands fronting Braunton Burrows across the river, are popular with summer holiday-makers, and water sports are popular around the estuary mouth; these increase disturbance to wildlife. Parts of the lower estuary, especially around Braunton Burrows, are used for military exercises at times.

SPECIES

This large estuary supports the area's third largest wader population after the Exe and Tamar, although it has large numbers of certain species rather than

Devon (north coast and inland)

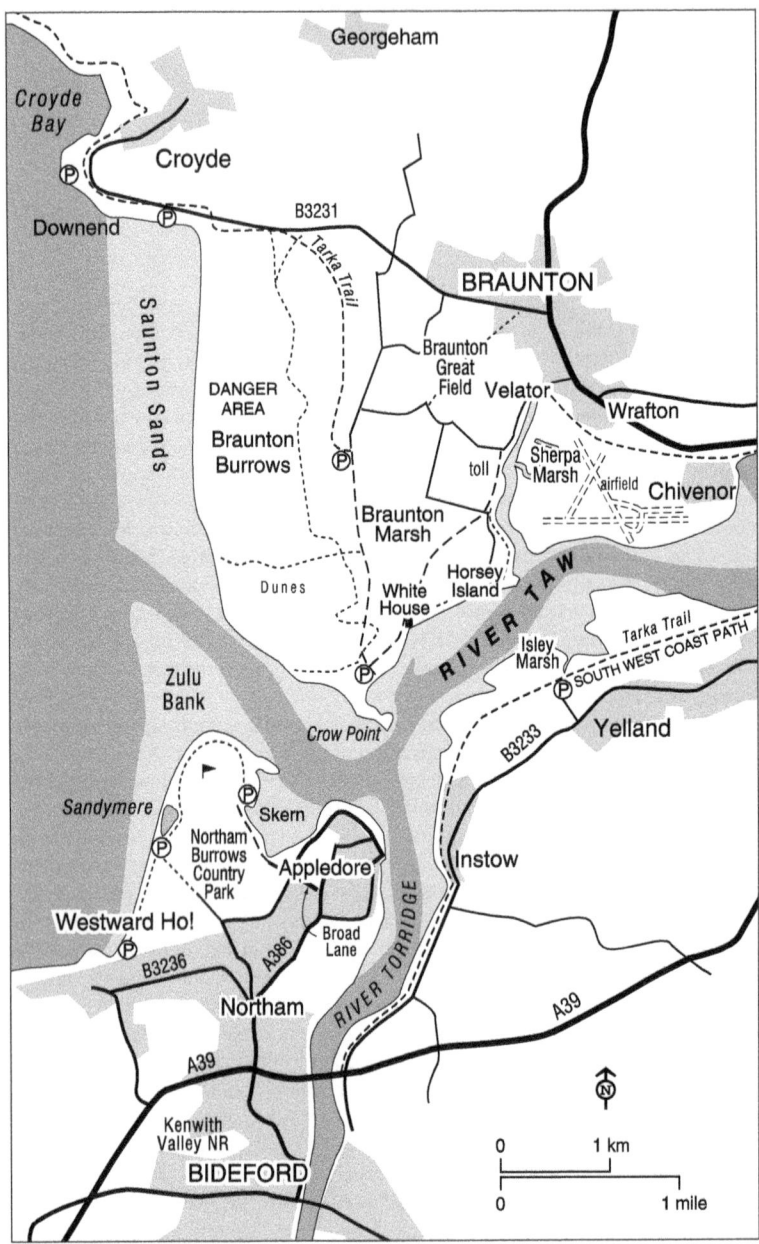

variety. Peripheral dunes and marshland attract a number of species of interest, including some uncommon winter visitors.

Low-lying Braunton Marshes and adjacent Horsey Island, on the upriver side of the dunes, may hold large flocks of up to 3,000 each of Lapwing and Golden Plover early in the year, perhaps accompanied by a few Ruff; Snipe are regular, well over

Devon (north coast and inland)

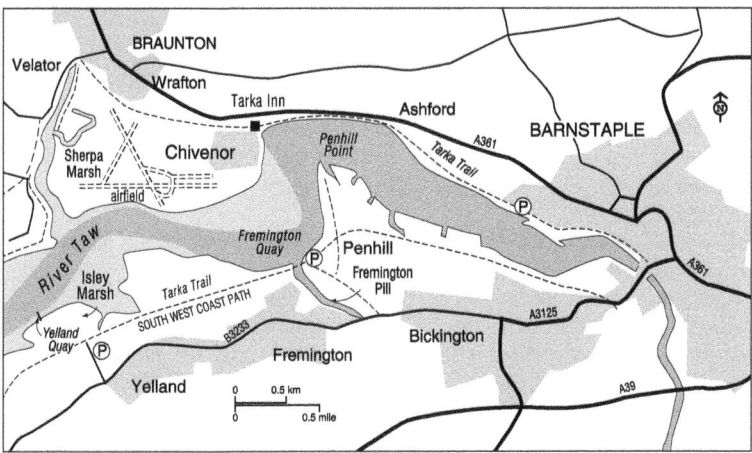

200 scattered around marsh dykes and rushy areas. A few Jack Snipe are also detected at more regularly watched areas. The large flocks of plovers are often targets for a Peregrine circling overhead, while Merlin is also possible, hunting larks and pipits over fields or swerving over saltings after smaller waders such as Dunlin. Around estuary mouth beaches, there are often over 150 Sanderling running along tidelines; muddier stretches hold up to 1,000 Dunlin, and flocks of up to 60 Ringed Plover are among the region's largest winter gatherings of this species. Large waders are conspicuous, with midwinter counts of over 1,000 Oystercatcher, 200 Curlew and 100 Black-tailed Godwit. The main roosts for estuary waders are on either side of the estuary mouth, at Crow Point and Horsey Island on the north side, at the tip of Braunton Burrows, or at Northam Burrows on the south side, by sheltered Skern saltmarsh and at Isley Marsh. Other waders may be seen: up to 250 Redshank, perhaps 100 Grey Plover and half that number of Turnstone, together with a few Knot and Bar-tailed Godwit.

The wildfowl population of the 'Two Rivers' estuary, although perhaps lacking in variety, may increase considerably in cold weather. 'Grey' geese, now usually Pink-footed, may arrive, as may a family party of Whooper Swans. Single Whooper Swans have also wintered regularly with Mute Swan, away from the estuary on the upper Torridge. Dark-bellied Brent Geese were formerly almost unknown in north Devon but have become regular on the saltmarshes; up to 300 can now be encountered, including occasional individuals of the Pale-breasted form and once an American Black Brant. Shelduck is widespread, reaching late winter peaks of well over 250 most years. Regular ducks include up to 800 Wigeon, mostly on the lower estuary basin, and often 400 or more Teal, which may be scattered in groups over the marshes. Up to 100 Pintail occur, Shoveler may gather on muddy pools where there is standing water and Wrafton Pond is a likely location for Gadwall. Diving ducks are limited on the open estuary, although two or three Goldeneye and single-figure counts of Goosander or Red-breasted Merganser occur; the sheltered waters of Kenwith and Wrafton Pond have attracted small flocks of Tufted and Pochard, plus an occasional rarer visitor such as Scaup and, once, a Ring-necked Duck. A long list of unusual ducks seen at Kenwith includes Green-winged Teal, this species having occurred several times on the estuary along with American Wigeon. Dozens of Common Scoter are often present in Bideford Bay, perhaps viewable off

Devon (north coast and inland)

Westward Ho! or Downend rocks beyond Braunton – locations where a few Purple Sandpipers may be discovered feeding inconspicuously along the shore.

Baggy Point offers opportunities to see a few passing seabirds, plus winter records of divers and seaducks, especially Common Scoter, Eider or even rarer scoters. The most regular diver species here is Red-throated, with occasional winter sightings of dozens together probably linked to the larger Hartland Point gatherings (see site 44). As at Hartland, one or two Great Northern Divers may linger, feasting on crabs.

Rough weather offshore may force a Great Northern Diver to feed in the estuary, where single Black-necked Grebes are occasionally recorded. The browner Little Grebe, a marshland breeder here in very small numbers, may also be found diving on the tideway in winter. Colder months can bring increased interest to the marshes and freshwater pools, where a streaky-brown Bittern may lurk hidden in reedy margins, joining Water Rails. At sheltered spots such as Sherpa Marsh reedbeds east of Braunton, the *ping* calls of small parties of Bearded Tits have occasionally been heard over the noise of resident Cetti's Warblers, and Marsh Harrier increasingly overwinters.

Further upriver, in side creeks and bays, fishing Grey Herons are outnumbered by dozens of Little Egrets, which are present through the year, often in deep, sheltered saltmarsh channels. Glossy Ibis and Great White and Cattle Egrets are increasingly regular, the last often in flocks. Spoonbills have overwintered since the 1980s, with two to three regular. They are likely to be seen roosting at sheltered locations such as the saltmarsh at Isley, but at lower tides might be watched sweeping side to side through the shallows anywhere on the wide middle reaches of the estuary. This is one of the most regular UK wintering sites for the species. Immatures can be picked out in flight by their black wingtips. Sheltered areas hold wintering Greenshank, totalling up to half a dozen around the area; Spotted Redshank may occur in similar habitats but are much scarcer. Kingfishers are also regular visitors to the upper estuary, and the muddiest creeks or the riverside marshes above Barnstaple and Bideford may hold a Green or Common Sandpiper. The Landcross area, where the sheltered River Yeo enters the Torridge, can be productive for these species and lost wildfowl. Black-headed Gull, with an estuary total that can approach 10,000, and Herring Gull, usually less than 2,000, are sometimes joined by several hundred Great Black-backed Gulls after coastal gales. These flocks have hosted rarer species such as Glaucous and Iceland Gulls, and it was a regular site for Ring-billed Gulls when it used to occur more frequently in the region. Mediterranean Gulls are found regularly among flocks of commoner species on the estuary, and late summer peaks in three figures are expected. Among rarer species, American vagrants – Bonaparte's, Laughing and Franklin's Gulls – have been identified.

Spring wader passage is conspicuous, with dozens of whistling Whimbrel and many scattered Common Sandpipers stopping off. Garganey is regular in spring on adjacent marshes. Migrant parties of 30 or more pale grey-backed White Wagtails, stopping off on their way to Iceland, are seen on marshes near the estuary mouth, especially at Northam, and Yellow Wagtails appear alongside from April. Cetti's, Sedge, Reed and occasional Grasshopper Warblers sing from the marshes. Singing Whitethroats in thickets on Braunton Burrows are joined by one or two dark-masked Lesser Whitethroats, a species on the edge of its breeding range. Later, in the ancient Great Field system, Quail might be heard calling; this is a regular site for the scarce migrant gamebird. Other interesting vagrants in spring have included Greater Yellowlegs, Stone-curlew and Red-footed Falcon. The Skern area on the south side of the estuary mouth has produced surprise spring finds such as Short-toed Lark and Red-throated Pipit; Kentish Plover has turned up at the roost. A Black Stork visited the marshes briefly and a Collared Pratincole made repeat visits. More common but perhaps unexpected at sea level are breeding Wheatears in the shingle and dunes around the estuary mouth, utilising rabbit burrows and artificial pipes or debris for nest-holes; good views can be obtained especially along the Northam Burrows ridge. Several pairs of Oystercatcher lay their well-camouflaged eggs on quieter stretches of the estuary, but successful breeding is limited to quiet sites such as a regularly used wrecked boat on the exposed mudflats. A combination of erosion and disturbance has removed breeding areas for Ringed Plover.

Autumn brings varied wader passage. Sheltered bays and creeks where streams flow in, known locally as 'pills', may hold Little Stint or Curlew Sandpiper, but generally fewer than six of each; they are seen particularly at muddy feeding areas near the estuary mouth, such as the Northam Burrows tip road pool or the River Caen outlet at Braunton Pill behind the Burrows. Occasionally an American vagrant such as Pectoral Sandpiper or Long-billed Dowitcher is found. American Golden Plover has been discovered following careful searching through the Golden Plover flock at The Skern. Other passage waders such as Green and Wood Sandpipers may be discovered at Bradiford or Horsey Island. Passerine migrants move through the dune-slack bushes where damp conditions encourage rich insect life, and among commoner birds a scarcer migrant such as a Wryneck might be seen. Icterine and Yellow-browed Warblers have both been reported in the Kenwith Valley bushes. The presence of an unusually obliging, rare Dusky Warbler, which stayed on to winter here, along with a Yellow-browed Warbler (alongside the regular Chiffchaffs and Blackcaps) attracted large numbers of birdwatchers. Feeding hirundines, often in hundreds over the marshes, may attract a passing Hobby. Late summer brings buildups of Mediterranean Gull at roost areas.

A few Sandwich, Common and sometimes Little Terns feed out around the estuary mouth, but numbers on this coast are usually small, although Sandwich may peak at 20 or so. Little Terns occur most years, with small flocks visiting in spring, late summer and autumn. Common Tern, if seen closely, may be checked for individuals of the scarcer Arctic Tern, seen most years in autumn. Rarities have included Caspian, Gull-billed and White-winged Black Terns.

The lower estuary also attracts considerable gatherings of noisy Greenshanks, with frequent counts of more than 20, and perhaps a group of passing Bar-tailed Godwits. The upper Taw Estuary is also likely to attract a few Black-tailed Godwits. Ospreys may be seen on both spring and autumn passage, often lingering during August and September.

Migrants on the downland at Baggy Point have included Shore Lark, and a small area of bushes at the south flank has held Barred Warbler among commoner warblers and flycatchers. Late autumn is often interesting on the estuary. When Peregrine and Merlin return to harry wintering flocks, there could be a Short-eared Owl in the coastal dunes, and a Hen Harrier, usually a ringtail, may quarter the marshes. Late season also brings specialities such as regular Snow Bunting, seen flashing white wing-patches particularly along Northam pebble ridge, sometimes in parties up to a dozen, although twos and threes are more normal. Lapland Bunting may also join them some winters. A gale at sea may bring in an exhausted Grey Phalarope to spin on one of the pools, and winter evenings may bring a Barn Owl floating across riverside pastures.

TIMING

At low tide, the vastness of the estuary system defeats close watching of ducks or waders; there is a very large tidal drop on this coast. Saltmarsh areas such as Isley, which can be productive, are difficult to view at low tides, when waders and wildfowl are mostly hidden in deep muddy channels. An incoming tide, particularly about halfway into creeks and bays, is more likely to bring success, as is a visit to the main roosts on either side of the estuary mouth two hours or so up to high tide as birds fly in. Very high tides are less easy to watch as few secure roost areas remain, especially at Skern, and waders may be flushed by disturbance. Snow and ice in other regions are likely to increase flocks of open-ground species considerably and perhaps bring White-fronted or even Tundra Bean Geese. Look for American waders after strong, persistent west winds in autumn, and Grey Phalarope after north-westerly or northerly gales have forced them into Bideford Bay in late autumn. Quail is more likely during a summer influx. The establishment of a well-maintained cycle path along old railway lines both sides of the Taw has improved viewing options. There is little shelter, and wind or rain may make observations tricky.

Water sports may disturb the lower estuary and its mouth, especially on sunny weekends; public use of Crow Point, Braunton and Northam Burrows increases at weekends. See the Access section for army restrictions.

ACCESS

Barnstaple, reached by the A377 from Exeter, is the usual starting point, at the head of the Taw estuary. It is linked by the A39 west to Bideford, or the B3233 takes a less direct route along the side of the estuary.

Large areas of the estuary are difficult to approach but probably not outstanding for birds. The local council has allocated old branch railway tracks on both banks of the Taw Estuary (Tarka Trail) as public amenity areas for walking and cycling; they run from Barnstaple along the south bank through Instow towards Bideford and on the north bank past Chivenor airfield. They form convenient access points for some of the sites below. The south bank walk can be started in the Sticklepath area, just south of Barnstaple Bridge on the A3125 signposted towards Fremington and Instow; footpath signs lead off the main road. Alternatively, go off at the second roundabout south of the bridge into Station Road, adjacent to the existing railway station. You can join the trail from the far end of the car park. The area of damp thickets to the left of the path has held a winter Long-eared Owl roost and once a wintering Hoopoe. After another five-minute walk there are open views over the upper estuary and saltmarsh towards Penhill. The total walk to Bideford for the energetic is just short of 9 miles (14.4km). It may be better to start the north bank walk midway, near Ashford, from which a wide view of the estuary can be gained, then walk in either direction. Those wishing to leave their car and do a circular walk can pick up a bus on the main roads past the access points.

The following are probably the best bird areas.

NORTH SIDE:
Braunton Burrows (EX33 2NU, years.workers.something) For access to the front of the Burrows, drive west on the A361 from Barnstaple, signposted towards Ilfracombe, then turn left at Braunton town centre towards Saunton and Croyde. After 1 mile (1.6km), take a minor road left (not conspicuously signposted) to the Burrows. The Great Field area, surrounded by minor roads, is on your left. Drive down the lane behind the dunes; you can stop in signposted car parks, complete with map boards. From here, continue on foot down a rough track (known locally as the Yankee Road) towards the estuary mouth. After 2 miles (3.2km) of track, you reach Crow Point at the tip for resting waders and views up the estuary; or right across the dunes by a duckboard path to the beach and river mouth. Snow Buntings might be in the area in late autumn or winter. Stops to check the bushes may be profitable, especially at migration periods. Eider may be in sight off either the beach or river side of the dunes.

For access to the rear of the Burrows and the estuary marshes, turn off the A361 just east of Braunton (in Wrafton village) at signposts to Crow Point, initially driving down Velator Way for 200m past a mini-roundabout, and continue through a toll booth onto the narrow private road. At the end, a car parking area near the isolated White House enables access through the seawall for wide estuary views. From here you can walk out to Crow Point. A circuit of the dune and marsh peninsula gives chances to see varied ducks, waders and perhaps hunting raptors; do not forget to look in the sheltered River Caen channel for autumn passage waders.

For Wrafton Pond and Sherpa Marsh, having turned off the A361 east of Braunton at the Crow Point signpost, it is best to park on minor roads leading off Velator Way near the mini-roundabout; paths are signposted from here.

Sherpa Marsh Across the pill from Braunton lie further extensive grazing marshes, less disturbed by public access. A signposted public footpath, starting beside the cottages just beyond the mini-roundabout, leads along the seawall on the east side of the embanked River Caen. This path has to be retraced to the road following your visit. A narrow, reed-lined lagoon extends across the grazing marshes. Geese may use the fields, and the reedy pond can shelter marsh birds such as Water Rail or Bittern; a few Cetti's Warblers are usually present. Greater Yellowlegs has visited briefly, and various other freshwater migrant waders including Pectoral Sandpiper and Temminck's Stint have been reported. Little Ringed Plover now occurs most years in spring and autumn.

Wrafton Pond (EX33 2BG, denoting.linked.cheeses) By taking the Tarka Trail left (eastward) from the mini-roundabout, after 200m you reach the access point through surrounding trees and bushes to Wrafton Pond on the left. The partly enclosed pond backs onto a housing development. The wooden boardwalk is signposted. A surprising variety of ducks have been seen over the years, and Water Rails often lurk in the margins in winter.

The extension of the level Tarka Trail footpath system along the length of the estuary means that you can cross the River Caen by the mini-roundabout (Crow Point road) and continue on foot from here out to the estuary mouth, following the seawall throughout.

Downend (EX33 1PX, burst.flinches.coil) By continuing past Braunton Burrows for another mile (1.6km) towards Croyde Bay, you reach exposed Downend, on a sharp corner with parking on the left. A wide view of the shallow sea off the Burrows can be obtained. Common Scoter are often seen from here and Eider might be visible; seabirds are sometimes seen in rough weather. Purple Sandpiper may be with the Turnstone on the end rocks in winter.

Pottington (EX31 1LX, rising.metro.venue) Turn off the main A361 at the traffic lights just west of Barnstaple, signposted to Pottington Industrial Estate. Proceed to the end of the road then turn left along Riverside Road until it bends away from the river. Park here and join a signposted path. From there you can check with a telescope across the far bank towards Penhill. Visibility over the mudflat channels and saltmarsh creeks may be better from this vantage point than from the south side because of the deep tidal drop.

Bradiford Water At Pottington, continue along Riverside Road until it finishes at the end of the industrial estate. Park by the roadside, taking care not to block factory exits during working hours. View from the gate at the end of the road; there is no access onto the marsh at present. Snipe and other waders are generally present in winter, with a chance of a wider range of wader species on passage.

SOUTH SIDE:
Penhill/Fremington (EX31 2QF, quietly.plod.remaining) Drive west on the B3233 from Barnstaple. Between Bickington and Fremington villages, a small road leads off right alongside Fremington Pill, towards the disused rail halt, now a café. Park here or by the main road and walk down the lane for feeding waders (Greenshank, or maybe Spotted Redshank or Glossy Ibis), then turn left over the bridge for Home Farm Marsh or right along the estuary bank to view Penhill Point bend after 1 mile (1.6km).

Isley Marsh (EX31 3HB, koala.merge.seats) At the west end of Lower Yelland village, a lane runs for 300m north towards the estuary. This is a widely used access point onto the Tarka Trail for walkers and cyclists; from here, it is 4 miles (6.4km) to Bideford and about 5 miles (8km) to Barnstaple. Taking the footpath to the right, Isley Marsh lies adjacent to the cyclepath after 100m. Either view the area from the path by walking on eastward or, as you reach the bay, cross a stile to the left and take a coastal footpath around the western perimeter of the bay on a raised bank. Do not walk onto the marsh. The raised path provides a good vantage point, and watching on a rising tide will enable birds to be seen moving in closer. From the perimeter path you can walk west towards the old Yelland Quay; terns may feed off there in autumn and good views of the lower estuary are possible using a telescope.

Northam Burrows and The Skern (EX39 1NL, parked.norms.jabs) Drive to Bideford and cross the bridge, turning right on the A386 for Northam and Westward Ho! For the road past Skern saltmarsh and freshwater pools, providing views over the lower estuary, turn right towards Appledore then second left (Broad Lane) off the main road. Continue across minor road junctions and on down the mile-long (1.6km) road with close views from your car windows of the estuary mudflats and freshwater pools. After crossing the small bridge near the entrance, it is worth walking left across the wet boggy ground in winter (access unrestricted) to check patches of *Juncus*, which may shelter both Snipe and Jack Snipe. On a rising tide, the car park at the end provides a good vantage point for winter ducks and waders on the estuary, with terns in spring or autumn and Mediterranean Gull particularly in late summer. Walking across the dunes beyond this gives a wide view of the estuary mouth (telescope helpful). Check the far tip of the dunes in late autumn/winter for Snow Bunting. Other open-ground species might include pipits, larks and finches on nearby turf areas, with a chance of scarcer species among them. Walking behind the grassed-over former rubbish tip away from the car park, check areas of cover, which might attract migrant warblers.

For Northam pebble ridge, follow signs towards Westward Ho! on the B3236 and turn right (following brown tourist signs) down Sandymere Road to the country park entry points. Drive past the golf course and pastures, watching again for plovers, out to Sandymere Pool depression beside the pebble ridge. This area has attracted Lapland and Snow Buntings in late autumn and winter but tends to be heavily visited.

Westward Ho! (EX39 1JS, crib.pencil.spillage) Continue on the B3236 through the resort and turn down Merley Road at the west end of the town, where the road makes a sharp uphill left turn. Continue for 300m along Merley Road past holiday camps to a parking area with a public footpath signposted to Abbotsham Cliffs. View the rocks in winter for Purple Sandpiper and Black Redstart, and out to sea for divers and seaducks on calm days. The path continues west past gorse slopes and small coastal fields.

Kenwith Valley (EX39 3NG, pink.month.shaky) Driving through Bideford town centre towards Westward Ho!, turn sharp left at Raleigh Garage, then pass the reserve notice after 200m on the right; park 400m along this road (Northam Road) and walk back to the entrance. Public paths are laid out around this small area; walk past the first lake to overlook the sheltered second lake. A path leads across boardwalks to left and on to the south side of the valley, exiting into a housing estate.

Landcross (EX39 5JA, thread.willpower.streak) Drive south from Bideford for 2 miles (3.2km) on the main A386 Torrington road. The road crosses the River Yeo where it meets the main estuary. Park near the road bridge and walk to the nearby road junction, then follow the minor road for a few hundred metres along the roadside towards Whitehall, checking the narrow semi-tidal creek banks for Green and Common Sandpipers in winter. There is no safe parking on this minor road and walkers must take care as there is no pavement.

Seafront roads at Appledore and Instow, adjacent to Bideford, provide wide estuary mouth views and may enable sightings of divers and seaducks, especially at higher tides.

The Bideford end of the Tarka Trail walk can be reached by turning right after crossing old Bideford Bridge eastward; park in the signposted area.

CALENDAR

Resident: Little Grebe, Cormorant, Grey Heron, Little Egret, Shelduck, Sparrowhawk, Buzzard, Oystercatcher, Water Rail, Barn Owl, Raven, Cetti's Warbler.

December–February: Red-throated and Great Northern Divers, Spoonbill, Cattle Egret, maybe Glossy Ibis or Bittern, 'grey' geese and Whooper Swan, especially after cold weather, Dark-bellied Brent Goose, Teal, Wigeon, Shoveler, Pintail, Gadwall, Tufted Duck, probable Pochard and Goldeneye, Red-breasted Merganser, Eider, Common Scoter, Marsh Harrier, Peregrine, Merlin, Lapwing, Grey and Golden Plovers, Snipe, Bar-tailed and Black-tailed Godwits, Green and Common Sandpipers, Greenshank, Sanderling, Dunlin, Turnstone, Knot, maybe Spotted Redshank or Ruff, Kingfisher, possible Snow Bunting.

March–May: Wheatear; later wader passage includes Whimbrel, shanks, Sandwich Tern, chance of Little Tern from mid-April; White and Yellow Wagtails, mostly April; wintering Spoonbill or other southern heron may still be present; commoner warblers arrive mostly from mid-April, including Lesser Whitethroat; Glaucous or Iceland Gulls may still appear; scarce migrant, e.g. Hoopoe, possible in dunes.

June–July: Breeding species, including Shelduck, Water Rail, Oystercatcher, Quail in some years, Reed and Sedge Warblers, Wheatear; returning Black-headed and passage Mediterranean Gulls and first waders, e.g. Common Sandpiper, shanks and Whimbrel from late July; terns may appear throughout.

August–November: Hirundines feeding, August–September, perhaps attracting Hobby; Osprey, especially Aug-Sept; terns, August–September, possibly including Arctic and Little; Yellow and White Wagtails, passage of commoner warblers; passage wader peak in September, with Little Stint and Curlew Sandpiper likely in good conditions and perhaps a Pectoral Sandpiper or other American species; Merlin from late September; probable Snow Bunting and chance of Hen Harrier, Short-eared Owl, Grey Phalarope, Lapland Bunting, late October–November.

47 NORTH DEVON COAST (MORTE POINT – LYNTON)

OS LANDRANGER MAP 180
OS grid ref: SS5248
Postcode: **Morte Point** – EX34 7DR **Chapel Wood** – EX33 1JA
Wistlandpound Reservoir – EX31 4SJ
what3words: **Morte Point** – whispers.huts.splendid
Chapel Wood – jugs.pictured.annoys
Wistlandpound Reservoir – accordion.snowmen.decimals

HABITAT

A highly scenic, exposed coastline of cliffs and a few rocky coves runs directly east-west along the Bristol Channel coast until an abrupt southward turn at long, jagged Morte Point on the edge of Bideford Bay. Coastal resort towns such as Ilfracombe, Combe Martin and Lynton are encircled by steep, rocky slopes and backed by high ground, rising especially to the east, on the fringe of Exmoor. Over much of the area, although sheer cliffs are limited and often under 50m, the land rises very steeply, reaching 300m only half a mile (800m) inland.

Inland, behind the high, open coastal downs, steep sheltered valleys (combes) hold belts of mainly deciduous woodland. Chapel Wood in the west of the area is an RSPB reserve. Arlington Court estate (National Trust), further east, has a 2.4ha lake set in mature mixed wood and parkland. On the edge of Exmoor, nearby, 17.4ha Wistlandpound Reservoir is extensively used for sailing and fishing. The whole area is popular with summer holiday-makers.

SPECIES

Although much of this area is not regularly visited by birdwatchers, it offers attractive birdwatching potential with a variety of typical Devon breeding birds, seabird colonies and coastal migration. Through spring and summer, the coastline is occupied by large numbers of breeding seabirds, with widespread Herring

Gulls and a number of Great Black-backed Gulls nesting on rocky promontories. Fulmar is one of the commonest coastal species, sitting on cliff ledges or veering past on stiff, outstretched wings. Breeding Razorbills are scattered along the eastern half of this coastline, particularly in the Heddons Mouth–Martinhoe–Woody Bay district, where small groups gather off the towering coast from early spring. The population is challenging to census, but up to 400 pairs have been estimated, the region's largest mainland colony. Guillemots are also present but less widespread, with counts of up to 200 individuals in the nesting period around Woody Bay. Kittiwakes, becoming less common, have small colonies of two or three dozen pairs at Bull Point, further west, and Woody Bay. All through summer, lines of Manx Shearwaters can be seen passing west from protruding headland lookout points, and in onshore gales there is often a European Storm Petrel or two pattering low over wave troughs off Ilfracombe or Combe Martin.

Breeding species include one of Devon's larger heronries, at Arlington Court, where a mix of common woodland passerines may also be found. Coastal valleys, and even scrubby trees on steep clifftop slopes, also hold small populations of interesting summer migrant passerines such as Whitethroat and Redstart. Pied Flycatcher has increased its population, becoming established in nest-boxes in several woodlands, and smart male birds turn up to sing in clifftop copses. Valleys overlooking the sea hold a few breeding Whinchats and regular 'reeling' Grasshopper Warblers, unobtrusive and usually unseen. Passing spring migrants can include a party of Ring Ouzels pausing to feed on coastal downs on their way north. Scarcities such as Hoopoe and Shorelark have been on Morte Point's turfy slopes, and coastal gorse thickets hold breeding Stonechat and Linnet. The high line of downs may prove a suitable thermalling path for a migrant raptor such as

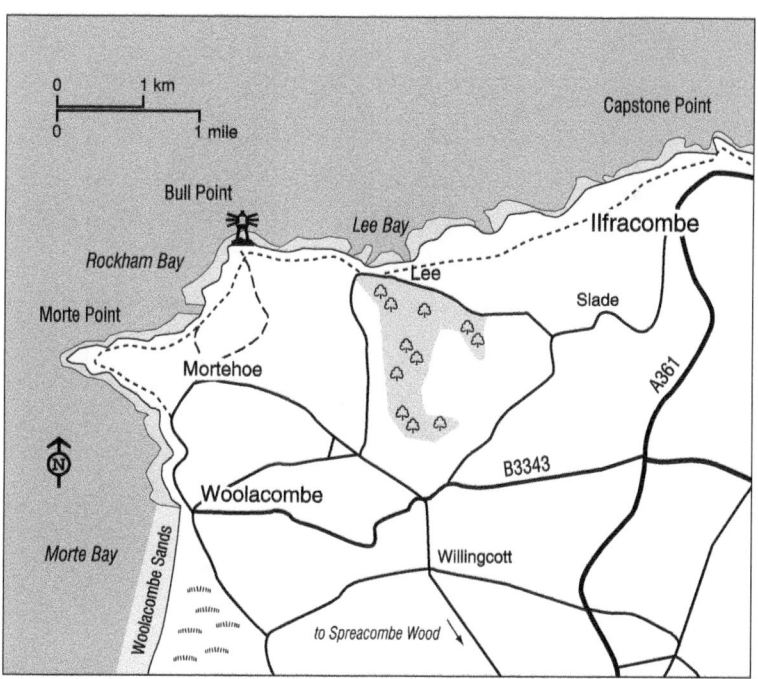

Devon (north coast and inland)

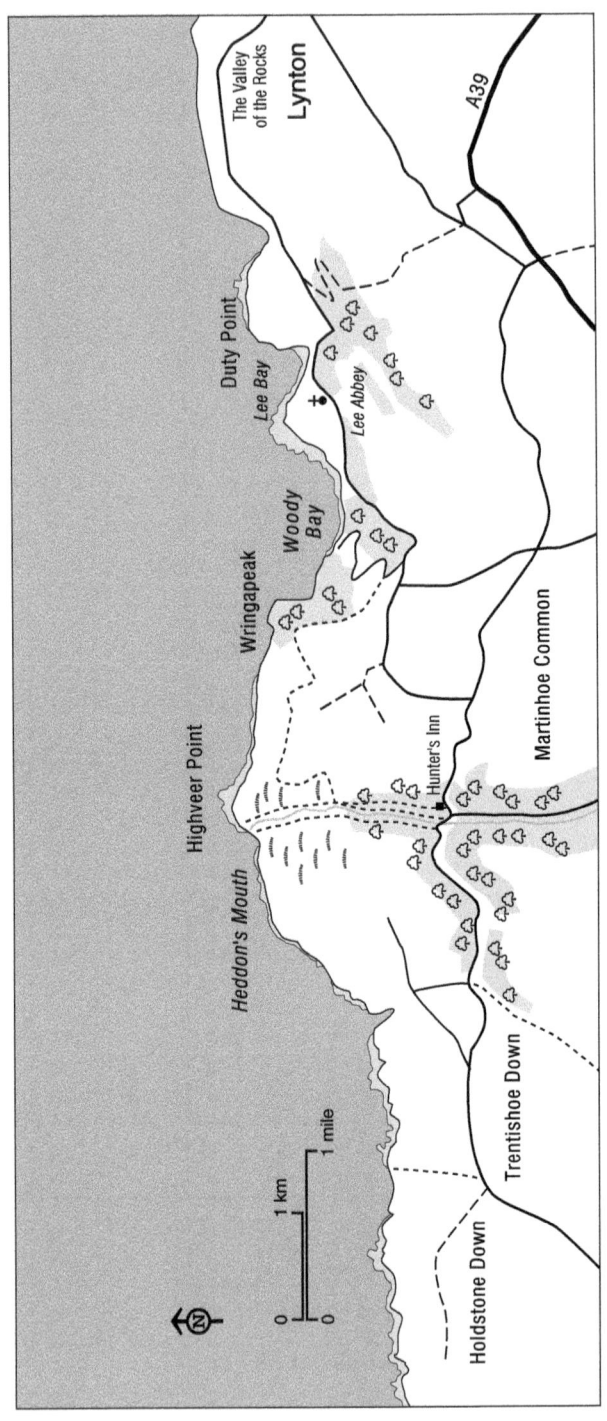

Red Kite or Marsh Harrier; less common birds such as the intricately marked Honey Buzzard have been watched soaring over. Ravens breed in many woods, such as Chapel, often choosing large old conifer trees and sometimes competing for territory with mewing Buzzards. Sometimes a dozen or more of the latter can be seen in the air at once. The attractive tail-flicking Grey Wagtail, flashing sulphur-yellow underparts, is a frequent sight by hill streams, many of which will also have a resident pair or two of Dippers.

As with Hartland Point, westward offshore movements of seabirds departing the Severn basin are noted; these include shearwaters, skuas and terns in autumn. An occasional Arctic or even Pomarine Skua and a trickle of terns, usually Sandwich, might be seen in spring. Bull Point and Capstone Point at Ilfracombe have proved to be suitable lookout points in summer, autumn and winter, and Morte Point may be good, especially in spring. Despite the lack of regular watchers, astonishingly Devon's first Black-browed Albatross and White-billed Diver were both reported from here. Movements of more than half a dozen skuas and a couple of dozen terns, usually moving west, are unusual even in autumn. Spring up-channel movements involve similar numbers but both are heavily weather dependant. Scarcer species such as the oceanic Sooty Shearwater are more likely through late summer and autumn, when a handful of birds probably pass westward each year although, surprisingly, this wanderer has also been seen off the coast in spring. Brownish Balearic Shearwaters are also annual in varying numbers but are less frequent here than off the region's southern and western extremities. Divers of all three species have been noted moving past in winter and especially in spring, although (as usual in Devon) Black-throated is least regular. Divers appear not to feed regularly along this stretch, however, although a Great Northern has sometimes turned up at Wistlandpound Reservoir in winter.

Autumn has brought large coasting movements of hirundines along the clifftops, followed later in the season by other diurnal migrants concentrated into a stream by the straight coastal escarpment. A passage of larks, pipits and finches is regularly recorded; sometimes several thousand have moved west in a day in late autumn, the vast bulk being Chaffinches, perhaps bound for Ireland, although some flocks certainly continue down the north Cornwall coast. The flocks might be seen passing over at any point along the coastal downs. The 'pinking' calls of Chaffinches are accompanied by a few harsher-voiced Bramblings and other finches or buntings, such as Lapland or Snow. Cold weather may bring a party of Snow Buntings to rest and feed on open down or moorland, such as Holdstone Down near Trentishoe, and predators such as Merlin often pass down the coast in pursuit of travelling flocks of passerines.

Winter does not bring major gatherings of birds inland, but in cold weather fields can be covered with Golden Plover or Fieldfare and, depending on disturbance levels, ducks (mostly diving species) visit Wistlandpound Reservoir, with a dozen Tufted Duck and four or five Goosander at times; small groups also appear on nearby Arlington Lake. Less common diving ducks such as Scaup are seen on either lake in most winters, and Ring-necked Duck has wintered. The small wooded areas bordering Wistlandpound and in other hidden valleys are also worth a look if undisturbed; harsh nasal calls draw attention to Willow Tits, and a Woodcock may burst out from ground cover.

Devon (north coast and inland)

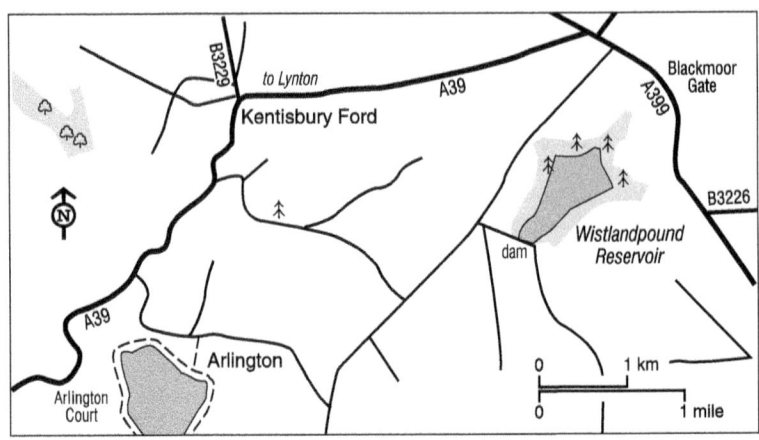

TIMING

At any time of day, highly scenic woodland and coastal walks can bring views of characteristic local birds. Woodland bird song in spring and summer will be most obvious in the mornings, which are also best for coastal migrant passerines. Fall conditions might leave resting migrants around Morte or Bull Points at dawn; autumn coasting movements of hirundines and finches, commencing soon after daybreak, are most prominent up to mid-morning, especially in light westerly winds. Occasional larger raptors circling over the coast are most likely on warm anticyclonic days, later in the morning than other migrants, when thermal currents have had time to develop. At this time of day local Buzzards and Ravens can be seen in good numbers.

Seawatching is best when seabirds are pushed towards the coast by mist, rain or onshore winds. Strong north-westerlies are often interesting, especially after a period of stong south-westerlies, and are likely to produce numbers of passing birds, mostly early in the day. Seabirds breeding locally pass at any time of day, with shearwaters often on the move late in the day.

Wistlandpound Reservoir and Arlington Lake are vulnerable to disturbance and are best visited at off-peak periods such as weekday mornings.

ACCESS

The A39 (Barnstaple–Lynton) and A399 (Ilfracombe–Combe Martin) serve the main holiday resort towns. Minor roads cross the hinterland, running south through wooded valleys towards the Taw Valley and Barnstaple; relatively few minor roads give access to the larger expanses of coastal down and cliff. Public footpaths are the best way to cover these areas. West from Lynton, for example, good signposted paths lead from Heddon Valley woods near Hunter's Inn either way along the clifftops for views of seabirds breeding far below and clifftop passerine migrants. This area can be reached by leaving Lynton southwards on the A39 and taking narrow right turns to Martinhoe and Hunter's Inn. Park by roadsides near the inn (which can be congested later on summer days), and choose your path beside the inn. West takes you across high ground towards Holdstone Down; east leads back towards Lynton via Woody Bay. The area is worth at least two or three hours' walk in either direction.

The Capstone seawatching point is clearly visible as a high, grassed headland beside Ilfracombe seafront. From this town, the B3231 and B3343 lead west towards Woolacombe and little-watched Morte Point, which is worth a try. South of the Morte–Woolacombe area, a left turn (eastward) off the B3231, half a mile (800m) before Georgeham village, takes you to Chapel Wood, a small RSPB reserve.

Morte Point is reached via Mortehoe village west of Ilfracombe. From the A361 between Ilfracombe and Barnstaple take the B3343 west at Mullacott Cross roundabout towards Woolacombe; after 2 miles (3km) follow a minor road to Mortehoe. Park in the village and follow the tarmac lane beside the church. This lane passes the cemetery then leads onto well-marked tracks across the headland. For seawatching take the lower (left-hand) track to get down towards sea level for closer views of passing birds, and follow it out towards the tip of the Point, finding limited shelter under rocks where possible in rough weather. Passerines are more likely to be seen from the higher tracks across the ridge where there are more thickets and rocky outcrops.

Wistlandpound Reservoir can be reached off the A39 Barnstaple–Lynton road, turning south onto the B3226 (signposted to South Molton) at the Blackmoor Gate junction; then turn right onto a minor road after half a mile (800m).

CALENDAR

Resident: Sparrowhawk, Buzzard, Grey Heron, Oystercatcher, Great Black-backed Gull, Grey Wagtail, Dipper, Rock Pipit, Stonechat, Willow Tit, Raven.

December–February: A few divers pass; Purple Sandpiper, Peregrine; Hen Harrier or Merlin possible over downs; Tufted Duck, Goosander, maybe Scaup or Pochard at Wistlandpound; Teal and Wigeon irregular; Woodcock possible; Fulmar, Grey Heron and Raven start breeding cycle as spring arrives.

March–May: Passerine migration along coast. Wheatear and probable Ring Ouzel from mid–late March; breeding visitors and passerine migrants, including warblers, Pied Flycatcher, Redstart from mid–late April; seabirds at colonies from mid-April (Fulmar earlier); maybe raptors or other overshooting migrants especially from late April; Manx Shearwater pass from April, maybe European Storm Petrel from May; divers, Sandwich Tern, maybe Arctic Skua pass.

June–July: Summer breeding passerines and seabirds, including Fulmar, Kittiwake, Razorbill, Guillemot; passing Manx Shearwater, occasional European Storm Petrel, Gannet offshore; Sandwich and Common Terns from July; woodland birdsong decreases from late June; auks leave mid-July.

August–November: Summer breeding passerines depart from August; migration 'falls' possible on coast; Balearic and possibly Sooty Shearwater, Arctic and Great Skuas, terns with possible Black (mainly August); chance of waders at Wistlandpound, e.g. Greenshank or Green Sandpiper, August–September; coastal movement of finches (peaking late October–early November) and northern migrants; winter visitors return November.

48 RACKENFORD, KNOWSTONE AND HARE'S DOWN

> OS LANDRANGER MAP 181
> OS grid ref: SS8521
> Postcode: **Rackenford** – EX36 4SB
> what3words: **Rackenford** – padding.triangles.shovels

HABITAT
In the north-east corner of Devon, flanking the southern edge of Exmoor, lies a strip of rough hill farmland and wet heath that represents some of the original Culm Measures heathland of mid- and north Devon. The heathland has been encroached upon and fragmented by agriculture and road building. Rackenford Moor (55ha) is a DWT reserve.

SPECIES
The birds of the Culm include some specialised breeders of marginal agricultural land, and visitors from nearby moorland areas, including predators. In winter, the heaths can appear bleak and birdless; a Hen Harrier or Merlin may come down from the moors to hunt, and the wet areas may hold a scattering of Snipe and one or two scarce Jack Snipe. A Woodcock might be flushed from scrub. Flocks of 200–300 Golden Plover and winter thrushes feed on nearby farmland. Resident Lesser Redpoll and Willow Tit are present in trees and encroaching damp scrub on the edge of the heaths. Occasionally a Great Grey Shrike is reported. Summer brings a wider range of interest: Nightjar has been recorded, and summer visitors also include Grasshopper Warbler, Cuckoo and Tree Pipit.

TIMING
In open areas such as this, fine bright days produce maximum activity and the likelihood of raptors hunting in winter; Grasshopper Warbler and Nightjar are most likely to be singing at dusk in summer.

ACCESS
From Tiverton on the A361 North Devon Link Road, turn left towards Rackenford village on the B3221. Do not turn left off the B3221 to go into the centre of Rackenford, but continue west for another mile (1.6km) to Knowstone Cross, turning right towards Knowstone and Molland. After half a mile (800m), passing open heath areas on the left, cross a flyover over the A361. Stop at a lay-by immediately on the right; the entry to Rackenford Moor DWT reserve is through the gate. The area can be scanned from the roadside for larger birds. The open, unfenced heath to the left of this road is part of the Hare's Down area. By continuing on this road and taking left turns back through Roach Hill hamlet you pass Knowstone Moor to the left, immediately before arriving back on the A361.

CALENDAR
Resident: Stonechat, Lesser Redpoll, Willow Tit, Raven, Yellowhammer.

December–February: As above plus Golden Plover, Snipe, occasional raptors, winter thrushes, possible Great Grey Shrike.

March–May: Warblers including Grasshopper, Tree Pipit, Cuckoo from end of April; Nightjar, late May.

June–July: Breeding species as above.

August–November: Apart from residents, quiet until cold weather arrives.

49 MEETH QUARRY, HATHERLEIGH

OS LANDRANGER MAP 191
OS grid ref: SS8501
Postcode: EX20 3QD
what3words: depth.totals.guardian

HABITAT

The market town of Hatherleigh lies in the Lew Valley, 7 miles (11.2km) north of Okehampton. It is surrounded by areas of Culm grassland in rolling agricultural land. Until the late 1990s, Meeth was a busy industrial site producing ball clay for export but is now a 150ha DWT nature reserve. The quarry is now a series of deep-water lakes with two hides, surrounded by grassland. The adjacent Ashmoor DWT reserve has scrub and mature woodland. Wood White butterfly has one of its national strongholds around the quarry.

SPECIES

The creation of this new island of habitat has significantly increased the bird-watching potential of this area. Whooper Swans have visited in winter, when the lakes hold up to 400 Canada Geese, the occasional wild or escaped goose joining them. Dabbling ducks fringe the edges in the same season, with 100 Teal and Mallard joined by 20 Wigeon and a few Gadwall and Shovelers. Little Grebe also favours areas of overhanging vegetation, while a dozen Great Crested Grebes and over 100 Coot prefer open areas.

Glebe Lake hosts around 40 wintering Tufted Duck, often with scarce species such as Pochard, Scaup or Goldeneye among them. Ring-necked Duck has wintered several times, as has a Tufted x Ring-necked Duck hybrid. The quarry has the largest Goosander roost in the region, at times peaking at more than 60 birds; most depart early each morning although a few remain all day before being rejoined at sunset. Water levels are often too high for waders in winter, but several dozen Snipe and occasionally a Jack Snipe may be around reedy bays. Woodcock roost unseen in the woodland and winter thrushes feed on nearby farmland. Gulls often drop in to bathe and preen in low numbers but with winter peaks of 300 Lesser Black-backed noted. Barn Owl, Peregrine and Merlin have also been seen around the reserve.

As spring arrives, resident species start to breed, with Great Crested Grebe conducting its weed-waving display and Coot and Moorhen building nests. Kingfishers breed in the area and may be seen dashing between waterside perches.

Devon (north coast and inland)

The area is well known for Willow Tit, most vocal early in spring; they can be found across the reserve, often right by the car park with Lesser Redpoll buzzing overhead. Spring migrants appear as the first hirundines feed low over the water on their way north. Ospreys pass through, occasionally lingering in autumn. At the same time, a few pairs of Willow and Sedge Warblers sing around the lakes with Tree Pipits on Ash Moor and a few Spotted Flycatchers.

Autumn may bring a few more waders, especially if water levels are low, and wildfowl return.

TIMING

Fine bright days produce maximum activity, with woodland residents most active in early mornings. Migrants may drop in any time, especially after rain. A dusk visit is required to witness the Goosander roost.

ACCESS

The A386 runs roughly north-south just pass the entrance road to the reserve car park, but the entrance is is not well signposted and is easily missed. If you are travelling from the town of Hatherleigh, just as you reach the small village of Meeth turn left into a road that takes you to a car park. A series of colour-coded trails allows access; the red way-marked trail is suitable for wheelchairs and mobility scooters.

Note: The gates to the car park are locked each evening at 5.00 p.m. re-opening at 9.00 a.m. This does not affect pedestrian or cycle access to the reserve.

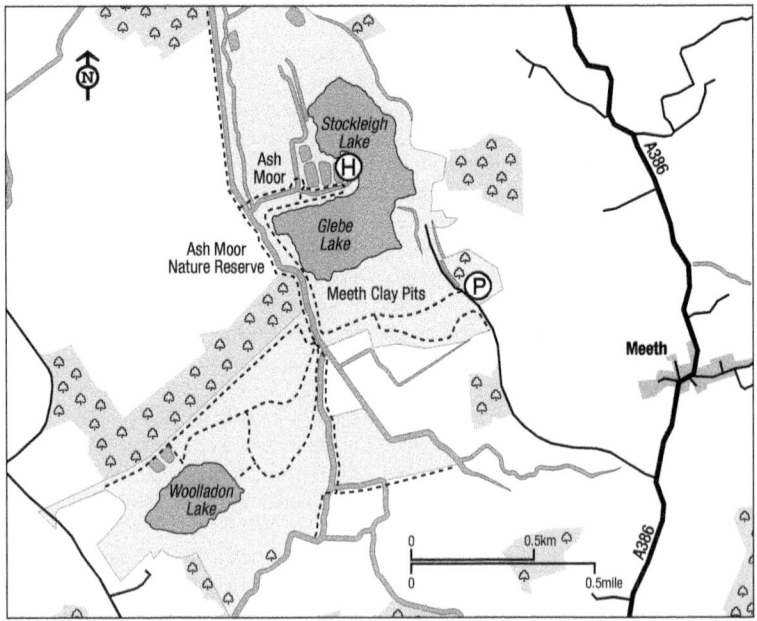

CALENDAR

Resident: Tufted Duck, Little and Great Crested Grebes, Cormorant, Little Egret, Coot, Barn Owl, common woodland species, Lesser Redpoll, Willow Tit, Raven.

December–February: Goosander, Goldeneye, occasional Pochard and Scaup, Wigeon, Teal, Gadwall, occasional rarer ducks, possible Merlin, Snipe, Woodcock, Lesser Black-backed Gull, winter thrushes.

March–May: Diving ducks remain into March; in April–May, migrants include possible Garganey, Red Kite, Common Sandpiper, perhaps Little Ringed Plover, hirundines, Willow Warbler, Tree Pipit.

June–July: A few summering ducks, breeding passerines and other resident species, possibly Hobby.

August–November: Waders including Green and perhaps Wood Sandpipers, August–September; duck numbers build in November.

49A SHOBROOKE PARK, CREDITON

OS LANDRANGER MAP 191
OS grid ref: SS8501
Postcode: EX17 1DG
what3words: nappy.foil.protester

HABITAT

The market town of Crediton lies in the Creedy Valley, almost 9 miles (14.4km) north-west of Exeter, surrounded by rolling agricultural land. The Raddon Hills rise to over 250m to the east. Immediately north-east of the town is Shobrooke Park estate, with two ornamental lakes totalling 5ha in area, which are set in open parkland with mature deciduous trees. The park is a popular with the general public.

SPECIES

This is a convenient area to see a range of woodland and waterside species, including some localised breeders. It may have general birdwatching interest all year, although winter visits are the most productive for a range of species including residents, winter-visiting passerines and waterfowl. The lakes are dominated by a large population of feral Canada Geese, one of the region's largest, exceeding 400 birds at times; flocks from here travel all over east and south Devon. Wooded islets in the lower lake provide nesting refuges for a number of pairs. The Canada Geese act as a decoy for geese of various other species, which may spend several weeks at a time accompanying the flocks; such stragglers have included (usually lone) Tundra Bean, White-fronted and Pink-footed Geese. The origin of these birds, especially in summer is unknown, but some are likely to be escapes, as Bar-headed and Snow Geese are also seen. Other wildfowl include a few midwinter Tufted Duck and Mallard, which may approach 60. Other dabbling ducks include up to 40 Teal; Wigeon and Shoveler may visit in small parties, especially in prolonged cold weather. Such conditions may produce a visit from a Goosander, Smew or Goldeneye. Ducks and geese resting on the less disturbed west bank of the lakes may be joined by up to 20 Coot, a few of which stay to nest, together with Moorhens.

Shobrooke is one of the region's few localities where Great Crested Grebes breed annually; Little Grebes also breed, although they are not always present. Lack of suitable habitat severely limits the region's populations of these two species. Cormorants are far more conspicuous visitors, especially outside the summer breeding season, resting on the west banks when not fishing or roosting in tall trees on the islets. Ten to 20 birds can be expected regularly, including some white-bellied immatures; breeding has also been attempted. Grey Herons are similarly conspicuous, with a long-established heronry of three to five pairs in the park, and often a few birds rest along a quieter stretch of lake bank, although breeding birds feed widely along local river valleys.

The parkland hosts a good range of commoner species characteristic of Devon lowlands: Green and Great Spotted Woodpeckers are often seen and heard, while Buzzards and Sparrowhawks pass over. Stock Doves and Jays frequent the old oaks, while Ravens fly above, and there is an active rookery on the edge of the park. Small birds may include up to 50 Siskins and a few Lesser Redpolls in waterside trees in winter, when flocks of Redwings and Fieldfares are usually present, and Bramblings may be found among the Chaffinches. Grey Wagtails often feed along the water's edge, where a Kingfisher may sit outside the breeding season. Commoner breeding warblers are present in good numbers through summer. Wader passage is not very marked this far inland, although a Common or Green Sandpiper may stop off by the lakes. In late summer a Hobby may dart in to attack hirundines feeding over the water.

TIMING

Freezing weather elsewhere brings more ducks to the lakes. Fine, bright days give the best winter watching conditions, being suitable all day, although there will probably be more activity in the mornings. Sunny weekends bring increased public visits and more disturbance.

ACCESS

Crediton is reached via the A377 from Exeter; turn right in the town centre towards Tiverton (A3072). After a mile (1.6km) turn right, following the Shobrooke sign. After 100m, park in a lay-by on the left and walk through the gate into the park, following public footpath signs. The path follows the right (east) bank of both lakes. Sheep may be grazing and dogs must be kept on leads.

CALENDAR

Resident: Great Crested and Little Grebe, Stock Dove, Grey Wagtail, Bullfinch.

December–February: Small numbers of dabbling and diving ducks, Kingfisher, Siskin.

March–May: Returning summer migrants.

June–July: Breeding species.

August–November: Quieter period, until winter visitors return.

TOP SITES FOR DISABLED ACCESS

There is a problem in trying to evaluate the suitability of a site for disabled birders, as each disability is different. However, the sites below are deemed accessible to people with walking difficulties or using wheelchairs.

1. Axe Estuary (1). The estuary is viewable from a vehicle. Trails accessible for wheelchair users on marshes, including Island Hide at Black Hole Marsh.
2. Exe Estuary (4). The estuary is viewable from cycle track on east side and around Powderham (4E) on the west. The hide at Bowling Green Marsh (4B) is wheelchair accessible.
3. Tor Bay and Berry Head (9). Car parks at Preston, Goodrington and Shoalstone offer views across the bay. Berry Head is flat with tarmacked routes on top.
4. Torpoint and Millbrook Lake (22). The sites are viewable from the car as roads follow the estuary.
5. Looe (23). Seawatching is possible from Marine Drive, Hannafore.
6. Siblyback Lake (24). A Tramper mobility scooter is available for hire at £5 for two hours, which allows less mobile visitors to explore the lake. Advance booking is essential to guarantee use of the Tramper. Call the South West Lakes Head Office on 01566 771930 before 5.00 p.m. on the Monday before you wish to hire it (or earlier if possible). Tramper hire may be possible on arrival if staff are present, but this cannot be guaranteed.
7. Colliford Lake (24). This water is viewable from the car parks.
8. Goss Moor (26A). The trail is accessible from the St Dennis car park; it is recommended that wheelchair users are accompanied as there are gates along the trail.
9. Boscawen Park (29A). There is level access by the Truro River to Sunny Corner to view waders and water birds.
10. Marazion Marsh (33). The Parade car park, Mousehole, for sea watching.
11. Taw-Torridge Estuary (46). The Skern high-tide roost and Fremington Pill can be readily viewed from a vehicle. The cycle path around the estuary also allows for good viewing opportunities.
12. Meeth Quarry (49). The red way-marked trail, which links to the lookout over Stockleigh Lake, is suitable for wheelchairs and mobility scooters.

TOP SITES FOR PUBLIC TRANSPORT

DEVON SITES

1. Exe Estuary (4) is embanked around much of its length by a railway, with stations at Dawlish Warren, Exmouth, Exton, Starcross and Topsham.
2. Aylesbeare Common (3) is accessed by buses from Exeter. Ask for the request stop at Joney's Cross.
3. Taw-Torridge Estuary (46). Trains run to Barnstaple with local bus routes to Bideford, Braunton and Ifracombe.
4. Haytor (19A). Buses run from Newton Abbot with a stop at Haytor lower car park and, for Emsworthy Mire, at Hemsworthy Gate.
5. Plymouth (19). The city can be reached by coach and train from many places. Sites in and around the city are accessible using regular buses; for routes and timetables visit plymouthbus.co.uk.

CORNWALL SITES

1. Goss Moor (26A) can be reached by bus from many towns and villages.
2. The Lizard (32) can be reached by bus from Helston and Penzance.
3. Pendeen (35A). Regular buses run between Penzance and Pendeen.
4. St Ives (36) can be reached by train and bus from several destinations.
5. Hayle (38) can be reached by train, and it is possible to view the estuary from two station platforms, Lelant and Lelant Saltings.
6. Isles of Scilly (35). Trains and coaches run to Penzance, from where a ferry steams to St Mary's; there is no need for transport on the islands.

For more information about public transport in the South West, including timetables and tickets, visit the Traveline South West website (travelinesw.com) or phone 0871 22 22 33.

THIRTY SPECIES TO SEE IN DEVON AND CORNWALL

In this section we outline 30 species people might most hope to encounter in Devon and Cornwall. The list includes personal favourites that are always a joy to see and some migrants that are regular; the species chosen are very much 'of today' and will obviously change over time.

BRENT GOOSE

Two races of Brent winter in Devon and Cornwall, the Dark-bellied subspecies that breeds in Siberia and the Pale-bellied subspecies that breeds in Greenland, Svalbard and Canada. Dark-bellied are the most numerous and the Exe Estuary (site 4) is one of the best places to view these winter visitors; be aware, though, that they do move around with the tide. Occasional Pale-bellied forms winter but April and September are the best times to catch up with them on migration. In Cornwall they only occur in small numbers, but in recent years a mixed flock has wintered on St John's Lake (site 22).

GOOSANDER

There are a few places where this sawbill can be seen flying in to winter roosts around dusk. In Devon, Venford Reservoir (site 21B) or Meeth (site 49) will afford good views, although it can also be seen at many other locations, e.g. Burrator (site 21G). It is harder to see in Cornwall but often present during winter on the Hayle Estuary (site 38), Loe Pool (site 32A) and Tamar Lakes (site 42).

NIGHTJAR

The heathlands of both counties play summer host to the crepuscular displays of this species. Favoured sites include the Pebblebed Heaths, including Aylesbeare Common (site 3), Haldon and Little Haldon (site 6), the Dartmoor plantations (sites 21C, D and G), Dozmary Pool (site 25) and Goss Moor (site 26A). Any area of heathland or harvested forestry plantation may prove fruitful.

CUCKOO

This is considered a short-staying summer visitor since adult birds arrive in April, breed and are generally gone by the end of June, leaving the young to find their own way to Africa before the end of September. A declining species, it can still be found on moorland and other semi-natural habitats such as the Pebblebed Heaths (site 3), Emsworthy (site 21A) and Burrator (site 21G) in Devon, and Goss Moor (site 26A), The Lizard (site 32) and Porthgwarra and Lands' End (site 34) in Cornwall.

AVOCET

There are two nationally important wintering sites for this iconic bird in Devon and Cornwall, the Exe Estuary (site 4) in Devon and the Tamar Estuary (sites 22–22C) straddling the border of the two counties. Up to 600 can be seen on the Exe and around 200 on the Tamar; birds distribute themselves around the estuaries depending on weather and tide conditions and where their prey items are. They may appear as early as August, but the bulk of the flocks arrive in November and stay into February, with the occasional straggler hanging on until April.

BLACK-TAILED GODWIT

The Exe Estuary (site 4) holds internationally important numbers of this local winter visitor and passage migrant during the winter. They can be viewed from several points around the estuary but Bowling Green Marsh (site 4B) at high tide will give excellent close views of the species. In Cornwall, the Camel Estuary holds up to 300 during winter, again readily viewed from several places including Walmsley (site 40).

SANDERLING

In winter, flocks of these white-and-black dervishes play chicken with the waves on some of our beaches, with the largest flocks scurrying over the sand at Dawlish Warren (site 4F), Braunton (site 46), Marazion (site 33) and the Isles of Scilly (site 35). More widespread on late spring passage when the winter ermine is replaced by rich, brick-red spangled plumage, peak counts come from the sites listed.

PURPLE SANDPIPER

A winter visitor to the region's rockiest shorelines, this wader shuns the food-rich estuaries to forage on wave-splashed rocks, superbly camouflaged amongst the seaweed. Favoured sites include Hope's Nose (site 8) and Brixham Harbour (site 9) in the east; Jubilee Pool, Penzance (site 33), St Ives (site 36) and scattered spots around the many small islets in the Isles of Scilly (site 35) in the west; and Newquay (site 39) and Westward Ho! (site 46) in the north.

BUFF-BREASTED SANDPIPER

This North American species is a regular but scarce visitor to Britain, particularly Devon and Cornwall, during September. Preferring short, rough grass, it is regularly noted at Davidstow Airfield (site 26), Porthgwarra (site 34) and the Isles of Scilly (site 35). It has also been recorded from many other suitable coastal sites.

JACK SNIPE

A regular winter visitor in small numbers to around 20 selected sites in the region but no doubt more widespread, especially when hard weather pushes more birds to the area. Most birds are recorded in October to February. The hides at Porthellick and Lower Moors on St Mary's, Isles of Scilly (site 35), are renowned for providing excellent views of this elusive species. Black Hole Marsh (site 1) and the Exe Estuary (site 4) in Devon hold sometimes-visible wintering birds. Stithians Reservoir (site 31), Marazion (site 33), Amble Marshes (site 40) and Tamar Lakes (site 42) are good places to check for these bobbing beauties in Cornwall.

SANDWICH TERN

Always a joy to hear as it means winter must be over when they first appear around the coasts of Devon and Cornwall, Sandwich Tern's peak migration months are March and August. During these months, they are likely to be seen at any seawatching point in either county. Dawlish Warren (site 4F) and Slapton (site

11) are good places to try in Devon, while Marazion (site 33) and the mouth of the Camel Estuary (site 40) are good in Cornwall.

PUFFIN
Having been lost from the mainland in the South West, the only two reliable breeding populations are on Lundy (site 45) and rat-free areas of the Isles of Scilly (site 35). Otherwise, they are often seen on passage from as early as February in spring and as late October in autumn off Porthgwarra (site 34), St Ives (site 36) and Pendeen (site 37). Devon sees lower numbers during the same periods with Berry Head (site 9), Start Point (site 12) and Prawle Point (site 13) favoured sites.

EUROPEAN STORM PETREL
This tiny pelagic seabird is most often seen when driven closer inshore by inclement weather, with largest numbers seen from well-watched headlands, although night-time ringing efforts show it is likely just offshore around much of the region during the breeding season. Sites with the best chance of success include Berry Head (site 9), Start Point (site 12), Porthgwarra (site 34), St Ives and Pendeen (sites 36 and 37) and Hartland (site 44). For the best views, pelagic trips are recommended and to hear 'Mother Carey's chicken' a night on Lundy (site 45) or St Agnes (site 35) may pay dividends.

CORY'S SHEARWATER
One of the large shearwaters, much sought after by visiting birdwatchers, the headlands of the far west of Cornwall (sites 34, 36 and 37) offer the best chance for land-based observers in the right conditions in late summer. Pelagics off Scilly (site 35) often enable closer views. Increasingly, they are also seen from headlands further east such as Prawle Point (site 13), Start Point (site 12) and Berry Head (site 9) on their migrations from breeding islands off North Africa.

GREAT SHEARWATER
The other much-sought large shearwater breeds on remote islands in the South Atlantic, but its loop migration around the North Atlantic brings it to our region, usually slightly later in autumn than Cory's, although both species often occur alongside each other in good seawatching conditions. Sites as for Cory's.

MANX SHEARWATER
A constantly banking flock stretched out in a stiff-winged line may be seen from almost any section of the region's coast between April and September. Peak counts come from Berry Head (site 9), Start Point (site 12), Porthgwarra (site 34) and Pendeen (site 37), when tens of thousands may stream past in just a few hours, but large feeding movements can also be seen off the north Devon coast (site 44 and 47) in calmer conditions. To fully experience the species and its eerie nocturnal song, spend a night on Lundy (site 45) or St Agnes (site 35).

BALEARIC SHEARWATER
Internationally important numbers of this Critically Endangered seabird are regularly seen feeding and on passage from coastal seawatching sites in both counties from June to November. Start Point (site 12) has seen record UK counts, with Berry Head (site 9) and Dawlish Warren (site 4F) also recording good numbers. In Cornwall, Lizard Point (site 32), Porthgwarra and Land's End (site 34) regularly

record birds. Strong winds are not necessary for sightings as birds often linger to feed, but mist and rain at sea can provide closer views. On the north coast, St Ives (site 36) and Pendeen (site 37) are both good bets. Here the birds are often seen in the company of other species after gales.

OSPREY

As the UK population has increased, so has the chance of encountering this spectacular bird of prey on migration over any open area of water. It may be seen fishing on many of the region's estuaries but the Axe (site 1), Exe (site 4), Dart (site 10), Tamar/Tavy (sites 22A-D), Fal (site 29), Camel (site 40) and Taw (site 46) regularly host lingering birds in autumn. With ongoing introductions in Dorset and proposals for more in the region, it may become a summer resident over time.

WRYNECK

A scarce migrant, this uniquely patterned woodpecker might be encountered on any ant-rich turf around the region. As with many scarce migrants, coastal areas are favoured, although it regularly turns up inland in gardens. An autumn visit to the Isles of Scilly (site 35) provides the best chance to encounter the species, but other sites such as Porthgwarra (site 34), The Lizard (site 32), Prawle Point (site 13), Dawlish Warren (site 4F), Thurlestone (site 16) and Lundy (site 45) are also favoured.

CHOUGH

An emblem of Cornwall, this species died out in the county in 1973. After several failed reintroduction projects, five birds arrived near Newquay in early 2001. Subsequent DNA testing indicated the birds were of Irish descent. Three settled in The Lizard area and in 2002 fledged the first Cornish Chough for over 50 years. By 2023, 55 pairs were found across Cornwall, 39 of which bred, raising 112 young. Lizard Point (site 32) and the surrounding area is one of the best places to see the resident birds. They can also be found around Land's End (site 34) and Pendeen Watch (site 37) and are slowly spreading around the north Cornish coast. It remains a rare bird in Devon, but birds have wintered on both coasts and their arrival is surely just a matter of time.

WILLOW TIT

Holding the unfortunate title of the fastest declining UK resident bird, Willow Tit has one of its few remaining strongholds in the region – and the only one south of the line from The Wash to the Severn Estuary. Best separated from the near-identical Marsh Tit by call, with habitat often a good indicator, Willow Tit favours wet, scrubby woodland containing dead standing trees in which to excavate its own nest-holes. It can still be found across the Culm Measures in north-west Devon/north-east Cornwall, with outlying populations in similar Rhôs pasture habitat around Bodmin and Dartmoor. Tamar Lakes (site 42) and Meeth Quarry (site 49) offer the best chance of seeing Willow Tit, with birds also possible at Rackenford (site 48), Roadford Reservoir (site 43) and Upper Fowey Valley (site 25).

CETTI'S WARBLER

A resident bird of reedbeds and dense scrubby vegetation, usually near water, this warbler is unique among British birds as it has only 10 tail feathers instead of the usual 12. Often heard before being seen, it can be found at around 70 sites in Devon and three, reliably, in Cornwall. Slapton Ley (site 11) and Exminster Marshes (site 4C) are the most reliable locations in Devon while Marazion Marsh (site 33) and Loe Pool (site 32A) are the best in Cornwall, but look out for migrant and dispersing birds away from the primary areas.

YELLOW-BROWED WARBLER

The arrival of this diminutive warbler from Siberia is eagerly anticipated each autumn, with birders searching through tit flocks and listening out for the distinctive *swhooet* call at familiar migration points. The Isles of Scilly (site 35) are particularly favoured, and Porthgwarra and Cot Valley (site 34), Berry Head (site 9) and Lundy (site 45) also have good track records. As autumn progresses, birds filter through the country and turn up at more inland sites, especially scrub-fringed wetlands and even sewage works, where they may overwinter.

DARTFORD WARBLER

This species is very susceptible to hard winters, which can wipe out entire populations. However, they seem to recover and spread on heathlands, south-facing moorland fringes and gorse-clad coastal areas. Dartfords are easiest to find when conditions are calm and warm; the Pebblebed Heaths, including Aylesbeare (site 3) in Devon hold resident birds as do some other heathland and coastal areas. In Cornwall, areas on The Lizard (site 32) with suitable habitat hold small numbers. Migrants and wintering birds regularly wander away from core areas.

FIRECREST

This stunning kinglet is now a regular, and increasing, breeder in Devon where numbers are boosted in winter by birds from the Continent. Wintering birds are regular at Broadsands (site 9) but any sewage works where Chiffchaffs congregate is likely to attract this species. Passage birds are widespread, with peak counts usually from Berry Head (site 9), Prawle Point (site 13), Soar (site 15) and Lundy (site 45) in Devon, and Porthgwarra (site 34) and West Penwith valleys such as Cot (site 34) in Cornwall. Good numbers are also seen on the Isles of Scilly (site 35).

RING OUZEL

Previously a highlight of a spring morning on Dartmoor, climate change and, at some sites, disturbance mean the 'mountain blackbird' sadly no longer breeds in the region. However, it can still be found on migration, especially in autumn when flocks often gather at favoured sites. Prime locations to search out this species in autumn include Soar (site 15), Porthgwarra (site 34), the Isles of Scilly (site 35) and Lundy (site 45). The largest numbers, though, are often around Dartmoor, arriving with winter thrushes. Emsworthy Mire (site 21A) is particularly frequented.

PIED FLYCATCHER

The cause of the decline of this stunning little bird is not clear, but it is still holding on as a passage migrant in the region and a summer resident in Devon. Visits to woods such as Yarner or Emsworthy (site 21A) afford good views as nest-boxes are provided to encourage breeding. Lundy (site 45), The Lizard (site 32), Porthgwarra (site 34) and the Isles of Scilly (site 35) are notable for passage birds in both spring and autumn.

Thirty species to see in Devon and Cornwall

DIPPER

Widespread on many moorland rivers, Dippers are even found in urban areas and on some fast-flowing rivers in coastal areas. They are generally resident but do move downstream in adverse weather conditions. The Otter in Devon (site 2), along with the Dartmoor sites of Postbridge (site 21C), Tavy Cleave (site 19F) and Burrator (site 21G), usually provide good views of the species. Plymbridge (site 20) is another reliable place to view them. In Cornwall, the Upper Fowey Valley (site 25) and the Newquay district (site 39) are good areas to search.

ROCK PIPIT

Often overlooked by locals, these charismatic little birds can be found on almost any section of the region's coastline despite being scarce breeders elsewhere in southern England. Rarely venturing far inland, they are joined by Scandinavian birds in winter and flocks gather in sheltered coves feeding along the strandline. Good numbers can be found at Hope's Nose (site 8), Prawle Point (site 13), Wembury (site 18), Looe (site 23) and Mount's Bay (site 33).

CIRL BUNTING

Thanks to farmers and dedicated conservation work, this stunning bunting can still be found in both Devon and Cornwall. In the former, it can be found at Wembury (site 18) and through the South Hams (sites 10–18), Labrador Bay (site 7a) and the Exe Estuary (sites 4F and 4D). A winter-feeding station is maintained at Broadsands car park (site 9) where great views can be obtained. There are small populations in Cornwall at Rame Head (site 23), Portscatho (site 28) and Rosemullion (site 30); listen out for a song similar to that of a Yellowhammer but without the *cheeeese*.

LIST OF ORGANISATIONS AND REFERENCES

Abbreviations used in the text are indicated in brackets.

Records of unusual species should be sent to the relevant County Recorder. See the websites below for the latest contact details.

Cornwall Bird Watching and Preservation Society (CBWPS) – cbwps.org.uk

Cornwall Wildlife Trust (CWT) – cornwallwildlifetrust.org.uk

Isles of Scilly Wildlife Trust – ios-wildlifetrust.org.uk

Isles of Scilly Bird Group – scilly-birding.co.uk

Dartmoor National Park – dartmoor.gov.uk

Devon Birds – devonbirds.org

Devon Wildlife Trust (DWT) – devonwildlifetrust.org

Forestry England – forestryengland.uk

National Trust – nationaltrust.org.uk

Royal Society for the Protection of Birds (RSPB) –rspb.org.uk

South West Lakes Trust – swlakestrust.org.uk

REFERENCES

Annual reports produced by Devon Birds, Cornwall Bird Watching and Preservation Society and Isles of Scilly Bird Club.

Beavan, S. & Lock, M. (2016). *Devon Bird Atlas*. Devon Birds, Devon.

Davies, T. & Jones, T. (2007). *The Birds of Lundy*. Devon Birds, Devon.

Jones, R. (1998). *The Birds of Roadford Lake*. Published privately.

Lakin, I. & Rylands, K. (2000). *The Birds of Dawlish Warren*. Published privately.

Macklin, R. (2019). Birds of Soar. Published privately.

Mayer, P. (1993). *The Birds of Prawle*. Published privately.

McMahon, S. & Hudson N. (2008). *Best Birdwatching Sites in Cornwall & The Isles of Scilly*. Buckingham Press, Peterborough, Cambridgeshire.

Smaldon, R. (2005). *The Birds of Dartmoor*. Isabelline Books, Penryn, Cornwall.

Tucker, V. (1995). *The Birds of Plymouth*. Devon BWPS, Devon.

GLOSSARY

ACTIVITY TIMES

Crepuscular Active in dim light at dawn and especially dusk, e.g. Nightjar.

Diurnal Active in full daylight.

Nocturnal Active at night, e.g. most owls; many small insect-eating passerines are nocturnal fliers (navigating by the stars) when migrating.

BIRD TERMS

Auk A seabird of the family Alcidae, including guillemots, Puffins and murrelets.

Brown-head/red-head A female or immature of certain northern ducks, usually Goldeneye, Smew, Red-breasted Merganser, Goosander. Not to be confused with the Redhead *Aythya americana* – a rare vagrant duck from North America.

Coasting Diurnal movement against the wind by groups of migrants, e.g. Swallows and pipits, following major landmarks and coastlines. Most noticed on autumn days with a light to moderate wind from south-west or west.

Commic tern A sea tern, Common or Arctic, not specifically identified.

Common woodland passerines Those small songbirds resident in most English woods, e.g. Dunnock, thrushes, tits, Nuthatch, Treecreeper.

Corvid A member of the crow family.

Ducks, dabbling Surface-feeders such as Mallard and Teal.

Ducks, diving Species which seek food entirely by swimming underwater, e.g. Tufted Duck, Pochard.

Fall A mass arrival of night-flying migrants, e.g. warblers, flycatchers, along the coastline when conditions prevent them from continuing their journey. Winds from fine high-pressure weather areas on the Continent, combined with cloud, mist or drizzle at our end, are most likely to cause this, as large numbers of birds set off in fine conditions for migration and are then forced down.

Feral A bird that has escaped or been introduced into the wild from captivity and is now living in a wild state.

Grey geese Greylag, Pink-footed, Bean and White-fronted Geese

Hirundine A bird of the swallow and martin family.

Irruption An arrival of certain specialised feeders from the Continent, e.g. Waxwing or Crossbill, which occurs when their population is high and food runs short in their native areas. Irruptions vary in size from year to year and are more marked in eastern Britain; only very significant arrivals affect the South West.

Movement A long-distance, purposeful journey, e.g. migration or search for food, rather than a routine local activity.

Movement, weather A mass movement of wintering species, e.g. wildfowl, open-ground species such as Lapwing or winter thrushes, into our region when ice and snow prevent feeding in other parts of Britain and the adjacent Continent.

Naturalised Birds whose present wild breeding populations are entirely derived from escaped or artificially introduced ancestors, e.g. Canada Goose.

Off-passage Used to describe a migrant which makes an extended stop-over to rest and feed, maybe for weeks, before resuming its journey.

Open-ground species Species which tend to use treeless expanses, open fields, moors and downs, e.g. plovers and larks.

Overshoot In spring and early summer, individuals of migratory species that travel north from Africa and normally breed in southern Europe, such as Alpine Swift, Hoopoe and Golden Oriole, may overshoot their normal range and be carried to Britain by high pressure with following winds.

Passage migrant A bird that occurs only when passing through on migration between its summer and winter quarters.

Passerine A taxonomic grouping of perching songbirds; includes most small landbirds.

Pelagic Feeding over areas of deep sea and not normally seen near the coast except when visiting nest sites, e.g. small petrels, or when displaced by gales.

Raptor A diurnal bird of prey, e.g. Kestrel, buzzards; excludes owls.

Ringtail A female or immature Hen, Pallid or Montagu's Harrier.

Sawbill A duck of the genera *Mergus* or *Mergellus* (i.e. Red-breasted Merganser, Goosander and Smew), with a serrated bill edge to grasp fish.

Seabird Any of the mainly pelagic or coastal species or groups of birds, not normally seen inland, e.g. shearwaters, Gannet, skuas, most gulls.

Seaducks Marine diving ducks not normally seen on fresh water, e.g. Eider, scoters.

Seawatch A prolonged watch over an area of sea through binoculars or telescope from a coastal headland, scanning to pick out passing seabirds. Views can be distant and considerable skill is needed to make accurate identifications. Most likely to be productive in poor visibility or onshore winds. In the wrong conditions, can be unrewarding, but on good days thousands of birds may pass.

Shank A medium-sized wader of the *Tringa* genus, e.g. Redshank, Spotted Redshank, Greenshank.

Vagrant A rare, accidental visitor from other countries, mainly at migration times.

Waders Also known as shorebirds, a diverse group of often long-billed, long-legged, medium-sized birds, most of which feed in mud, water or marshland, e.g. Dunlin, Curlew, plovers.

Warbler, *Phylloscopus* A 'leaf warbler' of the genus *Phylloscopus* e.g. Willow and Wood Warblers, Chiffchaff and scarcer related species. Often shortened by birdwatchers in the field to 'Phyllosc'. (Note: The other main warbler groups have fewer species and we have named these individually in the text.)

Wild swans Whooper or Bewick's Swans, uncommon winter visitors to our region, rather than the introduced Mute Swan.

Winter thrushes Those which come across from northern Europe in winter; chiefly Fieldfare and Redwing, but Blackbirds and Song Thrushes also arrive to join local birds.

Glossary

Wreck An arrival of exhausted and hungry seabirds, e.g. petrels or auks, after prolonged severe gales at sea, occasionally driven far inland.

WEATHER

Anticyclone (or High) An area of high barometric pressure, where fine clear conditions predominate, from which winds flow out to neighbouring regions. High pressure is defined as over 1,000 millibars, sometimes reaching 1,040mb in strong anticyclones. Such conditions encourage migrants to begin or continue their journeys.

Depression (or Low) A system of low pressure, generally originated over the Atlantic and drifting eastward towards Britain unless pushed back by high pressure over the Continent. As it drifts, with winds revolving in an anticlockwise direction and strong at times, water is drawn in to create an unstable weather zone with rain and cloud. Low pressure is defined as under 1,000 millibars and may drop to 950mb (rarely lower) in deep depressions, with strong gales.

Front A sharp division between two air masses of different temperature and humidity, drawn together in a depression. Fronts passing overhead are often accompanied by rainfall and poor visibility. They usually herald a change in temperature, wind direction and humidity as the new air mass arrives. Passerine migrants tend to land and seabirds may fly close inshore to avoid the front. A cold front precedes the arrival of cold, clear polar air, often with intermittent heavy showers, and characteristically with west or north-west winds. A warm front brings milder, cloudy and damp conditions, often with south-west winds. In a normal depression, warm fronts arrive first, and the wind veers towards north-west when cold fronts arrive later.

Thermal A rising current of warm air over land, often used by soaring raptors and other large birds to gain height without exertion.

GEOGRAPHY

Brake A dense area of trees and bushes, often on sloping ground.

Carn (Cornwall) An open hilltop vantage point.

Combe or Coombe (mostly Devon) A steep-sided valley, often wooded.

Dyke An embanked marsh-drainage ditch.

Escarpment A prominent edge of a hill or ridge from which the land drops away steeply.

Leat Artificial freshwater channel fed off a stream to supply water to a village.

Pill (mostly north Devon) A very narrow tidal creek or channel.

Tor (chiefly Devon) A mass of granite boulders on a moorland hilltop.

CODE OF CONDUCT FOR BIRDWATCHERS

Today's birdwatchers are a powerful force for nature conservation. The number of people interested in birds rises continually and it is vital that we take seriously our responsibility to avoid any harm to birds.

We must also present a responsible image to non-birdwatchers who may be affected by our activities, particularly those on whose sympathy and support the future of birds may rest.

There are 10 points to bear in mind:

1. The welfare of birds must come first.
2. Habitat must be protected.
3. Keep disturbance to birds and their habitat to a minimum.
4. When you find a rare bird think carefully about whom you should tell.
5. Do not harass rare migrants.
6. Abide by the bird protection laws at all times.
7. Respect the rights of landowners.
8. Respect the rights of other people in the countryside.
9. Make your records available to the local bird recorder.
10. Behave abroad as you would when birdwatching at home.

WELFARE OF BIRDS MUST COME FIRST

Whether your particular interest is photography, ringing, sound recording, scientific study or just birdwatching, remember that the welfare of the bird must always come first.

HABITAT PROTECTION

Their habitat is vital to all birds, and therefore we must ensure that our activities do not cause damage.

KEEP DISTURBANCE TO A MINIMUM

Birds' tolerance of disturbance varies between species and seasons. Therefore, it is safer to keep all disturbance to a minimum. No birds should be disturbed from the nest in case opportunities for predators to take eggs or young are increased. In very cold weather, disturbance to birds may cause them to use vital energy at a time when food is difficult to find. Wildfowlers already impose bans during cold weather; birdwatchers should exercise similar discretion.

RARE BREEDING BIRDS

If you discover a rare bird breeding and feel that protection is necessary, inform the appropriate county recorder. Otherwise it is best in almost all circumstances to keep the record strictly secret in order to avoid disturbance and attacks by egg collectors. Never visit known sites of rare breeding birds unless they are adequately protected. Even your presence may give away the site and cause so many visitors that the nest fails.

Disturbance at or near the nest of species listed in Schedule 1 of the Wildlife and Countryside Act 1981 is a criminal offence.

RARE MIGRANTS

Rare migrants or vagrants must not be harassed. If you discover one, consider the circumstances carefully before telling anyone. Will an influx of birdwatchers disturb the bird or others in the area? Will the habitat be damaged? Will problems be caused with the landowner?

THE LAW

The bird protection laws (now embodied in the Wildlife and Countryside Act 1981) are the result of hard campaigning by previous generations of birdwatchers. As birdwatchers, we must abide by them at all times and not allow them to fall into disrepute.

RESPECT THE RIGHTS OF LANDOWNERS

The wishes of landowners and occupiers of land must be respected. Do not enter land without permission. Comply with permit schemes. If you are leading a group, do give advance notice of the visit, even if a formal permit scheme is not in operation. Always obey the Country Code.

RESPECT THE RIGHTS OF OTHER PEOPLE

Have proper consideration for other birdwatchers. Try not to disrupt their activities or scare the birds they are watching. There are many other people who also use the countryside. Do not interfere with their activities and, if it seems that what they are doing is causing unnecessary disturbance to birds, do try to take a balanced view. Flushing gulls when walking a dog on a beach may do little harm, while the same dog might be a serious disturbance at a tern colony. When pointing this out to a non-birdwatcher be courteous, but firm. The non-birdwatchers' goodwill towards birds should not be destroyed by the attitudes of birdwatchers.

KEEPING RECORDS

Much of today's knowledge about birds is the result of meticulous record keeping by our predecessors. Make sure you help to add to tomorrow's knowledge by sending records to your county bird recorder, either directly or via Birdtrack/eBird.

This code has been drafted after consultation between The British Ornithologists' Union, British Trust for Ornithology, the Royal Society for the Protection of Birds, the Scottish Ornithologists' Club, the Wildfowl and Wetlands Trust and the Editors of *British Birds* magazine.

DEVON, CORNWALL AND THE ISLES OF SCILLY BIRD LIST

Checklist of birds recorded in Devon, Cornwall and the Isles of Scilly. **Bold** indicates species most likely to be recorded in the region, including annually occurring scarce migrants.

1	Ruddy Duck	32	**Ring-necked Duck**
2	**Mute Swan**	33	**Tufted Duck**
3	Bewick's Swan	34	Lesser Scaup
4	**Whooper Swan**	35	**Scaup**
5	**Dark-bellied Brent Goose** *bernicla*	36	**Garganey**
		37	Blue-winged Teal
5.1	**Pale-bellied Brent Goose** *hrota*	38	**Shoveler**
5.2	Black Brant *nigricans*	39	Falcated Duck
6	Red-breasted Goose	40	**Gadwall**
7	**Canada Goose**	41	**Wigeon**
8	**Barnacle Goose**	42	American Wigeon
9	**Greylag Goose**	43	**Mallard**
10	**White-fronted Goose** *albifrons*	44	American Black Duck
10.1	Greenland White-fronted Goose *flavirostris*	45	**Pintail**
		46	**Teal**
11	Tundra Bean Goose	46.1	**Green-winged Teal** *carolinensis*
12	**Pink-footed Goose**	47	**Red Grouse**
13	Taiga Bean Goose	48	Black Grouse (extinct in region)
14	**Mandarin Duck**	49	Grey Partridge (extinct in region?)
15	**Egyptian Goose**		
16	**Shelduck**	50	**Pheasant**
17	**Long-tailed Duck**	51	**Quail**
18	King Eider	52	**Red-legged Partridge**
19	**Eider**	53	**Little Grebe**
20	**Common Scoter**	54	Pied-billed Grebe
21	**Surf Scoter**	55	**Slavonian Grebe**
22	**Velvet Scoter**	56	**Red-necked Grebe**
23	Bufflehead	57	**Great Crested Grebe**
24	**Goldeneye**	58	**Black-necked Grebe**
25	Smew	59	Great Bustard
26	**Red-breasted Merganser**	60	Little Bustard
27	**Goosander**	61	Great Spotted Cuckoo
28	Red-crested Pochard	62	Yellow-billed Cuckoo
29	Ferruginous Duck	63	Black-billed Cuckoo
30	**Pochard**	64	**Cuckoo**
31	Canvasback	65	Pallas's Sandgrouse

66	Mourning Dove (subject to acceptance)	115	**Snipe**
		116	Terek Sandpiper
67	Oriental Turtle Dove	117	**Common Sandpiper**
68	**Turtle Dove**	118	Spotted Sandpiper
69	**Collared Dove**	119	Wilson's Phalarope
70	**Woodpigeon**	120	**Grey Phalarope**
71	**Rock Dove/Feral Pigeon**	121	Red-necked Phalarope
72	**Stock Dove**	122	**Green Sandpiper**
73	Crane	123	Solitary Sandpiper
74	**Water Rail**	124	Marsh Sandpiper
75	Corncrake	125	**Wood Sandpiper**
76	Sora	126	**Redshank**
77	**Spotted Crake**	127	Lesser Yellowlegs
78	**Moorhen**	128	**Spotted Redshank**
79	**Coot**	129	**Greenshank**
80	American Purple Gallinule	130	Greater Yellowlegs
81	Little Crake	131	**Turnstone**
82	Baillon's Crake	132	**Knot**
83	Stone-curlew	133	**Ruff**
84	**Avocet**	134	Sharp-tailed Sandpiper
85	Black-winged Stilt	135	Broad-billed Sandpiper
86	**Oystercatcher**	136	**Curlew Sandpiper**
87	**Grey Plover**	137	Temminck's Stint
88	**Golden Plover**	138	Long-toed Stint
89	**American Golden Plover**	139	**Buff-breasted Sandpiper**
90	Pacific Golden Plover	140	**Sanderling**
91	**Dotterel**	141	**Dunlin**
92	Killdeer	142	**Purple Sandpiper**
93	**Ringed Plover**	143	Baird's Sandpiper
94	Semipalmated Plover	144	**Pectoral Sandpiper**
95	**Little Ringed Plover**	145	Semipalmated Sandpiper
96	**Lapwing**	146	Western Sandpiper
97	Sociable Plover	147	**Little Stint**
98	Caspian Plover	148	Least Sandpiper
99	Greater Sand Plover	149	White-rumped Sandpiper
100	Kentish Plover	150	Cream-coloured Courser
101	Upland Sandpiper	151	Black-winged Pratincole
102	Eskimo Curlew (globally extinct)	152	Collared Pratincole
103	Hudsonian Whimbrel	153	**Arctic Skua**
104	**Whimbrel**	154	**Long-tailed Skua**
105	**Curlew**	155	**Pomarine Skua**
106	**Bar-tailed Godwit**	156	**Great Skua**
107	**Black-tailed Godwit**	157	South Polar Skua
108	Hudsonian Godwit	158	**Puffin**
109	Long-billed Dowitcher	159	Ancient Murrelet
110	Short-billed Dowitcher	160	Long-billed Murrelet
111	**Jack Snipe**	161	**Black Guillemot**
112	**Woodcock**	162	**Razorbill**
113	Great Snipe	163	**Little Auk**
114	Wilson's Snipe	164	**Guillemot**

165	Sooty Tern
166	Bridled Tern
167	Little Tern
168	Caspian Tern
169	Gull-billed Tern
170	Whiskered Tern
171	White-winged Black Tern
172	**Black Tern**
173	**Sandwich Tern**
174	Elegant Tern
175	Royal Tern
176	Lesser Crested Tern
177	Forster's Tern
178	**Arctic Tern**
179	**Common Tern**
180	**Roseate Tern**
181	**Little Gull**
182	Ross's Gull
183	**Kittiwake**
184	**Sabine's Gull**
185	Ivory Gull
186	Bonaparte's Gull
187	**Black-headed Gull**
188	Laughing Gull
189	Franklin's Gull
190	Great Black-headed Gull
191	Audouin's Gull
192	**Mediterranean Gull**
193	Ring-billed Gull
194	**Common Gull**
195	**Caspian Gull**
196	American Herring Gull
197	**Herring Gull**
198	**Yellow-legged Gull**
198.1	Azorean Yellow-legged Gull *atlantis*
199	**Great Black-backed Gull**
200	**Glaucous Gull**
201	**Lesser Black-backed Gull**
202	**Iceland Gull** *glaucoides*
202.1	Kumlien's Gull *kumlieni*
203	Red-billed Tropicbird
204	**Red-throated Diver**
205	**Great Northern Diver**
206	White-billed Diver
207	Pacific Diver
208	**Black-throated Diver**
209	Black-browed Albatross
210	**Wilson's Storm Petrel**
211	**European Storm Petrel**
212	Band-rumped Storm Petrel sp.
213	Swinhoe's Storm Petrel
214	**Leach's Storm Petrel**
215	**Fulmar**
216	Scopoli's Shearwater
217	**Cory's Shearwater**
218	**Sooty Shearwater**
219	**Great Shearwater**
220	**Manx Shearwater**
221	Mediterranean Shearwater
221.1	**Balearic Shearwater** *mauretanicus*
222	Barolo Shearwater
223	Zino's Petrel
223.1	Desertas/Fea's Petrel
224	Black Stork
225	White Stork
226	Frigatebird sp.
227	**Gannet**
228	Red-footed Booby
229	Brown Booby
230	**Shag**
231	**Cormorant**
232	**Glossy Ibis**
233	**Spoonbill**
234	Dalmatian Pelican
235	**Bittern**
236	American Bittern
237	Little Bittern
238	**Little Egret**
239	**Night-heron**
240	Green Heron
241	Squacco Heron
242	**Great White Egret**
243	**Cattle Egret**
244	**Purple Heron**
245	**Grey Heron**
246	Great Blue Heron
247	Common Nighthawk
248	**Nightjar**
249	Chimney Swift
250	Alpine Swift
251	Little Swift
252	**Swift**
253	Pallid Swift
254	**Barn Owl**
255	**Little Owl**
256	Hawk Owl
257	Scops Owl
258	**Short-eared Owl**

Devon, Cornwall and the Isles of Scilly bird list

259	**Long-eared Owl**	309	**Great Grey Shrike**
260	Snowy Owl	309.1	Steppe Grey Shrike *pallidrostris*
261	**Tawny Owl**	310	Masked Shrike
262	**Osprey**	311	Lesser Grey Shrike
263	Egyptian Vulture	312	**Woodchat Shrike**
264	**Honey Buzzard**	312.1	Balearic Woodchat Shrike *badius*
265	Short-toed Eagle	313	Daurian Shrike
266	Spotted Eagle	314	**Red-backed Shrike**
267	Booted Eagle	315	Turkestan Shrike
268	Golden Eagle	316	Brown Shrike
269	**Sparrowhawk**	317	**Chough**
270	**Goshawk**	318	**Jay**
271	Pallid Harrier	319	**Magpie**
272	**Hen Harrier**	320	Nutcracker
273	Northern Harrier	321	**Jackdaw**
274	Montagu's Harrier	322	**Rook**
275	**Marsh Harrier**	323	**Raven**
276	**Red Kite**	324	**Carrion Crow**
277	Black Kite	324.1	**Hooded Crow** *cornix*
278	White-tailed Eagle	325	Penduline Tit
279	Rough-legged Buzzard	326	**Blue Tit**
280	**Buzzard**	327	**Great Tit**
281	**Hoopoe**	328	**Coal Tit**
282	Roller	328.1	Continental Coal Tit *ater*
283	**Bee-eater**	329	Crested Tit
284	Blue-cheeked Bee-eater	330	**Marsh Tit**
285	**Kingfisher**	331	**Willow Tit**
286	Belted Kingfisher	332	**Bearded Tit**
287	**Wryneck**	333	**Woodlark**
288	Yellow-bellied Sapsucker	334	**Skylark**
289	**Green Woodpecker**	335	Crested Lark
290	**Great Spotted Woodpecker**	336	Shore Lark
291	**Lesser Spotted Woodpecker**	336.1	Horned Lark *alpestris/praticola/hoyti*
292	Lesser Kestrel		
293	**Kestrel**	337	Short-toed Lark
294	American Kestrel	338	Bimaculated Lark
295	Red-footed Falcon	339	Calandra Lark
296	Amur Falcon	340	**Icterine Warbler**
297	**Merlin**	341	**Melodious Warbler**
298	Eleanora's Falcon	342	Booted Warbler
299	**Hobby**	343	Syke's Warbler
300	**Peregrine**	344	Eastern Olivaceous Warbler
301	Gyr Falcon	345	**Sedge Warbler**
302	**Ring-necked Parakeet**	346	Aquatic Warbler
303	Eastern Phoebe	347	Paddyfield Warbler
304	Alder Flycatcher	348	Blyth's Reed Warbler
305	Philadelphia Vireo	349	Marsh Warbler
306	Red-eyed Vireo	350	**Reed Warbler**
307	Yellow-throated Vireo	351	Great Reed Warbler
308	**Golden Oriole**	352	Lanceolated Warbler

Devon, Cornwall and the Isles of Scilly bird list

353	Savi's Warbler	399	**Nuthatch**
354	**Grasshopper Warbler**	400	**Treecreeper**
355	**Sand Martin**	401	**Wren**
356	Tree Swallow	402	Grey Catbird
357	Crag Martin	403	Northern Mockingbird
358	**Swallow**	404	**Starling**
359	**House Martin**	405	**Rose-coloured Starling**
360	**Red-rumped Swallow**	406	**Dipper**
361	American Cliff Swallow	407	White's Thrush
362	**Long-tailed Tit**	408	Varied Thrush
363	**Cetti's Warbler**	409	Wood Thrush
364	**Wood Warbler**	410	Swainson's Thrush
365	Western Bonelli's Warbler	411	Veery
366	Eastern Bonelli's Warbler	412	Grey-cheeked Thrush
367	**Yellow-browed Warbler**	413	Hermit Thrush
368	Hume's Warbler	414	Siberian Thrush
369	Pallas's Warbler	415	**Mistle Thrush**
370	Radde's Warbler	416	**Song Thrush**
371	Sulphur-bellied Warbler	417	**Redwing**
372	Dusky Warbler	418	**Blackbird**
373	Willow Warbler	419	**Fieldfare**
374	Iberian Chiffchaff	420	**Ring Ouzel**
375	**Chiffchaff**	421	Black-throated Thrush
375.1	**Siberian Chiffchaff** *tristis*	422	Dusky Thrush
376	Green Warbler	423	Eyebrowed Thrush
377	Two-barred Greenish Warbler	424	American Robin
378	Greenish Warbler	425	Rufous-tailed Scrub Robin
379	Pale-legged Leaf Warbler	426	**Spotted Flycatcher**
380	Arctic Warbler	427	**Robin**
381	**Garden Warbler**	428	Thrush Nightingale
382	**Blackcap**	429	**Nightingale**
383	**Barred Warbler**	429.1	Eastern Common Nightingale *golzii*
384	**Lesser Whitethroat**	430	**Bluethroat**
384.1	**Siberian Lesser Whitethroat** *blythi*	430.1	White-spotted Bluethroat *cyanecula*
385	Eastern Orphean Warbler	431	**Red-breasted Flycatcher**
385.1	Orphean Warbler sp.	432	Collared Flycatcher
386	Asian Desert Warbler	433	**Pied Flycatcher**
387	**Whitethroat**	434	Red-flanked Bluetail
388	Spectacled Warbler	435	**Black Redstart**
389	**Dartford Warbler**	435.1	Eastern Black Redstart *phoenicuroides/rufiventris*
390	Ruppell's Warbler		
391	Sardinian Warbler	436	**Redstart**
392	Moltoni's Subalpine Warbler	437	Rock Thrush
393	Western Subalpine Warbler	438	Blue Rock Thrush
394	Eastern Subalpine Warbler	439	**Whinchat**
395	Cedar Waxwing	440	Siberian Stonechat
396	Waxwing	440.1	Caspian Stonechat *hemprichii*
397	**Firecrest**	441	**Stonechat**
398	**Goldcrest**		

442	Desert Wheatear	478.2	Hornemann's Arctic Redpoll *hornemanni*
443	Western Black-eared Wheatear		
444	Pied Wheatear	478.3	Coues's Arctic Redpoll *exilipes*
445	Eastern Black-eared Wheatear	479	Two-barred Crossbill
446	**Wheatear**	480	Parrot Crossbill
446.1	Greenland Wheatear *leucorhoa*	481	**Crossbill**
447	Isabelline Wheatear	482	**Goldfinch**
448	Alpine Accentor	483	**Serin**
449	**Dunnock**	484	**Siskin**
450	Tree Sparrow	485	**Snow Bunting**
451	Spanish Sparrow	486	**Lapland Bunting**
452	**House Sparrow**	487	**Reed Bunting**
453	**Grey Wagtail**	488	Yellow-browed Bunting
454	**Yellow Wagtail** *flavissima*	489	Yellow-breasted Bunting
454.1	**Blue-headed Wagtail** *flava*	490	**Little Bunting**
454.2	Iberian Yellow Wagtail *iberiae*	491	Rustic Bunting
454.3	Ashy-headed Wagtail *cinereocapilla*	492	Black-faced Bunting
		493	Black-headed Bunting
454.4	Black-headed Wagtail *feldegg*	494	Corn Bunting
454.5	Grey-headed Wagtail *thunbergii*	495	**Ortolan Bunting**
		496	**Cirl Bunting**
455	Citrine Wagtail	497	Pine Bunting
456	Eastern Yellow Wagtail	498	**Yellowhammer**
457	**Pied Wagtail**	499	Dark-eyed Junco
457.1	**White Wagtail** *alba*	500	White-throated Sparrow
458	Blyth's Pipit	501	White-crowned Sparrow
459	Tawny Pipit	502	Eastern Towhee
460	**Richard's Pipit**	503	Bobolink
461	Pechora Pipit	504	Baltimore Oriole
462	**Tree Pipit**	505	Ovenbird
463	Olive-backed Pipit	506	Northern Waterthrush
464	Red-throated Pipit	507	Black-and-White Warbler
465	Buff-bellied Pipit	508	Common Yellowthroat
466	**Meadow Pipit**	509	American Redstart
467	**Rock Pipit**	510	Hooded Warbler
467.1	**Scandinavian Rock Pipit** *littoralis*	511	Northern Parula
		512	Magnolia Warbler
468	**Water Pipit**	513	Blackburnian Warbler
469	**Brambling**	514	Blackpoll Warbler
470	**Chaffinch**	515	Bay-breasted Warbler
471	**Hawfinch**	516	Chestnut-sided Warbler
472	**Common Rosefinch**	517	Cape May Warbler
473	**Bullfinch**	518	Yellow-rumped Warbler
474	Trumpeter Finch	519	Wilson's Warbler
475	**Greenfinch**	520	Rose-breasted Grosbeak
476	**Twite**	521	Indigo Bunting
477	**Linnet**	522	Scarlet Tanager
478	**Redpoll**		
478.1	**Lesser Redpoll** *caberet*		

INDEX TO SPECIES

Species index listed by site number

Albatross, Black-browed 13, 32, 34, 35A, 37, 47
Auk, Little 4A, 4C, 4F, 8, 9, 13, 30, 33, 36, 39, 39A, 44
Avocet 4, 4A, 4B, 4C, 4E, 4F, 7, 19, 22A, 22B, 22C, 22D, 29, 29A, 43

Bee-eater 2, 3, 8, 13, 26A, 32, 44
  Blue-cheeked 2
Bittern 4C, 7B, 9, 11, 14, 22D, 27, 32A, 33, 40, 41, 46
  American 40
  Little 4A, 11, 19, 30
Blackbird 44, 45
Blackcap 2, 5, 6, 10, 13, 14, 15, 17, 17A, 18, 19, 20, 21G, 23, 25, 29, 30, 34, 35, 40, 46
Bluetail, Red-flanked 9, 23, 45
Bluethroat 9, 11, 16, 19
Bobolink 15
Booby
  Brown 9, 32, 35, 36
  Red-footed 35
Brambling 3, 4A, 4F, 5, 6, 7B, 9, 12, 13, 15, 18, 20, 21C, 21D, 21G, 23, 32, 34, 44, 45, 47, 49A
Brant, Black 4A, 4F, 14, 46
Bufflehead 31, 43
Bullfinch 6, 6A, 7A, 17, 49A
Bunting
  Black-faced 45
  Black-headed 23
  Cirl 2, 4D, 4F, 7, 7A, 9, 11, 12, 13, 14, 15, 16, 17A, 18, 23, 28, 30
  Corn 2, 23, 39, 39A
  Lapland 2, 4A, 4F, 12, 26, 32, 34, 34A, 35, 37, 39, 39A, 41, 44, 45, 46, 47
  Little 1A, 9, 11, 16, 23, 26A, 35, 45
  Ortolan 1, 8, 12, 13, 23, 32, 34, 35, 39A, 45
  Pine 18
  Reed 1, 1A, 2, 3, 4B, 4C, 4F, 6A, 9, 11, 16, 17, 21B, 21C, 21E, 25, 26A, 27, 31, 32, 33, 34, 41, 42, 43
  Rustic 34, 35, 45

Snow 2, 4F, 11, 16, 21E, 23, 26, 32, 34, 34A, 36, 37, 39, 39A, 41, 44, 45, 46, 47
  Yellow-breasted 15, 45
  Yellow-browed 35
Bushchat, Rufous 13
Bustard, Little 32
Buzzard 1, 3, 4E, 5, 6, 7, 7A, 9, 10, 13, 16, 17, 18, 19, 20, 21, 21A, 21B, 21C, 21E, 21F, 21G, 21H, 23, 25, 26, 29, 32, 33, 34, 38, 42, 44, 46, 47, 49A
  Honey 6, 11, 23, 29, 34, 35, 47
  Rough-legged 45

Catbird, Grey 34
Chaffinch 3, 4F, 15, 18, 20, 21B, 21C, 21D, 32, 34, 39A, 44, 45, 47, 49A
Chiffchaff 1, 2, 4C, 4F, 5, 7, 7B, 8, 9, 10, 11, 12, 13, 14, 15, 16, 17, 17A, 18, 19, 21D, 21G, 23, 25, 29, 30, 32, 34, 35, 40, 41, 44, 45, 46
  Iberian 1, 12, 21J, 32
  Siberian 1, 4F, 11, 13, 16, 30, 37
Chough 32, 34, 37
Coot 4F, 7, 7B, 9, 11, 19, 21G, 22D, 24, 25, 27, 30A, 31, 32A, 33, 35, 42, 43, 49, 49A
Cormorant 1, 2, 4A, 4E, 4F, 5, 7, 7B, 8, 10, 11, 14, 17, 18, 21B, 21D, 21E, 22A, 22B, 22C, 22D, 23, 24, 26, 28, 29, 31, 33, 34, 35, 36, 39, 40, 42, 43, 45, 46, 49, 49A
Corncrake 34
Crake
  Baillon's 31, 34
  Little 33
  Spotted 1, 14, 16, 27, 33, 35, 42
Crane, Common 32, 40
Crossbill 3, 6, 6A, 7B, 9, 20, 21, 21C, 21D, 21G, 25, 26, 45
Crow, Carrion 7, 21E, 35
Cuckoo 3, 6, 20, 21A, 21B, 21C, 21E, 21F, 21G, 21H, 25, 26, 26A, 32, 34, 48
  Black-billed 45

Index to species

Great Spotted 1, 4F
Yellow-billed 45
Curlew 1, 2, 3, 4B, 4C, 4E, 4F, 7, 10, 13, 14, 17, 18, 19, 22D, 23, 24, 29, 29A, 38, 39, 40, 41, 46

Dipper 2, 5, 7, 10, 19, 20, 21, 21A, 21B, 21C, 21D, 21E, 21F, 21G, 21H, 21J, 21K, 25, 27, 39, 47
Diver
 Black-throated 4F, 8, 9, 11, 13, 19, 22A, 23, 24, 27, 27A, 28, 29, 30, 31, 32, 32A, 33, 34, 36, 38, 39, 40, 47
 Great Northern 1, 2, 4F, 7, 7A, 8, 9, 11, 12, 13, 14, 16, 19, 22A, 22B, 22C, 22D, 23, 24, 27, 27A, 28, 29, 30, 31, 32, 33, 34, 35, 36, 38, 39, 39A, 40, 43, 44, 46, 47
 Pacific 9, 28, 33
 Red-throated 1, 2, 4C, 4F, 8, 9, 11, 22A, 23, 27, 27A, 28, 29, 33, 34, 36, 39, 39A, 40, 41, 43, 44, 46, 47
 White-billed 9, 12, 27A, 37, 38, 47
Dotterel 1, 9, 13, 15, 21B, 21E, 21H, 24, 26, 31, 34, 34A, 35, 39, 39A, 45
Dove
 Stock 1, 2, 4E, 4F, 5, 13, 15, 17, 19, 20, 21C, 21F, 34, 35, 49A
 Turtle 3, 13, 34, 35
Dowitcher
 Long-billed 4B, 26, 31, 33, 33A, 38, 40, 42, 46
 Short-billed 35
Duck
 American Black 11, 14, 31, 35
 Falcated 4B
 Ferruginous 11
 Long-tailed 2, 4A, 4C, 4F, 11, 14, 19, 21D, 22A, 25, 27A, 28, 29, 32A, 33, 34A, 35, 38, 39A, 40, 42, 43
 Mandarin 4F, 7, 7B, 10, 19, 20, 21A, 21B, 21J, 21K
 Ring-necked 6A, 7B, 11, 21G, 22C, 22D, 24, 25, 26, 32A, 33A, 39, 42, 43, 46, 47, 49
 Tufted 1, 4B, 4E, 4F, 6A, 7, 7B, 9, 11, 14, 19, 21D, 21G, 22C, 22D, 24, 25, 26, 27, 30, 30A, 31, 32A, 33, 35, 39, 40, 42, 43, 46, 47, 49, 49A

Dunlin 1, 2, 4C, 4E, 4F, 7, 11, 13, 14, 16, 17, 18, 19, 21, 21E, 22A, 22B, 22C, 22D, 24, 26, 27, 29, 29A, 31, 33, 35, 37, 38, 40, 41, 42, 43, 45, 46
Dunnock 35, 45

Eagle, Short-toed 4F, 35
Egret
 Cattle 1, 2, 4C, 4E, 7, 11, 14, 17, 19, 22, 22A, 22B, 22C, 22D, 24, 26A, 27, 29, 29A, 32, 32A, 33, 33A, 39, 40, 41, 46
 Great White 4E, 11, 14, 19, 22, 22B, 29, 31, 32, 32A, 33, 33A, 38, 39, 40, 41, 46
 Little 1, 2, 4A, 4B, 4E, 4F, 5, 7, 10, 11, 13, 14, 17, 19, 22, 22A, 22B, 22C, 22D, 23, 29, 29A, 33, 33A, 35, 38, 39, 40, 41, 43, 46, 49
Eider 4A, 4F, 8, 9, 11, 13, 14, 19, 23, 27A, 28, 29, 30, 33, 36, 39, 39A, 40, 41, 46
 King 28, 33, 39

Falcon
 Amur 34
 Gyr 9, 18, 23, 34, 39A
 Red-footed 4C, 13, 15, 25, 32, 44, 46
Fieldfare 1, 4C, 20, 21, 21B, 21C, 25, 26, 42, 44, 45, 47, 49A
Finch, Trumpeter 45
Firecrest 1, 2, 4C, 4F, 6, 7, 7A, 8, 9, 11, 12, 13, 14, 15, 16, 17A, 18, 19, 23, 29, 30, 32, 34, 35, 37, 39A, 40, 44, 45
Flycatcher
 Pied 1, 3, 6, 12, 21, 21A, 21B, 21D, 21E, 21G, 21J, 21K, 22D, 23, 32, 34, 37, 44, 45, 47
 Red-breasted 9, 13, 15, 23, 32, 34, 35, 39, 39A, 41, 44
 Spotted 6A, 7A, 7B, 12, 17, 18, 21A, 21B, 21D, 21G, 23, 25, 26, 32, 34, 49
Fulmar 1, 2, 4F, 8, 9, 11, 12, 13, 15, 16, 17A, 18, 19, 23, 27A, 28, 30, 32, 34, 34A, 35, 35A, 36, 37, 39, 39A, 41, 44, 45, 47

Index to species

Gadwall 1, 4F, 7B, 9, 10, 11, 14, 16, 17, 26, 27, 31, 32A, 33, 35, 40, 42, 43, 46, 49
Gannet 4F, 7A, 8, 9, 11, 12, 13, 15, 23, 27A, 32, 34, 34A, 35, 35A, 36, 37, 39, 39A, 41, 44, 45, 47
Garganey 1, 4B, 4C, 4F, 11, 14, 16, 19, 22C, 26A, 31, 33, 40, 41, 43, 46, 49
Godwit
    Bar-tailed 1, 4F, 11, 12, 13, 14, 16, 18, 19, 22A, 22B, 22C, 22D, 23, 29, 33, 36, 38, 40, 46
    Black-tailed 1, 2, 4, 4B, 4C, 4E, 4F, 19, 22A, 22B, 22C, 22D, 29, 29A, 38, 40, 46
    Hudsonian 4C
Goldcrest 6, 12, 13, 15, 17A, 19, 20, 21C, 21G, 23, 34, 39A, 45
Goldeneye 4B, 4C, 4F, 6A, 11, 14, 19, 21G, 22C, 24, 25, 26, 27, 29, 30A, 31, 32A, 33A, 35, 39, 42, 43, 46, 49, 49A
Goldfinch 13, 39A
Goosander 1, 2, 4F, 5, 6A, 7B, 10, 11, 19, 21, 21B, 21D, 21G, 21J, 21K, 24, 25, 26, 29, 29A, 30A, 31, 33A, 38, 39, 40, 41, 42, 43, 46, 47, 49, 49A
Goose
    Bar-headed 49A
    Barnacle 19, 36, 43
    Brent 4A, 4B, 4E, 4F, 7, 8, 14, 16, 17, 36, 38
    Canada 2, 4B, 5, 7, 19, 21B, 21E, 27, 38, 42, 43, 49, 49A
    Dark-bellied Brent 4, 4F, 22A, 22B, 22C, 22D, 46
    Egyptian 4E
    Greylag 4B, 31
    Pale-bellied Brent 4C, 22A, 22B, 22C, 22D, 46
    Pink-footed 24, 26, 31, 35, 45, 49A
    Red-breasted 4A
    Snow 43, 49A
    Tundra Bean 4C, 5, 46, 49A
    White-fronted 4C, 5, 16, 17, 24, 26, 31, 40, 46, 49A
Goshawk 6, 16, 21A, 25, 26, 44

Grebe
    Black-necked 4A, 9, 11, 14, 19, 22A, 23, 24, 27A, 28, 29, 33, 40, 43, 46
    Great Crested 1, 4F, 6A, 7, 7B, 8, 9, 11, 14, 19, 21B, 21D, 21G, 22A, 22C, 23, 26, 27A, 28, 29, 30A, 31, 32A, 33A, 39, 40, 42, 43, 49, 49A
    Little 1, 2, 4B, 4F, 7, 7B, 9, 10, 14, 17, 19, 22A, 22C, 22D, 23, 24, 26, 27, 29, 30, 31, 32A, 33, 33A, 38, 39, 42, 46, 49, 49A
    Pied-billed 32A
    Red-necked 4F, 8, 9, 11, 19, 22B, 23, 24, 27, 27A, 28, 29, 30, 32A, 33, 36, 40, 43
    Slavonian 4F, 19, 22A, 23, 27, 27A, 28, 29, 30, 33, 36, 38, 39, 40, 43
Greenshank 1, 2, 4B, 4E, 4F, 7, 10, 11, 14, 17, 19, 21D, 22A, 22B, 22C, 22D, 23, 24, 29, 29A, 31, 32A, 35, 38, 39, 40, 42, 46, 47
Grosbeak, Rose-breasted 35
Grouse, Red 21, 21E
Guillemot 4F, 7, 8, 9, 28, 29, 32, 34, 36, 39A, 45, 47
    Black 9, 12, 18, 19, 28, 29, 30
Gull
    American Herring 1, 2, 35
    Audouin's 1
    Azores 34A
    Black-headed 2, 4C, 4E, 5, 7, 8, 9, 17, 19, 21D, 22A, 22B, 22C, 22D, 24, 26, 27, 29, 30, 31, 38, 39, 40, 41, 42, 43, 46
    Bonaparte's 1, 2, 7, 19, 22A, 28, 30, 32A, 33, 33A, 38, 39, 46
    Caspian 1, 2, 4F, 9, 11, 19, 24, 33, 33A, 38
    Common 4C, 5, 7, 9, 11, 17, 19, 21D, 22A, 22D, 23, 27, 29, 30, 32A, 33, 38, 39, 40, 41, 42
    Franklin's 4B, 7, 9, 19, 26, 32A, 33, 38, 39, 46
    Glaucous 1, 2, 4F, 7, 8, 9, 11, 16, 18, 19, 23, 24, 27, 30, 32, 32A, 33, 33A, 34A, 36, 37, 38, 40, 41, 46
    Great Black-backed 5, 7, 8, 9, 11, 12, 13, 18, 19, 27, 30, 32A, 35, 36, 38, 39, 40, 43, 44, 45, 46, 47

Index to species

Herring 7, 8, 9, 18, 19, 27, 30, 34A, 36, 38, 39, 39A, 40, 41, 42, 43, 44, 45, 46
Iceland 1, 7, 8, 9, 11, 16, 18, 19, 23, 24, 27, 30, 32, 32A, 33, 33A, 34A, 36, 37, 38, 39, 40, 41, 46
Kumlien's 19, 32A, 38
Laughing 1, 4C, 7, 7B, 9, 14, 19, 33, 33A, 35, 36, 39, 41, 46
Lesser Black-backed 5, 7, 8, 11, 13, 17, 23, 24, 25, 26, 27, 29, 32A, 33, 34, 35, 36, 38, 39, 40, 41, 43, 45, 49
Little 1, 4C, 4F, 8, 11, 15, 16, 19, 22A, 24, 27, 30, 31, 33, 34A, 36, 38, 39, 39A, 40, 43
Mediterranean 1, 2, 4B, 4E, 4F, 5, 7, 8, 9, 11, 16, 17, 19, 22A, 22B, 22C, 22D, 23, 27, 29, 29A, 30, 30A, 31, 32A, 33, 33A, 34A, 36, 38, 39, 39A, 40, 41, 46
Ring-billed 7, 9, 19, 22A, 23, 27, 30, 30A, 32A, 33, 33A, 35, 38, 39, 40, 46
Ross's 11, 16, 19, 22D, 32, 33
Sabine's 4F, 8, 9, 13, 16, 18, 32, 34A, 35, 35A, 36, 37, 39, 39A, 44
Yellow-legged 1, 4E, 4F, 19, 23, 24, 26, 27, 31, 33, 33A, 38

Harrier
  Hen 3, 12, 13, 15, 17, 21, 21A, 21C, 21E, 21F, 21H, 24, 25, 26, 26A, 31, 32, 34, 39, 43, 44, 45, 46, 47, 48
  Marsh 1, 4B, 4C, 4F, 6, 11, 14, 16, 17, 21C, 24, 26, 32, 33, 39, 40, 44, 46, 47
  Montagu's 11, 21C, 25, 26, 32, 34, 39, 45
  Northern 32
  Pallid 3, 34, 34A
Hawfinch 4F, 6, 9, 12, 15, 45
Heron
  Great Blue 35
  Grey 1, 2, 4E, 4F, 5, 7, 7B, 10, 11, 14, 17, 19, 20, 21B, 21C, 21D, 21E, 21F, 21G, 22A, 22B, 22C, 22D, 23, 24, 26, 27, 29, 29A, 33, 38, 39, 40, 42, 43, 46, 47, 49A

Night 1, 4A, 7, 7B, 11, 14, 17, 19, 27, 30A, 40
Purple 1, 7B, 11, 16, 17, 30A, 32, 33, 39, 41
Squacco 1, 11, 13, 17, 35, 41
Hobby 1, 3, 4A, 4C, 4E, 4F, 5, 6, 6A, 9, 11, 13, 21A, 21B, 21C, 21D, 21E, 21F, 21H, 23, 26, 26A, 31, 32, 33, 34, 39A, 40, 43, 46, 49, 49A
Hoopoe 1, 2, 4F, 9, 11, 12, 15, 16, 17, 18, 21D, 23, 26A, 32, 32A, 33, 34, 35, 39, 45, 46, 47

Ibis, Glossy 2, 4C, 9, 17, 19, 22C, 26A, 32, 32A, 33, 40, 41, 46

Jackdaw 4F, 32
Jay 49A

Kestrel 1, 2, 3, 4E, 6, 7A, 12, 13, 15, 17, 17A, 20, 21A, 21C, 21E, 21F, 21G, 21H, 35, 39A
  Lesser 8, 35
Killdeer 17, 35, 45
Kingfisher 1, 2, 4A, 4B, 4C, 4E, 4F, 5, 7, 7B, 9, 10, 11, 14, 17, 19, 20, 21J, 22D, 23, 25, 27, 29, 29A, 30A, 38, 39, 40, 41, 42, 43, 46, 49, 49A
  Belted 35
Kite
  Black 11, 13, 15, 19, 26A, 32, 34, 35, 45
  Red 1, 3, 4C, 4F, 6, 16, 19, 21H, 24, 31, 32, 34, 47, 49
Kittiwake 4A, 4F, 7, 8, 9, 11, 12, 13, 30, 32, 33, 34, 34A, 35, 35A, 36, 37, 39, 39A, 41, 44, 45, 47
Knot 4C, 4F, 22A, 22B, 22C, 22D, 38, 40, 45, 46

Lapwing 1, 2, 4B, 4C, 4D, 4F, 5, 7, 13, 17A, 21A, 24, 25, 26, 29, 31, 38, 40, 41, 42, 45, 46
Lark
  Shore 9, 39A, 46, 47
  Short-toed 4F, 9, 15, 35, 45, 46
Linnet 1A, 3, 4F, 6A, 7A, 8, 12, 13, 15, 17A, 18, 21A, 21J, 23, 35, 39A, 47

Magpie 18

Index to species

Mallard 4E, 7, 7B, 9, 11, 14, 16, 17, 19, 21B, 21D, 21G, 22C, 24, 25, 26, 27, 29, 30A, 31, 32A, 33, 33A, 38, 39, 40, 41, 42, 43, 45, 49, 49A
Martin
  Crag 31, 35
  House 4C, 17, 21G, 24, 33, 44
  Sand 1, 2, 4C, 5, 7, 7B, 11, 16, 17, 24, 25, 32, 33, 42, 44
Merganser, Red-breasted 4A, 4B, 4C, 4E, 4F, 7, 14, 19, 29, 29A, 38, 40, 46
Merlin 1, 3, 4F, 7A, 9, 12, 13, 15, 16, 17A, 21, 21A, 21B, 21C, 21E, 21F, 21H, 23, 24, 25, 26, 26A, 31, 32, 34, 35, 39, 39A, 40, 41, 42, 43, 44, 45, 46, 47, 48, 49
Moorhen 9, 19, 22D, 27, 30A, 31, 32A, 33, 35, 42, 49, 49A
Murrelet
  Ancient 45
  Long-billed 4F

Nighthawk, Common 35
Nightingale 8, 11
  Thrush 45
Nightjar 1A, 3, 6, 6A, 7B, 20, 21A, 21C, 21D, 21G, 21K, 25, 26A, 44, 48
Nuthatch 5, 7B, 10, 19, 20, 21G, 21J, 29A

Oriole
  Golden 3, 21H, 21K, 32, 34A, 35, 39A, 45
  Northern 45
Osprey 1, 4A, 4B, 4C, 4E, 4F, 6, 7, 10, 14, 16, 17, 17A, 19, 21B, 21D, 22A, 22B, 22C, 22D, 24, 29, 29A, 31, 33A, 34, 35, 38, 39, 40, 43, 44, 45, 46, 49
Ouzel, Ring 1, 8, 9, 13, 15, 17A, 21A, 21C, 21E, 21G, 23, 32, 34, 35, 37, 41, 45, 47
Ovenbird 18
Owl
  Barn 1, 2, 3, 4C, 4F, 11, 17, 25, 26, 26A, 42, 43, 44, 46, 49
  Long-eared 46
  Scops 41, 44

Short-eared 3, 4A, 4C, 4F, 9, 12, 13, 15, 21A, 21C, 24, 25, 26, 26A, 31, 32, 34, 35, 39, 39A, 43, 44, 45, 46
Snowy 34
Tawny 2, 20, 21A, 21G
Oystercatcher 1, 2, 4A, 4F, 7, 8, 9, 12, 13, 14, 17, 17A, 18, 19, 22A, 22B, 22C, 22D, 27, 29, 29A, 34A, 35, 36, 38, 39, 39A, 40, 41, 44, 45, 46, 47

Parakeet, Ring-necked 19
Parula, Northern 23
Peregrine 4A, 4B, 4C, 4E, 4F, 6, 7, 7A, 8, 9, 11, 12, 19, 20, 21B, 21E, 21F, 22A, 22B, 22C, 22D, 24, 25, 26, 29, 31, 32, 34, 35, 38, 39, 40, 41, 42, 43, 44, 46, 47, 49
Petrel
  Desertas-type 9, 12, 13, 32, 34, 37
  European Storm 1, 4F, 8, 9, 12, 13, 30, 34, 35, 35A, 36, 37, 39, 44, 45, 47
  Leach's Storm 1, 15, 35, 36, 39, 44
  Swinhoe's 35
  Wilson's Storm 12, 32, 34, 35, 35A, 37, 39
  Zino's 35
Phalarope
  Grey 1, 4A, 4C, 4F, 8, 9, 11, 13, 16, 22D, 30, 33, 35, 36, 37, 39, 39A, 41, 45, 46
  Red-necked 11, 24, 41
  Wilson's 4C, 11, 24, 26, 31, 32A, 35, 38, 40, 41, 42
Pintail 1, 4A, 4B, 4C, 4E, 4F, 5, 14, 16, 17, 22B, 26, 46
Pipit
  Blyth's 34
  Buff-bellied 13, 32, 34
  Meadow 1A, 2, 6A, 7A, 12, 13, 15, 17A, 18, 21, 21A, 21B, 21C, 21E, 21H, 23, 25, 26, 31, 34, 39, 39A, 44, 45
  Olive-backed 13, 35
  Pechora 34
  Red-throated 4A, 13, 34, 35, 45, 46
  Richard's 2, 4A, 4F, 9, 13, 15, 18, 32, 34, 34A, 35, 37, 39, 39A, 41, 44, 45

Index to species

Rock 1, 2, 8, 9, 12, 13, 16, 17, 18, 19, 23, 27, 34, 35, 36, 37, 39, 39A, 41, 44, 45, 47
Tawny 13, 17A, 32, 34, 35, 39A
Tree 1A, 3, 6, 6A, 9, 12, 13, 20, 21A, 21B, 21D, 21E, 21F, 21G, 21H, 21J, 23, 25, 32, 34, 37, 43, 45, 48, 49
Water 1, 2, 4B, 9, 13, 16, 17, 18, 33, 39, 40, 41
Plover
American Golden 4C, 14, 24, 25, 26, 31, 34A, 35, 40, 41, 46
Caspian 35
Golden 4B, 4C, 4F, 13, 14, 17A, 19, 21, 21A, 21B, 21C, 21D, 21E, 21F, 21H, 24, 25, 26, 29, 31, 35, 40, 41, 42, 45, 46, 47, 48
Greater Sand 4F
Grey 4C, 4F, 14, 18, 22A, 22B, 22C, 22D, 23, 26, 27, 33, 34A, 38, 39A, 40, 43, 46
Kentish 4F, 15, 16, 27, 33, 46
Little Ringed 1, 2, 4B, 4C, 4F, 5, 14, 16, 19, 22C, 24, 27, 31, 33, 38, 41, 42, 43, 46, 49
Pacific Golden 4B, 24, 25, 31
Ringed 2, 4F, 7, 11, 17, 18, 19, 22A, 22B, 22C, 22D, 24, 26, 27, 29, 31, 33, 35, 38, 40, 42, 43, 46
Semipalmated 4F
Sociable 26, 41
Pochard 6A, 7, 7B, 11, 21G, 22C, 24, 25, 27, 31, 32A, 35, 43, 46, 47, 49
Pratincole
Black-winged 26, 34A
Collared 32, 40, 46
Puffin 8, 9, 12, 13, 27A, 32, 34, 35, 36, 39, 45

Quail 9, 39, 46

Rail
Sora 7B
Water 1, 2, 4F, 7, 7B, 9, 10, 11, 16, 17, 27, 30, 32A, 33, 34, 35, 41, 45, 46
Raven 1, 1A, 2, 5, 6A, 7A, 8, 9, 10, 11, 12, 13, 14, 15, 16, 17, 17A, 18, 19, 20, 21, 21A, 21B, 21C, 21D, 21E, 21F, 21G, 21H, 21K, 23, 25, 26, 29, 32, 34, 35, 39, 39A, 41, 44, 45, 46, 47, 48, 49, 49A
Razorbill 4F, 7, 8, 9, 23, 28, 29, 32, 34, 35, 36, 39A, 45, 47
Redpoll
Arctic 35
Coues's Arctic 39A
Lesser 3, 4F, 5, 6, 6A, 7, 7B, 10, 13, 15, 20, 21, 21A, 21B, 21C, 21D, 21G, 25, 26, 26A, 27, 43, 44, 45, 48, 49, 49A
Redshank 1, 2, 4B, 4E, 4F, 7, 10, 13, 14, 17, 18, 19, 22A, 22B, 22D, 23, 24, 26, 29, 29A, 31, 38, 40
Spotted 4B, 4E, 14, 19, 22A, 22B, 22C, 27, 29, 29A, 31, 38, 40, 46
Redstart 1, 3, 5, 6A, 7A, 9, 12, 13, 15, 21, 21A, 21B, 21C, 21D, 21E, 21F, 21G, 21H, 21J, 23, 25, 26, 32, 34, 45, 47
American 34
Black 1, 2, 4F, 8, 9, 11, 12, 13, 14, 15, 16, 18, 19, 23, 29, 30, 32, 33, 34, 34A, 35, 36, 39, 39A, 41, 44, 45, 46
Redwing 1, 4C, 17A, 20, 21B, 21C, 26, 42, 45, 49A
Robin 15, 34, 35
American 4C, 45
Rufous-tailed Scrub 32
Roller 3, 23
Rook 7, 17, 42
Rosefinch, Common 9, 13, 45
Ruff 1, 2, 4C, 4F, 14, 16, 24, 26, 29, 30A, 31, 33, 33A, 38, 40, 42, 46

Sanderling 4F, 18, 27, 33, 35, 40, 46
Sandpiper
Baird's 1, 4B, 4F, 26, 29, 31, 33, 38, 39
Broad-billed 4C, 4F, 38
Buff-breasted 1, 4F, 13, 15, 16, 24, 26, 34, 35, 39, 41, 45
Common 1, 2, 4B, 4C, 4E, 4F, 5, 6A, 7, 10, 11, 14, 17, 18, 19, 21D, 21G, 22A, 22B, 22C, 22D, 23, 24, 29, 29A, 30A, 31, 32A, 35, 38, 39, 40, 42, 43, 45, 46, 49, 49A

Index to species

Curlew 4B, 4C, 4E, 4F, 7, 17, 18, 22A, 22B, 22C, 22D, 24, 26, 27, 29, 31, 33, 33A, 35, 38, 40, 42, 46
  Green 1, 2, 4B, 4C, 4E, 4F, 5, 7, 9, 10, 14, 17, 21G, 22A, 22B, 22C, 22D, 23, 24, 27, 29, 30A, 31, 32A, 33, 33A, 38, 39, 40, 42, 43, 45, 46, 47, 49, 49A
  Least 1, 16, 28, 30A, 38, 45
  Marsh 17
  Pectoral 4B, 4F, 9, 11, 13, 14, 16, 17, 22C, 24, 26, 29, 30A, 31, 32, 33, 33A, 35, 38, 39, 40, 41, 42, 45, 46
  Purple 2, 4A, 4F, 8, 9, 13, 16, 18, 19, 23, 27, 30, 32, 33, 34A, 35, 36, 37, 39, 39A, 41, 44, 45, 46, 47
  Semipalmated 1, 4F, 22A, 31, 33A, 40, 41, 45
  Sharp-tailed 33A
  Solitary 1, 31, 35
  Spotted 4A, 7, 10, 19, 22D, 33A, 35, 42
  Terek 4B
  Upland 32, 34, 41
  Western 1
  White-rumped 4B, 14, 26, 38, 45
  Wood 1, 4B, 4C, 4E, 4F, 5, 9, 14, 16, 24, 27, 29, 30A, 31, 32A, 33, 33A, 38, 40, 41, 42, 43, 46, 49
Scaup 4F, 7, 10, 11, 14, 19, 22A, 22C, 22D, 24, 25, 26, 27, 30A, 31, 32A, 33, 33A, 39, 42, 43, 46, 47, 49
  Lesser 4C, 11, 24, 25, 31, 32A, 33A, 42, 43
Scoter
  Common 1, 2, 4F, 7, 7A, 8, 9, 11, 13, 17, 19, 23, 27, 27A, 28, 29, 32, 33, 34, 34A, 36, 37, 39, 39A, 40, 43, 46
  Surf 1, 4F, 9, 14, 27A, 28, 32A, 34A, 36, 39
  Velvet 1, 2, 4A, 4F, 9, 11, 14, 22A, 23, 27, 28, 29, 30, 33, 36, 39, 39A, 40
Serin 2, 9, 12, 13, 32, 34
Shag 1, 2, 4A, 4F, 7, 7A, 8, 9, 10, 11, 12, 13, 14, 17A, 18, 28, 29, 30, 32, 33, 34, 35, 36, 37, 39, 39A, 40, 41, 44, 45

Shearwater
  Balearic 1, 4A, 4F, 7, 8, 9, 11, 12, 13, 23, 30, 32, 34, 36, 37, 39, 39A, 41, 44, 47
  Cory's 8, 9, 12, 13, 23, 30, 32, 34, 35, 35A, 36, 37, 39, 39A, 44
  Great 8, 9, 12, 13, 23, 30, 32, 34, 35, 35A, 36, 37, 39A, 44
  Little 9, 12, 35A
  Manx 1, 7, 8, 9, 11, 12, 13, 15, 17A, 23, 30, 32, 34, 34A, 35, 36, 37, 39, 39A, 41, 44, 45, 47
  Scopoli's 35, 37
  Sooty 8, 9, 11, 12, 13, 23, 32, 34, 35, 35A, 36, 37, 39, 39A, 41, 44, 47
  Yelkouan 9
Shelduck 1, 2, 4C, 4E, 4F, 5, 7, 10, 13, 14, 17, 17A, 18, 19, 22A, 22B, 22C, 22D, 23, 24, 29, 29A, 38, 40, 46
Shoveler 1, 2, 4B, 4C, 4E, 4F, 5, 7B, 9, 11, 14, 16, 17, 19, 27, 29A, 31, 32A, 33, 35, 40, 41, 42, 43, 46, 49, 49A
Shrike
  Brown 32, 37
  Great Grey 3, 4F, 21A, 21C, 21D, 26A, 42, 44, 48
  Isabelline 9, 16, 18
  Lesser Grey 4F, 19, 28
  Masked 35
  Red-backed 9, 13, 15, 19, 21, 24, 32, 34, 35, 37, 39, 45
  Woodchat 4F, 8, 9, 11, 12, 13, 15, 16, 17A, 18, 19, 24, 32, 34, 35, 37, 39A, 45
Siskin 3, 5, 6, 6A, 7, 7B, 10, 12, 13, 15, 17, 20, 21, 21A, 21B, 21C, 21D, 21G, 25, 26, 27, 29, 30, 34, 39, 39A, 40, 44, 45, 49A
Skua
  Arctic 1, 4A, 4F, 8, 11, 12, 13, 16, 23, 30, 32, 34, 36, 37, 39, 44, 47
  Great 1, 4F, 8, 9, 12, 13, 23, 30, 32, 34, 36, 37, 39, 44, 47
  Long-tailed 1, 8, 9, 13, 18, 36, 37, 39, 44
  Pomarine 1, 4F, 8, 9, 12, 13, 15, 23, 30, 32, 34, 36, 37, 39, 44, 47

Index to species

Skylark 2, 4A, 4F, 7A, 12, 13, 17A, 18, 21, 21B, 21E, 23, 26, 31, 34, 39, 39A, 41, 45
Smew 10, 11, 19, 22D, 24, 25, 26, 49A
Snipe 1, 2, 3, 4C, 4F, 5, 6, 7B, 9, 10, 16, 17, 20, 21, 21A, 21B, 21C, 21D, 21E, 22B, 24, 25, 26, 29, 31, 33, 34, 38, 39, 40, 41, 42, 43, 45, 46, 48, 49
  Jack 1, 3, 4C, 4F, 16, 22B, 24, 31, 33, 34, 35, 38, 40, 41, 42, 45, 46, 48, 49
Sparrow
  House 35, 45
  Spanish 23
  Tree 9, 34
Sparrowhawk 1, 2, 3, 4E, 5, 6, 7, 7A, 8, 9, 11, 13, 16, 18, 19, 20, 21A, 21C, 21F, 21G, 23, 25, 26, 29, 32, 33, 34, 42, 44, 46, 47, 49A
Spoonbill 1, 2, 4B, 4C, 7, 14, 19, 22A, 22B, 22C, 22D, 24, 29, 29A, 33, 35, 38, 40, 46
Starling 11, 12, 13, 16, 26, 27, 32, 33, 35, 41, 44, 45
  Rose-coloured 11, 35, 37, 44, 45
Stilt, Black-winged 4C, 14, 16, 19, 22A, 23, 27, 32, 38, 39, 40, 41
Stint
  Little 1, 4B, 4C, 4F, 7, 17, 18, 22A, 22B, 22C, 22D, 24, 26, 27, 29, 31, 32A, 33, 33A, 35, 38, 40, 41, 42, 46
  Temminck's 4B, 4C, 24, 38, 40, 41, 46
Stone-curlew 4F, 24, 39, 46
Stonechat 1A, 2, 3, 4F, 5, 6, 6A, 7A, 8, 9, 11, 12, 13, 14, 16, 17, 18, 19, 21, 21A, 21B, 21C, 21F, 21H, 21J, 23, 28, 32, 33, 34, 35, 37, 39, 39A, 41, 43, 44, 47, 48
  Eastern 12
Stork
  Black 16, 22D, 40, 46
  White 1
Swallow 4C, 7A, 11, 12, 16, 17, 27, 32, 33, 38, 41, 44
  Cliff 35
  Red-rumped 9, 11, 16, 28, 41

Swan
  Bewick's 17, 25, 31
  Mute 7, 7B, 17, 19, 22A, 24, 27, 38, 40, 42, 46
  Whooper 4C, 4F, 17, 24, 25, 35, 40, 42, 45, 46, 49
Swift 5, 11, 24, 32, 42
  Alpine 1, 9, 15, 32, 41, 44
  Chimney 1, 9, 23, 34
  Little 11
  Pallid 9

Teal 1, 2, 4A, 4B, 4C, 4E, 4F, 5, 7, 7B, 9, 10, 11, 14, 16, 17, 19, 21D, 21G, 22A, 22D, 24, 25, 26, 29, 29A, 31, 32A, 33, 33A, 35, 38, 39, 40, 41, 42, 43, 45, 46, 47, 49, 49A
  Blue-winged 9, 17, 30A, 31, 32A, 42, 43
  Green-winged 4B, 22A, 22B, 22C, 22D, 24, 30A, 31, 32A, 38, 41, 42, 43, 46
Tern
  Arctic 4B, 4C, 4F, 8, 11, 16, 19, 22A, 22B, 22C, 22D, 28, 29, 30, 33, 34, 35, 36, 38, 39, 40, 41, 46
  Black 4A, 4C, 4F, 8, 11, 15, 16, 19, 22A, 22C, 24, 26, 30A, 31, 33, 36, 38, 39, 40, 41, 42, 43, 47
  Caspian 4B, 4F, 46
  Common 4C, 4E, 4F, 8, 10, 11, 16, 18, 19, 22A, 22B, 22C, 22D, 23, 28, 29, 30, 33, 34, 34A, 35, 36, 38, 39, 40, 46, 47
  Elegant 4F
  Forster's 22B, 27, 30
  Gull-billed 1, 4B, 7, 19, 29, 38, 40, 46
  Lesser Crested 4F
  Little 4E, 4F, 11, 16, 17, 19, 22A, 27, 33, 38, 39, 40, 41, 46
  Roseate 4A, 4B, 4C, 4F, 11, 17, 19, 22A, 27, 33, 34, 35, 39, 40
  Royal 35
  Sandwich 2, 4C, 4E, 4F, 7, 8, 9, 11, 12, 13, 16, 17, 18, 19, 22A, 22B, 22C, 22D, 23, 27, 28, 29, 30, 32, 33, 34, 34A, 35, 36, 37, 38, 39, 40, 41, 46, 47
  Whiskered 11, 16, 38, 40

Index to species

White-winged Black 11, 19, 31, 33, 38, 39, 42, 46
Thrush
  Black-throated 35
  Dusky 35, 41
  Eye-browed 35
  Grey-cheeked 35
  Hermit 35
  Mistle 4E, 4F, 6A, 7, 7A, 9, 21B, 21C, 21E
  Rock 21H, 35
  Siberian 35
  Song 35
  Swainson's 34, 35
  Varied 34
  White's 35, 45
  Wood 35
Tit
  Bearded 2, 4C, 4F, 11, 16, 33, 41, 46
  Blue 35
  Coal 6, 21C, 21D, 21G, 25, 26
  Great 35
  Marsh 5, 6, 6A, 7, 7B, 20, 21A, 21J, 21K, 25, 31, 42
  Penduline 4A, 4B, 9, 11, 16, 34
  Willow 25, 26A, 42, 43, 44, 47, 48, 49
Treecreeper 5, 7B, 19, 20, 21J, 25
Turnstone 2, 4A, 4F, 7, 8, 9, 11, 12, 13, 14, 16, 17, 17A, 18, 19, 22A, 22B, 22C, 22D, 23, 27, 30, 32, 33, 34A, 35, 36, 38, 39, 39A, 43, 45, 46
Twite 34

Veery 34, 45
Vireo
  Red-eyed 4F, 13, 18, 32, 34, 35, 41, 45
  Yellow-throated 34
Vulture, Egyptian 35

Wagtail
  Black-headed 14, 16, 41
  Blue-headed 16, 33, 41
  Citrine 32, 33, 38, 40, 41
  Eastern Yellow 1, 35
  Grey 1, 2, 5, 7, 9, 10, 13, 14, 16, 17, 19, 20, 21, 21A, 21B, 21C, 21D, 21E, 21F, 21G, 21H, 21J, 21K, 22D, 23, 25, 29A, 32, 34, 35, 41, 44, 47, 49A
  Grey-headed 16
  Pied 16, 17, 21B, 26, 27, 29A, 38, 45
  White 11, 16, 17, 27, 32, 33, 34, 38, 45, 46
  Yellow 1, 2, 4B, 4C, 5, 11, 12, 13, 15, 16, 17, 23, 26, 27, 32, 33, 34, 37, 39, 41, 45, 46
Warbler
  Aquatic 11, 15, 16, 32, 33
  Arctic 12, 32, 34
  Barred 4F, 8, 9, 13, 34, 35, 41, 45, 46
  Bay-breasted 34
  Black-and-white 13, 35
  Blackpoll 13, 34, 35
  Blyth's Reed 1, 9, 35
  Booted 12, 35
  Cetti's 1, 2, 4C, 4F, 5, 7, 9, 11, 16, 27, 32, 32A, 33, 35, 41, 46
  Chestnut-sided 13
  Dartford 3, 6, 9, 23
  Desert 19
  Dusky 1, 4A, 4F, 9, 12, 13, 15, 32, 33A, 34, 35, 39, 41, 46
  Garden 5, 6, 6A, 7A, 10, 20, 21A, 21C, 21G, 23, 24, 25, 26A
  Grasshopper 1A, 3, 4C, 6A, 7, 8, 12, 13, 15, 21A, 21B, 21C, 21E, 21F, 25, 26, 26A, 32, 34, 39, 43, 44, 46, 47, 48
  Great Reed 4F, 11, 16, 32
  Green 35
  Greenish 34
  Hume's 19
  Icterine 11, 13, 15, 16, 17A, 32, 34, 35, 41, 46
  Marsh 4A, 32
  Melodious 11, 13, 15, 19, 23, 32, 34, 35, 45
  Myrtle 45
  Paddyfield 32, 33, 35, 45
  Pallas's 1, 4A, 4F, 9, 13, 15, 23, 30, 32, 34, 35, 40
  Radde's 4F, 12, 13, 15, 34
  Reed 1, 2, 4A, 4C, 4F, 7, 9, 11, 13, 16, 26, 27, 30, 32, 32A, 33, 35, 40, 41, 42, 46
  Rüppell's 45

Index to species

Sardinian 4A, 9, 13, 39A, 41
Savi's 27, 32
Sedge 1, 2, 4A, 4C, 4F, 5, 7, 11, 12, 13, 15, 16, 24, 25, 26, 27, 30, 32, 33, 33A, 34, 35, 39, 40, 41, 42, 44, 46, 49
Subalpine 16, 32, 34
Sulphur-bellied 45
Sykes's 35
Two-barred Greenish 35
Western Bonelli's 9, 15, 32
Willow 2, 4F, 5, 6, 6A, 7A, 7B, 12, 13, 15, 17, 18, 19, 21C, 21D, 21G, 21H, 23, 25, 26A, 32, 33A, 34, 35, 43, 45, 49
Wilson's 23
Wood 21A, 44
Yellow-browed 1, 4C, 4F, 9, 11, 12, 13, 14, 17A, 18, 19, 23, 27, 30, 32, 34, 35, 37, 39, 41, 44, 46
Waxwing, Cedar 35
Wheatear 1, 2, 4C, 4F, 6, 6A, 7A, 8, 9, 11, 12, 13, 15, 16, 17, 17A, 18, 19, 21, 21A, 21B, 21C, 21D, 21E, 21F, 21G, 21H, 23, 25, 26, 32, 33, 34, 35, 37, 39, 39A, 41, 44, 45, 46, 47
  Black-eared 25
  Desert 9, 11, 13, 16
  Isabelline 1, 32
  Pied 9
Whimbrel 1, 2, 4B, 4C, 4E, 4F, 7, 8, 11, 12, 13, 14, 16, 17, 18, 19, 22A, 22B, 22C, 22D, 23, 26, 27, 28, 29, 29A, 33, 34, 36, 37, 38, 39, 39A, 40, 41, 43, 45, 46

Whinchat 1, 5, 7A, 9, 12, 13, 17A, 21, 21A, 21B, 21C, 21E, 21F, 21H, 23, 24, 25, 32, 34, 45, 47
Whitethroat 2, 4F, 6A, 7, 7A, 8, 10, 11, 12, 13, 15, 17, 18, 20, 23, 26A, 32, 34, 44, 45, 46, 47
  Lesser 7A, 8, 13, 32, 39, 44, 46
Wigeon 1, 2, 4A, 4B, 4C, 4F, 5, 7, 8, 11, 14, 16, 17, 19, 22A, 22B, 22C, 22D, 24, 25, 26, 29, 29A, 30A, 31, 32A, 33A, 35, 38, 39, 40, 41, 42, 43, 46, 47, 49, 49A
  American 4B, 4F, 16, 19, 32A, 38, 40, 43, 46
Woodcock 3, 5, 6, 6A, 7B, 15, 20, 21A, 21C, 21D, 21E, 21F, 21G, 21H, 26, 26A, 34, 35, 44, 45, 47, 48, 49
Woodlark 4F, 9
Woodpecker
  Great Spotted 4E, 17, 19, 20, 25, 26, 29A, 31, 39, 49A
  Green 3, 4E, 7A, 8, 13, 17, 19, 20, 21B, 25, 34, 39, 49A
  Lesser Spotted 21A
Woodpigeon 4F, 12, 21C, 34
Wren 35, 45
Wryneck 3, 6, 8, 9, 11, 13, 15, 16, 24, 32, 34, 34A, 35, 37, 41, 45, 46

Yellowhammer 1, 3, 6, 6A, 7A, 9, 12, 13, 14, 15, 17A, 18, 21A, 21H, 21J, 48
Yellowlegs
  Greater 40, 46
  Lesser 4B, 17, 19, 31, 32, 32A, 33A, 38, 39, 43